MIRACLES
— of the —
OLD
TESTAMENT

A GUIDE TO THE SYMBOLIC MESSAGES

ALONZO L. GASKILL

CFI, AN IMPRINT OF CEDAR FORT, INC.
SPRINGVILLE, UTAH

ISBN 13: 978-1-4621-4250-7

Published by CFI, an imprint of Cedar Fort, Inc., 2373 W. 700 S., Springville, UT 84663
Distributed by Cedar Fort, Inc., www.cedarfort.com

The Library of Congress cataloged the hardback edition as follows:

Names: Gaskill, Alonzo L., author.
Title: Miracles of the Old Testament : a guide to the symbolic messages / Alonzo L. Gaskill.
Description: Springville, UT : CFI, an imprint of Cedar Fort, Inc., [2017] | Includes bibliographical references and index.
Identifiers: LCCN 2017033068 (print) | LCCN 2017034426 (ebook) | ISBN 9781462127818 (ebook) | ISBN 9781462120253 (hardback : alk. paper)
Subjects: LCSH: Miracles--Biblical teaching. | Bible. Old Testament--Criticism, interpretation, etc.
Classification: LCC BS1199.M5 (ebook) | LCC BS1199.M5 G37 2017 (print) | DDC 2221.6/4--dc23
LC record available at https://lccn.loc.gov/2017033068

Cover design by Shawnda T. Craig
Cover design © 2017 by Cedar Fort, Inc.
Edited and typeset by Chelsea Holdaway

Printed in the United States of America

10 9 8 7 6 5 4 3 2 1

Printed on acid-free paper

In memory of Mormonism's most gifted preachers—from the Prophet Joseph down to the current General Authorities and General Officers of the Church—whose wit and wisdom provoke the Spirit and invite us to seek true conversion.

And to all those who, week after week, give their all in preparing and presenting the word of God in such powerful and Spirit-directed ways that their hearers are motivated to sup more earnestly from the words of the prophets and to obey God's laws.

CONTENTS

Contents

Acknowledgments

I express my sincere appreciation to the many individuals who have helped me with this final volume of my Miracles trilogy.

I am grateful to my several formative and summative peer reviewers who each took the time to read this very long manuscript and offer helpful suggestions for improving what I had written. The hours they have given—without compensation—are a testament to their consecrated and giving hearts.

I also express appreciation to Judson Burton who, when I started this project in 2009, was serving as my research assistant, and who began the work of gathering sources from which I would eventually draw many of my insights.

In perpetuum, I am indebted to Jan Nyholm for her editorial assistance when this manuscript was in its working stages. She has given countless hours over the years reading and rereading what I have written. My publications have been greatly improved because of Jan's eye for details. I can never repay this good sister for all she has done for me and my family.

INTRODUCTION

A good, universal definition of what constitutes a "miracle" is difficult to come by. By that I mean, while most people will acknowledge that miracles are those events that are largely unexplainable by *known* natural laws, what falls into that category is not always agreed upon. Should, for example, visions be included in a list of scriptural miracles? For surely they are miraculous events. Or what about the manifestation of any of the gifts of the Spirit, such as speaking in tongues or prophesying? Those are also quite miraculous. If we speak technically, must we not acknowledge that events largely taken for granted—such as the birth of a human being—are miracles also? Thus, the definition of what constitutes a miracle is not always cut-and-dried, and the ability to create a complete list of Old Testament miracles is therefore difficult.

That being the case, the list of miracles we will examine here largely ignores traditional life events, such as giving birth or using the human brain to think and reason—even though most readers will feel a measure of awe at God's handiwork manifest through such events. Instead, our focus will be on that which most would acknowledge as extraordinary; on those events in the Old Testament that confront us with a sense that God's power is absolutely incomprehensible and unexplainable to finite humans. We will look at stories where prophets and patriarchs employ the powers of heaven to change lives, heal the hopeless, and cast out demons. We will examine miracles that provide evidence that God is in charge and that what He wills certainly comes to pass.

One of the difficulties in a study such as this has to do with the approach that should be used. Is there a place for a systematic look at the miracles? Surely there is. But which *approach* or *system* should be employed? Of course, how one person reads Old Testament symbolism will be dramatically affected by how they perceive the Hebrew Bible. Some, for example, see the

Old Testament as a sub-Christian text, others as a non-Christian (or Jewish) text. Some, on the other hand, see it as pre-Christian, while many in early Christianity and within the restored gospel see it as decidedly Christian.[1] That person's view on this matter will determine how they approach Old Testament symbolism, and also how they read the miracles recorded in the Hebrew Bible. Similarly, it is no secret that the Old Testament contains several genres of scripture (e.g., prophetic, historical, wisdom, and legalistic texts, to name the obvious). While some symbols are used in similar ways across genres, many are not. For example, the way the temple is discussed in Mosaic texts is not the same way it is discussed in Solomonic texts. Or, while Isaiah often uses symbols in very historic and prophetic ways, texts attributed to Moses sometimes use similar symbols in very practical ways. Thus, genre and authorship greatly influence how symbols are employed in the Old Testament. Because there is not a consistency across the Hebrew Bible—or even across genres—our approach here will be to examine each of the miracles individually and aside from any overarching structure that one scholar or another has proposed. While we acknowledge the value of structured approaches, for what we are seeking to do here it will be best to look at the smaller picture rather than the larger one.

The reader should be aware that, by looking for symbolic applications, we are not challenging the historicity of the stories or miracles described in the Old Testament. Though we will examine these for their symbolic value—for their application—we take the position of Augustine (AD 354–430), who said: "We do not, because we allegorize facts, however, lose our belief in them as facts."[2]

While all scriptural miracles *are* testaments to the power of God, the plethora of miracles in the Bible—in both the Old and New Testaments—seems to suggest that something is intended by them (in addition to witnessing that God is a real and powerful being). In other words, the miracles certainly testify of His supremacy, but what else might they testify of? What else might they communicate to the reader? As we study the various miracles of the Old Testament, it becomes evident that the miracles serve well as great teaching devices that can help us understand gospel truths buried within the miraculous events. One commentator penned this explanation, "Bible miracles were designed to symbolize the spiritual blessings that God is able and willing to bestow upon our needy hearts. The majority of miracles were acts of mercy and are conspicuous as emblems of redemption."[3] In other words, through His appointed prophets and patriarchs, God performed many mighty miracles in the lives of the *ancients*, but each of those miracles can symbolize blessings He has in store for you and me *today*! One of my colleagues here at BYU put it this way:

> It is interesting that while people are concerned about the historicity of symbols, rarely do they concern themselves with the symbolism of history. Just as symbols can correspond to actual events, actual events can be symbolic. I am not just referring to ritual and ceremony, such as the sacrament or temple worship, which are by definition symbolic actions. I am referring to events in everyday life that . . . actually point to meaning outside of themselves.[4]

The trick is learning to see symbolically so that we might draw out of the historic miracles applications for our lives today.

It is well known that in antiquity there were a variety of approaches to reading and applying scripture. For example, the exegetical[5] school of Antioch tended to look for the literal or historic sense of scripture, whereas the Alexandrian school very much fostered an allegorical approach to the Bible.[6] Which approach was right? I suppose the answer largely depends on your school of thought and what it is you feel you need from scripture. As one scholar pointed out:

> Every text is capable of different levels of apprehension. At the most elementary level, early Rabbis made a distinction between what was "written" (*kitab*) and what was "read" (*qere*) in the text of Torah; more elaborate distinctions between *peshat* ("literal meaning"), *darash* ("applied or extended meaning"), and *sod* ("mystical meaning") were to follow. Christianity would develop similar distinctions between literal, moral, and allegorical readings of its texts.[7]

Contingent upon what you are using scripture for, or what you need personally from the text, there are a variety of ways to approach the reading and applying of scripture. So, for example, a word study (of the Hebrew terms employed) attempts to do something entirely different than drawing a homily out of one of the Old Testament narratives. Neither approach is necessarily wrong, but each has a different purpose and different "rules of engagement," *per se*. Elder Dallin H. Oaks made this point:

> For us, the scriptures are not the ultimate source of knowledge, but what precedes the ultimate source. The ultimate knowledge comes by revelation. . . .
>
> The word of the Lord in the scriptures is like a lamp to guide our feet (see Ps. 119:105), and revelation is like a mighty force that increases the

lamp's illumination manyfold. We encourage everyone to make careful study of the scriptures and . . . to prayerfully seek personal revelation to know their meaning for themselves. . . .

Such revelations are necessary because, as Elder Bruce R. McConkie of the Quorum of the Twelve observed, "Each pronouncement in the holy scriptures . . . is so written as to reveal little or much, depending on the spiritual capacity of the student" (*A New Witness for the Articles of Faith*, Salt Lake City: Deseret Book Co., 1985, p. 71). . . .

. . . Elder Bruce R. McConkie [also] said, "I sometimes think that one of the best-kept secrets of the kingdom is that the scriptures open the door to the receipt of revelation" (*Doctrines of the Restoration*, ed. Mark L. McConkie, Salt Lake City: Bookcraft, 1989, p. 243). This happens because scripture reading puts us in tune with the Spirit of the Lord. . . .

. . . Many of the prophecies and doctrinal passages in the scriptures have multiple meanings. The Savior affirmed that fact when he told his disciples that the reason he taught the multitude in parables was that this permitted him to teach them "the mysteries of the kingdom of heaven" (Matt. 13:11) while not revealing those mysteries to the multitude. His parables had multiple meanings or applications according to the spiritual maturity of the listener. They had a message for both children and gospel scholars. . . .

Those who believe the scriptural canon is closed typically approach the reading of scriptures by focusing on what was meant at the time the scriptural words were spoken or written. In this approach, a passage of scripture may appear to have a single meaning and the reader typically relies on scholarship and historical methods to determine it.

The Latter-day Saint approach is different. . . .

. . . "In the wise words of St. Hilary, . . . 'Scripture consists not in what one reads, but in what one understands.'" . . .

. . . One trouble with commentaries is that their authors sometimes focus on only one meaning, to the exclusion of others. As a result, commentaries, if not used with great care, may illuminate the author's chosen and correct meaning but close our eyes and restrict our horizons to other possible meanings. Sometimes those other, less obvious meanings can be the ones most valuable and useful to us as we seek to understand our own dispensation and to obtain answers to our own questions. This is why the teaching of the Holy Ghost is a better guide to scriptural interpretation than even the best commentary.[8]

Elder Oaks added that "scripture is not limited to what it meant when it was written but may also include what that scripture means to a reader today."[9]

I could not agree more with Elder Oaks's point. While there is value in scholarly commentaries (and we shall draw upon many in this text), there is also great value in an openness to applications beyond "what was meant at the time the scriptural words were spoken or written."[10] Thus, our purpose here will be to find meaning and personal application in the stories of the miracles preserved for us on the pages of the Old Testament. I will *not* seek a singular dogmatic interpretation or application. *Nor* will it be my intention to suggest what the ancients necessarily saw in or meant by a given miracle. Rather, we will look at various potential applications of the miracles and their surrounding storylines and how they relate to the lives of those of us living in "the dispensation of the fulness of times" (D&C 124:41). My target audience is the laity of the Church—not the scholars. And instead of a scholarly or academic treatment of these miracle narratives, what I offer here is a series of homilies—ways to apply the passages to our lives—fodder for the teacher and preacher. I acknowledge that this is but one approach to these miraculous events; but it is one that many have personally found meaning and benefit from.[11] Remember the prophet Nephi's familiar declaration, "I did liken all scriptures unto us, that [they] might be for our profit and learning" (1 Nephi 19:23). This is the task in which I seek to engage. Thus, the following should be understood and kept in mind as you digest the concepts presented in the pages of this book:

- What I am offering here is a modern application of an ancient story. In other words, while the original author may not have intended for us to see symbolism in a given miracle story, there are some interesting and thought-provoking analogies which can be drawn from these miracles. Thus, what this book seeks to present is not necessarily what the ancients saw in these stories; but, instead, what you and I can draw from them by way of modern applications. As one commentator pointed out, "So long as we claim this only as an illustration of a great biblical truth, and not as an exegesis of the passage before us, this is fair enough."[12] This is important for you to understand, both as you read this book, and as you look for applications for yourself.[13]

- In addition, as Elder Oaks suggested, the commentary from various authors that I have offered herein should not be seen as the *only* way to apply these miracles, nor should it necessarily be seen as the best or most correct way. But what others have said about these miracles and their applications serves the purpose of getting you and me to think about these stories and what they might potentially offer by way of application to the lives of those of us living thousands of years after these stories were initially penned.

- As to sources, I've relied on several types of sources. I have drawn freely from scholarly commentaries for insights into the historical and linguistic portions of the miracles. I've depended on modern homiletic commentators for their applications of these events to our day.[14] And I've often pulled from the writings of the fathers of the early Church because of their tendency to see symbolic applications in the miracles of the Bible. While I do not hold any of these texts as necessarily authoritative, I offer them here because of the profundity of their insights and applications. I have not drawn on non-LDS sources for doctrine, nor do I present non-LDS views regarding the symbolism and application of these miracles as dogmatic interpretations—only as insights worthy of consideration.

- A distinction should be made between the historical meaning of an event, what that event symbolizes, and what analogies or allegories might be drawn from that event. The historical meaning is what the event meant for those of the pre-Christian era who actually witnessed the miracle. (This is not so much our focus herein.) The symbolic meaning would be what the author who penned the story was trying to teach his audience. (I have occasionally pointed these out, particularly as other commentators have highlighted such meanings.) Analogies and allegories are those things that you and I may draw from these stories as personal applications. (These are the primary focus of this text.) Our modern analogies and allegorizations may be such that they would be completely foreign to those living in Old Testament times. To say that they are what was meant by the original author would in some circumstances be inaccurate at best and dishonest (or misrepresentative) at worst. Thus, we are careful to emphasize here that the analogies and allegories presented in this book are simply modern applications. This book is largely *not* about how the ancients saw these events, nor about what they meant for those living in the pre-Christian era. We are simply asking the questions: "How can a given miracle apply to my life today?" or "How can it teach me principles for the twenty-first century?" But, as the reader, you should be careful to distinguish between the historical event, the ancient symbolic connotation, and the modern applications and allegorizations offered herein.

• The commentary on each miracle follows a consistent pattern. In order, we will look at the following things for each of the narratives examined:

> SCRIPTURAL CITATIONS: At the beginning of each section, I have offered the scriptural references where the miracle is recorded in the Old Testament. When a miracle is recorded in multiple places, or is referred to in a significant way in the New Testament, I have listed each of the scriptural references at the beginning of a given section.

> SUMMARY OF THE MIRACLE: Rather than citing the actual scriptural text, I have summarized each miracle. This became necessary for two reasons. First, some of the miracles appear in more than one Old Testament book—and not all scriptural authors give all of the details. Thus, it seemed important to offer a harmony or summary of each miracle that included the insights of each of those who recorded it. Second, a summary seemed helpful in the case of those miracles where the King James Version (commonly used by Latter-day Saints) was not very clear. Thus, we summarized the text and, in so doing, sought to present the more difficult sections in clearer language.

> BACKGROUND ON THE MIRACLE: This section deals less with the symbolism and more with the historic, geographic, cultural, or linguistic insights into each miracle. This is offered more by way of clarification and less with the intent of seeking application.

> SYMBOLIC ELEMENTS: In this section, I list various common symbols employed in the miracle under examination: symbols that appear in the story but that have familiar or well-known meanings aside from the miracle being discussed.

APPLICATION AND ALLEGORIZATION: This portion of the commentary offers insights into what ancient, medieval, and modern commentators have seen by way of personal application in these miracles. These are offered nondogmatically. They are intended only as springboards to encourage you to think about ways you might apply these miracles to your personal life or to the lives of those whom you teach.

Now, before we begin our foray into a study of the symbolic meaning of the Old Testament miracles, I need to impress upon the reader my personal witness that the greatest of all miracles is the Atonement of the Lord Jesus Christ. Unfathomable as God's love is, and as incomprehensible as Christ's passion is, they encompass all other miracles and supersede them all. In many ways, we will discuss the Atonement in the pages of this book, and in the context of the other miracles examined here. But, unlike so many of the miracle stories of the Old Testament, the application of Jesus's Atonement—wrought on our behalf—is not metaphorical. It is real, necessary, and salvific; and because of its sacred nature, we will make no attempt to allegorize or spiritualize it here. But it is my hope that our discussion of the many other miracles Jesus brought to pass (through the prophets and patriarchs of the Hebrew Bible) will bring a greater sense of appreciation for that Ultimate Miracle in the lives of all who read this work.

NOTES

1. See Sidney Greidanus, *Preaching Christ from the Old Testament: A Contemporary Hermeneutical Method* (Grand Rapids, MI: Eerdmans, 1999), 39. The Book of Mormon speaks of Christians many decades before the birth of Jesus (see Alma 46:13–16 and Alma 48:10). To many, these passages imply a "Christian view" of the pre-New Testament Church and, thus, of the people of the Hebrew Bible.

2. Augustine, "On Eighty-Three Varied Questions," 65, quoted in Joel C. Elowsky, ed., *New Testament 4b; John 11–21*, in *Ancient Christian Commentary on Scripture* (Downers Grove, IL: InterVarsity Press, 2007), 25.

3. Herbert Lockyer, *All the Miracles of the Bible: The Supernatural in Scripture— Its Scope and Significance* (Grand Rapids, MI: Zondervan, 1961), 15. Lockyer also noted that the miracles were visible emblems of what Jesus is and what He came to do for each of us. (See Lockyer, *All the Miracles of the Bible*, 15.)

4. Charles L. Swift, doctrinal dissertation, *"I Have Dreamed a Dream": Typological Images of Teaching and Learning in the Vision of the Tree of Life* (Provo, Utah: Brigham Young University, 2003), 115n33.

5. "Exegesis" means to "draw out" the meaning of a text. An "exegetical" approach, therefore, is one that seeks to "draw out" of a text the meaning and/or application intended by the original author who penned the text. (See *Encyclopedia of Christianity*, ed. John Bowden [New York: Oxford, 2005], 1332.)

6. See Greidanus (1999), 80–96; *The Oxford Dictionary of the Christian Church*, eds. Frank Lloyd Cross and Elizabeth A. Livingstone, 2nd ed. (New York: Oxford University Press, 1990), s.v. "exegesis"; *Encyclopedia of Christianity*, ed. John Bowden (New York: Oxford, 2005), 552; Joseph W. Trigg, "Allegory," in *Encyclopedia of Early Christianity*, ed. Everett Ferguson (New York: Garland Publishing, 1990); Fredrick W. Norris, "Antioch," in Ferguson *Encyclopedia of Early Christianity*, 54.

7. Luke Timothy Johnson, *Sacra Pagina: The Acts of the Apostles* (Collegeville, Minnesota: The Liturgical Press, 1992), 155. While I acknowledge that a fifth- or sixth-century source does not tell us how the first-century Church read scripture, it does seem quite clear that the New Testament Church read the Old Testament—which was their "scripture"—in very symbolic and Christocentric ways, thus giving us some sense of their tendency to see scripture as symbolic and typological. That being said, we are not here arguing for an ancient interpretation. What we are saying is that, just as many ancients read the scriptures symbolically—as the New Testament often does of the Old, the Rabbis did of the Hebrew Bible, and the early post-New Testament Christians did of the Bible generally—we too will look for messages of application that can be drawn from the texts generally, and from their symbols specifically.

8. Dallin H. Oaks, "Scripture Reading and Revelation," *Ensign*, January 1995. See also Charles L. Swift, "Three Stories," in *My Redeemer Lives!* eds. Richard Neitzel Holzapfel and Kent P. Jackson (Provo, UT: Brigham Young University Religious Studies Center and Deseret Book, 2011), 125–46.

9. Oaks, "Scripture Reading and Revelation."

10. Oaks, "Scripture Reading and Revelation." Regarding sources, we have largely drawn upon two types of commentaries for the writing of this text: homiletic and scholarly. Some of our homiletic commentators are ancient or medieval, and some are modern. (Authors from very early on in the history of the Christian church saw the value in a homiletic and symbolic reading of these miracle stories.) While academicians sometimes don't like—or don't see as legitimate—homiletic commentaries, because of our stated purpose in this book, those really *are* the most appropriate for engaging in a discussion about modern applications. We have also employed a handful of scholarly commentaries, in part because of their historical, cultural, or linguistic insights into the text, but also because they too sometimes offer symbolic insights into the text. Hence our mixture of sources, which to some, no doubt, seem like rather strange bedfellows.

11. One commentator noted: "In some circles these days, it has fallen out of style to speak of biblical types. . . . The abuse of typology in former generations, where

every spiritual lesson one might derive from a text was declared to be a 'type,' has led to a gradual but sure reaction against typology of any kind. Yet the idea of typology is a factor of the text of Scripture, not an innovation of 'creative' interpretation." (Ronald B. Allen, "Numbers," in Frank E. Gaebelein, ed., *The Expositor's Bible Commentary*, vol. 2 [Grand Rapids, MI: Zondervan, 1990], 2:878–79.) Indeed, for this very reason, the Book of Mormon declares: "Therefore, if ye teach the law of Moses, also teach that it is a shadow of those things which are to come" (Mosiah 16:14).

12. R. Alan Cole, *Exodus*, in *Tyndale Old Testament Commentaries* (Downers Grove, IL: InterVarsity Press, 1973), 129.

13. While we will offer occasional points of clarification as they relate to language, culture, or history surrounding these miracles, this work is *not* intended as a historical analysis of the facts, nor as a scholarly examination of the miracles. To read what we've done here as such would be to entirely miss the point of this work. We acknowledge that for some academics such an approach will be frustrating. Nevertheless, we personally see value in asking "How does this speak to me personally, owing to the circumstances in my life today?" And so, rather than asking "What did this mean for the first-century Church?" our question will be "What can I see in this for my life *today*?"

14. A number of the scholarly commentaries I used also interpreted these miracle stories in symbolic ways—occasionally finding modern application in the ancient accounts and with the intent of promoting application among readers of the scriptural texts.

Sarah's Conception

Genesis 17:15–19; 18:10–14; 21:1–8

The Miracle

In his hundredth year of life—and when his wife was ninety years of age—Abraham received a promise from God that He would bless Sarah that she would deliver a son and would become "a mother of nations" (Genesis 17:16).

Upon hearing God's promise, Abraham fell upon his face and "rejoiced" (JST Genesis 17:23) that a child would be born to them when they were of such advanced years. Sarah, on the other hand, "laughed within herself" when she heard God's pledge (Genesis 18:12. See also Genesis 18:10; 19:6), forgetting that nothing is "too hard for the Lord" (Genesis 18:14. Cf. Luke 1:37).[1]

Upon revealing His intent, God commanded Abraham to name the child Isaac, and the Lord promised to establish His "everlasting covenant" (Genesis 17:7) with the patriarch's soon-to-be-born son and with his posterity after him.

Background

God's promise that Sarah "shall be a mother of nations" (Genesis 17:16) was quite literally fulfilled via Ishmael (through whom the Arabs are traditionally believed to have descended) and through Isaac (from whence the Jews are believed to have sprung). But, more important, God's promise that "kings of people shall be of her" (Genesis 17:16) was fulfilled, not only in the life of men like King David, but also through the King of the Jews—even Jesus the Christ. Both of these men were literal descendants of Abraham and Sarah. Perhaps Sarai's new name,[2] "Sarah" (meaning "princess," "priestess," or "chieftainness"), foreshadowed this.[3]

The King James Version (KJV) states that Abraham "laughed" at the announcement that ninety-year-old Sarah would have a baby. However, the Joseph Smith Translation (JST) changes the verb to "rejoiced," which is in harmony with the sense of the Hebrew. Ambrose, the fourth-century bishop of Milan, explained it this way: "The fact that Abraham laughed when he had been promised a son through [Sarah] was an expression not of unbelief but of joy. Indeed, he 'fell on his face'—in worship, which means he believed."[4]

While both Abraham and Sarah are depicted as "laughing" (in the KJV), only Sarah's "laughter was met with divine disapproval," confirming what most commentators suspect; namely that Abraham "rejoiced," while Sarah initially laughed in "doubt."[5]

Symbolic Elements

Barrenness is a standard symbol in scripture. The ancients believed that to be barren was to be cursed. Symbolically, to be fruitful is to be blessed. One dictionary of biblical imagery explains:

> Barrenness in the Bible is an image of lifelessness, where God's redemptive blessing is absent. . . .
>
> The image of the barren wife is one of the Bible's strongest images of desolation and rejection. . . .
>
> Conversely, few images of joy can match that of the barren wife who becomes pregnant. To the psalmist a supreme blessing of God is his settling "the barren woman in her home as a happy mother of children. Praise the Lord" (Ps 113:9). . . .
>
> In the covenant with ancient Israel, God pronounced blessing for the covenant obedience in terms of fertility, and curse for covenant disobedience in terms of barrenness:
>
>> If you fully obey the Lord your God and carefully follow all his commands I give you today, . . . The fruit of your womb will be blessed, and the crops of your land and the young of your livestock. . . . However, if you do not obey the Lord your God . . . The fruit of your womb will be cursed, and the crops of your land, and the calves of your herds and the lambs of your flocks. (NIV Deut 28:1–4, 15–18)
>
> The prophets later use the imagery of barrenness to indict God's people for their sin of disobeying the covenant. . . .

Jesus Christ is the consummation of God's plan to resurrect humanity from the lifelessness of sin. His lineage is traced through unexpected births to barren women, starting with Sarah . . . and finally from the innocent barrenness of his virgin mother, Mary (Mt 1:1–16). Throughout redemptive history God transforms barrenness and frustrated fertility into the fruit of eternal life.[6]

Thus, in this narrative, Sarah is a perfect image for how Christ reaches into the lives of God's children and performs miracles so that their spiritual barrenness might be cured and the fruitfulness of faith might be developed in them.

The name Isaac is most commonly translated as "he laugheth" or "to laugh."[7] That being said, the word "Isaac" and the word "rejoice" come from the same Hebrew root, and the name Isaac carries the connotation of rejoicing.[8] Thus, the boy was appropriately named, as his birth gave Abraham and Sarah reason to rejoice that God's promises to them had been fulfilled.

APPLICATION AND ALLEGORIZATION

An obvious application is to be found in the reality that Sarah desperately wanted children, and had been given a promise from God that she *would* be a mother, and yet she was still childless many years past menopause. It seemed that God's promises to one as faithful as Sarah would certainly go unfulfilled. And yet God kept His word. Much later than she expected, she bore a son—and billions upon billions were descendants of Sarah and Abraham. And so, for those women who themselves doubt God's promises of posterity, this miracle reminds us that if we—like Sarah—remain faithful, God will provide.[9] Those who are barren in this life, if faithful to covenants, have the promise that they will be the mother or father of nations and kings. One sister who struggled with infertility pointed out that the scriptures enabled her to put her personal trial in a gospel context. She wrote:

> From Abraham's wife, Sarah . . . I learned that miracles do happen, that nothing is "too hard for the Lord" (Genesis 18:14), and that the Lord's timing is critical. I learned that even when we think the time has completely passed for a miracle to occur in our lives, it still can: "For Sarah conceived, and bare Abraham a son in his old age, at the set time of which God had spoken to him" (Genesis 21:2).
>
> From Isaac's wife, Rebekah, I learned I needed to keep trusting in the words of my patriarchal blessing, recognizing that blessings aren't always fulfilled in mortality or in the ways we expect. . . .

From Elkanah's wives, Hannah and Peninnah, I learned some unexpected lessons (1 Samuel 1:1–21). I instantly empathized with Hannah because of her childlessness, but I soon realized she wasn't the only one suffering. I was moved by Hannah's pain in her barrenness, Elkanah's pain in Hannah's unhappiness, and Peninnah's pain in her loneliness, which dese her many children must have been great as she understood she was less loved by her husband than was Hannah. From Hannah and Peninnah, I understood that we each have trials and challenges; we each have secret sorrows and pain. Was Hannah's pain in her barrenness greater than Peninnah's pain in her loneliness? . . . I suddenly realized that I wouldn't trade trials with Peninnah. For me, it was a revelation.

I learned from Hannah's despair that it makes no sense to let gratitude for the blessings we do have be crowded out by sorrow over the one thing we lack. I wondered if Hannah recognized how blessed she was in her marriage, despite her childlessness. Her husband, Elkanah, wondered the same: "Hannah, why weepest thou? and why eatest thou not? and why is thy heart grieved? am not I better to thee than ten sons?" (1 Samuel 1:8). We each have joys in life despite our trials; what a waste to fail to notice or cherish or celebrate all the reasons we do have to rejoice. . . .

From Zacharias's wife, Elisabeth, I learned that infertility was not God's punishment for my imperfections, weaknesses, or unworthiness to be a mother. In Luke, we find that Zacharias and Elisabeth "were both righteous before God, walking in all the commandments and ordinances of the Lord blameless. . . ." (Luke 1:6–7).

Elisabeth remained steadfast and immovable despite the fact that her dreams of motherhood went unfulfilled for so many years. How could Elisabeth have known during those long years of waiting that she would one day become the mother of the forerunner to Jesus Christ? From Elisabeth, I learned patience and faithful endurance, and I learned that God's plan for our lives might just be greater than we could ever imagine.

From all of these women in the scriptures, I learned that I was not alone in my heartache; other women who had gone before knew just how I felt, and surely there were others surrounding me who knew as well. Most of all, the Savior knew; not only could He comfort me in my burden of sorrow, but He could ease it for me as Isaiah promised: "Surely he hath borne our griefs, and carried our sorrows" (Isaiah 53:4).

Further, Isaiah 54 taught me about joy. I knew this passage of scripture had a larger, deeper meaning encompassing the redemption of Zion, but as I searched for understanding and continued to liken the scriptures to myself, I learned that it would still be possible to find joy *even if I never had children.* I clung to the fact that the Lord spoke of mercies and kindnesses—and above all, peace—for both the barren woman and the children her future eventually held.[10]

As crushing as the trial of infertility is, God's promises are sure, and this miracle is a testament to that fact! The Prophet Joseph promised: "All your losses will be made up to you in the Resurrection, provided you continue faithful. By the vision of the Almighty I have seen it."[11] Appropriately, one Talmudic scholar wrote: "The birth of Isaac was a happy event, and not in the house of Abraham alone. The whole world rejoiced, for God remembered *all* barren women at the same time with Sarah."[12]

Barrenness is not only a meaningful symbol for the childless mother, but also for each of us who struggle with sin and obedience. One commentary on this passage states:

> There are times in our lives when we are barren. We may be spiritually unfruitful. But Christ has power to engender new life within us. He can bring to pass miracles in lives that seem past their time. He can take us from spiritual sterility to surprising fertility. "In the barren deserts" he can bring forth "pools of living water," and the "parched ground" of our souls "shall no longer be a thirsty land" (D&C 133:29).[13]

Sarah's infertility can serve as a great symbol for the struggles that each of us has at times with spiritual barrenness. Just as she struggled to have offspring, there are times in each of our lives when we struggle to connect with the Lord and, thus, we do little to build the kingdom and our own testimonies. But God was able to heal Sarah's womb, and He has the power to heal our souls too—enabling us to give birth to much good in the world, in the Church, and in our own lives. When overwhelmed by addictive sins and the consequent hopelessness that we feel that we will never overcome, rather than doubting, we must believe that nothing is "too hard for the Lord" (Genesis 18:14. Cf. Luke 1:37). If God could enable Sarah to overcome her barrenness, He can do the same for each of us in our spiritual barrenness. He can make us spiritually fruitful.

In the late fourth century, John Chrysostom tackled the symbolism in this miracle, explaining what he saw as the ultimate meaning of Sarah's barrenness. He wrote: "Do you wish to learn the symbolic meaning of Sarah's sterility? The church was to bring forth the multitude of believers. . . . Sarah became a type of the Church. For just as she gave birth in her old age when she was barren, so too the church, though barren, has given birth for these, the final times."[14] Latter-day Saints might find particular significance in Chrysostom's application, as we often see Christianity as having gone through a long period during which the fulness of the gospel was absent. In that sense, it might be appropriate to symbolically see Christianity's barrenness depicted. But then, when the gospel was some 1,800 years of age, God restored it, and the Church became fruitful again. Now the Church brings forth "multitudes." While the Church was required to wait many years for the day when it would see the fulfillment of the promises of God, because of the Restoration, those divine assurances are being fulfilled and the bride of Christ is no longer barren.

NOTES

1.   See Ramban Nachmanides, *Commentary on the Torah* (New York: Shilo Publishing House, 1971), 1:221.

2.   The concept of a new "name" (*shêm*) in Hebrew suggests a "memorial, mark, token, and sign of true identity; a revelatory token of the divine essence, meaning, and purpose of one's life and true identity standing before God." Kent J. Hunter, personal correspondence, May 26, 2017.

3.   See Francis Brown, S. R. Driver, and Charles A. Briggs, *The Brown-Driver-Briggs Hebrew and English Lexicon* (Peabody, MA: Hendrickson Publishers, 1999), 979; Ellen Frankel and Betsy Platkin Teutsch, *The Encyclopedia of Jewish Symbols* (Lanham, MD: Rowman & Littlefield Publishers, 1995), 143. See also D. Kelly Ogden and Andrew C. Skinner, *Verse By Verse—The Old Testament Volume One: Genesis through 2 Samuel, Psalms* (Salt Lake City, UT: Deseret Book, 2013), 1:102; John H. Sailhamer, "Genesis," in Frank E. Gaebelein, ed., *The Expositor's Bible Commentary*, vol. 2 (Grand Rapids, MI: Zondervan, 1990), 2:139. Kent Hunter suggested, "Although translators have used 'princess' [as the primary meaning of the name Sarah], it doesn't really capture what is meant to be conveyed by the Hebrew. According to some [Jewish sources], "chieftainess" or "priestess" reflect much better the idea being conveyed [by the Hebrew], and [these alternate renderings of the name] fit beautifully with Sarah's ancient designation as a 'seeress' and [they offer] fascinating hints to her service, with Abraham, as something of a temple matron." (Kent J. Hunter, personal correspondence, April 19, 2017.)

4.   Ambrose, "On Abraham," 1.4.31, quoted in Mark Sheridan, ed., "17:15–21 The Promise of Isaac," in *Genesis 12–50*, in *Ancient Christian Commentary on Scripture* (Downers Grove, IL: InterVarsity Press, 2002), 58.

5.   See Sailhamer, in Gaebelein, *The Expositor's Bible Commentary*, 2:139–40.

6.   Leland Ryken, James C. Wilhoit, and Tremper Longman III, eds., *Dictionary of Biblical Imagery* (Downers Grove, IL: InterVarsity Press, 1998), 75.

7.   See Judson Cornwall and Stelman Smith, *The Exhaustive Dictionary of Bible Names* (Alachua, FL: Bridge-Logos Publishers, 1998), 84; Brown, Driver, and Briggs, *The Brown-Driver-Briggs Hebrew and English Lexicon*, 850.

8.   See E. A. Speiser, *The Anchor Bible: Genesis*, vol. 1 (New York: Doubleday, 1962), 125; J. H. Hertz, *The Pentateuch and Haftorahs*, 2nd edition (London: Soncino Press, 1962), 59; Nachmanides, *Commentary on the Torah*, 1:221–22; Ogden and Skinner, *Verse By Verse—The Old Testament*, 1:103.

9.   Sister Patricia Holland wrote, "As I tenderly acknowledge the very real pain that many single women, or married women who have not borne children, feel about any discussion of motherhood, could we consider this one possibility about our eternal female identity—our unity in our diversity? Eve was given the identity of 'the mother of all living'—years, decades, perhaps centuries before she ever bore a child. It would appear that her *motherhood preceded her maternity*, just as surely as the perfection of the Garden preceded the struggles of mortality. I believe *mother* is one of those very carefully chosen words, one of those rich words—with meaning after meaning after meaning. We must not, at all costs, let that word divide us. I believe with all my heart that it is first and foremost a statement about our nature, not a head count of our children." (Patricia T. Holland, "'One Thing Needful': Becoming Women of Greater Faith in Christ," *Ensign*, October 1987; emphasis in original.)

10.   Carolynn R. Spencer, "Learning to Cope with Infertility," *Ensign*, June 2012; emphasis in original.

11.   Joseph Smith, in *Teachings of the Prophet Joseph Smith*, comp. Joseph Fielding Smith (Salt Lake City, UT: Deseret Book, 1976), 296. See also Andrew F. Ehat and Lyndon W. Cook, comps., *The Words of Joseph Smith* (Provo, UT: Religious Studies Center, Brigham Young University, 1980), 195–97.

12.   Louis Ginzberg, *The Legends of the Jews*, vol. 1 (Philadelphia: The Jewish Publication Society of America, 1967), 1:261; emphasis added.

13.   Donald W. Parry and Jay A. Parry, *Symbols and Shadows: Unlocking a Deeper Understanding of the Atonement* (Salt Lake City, UT: Deseret Book, 2009), 104.

14.   John Chrysostom, "Do Not Despair," quoted in Mark Sheridan, ed., "21:1–7 The Birth of Isaac," *Genesis 12–50*, in *Ancient Christian Commentary on Scripture* (Downers Grove, IL: InterVarsity Press, 2002), 90.

THE SODOMITES
Are BLINDED

GENESIS 19:9–11

THE MIRACLE

Lot encountered three messengers of the Lord who had entered the city of Sodom. Worried about their safety overnight in this city of sin, Lot entreated them to spend the night in his home. The heaven-sent messengers accepted his invitation, and so he brought them into his abode and fed them.

Before the visitors and the family of Lot had retired to sleep, the "men of Sodom compassed the house" (Genesis 19:4) and began to bang on the door, demanding that Lot bring his three guests out to them that they might "know" them (Genesis 19:5). Lot went outside, shutting the door behind him, and told the sinful men of the city, "I pray you, brethren, do not so wickedly" (Genesis 19:7).

The men ordered Lot to get out of their way (JST Genesis 19:9). Offended by what they perceived as condescension, they essentially said, one to another, "Lot has come to dwell among us, and now he makes himself a judge of us. Well, we will deal more harshly with him than with his guests! And we shall do with Lot's daughters as seemeth us good!" (see JST Genesis 19:10–11).[1]

Lot, shocked by their wickedness—and fearful for the well-being of his family and his guests—begged the threatening men who surrounded his home to not do such wicked things to his daughters or his guests: "For God will not justify his servant in this thing" (JST Genesis 19:14. See also JST Genesis 19:13).

Lot's words only served to increase the anger of the already unruly mob. As they pressed forward to break down the door to Lot's home, the three messengers of God "pulled Lot into the house . . . and shut the door" behind them (JST Genesis 19:15).

Having secured Lot and his family within the house, the three messengers of God "smote the men that were at the door of the house with blindness . . . so that they wearied themselves to find the door" (Genesis 19:11).

BACKGROUND

The Joseph Smith Translation changes the King James Version from "two angels" to three "angels of God, which were holy men" (JST Genesis 19:15).

It has traditionally been assumed that the sister cities of Sodom and Gomorrah were situated somewhere on the southern coast of the Dead Sea, though the biblical text is silent on their exact location.[2] One commentator wrote, "There appears to be much evidence for the assertion that Sodom stood on the ground now covered by the Dead Sea, or Salt Sea."[3] Another wrote that Sodom "is usually thought to have lain south of the Lisan (the tongue-shaped peninsula on the eastern shore of the Dead Sea)."[4] Of course, all of this is conjecture. The text is simply unclear on the exact location of the famed sister cities.

While it is certain that homosexuality was one of the vices of Sodom,[5] there were other sins too. One commentary on scriptural symbolism points out that Sodom and Gomorrah,

> Are also cited explicitly as paradigms of what is ungodly. Most often a particular sin of Genesis 19 is not mentioned; rather, Sodom and Gomorrah serve as a byword for evil. They represent what is unnatural (Deut 32:32). Jerusalem is like them because of oppression and hollow religiosity (Is 1:10; 3:9; Jer 23:14). Jesus says that the nation's rejection of his message and person makes his audience guiltier than Sodom and Gomorrah (Mt 10:11–15; 11:20–24). For killing its divine messengers, the city of David in the future will be called Sodom (Rev 11:8). In two passages the comparison with Sodom and Gomorrah is based on a list of sins (Ezek 16:46–56; Jude 7). Sexual perversion does not appear in the prophetic list, but in the context the idolatrous activity of Israel and Judah is repeatedly pictured as promiscuity (Ezek 16:15–43). In Jude the sexual sin is clearly alluded to. So Sodom and Gomorrah represent self-destructive depravity, although the nature of the sin that is denounced varies from passage to passage.[6]

Sodom largely functions as an archetype for willful sin, rebelliousness, and evil. Book after biblical book draws upon its reader's memory of that city's sin in order to highlight and condemn evil.

The Hebrew word for "blindness" that is employed in this miracle appears in only one other place in the Bible (2 Kings 6:18), and it means a "sudden" and "temporary blindness," rather than a permanent blindness.[7] One commentator explained, "The rare word for blindness [used here] probably indicates a dazzled state, as of Saul on the Damascus Road."[8] Elsewhere we read: "The people who were at the entrance of the house, one and all, they [were] struck with blinding light . . . having extraordinary brightness. . . . A blinding flash emanating from angels . . . would induce immediate, if temporary, loss of sight, much like desert or snow blindness."[9]

SYMBOLIC ELEMENTS

One of the Lord's most common miracles was to heal blindness. Here, however, He does the exact opposite (via His appointed messengers). Where sight implies knowledge and perspective, blindness is a commonly employed symbol of being spiritually lost or deceived. One commentator noted: "Blindness had a special, symbolic meaning. . . . It symbolized moral and spiritual decay and apostasy."[10] *The Dictionary of Biblical Imagery* similarly states, "Figuratively, blindness refers to an inability to recognize the truth, usually a culpable condition."[11] Consequently, in scripture sin is frequently equated with "moral blindness"[12] and, thus, freedom from blindness is a symbol of redemption from sin. Receiving one's sight represents being born again. Jesus is the "light of the world" (John 8:12) to those who are in "darkness" (D&C 38:8), but only if they desire the "light." Clearly the men of Sodom were *not* seeking light, but rather, desired to propagate the darkness in which they happily dwelt.

APPLICATION AND ALLEGORIZATION

Willfull rebellion against God and one's covenants causes spiritual blindness. We all sin, and though we may not have recognized it at the time, we have all experienced, to some degree, the dulling effect that Lucifer's influence has upon our spiritual sensitivities. If we willfully sin, we—like the men in this miracle—will struggle to see and recognize the errors of our ways and the evils of our choices. One Jewish source interpreted the moral of the miracle this way: "Be not like Sodom, my children, which recognized not the angels of the Lord, that ye be not delivered into the hands of your enemies."[13] One of the most oft repeated concerns in the scriptures is this: "Eyes have they, but they see not" (Psalm 135:16. See also Isaiah 44:18; Jeremiah 5:21; Ezekiel 12:2; Matthew 13:15; Acts 28:27; Moses 6:27). Elder D. Todd Christofferson taught,

> The importance of having a sense of the sacred is simply this—if one does not appreciate holy things, he will lose them. Absent a feeling of reverence, he will grow increasingly casual in attitude and lax in conduct. He will drift from the moorings that his covenants with God could provide. His feeling of accountability to God will diminish and then be forgotten. Thereafter, he will care only about his own comfort and satisfying his uncontrolled appetites. Finally, he will come to despise sacred things, even God, and then he will despise himself.
>
> On the other hand, with a sense of the sacred, one grows in understanding and truth. The Holy Spirit becomes his frequent and then constant companion. More and more he will stand in holy places and be entrusted with holy things. . . .
>
> Be wise with what the Lord gives you. It is a trust.[14]

Just as the sinners in this miracle were struck blind, you and I can lose the ability to see clearly if we rebel against God, or if we ignore that light that is native to each of us from our birth. Nephi asks his brothers, Laman and Lemuel:

> How is it that ye are so hard in your hearts, and so blind in your minds . . . ?
>
> How is it that ye have not harkened unto the word of the Lord?
>
> How is it that ye have forgotten that ye have seen an angel of the Lord?
>
> Yea and how is it that ye have forgotten what great things the Lord hath done for us . . . ? (1 Nephi 7:8–11)

The answer to each of Nephi's questions is simply this: sin! Sin is how we forget, because sin *always* makes us blind to reality. It blinds us so that we cannot see the error of our ways, and it blinds us so that we forget the feelings and miracles we've experienced in the past. Sin prevents us from seeing things "as they really are" (Jacob 4:13); and, therefore, it entices us to live in abhorrent, unkind, immoral, and selfish ways. So this miracle attests, and so each of our lives has shown.

Lot had moved to "the cities of the plain, and pitched his tent toward Sodom" (Genesis 13:12) because "all the plain of Jordan . . . was well watered every where [*sic*]" and it was "even as the garden of the Lord" known as

Eden (Genesis 13:10). Of Lot's conscious choice to move there, one commentator noted, "Like Eve in Eden, [he] is tempted by what is 'pleasing to the eye' (Gen 3:6 NIV)."[15] An obvious application of this component of the miracle is the reality that you and I must never allow ourselves to dwell in or around sin—no matter how strong we believe ourselves to be. If we tolerate that which God rejects, eventually it will make its way into our lives. "First we kick it out the door, and then we let it sit on the porch. Soon enough, sin is inside warming itself by the fire, and our home is corrupted."[16] I am reminded of a young man I knew who, confident in his own strength, began to "hang out" with those having much lower standards than his own. His self-proclaimed purpose was to "Save the sinner!" However, over time he became enticed and sin entered his life. Today he is far from the Church and in violation of his covenants. Lot's choice to move toward (and eventually into) Sodom, placed him and his family in spiritual danger. We must learn the lesson of Lot, and be careful to what degree we allow the world into our lives and into the lives of those we love and have a duty to protect.[17]

One other application of this miracle seems evident and appropriate. The enemies of Lot are divinely prevented from seeing; and, thus, they grope along looking to destroy Lot, his family, and their friends. However, they fail because God intervened. For generations Latter-day Saints have declared, "Truth Will Prevail!" Just as God intervened on behalf of Lot and his family, God can intervene in our own lives. The Prophet Joseph Smith taught, that

> The Standard of Truth has been erected; no unhallowed hand can stop the work from progressing; persecutions may rage, mobs may combine, armies may assemble, calumny may defame, but the truth of God will go forth boldly, nobly, and independent, till it has penetrated every continent, visited every clime, swept every country, and sounded in every ear, till the purposes of God shall be accomplished, and the Great Jehovah shall say the work is done.[18]

He too can perform miracles for us, wherein our enemies are thwarted in their attempts to destroy God's work and harm our individual lives. While angels may not send a "flash of light" to impede our enemies, nevertheless, they can be blinded in other ways wherein they do not see, and, thus, cannot harm.[19] We must trust that God will accomplish this miracle, if and when it is needed. Indeed, "truth *will* prevail!"

Most of us, when we think of Sodom and Gomorrah, think of immorality and sexual sin. In referencing the lewd and pornographic society in which we live—a society in which men are governed by the lust of their eyes—Elder Neal A. Maxwell wrote:

> The spreading oil slick of pornography . . . carries with it terrible consequences such as bizarre and oppressive sexual behavior, child and spouse abuse, and ultimately a loss of the capacity to love. Unfortunately, there is no "superfund" available to underwrite the cleanup of this destructive ooze. In fact, the funding flows in just the opposite direction, as that ancient cartel of lust and greed has significant sway once again. Meanwhile those coated in the awful ooze of pornography are effectively beached, and on filthy shores. Spiritually speaking, they can never take wing again until the ooze is finally cleaned off—"every whit"![20]

Just as the "men of Sodom compassed [Lot's] house" and began to bang on the door, pornography is no longer a passive enemy. It aggressively seeks entrance into our homes and lives through many means. And like the oil slick that takes the unaware fowl by surprise—by potentially blinding, if not killing it—men and women who traverse (without caution) the wildlands of the Internet will surely be caught in the destructive filth that Elder Maxwell described as an "awful ooze" in our contemporary society, and the spiritual consequence will be no less destructive.

NOTES

1. The KJV suggests that Lot offered the mob his two virgin daughters if they would but leave his guests alone. This has caused many commentators to look upon Lot with a great deal of derision. While the JST resolves this issue, one commentator on the KJV has suggested that Lot may have been offering his daughters only rhetorically. In other words, it has been suggested that Lot had no intention to turn his virgin daughters over to the mob. He may have only been seeking to shock the men and, thereby, wake them up to the morally unthinkable nature of their proposed actions. "Was . . . the host's offer meant literally? Or was it meant rhetorically to shock the local men to their moral senses? . . . It may be—but we cannot be sure—that Lot in Gen. 19:8 seeks to shock the men of the city to their senses, by apparently offering for gang rape two young women whom they as 'my brothers' should recognize and treat as the daughters of a neighbor. . . . Lot's apparent offer would aim to show up the city dwellers' intentions against the visitors as even worse than the 'altogether' morally unthinkable act of the gang rape of a neighbor's daughter. Thus, by offering his daughters to those who should view them as their sisters, Lot may hope to awaken his neighbors to the common humanity they share with those whom they view only as strangers, therefore enemies, and therefore fit objects of their power." (J. Gerald Janzen, *Abraham and All the Families of the Earth: A*

Commentary on the Book of Genesis 12–50, in *International Theological Commentary* [Grand Rapids, MI: Eerdmans, 1993], 63–64.)

2. See Martin J. Mulder, "Sodom and Gomorrah," in David Noel Freedman, ed., *The Anchor Bible Dictionary: Judges*, vol. 6 (New York: Doubleday, 1992), 6:99, 101.

3. Herbert Lockyer, *All the Miracles of the Bible: The Supernatural in Scripture— Its Scope and Significance* (Grand Rapids, MI: Zondervan, 1961), 41. See also D. Kelly Ogden and Andrew C. Skinner (*Verse By Verse—The Old Testament Volume One: Genesis through 2 Samuel, Psalms* [Salt Lake City, UT: Deseret Book, 2013], 1:106), who state that this theory is "widely supported."

4. Joseph A. Fitzmyer, *The Anchor Bible: The Gospel According to Luke X–XXIV*, vol. 28 (New York: Doubleday, 1985), 1171.

5. See Daniel H. Ludlow, *A Companion to Your Study of the Old Testament* (Salt Lake City, UT: Deseret Book, 1981), 128; Leland Ryken, James C. Wilhoit, and Tremper Longman III, eds., *Dictionary of Biblical Imagery* (Downers Grove, IL: InterVarsity Press, 1998), 802–3; Janzen, *Abraham and All the Families of the Earth: A Commentary on the Book of Genesis 12–50*, 62.

6. Ryken, Wilhoit, and Longman, *Dictionary of Biblical Imagery*, 803.

7. J. H. Hertz, *The Pentateuch and Haftorahs*, 2nd edition (London: Soncino Press, 1962), 67; Francis Brown, S. R. Driver, and Charles A. Briggs, *The Brown-Driver-Briggs Hebrew and English Lexicon* (Peabody, MA: Hendrickson Publishers, 1999), 703.

8. Derek Kidner, *Genesis*, in *Tyndale Old Testament Commentaries* (Downers Grove, IL: InterVarsity Press, 1967), 145.

9. E. A. Speiser, *The Anchor Bible: Genesis*, vol. 1 (New York: Doubleday, 1962), 136, 139–40.

10. E. Keith Howick, *The Miracles of Jesus the Messiah* (St. George, UT: WindRiver Publishing, 2003), 182.

11. Ryken, Wilhoit, and Longman, *Dictionary of Biblical Imagery*, 99. This same source explains: "As such, it describes judges whose judgment is perverted because of bribes (Ex 23:8; Deut 16:19; Job 9:24), idolaters whose worship is illogical as well as wrong (Is 44:9–10) and people who simply do not want to know (Is 43:8). Such blindness to the truth and mental confusion could actually be the result of God's judgment on those who did not want to admit the truth and who therefore forfeit the ability to perceive it at their cost (Deut 28:28–29; Is 6:9–10; 29:9–10). This is true of the Israelites, both leaders (Is 56:10) and followers (Is 42:18–19). Only God in his mercy can reverse this condition (Is 29:18; 35:5; 42:16). Paul describes gradual blindness when he writes of those whose 'foolish hearts were darkened' (Rom 1:21). In another vein he talks of seeing poorly now in contrast to seeing perfectly in the life to come (1 Cor 13:12)."

12. The imagery of sight and blindness is especially prominent in the account of Jesus' earthly ministry. . . . Jesus performed miracles of giving sight to the blind. . . . Jesus described the religious leaders and teachers of his own generation in terms of blindness (Mt 15:14; 23:16–17, 19, 24, 26). . . . Those who rejected Jesus' words came under a judgment similar to that of Israel—a state of permanent blindness (Jn 12:40; cf. Rom 11:7–10). Although metaphorically blindness may describe mere ignorance (Rom 2:19), it usually carries the overtones of an unwillingness to face up to the truth (Jas 1:23–24). . . . Similarly, Christian believers who revert to their pre-Christian way are described as blind, not perceiving the contradiction expressed in their behavior (2 Pet 1:9; 1 Jn 2:11)." E.g., Deuteronomy 28:29; Job 12:25; Isaiah 59:10; Zephaniah 1:17; 1 Nephi 7:8; 13:27; 2 Nephi 9:32; D&C 38:7; Moses 6:27.

13. Louis Ginzberg, *The Legends of the Jews*, vol. 2 (Philadelphia: The Jewish Publication Society of America, 1967), 2:219.

14. D. Todd Christofferson, "A Sense of the Sacred," *CES Young Adult Fireside*, November 7, 2004, speeches.byu.edu/talks/d-todd-christofferson_sense-sacred/.

15. Ryken, Wilhoit, and Longman, *Dictionary of Biblical Imagery*, 803.

16. See Ogden and Skinner, *Verse By Verse—The Old Testament*, 1:105.

17. I am in no way suggesting that we ostracize those who believe differently than we do. I am only saying that one needs to be cautious to not place one's self in situations that might lead to temptation or sin. Regardless of whether those around us are LDS or not, we should each be conscious of the influence our surroundings have on our spirituality. And, where our environment—or those in it—might place us in a spiritually precarious situation, we should have the wisdom to withdraw, so that the Spirit of the Lord has no need to.

18. Joseph Smith, in *History of the Church of Jesus Christ of Latter-day Saints*, rev. ed., B. H. Roberts, ed., vol. 4 (Salt Lake City, UT: Deseret Book, 1978), 4:540.

19. It seems significant that, just as Lot's enemies were temporarily blinded, God also only temporarily blinds our enemies, as He ultimately desires their repentance and change. If they are willing to repent, He will grant them their spiritual sight again. If not, they will remain "blind" and will ultimately bring about their own destruction—as those of Sodom did.

20. Neal A. Maxwell, *That Ye May Believe* (Salt Lake City, UT: Bookcraft, 1992), 99.

Lot's Wife *Is* Turned *to* Salt

Genesis 19:15–28
Luke 17:28, 32

The Miracle

As mentioned previously, the name of the infamous city of Sodom has become synonymous with sin and depravity. So gross and blatant was their wickedness that God determined He could not save the community. Hence, Sodom was destroyed by fire that rained down from heaven.

Abraham's nephew, Lot, lived in Sodom, along with his wife and daughters. Just before the city's divine destruction, they were admonished by three angels (JST Genesis 19:1) to flee the city. The angels gave them a warning as they fled; namely, head to the mountains, but *do not* look back at Sodom or you will be consumed (Genesis 19:17).

As God's destruction of the city began, and as Lot's family fled their home, Lot's wife looked back upon Sodom and, consequently, was turned into "a pillar of salt" (Genesis 19:26).

Background

Lot was the son of Haran, Abraham's brother (Genesis 11:27). Thus, Lot was the patriarch's nephew. Abraham took Lot with him when he left Mesopotamia, and together they traveled to Canaan. After stays in Shechem, Bethel, Egypt, and then again in Bethel, Lot parted company with his uncle and went to the Jordan Valley (Genesis 13:11) prior to relocating to Sodom.[1]

The sixteenth-century *Sefer ha Yasher*[2] (19:52) refers to Lot's wife by the name of *Ado*—meaning "beautiful." However, even earlier, the thirteenth-century Jewish philosopher and exegete, Ramban Nachmanides, indicated that her name was *Edis* (i.e., Edith)—typically translated "prosperous in war."[3] Of course, the Bible offers no such detail, referring to her only as "Lot's wife."

The ancients often claimed to have seen Lot's wife's salinized corpse: the pillar of salt that was once a woman. Sometime in the first century of the Common Era, the Jewish historian, Flavius Josephus, wrote: "Lot's wife . . . was changed into a pillar of salt; for I have seen it, and it remains at this day."[4] Also in the first century, Clement of Rome—the first apostolic father of the Church—spoke of the pillar of salt that was once Lot's wife as still extant.[5] Likewise, in the second century, the Christian theologian Irenaeus wrote that the pillar "still endures," implying that he too had firsthand knowledge of the ancient monument to sin.[6] Today, nearly four thousand years after her salinization, there exists at Mount Sodom (along the southwestern side of the Dead Sea) a pillar of salt, limestone, and clay commonly referred to as "Lot's Wife." One would assume that the pillar thought by so many in the first century to be the remains of "Edith" was also a similar natural mineral formation, merely having the appearance of a human figure.

D. Kelly Ogden and Andrew Skinner offer an interesting conjecture as to the source of the fire that destroyed the city of Sodom. They write,

> Apparently Sodom and Gomorrah were destroyed by the Lord and/or other celestial beings appearing with their glory and consuming the depraved citizens of these cities. Jude 1:7 records simply that they were destroyed by "eternal fire." The prophet Joseph Smith used the phrase "eternal fire" to describe the unparalleled glory God possesses as well as the environment in which he dwells in order to teach that all corruption is consumed by it: "God Almighty Himself dwells in eternal fire. . . . 'Our God is a consuming fire.'"[7]

In other words, rather than this destruction being caused by a volcanic eruption or earthquake—as some have conjectured[8]—Ogden and Skinner see it as being caused by the same destructive force that will extinguish the wicked at the Second Coming: namely, the glory of God. The Jewish Talmudic scholar, Louis Ginzberg, made a similar argument, indicating that "the Shekinah," or glory of God, "had descended to work the destruction of the cities" of Sodom and Gomorrah.[9] While I do not know if their conjecture is correct, it would make sense in light of the fact that this miracle is traditionally seen as a type for the destruction of the wicked at Christ's return.

Finally, one commentary states that a careful reading of Luke 17:29–32 may suggest that Lot's wife didn't simply "look back" at Sodom, but may have actually "returned" to Sodom.[10] The Qur'an implies something similar, suggesting that she "lagged behind" (Surah 27:57).

Symbolic Elements

At the beginning of Genesis 19, the wickedness of Sodom is set in the darkness of night (Genesis 19:4–5). However, the rescue of Lot and his family takes place at daybreak (Genesis 19:15). Thus, the passage employs a symbolic image of light dispelling darkness.[11] The city had been saturated in sin and a dark spirit enveloped it. Still, by following the directions of their angelic guides, Lot and his family were able to break through the dark and follow the light.

The destruction of Sodom's wicked by fire raining down from heaven has been seen as a standard symbol of the destructive outpouring upon the unrighteous at the Second Coming of Christ.[12] Indeed, Jesus's counsel that we "Remember Lot's wife" (Luke 17:32) was given in a discourse about the destruction of the corrupt at His return.

Lot and his family are commanded to flee Sodom and run to the mountain (Genesis 19:17, 19). In scripture, mountains are often symbols for the temple.[13] Thus, fleeing to the "mountain" can symbolically remind us of our need to head to God's temple so that we might have protection from the world.

"Looking back" often symbolizes longing for something lost, or something given up. Hence, Lot's wife's glance back was more than a simple look, but a longing for what once was. One commentator noted: "God read the motive of her heart (19:26) and knew of her regret on having to leave the sinful pleasures of Sodom. . . . She left Sodom as a city, but Sodom was very much in her heart. She was deeply attached to the life she was compelled to relinquish."[14] Thus, though she headed toward the temple (or mountain), she had in no way come to love it as she loved the world (or Sodom).

Anciently, pillars often carried the connotation of spiritual strength and steadfastness.[15] Obviously Lot's wife was neither spiritually strong nor steadfast. *The Dictionary of Biblical Imagery* suggests that pillars that are freestanding bear "witness to [an] encounter with God."[16] The pillar of salt into which Lot's wife was turned was a "variation on this motif of the pillar as a memorial," suggesting that Lot's wife would stand as a testament to her own sins and the dangers of the path she chose.[17] She was a memorial to, or a reminder of, the dangers of sin and the need for spiritual strength and steadfastness.

Salt was an ancient symbol of preservation and covenant-making (Leviticus 2:13; Numbers 18:19; 2 Chronicles 13:5; Ezra 6:9; Ezekiel 16:4).[18] It was a required component of the meal offering and burnt offering under the law of Moses. As one commentator noted: "While leaven and honey cause corruption, salt is that which prevents it."[19] In antiquity, salt was used as a flavorer, an antiseptic, and also as a preservative. Those who were Christ's covenant people were called to make covenants that would preserve themselves and those they took the gospel to. For this reason, Christ commissioned His followers to be the "salt of the earth" (Matthew 5:13; 3 Nephi 12:13; D&C 101:39–40), and to have "salt in themselves" (Mark 9:49–50). Thus, salt is a symbol of covenants and also of permanence. In the case of Lot's wife, it was a symbol of covenants she had made and broken, and the permanence of the consequences of her choice. Thus, one commentator points out that, "In ancient treaty texts, salination of the earth is a symbol of judgment."[20] Salt was often associated with life, incorruptibility, fidelity, wisdom, the elect, purity, discretion, and strength.[21] Ironically, Lot's wife turned out to be the opposite of each of these attributes; and, thus, the pillar of salt that she was turned into stood as a memorial of her life of contradiction—running toward the temple but longing for the world. As one typologist suggested, the story of the Lord turning Lot's wife into salt symbolizes "God's power to change a blessing [represented by the salt] to a curse."[22] Such is what all covenants will become for those who willingly enter into them and then consciously break them.

APPLICATION AND ALLEGORIZATION

Lot's wife was not the only one to look back at Sodom. Abraham also looked back (Genesis 19:27–28), but without being destroyed. Thus, the way or reason for which Lot's wife looked back explains her destruction. As suggested above, looking wasn't the problem; but looking longingly was![23] Elder Neal A. Maxwell wrote: "Laman and Lemuel, like Lot's wife, looked back over their shoulder at Jerusalem, regretting the decision to leave— doubting the prophesied and impending fall of such a strong and seemingly invincible city."[24] One non-LDS source states: "Her disobedience seems partly to have arisen from an excessive attachment to the conveniences and enjoyments of this life."[25] Like Lot's wife, there is a percentage of Latter-day Saints who are never quite able to make a break with Babylon. They profess a love for the Lord, but they have a lingering desire to be part of the fallen, telestial world. They "decide to leave Babylon," but they "endeavor to keep a second residence there, or [they] commute on weekends."[26] This seemingly negative miracle story reminds all those who have made covenants that they cannot move toward God if they are looking longingly at the world. Each of us must get to the point that we can overcome the temptation that comes so natural to man—to look longingly at sin. We must focus our eyes on "the mountain of the Lord's house" (Isaiah 2:2) and the standards it represents. One commentator wrote: "Burnt and suffocated to death, [Lot's wife's] story remains as a solemn warning against disobedience of divine commands."[27] Converted Christians must break their heart of its longing for the world and sin, or their testimonies will not last and their exaltation will not be assured. Lot's wife well represents those who have been blessed with spiritual experiences, but who (at least to some degree) "[love] darkness rather than light, because their deeds [are] evil" (John 3:19).[28]

Focusing on the physical change of Lot's wife, one commentator wrote, "The ruling desires of the mind will be expressed in the transformation of the body."[29] In other words, the more we love the world, the more we take upon ourselves its countenance, whether that be darkness, worldliness, lasciviousness, or some other trait of that which we love. Similarly, if we love the Lord, it is His image that we will begin to develop in our countenance (Alma 5:14, 19). It is a telltale sign when a young man or young woman returns from a full-time mission and almost immediately slides back into the grooming standards of the world. When the gospel finds a place deep within our hearts, it changes us—even in our appearance and countenance. When our commitment to Christ is but superficial, that shallow level of conversion is evident even on the surface.

As we have noted above, pillars are testaments or memorials. The Apocrypha speaks of Lot's wife as "a standing pillar of salt [which] is a monument of an unbelieving soul" (Wisdom of Solomon 10:7). Such tends to be the case with all who give in to serious sin. Their lives become pillars, testaments, or memorials to the sins they have embraced and the consequences of those actions. Each of our lives, once over, will stand as a memorial to what we truly loved. So it was with Lot's wife, and so it will be for you and me. "Lot's wife was condemned for a *look*, but that look expressed [her] preference of her own will to the will of God."[30] You are writing your own biography by the way you live, and you have the opportunity to show your posterity that you love God and His ways. You can make yours a story that will influence those who come after you for good. Make it a story that God would want to read.

It has been said that Lot's wife "was a woman without decision, finding it hard to make decisions without looking back on what she had decided."[31] Many of us are this same way. Applying this miracle to the lives of the Saints, Elder Orson F. Whitney said, "Look to the future. Remember the past and its lessons, but do not live in it nor worship it, nor look longingly backward, as did Lot's wife, to her destruction. Look ahead! Do not think too much of the present, but wisely use it and improve it."[32] Often one of Satan's most functional tools is to get you and me to focus so much on what is behind us that we either don't accomplish much in the future, or can't forgive ourselves for the past. Thus, as Elder Whitney suggested, we must remember the lessons, but don't keep looking back; lest, like Lot's wife, we become paralyzed, incapable of moving forward.

The emphasis on salt in this miracle reminds us of another common application. As was noted earlier, salt is highly symbolic, and often associated with making covenants. One text notes: "References to salt's positive qualities emphasize its seasoning, preserving and purifying properties."[33] Since the Saints are to be "the salt of the earth," it seems appropriate to examine how we are to be the seasoning or flavoring, antiseptic or purifiers, and preservatives to the world.

- We are to bring "seasoning" to the world around us by adding spice and beauty to the communities in which we live. In addition, the gospel certainly gives our lives spice and beauty, as it does to the lives of all those with whom we share it. In Psalm 144:15 we read: "Happy is that people . . . whose God is the Lord." Jesus informed us: "I am come that they might have life, and that they might have it more abundantly" (John 10:10). Christ desires that we have the "abundant life," and the gospel was designed to bring us just that. As we live the gospel, we make the world around us a better place, and our lives also dramatically improve.

- The Saints are to function as an "antiseptic" or "purifier" in the world, in that one of our goals is to cleanse the world around us by the way we live and by the things we stand for. Doctrine and Covenants 123:13 states: "Therefore . . . we should waste and wear out our lives in bringing to light all the hidden things of darkness, wherein we know them; and they are truly manifest from heaven."

As we do this in our communities and in our country, we have the power to cleanse much of the evil that is readily accepted today. If we do not stand for what we know to be right, the spiritual diseases that are taking over our world will continue to grow and infect more and more people until you and I will find ourselves suffocated by that which we have allowed to grow around us.

- Christ's covenant people are also called to be "preservatives" in the world. We preserve ourselves and our families by living the gospel, but we also seek to preserve others by sharing the gospel with them, and by doing vicarious temple work for our deceased ancestors. Doctrine and Covenants 103:9 states: "For they were set to be a light unto the world, and to be the saviors of men." We are to be "saviours . . . on mount Zion" (Obadiah 1:21). If we don't redeem our dead, neither they nor we can be saved! (see D&C 128:15).

The Lord stated of His covenant people: "Verily, verily, I say unto you, I give unto you to be the salt of the earth; but if the salt shall lose its savor wherewith shall the earth be salted? The salt shall be thenceforth good for nothing, but to be cast out and to be trodden under foot of men" (3 Nephi 12:13). "Savor" is a food's designated or specified flavor or taste. The only way in which salt can lose its savor is by being contaminated. Similarly, if we allow ourselves to become contaminated, we will not be useful to the Lord. Lot's wife is a prime example of someone who had lost her savor. She was no longer a preservative, an antiseptic, or a flavorer in the world. Rather, she longed for Sodom more than she longed to be a Saint. Thus, rather than being the "salt of the earth," she was turned into a "pillar of salt" to memorialize her bad choice and the dangers set for each of us if we choose to follow her example.

Commenting on the Hebrew (Genesis 19:26 is often translated as, "His wife looked back *from behind him*"), the thirteenth-century Jewish exegete Ramban Nachmanides explained that Lot's wife looked back "from behind Lot, who was following them, acting as a rearguard for all his household, who were hurrying to be saved."[34] In this there is a message about parents. Parents have a duty to protect their families from the spiritual dangers in the world. We must live our lives in such a way that the Spirit of the Lord can direct us as we attempt to do so. And, like Lot—who brought up the rear— we need to be looking for the dangers, giving warnings as we see them, and doing all that we can to ensure that our families are protected from them.

In the story of this miracle, the messengers of God warn Lot and his family. Indeed, they urge them to remove themselves from the pending dangers of Sodom (Genesis 19:15–17). If we are striving to live in accord with God's commands and the dictates of His Spirit, His messengers will always warn us too. Whether those urgings come through the Holy Ghost or His living prophets, we will be warned of the dangers and pressed upon to flee them. President Boyd K. Packer taught: "It is not expected that you go through life without making mistakes, but you will not make a major mistake without first being warned by the promptings of the Spirit. This promise applies to all members of the Church."[35] Of course, it is our decision to make; will we obey?

Perhaps one last application should be drawn from the miracle of Lot's wife. She made a mistake. She did a very human thing, and thousands of years later we still talk about it. As suggested above, our choices haunt us—they follow us, even beyond the grave. However, because we are Christians, and because we seek to pattern our lives after our Savior, we need to be cautious that we do not turn others into Lot's wife. When a friend, acquaintance, spouse, child, or family member sins, we *must not* keep those sins alive by never letting them be forgotten. Jesus taught: "I, the Lord, will forgive whom I will forgive, but of you it is required to forgive all men" (D&C 64:10). The memory of Lot's wife's sin has made her ability to "move on" and seek forgiveness a virtual impossibility. To hold such things over the head of the repentant sinner is to deny the Atonement of Christ and His infinite grace. If we are to pattern our lives after the Lord's, we must learn to forgive and forget the mistakes of the past, just as He does. Let us never make it difficult for others to move on from their mistakes. When one repents, let us—with the Lord—remember those sins "no more" (D&C 58:42).

NOTES

1. Joseph A. Fitzmyer, *The Anchor Bible: The Gospel According to Luke X–XXIV*, vol. 28 (New York: Doubleday, 1985), 1170–71.

2. The *Sefer ha Yashar* (first published in 1552) is a Hebrew *midrash*, also known by the names *Toledot Adam* and *Dibre ha-Yamim be-'Aruk*. Scholars conjecture that it was likely written by a Jew in Spain or southern Italy in the early sixteenth century. It is certainly not the same text referred to in Joshua 10:13 and 2 Samuel 1:18.

3. See Ramban Nachmanides, *Commentary on the Torah*, vol. 1 (New York: Shilo Publishing House, 1971), 1:259. See also Isidore Singer, ed., *The Jewish*

Encyclopedia, vol. 8 (New York: Funk and Wagnalls Company, 1906), 8:186. The name *Edis* or *Edith* is variously translated: "prosperous in war," "riches of war," "spoils of war," "happy warfare," "rich gift," and even "joyous."

4.   Flavius Josephus, "Antiquities of the Jews," bk. 1, chap. 11 in William Whiston, trans., *The Complete Works of Josephus* (Grand Rapids, MI: Kregel Publications, 1999), 65.

5.   Clement of Rome, "The First Epistle of Clement to the Corinthians," in Alexander Roberts and James Donaldson, eds., *The Ante-Nicene Fathers*, vol. 1 (Peabody, MA: Hendrickson Publishers, 1994), 1:8.

6.   See Irenaeus, "Irenaeus Against Heresies," in Roberts and Donaldson, *The Ante-Nicene Fathers*, 1:505.

7.   D. Kelly Ogden and Andrew C. Skinner, *Verse By Verse—The Old Testament Volume One: Genesis through 2 Samuel, Psalms* (Salt Lake City, UT: Deseret Book, 2013), 1:106–7.

8.   See, for example, Fitzmyer, *The Anchor Bible: The Gospel According to Luke X–XXIV*, 1171.

9.   Louis Ginzberg, *The Legends of the Jews*, vol. 1 (Philadelphia: The Jewish Publication Society of America, 1967), 1:255.

10.   See Ogden and Skinner, *Verse By Verse—The Old Testament*, 1:105.

11.   See John H. Sailhamer, "Genesis," in Frank E. Gaebelein, ed., *The Expositor's Bible Commentary*, vol. 2 [Grand Rapids, MI: Zondervan, 1990], Sailhamer, in Gaebelein (1990), 2:156–57. See also Deuteronomy 29:23; Job 18:15; Psalm 11:6; Isaiah 9:2; 34:9; Ezekiel 38:22; Luke 17:29; Revelation 9:17–19; 14:10; 19:20; 20:10; 21:8.

12.   See Sailhamer, in Gaebelein, *The Expositor's Bible Commentary*, 2:157.

13.   See Hugh Nibley, *Enoch the Prophet* (Salt Lake City, UT: Deseret Book, 1986), 224; Leland Ryken, James C. Wilhoit, and Tremper Longman III, eds., *Dictionary of Biblical Imagery* (Downers Grove, IL: InterVarsity Press, 1998), 573; J. C. Cooper, *An Illustrated Encyclopaedia of Traditional Symbols* (London: Thames and Hudson, 1995), 110; Jack Tresidder, *Symbols and their Meanings* (London: Duncan Baird Publishers, 2000), 116.

14.   Herbert Lockyer, *All the Miracles of the Bible: The Supernatural in Scripture—Its Scope and Significance* (Grand Rapids, MI: Zondervan, 1965), 41.

15.   James Hall, *Dictionary of Subjects & Symbols in Art*, rev. ed. (New York: Harper & Row, 1979), 247; Tresidder, *Symbols and their Meanings*, 125.

16.   See Ryken, Wilhoit, and Longman, *Dictionary of Biblical Imagery*, 645.

17.   Ibid., 645.

18.   Patrick Fairbairn, *Typology of Scripture* (Grand Rapids, MI: Kregel Publications, 1989), 2:313; Kevin J. Conner, *Interpreting the Symbols and Types*, rev. ed. (Portland, OR: City Bible Publishing, 1992), 165. It should be noted, however, that "salt can

be used negatively or positively" in scripture, though the majority of its uses are positive. (See Ryken, Wilhoit, and Longman, *Dictionary of Biblical Imagery*, 752.)

19. Ada R. Habershon, *Study of the Types* (Grand Rapids, MI: Kregel Publications, 1974), 98.

20. J. Gerald Janzen, *Abraham and All the Families of the Earth: A Commentary on the Book of Genesis 12–50* (Grand Rapids, MI: Eerdmans, 1993), 64.

21. Cooper, *An Illustrated Encyclopaedia of Traditional Symbols*, 144. Another source states: "Salt" can be "a symbol of sterility or barrenness, often as a result of a curse due to a covenantial breach. . . . On the one hand there is Lot's unnamed wife, who bears children . . . but who becomes the very epitome of sterility and barrenness: a pillar of salt (Gen 19:26; cf. Lk. 17:32); on the other hand there is Abraham's wife Sarah, who is initially infertile but who ultimately becomes a 'mother of nations' (Gen 17:16)." (Ryken, Wilhoit, and Longman, *Dictionary of Biblical Imagery*, 557.)

22. Walter L. Wilson, *A Dictionary of Bible Types* (Peabody, MA: Hendrickson, 1999), 356. Said one source: "The Salt Sea (Dead Sea), the Valley of Salt and the City of Salt all connote death, desolation, despair and deserts. . . . Jeremiah associates . . . salt with a person who turns away from God (Jer 17:6)." (Ryken, Wilhoit, and Longman, *Dictionary of Biblical Imagery*, 752.) This interpretation of the salt applies well to Lot's wife.

23. See Neal A. Maxwell, *We Talk of Christ—We Rejoice in Christ* (Salt Lake City, UT: 1984), 120.

24. Ibid., 120. Similarly, Reynolds and Sjodahl penned this: "In addition to the frequency with which King Benjamin's reign was troubled with false prophets, there was another class, who, moved by the spirit of unrest, were also a source of perplexity to the king. They were those who left the Land of Lehi-Nephi with the righteous under Mosiah and still permitted their thoughts and affections to be drawn toward their former homes and old associations. Like Lot's wife they hankered for that which they had left behind. The natural consequence was that they were constantly agitating the idea of organizing expeditions to visit their old homes." (George Reynolds and Janne M. Sjodahl, *Commentary on the Book of Mormon*, vol. 2 [Salt Lake City, UT: Deseret Book, 1955–61], 107.)

25. Richard C. Trench, *Miracles and Parables of the Old Testament* (Grand Rapids, MI: Baker Book House, 1974), 2.

26. Neal A. Maxwell, *The Neal A. Maxwell Quote Book*, Cory H. Maxwell, comp. (Salt Lake City, UT: Deseret Book, 1997), 25.

27. Lockyer, *All the Miracles of the Bible: The Supernatural in Scripture—Its Scope and Significance*, 41

28. In a similar vein, one early Christian interpreted the sin of Lot's wife in a metaphorical way. He said of Lot's wife, "[She] represents the flesh. The flesh always looks to vices. When the soul is going toward salvation, it looks backward

and seeks pleasures. Concerning this, the Lord also said, 'No man putting his hand to the plow and looking back is fit for the kingdom of God.' He adds, 'Remember Lot's wife.' The fact that 'she became a little statue of salt' appears to be an open indication of her foolishness. Salt represents the wisdom that she lacked." ("Homilies on Genesis," 5.2, in Arthur A. Just Jr., ed., *Luke*, in *Ancient Christian Commentary on Scripture* [Downers Grove, IL: InterVarsity Press, 2003], 273–74.) In other words, you and I must not let our flesh reign over our spirit. To do so is not only foolish, but spiritually dangerous. The story of Lot's wife teaches us to "flee excess and shun extravagance." (Ambrose, "Exposition of the Gospel of Luke 8.45," in Just, *Luke*, 273.) Her longing for Sodom was, at least in part, a longing for the comforts that that city provided her. She was being called by God to give up the world, but though she moved toward the mountain (or temple) her heart was still saturated in the world, disqualifying her to be with God. Elder Neal A. Maxwell wrote: "Many today are as indecisive about the evils emerging around us—are as reluctant to renounce fully a wrong way of life—as was Lot's wife. Perhaps in this respect, as well as in the indicators of corruption of which sexual immorality is but one indicator, our present parallels are most poignant and disturbing. It was Jesus himself who said, 'Remember Lot's wife.' Indeed we should—and remember too all that the Savior implied with those three powerful words. While it was tragic for Lot's wife to look back, for our generation a hard look back at Sodom could save us from impending tragedies!" (Neal A. Maxwell, *Look Back at Sodom* [Salt Lake City, UT: Deseret Book, 1975], Introduction.) He also wrote: "The reasons prompting Lot's wife to take one more tempting look back at Sodom and Gomorrah, instead of being obedient to the command she and Lot had received, were inconsequential in comparison with the consequences of her disobedience. Looking back, said Jesus, will not do for us either. Wistfulness or uncertainty over leaving the ways of the world brought the Master's stern advice to 'Remember Lot's wife.' (Luke 17:32.)" (Neal A. Maxwell, *We Will Prove Them Herewith* [Salt Lake City, UT: Deseret Book, 1982], 27.) President John Taylor said of Lot's wife that she "was a little tinctured with gentilism." (John Taylor, discourse delivered December 14, 1884. See *Journal of Discourses*, 26:36.) She was stained by the world. She was a "saint" who really loved sin! Of those like-minded, Elder Bruce R. McConkie wrote: "As for Lot's wife, she looked back; that is, she turned again to the things of the world, and she too was destroyed with the wicked. So also shall it be at the end of the world. Even now the generality of men love Satan more than God; even now sodomic practices—immorality, homosexuality, and all manner of perversions—are found among great segments of our society; even now the righteous are leaving the world and finding place in the stakes of Zion. And as the residue of men go forward in their normal activities, reveling in their wickedness as did they of old, the day of burning, coming, as it were, from the midst of eternity, shall come upon them. And should any of the saints look back as did Lot's wife, they will be burned with the wicked." (Bruce R. McConkie, *The Promised Messiah* [Salt Lake City, UT: Deseret Book, 1982], 362.) In the *History of the Church* we find this: "And some that came [to Zion] have turned away, which may cause thousands to exclaim, amid the general confusion and fright of the times, 'Remember Lot's wife.'" (W. W. Phelps, in *History of the Church*, 2:132.)

29. Trench, *Miracles and Parables of the Old Testament*, 2.

30. Trench, *Miracles and Parables of the Old Testament*, 3; emphasis in original.

31. Maxwell, *Look Back at Sodom*, 10.

32. Orson F. Whitney, "Zion and Her Redemption," *The Deseret Weekly*, discourse given September 22, 1889, in *The Deseret Weekly*, vol. 40 (Salt Lake City, UT: Deseret News Co., 1980), 79.

33. Ryken, Wilhoit, and Longman, *Dictionary of Bible Imagery*, 752.

34. Nachmanides, *Commentary on the Torah*, 1:261. See also Speiser, *The Anchor Bible: Genesis*, 137, note e, and 141.

35. Boyd K. Packer, "Counsel to Youth," *Ensign*, November 2011.

THE BURNING BUSH

EXODUS 3:1–5

THE MIRACLE

Moses had been tending his father-in-law's flock of sheep in the desert near Mount Horeb. One day, having ascended the mount, he saw a bush that was on fire, but was not consumed or destroyed by the flames—a miraculous event by any man's standards. As Moses drew near the bush to investigate this seemingly impossible occurrence, he heard God's voice from within the bush telling him to take off his shoes, for Moses—in approaching this symbol of God's presence—was treading holy ground.

BACKGROUND

Moses lived some 120 years. The first forty of those were spent in Pharaoh's house. The next forty years were spent as an exile in Arabia.[1] For the last forty years of his life, he functioned as the prophet and leader of God's people—Israel. The miracle of the burning bush took place when Moses was in the second of these three stages of his life.

Near his fortieth birthday, Moses became aware that, as a child, he had been adopted by the daughter of the Pharaoh, and that he was actually an Israelite by birth. That realization caused him to take a hard look at how his *actual* people, the Israelites, were treated by the Egyptians (i.e., they who had adopted him in his infancy). Repulsed by the slavery of the Israelites, Moses made efforts to free them from the bondage, mistreatment, and neglect they were suffering under Egyptian rule. However, he was unsuccessful in his efforts and was eventually banished because of his activism on behalf of the Israelites.

This miracle took place (at *Har 'Elohim*) in a desert region called Horeb,[2] which literally means "wasteland" or "desolation." It was called such because there was nothing around for many miles. At the time of this miracle, Moses had not yet been called by God as a prophet; but, rather, was an ordinary man engaged in an ordinary day's work. Indeed, setting aside the miracle, there was nothing significant about the day nor the setting of this event.

SYMBOLIC ELEMENTS

Moses was a shepherd when he encountered the burning bush. As such, he not only typified Christ—who is the "good shepherd" (John 10:11)—but he also symbolized a leader of God's people (e.g., Ezekiel 34:23), which he was shortly to become.

> In keeping with the shepherd's role as a leader and provider, biblical pastoral writings often picture civil and religious leaders as shepherds and the people as sheep. In a sense the patriarchs fit the pattern, inasmuch as they were both shepherds by vocation and the progenitors of the nation of Israel. The first decisive example is Moses, who was a shepherd before becoming leader of the Israelites (Ex. 2:15–3:1), leading one of the psalmists to speak of God's leading his people "like a flock by the hand of Moses and Aaron" (Ps. 77:20 RSV).[3]

As we have noted, Moses's miracle took place on a mountain. In scripture, mountains are standard symbols for the temple, or the abode of God.[4] Thus, the imagery present in the miracle implies that the location of this miracle was equivalent to the holy temple. It highlights the sacred nature of what happened there. It suggests this was not a temporal event but, rather, something entirely divine.

The miracle took place when Moses was leading "the flock to the backside of the desert" (Exodus 3:1). One commentator noted, "As usual in Semitic thought, one faces east when giving compass directions; 'behind' is therefore 'west'."[5] The fact that Moses was traveling westward instead of eastward implies that he was *not* looking for God nor seeking to move toward God at the time of the miracle.[6] He was quite literally just going about his business when the burning bush and God's will were revealed to him. This does not imply that Moses was wicked or void of spirituality at the time of the miracle. It only suggests he had not set out that day with the intent or hope of encountering the divine. He was quite literally "surprised by joy," to borrow a line from C. S. Lewis.[7]

Flames or fire can have a number of symbolic meanings. They are often associated with the glory of God or other celestial beings. But they can also represent our trials or afflictions. Of course, because of their connection with the Holy Ghost, they can sometimes symbolize sanctification or cleansing. Not surprisingly, these are all related ideas. Our trials, if endured gracefully, can sanctify us, which qualifies us to be endowed by the Father with celestial glory at the Day of Judgment. Thus, in this miracle, the flames of the burning bush are not three separate symbols but, rather, one intricate and interrelated symbol.

The bush or tree, central to this miracle, can also have several symbolic meanings. Bushes or trees can represent "the despised and oppressed people of God," as some commentators suppose this bush does.[8] Green trees often represent the righteous, whereas dry trees can symbolize the wicked.[9] Though it is not explicitly stated in this miracle whether the burning bush is green or dry, the fact that it is not consumed by the fire suggests it is green, and thus that it stands as a symbol for that which is good or righteous. BYU's M. Catherine Thomas noted: "Most often in scripture . . . the tree is an anthropomorphic symbol. A tree serves well as such a symbol because it has, after all, limbs, a circulatory system, the bearing of fruit, and so forth. Specifically, scriptural trees [can] stand . . . for Christ and his attributes."[10] Elsewhere we read, "In ancient times, sacred trees . . . were [the] attributes of the gods."[11] Professor Susan Easton Black wrote: "The tree of life is connected with the cross, the two having somewhat the same significance. Both relate to the resurrection, eternal life, the Lord, and the 'love of God.' . . . Before the crucifixion of Christ, the *tree of life* symbol was used extensively. After the crucifixion the cross seems to have replaced it to a degree."[12] Thus, while the burning bush can represent humans (particularly the covenant people), it is also a perfect symbol for God. The multiplicity of meanings for trees or bushes may be appropriate here, in light of the many significant symbols seemingly present in this story. Finally, a number of commentators, ancient and modern, have suggested that the dual nature of the bush—flames representing its celestial nature and an earthly plant symbolizing its mortal or temporal nature—might be designed to highlight the dual makeup of Christ. He had a divine side, which He inherited from His Father, and a mortal side, which He inherited from His mother. "The flame of fire in the lowly desert bush can also typify the combination of deity and humanity in Christ who was the great 'I Am' . . . revealing His power to Moses."[13]

In the miracle, the Lord tells Moses to remove his shoes because the ground on which he was walking was holy. The Lord Himself then explains the symbolism behind footwear. Shoes and sandals represent the opposite of holiness, primarily because of their contact with the filth of the earth.[14] One source notes, "Putting off shoes on entering a holy place represents leaving earthly contact outside, to enter in submissiveness and reverence, and to divest oneself of vice."[15] Removing his shoes in this miracle symbolizes Moses's need to free himself of the world and its attachments and ways.[16] Augustine put it this way:

> What are the shoes? Well, what are the shoes we wear? Leather from dead animals. The hides of dead animals are what we protect our feet with. So what are we being ordered to do? To give up dead [or insincere] works [we so often perform]. This is symbolically what he instructs Moses to do . . . when the Lord says to him, "Take off your shoes. For the place you are standing in is holy ground." There's no holier ground than the church of God, is there? So as we stand in it let us take off our shoes, let us give up dead [or insincere] works.[17]

The Lord does not want Saints who are really only sinners in camouflage. As the Apostle Paul put it, "For they are not all Israel, which are of Israel" (Romans 9:6). Some who claim the name of Christ do not walk the way He set out. If we are to approach Him and His work, we must set aside the feigned and insincere: the dead works we do for show, but are contrary to our hearts. For, though we may fool our friends, the Lord knows who we really are in our hearts, and He seeks no sinful Saints.

APPLICATION AND ALLEGORIZATION

The symbolic message of this miracle has application to Moses, ancient Israel, the Church as a whole, and to individuals who seek to follow Christ.

On the day this miracle took place, Moses had been out grazing his father-in-law's sheep. One commentator described, in his own words, what happened next:

> Glancing from his monotonous task of watching the sheep, he saw a frail bush aflame. It made a very small impression. Soon its gray ashes would be blown away on the desert winds. But when he looked again, the bush was still burning. That gripped his attention. He knew there must be a reason. Therefore, he turned aside [from minding the sheep], and turning, he heard the voice of God. "Once you burned like that," said that voice. "You were all aflame with enthusiasm. You were aglow with the high purpose of delivering your people. But now the fire is utterly dead. You even tell yourself that you were a bit of a fool for ever being so hotly interested in what was none of your business." But this fire that failed to go out had another word for Moses. "What does that frail bush have that

you lack?" came the inevitable question. "God" was the answer. "You set yourself to an impossible task. You were going to work deliverance with your own strength, work it with the power that came from the throne of Egypt. Trusting thus in yourself, you made failure inevitable." "Here," said God, "is another chance. Here you have an opportunity to reaffirm that choice of the long ago. I am going to send you to Egypt. When they ask you this time for your credentials, you will have an answer." Thus with nothing but a staff in his hand and God in his heart, Moses set himself to the accomplishment of one of the greatest achievements of human history.[18]

For Moses, this miracle constituted his call to free Israel from the bondage in which they were being held in Egypt. As noted in the aforementioned quote, Moses had already sought to free his friends when he had lived in Pharaoh's court, though he did not succeed. This time, however, he would have God's help; and, thus, he could not fail. This is not to suggest that Moses would not have trials. On the contrary, part of what is symbolized by the burning of the bush is the idea that God would try Moses. As the Lord said: "Behold, I have refined thee . . . I have chosen thee in the furnace of affliction" (Isaiah 48:10). The trials that God was about to give Moses would test him, would improve him, and (via their sanctifying influence) would prepare him to inherit celestial glory.

There is certainly a message in all of this for the Lord's chosen people.[19] Notice that the bush was not on fire. Rather, the fire was in the bush. This ordinary thornbush,[20] with God in its midst, foreshadowed what He was about to do with Israel, His covenant people.[21] They were common, like the bush, but like that plant that revealed God's will to Moses, the covenant people would be the means by which God would reveal His will to mankind in that dispensation.[22] Just as no power on earth can destroy that in which God's light is allowed to dwell, so also, no power would be able to overcome God's people (in any dispensation) so long as they retain that light within.[23] Of course, the sad history of God's people is that they so often *have* forfeited His Spirit; and, consequently, they have been left to themselves, to suffer at the hands of their enemies *because* they have forgone the protection that God promised to give them. But this miracle informs us that this need not be *our* lot.

Of course, none of this is to suggest that being part of the covenant people means to be without trials. Moses's call (through this miracle) made no promises that his work would be easy. As we noted with Moses, it is also so with ancient Israel, the Christians of the Common Era, and the Mormons of modernity. Those who choose to follow Christ *must* know that this call will require some sanctification, and sanctification usually comes through trials and tests.

> The Church of God, like Israel, has at all times suffered by persecution. Yet it has survived many a fiery trial and, in spite of all worldly powers confederated against it, is as great and powerful as ever. . . . She has worn out many an anvil of antagonism. . . . Conflict without and corruption within have not destroyed her. Indwelt by the invincible Lord, the Church continues by a power greater than her own.[24]

The covenant people are often surrounded by the "fire of affliction."[25] In every dispensation, the godly have had to suffer through trials and persecutions (see 2 Timothy 3:12). But just as the bush in Moses's miracle was not consumed by the fire but, rather, drew those whose hearts were holy to it, when Saints are called into the "furnace of affliction," they are purified and refined by it (Isaiah 48:10. See also Romans 5:3–5), rather than being destroyed by it. Those who have holy hearts will typically be drawn to the Saints and the message they bear. So long as we keep the Lord's light within us (just as the burning bush had God within it), our Savior will preserve us for, "Lo, [He is] with [us always], even unto the end of the world" (Matthew 28:20).[26]

Part of the symbolism of the hallowed ground on which Moses walked suggests that Christians are all called to live as Jesus lived. If we are *truly* His disciples, then we must discipline ourselves to "think what he thinks, know what he knows, say what he would say, and do what he would do in every situation."[27] One sixth-century source found the following application in this element of the miracle:

> See what the Lord said to Moses and Joshua: "Remove the strap of your shoe, for the place where you stand is holy ground." . . . How could that ground upon which they trod be holy, since doubtless it was like the rest of the earth? However, notice carefully what was said: "For the place whereon you stand is holy ground." That is to say, Christ whose figure you bear and of whom you seem to be a type, is holy ground. True holy ground is the body of our Lord Jesus Christ through whom everything heavenly and earthly is sanctified.[28]

Thus, since all things good typify of Him[29]—including *all* Christians—we must consider it a sacred duty, or holy ground, to be called after His name and to be members of His Church and representatives of His will. We must not be cavalier about what we have been called to be and do. We must sense the sacred trust that has been placed in us and live and act accordingly. The ground Moses was on was not itself holy, though God's presence always sanctifies the place or the person to whom He appears. However, the act in which Moses was engaging was holy, and so is any attempt on our part to commune with God. Praying, partaking of the sacrament, giving or receiving blessings, and participating in temple rites are all holy acts because of what they represent, and you and I should approach each with a sense of awe and sacredness if they are to transition from mundane experiences to the spiritual experiences they were designed to be.

The setting of this miracle has something to teach us about the personal burning bushes in our lives. Just as Moses was an ordinary man, in an ordinary place, doing an ordinary job at the time of the miracle, you and I can be recipients of God's miracles even though we are not prophets and apostles. We do not necessarily live in some special place, and we may live a rather mundane existence doing rather average things day in and day out. Similarly, just as Moses had to "turn aside" from his worldly distractions to view or experience the miracle, you and I must "turn aside" from our worldly distractions, our petty sins, and even our faithless reasoning, if we are to view the miracles God has for us.[30] It is curious that God only called out to Moses once He saw that Moses was interested in understanding what was taking place within the bush. It may well be that, had Moses turned from the miracle bush, God would not have spoken to him. How many miracles in our own lives do we miss because we are distracted from the things of the Spirit, or we do not take the time to investigate what God is doing in the world or in our lives? God called to Moses only after he looked. He can only call to us if we too look searchingly for Him.[31] Thus, one commentator wrote: "God [chose] the small and despised burning bush as his medium of revelation, and he [waited] to see how sensitive Moses [was] toward the insignificant and small things of life before he [invested] him with larger tasks. . . . [God wanted] to use this bush for a lesson to make an impression on Moses."[32] If we want God to trust us in the big things, then we must first prove to Him that we can be sensitive to His presence in the small things.

One commentator drew from the miracle of the burning bush that any message God reveals to us is given to us based on the spiritual level we are at during the time of the given revelation. He takes our spiritual and intellectual maturity into consideration, and tailors His message to our ability to receive and grasp it. "The thorn-bush was a familiar object to Moses, and the revelation through it, though awe-inspiring, was not so overwhelming as to deprive him of the power of receiving it. So the manifestation of God in the babe of Bethlehem, the carpenter of Nazareth, the human son of man dying upon the cross."[33] As the Prophet Joseph said, if Jesus "comes to a little child, he will adapt himself to the language and capacity of a little child."[34] The bush was the way Moses needed to receive his calling and revelation from God; the grove was the way Joseph Smith needed to receive his. God will speak to you and me in the way we best can hear, and in the spiritual language we are able to understand.

President Gordon B. Hinckley found an interesting application of this miracle. In emphasizing the importance of reverence, he stated:

> Socializing is an important aspect of our program as a Church. We encourage the cultivation of friends with happy conversations among our people. However, these should take place in the foyer, and when we enter the chapel we should understand that we are in sacred precincts. All of us are familiar with the account in Exodus of the Lord's appearance to Moses at the burning bush. When the Lord called, Moses answered, "Here am I" (Exodus 3:4).
>
> And the Lord said, "Draw not nigh hither: put off thy shoes from off thy feet, for the place whereon thou standest is holy ground" (Exodus 3:5).
>
> We do not ask our people to remove their shoes when they come into the chapel. But all who come into the Lord's house should have a feeling that they are walking and standing on holy ground and that it becomes them to deport themselves accordingly.[35]

Mormonism is a social religion. However, as President Hinckley pointed out, once we enter the actual chapel portion of our church houses, a spirit and feeling of reverence should be sought for. (The same could be said of the temple.) If we are to fully feel the Lord's Spirit, we must seek for a sense of the holy when we are in His house. Metaphorically, we must remove the sandals of the world, and don the things of the Divine.

NOTES

1. "The years serving as a humble shepherd were essential for the training and preparing of this former prince of Egypt to be a shepherd-prophet." (Kent J. Hunter, personal correspondence, May 26, 2017.)

2. Commentators commonly note: "'Horeb' is found in the Elohistic and Deuteronomistic material, while 'Sinai' is the name used in Yahwistic and Priestly material. We do not know why the two names are used, seemingly interchangeably. It has been suggested that Horeb is part of Sinai, but this is pure guess-work." (R. Alan Cole, *Exodus*, in *Tyndale Old Testament Commentaries* [Grand Rapids, MI: Eerdmans, 1973], 62.)

3. Leland Ryken, James C. Wilhoit, and Tremper Longman III, eds., *Dictionary of Biblical Imagery* (Downers Grove, IL: InterVarsity Press, 1998), 782–83.

4. See Hugh Nibley, *The Collected Works of Hugh Nibley: Enoch the Prophet*, vol. 2 (Salt Lake City: UT, Deseret Book, 1986), 224; Ryken, Wilhoit, and Longman, *Dictionary of Biblical Imagery*, 573; J. C. Cooper, An Illustrated Encyclopaedia of Traditional Symbols (London: Thames and Hudson, 1995), 110; Jack Tresidder, *Symbols and their Meanings: The Illustrated Guide to More than 1,000 Symbols— Their Traditional and Contemporary Significance* (London: Duncan Baird Publishers, 2006), 116.

5. Cole, *Exodus*, in *Tyndale Old Testament Commentaries*, 62.

6. See Alonzo L. Gaskill, *The Lost Language of Symbolism: An Essential Guide for Recognizing and Interpreting Symbols of the Gospel* (Salt Lake City, UT: Deseret Book, 2003), 166–70.

7. See C. S. Lewis, *Surprised by Joy: The Shape of My Early Life* (New York: Harcourt Brace, 1955).

8. Walter C. Kaiser Jr., "Exodus," in Frank E. Gaebelein, *The Expositor's Bible Commentary* (Grand Rapids, MI: Zondervan, 1976–1992), 2:315.

9. Joseph Fielding McConkie, *Gospel Symbolism* (Salt Lake City, UT: Deseret Book, 1985), 274. See also, Cooper, *An Illustrated Encyclopedia of Traditional Symbols* (London: Thames and Hudson, 1987), 178.

10. M. Catharine Thomas, "Jacob's Allegory: The Mystery of Christ," in Stephen E. Ricks and John W. Welch, *The Allegory of the Olive Tree* (Salt Lake City, UT: Deseret Book, 1994), 13.

11. Nadia Julien, *The Mammoth Dictionary of Symbols: Understanding the Hidden Language of Symbols* (New York: Carroll & Graff Publishers, 1996), 462; See also J. E. Cirlot, *A Dictionary of Symbols*, 2nd ed. (New York: Routledge & Kegan Paul, 1971), 347.

12. Susan Easton Black, "Behold, I Have Dreamed a Dream," in Monte S. Nyman and Charles D. Tate Jr., *The Book of Mormon: First Nephi, The Doctrinal Foundation* (Provo, UT: Religious Studies Center, Brigham Young University, 1988), 123, note 7; emphasis in original.

13. Herbert Lockyer, *All the Miracles of the Bible: The Supernatural in Scripture— Its Scope and Significance* (Grand Rapids, MI: Zondervan, 1961), 45. See also Richard C. Trench, *Miracles and Parables of the Old Testament* (Grand Rapids, MI: Baker Book House, 1959), 8; Prudentius, "The Divinity of Christ," 49–70, in Joseph T. Lienhard, ed., *Exodus, Leviticus, Numbers, Deuteronomy*, in *Ancient Christian Commentary on Scripture* (Downers Grove, IL: InterVarsity Press, 2001), 10–11.

14. One source states: "Shoes represent what is dead." (See Lienhard, *Exodus, Leviticus, Numbers, Deuteronomy*, 14.)

15. Cooper, *An Illustrated Encyclopaedia of Traditional Symbols*, 152.

16. Evagrius, "Chapters on Prayer," 4, in Lienhard, *Exodus, Leviticus, Numbers, Deuteronomy*, 14. "Holy—*qodesh*— Hebrew in its dominative verb form, *qadash*, denoting an invitation from the Lord to become holy—consecrated, set apart, purified, sanctified, dedicated—to become as holy as God is holy." (Kent J. Hunter, personal correspondence, May 26, 2017.)

17. Augustine, "Sermon," 101:7, in Lienhard, *Exodus, Leviticus, Numbers, Deuteronomy*, 14.

18. Clovis Gillham Chappell, *The Cross Before Calvary* (New York: Abingdon Press, 1960), 42–43.

19. "Just as the bush was burned but unconsumed, Moses would be [also]. He had much to face from the people he led: doubt, criticism, and rebellion were [to be] his lot from them. But because of God's power in him, the prophet was not destroyed by their attitudes. We, too, need not be consumed by the world if we trust in the Lord alone and seek to serve Him. Do we?" (Pamela McQuade, *The Top 100 Miracles of the Bible: What They Are and What They Mean to You Today* [Uhrichsville, OH: Barbour Publishing, 2008], 29.)

20. The Septuagint calls it a "blackberry bush." (See Herbert Lockyer, *All the Miracles of the Bible: The Supernatural in Scripture—Its Scope and Significane* [Grand Rapids, MI: Zondervan, 1961], 44.) Jewish midrash calls it a "thorn-bush." (See Louis Ginzberg, *The Legends of the Jews* [Philadelphia, PA: The Jewish Publication Society of America, 1967–1969], 2:303–4 & 3:66; J. H. Hertz, *The Pentateuch and Haftorahs: Hebrew Text English Translation and Commentary*, 2nd ed. [London: Soncino Press, 1960], 213.)

21. One Jewish commentator noted that "many of the Rabbis [saw] in the bush a symbol of Israel, and in the fire that could not consume it a symbol of Israel's enemies." (Ginzberg, *The Legends of the Jews*, 5:416n115.) Another commentator similarly explained: "The burning bush has often been taken as a symbol of Israel—small and lowly among the nations, and yet indestructible; because of the Divine Spirit that dwelleth within Israel." (Hertz, *The Pentateuch and Haftorahs*, 213.)

22. See Trench, *Miracles and Parables of the Old Testament*, 5. See also Caesarius of Arles, "Sermon," 96:1, in Lienhard, *Exodus, Leviticus, Numbers, Deuteronomy*, 12. "In spite of all their afflictions under Pharaoh, the Jews could not be destroyed (see II Corinthians 4:8–10). Groaning under the rigorous burden of their taskmasters, the Jews, like the bush, were never reduced to ashes. The flame was in the bush, not the bush in the flame. . . . Being in her, He protected her, not *from* suffering, but preserved her *in* and *through* 'the flame of fire' of Egyptian persecution (Exodus 1:9–22), as He has all down the ages. The indestructible Jew is the miracle of history. In spite of all means to destroy God's ancient people, they have multiplied." (Lockyer, *All the Miracles of the Bible*, 44–45.)

23. See Trench, *Miracles and Parables of the Old Testament*, 6.

24. Lockyer, *All the Miracles of the Bible*, 45.

25. "As the bush while it burned with the presence of the Lord assumed a grandeur of appearance until then unseen, so will the Christian character, refined by suffering" (Trench, *Miracles and Parables of the Old Testament*, 7). As Peter taught: "Beloved, think it not strange concerning the fiery trial which is to try you, as though some strange thing happened unto you: But rejoice, inasmuch as ye are partakers of Christ's sufferings; that, when his glory shall be revealed, ye may be glad also with exceeding joy" (1 Peter 4:12–13).

26. See Lockyer, *All the Miracles of the Bible*, 45.

27. Bruce R. McConkie, *Doctrinal New Testament Commentary* (Salt Lake City, UT: Bookcraft, 1965–1972), 2:322.

28. Caesarius of Arles, "Sermon," 96:4, in Lienhard, *Exodus, Leviticus, Numbers, Deuteronomy*, 14.

29. Nephi wrote: "Behold . . . *all things* which have been given of God from the beginning of the world, unto man, are the typifying of him" (2 Nephi 11:4; emphasis added). Nephi's brother Jacob recorded: "Behold, I say unto you that *none* of the prophets have written, nor prophesied, save they have spoken concerning this Christ" (Jacob 7:11; emphasis added). And in the Book of Moses, the Lord Himself stated: "And behold, *all* things have their likeness, and *all* things are created and made to bear record of me." (Moses 6:63; emphasis added). Thus, from these prophetic utterances it appears that (1) *all* things given by God symbolize or typify Christ, (2) *all* prophets have prophesied and testified of Christ, and (3) potentially *all* things can remind us of Christ. Indeed, one modern typologist remarked: "The red line of [Christ's] blood runs all through the Old Testament, and . . . thus we are constantly reminded of the shed blood, without which there is no remission." (Ada R. Habershon, *Study of the Types* [Grand Rapids, MI: Kregel Publications, 1974], 35.)

30. See Trench, *Miracles and Parables of the Old Testament*, 8.

31. See Terence Fretheim, *Interpretation: A Bible Commentary for Teaching and Preaching—Exodus* (Louisville, Kentucky: John Knox Press, 1991), 54; Avivah Gottlieb Zornberg, *The Particulars of Rapture: Reflections on Exodus* (New York: Doubleday, 2001), 79–80; Origen, "Homilies on Genesis," 12:2 in Lienhard, *Exodus, Leviticus, Numbers, Deuteronomy*, 12; Ambrose, "Concerning Repentance," 1.14.74 & 2.11.107, in Lienhard, *Exodus, Leviticus, Numbers, Deuteronomy*, 12 & 13; Jerome, "Homilies on the Psalms," 51, in Lienhard, *Exodus, Leviticus, Numbers, Deuteronomy*, 12; Gregory the Great, "Moral Interpretation of Job," 15.57.68, in Lienhard, *Exodus, Leviticus, Numbers, Deuteronomy* 12–13; Ambrose, "Flight from the World," 5.25, in Lienhard, *Exodus, Leviticus, Numbers, Deuteronomy*, 13.

32. Kaiser, "Exodus," in Gaebelein, *The Expositor's Bible Commentary*, 2:315.

33. See Trench, *Miracles and Parables of the Old Testament*, 6.

34. Joseph Smith, *Teachings of the Prophet Joseph Smith*, Joseph Fielding Smith, comp. (Salt Lake City, UT: Deseret Book, 1976), 162.

35. Gordon B. Hinckley, "Reverence and Morality," *Ensign*, May 1987.

Three Miracles *for* Moses Involving *His* Staff, *His* Hand, *and the* Water of the Nile

EXODUS 4:1–9

THE MIRACLE

Moses had been called by God to return to Egypt to free the Israelites from Egyptian bondage. God promised him that, though the Pharaoh would initially resist Moses's request to let the Israelites go, God would smite the Egyptians with "wonders" that would eventually cause them to let the Israelites go free (Exodus 3:19–20).

Moses's reply to God's promise was to ask, "What if they don't believe me? What if they won't listen to me? And what if they say that I haven't really seen you?" (see Exodus 4:1). In response to Moses's doubts, God explained to him what exactly He was going to do so as to convince the doubters that Moses really had been commissioned and sent by God.

Thus, at the onset of this miracle, God told Moses to throw his shepherd's crook or staff on the ground which, when he did, became a snake. Out of fear, Moses ran from it. But God then commanded Moses to pick it up by the tail, and, when Moses did, it became his staff again. God told Moses that he should do this before Pharaoh and it would serve as a sign that the God of Abraham, Isaac, and Jacob was with him (see Exodus 4:2–5).

Next, Moses was told to put his hand into his cloak and then pull it out again. When Moses did so his hand turned leprous. The newly called prophet was then told to do the same thing again, and, when he did, his hand was healed. God told Moses that if the Egyptians reject the first sign, they might not disbelieve the second one (see Exodus 4:6–8).

Finally, Moses was told that, should the Egyptians reject the first *and* second sign, a third miracle should be performed. God instructed Moses that he should take some water from the Nile and pour it out on the ground. God would cause it to turn to blood and, no doubt, that would have a convincing power over the Egyptians (see Exodus 4:9).

BACKGROUND

Though this specific passage does not record Moses manifesting these three promised powers, Exodus 7:9–12 informs us that Moses *did* turn his staff into a snake—one which actually consumed the staffs of Pharaoh's magicians. Also, Exodus 7:14–25 tells us that Moses turned the waters of the Nile to blood. Though nowhere in scripture are we clearly told that Moses ever turned his hand leprous as a sign to the Egyptians, since the *first* sign was to turn the staff to a serpent and the *third* sign was to turn the water of the Nile to blood, it is assumed that Moses must have performed the *second* miracle of leprosy, even though our current biblical text does not record the event.[1]

The Lord's declaration to Moses that his miracles would prove to the Egyptians that he had been visited by the God of Abraham, Isaac, and Jacob (Exodus 4:5) is not a passing comment; but, rather, it is foundational to understanding this miracle and the one that follows (see Exodus 7:15–12:30). Each of the miraculous plagues Moses brought down upon Egypt—including the three signs listed in this miracle—symbolized Jehovah's power over the gods of Egypt. Thus, the Lord's words to Moses were a testament to the message that would be sent; namely, the God of Israel is real and powerful, but the gods of Egypt are neither.[2]

SYMBOLIC ELEMENTS

The snake is a curious symbol. In contemporary Christian thinking, it is often associated with Satan—the devil, the adversary and tempter of man. However, that is not what it originally symbolized, and that is not the primary symbolic message intended in this miracle. Prior to the Fall of Adam and Eve—and certainly during the early portions of the Hebrew Bible—the snake was a symbol for Christ, not the devil.[3] Medical doctors today use the symbol of the serpent on the staff because of the scriptural story associating the snake with healing powers (see Numbers 21:8, Alma 33:19–20, and

Helaman 8:13–15).[4] Because of the snake's practice of shedding its skin, the serpent is also a standard symbol of healing, the Resurrection, or immortality.[5] So, when the devil appeared to Adam and Eve in Eden in the form of, or through the use of, a serpent, he was actually seeking to appear as an "angel of light" (2 Nephi 9:9). In other words, he had chosen that symbol because he knew that the snake represented the Messiah, and that was what he wished to be viewed as.[6] When God informed Moses that his staff would turn into a snake, the snake was a symbol of Jehovah, not of Satan. Perhaps it would be appropriate to see the staffs of Pharaoh's magicians—which also turned into snakes, but were then eaten by Moses's staff[7]—as symbols of the devil and his attempts to imitate the power and role of Christ. Regardless, Moses's snake was definitely intended to be a positive symbol. It is curious that the staff of Moses used to bring down Jehovah's plagues upon Egypt "had more than passing similarities to the 'rod' of affliction used by the Egyptian slave masters" to punish the Israelites.[8] It is as though Jehovah was saying the tables have been turned, and we have a new set of slaves and a new Master. Thus, the miracle of the staff turned serpent highlights the power of Jehovah over the false gods and corrupt leaders of the Egyptians, who pretend power, but are really only imitators of the true and living God.

Leprosy is a common scriptural symbol for sin or spiritual sickness.[9] But it was also commonly perceived as a sign of God's punishment; hence it was often called by the Jews "the finger of God."[10] Of the symbolism behind this miracle, one text states: "The instantaneous cure [was] . . . to reflect the greatness and majesty of God's power. The significance of this power to take away the health of the body and then restore it again . . . [was] to warn Pharaoh that this God who had sent Moses [had] the power to inflict or to save what he [would] with just a word or a gesture from his ambassador."[11] Thus, the miracle of the given and taken leprosy symbolizes Jehovah's power over all things—temporal and spiritual. He can in an instant smite with a curse, and just as quickly retract or heal that curse. We must but accept and follow Him.[12]

The turning of the Nile to blood was symbolically significant on two levels. First of all, the Nile was considered holy by the ancient Egyptians, and it was the residence of several of their gods, such as Sobek, Hep, and Heket.[13] Because it sustained the lives of the people and the land, the Nile was seen as the means by which the gods blessed their faithful followers. Thus, to turn the water of the Nile to blood was tantamount to bringing defilement and death to the Egyptian gods and their heavens. In addition, it suggested that death would also come to all that placed their dependence upon these deceased deities.[14] A second but related point potentially found in the symbolism of the blood, is this; in ancient times, blood was often associated with death, impurity, guilt, or sin.[15] Moses's act, therefore, would suggest all of these things about the Egyptian gods. Therefore, this final of the three signs would have been quite offensive, and would have made a rather bold and dramatic statement to the Egyptians who witnessed it.

APPLICATION AND ALLEGORIZATION

More than anything else, the three miracles that Moses was empowered to preform symbolized the power of Jehovah over the gods and divine leader of Egypt. In each case, in very symbolic ways that would be understood by the Egyptians, the God of Abraham, Isaac, and Jacob was saying that He was more powerful than any man, any nation, or any god in Egypt. Thus, this series of miracles was designed to invite Pharaoh and his people to believe in the true and living God, and to reject their false gods that would, in symbolic terms, be painted as dead. We too must remember that the God of Moses is the only true and living God—and that we must "have no other gods" before Him (Exodus 20:3). While practicing Latter-day Saints are unlikely to worship other deities, we are as susceptible as anyone else to having idols—things that we love more than the true and living God. Wealth, power, fame, looks—these, and many other false gods, may entice us. Yet, they are as unreal as the gods of Pharaoh—incapable of bringing life, meeting needs, or saving souls. Is there anything in your life that comes before God? If so, like Moses, you must destroy those false gods.

On a different note, Moses is well known to have been a type for Christ.[16] Just as he was the source of these three miracles in the lives of ancient Israel, Jesus is the source of what each of these miracles symbolize. Thus, one early third-century father wrote that the three signs of this miracle symbolize the "threefold power of God."[17] The grasping of the snake and turning it back into a dead piece of wood symbolizes how God has power over, and will eventually destroy, the influence of the devil, not only in the world, but in our individual lives. The healing of the hand that had become corrupted by leprosy foreshadowed the Resurrection, when all of our physical corruption, deformities, and death shall be reversed. And the turning of the water of the Nile to blood reminds us of the sins of mankind that must be atoned for by the blood of Christ.[18] Thus, the Savior was sent to empower us to overcome our adversary, resurrect us from the dead, and apply His atoning blood to the sins and sicknesses of fallen mankind.

As to God equipping Moses with proofs of his calling, one source noted: "The servants of God must be able to produce evidence that they are what they profess to be. Moses and Aaron were enabled to prove their authority by the power of transforming a dead stick into a living serpent."[19] Joseph Smith performed a number of miracles, including healings, prophetic utterances, the receipt of visions and angels, etc. However, one of the greatest miracles he performed—one of the greatest "evidences" of his divine calling that he produced—was the translation and publication of the Book of Mormon. No explanation as to its origins, other than the one the Prophet Joseph gave, has been able to stand the test of time. "Although all kinds of divine working will find themselves face to face with imitations, yet it is always possible to distinguish the real from the false."[20] The Book of Mormon suggests that prayer can reveal the divine from the demonic (Moroni 10:3–5). The New Testament, as well as the Book of Mormon, suggests that the "fruits" of a movement and its people can also enable us to distinguish between the saintly and the satanic (Matthew 7:16; 3 Nephi 14:16). We too must have "fruits" as "evidence" that we are God's covenant people and that the message we bear is His revealed word. As one commentator wrote: "Christians must prove their right to their name by showing a power to become transformed in character (Rom. xii, 2; 2 Cor. iii. 18)."[21] If we, like Moses, have God with us, He will endow us with His power to do His work. Miracles will be ours. The Church will grow. Satan, and his servants, will be thwarted in their efforts against us. And the world will sense that The Church of Jesus Christ of Latter-day Saints has God's blessings upon its sacred work (D&C 45:66–71).

Moses's grasping of the snake (thereby turning it into a staff) reminds us of the prophet's typological foreshadowing of Christ, and also of Mose's eventual power over Pharaoh. One commentator noted the connection between the snake Moses's staff became and the cobra worn on the headdress of the Egyptian Pharaoh: "As though Moses [had], so to speak, Egypt's king by the tail."[22] Similarly, another said, "The rod that was turned into a serpent, and when grasped by Moses once more became a rod, tells of God's power over Satan."[23] You and I certainly don't have the power, in and of ourselves, to defeat the adversary. But through Christ and His prophets, we can overcome all things. Christ is the way, and His prophets are ever pointing us in the right direction. If we heed the Lord's commandments and the prophets' advice, we will find Satan about as threatening as the serpent Moses turned into a staff. In his book, *All The Miracles of the Bible*,

Dr. Herbert Lockyer wrote: "The rod in Moses' hand was possibly . . . one which, as a shepherd of eighty years of age, he needed for support."[24] As we noted above, that rod symbolized Jesus.[25] And just as Moses needed something to lean on to keep him stable in his advanced years, so also it was Jesus upon whom he needed to rely for stability as he sought to rebuke Pharaoh and free Israel. We too must rely upon that rod for the support necessary to make it through this difficult mortal experience.

The miraculous curing of Moses's leprous hand mirrors the power of the Atonement to take away sins and to restore one to spiritual health. "*The hand turned leprous* speaks of divine power to cleanse from sin—a disease more loathsome and incurable than leprosy. The mission of Moses was to punish and to save. Power can be ours not only over Satan, but over the sin he introduced."[26] Similarly, the Prophet Joseph noted: "The devil has no power over us only as we permit him. The moment we revolt at anything which comes from God, the devil takes power."[27] Like Moses, we will all have times when we see the signs of sin and spiritual sickness evident in our lives. But just as God gave Moses the ability to overcome his leprosy (via trusting in God's power), He has given you and I the ability to overcome sin and spiritual decay through trusting in that same power. It is as real for us today as it was for Moses millennia ago, and being healed from sin is no less miraculous than being cured from a physical disease. Indeed, while brilliant scientists and physicians may have figured out how to cure physical sickness, only God can cure spiritual sickness and death. Thus, could there be any greater miracle?

Finally, one text notes the fear that leprosy brought to all who were familiar with it, and suggests that there is a message in this second of the three signs of this narrative.

> God commanded that anyone with leprosy was unclean—separated from others so the illness would not spread. Such a person was also a picture of spiritual unbelief or failure. Anyone who could work this miracle [of instantly healing leprosy] would be someone to follow and respect, for surely this would be God's representative. Does God have to make us fear Him before we obey? Will only the unpleasant get our attention? [If so,] then He will use such a method. But He would rather woo us, calling us into obedience with a gentle voice. Are we listening?[28]

"Are we listening," indeed. As President Ezra Taft Benson noted: "God will have a humble people. Either we can choose to be humble or we can be compelled to be humble."[29] God wishes our willing hearts. He desires that we obey because we love Him and His law. However, if we need the nudging that comes through the unpleasant, He will provide that too—not in some punitive way, but out of love for our souls, and because of His sincere desire to save each one of us. May we choose obedience out of love, rather than fear, and thereby reap the rich blessings of the Lord.

As a final application, one author suggested this: "God doesn't always prove Himself in miraculous physical ways, as He did in this instance. But He often uses the things that are right in our hands to show His faithfulness to us. With them, we can always be ready to show forth God's truth to those who doubt. In His hand, the common becomes uncommon, and amazing events can happen."[30] God desperately desires to use us as instruments, thereby converting the unconverted, while increasing our own faith in significant ways. Are we living as we need to so that He can use us? While the miracles performed through us might seem small and insignificant in comparison to those that Moses performed, for those whose lives will be changed by them, they will be just as big and just as profound. For those sensitive to the reality that God is active in the little details of life, there are no insignificant miracles—regardless of their size and scope.

NOTES

1. See Alan R. Cole, *Exodus*, in *Tyndale Old Testament Commentaries*, 74; Pamela McQuade, *The Top 100 Miracles of the Bible: What They Are and What They Mean to You Today* (Uhrichsville, OH: Barbour Publishing, 2008), 31. One text states: "The [Jewish] midrash identifies the Egyptian boils with the leprosy that afflicts Moses . . . at the Burning Bush: 'Moses put his hand into his bosom and brought it forth leprous as snow. They [the magicians] too put their hands in their bosoms and brought them out leprous as snow. *But they were not healed till the day of their death.*' The sign that Moses is taught to perform is immediately imitated by the magicians. . . . The triumph of their success is marred, however, by the fact that they cannot revert to health. From this point on, they are afflicted with leprosy/boils." (Avivah Gottlieb Zornberg, *The Particulars of Rapture: Reflections on Exodus* [New York: Doubleday, 2001], 109. See also Terence E. Fretheim, *Interpretation: A Bible Commentary for Teaching and Preaching—Exodus* [Louisville, KY: John Knox Press, 1991], 70.) It is worth noting that Moses does play a role in healing the leprosy of his sister, Miriam. (See Numbers 12:10–16.)

2. One commentator noted: "The close connection between these [three] signs and the plagues [of Exodus chapters 7 through 12] should be noted. This is seen in specific matters (staff/snakes; leprosy/boils; water/blood), their ominous character, their relationship to the realm of nature, and the fact that both are called signs

('*ot*)." (Fretheim, *Interpretation: A Bible Commentary for Teaching and Preaching—Exodus*, 70.)

3.   See Andrew Skinner, "Savior, Satan, and Serpent: The Duality of a Symbol in the Scriptures," in Stephen D. Ricks, Donald W. Parry, and Andrew H. Hedges, eds., *The Disciple as Scholar: Essays on Scripture and the Ancient World in Honor of Richard Lloyd Anderson* (Provo, UT: Neal A. Maxwell Institute for Religious Scholarship, 2000), 359–84; Andrew C. Skinner, "Serpent Symbols and Salvation in the Ancient Near East and the Book of Mormon," in *Journal of Book of Mormon Studies* 10, no. 2 (2001): 42–55; Walter L. Wilson, *A Dictionary of Bible Types: Examines the Images, Shadows, and Symbolism of Over 1,000 Biblical Terms, Words, and People* (Peabody, MA: Hendrickson, 1999), 363.

4.   Herbert Lockyer, *All the Miracles of the Bible: The Supernatural in Scripture—Its Scope and Significance* (Grand Rapids, MI: Zondervan, 1961), 77. There is actually some controversy as to why the medical profession uses this symbol, and what its origins are. Some associate it with the Mesopotamian caduceus (a staff that had two serpents intertwined on it). Others with the Rod of Asclepius, the son of Apollo (a staff with a singular snake wrapped around it). However, the Mosaic copper snake on a pole, or the *nekh-o'-sheth naw-khawsh'*, is most likely the origin of the medical symbol, in part because the medical insignia typically has the pole and the serpents, but also the wings of the "fiery flying serpents" of the story of Moses. (See Numbers 21:8; 1 Nephi 17:41; Alma 33:19–20; Helaman 8:13–15.) Thus, the latter of these three is most likely the source of the symbol.

5.   See Bruce Vawter, *On Genesis: A New Reading* (New York: Doubleday, 1977), 78.

6.   On a related note, the Hebrew word translated as *serpent* in the Genesis account of the Fall is related to the Hebrew word for "luminous" or "shining." Thus, some have suggested that the Genesis account should not read "serpent" but rather "angel of light." (See, for example, Victor P. Hamilton, *Handbook on the Pentateuch* [Grand Rapids, MI: Baker Academic, 1982], 42. See also "Revelation of Moses," in Alexander Roberts and James Donaldson, eds., *Ante-Nicene Fathers* [Peabody, MA: Hendrickson Publishers, 1994], 8:566.) Ginzberg records: "Satan assumed the appearance of an angel." (Louis Ginzberg, *The Legends of the Jews* [Philadelphia, PA: The Jewish Population Society of America, 1912–1938], 1:95; see also "Life of Adam and Eve," Latin version 9:1 and Greek version 17:1–2 and 29:15, in James H. Charlesworth, ed., *Old Testament Pseudepigrapha* [New York: Doubleday, 1983–1985], 2:260, 261, and 277; Robert Jamison, Andrew Robert Fausset, and David Brown, *Jamieson, Fausset and Brown's Commentary on the Whole Bible* [Grand Rapids, MI: Zondervan, 1999], Old Testament page 19; Adam Clarke, *The Holy Bible, Containing the Old and New Testaments . . . with a Commentary and Critical Notes. . . .* [New York: T. Mason & G. Lane, 1837], 1:48.)

7.   Curiously, the Hebrew word translated "snake" in the King James Version of the Bible means basically a crocodile, which is significant because Sobek (or Sebek) was the crocodile god of the Egyptians. (See "A Facsimile from the Book of Abraham, No. 1, Fig. 9," in the Pearl of Great Price.) Thus, whether Moses's staff became a crocodile, or whether he was just using an interesting bit of wordplay for his readers, the message behind saying "the staff became a crocodile" seems to be that the crocodile god of the Egyptians was only an imitator of the true God—Jehovah. (See Cole, *Exodus*, in *Tyndale Old Testament Commentaries*, 74; Walter C. Kaiser Jr., "Exodus," in Gaebelein, *The Expositor's Bible Commentary* [Grand Rapids, MI: Zondervan, 1976–1992], 2:326; J. H. Hertz, *The Pentateuch and Haftorahs: Hebrew Text English Translation and Commentary*, 2nd ed. [London: Soncino Press, 1960], 236.)

8.   Kaiser, "Exodus," in Gaebelein, *The Expositor's Bible Commentary*, 2:327.

9.   See J. C. Cooper, *An Illustrated Encyclopaedia of Traditional Symbols* (London: Thames and Hudson, 1987), 96; Kevin J. Conner, *Interpreting the Symbols and Types*, rev. ed. (Portland, OR: City Bible Publishing, 1992), 152; Charles H. Spurgeon, *Spurgeon's Sermons* (Grand Rapids, MI: Baker Books, 1996), 7:311–27; Leland Ryken, James C. Wilhoit, and Tremper Longman III, *Dictionary of Biblical Imagery* (Downers Grove, IL: InterVarsity Press, 1998), 507; Richard C. Trench, *Miracles and Parables of the Old Testament* (Grand Rapids, MI: Baker Book House, 1959), 134–35. "The biblical word traditionally translated 'leprosy' does not (at least usually) refer to what we call leprosy (Hansen's disease) but rather covers a variety of skin diseases, including the different forms of psoriasis and vitiligo (both of which make the skin white, cf. 2 Kings 5:27). The leprosy in Leviticus that contaminates clothing or a house is mold or mildew (Lev 13:47–59; 14:33–57)." (Ryken, Wilhoit, and Longman, *Dictionary of Biblical Imagery*, 507. See also Douglas R. A. Hare, *Interpretation: A Bible Commentary for Teaching and Preaching—Matthew* [Louisville, KY: John Knox Press, 1993], 89.)

10.   Lockyer, *All the Miracles of the Bible*, 172; Trench, *Miracles and Parables of the Old Testament*, 135.

11.   Kaiser, "Exodus," in Gaebelein, *The Expositor's Bible Commentary*, 2:326. See also Ada R. Habershon, *The Study of the Miracles* (London: Morgan & Scott, 1911), 87.

12.   In this spirit, one early Christian source mused: "Moses [as a symbol of Christ] . . . was ordered to thrust his hand into his bosom, and when it was brought out again it was found to be leprous; at once healed. This indicates that the Jewish people [were] to become impure by abandoning the Lord Christ but that [they] would recover [their] former health by returning to him." (Cassiodorus, "Exposition of the Psalms," 73:11, in Joseph T. Lienhard, ed., *Exodus, Leviticus, Numbers, Deuteronomy*, in *Ancient Christian Significance* [Grand Rapids, MI: Zondervan, 1961], 26.)

13. See John R. Huddlestun, "Nile (OT)," in David Noel Freedman, ed., *The Anchor Bible Dictionary* (New York: Doubleday, 1992), 4:1108–12; Bruce B. Williams, "Nile (Geography)," in Freedman, *The Anchor Bible Dictionary*, 4:1115; E. A. Wallis Budge, *Osiris: The Egyptian Religion of Resurrection* (New York: University Books, 1961), 1:19 & 2:295–96; Evelyn Wells, *Nefertiti* (New York: Doubleday, 1964), 130; J. R. Dummelow, *The One Volume Bible Commentary* (New York: Macmillan, 1965), 55; "A Facsimile from the Book of Abraham, No. 1, Fig. 9," in the Pearl of Great Price.

14. "As the Nile was worshiped as a god, and as its water was the life-blood of Egypt, while fish was a most important food, this blow was devastating," beyond the loss of the fish! (Cole, *Exodus*, in *Tyndale Old Testament Commentary*, 90.)

15. See Maurice H. Farbridge, *Studies in Biblical and Semitic Symbolism* (London: Routledge, 1923), 228; Cooper, *An Illustrated Encyclopaedia of Traditional Symbols*, 22; Ryken, Wilhoit, and Longman, *Dictionary of Biblical Imagery*, 100; Paul Ricoeur, *The Symbolism of Evil* (Boston, MA: Beacon Press, 1969), 36; Joseph Fielding McConkie and Donald W. Parry, *A Guide to Scriptural Symbols* (Salt Lake City, UT: Deseret Book, 1990), 22; Patrick Fairbairn, *The Typology of Scripture*, 1:182–83; Joseph Fielding McConkie, *Gospel Symbolism* (Salt Lake City, UT: Bookcraft, 1985), 253.

16. See Alonzo L. Gaskill, *The Lost Language of Symbolism: An Essential Guide for Recognizing and Interpreting Symbols of the Gospel* (Salt Lake City, UT: Deseret Book, 2003), 185–88.

17. Tertullian, "On the Resurrection of the Flesh," 28:1–2, in Lienhard, *Exodus, Leviticus, Numbers, Deuteronomy*, in *Ancient Christian Commentary on Scripture*, 25.

18. Ibid.

19. Trench, *Miracles and Parables of the Old Testament*, 20.

20. Ibid. Just as the magicians of Pharaoh sought to imitate each of the divine manifestations that God gave through Moses, so also Satan seeks to imitate the divine today, all in an effort to keep people away from the truth. And just as the Egyptians copied many elements from the true gospel, including elements of the rites of the temple, so also today the devil copies bits of the true gospel and its rites in an effort to confuse people and keep them from the restored gospel.

21. Ibid.

22. See Kaiser, "Exodus," in Gaebelein, *The Expositor's Bible Commentary*, 2:325–26. See also Ogden and Skinner, *Verse By Verse—The Old Testament Volume One: Genesis through 2 Samuel, Psalms*, 1:185.

23. Habershon, *Study of the Types* (Grand Rapids, MI: Kregel Publications, 1974), 24. See also Lockyer, *All the Miracles of the Bible*, 46.

24. Lockyer, *All the Miracles of the Bible*, 46.

25. We are reminded of the Book of Mormon's declaration that the "iron rod" of Lehi's vision was the "word of God" (1 Nephi 11:25). So it is that our fullest access to Christ will be through reading, coming to know, and faithfully living His words, as found in the holy scriptures and the teachings of the living prophets.

26. Lockyer, *All the Miracles of the Bible*, 46. One Jewish source states: "The plague on his hand was to teach him that as the leper defiles, so the Egyptians defiled Israel, and as Moses was healed of his uncleanness, so God would cleanse the children of Israel of the pollution the Egyptians had brought upon them." (Ginzberg, *The Legends of the Jews*, 2:321.)

27. Joseph Smith, *Teachings of the Prophet Joseph Smith*, Joseph Fielding Smith, comp. (Salt Lake City, UT: Deseret Book, 1976), 181.

28. McQuade, *The Top 100 Miracles of the Bible*, 32.

29. Ezra Taft Benson, "Beware of Pride," *Ensign*, May 1989.

30. McQuade, *The Top 100 Miracles of the Bible*, 31.

THE PLAGUES in EGYPT

EXODUS 7:15–12:30

THE MIRACLE

God sent Moses and Aaron to Pharaoh to perform a number of miracles in the form of plagues. The goal of these miracles was not to convert Pharaoh by showing him signs; but, rather, to break him by providing him with plagues. God desired repentance and compliance, but Pharaoh was interested in offering neither.

Thus, time and again Moses and Aaron approached Pharaoh with various plagues, sending nine in a row. However, none of them softened Pharaoh's heart.

Finally, God sent a tenth plague—the ultimate plague—the death of the firstborn son. This last plague broke Pharaoh's will, and he allowed the Israelites to go free.

BACKGROUND

The English word "plague" comes from a Greek word, which means literally to strike a "blow" toward someone or something.[1] Thus, each of these plagues were "blows" struck by God against or upon Pharaoh.

The plagues of Egypt would have been seen by the Egyptians, or anyone from the ancient Mediterranean, as visible attacks and divinely poured out judgments on the gods of Egypt. The plagues would have implied to observers that the gods of Pharaoh were inferior to the God of Moses. Hence, one witness to the series of plagues declared: "Now I know that the Lord [Jehovah] is greater than all gods" in Egypt (Exodus 18:11).[2]

Scholars traditionally hold that each of the plagues symbolized some aspect of Pharaoh's religion. Thus, through them, Jehovah metaphorically defeated these false gods and the faith that they presided over. One LDS text noted: "Through the plagues, God showed his power over all the principal gods that were worshiped in the Nile Valley, discrediting them and their presumed power. . . . Through the plagues, every Egyptian god and every sign of the gods became a horror and a torment to the people."[3] One non-LDS text put it this way: "It has long been maintained that . . . a specific degrading of Egyptian deities [is] evident in the plague narratives. Exodus 12:12 and Numbers 33:4 point out that plagues and exodus were God's executing judgment on 'the gods of Egypt.' . . . Plagues were considered to be divine in origin. . . . Indeed the gods of Egypt were shown to be impotent through Yahweh's 'signs and wonders.'"[4] Thus, understanding the symbolism behind each of the plagues will explain why God selected the particular plagues that He did.

SYMBOLIC ELEMENTS

The plagues were sent in three cycles of three.[5] The first plague of each cycle was "announced to the Pharaoh, at the river, in the morning" (see Exodus 7:15). The second plague of each cycle was announced with a warning. The third plague of each cycle was inflicted without warning. Of course, anciently, the number three was an indicator that something was of divine influence or origin. Thus, to send the plagues in cycles of three would have sent a message to all in Egypt that this was God's doing—that divine displeasure was being manifest.

The first of the plagues is recorded in Exodus 7:14–25. Moses turned the Nile to blood, and consequently brought about the death of all the creatures that lived in that body of water. As a result, the Egyptians had no water to drink, bathe in, or irrigate with. In addition, a great deal of their food was lost. Some have seen this as an ironic twist of fate. As one commentator noted: "The punishment of this plague was retaliatory. The Egyptians had made the Nile the means of destroying Hebrew infants ([Exodus] 1:22), so that Hebrew parents loathed to drink of it, as though it had been stained with the blood of their children; so is it now made by means of blood undrinkable for the Egyptians."[6] More importantly, the Nile waters were considered holy to the Egyptians. Indeed, some saw them as a symbol of the heavens, and as the residence of gods like Sobek, Hep and Heket, while others saw the waters themselves as divine.[7] Therefore, this plague symbolized the defilement of the heavens and the killing of some of Egypt's gods. One commentary records: "As the Nile was worshiped as a god, and as its water was the life-blood of Egypt, while fish was a most important food, this blow was devastating" beyond the loss of the fish![8] Through this plague, the Egyptians were taught not only about the power of Jehovah over their own gods, but also about who was truly the source of water, and, thus, the source of life![9]

Plague number two is recorded in Exodus 8:1–15. Moses caused frogs to infest the land. The frog was a standard Egyptian symbol of reproduction, and an emblem of the goddess Heket and the god Osiris.[10] Thus, in this plague, the Egyptians are overrun and plagued by their own gods. The book of Exodus informs us that Moses granted Pharaoh the opportunity to name the time when the second plague would be withdrawn (see Exodus 8:9–11, 13–14). This symbolizes the idea that the God of Moses was omnipotent, but also that He was the source for the plague.[11] The means of withdrawing the frogs was not having them return to the Nile, but, rather, to cause them to drop dead on the spot at the appointed hour. Their death by Moses's command symbolized the death of the gods Heket and Osiris, and implied that Israel's God and prophet had the power to both control and kill Egypt's gods.[12]

Plague number three is recorded in Exodus 8:16–19. This plague came in the form of an infestation of gnats or lice.[13] This was the first plague that Pharaoh's magicians could not imitate. Thus, through this miracle we are symbolically shown that Satan's power is limited.[14] The book of Exodus indicates that the gnats or lice came from the "dust."

> The key word for the sign here is the repeated word "dust" (*'apar*), the loose topsoil. "The dust of the earth" has been turned into gnats. Dust is that from which human beings have come and to which they return upon death. . . . In fact, it can refer to the grave or the nether world (Job 17:16; 21:26; Ps. 22:29; Isa. 26:19). The image thus suggests the end of the Egyptians; they will be no more, for their source and goal have been taken away. It is also an image used to speak of the humiliation of those who oppose the God of Israel, including kings of the earth (Isa. 26:5; 41:2; 49:23; Micah 7:17; Job 40:13; Ps. 72:9). Dust is the creation of God . . . , and in this sign God displays control of it. But its use as a prominent image of human morality and humiliation is a sign which Pharaoh ignores at his peril.[15]

One commentator suggested: "The dust of the earth was worshiped in Egyptian pantheism as Seb, the earth god, or father of the gods."[16] If this is the case, then the source of the plague upon the Egyptians was one of their own gods. In other words, one of their own deities was tormenting them.

This could only be taken by the Egyptians as a sign that their own divinity was displeased with their behavior.

Plague number four is recorded in Exodus 8:20–32. It brought an infestation of flying insects that some scholars believe were likely scarab beetles.[17] If the swarming insects were indeed beetles, then they likely represented the Egyptian sun god, Re/Ra or Khepera.[18] Thus, symbolically speaking, this major Egyptian deity had become a plague to its worshipers.[19] "Beetles were deemed sacred and were seldom destroyed."[20] Thus, an infestation of this magnitude, coupled with an inability to kill the insects, made this a frustrating plague, to say the least.

Plague number five is described in Exodus 9:1–7. This plague brought a pestilence that killed most of the animals,[21] but only the animals of the Egyptians! The livestock that were killed by this plague are symbolically significant, so as to send a message to Pharaoh that would have been unmistakable. Scholars indicate that each of the animals killed in this plague were worshiped as a god by the Egyptians.[22] "Another part of Egypt's wide array of gods was hard hit: the Apis, or sacred bull Ptah; the calf god Ra; the cows of Hathor; the jackal-headed god Anubis; and the bull Bakis of the god Mentu. The evidence was too strong to be mere coincidence."[23] Rather plainly, Moses is informing Pharaoh that Jehovah has power over Egypt's gods. If he will not submit to the demands of the God of Israel then the sacrifice of all that is sacred in Egypt will be the penalty.[24]

In Exodus 9:8–12 we find the details of plague number six. This outpouring of God's power consisted of giving boils or (as some have interpreted the Hebrew), leprosy to what animals remained, and to the Egyptian people also. The people likely contracted the bacteria, which caused the boils or leprosy on the cattle, which were symbols of one of Pharaoh's gods. Thus, the deity proved to be a curse to its people; it brought them sickness, pain, and death, just as the worship of false gods brings spiritual sickness, pain, and death to those who practice idolatry.[25] As with so many of the plagues before this one, the symbolic message was that the gods of Pharaoh and the people of Egypt were under the control of the God of Israel, who was in *all ways* more powerful than them, and who held their collective and individual destinies in His hands. Pharaoh's gods had no power to save, but, as the symbolism implies, had an ability to bring sickness and sorrow to their people.[26]

> The ashes of the furnace which Moses sprinkled toward the heavens and God turned into the boils provide an interesting aspect. One expositor

suggests that the furnace in question was the one where human victims to an Egyptian god were burnt alive and that Pharaoh possibly was standing before the furnace. Moses in the sight of the king cast ashes heavenward, presenting it, as it were, to God in evidence of His people's [victimization at the hands of Pharaoh]. This fact is evident that if the living sacrifices offered by the Egyptians were meant to avert the plagues, the ashes, instead of doing so, brought a fresh one.[27]

The seventh of the plagues is recorded in Exodus 9:13–35. It consisted of hail coupled with fire and thunder.[28] Yahweh was known as the "Storm God."[29] Thunder, fire, and hail were all associated with Him; representing His weapons of war against His enemies.[30] "The [seventh] miracle . . . was directed against Shu, god of the atmosphere, and the two gods, Iris and Osiris. How utterly helpless these atmospheric gods were to help the land and its people when smitten by atmospheric forces!"[31] Through this miracle, Jehovah is symbolically represented as personally plaguing the Egyptians, and showing that He had more power than the Egyptian gods who were believed to control the weather.[32]

The eighth plague that Moses was commanded to bring down upon Egypt is described in Exodus 10:1–20, and consisted of myriads of swarming locusts from the east. These pests destroyed the crops of the Egyptians, leaving them no plants to eat.[33] They had lost their drinking, bathing, and irrigation water in plague number one, along with the meat they would have gained from any of the fish that died during that plague. Then, in plague number five, their livestock died, leaving them without any other potential source of meat.[34] Now all grain, vegetable, and plant life was taken from them, leaving them with literally nothing to eat. The fact that these locusts came from the east was a symbolic message that they were not some coincidental inconvenience. Rather, because east was the sacred direction that represented the presence of God, the Egyptians would have understood these flying faunae as God's messengers, come to pour out His displeasure upon them.[35] "The god, Serajia, was reckoned to be the protector of the land from locusts. How the religious belief of the [Egyptian] people must have been shattered as they saw how helpless their deity was against [Jehovah's] invading host!"[36]

The ninth plague was the last to symbolize Egypt's gods. It is recorded in Exodus 10:21–29. It consisted of three days of darkness that covered all of Egypt. The darkness was of such a nature that it even prevented fires from being lit (very reminiscent of 3 Nephi 8:21–22). As with the other plagues poured out upon the Egyptians, the Israelites appear to be unaffected by this one. We are told that they had light in their homes (Exodus 10:23). "The period of *three days* may be symbolic."[37] Certainly the number three implies that something is from God. Thus, the length of the darkness may have been one more reminder to Pharaoh that the God of Israel was behind these awful events. It is traditionally believed that this thick darkness represented the death of Re/Ra, the Egyptian sun god. One commentator wrote: "The obscuring of the sun in connection with the 9th plague has been regarded as the triumph of the Hebrew God over the head of the Egyptian pantheon."[38] Another penned this:

> The worship of the *sun* was common in Egypt and in Eastern lands generally. One of the principle cities, called *On*, meaning "house of the sun," was the seat of the idolatrous form of sun-worship. The plague of darkness, therefore, robbed the Egyptians of their supreme god, *Ra*, the sun god, and proved Jehovah to be the God of gods. *Ra* was among the principle objects of heathen worship in the delta, where the cities of Heliopolis and Pithom were dedicated to him. Darkness was a creation of *Set*—the evil principle, the destroyer of Osiris—and of *Apophis*, the great serpent, the impeder of souls in the lower world. It must have been a crushing blow to the religion of Egypt when darkness covered it. Had *Ra* died? Had *Set* triumphed over his brother, or had *Apophis* encircled the world with his dark folds and plunged it into eternal night?[39]

The tenth plague consisted of the death of the firstborn son of all families living within the boundaries of the land of Egypt. It was the Passover plague, and did not come in a cycle of three, as had the other nine plagues. Whereas the first nine plagues symbolized some aspect of Egypt's religion or gods, the tenth plague represented the God of Israel—Jehovah, the Atoning Christ! As we have already noted, the first nine plagues only influenced the lives of the Egyptians, but the tenth plague had power and influence over both the Egyptians and the Israelites. This implies the limited power of the false gods of Pharaoh, but the universal power of the God of Israel. Jesus not only has power over all the earth, and over *all* peoples, but His Atonement (symbolized by this tenth miracle) is also universally applicable and powerful. Just as the death of the firstborn son finally freed the Israelites from Egyptian bondage, so also the death of God's firstborn frees you and me from the bondage of Satan (whom Pharaoh symbolizes).[40]

APPLICATION AND ALLEGORIZATION

Ultimately, the message of this series of ten miracles was this: The God of Israel was the only true and living God. Each of these miraculous plagues showed in some symbolic way the weakness or death of one or more of the Egyptian gods. Each plague figuratively suggested that Pharaoh's gods were weaker than, and subject to, the God of Moses.[41] "It was obvious that these terrible plagues weren't mere coincidence: Moses announced most of them before they happened, and Pharaoh pleaded with Moses to intreat [sic] God for relief."[42] Whereas the Israelites were consistently protected from these plagues, the Egyptians suffered terribly because of them. But they didn't have to. God, through Moses, continually offered them a way out of their suffering; namely, repentance and obedience. So it is with you and me and sin. If we repent and obey, we need not suffer. If, on the other hand, we choose to act like Pharaoh, then we should expect the discomfort symbolized by the plagues of this story. The Egyptian gods were impotent in their battle with the God of Israel. Likewise, all of the world's "gods" are also impotent when compared with the true and living God. They are impotent in their ability to save, in their ability to bring peace and joy, and in their ability to bless the lives of those who worship them.

Something typological may be meant by the miracle of the staff that turned into a snake. One text suggests: "The swallowing of the magicians' staffs by Aaron's . . . functions as a sign of things to come in a very specific way: the fate of the Egyptians at the Red Sea."[43] In other words, just as Moses and Aaron's rod turned into a snake (or a crocodile, as some translate the Hebrew), and then swallowed the staffs of the Egyptians, so also the water of the Red Sea would swallow up the Egyptians when they pursued the Israelites across it. It may not be coincidental that Sobek (or Sebek), the crocodile god of the Egyptians, lived in the waters of the region. Though most of the Egyptian army was swallowed by the sea (metaphorically fulfilling the type), perhaps a few were even eaten by Sobek (thereby quite literally fulfilling it)![44]

One early Christian source noted that the plagues listed in this miracle were physically brought down upon Egypt, but are spiritually present in our own lives. "Egypt is the figure of this world."[45] It represents the sin-laden society in which you and I are forced to dwell. In the first Mosaic plague, the waters were turned to blood, and just as the waters of the Nile were "erratic," the dogmas, morals, and teachings of this world are inconsistent and chaotic. Likewise, just as the water was turned to blood in the miracle, when the philosophers and "wise men" of our day ponder life's questions, they "think carnally," and consequently increase the sins of society via their teachings.[46]

Of turning the waters of the Nile to blood, one ancient source suggested the following connection; John depicted Jesus turning water to wine, which symbolized that people were being changed for the better. But in this plague the water turns to blood, which is a negative symbol, and suggests that the religion of Egypt did not make people better, but rather more sinful.[47] Similarly, one modern author saw this in the miracle: "How striking the contrast between this and the first miracle performed . . . at Cana in Galilee. . . . Do they not mark the difference between the two dispensations? . . . One spoke of death, the other of joy."[48] Regarding the infestation of frogs that Jehovah sent and then removed, one book on miracles suggests: "Whatsoever any man makes his god, beside the true one, shall be once his tormentor."[49] In other words, the very things Pharaoh and his people worshiped ended up being their tormentors. Likewise, if your god is drugs or alcohol, they will eventually torment or punish you. If your god is money, it will eventually serve to be the primary source of your torment or frustration. If your god is sex or pornography, it will eventually be the means by which you're tormented and enslaved. That which we worship becomes our god. Thus, if we wish to be happy, we had better place the God of Israel as our master, because He will bless us, while all other false gods will torment us. Another commentator found the following application for the miracle of the amphibian affliction.

> Pharaoh probably didn't see the eruption of frogs into his life as a miracle, but he could certainly appreciate their sudden removal. But once the frogs were dead, maybe it didn't seem like such a big thing. We can relate to Pharaoh's about-face, can't we? For we, too, have begged God for relief from a problem, only to forget all He's done for us when our pain is relieved. Do we forget God's graces too easily? Is He truly Lord of our lives?[50]

Do we remember God in times of need, but ignore Him when life is going well? Are we guilty of begging for blessings, but then, after our prayers are answered, marginalizing the miracle? When we do this, we act like Pharaoh did in response to the removal of his trials.

Of the gnats or lice of the third plague, one text noted how they fly through the air "so subtle and minute" that they entirely escape notice, except by those who look closely. But when the gnat or lice land on your body and bite or sting you, the pain of their action is immediately noticeable. So it is with "the subtlety of heretics, who drill into souls with the subtle stings of their words" and false doctrines. "They attack with such cunning that one who is deceived [by them] neither sees nor understands the source of his deception."[51] We must ever be on guard against the falsehoods and damnable doctrines of heretics. Just as they caused the great Apostasy of the first century, they can cause the individual apostasy of any believer today.[52] Another commentator interpreted the miracles of the gnats or lice this way: "Insidious as the bugs were, they should have given Pharaoh a message that God was determined to get through to him. We've seen this determination in our own lives, when God has wanted us to understand that the life we've been living is not what He wants. He will continually redirect us until we finally listen. Is God redirecting [you] today?"[53]

In the fifth miracle—that of the flies or beetles—we learn that Pharaoh sought to "make a deal" with God. The Israelites had wanted to leave Egypt to make sacrifices outside of that land. Pharaoh, sensing that the God of Israel was real, offered to let the children of Israel sacrifice *in* Egypt, as though God would make concessions with him. Jehovah said, *no*! From this experience, we can learn an important lesson: "God is not One to be bargained with, as Pharaoh would discover. Just as he could not turn God from His purpose, neither can we. Do we try to cheat [or strike bargains with] Him?"[54] Ironically, only a short time later—in the miracle of the locusts—Pharaoh again sought to make concessions with God. In light of how Jehovah punished the king and his people for their last attempt at "bargaining with God," it seems rather puzzling that they would try the same "trick." Does God change His mind? Does He forget what happened in the past? To what degree are you and I like Pharaoh in how we deal with God?[55] Do we consistently make promises to Him that we've made and broken in the past, as though He'll think "this time might be different"?

Though God had turned the water in the land to blood, sent frogs everywhere, brought gnats or lice, and beetles or flies, to afflict and torment Pharaoh and his people, nevertheless, the king's heart seemed untouched. He stood firm and defiant against Israel's God and His emissaries, and thus brought an additional plague—the death of most of Egypt's livestock.[56] Note how this miracle seems to highlight the inability to sin "in a vacuum," *per se*. All of our lives touch or influence the lives of others. One text notes: "All Pharaoh's people suffered from their relationship to him as his subjects. This principle extends to creatures below man. The cattle of Egypt suffered because their masters sinned."[57] Too often we hear those who disobey God's commands reason, "I'm not hurting anyone," or "It's my body; what do you care what I do with it?" What we learn here is that Pharaoh's stubbornness brought pain, suffering, and even death upon his own people, *and* their animals. None of us can sin without harming others—even though we may not realize at the time the degree of negative influence our choices have.

It has been suggested that the boils, or leprous swollen cysts and fever, of the sixth plague have a parallel in modern society. In these sores, the "troubled and purulent evil of this age" is symbolized. The swollen sores remind us of the swells of pride we so commonly suffer from. The fevers that accompanied these sores can symbolize the madness and insanity of our day.[58] Likewise, the thick darkness of the tenth plague has been said to represent the "blindness of their minds"[59] and the accompanying mistakes that come to a nation that walks without God's light to guide them. It was true of Egypt of old, and it is becoming increasingly true of the society in which we live today.[60] Of these boils or sores, one book states: "Anyone who consistently stands against God will suffer increasing pain, spiritual or physical. Here God made Pharaoh and his people feel the pain of their sin in their own bodies. There was no way to escape or forget about God's message."[61] While certainly not all physical problems or ailments are the result of sin, nevertheless, this miracle invites us to ask ourselves during our times of trial, "Have we brought it on ourselves by our bad habits or bad attitudes? Do we need to seek Him and ask for clean hearts, as well as clean bodies?"[62]

In the plague of hail, fire, and thunder, we read that Pharaoh seemed to soften his heart because of the plague. Moses recorded:

> And Pharaoh sent, and called for Moses and Aaron, and said unto them, I have sinned this time: the Lord is righteous, and I and my people are wicked.
>
> Entreat the Lord (for it is enough) that there be no more mighty thunderings and hail; and I will let you go, and ye shall stay no longer. (Exodus 9:27–28)

But almost immediately after the plague had ceased, Pharaoh again hardened his heart and refused to keep his promise to let the children of Israel go (Exodus 9:34–35). "Real repentance does not come and go. One who turns to the Lord in faith will not quickly decide it was all a mistake or return to former hard-heartedness. Sure, we all make mistakes, but a heart touched by God will always show."[63] As one commentator wisely noted:

There are vessels belonging to our navy which are past repair or improvement, and are therefore unfit for sea. Yet they are retained as light-ships along the coast, that they may be the means of preventing better ships from going to pieces on the rocks. So it was with Pharaoh, and so it has been with many men since. Long and obstinate resistance to the commands of God would seem at last to deprive men of the capacity to receive Divine influence, and they are only useful as beacons [or examples] to others.[64]

In the example of Pharaoh, we are reminded of the dangers of fighting against God. Will you and I be used by Him to further His purposes? Or will He have to use us as an example of what not to do, and what not to become?

Of the locusts, one text noted that something seemingly insignificant or powerless in and of itself can be nearly omnipotent, if combined with many others with the same mindset or will. Just as one locust could be readily crushed under Pharaoh's foot, but millions overwhelmed him, so also can one faithful Saint have limited influence in converting or changing the world, but if millions of Saints can have the same mindset, they would be a force to be reckoned with. This miracle reminds us that "unity of action increases immensely the power of numbers."[65]

The ninth plague—the plague of darkness—sent an unmistakable message to Pharaoh and his people. "The Egyptians would have understood the meaning of this plague, for they worshiped Ra, the sun god."[66] Jehovah had sent a message, loud and clear. This powerful god of the Egyptians was not there for them. He could not hear their pleas for relief. The God of Israel "was showing the people [of Egypt] that He was more powerful than their pagan deity."[67] So many signs had been given to them. This was not the first plague to suggest that their god was powerless, if not dead. But they would not believe, no matter how overwhelming the evidence was. One commentator offered this modern application of this miracle:

Those who are blinded by unbelief live in darkness as black as the ninth plague. As Christians, who enjoy the benefits of the Light, we often wonder why people will not turn to Him. Their darkness is not the ordinary middle-of-the-night sort, but one that so thoroughly covers the eyes that they have no inkling of the Light. What lifts this darkness? Only repentance and faith in Jesus. We can discuss faith with unbelievers until we turn blue in the face, but until they trust in Him, they cannot fully understand.[68]

The darkness that reigned in Egypt was a symbol of the spiritual darkness that Pharaoh labored under.[69] The Israelites had light in their dwellings while the Egyptians did not (see Exodus 10:23). So also, those who have and follow the truth will have light in their lives while others around them may walk in darkness. One commentator wisely noted, you can make darkness in your own house, but you can't make it outside.[70] So it is with each man or woman, we can choose to live in spiritual darkness, but we cannot force that same darkness upon those who reject it. Pharaoh wished to live in darkness, even though he had clearly seen the light. But he could not force the Israelites into his darkness. They had light because they sought to embrace the light—to live in it. We too get to choose whether our lives are filled with darkness or light.

> Like many people today, Pharaoh was comfortable in his unbelief. The world seemed to revolve around him, and he liked it that way. There was little room in his life for real truth that confronted his false reality. When we witness [or bear testimony] to people who refuse to believe, let's understand that they are caught in Pharaoh's trap. Only God can release them from the hardness of their own hearts. Before we seek to bring the Word to them, we'd be wise to spend time in prayer that seeks to open hearts to Him.[71]

Is your heart ever hardened like Pharaoh's? Are the things you love "plagues"[72] that will come back to haunt you when Christ returns—or, perhaps, even sooner? "If we look inward, and see how we have withstood the commands of God, and how little effect either His judgments or His mercies have produced on us, we should find little occasion to exult over Pharaoh."[73]

Egypt was a representation of all heathendom: the kingdom of the devil. The battle between Moses and Pharaoh was a symbolic representation of all warfare between the bride of Christ and the adversary of all mankind—Satan.[74] Though Moses eventually won the battle, it took time, perseverance, and the Lord's intervention. So it is in all of our lives. If we persevere, we will eventually win the battle. But it will take the Lord's assistance, and a great deal of time.

NOTES

1. See Leland Ryken, James C. Wilhoit, and Tremper Longman III, *Dictionary of Biblical Imagery* (Downers Grove, IL: InterVarsity Press, 1998), 648.
2. Ibid.
3. Renee Vorhaus, in "I Have a Question," *Ensign*, September 1980.

4.   James K. Hoffmeier, "Egypt, Plagues In," in David Noel Freedman, ed., *The Anchor Bible Dictionary* (New York: Doubleday, 1992), 2:376–77. See also Stephen L. Harris, *Understanding the Bible: A Reader's Introduction*, 2nd ed. (Houston, TX: Mayfield Publishing Company, 1992), 22; Patrick Fairbairn, *The Typology of Scripture*, 2nd ed. (Philadelphia, PA: Smith & English, 1989), 1:38–50.

5.   See Ellis T. Rasmussen, *An Introduction to the Old Testament and Its Teachings* (Provo, UT: Brigham Young University, 1972), 1:78–79; Hoffmeier, "Egypt, Plagues In," in Freedman, *The Anchor Bible Dictionary*, 2:374–75; Ellis T. Rasmussen, *A Latter-day Saint Commentary on the Old Testament* (Salt Lake City, UT: Deseret Book, 1994), 93–94.

6.   Herbert Lockyer, *All the Miracles of the Bible: The Supernatural in Scripture— Its Scope and Significance* (Grand Rapids, MI: Zondervan, 1961), 49–50.

7.   E. A. Wallis Budge, *Osiris: The Egyptian Religion of Resurrection* (New York: University Books, 1961), 1:19 & 2:295–96; Evelyn Wells, *Nefertiti* (New York: Doubleday, 1964), 130; J. R. Dummelow, *The One Volume Bible Commentary* (New York: Macmillan, 1965), 55; "A Facsimile from the Book of Abraham, No. 1, Fig. 9," in the Pearl of Great Price; Pamela McQuade, *The Top 100 Miracles of the Bible: What They Are and What They Mean to You Today* (Uhrichsville, OH: Barbour Publishing, 2008), 34; Lockyer, *All The Miracles of the Bible*, 49.

8.   R. Alan Cole, *Exodus*, in *Tyndale Old Testament Commentaries* (Grand Rapids, MI: Eerdmans, 1973), 90. One text states of the Nile that it "was looked upon as identical with Osiris, the highest god." (Fairbairn, *The Typology of Scripture*, 1:41.) Elsewhere we read: "Their god was struck dead. The Nile was one of the principle divinities of Egypt. They worshiped it as a source of their national prosperity. . . . Now not only death had passed upon it, but corruption had set in." (Richard C. Trench, *Miracles and Parables of the Old Testament* [Grand Rapids, MI: Baker Book House, 1959], 12.)

9.   Exodus 7:22 suggests that the magicians imitated the Lord's miracle, although the specifics are not given. The Exodus account seems to suggest that Moses had already turned all of the water to blood, so where the magicians would have acquired clean Nile water is uncertain. Perhaps they simply took some of the water (which Moses had already changed), and using an opaque jar, pretended to change it to blood. The logical or miraculous thing would have been for them to have turned the water back to fresh or undefiled water. But that was clearly beyond their powers. (See Cole, *Exodus*, in *Tyndale Old Testament Commentaries*, 90; McQuade, *The Top 100 Miracles of the Bible*, 34.) Pharaoh's heart was not softened by this first Mosaic miracle (see Exodus 7:23).

10.   J. C. Cooper, *An Illustrated Encyclopaedia of Traditional Symbols* (London: Thames and Hudson, 1987), 72; Budge, *Osiris: The Egyptian Religion of Resurrection*, 1:279; Donald A. Mackenzie, *Egyptian Myth and Legend* (Whitefish, MT: Kessinger Publishing, 2006), 75; Hoffmeier, "Egypt, Plagues In," in Freedman, *The Anchor*

Bible Dictionary, 2:376; Dummelow, *The One Volume Bible Commentary*, 55; Lockyer, A*ll the Miracles of the Bible*, 50. One commentator wrote: "The frog was worshiped as a representative of their god *Osiris*, and *Ptha*, another of their deities, was represented with a frog's head." (Trench, *Miracles and Parables of the Old Testament*, 13; emphasis in original. See also Lockyer, *All the Miracles of the Bible*, 50.)

11. Exodus 8:7 indicates that the magicians of Egypt replicated this miracle too. Even though the magicians bore testimony that this plague was a manifestation of "the finger of God," Pharaoh's heart was not softened by it (see Exodus 8:15, 19).

12. See Lockyer, *All the Miracles of the Bible*, 50.

13. "Whether the lice in question were mosquitoes, sandflies, ticks, or fleas is a doubtful point. This we do know, that having created various insects, God can command them to execute judgment upon an idolatrous nation." (Ibid., 51.)

14. This same idea is taught in the book of Job (see Job 1:12; 2:6) and also in the book of Revelation (see Revelation 9:1).

15. Terence E. Fretheim, *Interpretation: A Bible Commentary for Teaching and Preaching—Exodus* (Louisville, KY: John Knox Press, 1991), 118.

16. Lockyer, *All the Miracles of the Bible*, 51.

17. While "there is no accompanying noun to tell of what insects the 'mixture' or 'swarm' consisted" (Cole, *Exodus*, in *Tyndale Old Testament Commentaries*, 93. See also Lockyer, *All the Miracles of the Bible*, 52) "it is generally held that a kind of beetle, injurious both to the persons and property of men, is meant." (Lockyer, *All the Miracles of the Bible*, 52. See, also J. H. Hertz, *The Pentateuch and Haftorahs: Hebrew Text English Translation and Commentary*, 2nd ed. [London: Soncino Press, 1960], 240; Walter C. Kaiser Jr., "Exodus," in Frank E. Gaebelein, *The Expositor's Bible Commentary* [Grand Rapids, MI: Zondervan, 1976–1992], 2:355; Vorhaus, in "I Have a Question.")

18. Budge, *Osiris: The Egyptian Religion of Resurrection*, 2:326; Mackenzie, *Egyptian Myth and Legend*, 5; Dummelow, *The One Volume Bible Commentary*, 55; Cooper, *An Illustrated Encyclopaedia of Traditional Symbols*, 145; Lockyer, *All the Miracles of the Bible*, 52.

19. If this is an ordinary house fly (though that is doubted), then it would still be an appropriate symbol, as the prophet Isaiah uses the house fly as a representation of the nation of Egypt (see Isaiah 7:18). See also, Kaiser, "Exodus," in Gaebelein, *The Expositor's Bible Commentary*, 2:355. As usual, we are told that Pharaoh's heart was not softened by this miracle (see Exodus 8:32). He told Moses that he would let the Israelites go into the wilderness to sacrifice, so long as the flying insects were removed. But when Moses and the Lord complied, Pharaoh didn't do as he had promised. Symbolically, this is an interesting point, because it is generally held by scholars and typologists that Pharaoh was a symbol for Satan. And like Pharaoh, the devil always offers what he cannot deliver. He did so in the pre-mortal life with

salvation—he offered what he had no power to give. He did it with Cain, promising him power and wealth—again, something he had no intention of providing. And Lucifer consistently does this to you and me every time he convinces us to sin. He knows full well that he intends on leaving us disappointed, rather than uplifted, by any and all of our interactions with him. Satan never keeps his promises, and never provides what he tempts us with.

20. Lockyer, *All the Miracles of the Bible*, 52.

21. The biblical text states: "All the cattle of Egypt died" (Exodus 9:6). However, this phrase is understood to mean "'all the cattle which is in the field,' that is, the open air at that time. Evidently those confined to stables and shade were not smitten ([Exodus] 9:3, 6). 'All cattle' signifies cattle of every kind. Cattle were affected by the next plague, too ([Exodus] 9:10)," and thus not "all cattle" could have died in this fifth plague. (Lockyer, *All the Miracles of the Bible*, 53.)

22. See Hoffmeier, "Egypt, Plagues In," in Freedman, *The Anchor Bible Dictionary*, 2:376. See also, Cooper, *An Illustrated Encyclopaedia of Traditional Symbols*, 26, 44–45; Mackenzie, *Egyptian Myth and Legend*, 69; Wells, *Nefertiti*, 91; Cole, *Exodus*, in *Tyndale Old Testament Commentaries*, 95; Trench, *Miracles and Parables in the Old Testament*, 19. "Sheep and cows were deemed sacred by the Egyptians and in the use of them for a sacrifice to God, the Israelites would have to 'sacrifice the abomination of the Egyptians.' Moses knew that to offer these animals in the sight of Egyptians, who abominated killing cattle, would result in a riot or a civil war, and so refused it, with the warning to Pharaoh to deal deceitfully no more." (Lockyer, *All the Miracles of the Bible*, 53.)

23. Kaiser, "Exodus," in Gaebelein, *The Expositor's Bible Commentary*, 2:358. "They worshiped Jupiter Ammon in a ram, Anubis in a dog, and Apis in a bull, and others, too, which Egypt admired as symbols of its gods. They believed that the divine splendor was present in these forms and offered pathetic acts of worship to them." (Isidore of Seville, "Questions on the Old Testament, Exodus," 14:10, in Joseph T. Lienhard, ed., *Exodus, Leviticus, Numbers, Deuteronomy*, in *Ancient Christian Commentary on Scripture* [Downers Grove, IL: InterVarsity Press, 2001], 49.) "The Egyptians would consider the sacrifice of a sacred animal as blasphemous. Animal sacrifice, as such, was not unknown in Egypt. . . . A bull with certain marks was sacred to Apis, cows to Isis, rams to Amon, and so forth, covering nearly every possible sacrificial animal. The Persians unfairly won a battle against the Egyptians in the days of Cambyses by driving a 'screen' of sacred animals ahead of them, at which on Egyptian bowman would shoot, just as ruthless modern man will use women, children, or prisoners of war as a 'screen.'" (Cole, *Exodus*, in *Tyndale Old Testament Commentaries*, 95. See also Lockyer, *All the Miracles of the Bible*, 54.)

24. As always, Pharaoh's heart was not softened by this miracle (Exodus 9:7).

25. Hoffmeier, "Egypt, Plagues In," in Freedman, *The Anchor Bible Dictionary*, 2:376; Cooper, *An Illustrated Encyclopaedia of Traditional Symbols*, 26, 44–45; Mackenzie, *Egyptian Myth and Legend*, 69; Wells, *Nefertiti*, 91.

26. This miracle did not soften Pharaoh's heart (see Exodus 9:12).

27. Lockyer, *All the Miracles of the Bible*, 54.

28. "The hailstones must have been of an enormous size and weight to kill men and cattle." (Lockyer, *All the Miracles of the Bible*, 55.)

29. Frank E. Eakin, Jr., *The Religion and Culture of Israel: An Introduction to Old Testament Thought* (Boston, MA: Allyn and Bacon, 1971), 89; Sidney B. Sperry, *The Spirit of the Old Testament*, 2nd ed. (Salt Lake City, UT: Deseret Book, 1980), 42; William H. C. Propp, *The Anchor Bible: Exodus 1–18* (New York: Doubleday, 1999), 301, 334, 339.

30. See Ryken, Wilhoit, and Longman, *Dictionary of Biblical Imagery*, 359; Ada R. Habershon, *The Study of the Miracles* (London: Morgan & Scott, 1911), 51, 55.

31. Lockyer, *All the Miracles of the Bible*, 56.

32. Exodus 9:34–35 tells us that Pharaoh's heart was not softened by this outpouring of God's power.

33. Rather than just eating the crops in the fields, these locusts were said to have also devoured food in the homes, the leather of the water jugs, and even the wood of their furniture and buildings. (See Lockyer, *All the Miracles of the Bible*, 57.)

34. As the reader likely knows, the Egyptians would not have eaten the flesh of many of these animals that died. But in desperation, some would likely have caved and eaten the flesh of something forbidden them, such as a sheep. However, this plague made even that an impossibility. (See Paterius, "Exposition of the Old and New Testament, Exodus 13," in Lienhard, *Exodus, Leviticus, Numbers, Deuteronomy*, in *Ancient Christian Commentary on Scripture*, 49.)

35. J. E. Cirlot, *A Dictionary of Symbols*, 2nd ed. (New York: Routledge & Kegan Paul, 1971), 245; Cooper, *An Illustrated Encyclopaedia of Traditional Symbols*, 59; Joel F. Drinkard, "East," in Freedman, *The Anchor Bible Dictionary*, 2:248; Joseph Fielding McConkie and Donald W. Parry, *A Guide to Scriptural Symbols* (Salt Lake City, UT: Deseret Book, 1990), 44; Allen C. Myers, *The Eerdmans Bible Dictionary* (Grand Rapids, MI: Eerdmans, 1987), 300; Ryken, Wilhoit, and Longman, *Dictionary of Biblical Imagery*, 225. Pharaoh's heart was not softened by this plague (see Exodus 10:20), so Moses was instructed to send another.

36. Lockyer, *All the Miracles of the Bible*, 57.

37. Cole, *Exodus*, in *Tyndale Old Testament Commentaries*, 100; emphasis added.

38. Hoffmeier, "Egypt, Plagues In," in Freedman, *The Anchor Bible Dictionary*, 2:376. See also, Propp, *The Anchor Bible: Exodus 1–18*, 339–40. "The ninth plague . . . was three days of darkness—probably an eclipse of the sun—that directly discredited the power of the Egyptian sun-god Ra." (Vorhaus, in "I Have a Question.") As with the previous eight symbols, Pharaoh's heart was not softened by this one (see Exodus 10:27). Indeed, somewhat fed up with all of the plagues, Pharaoh actually threatened Moses's life (see Exodus 10:28–29).

39. Lockyer, *All the Miracles of the Bible*, 57–58; emphasis in original.

40. Likewise, one commentator noted: "On that memorable night in Egypt, death visited each home throughout the land. There was death even in the huts of Israel, but it was the lamb that had died instead of the firstborn. In all other dwellings the firstborn was slain." (Habershon, *The Study of the Miracles*, 84–85.) So also, where an individual accepts Christ, the Lord's life is sufficient to pay for that person's sins. But where one rejects that offering, he or she must now be the sacrifice (see D&C 19:15–20).

41. Louis Ginzberg offers a curious interpretation of the plagues. He wrote that "The plagues that God sent upon the Egyptians corresponded to the deeds they had perpetrated against the children of Israel." So, for example, Ginzberg writes: "Because [the Egyptians] forced the Israelites to draw water for them, and also hindered them from the use of the ritual baths, He changed their water into blood." He also said: "Because [the Egyptians] would throw the Israelites into dungeons, God brought darkness upon them, the darkness of hell, so that they had to grope their way." Ginzberg finds such an application for each of the plagues. (See Louis Ginzberg, *The Legends of the Jews* [Philadelphia, PA: The Jewish Publication Society of America, 1910–1938], 2:343–47.)

42. Vorhaus, in "I Have a Question."

43. Fretheim, *Interpretation: A Bible Commentary for Teaching and Preaching—Exodus*, 113. Some scholars, such as Fretheim, believe that the crossing took place at the shallower Reed Sea, rather than at the Red Sea.

44. Today, crocodiles are mostly found in the southern section of the Egyptian portion of the Red Sea. Whether that was different in Moses's day is difficult to tell, though the Nile River certainly hosted crocodiles during that period of Israelite history.

45. See Isidore of Seville, "Questions on the Old Testament, Exodus," 14:1–2, in Lienhard, *Exodus, Leviticus, Numbers, Deuteronomy*, in *Ancient Christian Commentary on Scripture*, 44.

46. Ibid.

47. See Cassiodorus, "Exposition of the Psalms," 77:44 in Lienhard, *Exodus, Leviticus, Numbers, Deuteronomy*, in *Ancient Christian Commentary on Scripture*, 43–44. See also Trench, *Miracles and Parables of the Old Testament*, 13; Lockyer, *All the Miracles of the Bible*, 48–49.

48. Habershon, *The Study of the Miracles*, 62.

49. Trench, *Miracles and Parables of the Old Testament*, 14.

50. McQuade, *The Top 100 Miracles of the Bible*, 37.

51. See Isidore of Seville, "Questions on the Old Testament, Exodus," 14:1–2, in Lienhard, *Exodus, Leviticus, Numbers, Deuteronomy*, in *Ancient Christian Commentary on Scripture*, 46–47.

52. One LDS source said of the symbolic meaning of plague number three: "The third plague . . . affected every man and beast with lice (or sand flies or

gnats), proving that God's finger could touch everyone, no matter who they were." (Vorhaus, in "I Have a Question.")

53. McQuade, *The Top 100 Miracles of the Bible*, 38.

54. Ibid., 39.

55. See ibid., 44.

56. "Standing adamant against God is never profitable. Without His blessing, we harm our livelihoods and our spiritual well-being." McQuade, *The Top 100 Miracles of the Bible*, 40.

57. Trench, *Miracles and Parables of the Old Testament*, 19–20.

58. See Isidore of Seville, "Questions on the Old Testament, Exodus," 14:1–2, in Lienhard, *Exodus, Leviticus, Numbers, Deuteronomy*, in *Ancient Christian Commentary on Scripture*, 50.

59. Ibid., 53.

60. Of this plague, one LDS source suggested: "The sixth plague . . . afflicted every Egyptian and all remaining beasts with painful boils, showing that Israel's God even had power over personal health." (Vorhaus, in "I Have a Question.")

61. McQuade, *The Top 100 Miracles of the Bible*, 41.

62. Ibid.

63. Ibid., 42.

64. Trench, *Miracles and Parables of the Old Testament*, 22–23.

65. Ibid., 25.

66. McQuade, *The Top 100 Miracles of the Bible*, 45.

67. Ibid.

68. Ibid., 46

69. Trench, *Miracles and Parables of the Old Testament*, 27.

70. See ibid., 26.

71. McQuade, *The Top 100 Miracles of the Bible*, 35.

72. Elder Bruce R. McConkie wrote: "All men have a choice. They can repent, or they can suffer. They can believe and obey, or they can reject the truth and live in disobedience. They can prepare themselves to abide the day and to stand when he appeareth, or they can bow in submission to the plagues and pestilences that lie ahead; and, should they escape these, they can then be numbered with the great host who will be burned at his coming." (Bruce R. McConkie, *The Millennial Messiah: The Second Coming of the Son of Man* [Salt Lake City, UT: Deseret Book, 1982], 379.)

73. Lockyer, *All the Miracles of the Bible*, 57.

74. See Trench, *Miracles and Parables of the Old Testament*, 33.

THE CROSSING *of* *the* RED SEA

EXODUS 14

THE MIRACLE

After the series of plagues, which we have just discussed in the previous chapter, Pharaoh told Moses that the Israelites were no longer his slaves, and that they could leave Egypt if they so desired. But once they began their exodus, Pharaoh had another change of heart, as he had so many times before. He began to think of the economic loss his nation would incur by not having the slave labor of the Israelites, and so Pharaoh called together his armies and pursued the Israelites.

The Lord had warned Moses that this would happen, and suggested to him that it had a divine purpose; namely, to establish for the Egyptians that the God of Israel was the true and living God (see Exodus 14:4). Indeed, the Lord had actually commanded Moses to have the Israelites wander about in the land by the sea, as though they were confused and lost (see Exodus 14:1–3), knowing this would provoke Pharaoh, and likely cause his attempted attack.

Moses had apparently not informed the Israelites as to what the Lord was doing because when they saw the approaching Egyptians, and the Israelites were up against the Red Sea with no avenue of escape, they became terrified (see Exodus 14:10). Their lack of faith and tremendous fear was evident in their cries that they would have been better off if they had stayed in Egypt as slaves, than to die in the desert at the hands of the Egyptians. Moses rebuked them for their fear, and promised them that, if they would "fear not," they would that day "see the salvation of the Lord" (Exodus 14:13), and the end of their Egyptian enemies.

God then commanded Moses to stretch forth his hand and staff and part the Red Sea so that the Israelites could pass through on dry ground, and so that the Egyptians would seek to follow them. The east wind came, the sea was parted, and the pillar of fire that had been leading the Israelites through the wilderness moved to their rear, dividing them from the Egyptians, and giving them a bit of a head start crossing the Red Sea.

Eventually, the Egyptians were able to pursue the Israelites, but as they did so they encountered difficulties. The Lord "troubled" them or threw them into confusion (Exodus 14:24). Psalm 77:16–20 suggests that God sent a rather sudden thunderstorm or rainstorm upon the Egyptians. Also, we're told that He caused the wheels of their chariots to get stuck in the mud and then jam or fall off.[1] According to extracanonical Jewish tradition, Pharaoh's armies were also made physically ill by God.[2] All of this scared the Egyptians, who felt that the Lord was fighting for the Israelites, and so they turned around and headed out of the sea, back toward Egypt.[3]

The Lord commanded Moses to close up the Red Sea, which he did, and Pharaoh's entire army drowned in the midst of it.[4] "And Israel saw that great work which the Lord did upon the Egyptians: and the people feared the Lord, and believed the Lord, and his servant Moses" (Exodus 14:31).

BACKGROUND

At the time of the exodus, the Israelites numbered around two million souls.[5] Thus the army that Pharaoh would have needed to assemble in order to capture and return the Israelites to Egypt would have been significant in size. While some have suggested that Israel's lack of military training would have made it easy for Pharaoh to round them up with only a few soldiers,[6] it seems very unlikely that two million Israelites would simply surrender to an estimated five hundred thousand troops.

The Red Sea is, in its deepest parts, some six thousand feet deep. Its narrowest portion is miles wide.[7] Thus, the profound and divine nature of this miracle is highlighted by the magnitude of the body of water that Moses parted and Israel crossed.

It has been suggested that a sort of "tit for tat" is at play here in the taking of Egyptian lives by water. Some eighty years earlier, Pharaoh had taken the lives of the male Israelite children by drowning them in the Nile. Now Israel's God would drown Pharaoh's armies in the Red Sea. Ironically, the very man God used to bring to pass the watery destruction of the Egyptians was Moses, who himself was rescued by God from the Nile when he was but an infant.[8]

SYMBOLIC ELEMENTS

Symbolically speaking, the sea has a number of different, but related, meanings that seem applicable here. One typologist wrote: "It may be used to represent extremely difficult problems and situations which arise in the Christian's path and are impossible to conquer unless the Lord performs a miracle."[9] This certainly applies to the Israelite's situation in Exodus 14. Another referred to the sea as a symbol of the "restless masses of humanity, [and of] the wicked nations" of the earth.[10] Because the sea is commonly linked to chaos, death, disorder, and the abode of Satan, such an interpretation would make sense.[11] Thus, one text states, "It is only at the sea that the forces of chaos are decisively overcome and the world is reestablished on firm moorings. . . . The Egyptians . . . drown in the midst of a chaos of their own making. . . . Chaos, in all of its creational-historical manifestations, has been overcome."[12] Therefore, in this miracle, the sea is most likely a symbol of that which Satan uses to thwart God's plans and our righteousness. But, as the miracle suggests, God will always conquer, and whatever Satan seeks to use to move forward his wickedness, God can use to accomplish His good. Indeed, it appears that the very traps Satan sets for the Saints are the very devices Deity uses to destroy the devil.

Pharaoh, in this miracle, as in others, was a standard symbol of Satan and his influences in the world. He represents evil, and those who oppose the true and living God.[13] The land of Egypt, of course, represents this fallen world, spiritual death, and the bondage it provides to those who love the fallen world more than God.[14]

The pillar of fire or cloud protected God's covenant people from their enemies (see Exodus 14:19–20) just as Jesus can protect us from ours.[15] Thus, in Exodus 14:20 we are told that the pillar of fire, which represented Jehovah's presence, "was a cloud and darkness" to the Egyptians, though "it gave light by night" to the Israelites. Of this, one commentator wrote: "What was light for Israel became darkness for the Egyptians (v.20). Thus the double nature of the glory of God in salvation and judgment could not have been more graphically depicted."[16] The day of Christ's return is known as "the great and dreadful day of the Lord" (Malachi 4:5; 3 Nephi 25:5; D&C 110:16) because it will be great for the righteous and dreadful for the wicked. This is well depicted by the presence of God in this miracle that brought darkness to the Egyptians and light to the Israelites.[17]

The staff or rod of Moses is a common symbol of strength, authority, priesthood power, judgment, and divine guidance.[18] Moses used it, on

Israel's behalf, to exercise each of these elements against Pharaoh, just as Christ uses His strength, authority, priesthood, revelation, and judgment against the adversary, and on our behalf.

Anciently, the east wind was a common representation of God's influence or power. Things that came from the east were believed to have been sent by God, or to be representative of God.[19] As one commentator noted: "Winds . . . are often described poetically in the Bible as almost personified messengers of the God who controls them (Ps. 104:4)."[20] Thus, symbolically speaking, it is to be understood that it was God who divided the Red Sea, not some random or fortuitous wind.

The parting of the waters, while not an obvious standard symbol, actually has a well-established meaning. Throughout the Hebrew Bible, the phrase translated in English as "make a covenant" would be rendered more literally as "cut a covenant." Anciently, one did not "make" covenants, one "cut" them. Thus, when making a covenant, it was common in biblical times to take an animal and slay it in a ritualistic manner, and then to say (often while gripping the hand of the party that you were making the oath or covenant with), "If I break my covenant with you may this same thing (which we've done to this animal) happen to me." The concept behind the "cutting of a covenant" was that the individuals making promises would be reminded as they entered into a covenant that there are blessings for keeping an oath, but there are also penalties for breaking one. Thus, at Shechem, Joshua was directed by Moses to divide Israel into two groups (once they entered the promised land)—half on Mount Ebal and the other half on Mount Gerizim—and Moses would pass between them while he had them recite the blessings and curses for covenants kept or broken (Deuteronomy 27–29:1). Symbolically speaking, one would be rent in two, just as the animal that was used to make the covenant was rent. In a more literal sense, the person making the covenant knew that they would be forfeiting the promised blessings associated with the covenant if they did not keep their part of the covenant. Numerous times throughout the Bible this concept of "cutting a covenant" appears in situations and settings that do not seem innately covenantal. Of course, in this miracle, Moses divided the Red Sea and the people passed between the parts (see Exodus 14). Later, Joshua would part the Jordan River and have Israel pass through the parts (see Joshua 4). We learn that Israel was rent in two kingdoms because of their disobedience (see 1 Kings 11:29–40; 12:1–24). Mark informs us that at the death of Jesus the veil of the Jewish temple was rent in two, enabling individuals other than just the Jewish high priest to pass between the veil's parts (see Mark 15:38). When Christ returns He will split the Mount of Olives in two, and the Jews will run between the parts, where they will see their Messiah (see Zechariah 14:1–5; D&C 45:48–59). The episode at the Red Sea appears to have covenant-making elements as part of it. In every case of "cutting a covenant," the idea was that, if the person kept their covenants they would be protected, blessed, and exalted. If they broke their covenants, they would be "cut" (or penalized) by the covenant. In passing through the Red Sea, the Israelites passed through safely and were blessed to make it to the land on the other side, but the Egyptians were drowned in the depths (so that they didn't get to inherit the land on the other side). The former group were symbolic depictions of the faithful, and the latter were symbolic of the unfaithful. The dividing of the Red Sea, therefore, appears to symbolize the idea that there are blessings and penalties associated with the covenant-making process.

APPLICATION AND ALLEGORIZATION

As with many of the miracles we have examined in this book, the parting of the Red Sea has a number of symbolic applications. Perhaps the most important being that there are blessings when we keep our covenants with God and consequences if we do not keep them. If we are unfaithful to what we know to be right and true, as the Egyptians were, we should expect to drown in the chaos we will have created through our disobedience to the light. If, on the other hand, we seek to obey and trust in God, we will successfully make the long journey to the promised land—the celestial kingdom.

Pharaoh's anxious pursuit of departing Israel reminds us of an important principle in life: "Pharaoh . . . did not want to lose his slaves, and with a great army he began to pursue [them]. Satan never willingly gives up any of his servants."[21] As the time for Christ's return nears, Lucifer is more anxious than ever to place us in bondage and to enslave us to our desires and passions. Like Pharaoh, the devil worries about us following Christ (like Israel followed Moses), and consequently finding a means by which we can escape his power. Now, more than ever, we need to trust and follow the Lord.

With all of the miracles they had seen, as soon as things seemed to be going wrong, Israel doubted God and chastised Moses (see Exodus 14:10–20). Of this wishy-washy behavior, one commentator wrote: "We recognized ourselves again and again in Israel."[22] How often do you and I, when things seem to be going differently than had we wished for them to go, forget the many miracles and blessings God has performed in our lives? We are so quick to doubt; so apt to turn from the Lord. He still loved Israel, and He'll still love us. But we must ever be conscious of such faithless attitudes, and fight to suppress them.

Israel found themselves in a rather hopeless situation. Their backs were up against the Red Sea, so that they had nowhere to escape. Their archenemy was about to attack them. And yet it is important for you and me to remember that this miracle promises escape to those who follow the prophets. "We see . . . deliverance from our enemies in the crossing of the Red Sea."[23] This miracle teaches us that God will provide the way by which we can escape our most formidable enemies.

> Moses had commanded his people to stand firm and watch God fight for them, and they had seen Him do just that as the waters enveloped their pursuers. God has not stopped fighting for His people. He still protects them from their enemies and watches their backs. If the Israelites could trust Him when their backs were to the sea [leaving them seemingly nowhere to go], can we do any less? No matter what we face today, if we've trusted in Him, we are His children. He will never fail us. What enemy need we fear?[24]

God's deliverance of Israel out of Egyptian bondage and slavery typified Christ's deliverance of His Church out of this fallen, corrupt, and enslaved world.[25] "Moses in the baptism of the Red Sea shook off the powers and principalities of Egypt, and Christ, in the baptism of Calvary, made possible a perfect deliverance for a sin-bound race."[26]

It is a curious fact that there were other ways into the promised land other than through the Red Sea. Indeed, a number of commentators have pointed out that traversing the Red Sea was likely the most difficult way to the promised land—but it was the one the Lord chose for Israel.

> The attainment of moral ends is more important than physical convenience. The Israelites could have entered Canaan by a much nearer way than through the Red Sea, but that way was chosen for them to teach them many important truths in connection with God. The shortest way to attain an end is not always the best way. A short way to a fortune may not be so conducive to the formation of a character, as one which it takes much longer to travel. This truth is taught in the temptation of our Saviour [sic] (Luke iv:5–8). Satan proposed a short way to that universal dominion which our Lord knew could only be safely and truly attained through Gethsemane and Calvary.[27]

So it is in our lives; the easiest and quickest way is not necessarily the best or most beneficial way. Often we simply need to accept the Lord's path, and be willing to set aside the one we've charted. Just as Israel needed that miracle in their lives to convince them that God was there for them, watching over them, and providing for them, you and I need to remember that He knows what we need, but may want to show us from time to time just how very involved He is in the details of our lives. We need to be willing to let Him perform the miracles He wants to in our lives, even if that means taking a different or harder road.

One of the most commonly mentioned symbols in this miracle is that which the Apostle Paul highlighted in 1 Corinthians 10:1–2. He wrote:

> Moreover, brethren, I would not that ye should be ignorant, how that all our fathers were under the cloud, and all passed through the sea;
> And were all baptized unto Moses in the cloud and in the sea.

Paul saw the crossing of the Red Sea as ancient Israel's baptism or, more particularly, the need for covenant Israel to accept baptism, and thereby come unto Christ. Paul was not alone in seeing this symbol in the crossing of the Red Sea. One early Christian source states: "The very name of the Red Sea is not superfluous. Just as it is known as Red, so the baptismal water can be labeled red, for it came forth mixed with blood from the Lord Savior's side."[28] Elsewhere we read:

> According to the view of the inspired Paul, the people . . . , by passing through the Red Sea, proclaimed the good tidings of salvation by water. . . . For even now, whensoever the people [are] in the water of regeneration, fleeing from Egypt, from the burden of sin, it is set free and saved. But the devil with his own servants . . . is choked with grief and perishes, deeming the salvation of men to be his own misfortune.[29]

Just as the Red Sea made an end of Israel's enemies, baptism can also make an end of ours, if we are true to the covenant associated with it.[30]

Finally, in the sixth century, one church father noted how Moses used a rod—a piece of wood—to perform many of his miracles, including the parting of the Red Sea. In this story, he was commanded to "lift thou up" the staff or rod of wood (Exodus 14:16) that Israel's deliverance might be provided via the water. This was a typological reminder of how Christ would need to be "lifted up" upon a cross of wood (1 Nephi 11:33) in order that covenant Israel might be delivered from the bondage of sin, again, via the waters of baptism.[31]

NOTES

1. The Hebrew, Syria, and Septuagint are inconsistent, and can, therefore, have the meaning that the wheels were "bound," "jammed," "bogged down," or "came off." (See Walter C. Kaiser Jr., "Exodus," in Frank E. Gaebelein, ed., *The Expositor's Bible Commentary* [Grand Rapids, MI: Zondervan, 1976–1992], 2:390–91.)

2. See Avivah Gottlieb Zornberg, *The Particulars of Rapture: Reflections on Exodus* (New York: Doubleday, 2001), 213–14.

3. Kaiser, "Exodus," in Gaebelein, *The Expositor's Bible Commentary*, 2:391

4. The text never states that Pharaoh drowned, only that his entire army did. However, Psalm 136:15 states that God "overthrew Pharaoh and his host in the Red sea," implying that Pharaoh also drowned. (See also Paulus Orosius, "Seven Books of History Against the Pagans," 1:10, in Joseph T. Lienhard, ed., *Exodus, Leviticus, Deuteronomy*, in *Ancient Christian Commentary on Scripture* [Downers Grove, IL: InterVarsity Press, 2001], 76; Clement of Rome, "Letter to the Corinthians," 51, in Lienhard, *Exodus, Leviticus, Deuteronomy*, in *Ancient Christian Commentary on Scripture*, 77; Zornberg, *The Particulars of Rapture*, 89; Herbert Lockyer, *All the Miracles of the Bible: The Supernatural in Scripture—Its Scope and Significance* [Grand Rapids, MI: Zondervan, 1961], 63.) Josephus claimed that the wind blew the bodies of Pharaoh's army toward the eastern shore, where Moses and Israel were assembled, thereby enabling them to obtain their weapons and armor. (See Josephus, "Antiquities of the Jews" bk. II, ch. 16:6, in *The Complete Works of Josephus*, William Whiston, trans. [Grand Rapids, MI: Kregel Publications, 1981], 65. See also Kaiser, "Exodus," in Gaebelein, *The Expositor's Bible Commentary*, 2:390.)

5. See Kaiser, "Exodus," in Gaebelein, *The Expositor's Bible Commentary*, 2:387; Lockyer, *All the Miracles of the Bible*, 61.

6. See, for example, ibid.

7. See Lockyer, *All the Miracles of the Bible*, 62.

8. See ibid.

9. Walter A. Wilson, *A Dictionary of Bible Types: Examines the Images, Shadows, and Symbolism of Over 1,000 Biblical Terms, Words, and People* (Peabody, MA: Hendrickson, 1999), 361.

10. Kevin J. Conner, *Interpreting the Symbols and Types*, rev. ed. (Portland, OR: City Bible Publishing, 1992), 166.

11. John S. Kselman and Michael L. Barré, "Psalms," in Raymond E. Brown, Joseph A. Fitzmyer, and Roland E. Murphy, eds., *The New Jerome Biblical Commentary* (Englewood Cliffs, NJ: Prentice Hall, 1990), 541; Joseph A. Fitzmyer, *The Anchor Bible: The Gospel According to Luke I–IX* (New York: Doubleday, 1970), 28:739n31; C. S. Mann, *The Anchor Bible: Mark* (New York: Doubleday, 1986), 278–79; "Firmage," in David Noel Freedman, ed., *The Anchor Bible Dictionary* (New York: Doubleday, 1992), 6:1132; Lamar Williamson, Jr., *Interpretation: A*

Bible Commentary for Teaching and Preaching—Mark (Atlanta, GA: John Knox Press, 1983), 104; Adam Clarke, *The Holy Bible, Containing the Old and New Testaments . . . with a Commentary and Critical Notes. . . .* (New York: T. Mason & G. Lane, 1837), 5:420; Sean Freyne, "The Sea of Galilee," in Freedman, *The Anchor Bible Dictionary*, 2:900; Leon L. Morris, *Revelation*, in *Tyndale New Testament Commentaries*, rev. ed. (Grand Rapids, MI: InterVarsity Press, 1987), 171; Walter L. Liefeld, "Luke," in Gaebelein, *The Expositor's Bible Commentary*, 8:913; J. C. Cooper, *An Illustrated Encyclopaedia of Traditional Symbols* (London: Thames and Hudson, 1987), 121.

12. Terence E. Fretheim, *Interpretation: A Bible Commentary for Teaching for Preaching—Exodus* (Louisville, KY: John Knox Press, 1991), 153, 160.

13. See Leland Ryken, James C. Wilhoit, and Tremper Longman III, *Dictionary of Biblical Imagery* (Downers Grove, IL: InterVarsity Press, 1998), 639; Conner, *Interpreting the Symbols and Type*, 140; Richard C. Trench, *Miracles and Parables of the Old Testament* (Grand Rapids, MI: Baker Book House, 1959), 33.

14. See Conner, *Interpreting the Symbols and Types*, 140; Trench, *Miracles and Parables of the Old Testament*, 33; Ryken, Wilhoit, and Longman, *Dictionary of Biblical Imagery*, 639.

15. See Kenneth E. Trent, *Types of Christ in the Old Testament: A Conservative Approach to Old Testament Typology* (Bloomington, IN: CrossBooks, 2010), 46.

16. Kaiser, "Exodus," in Gaebelein, *The Expositor's Bible Commentary*, 2:389.

17. Ginzberg records: "To prevent the enemy from inflicting harm upon the Israelites, He enveloped the Egyptians in profound darkness, so impenetrable it could be felt. . . . Nevertheless, the Egyptians could see that the Israelites were surrounded by bright light. . . . and when they tried to speed darts and arrows against them, the missiles were caught up by the cloud . . . hovering between the two camps, and no harm came to Israel." (Louis Ginzberg, *The Legends of the Jews* [Philadelphia, PA: The Jewish Publication Society of America, 1912–1938], 3:21.)

18. Conner, *Interpreting the Symbols and Types*, 164, 170; Ryken, Wilhoit, and Longman, *Dictionary of Bible Imagery*, 733–34; Cooper, *An Illustrated Encyclopaedia of Traditional Symbols*, 140; Jack Tresidder, *Symbols and Their Meanings: The Illustrated Guide to More than 1,000 Symbols—Their Traditional and Contemporary Significance* (London: Duncan Baird Publishers, 2006), 139.

19. J. E. Cirlot, *A Dictionary of Symbols*, 2nd ed. (New York: Routledge & Kegan Paul, 1971), 245; Cooper, *An Illustrated Encyclopaedia of Traditional Symbols*, 59; Joel F. Drinkard, "East," in Freedman, *The Anchor Bible Dictionary*, 2:248; Joseph Fielding McConkie and Donald W. Parry, *A Guide to Scripture Symbols* (Salt Lake City, UT: Deseret Book, 1990), 44; Allen C. Myers, *The Eerdmans Bible Dictionary* (Grand Rapids, MI: Eerdmans, 1996), 300; Ryken, Wilhoit, and Longman, *Dictionary of Bible Imagery*, 225. Pharaoh's heart was not softened by this plague (Exodus 10:20), so Moses was instructed to send another.

20. R. Alan Cole, *Exodus*, in *Tyndale Old Testament Commentaries* (Grand Rapids, MI: Eerdmans, 1973), 121.

21. Ada R. Habershon, *Hidden Pictures in the Old Testament* (Grand Rapids, MI: Kregel Publications, 1982), 71.

22. Cole, *Exodus*, in *Tyndale Old Testament Commentaries*, 120.

23. Ada R. Habershon, *Study of the Types* (Grand Rapids, MI: Kregel Publications, 1974), 45.

24. Pamela McQuade, *The Top 100 Miracles of the Bible: What They Are and What They Mean to You Today* (Uhrichsville, OH: Barbour Publishing, 2008), 52.

25. See Lockyer, *All the Miracles of the Bible*, 63.

26. Ibid., 63.

27. Trench, *Miracles and Parables of the Old Testament*, 35–36.

28. Cassiodorus, "Exposition of the Psalms," 80:6, in Lienhard, *Exodus, Leviticus, Deuteronomy*, in *Ancient Christian Commentary on Scripture*, 71.

29. Gregory of Nyssa, "On the Baptism of Christ," in Lienhard, *Exodus, Leviticus, Deuteronomy*, in *Ancient Christian Commentary on Scripture*, 76.

30. See Augustine, "Explanation of the Psalms," 107:3, Lienhard, *Exodus, Leviticus, Deuteronomy*, in *Ancient Christian Commentary on Scripture*, 76. "Just as the Jews were saved and extricated through the waters of the Red Sea, so we are delivered from the land of Egypt, that is, from the sins of the flesh, and reborn through regeneration by the sacred water" which is baptism. (Cassiodorus, "Exposition of the Psalms," 80:6, in Lienhard, *Exodus, Leviticus, Deuteronomy*, in *Ancient Christian Commentary on Scripture*, 71.)

31. See Caesarius of Arles, "Sermon," 112:4, in Lienhard, *Exodus, Leviticus, Deuteronomy*, in *Ancient Christian Commentary on Scripture*, 74.

The Healing *of the* Waters *at* Marah

The Miracle

The Israelites had only some three days earlier crossed the Red Sea when they came upon the waters of Marah. They had been traveling in the desert, and were, no doubt, quite thirsty. Thus, the waters of Marah appeared to be an answer to their prayers. Nevertheless, they quickly learned that the waters were so bitter that they could not be partaken of. As Charles Haddon Spurgeon put it, "When they did arrive at a fountain, they found worse than no water, for it was so brackish, so altogether unfit for drinking, that even though they thought they would have drunk any thing [*sic*], they could not possibly drink this."[1]

Out of their thirst and their frustrations, the people began to murmur to Moses that he needed to resolve this problem. So the prophet of the people prayed to God, and Moses received a revelation. He was instructed by Jehovah to take a branch of a specific tree, and cast it into the waters of Marah. Moses was told that if he did so the waters would become sweet, and the people's pain would be alleviated. Moses did as the Lord had instructed him, and the waters were miraculously made drinkable.

Background

The word "marah" means "bitter," and thus, the place was so named because of the fame of its waters.[2] Its location is typically thought to be modern-day Ain Hawarah—a site a few miles inland from the Gulf of Suez.[3] The pool of water at Marah today is about six to eight feet in diameter and about two foot deep. "It's taste is unpleasant, saltish, and somewhat bitter. . . . The Arabs . . . consider it the worst water in all these regions."[4]

This miracle was connected to a promise or covenant that God was introducing to Israel. Exodus 15:25–26 indicate that obedience to God's commandments or statutes would "bring healing, both physically and morally."[5] This same covenant, that God would not "put . . . diseases upon" Israel (Exodus 15:26), is at the heart of the symbolism of this miracle.

SYMBOLIC ELEMENTS

Israel's need for water in this miracle was a symbol of their need to turn to God. Water, when not depicted as a destroyer, symbolizes the Holy Ghost and the gifts God sends through His Spirit.[6] Because Israel was without water, it can be implied that they were without God. When they finally turned to Him, the water was provided. Said one source, "These bitter waters were in the very path of the Lord's leading, and stand for the trials of God's people, which are educatory and not punitive."[7] In other words, God had sent them a drought, of sorts, to lead them back to Him, and to teach, rather than punish, Israel (see Exodus 15:26). Elsewhere we read that Israel's thirst, as depicted at the waters of Marah, "Was a sign of Yahweh's grace in that it drove the sensitive Israelite back to God."[8] Thus, in this miracle, the bitter waters, or the lack of drinkable water, symbolized trials or tests sent by God to bring a wayward or faithless people back to Him.

Bitterness is a common symbol for the "hard experience of life."[9] It can also represent the "contaminated" state of a person's heart, which causes their life to be hard.[10] Thus, God brought Israel to these bitter waters to see if Israel would exercise faith in a time of test and trial. He allows the waters to be bitter because such an experience can provide the opportunity for their growth, and the changing of their hearts.

As noted earlier in this text, "Scriptural trees [can] stand . . . for Christ and his attributes."[11] Elsewhere we read, "In ancient times, sacred trees . . . were [the] attributes of the gods."[12] Susan Easton Black indicated that anciently the tree of life was associated with Jesus's cross; and, thus, was associated with the Resurrection, the receipt of eternal life, and the love of God—all very Christocentric ideas.[13] Thus, the tree utilized here is most likely a symbol for Christ and His Atonement, which have the power to take away the bitterness of life's experiences.[14]

APPLICATION AND ALLEGORIZATION

One text notes that, "Medieval commentators delight to see here a reference to the cross, by which the bitterest of life's waters is sweetened."[15] Early Christian sources also drew this parallel. Tertullian, Ambrose, and Jerome all saw Christ's cross as the tree that makes the bitter sweet.[16] Maximus of Turin wrote:

> Arriving at Marah and being unable to draw the water because of its bitterness (for the well had water but not sweetness, and it was pleasing to the eye but polluted to the taste), drank water that became sweet and mild as soon as wood was thrown into it by Moses. . . . The wood removed the harshness that the noxious water bore. I believe that this happened as a sign, for I think that the bitter water of Marah is the Old Testament law, which was harsh before it was tempered by the Lord's cross.[17]

One modern commentator wrote of this miracle, "In the incident at Marah . . . we probably have another foreshadowing of . . . 'Him who was cast into the bitter waters of death in order that those waters might yield nought [*sic*] but sweetness to us for ever [*sic*].'"[18] Elsewhere we read: "The miracle at Marah affords a fitting type of all Christ [was] able to accomplish. Those bitter waters were healed by Him who came to bear the curse. Christ is the Branch who can sweeten the earth's waters. His cross is spiritually the tree which, when cast into the most bitter waters, sweetens and heals them (Galatians 3:13)."[19] Perhaps the most important lesson we can learn from this miracle is that when we experience our "Marahs" at various times in our life, we must remember to cast the "tree" (the Atonement of Christ) into the "waters" of our heart that we too might be healed.[20]

On a related theme, the miracle at Marah teaches us about trials and their place in, and their benefit to, our lives. The famed nineteenth-century exegete, Charles Spurgeon, wrote:

> It will become sometimes to the Christian a subject of joy that Marah is bitter. For suppose Marah had been sweet, then Moses had not prayed to God, and then the tree had not been cut down, and they had never known the power of God to sweeten bitter waters. It must be an awful thing to live an unafflicted life on earth. You say it must be a very delightful thing. . . . but a person who has had no sickness, how can he have a sympathetic heart? . . . If you never had any trials, I should suppose . . . that you would become harsh and untender. . . . Our trials are not sent to us alone and by themselves; there is a *quantum suff* of grace sent with

them, by which they are made available as means to sanctify us, and make us meet to be partakers of the inheritance of the saints in light.[21]

A life without trials means a life without growth. As Spurgeon noted, God sends us trials (1) so that we see that He is involved in our lives, (2) so that we will be sanctified and changed to become like Him, and (3) so that we can be instruments in the lives of others, blessing them because of what we have experienced and have thereby been equipped with.[22] What a blessing our trials can be, if we embrace them rather than murmur about them! As the Apostle Paul taught, we should "glory in tribulations" because they "worketh patience" in us, thereby serving as one of the greatest blessings of the mortal experience (Romans 5:3). And President David O. McKay reminded us that "Adversity . . . may lead toward and not away from God . . . ; and privation may prove a source of strength if we can but keep sweetness of mind and spirit."[23]

This miracle can also teach us an important truth about God's omniscience, and His prior preparation to respond to our prayers. Note that as soon as Israel cried out for help the remedy was ready. God did not need to plant a tree to meet their needs. The tree Moses was commanded to place in the waters to remove the bitterness had been growing for years before Israel arrived at Marah. So it is with you and me. Long before we encounter our individual trials (our waters of Marah), God has prepared the remedy for our troubles. He simply awaits our prayerful request, and then He can administer His remedy. Nothing is left to chance. All of the preplanning has been done by God. He is waiting to bless us in any and all of our afflictions if we will but turn to Him. This miracle is a subtle reminder of that fact![24]

There is a curious wordplay that appears to be present in the Hebrew text of this miracle. Of it, one commentator on Jewish midrash noted:

> The word for "rebellion"—*meri*—may not immediately draw our attention; but the Israelites . . . travel[ed] for three days [after they had crossed the Red Sea], without finding water, and [they finally] arrive at a place called *Marah* ('bitterness'), where they complain about the undrinkable, bitter water. At this point, we cannot avoid noticing the *mar*-root: it occurs four times in one verse (15:23).[25]

Moses, who recorded this episode, seems to be highlighting the rebellious spirit that is behind those who murmur and complain—those who do not notice, or are ungrateful for, the rich blessings God has endowed them with. One commentary on these verses states: "The people murmured . . .

explicitly against Moses, whom God had appointed as their leader, and thus implicitly against God Himself (Ex. 16:8). In so doing, they are typical of all humanity: that is why they can become both a lesson and a warning (1 Cor. 10:11)."[26] Do we forget our blessings only days after receiving them? Do we murmur, as signs of our rebellious spirits?

> They murmured against Moses. And have you ever noticed how . . . most of us, when we are in a murmuring vein, are not honest enough to murmur distinctly against God. No: the child is dead, and we form a conjecture that there was some wrong treatment on the part of [the] nurse, or surgeon. . . . Or we have lost money, and have been brought down from opulence to almost poverty; then some one person was dishonest [and brought this upon us]. . . . We deny, perhaps indignantly, that we murmur against God. . . . In our heart of hearts [however] our rebellion is against the Lord himself. We have not quite honesty enough to rail against God openly and avowedly, and so we hypocritically cover up our repining against him by murmuring against some person, occasion, or event. . . . Thus we blame an accidental circumstance, as if it were not part of the divine arrangement.[27]

Though we may comfort ourselves by trying to claim that we never reject God's will (only man's injustice), we really are murmuring against Him, and fighting against the customized curriculum He has specifically designed for our personal mortal experience when, as this quote suggests, we reject the things God sends our way.

In a completely different approach to this miracle, Spurgeon compared Israel immediately after they crossed the Red Sea to new converts to the Church who feel that, because of their conversion, they have reached the end of all of their trials. However, the reality is that their conversion will only bring more trials and tests. Remember, Israel sang praises to God after their passing through the Red Sea, which Paul says symbolized their baptism (see 1 Corinthians 10:2). But, three days after their personal miracle, they were doubting, murmuring, and feeling rather frustrated at God and His prophet. "Ah yes, with some of us our delight at conversion was very great, our exhilaration at finding the Savior was something never to be forgotten, and yet only a day or so after we were stumbled with great temptation, amazed at the discovery of the evil of our hearts, or tried by the coldness of our fellow Christians, or the cruelty of the outside world, so that we found we had come to Marah."[28] The Nile's waters were sweet when compared with those of Marah. So, some converts feel that life before their conversion was sweeter than the seemingly restrictive and occasionally painful life of a committed Christian. "It were better to die at Marah free, than live a slave by the sweet Nile. . . . And truly to be a slave of Satan is so degrading a thing, that if this mouth were for ever [*sic*] filled with Marah's bitterness, yet were it better to be so than to be enchanted with the pleasures of sin."[29]

Finally, there is a unique aspect to this miracle that should be highlighted: God performs the miraculous in not so miraculous ways.

> The reader ought not heighten Gods' work beyond what the text says. . . . The implication is that God assumes that Moses knows what to do with the piece of wood and that the wood has certain properties that enable it to sweeten water (the bark and the leaves of some trees have such capacities). God is here working in and through human knowledge and the "healing" properties of certain elements of the natural order. God's providence is shown in leading Moses to *help that is already available in the world of creation*.[30]

In other words, God had Moses preform a miracle by using the unmiraculous things available to him. Often He does the same thing in our own lives. For example, instead of a miracle healing by the laying on of hands, He may have us take a miracle drug that was created through the inspiration of a chemist. Instead of miraculously removing a debt, He may time our tax return so as to meet a financial need. As President Spencer W. Kimball once taught: "God does notice us, and he watches over us. But it is usually through another mortal that he meets our needs."[31] How many miracles does God perform every day in your life or mine, which, because of ingratitude and inattentiveness, we miss, and therefore, fail to express appreciation for?

NOTES

1.   Charles Haddon Spurgeon, *Spurgeon's Sermons* (Grand Rapids, MI: Baker Book Hosue, 1996), 9:383.

2.   One commentator suggested that the passive construction of the Hebrew implies that the name had been given to the place even before Israel had wandered upon it. See Walter C. Kaiser Jr., "Exodus," in Frank E. Gaebelein, ed., *The Expositor's Bible Commentary* (Grand Rapids, MI: Zondervan, 1976–1992), 2:399. See also R. Alan Cole, *Exodus*, in *Tyndale Old Testament Commentaries* (Grand Rapids, MI: Eerdmans, 1973), 128.

3.   See Cole, *Exodus*, in *Tyndale Old Testament Commentaries*, 128; Kaiser, "Exodus," in Gaebelein, *The Expositor's Bible Commentary*, 2:398.

4.   Kaiser, "Exodus," in Gaebelein, *The Expositor's Bible Commentary*, 2:398.

5.   Ibid., 2:399.

6. For example, see John 7:37–39; Numbers 8:7; Walter L. Wilson, *A Dictionary of Bible Types* (Peabody, MA: Hendrickson, 1999), 347 & 452; Leland Ryken, James C. Wilhoit, and Tremper Longman III, eds., *Dictionary of Biblical Imagery* (Downers Grove, IL: InterVarsity Press, 1998), 931; J. C. Cooper, *An Illustrated Encyclopaedia of Traditional Symbols* (London: Thames and Hudson, 1987), 189 Kevin J. Conner, *Interpreting the Symbols and Types*, rev. ed. (Portland, OR: City Bible Publishing, 1992), 163 & 179; Ada R. Habershon, *Hidden Pictures in the Old Testament* (Grand Rapids, MI: Kregel Publications, 1982), 237–38; James Hall, *Dictionary of Subjects & Symbols in Art*, rev. ed. (Boulder, CO: Westview Press, 1979), 128; Ada R. Habershon, *Study of the Types* (Grand Rapids, MI: Kregel Publications, 1974), 40, 143 & 152; Herbert Lockyer, *All the Miracles of the Bible: The Supernatural in Scripture—Its Scope and Significance* (Grand Rapids, MI: Zondervan, 1961), 68.

7. See Lockyer, *All the Miracles of the Bible*, 65

8. Ryken, Wilhoit, and Longman, *Dictionary of Biblical Imagery*, 221.

9. Ibid., 315.

10. See Wilson, *A Dictionary of Bible Types*, 41.

11. M. Catherine Thomas, in Stephen E. Ricks and John W. Welch, eds., *The Allegory of the Olive Tree* (Salt Lake City, UT: Deseret Book, 1994), 13.

12. Nadia Julien, *The Mammoth Dictionary of Symbols: Understanding the Hidden Language of Symbols* (New York: Carroll & Graf Publishers, Inc., 1996), 462; See also J. E. Cirlot, *A Dictionary of Symbols*, 2nd ed. (New York: Routledge & Kegan Paul, 1971), 347.

13. Susan Easton Black, "Behold, I Have Dreamed a Dream," in Monte S. Nyman and Charles D. Tate Jr., *The Book of Mormon: First Nephi, The Doctrinal Foundation* (Provo, UT: Religious Studies Center, Brigham Young University, 1988), 123, note 7; emphasis in original.

14. One typologist wrote: "The tree of Marah is probably more a type of the cross of our Lord Jesus Christ than of Christ Himself. Yet it is impossible to separate the power of the cross from the Christ of the cross. Apart from the Lord Jesus Christ, the cross is both powerless and meaningless. . . . Note the sequence: First, the Passover symbolizing redemption on the basis of the applied blood; second, crossing the Red Sea, typifying the passing from the old life into newness of life based a covenant relationship with the Lord [which comes through baptism]; and, third, encountering the bitter waters of Marah, which represents the testing of the Lord that comes upon all His children. It must be kept in mind that the bitter waters of Marah typify the testing of the Lord and not divine chastisement for disobedience. . . . Often a period of severe testing follows a spiritual mountaintop experience." (Kenneth E. Trent, *Types of Christ in the Old Testament: A Conservative Approach to Old Testament Typology* [Bloomington, IN: CrossBooks, 2010], 47.)

15. Cole, *Exodus*, in *Tyndale Old Testament Commentaries*, 129. Elsewhere we read: "The people in the wilderness . . . were no worse than we are. They are an example to us of what our heart is; and whatever we see in them we have but to watch a little, and we shall see it all in ourselves. It was not Jewish nature that God proved in the wilderness so much as human nature at its very best estate. Assuredly, the tendency of human nature is to murmur. . . . O that we might have grace rather to say with Job, 'Though he slay me, yet will I trust him!'" (Spurgeon, *Spurgeon's Sermons*, 9:389.)

16. See, for example, Tertullian, "On Baptism," 9:2, in Joseph T. Lienhard, ed., *Exodus, Leviticus, Deuteronomy*, in *Ancient Christian Commentary on Scripture* (Downers Grove, IL: InterVarsity Press, 2001), 83; Ambrose, "On the Mysteries," 3:14, in Lienhard, *Exodus, Leviticus, Deuteronomy*, in *Ancient Christian Commentary on Scripture*, 83–84; Jerome, "Letter," 69:6, in Lienhard, *Exodus, Leviticus, Deuteronomy*, in *Ancient Christian Commentary on Scripture*, 84. One Jewish source records: "The ways of the Holy One, blessed be He, differ from the ways of man: Man turns bitter to sweet by . . . some sweet stuff [like sugar], but God transformed the bitter water through the bitter . . . tree." (See Louis Ginzberg, *The Legends of the Jews* [Philadelphia, PA: The Jewish Publication Society of America, 1912–1938], 3:39.)

17. Maximus of Turin, "Sermon," 67:4, in Lienhard, *Exodus, Leviticus, Deuteronomy*, in *Ancient Christian Commentary on Scripture*, 84.

18. Habershon, *Study of the Types*, 42. See also Habershon, *Hidden Picture in the Old Testament*, 80. Spurgeon, a contemporary of Habershon, wrote this: "May not this tree cut down be an emblem of the Saviour? A glorious tree indeed was he, . . . but he must suffer the axe for our sakes. . . . The troubles of life and the troubles of death are sweetened by his dear cross, which, though it be a bitter tree in itself, is the antidote for all the bitterness that comes upon us here and hereafter." (Spurgeon, *Spurgeon's Sermons*, 9:394.) Joseph Fielding McConkie wrote: "Surely the story is a type of him who died upon a tree, being cast into the bitter waters of death that they might bring forth the sweet waters of everlasting life." (Joseph Fielding McConkie, *Gospel Symbolism* [Salt Lake City, UT: Deseret Book, 1985], 53.)

19. Lockyer, *All the Miracles of the Bible*, 65. One text states: "The Christ of the gospel is God's (1 Cor. iii. 22). He is the tree of life whose leaves are for the healing of the nations (Rev. xxii. 2). As the Lord showed Moses the tree (verse 25), so has he caused the gospel of salvation to be brought nigh to the children of men." (Richard C. Trench, *Miracles and Parables of the Old Testament* [Grand Rapids, MI: Baker Book House, 1959], 40.)

20. See Romans 5:3–4; Philippians 3:8; Acts 20:24; Lockyer, *All the Miracles of the Bible*, 65. "There is for us, as we pass each through his own wilderness, a Marah also. . . . So, like Israel, before they came to Marah, we plant this wilderness

with joyous springs, sweet to the taste. And even after the experience of many disappointments, we often look forward to some one especial point in life which we feel certain will bring felicity at last. Like the thirsty Israelites, we hasten forward, even at some sacrifice; we reach the spring, we stoop to taste. Alas! It is bitter. Thou who art brooding over thine own Marah, cry unto the Lord, as Moses did, and He will shew thee a tree. Plant His cross in thine embittered heart, and by His grace, this spring of disappointment shall become less and less bitter, till nothing but sweetness shall remain." (Trench, *Miracles and Parables of the Old Testament*, 41.)

21. Spurgeon, *Spurgeon's Sermons*, 9:396.

22. Ibid.

23. David O. McKay, *Gospel Ideals: Selections from the Discourses of David O. McKay* (Salt Lake City, UT: Bookcraft, 1955), 390. See also David O. McKay, "The Blessings of Adversity," *Ensign*, February 1998.

24. See Spurgeon, *Spurgeon's Sermons*, 9:392–93.

25. Avivah Gottlieb Zornberg, *The Particulars of Rapture: Reflections on Exodus* (New York: Doubleday, 2001), 232.

26. Cole, *Exodus*, in *Tyndale Old Testament Commentaries*, (1973), 128. "Hebrew—murmur—*lun*—taken from the sound a camel makes when it will not get up and move on, even to save its own life. It means to grudgingly remain behind, refuse to go forward. . . . Greek—*goggusmos*—*gogguzo*—low muttered words drenched in distain resentment, muffled undertone smoldering with resentment. Onomatopoetic words meant to mimic certain sounds—in this case, the sound of a camel that will not get up to move." (Kent J. Hunter, personal correspondence, May 26, 2017.)

27. Spurgeon, *Spurgeon's Sermons*, 9:390.

28. Ibid., 9:384.

29. Ibid. See also 9:388.

30. Terence E. Fretheim, *Interpretation: A Bible Commentary for Teaching for Preaching—Exodus* (Louisville, KY: John Knox Press, 1991), 177. See also Lockyer, *All the Miracles of the Bible*, 65.

31. Spencer W. Kimball, *The Teachings of Spencer W. Kimball* (Salt Lake City, UT: Bookcraft, 1982), 252.

THE GIVING *of* MANNA *in the* WILDERNESS

EXODUS 16:14–36

NUMBERS 11:7–9

THE MIRACLE

Israel was hungry as they traveled in the wilderness. Many of the Israelites feared for their temporal well-being if they did not soon find some source of nourishment. Moses promised them God's blessing, and the next day it arrived in the form of manna from heaven.

Each morning it appeared like frost or dew on the ground, and when the Israelites initially saw it, they said to each other "What is it?," so unfamiliar were they with the strange heaven-sent food.[1] The substance had the appearance of a "fine flake-like thing" or like "frost" (NASB Exodus 16:14), and would literally dissolve or melt in the sun. The color of the manna was white, like coriander seed, and its taste was honey-like (KJV Exodus 16:31). It apparently could be used like flour to bake something akin to bread—indeed, bread from heaven. Though later supplemented by heaven-sent quail, the manna met Israel's dietary needs for some four decades.

The Israelites were commanded by Moses to gather the manna each day, and only take as much as they needed for that day, because it would not keep overnight. On the Sabbath, there would be none to gather, so they were instructed to collect twice as much the day before the Sabbath, and were promised that only on that day would the manna not spoil if kept overnight.

Background

Manna literally means "What is it?," and since the Israelites could not figure out what the unknown edible substance was, for want of a better name, they called it manna.[2]

Symbolic Elements

While physical hunger was the problem the manna was sent to resolve, scripture often uses hunger as a symbol for a lack of spirituality, or a weak relationship with God. (See Deuteronomy 8:3; Isaiah 49:9–10; Matthew 5:6; John 6:35.) As one expert in symbolism suggested, hunger "represents a deep desire for God."[3] Thus, the message of this miracle, as it relates to Israel's hunger, was not that they might die, but, rather, that they were spiritually in need. They needed fed souls as much as they did fed stomachs. You and I, if we have that "deep desire for God," should also expect to be fed from heaven with that which no man could provide—the "bread of life."

Manna imagery is present in numerous places in the scriptures, and it is traditionally used to symbolically show God's ability and desire to provide for His children—even those who complain from time to time. In the Gospel of John, Jesus makes reference to the symbol of manna and states that it is a typological foreshadowing of His divine mission to sustain life—specifically eternal life.[4] The following chart shows some of the major parallels that exist between manna and Christ.

Manna	Jesus
Manna is a form of bread.	Jesus was the "Bread of Life" (John 6:35) who came from Bethlehem (which means the "house of bread").
Manna appeared miraculously from heaven, as a gift from God (Exodus 16; Deuteronomy 8:3).	Jesus was born into mortality in a most miraculous manner, having been sent by God as a gift to mankind. His second advent will be no less miraculous.
Manna sustained the life of ancient Israel for some forty years—forty being the standard Hebrew number for trials or tests.[5]	Jesus sustains us both physically and spiritually throughout this life and in the life to come. Only He can enable us to endure life's trials.

MANNA	JESUS
"Manna" is a Hebrew word meaning, "What is this?"[6]	Matthew records that Christ was asked, "Who is this?" (Matthew 21:10).
Manna was said to taste sweet like honey (Exodus 16:31).	Not only are the words of Christ sweet to those who love God, but so also are the life, teachings, and ministry of the *Logos*, the actual Word of God (John 1:1).[7]
Manna had a white color, which is a standard symbol for purity.	Christ's purity is known to be one of the elements that qualified Him to function as the Messiah.
Manna was sent to satisfy the physical hunger of the people.	Jesus was sent to satisfy the spiritual hunger of the people (John 6:35).
The sending of the manna glorified God, and established His "loving mercy toward His people and His provision for their needs."[8]	Jesus glorified God and stood as a testament of God's mercy and love for His people and His commitment to provide for their spiritual needs.
While the manna may have arrived in a miraculous way, it was quite normal in its appearance.	While Christ may have come to earth in a rather miraculous way, Isaiah suggests that there was nothing spectacular about His appearance (Isaiah 53:2).
Some read the text as saying that the manna needed to be individually appropriated.[9]	Certainly we must each individually develop a personal relationship to and dependence upon Christ.
One commentator suggested that the manna "[was] not to be . . . eaten in the form they [gathered it]; instead, it [was] to be prepared by milling and baking (cf. Num 11:8)."[10]	Similarly, it is not enough to have heard of Jesus, or to believe in Him. Rather, it is what we do with Him that determines whether or not we are true Christians.

MANNA	JESUS
The manna was freely available to everyone, regardless of position, rank, wealth, or race.	Christ, and His gifts, are freely available to everyone, regardless of position, rank, wealth, or race.
The manna was entirely undeserved by Israel, who had been murmuring even though they were the recipients of numerous miracles.	The gifts that Christ gives to us are entirely undeserved, and most of us are far guiltier than we realize of ingratitude for all that God has done for us.
If Israel did not gather their manna before the Sabbath it would be too late to do so once the Sabbath came (Exodus 16:22–30).[11]	When Christ returns, for the Sabbath of the earth's temporal existence (the Millennium), those who have not gathered of His heaven-sent nourishment prior to His arrival will ever remain unfilled (Alma 34:33–34; Matthew 25:1–13).[12]

As a summary of this symbol, one dictionary states that the manna, "Invites all to taste and touch and smell and see that the Lord is good, his gifts delicious, nutritious, abundant and free, unearned and undeserved."[13]

APPLICATION AND ALLEGORIZATION

The manna was Christ, and you and I must daily seek a relationship with Him. We must daily, as did Israel of old, take Him into our lives. We must ensure that it is He, and He alone, that fills our lives if we are to be spiritually sustained here, and gain eternal life in the presence of the Father.

Israel was commanded to take some of the manna and place it in a pot, and put that in the ark of the covenant so that future generations would know that the miracle of the manna actually did happen, and that God did take care of His own. (See Exodus 16:32–34). This has been seen as a message about the importance of recording the mercies and miracles of God in our own lives, whether in a journal or otherwise, so that future generations would know of how blessed we had been, and how many miracles God had performed in our lives.[14]

One text reminds us that the divinely supplied manna was given to Israel for the entire forty years that they traveled through the wilderness.

However, the very day they entered the promised land and ate of the fruits of Canaan, the miracle of the manna ceased. God no longer gave, as it was no longer needed. "God never wastes His power."[15] Nor should we. While we seek God's blessings, and even His intervention, we must be careful that we do not expect Him to do what we can do for ourselves.

Numerous commentators suggest that the manna may have literally been the seeds or by-product of some tree or plant that, though Israel was unfamiliar with it, was used by God to meet their needs in what appeared to be a miraculous occurrence. In other words, God was actually using the natural resources of the earth, which He had previously prepared, to meet the needs of His children. For example, on the Sinai Peninsula there is said to be, even to this day, a type of "plant lice" that bores into the fruit of the tamarisk tree that is so common in the region. Utilizing the fruit juices, the lice excrete a "yellowish-white flake or ball" which is said to disintegrate in the heat of the daytime sun, but is also known to congeal in the cooler hours of the day. This lice excrement, known to be filled with carbohydrates and sugar, is even today gathered by the natives of the region, who utilize it to make a type of bread that they call "manna." Like the manna of Moses's miracle, this plant "manna" is said to decay quickly and also to readily attract ants and flies.[16] Thus, in a number of ways, this sounds like a possible explanation for the miracle of manna. While I personally have no opinion on how God provided the manna of Exodus 16, the following insight seems valuable.

> It is important to stress the naturalness of the manna and the quail [miracles]. . . . It is precisely the "natural" that is seen as a gift from God. God's gifts to Israel are to be found not only in the unusual but also in the everyday. If the provisions of God in the wilderness are all subsumed under the extraordinary or miraculous, then the people of God will tend to look for God's providential care only in that which falls outside the ordinary. The all too common effect of this is to absent God from the ordinary and everyday and to go searching for God only in the deep sea and mountain top experiences. Consequently, the people of God will not be able to see in the very ordinariness of things that God is the one who bestows blessings again and again. The result will often be that, when the miraculous can no longer be discerned in one's life, there will be a profound experience of the absence of God altogether.[17]

This commentator is correct, most of the miracles God performs in our lives—and He does them daily—come in such a way that they don't seem that miraculous. But should we only receive His intervention in the strange or out of the ordinary way, we would be prone to always look for, and possibly only accept, a God who is manifest in the miraculous, but never in the mundane.

Ambrose, a bishop from the fourth century, compared the manna given to Israel in the wilderness to the "Word of God," which is detailed in the "words of God." He said that the scriptures, which teach us of Christ, "nourish the soul of the wise." They "illuminate" and "sweeten" our lives and person with "truths" that are "soothing" and "sweeter than honeycomb." The scriptures have, in Ambrose's opinion, the power to delight and illuminate those who have the faith to believe in them.[18] As one commentator put it: "The scriptures are manna given as from heaven to feed us in the desert of this world."[19] Another wrote: "The thoughts of God, revealed in His word, are the soul's manna."[20] Only those who have made it a practice to daily sup from God's words can truly understand and testify to the truth behind this description of scripture. When we read the scriptures so much that we love them, they become one of the richest and sweetest things that God has given to us to enjoy as mortals. They bring power, insight, direction, the Spirit, and numerous other blessings that only those who are well-versed can imagine.

One commentator suggested that Exodus 16:18, where Israel is commanded to gather enough manna that each family member has their needs met, "[Was] used by the apostle Paul as an illustration for Christians to share with one another just as [Israel] pooled the manna everyone collected (2 Cor. 8:15)."[21] Similarly, another wrote that Paul used the miracle of the manna "to enforce on the rich a charitable distribution of their means to the needy, so that there might be provided for all a sufficiency of these temporal goods."[22] The fact that those of a household each went out and gathered, but then placed their gleanings in a common pot to be shared by all, is a strong message to us of our need to consecrate all that we have to the building up of the kingdom, and to the blessing of the lives of God's children.

In a simple application of this miracle, one author noted that the manna disintegrated or evaporated once the sun came out; thus, Israel had to act early if they were to secure the blessing available to them. So it is with you and I. This miracle reminds us that we must be diligent in fulfilling our duties if we are to lay hold upon the blessings God has in store.[23] A mission postponed may turn into a mission never served. A prompting postponed may be disaster developing. A calling neglected may be a blessing bypassed.

God has many gifts and blessings for us, but if we are not diligent in our part, there may be a number of gifts we never get.

A friend of mine suggested that she sees in this miracle a message about the importance of gathering food storage and being prepared for emergencies.

Finally, the manna's propensity to rot or decay and to produce worms, if more was gathered than was needed, or if it was hoarded and stored (against God's commands), has been seen by many commentators as a symbol of the dangers of greed and covetousness. For example, John Chrysostom wrote: "Those who gathered in their houses more than the lawful quantity gathered not manna but worms and rottenness. Just so both in luxury and in covetousness, the gluttonous and drunken gather not more delicacies but more corruption."[24] Elsewhere we read that the corruption that came upon the hoarded manna reminds us of the importance of being contented with "that portion God has assigned for us."[25]

NOTES

1. One commentator has pointed out that, while Israel is clearly curious (Exodus 16:15) about the new food, "the people give no sign of amazement" and "the report of these developments is matter-of-fact" almost "downplaying" the miracle. See Terence E. Fretheim, *Interpretation: A Bible Commentary for Teaching for Preaching—Exodus* (Louisville, KY: John Knox Press, 1991), 182.

2. Bible Dictionary, "Manna," 684.

3. Walter L. Wilson, *A Dictionary of Bible Types* (Peabody, MA: Hendrickson, 1999), 234.

4. Leland Ryken, James C. Wilhoit, and Tremper Longman III, eds., *Dictionary of Biblical Imagery* (Downers Grove, IL: InterVarsity Press, 1998), 534.

5. One source states: "The manna was supplied throughout the entire sojourn of the Israelites and did not cease until they reached Cannan. [See Exodus 16:35] . . . The children of Israel were fed with the heaven-sent manna. . . . Christ, the true Bread of heaven, shall satisfy our spiritual hunger . . . until that day when we shall be like Him and hunger no more (1 John 3:2)." (Kenneth E. Trent, *Types of Christ in the Old Testament: A Conservative Approach to Old Testament Typology* [Bloomington, IN: CrossBooks, 2010], 50.)

6. Bible Dictionary, "Manna," 684.

7. "There is a legend among the Jews that the flavour of the Manna was just what each person liked best." (Ada R. Habershon, *Hidden Pictures in the Old Testament* [Grand Rapids, MI: Kregel Publications, 1982], 81; see also Herbert Lockyer, *All the Miracles of the Bible: The Supernatural in Scripture—Its Scope and Significance* [Grand Rapids, MI: Zondervan, 1961], 66.) It is interesting to note, even within

the Church, how varied peoples' approaches to and needs from Christ are. Just as the Apostle Paul said that he sought to be "all things to all men, that [he] might by all means save some" (1 Corinthians 9:22), so also Jesus's approach to His disciples is to meet their every need—and to meet them in the ways that are best for them individually. The gospel and the Atonement are very much tailored to meet individual needs. There is nothing "one size fits all" about Christ's work on behalf of His brothers and sisters. He knows us individually, and He addresses our needs individually.

8. Trent, *Types of Christ in the Old Testament*, 49.

9. See Richard C. Trench, *Miracles and Parables of the Old Testament* (Grand Rapids, MI: Baker Book House, 1959), 49–50.

10. Walter C. Kaiser Jr., "Exodus," in Frank E. Gaebelein, ed., *The Expositor's Bible Commentary* (Grand Rapids, MI: Zondervan, 1976–1992), 2:402. Another commentator wrote: "The manna needed to be ground in mills or beaten in a mortar. [This symbolizes] the sufferings of our Lord throughout His lifetime. . . . His whole life was one of suffering; and as we have this again and again brought before us in these types, we learn something of the meaning of the words, 'it pleased the Lord to bruise Him.'" (Ada R. Habershon, *Study of the Types* [Grand Rapids, MI: Kregel Publications, 1974], 30.)

11. One commentator put it this way: "Christ, the Bread of Life, is available to all who call upon Him, yet He must be accepted while we are in life's 'work week.' When the spiritual Sabbath (ceasing from earthly toil and labor) comes, Christ cannot be found by those who have previously rejected Him (Prov. 1:28 and Isa. 55:6). 'Now is the accepted time, today is the day of salvation.'" (Trent, *Types of Christ in the Old Testament*, 50.)

12. Lenet Hadley Read, *Unveiling Biblical Prophecy: A Summary of Biblical Prophecy Concerning Christ, the Apostasy and Christ's Latter-day Church* (San Francisco, CA: Latter-day Light Publications, 1990), 44.

13. Ryken, Wilhoit, and Longman, *Dictionary of Biblical Imagery*, 534.

14. See Trench, *Types of Christ in the Old Testament*, 46.

15. Lockyer, *All the Miracles of the Bible*, 66.

16. See Fretheim, *Interpretation: A Bible Commentary for Teaching for Preaching—Exodus*, 182; Patrick Fairbairn, *The Typology of Scripture*, 2nd ed. (Philadelphia, PA: Smith & English, 1989), 2:56–57; R. Alan Cole, *Exodus*, in *Tyndale Old Testament Commentaries* (Grand Rapids, MI: Eerdmans, 1973), 133; Lockyer, *All the Miracles of the Bible*, 66; Trench, *Types of Christ in the Old Testament*, 43–44; Katharine Doob Sakenfeld, *Journeying with God: A Commentary on the Book of Numbers*, in *International Theological Commentary* (Grand Rapids, MI: Eerdmans, 1995), 69.

17. Fretheim, *Interpretation: A Bible Commentary for Teaching for Preaching—Exodus*, 181–82.

18. See Ambrose, "Letter" 54 (64):2, in Joseph T. Lienhard, ed., *Exodus, Leviticus, Deuteronomy*, in *Ancient Christian Commentary on Scripture* (Downers Grove, IL: InterVarsity Press, 2001), 87.

19. Lockyer, *All the Miracles of the Bible*, 66.

20. Trench, *Types of Christ in the Old Testament*, 44.

21. Kaiser, "Exodus," in Gaebelein, *The Expositor's Bible Commentary*, 2:403.

22. Fairbairn, *The Typology of Scripture*, 2:58.

23. See Trench, *Types of Christ in the Old Testament*, 46.

24. Chrysostom, "Homilies on 1 Corinthians," 40:5, in Lienhard, *Exodus, Leviticus, Deuteronomy*, in *Ancient Christian Commentary on Scripture*, 88.

25. Trench, *Types of Christ in the Old Testament*, 45.

THE GIVING *of* QUAILS
in the WILDERNESS

EXODUS 16:12–13

NUMBERS 11:18–24, 31–34

THE MIRACLE

Though they had manna to sustain them in the wilderness, the children of Israel were unsatisfied. They desired more than that. And so they complained to Moses that they needed meat. They wanted "flesh to eat" (Numbers 11:18), as they had in Egypt.

The Lord told Moses that He had heard the murmurings of the people, and would send them flesh to eat (see Exodus 16:12); He would send so much flesh that it would come out of their nostrils and they would loathe it (see Numbers 11:20). This He would do to teach them to not reject Him or His will.

The east wind rose up, and the quails flew in, hovering about three feet above the ground, making them easily accessible to the people. There were quails everywhere, for about a day's journey in either direction. Many of the Israelites went out and gathered all that day, and throughout the night, and into the next day. The least that anyone gathered was ten homers of quail.[1]

The people spread the dead quail out to dry, but before they could consume the meat, God sent a plague upon those who had complained that the manna was not enough. Many died from the meat. Thus, the place where this miracle took place was called *Kibroth-hattaavah* ("graves of craving"), because it was there that they buried those who had "craved other food" (NIV Numbers 11:34).

Background

In the Numbers narrative, the people claim that they had such a good diet in Egypt when they were slaves, and they longed for the good life they had there. They lamented:

> We remember the fish, which we did eat in Egypt freely; the cucumbers, and the melons, and the leeks, and the onions, and the garlick:
> But now our soul is dried away: there is nothing at all, beside this manna, before our eyes. (KJV Numbers 11:5–6)

Truth be told, meat was likely not the common fare of slaves in ancient Egypt, neither would have been the fresh fruits and vegetables they described. The Israelites are here romanticizing the past, forgetting how truly miserable they were during that time of bondage in Egypt. By minimizing their discomforts in Egypt they can dramatize their inconveniences in the desert under Moses's leadership. Their behavior, unfortunately, is all too common among humans. Because we tend to be ungrateful beings, we can find bad in the most blessed of situations.[2]

The passage speaks of the quail as "two cubits high upon the face of the earth" (Numbers 11:31). This can mean that they flew in at about three feet off of the ground, where they could be readily caught,[3] or it can mean that there were so many quail that they were piled three feet high. The Hebrew is unclear as to which is meant. It is worth noting that the Numbers account says that the least amount of quail that anyone gathered was "ten homers" (Numbers 11:32), which is "nearly sixty bushels."[4] If that is the case, then the statement about the quail being "two cubits high upon the face of the earth" may actually mean that they were piled three feet high upon the ground, so many had been caught.[5]

The location of this miracle is given as *Kibroth-hattaavah*, which means literally "graves of craving," because it was their cravings for that which God thought best not to give that ended up killing them.[6]

Symbolic Elements

As we noted in a previous miracle, the manna was a typological symbol of Christ. Thus, Israel's rejection of the manna in preference for flesh was a strong metaphor of the dangers of loving the things of this world (symbolized by the meat) more than the things of God (represented by the manna).

The Hebrew indicates that it was the east wind that brought this fantastic flock of fowls into Israel's camp.[7] As we noted before, anciently, the east wind was a common representation of God's influence or power. Things that came from the east were believed to have been sent by God, or to be representative of God.[8] So the fact that the quails came from the east (in this miracle) was a sign to Israel that God had sent them. But when the flesh of the quails began to take the lives of those who ate them, it was also a sign to Israel that it was God who was now punishing them.

Quails are symbols for darkness, but also for lust, craving, or desire.[9] In this episode, they symbolize the spiritually darkened state of the Israelites who did not acknowledge God's constant miracles in their lives, and who sought for that which God had not seen fit to send them. It was their craving or lust for flesh, and the darkness that such lusting brought into their lives, that is symbolized by these birds.

The nose is a symbol for anger or temperament,[10] thus we read: "The wrath of the Lord was kindled . . . and the Lord smote the people" (Numbers 11:33). In parts of Europe, one occasionally hears the colloquial phrase, "You get up my nose," meaning, "You are angering me." One source reasons, "Excited breathing, with distentions of the nostrils when moved by indignation, led to the nose being used figuratively for anger."[11] So when the Lord informs Israel that they shall have so much quail that it will come out of their noses (Numbers 11:20; See also 2 Samuel 22:9 & 16), it may be a symbol of His anger with Israel, but also a representation of the frustrations they will feel when their misguided wishes are fulfilled.

APPLICATION AND ALLEGORIZATION

This miracle mirrors the Fall in Eden. God had given Adam and Eve ample supply for their needs, but they desired more than what He had given, so they ate of the "forbidden fruit" (Genesis 2–3). So also, the children of Israel had been given by God that which was ample for their needs, but they desired that which He had not given, so they demanded more (see Numbers 11). In the end, both stories end with the fallen foes' death—Adam and Eve die spiritually because they partook of the "forbidden fruit," and Israel died physically because they greedily partook of what they insisted God give them. This miracle teaches a strong lesson about trusting that God knows what's best for us, and that seeking to "get around" His will can only do us harm. When we place our wills above God's we will have regrets, as this miracle shows.[12] As we noted above, the location of this miracle is given as *Kibroth-hattaavah*, which means, "graves of craving," because it was their cravings that ended up killing them.[13] The message in this name is that we must not crave that which God has said is not best for us to have. It will be our spiritual death, and, in some cases, our physical death, to crave those things that God has kept from us, or forbidden us to partake of. We must believe and always remember that He knows what's best for us, and He always has our best interests in mind when He determines what gifts to shower us with, and which ones to hold back from us.[14]

On a related note, this miracle teaches us to be careful what we pray for because the Lord may grant our requests, and that may be to our detriment. One text on the miracles states: "We read a fable of a man who was so greedy of gain that he prayed that all he touched might turn to gold. His prayer was granted: his very food became gold, and he died of starvation."[15] As President Spencer W. Kimball counseled us: "Let us pray with the attitude always of the crucified One, 'nevertheless not my will, but thine, be done.' (Luke 22:42)"[16] Of the miracle of the quails, Ada Habershon wrote:

> We learn a solemn lesson from one of the wilderness incidents. When the children of Israel cried to God for flesh to eat, . . . He brought great flocks of quails. . . . "He gave them their own desire," "He gave them their request; but sent leanness to their soul." Here is a startling fact. Earnest desire causes strong crying to God. He hears and puts forth His power to work a wonder in their midst; but it proves no blessing, for it brings judgment and death upon them. There are some who teach that if we have faith enough we could get anything for which we chose to ask; but is not this [miracle] a warning that we should first find out whether the desire is in accordance with God's will?[17]

While God may grant unto us that which we ask for, only God's will is safe to seek. Obtaining our own will may actually bring us heartache instead of blessings! Those who are spiritually safe are those who have turned their lives and wills over to the Lord. The Brethren have warned us time and again about seeking after the "flesh pots of Egypt" (see Exodus 16:3). Only you know what your "flesh pot" is, but this miracle, and modern prophetic utterances, have made it quite clear that each of us must fight the temptation to seek the "flesh pot" over the "pot of manna." Anything we place before Christ will, in the end, serve to spiritually kill us, just as Israel's quail snuffed out their temporal lives.

NOTES

1. See Bible Dictionary, "Weights and measures," 742.
2. See Ronald B. Allen, "Numbers," in Frank E. Gaebelein, ed., *The Expositor's Bible Commentary* (Grand Rapids, MI: Zondervan, 1976–1992), 2:790. This same source states: "To spurn a regularly occurring, abundant, and nutritious food only

because it is boring is understandably human—a pitiable mark of our tendency toward ingratitude." (Ibid.)

3. See Gordon J. Wenham, *Numbers*, in *Tyndale Old Testament Commentaries* (Downers Grove, IL: InterVarsity Press, 1981), 109; Louis Ginzberg, *The Legends of the Jews* (Philadelphia, PA: The Jewish Publication Society of America, 1912–1938), 3:50.

4. Allen, "Numbers," in Gaebelein, *The Expositor's Bible Commentary*, 2:795.

5. See Allen, "Numbers," in Gaebelein, *The Expositor's Bible Commentary*, 2:795; Wenham, *Numbers*, in *Tyndale Old Testament Commentaries*, 109; Dennis T. Olson, *Interpretation: A Bible Commentary for Teaching and Preaching—Numbers* (Louisville, KY: Westminster John Knox Press, 1996), 69.

6. See Allen, "Numbers," in Gaebelein, *The Expositor's Bible Commentary*, 2:790.

7. R. Alan Cole, *Exodus*, in *Tyndale Old Testament Commentaries* (Grand Rapids, MI: Eerdmans, 1973), 131; Herbert Lockyer, *All the Miracles of the Bible: The Supernatural in Scripture—Its Scope and Significance* (Grand Rapids, MI: Zondervan, 1961), 67; Ada Habershon, *The Study of the Miracles* (London: Morgan & Scott, 1911), 47 & 171. See also Psalm 78:26–27.

8. J. E. Cirlot, *A Dictionary of Symbols*, 2nd ed. (New York: Routledge & Kegan Paul, 1971), 245; Cooper, *An Illustrated Encyclopaedia of Traditional Symbols*, 59; Joel F. Drinkard, "East," in Freedman, *The Anchor Bible Dictionary*, 2:248; Joseph Fielding McConkie and Donald W. Parry, *A Guide to Scriptural Symbols* (Salt Lake City, UT: Deseret Book, 1990), 44; Allen C. Myers, *The Eerdmans Bible Dictionary* (Grand Rapids, MI: Eerdmans, 1987), 300; Ryken, Wilhoit, and Longman, *Dictionary of Biblical Imagery*, 225.

9. See Cooper, *An Illustrated Encyclopaedia of Traditional Symbols*, 135.

10. B. O. Banwell, "Nose, Nostrils," in J. D. Douglas, ed., *The New Bible Dictionary* (Grand Rapids, MI: Eerdmans, 1967), 895.

11. W. Ewing, "Nose, Nostrils," in James Hastings, ed., *Dictionary of the Bible*, rev. ed. (New York: Charles Scribner's Sons, 1963), 701. See also, John L. McKenzie, *Dictionary of the Bible* (Milwaukee, WI: The Bruce Publishing Company, 1965), 620. The proverb warns, "Surely the churning of milk bringeth forth butter, and the wringing of the nose bringeth forth blood: so the forcing of wrath bringeth forth strife" (Proverbs 30:33). When God is depicted as being angry, we read of smoke coming forth from his nostrils (2 Samuel 22:9; Psalm 18:8; See also Job 41:20).

12. See Allen, "Numbers," in Gaebelein, *The Expositor's Bible Commentary*, 2:789.

13. Ibid., 2:790.

14. Thus, while the quails were a curse to ancient Israel, they were a blessing to modern Israel. President Young reminded us of a miracle that took place in the lives of those who were crossing the plains in 1846: "At one time, I was told, they would have perished from starvation, had not the Lord sent quails among them.

These birds flew against their wagons, and they either killed or stunned themselves, and the brethren and sisters gathered them up, which furnished them with food for days, until they made their way in the wilderness." (Brigham Young, *Discourses of Brigham Young*, John A. Widtsoe, comp. [Salt Lake City, UT: Bookcraft, 1954], 474.)

15. Richard C. Trench, *Miracles and Parables of the Old Testament* (Grand Rapids, MI: Baker Book House, 1959), 54.

16. Spencer W. Kimball, *The Teachings of Spencer W. Kimball* (Salt Lake City, UT: Bookcraft, 1982), 123.

17. Ada Habershon, *The Study of the Miracles* (London: Morgan & Scott, 1911), 219.

WATER *from* a ROCK

EXODUS 17:1–7

NUMBERS 20:1–13

THE MIRACLE

In the first water-from-a-rock miracle (see Exodus 17), the children of Israel had been traveling in the Desert of Sin when they came to a place called Rephidim. They were tired and thirsty, and yet the *wadi*, or gully, there had dried up, and so there was no water for them to drink.

In the preceding six months, they had seen Moses bring the ten plagues upon Egypt, a pillar of fire by night and a cloud by day lead them on their way, God part the Red Sea for them and close it on their enemies, the waters of Marah miraculously made drinkable, and bread and meat sent from heaven to sustain them on their trek. With all of that happening in such a short window, Moses records that they still murmured and asked, "[have you] brought us up out of Egypt, to kill us and our children and our cattle with thirst?" (Exodus 17:3). They demanded that Moses provide them with water. There is almost a spirit of entitlement about their statement, as though they were taking for granted that Moses had the power to perform these miracles and was somehow holding out on them.

Moses turned to the Lord with his problem, asking Him what he should do. The Lord's solution was that, as always, He would provide. He commanded Moses to take some of the elders of Israel with him, go to the rock at Horeb, and with his staff, smite the rock, and water would flow out for the people to drink (see Exodus 17:5–6).

Moses did as commanded, and the water came. However, because of the incident, Moses named the place *Massah* ("testing, trying, or proving") and *Meribah* ("strife, complaint"), because the people there tested the Lord and quarreled with Moses (see Exodus 17:7, footnotes *a* and *b*).

In the second water-from-a-rock miracle (see Numbers 20), the Israelites were camped in Kadesh, very near Canaan (the promised land). Moses's sister, Miriam, had died and was buried there.Again, there was no water, so the people began to murmur, saying: "Why have ye brought up the congregation of the Lord into this wilderness, that we and our cattle should die there?" (Numbers 20:4).

Moses and his brother, Aaron, entered the tabernacle and prostrated themselves before the Lord. His glory appeared to them (see Numbers 20:6), as it had to the elders of Israel in the first miracle of water-from-a-rock (see Exodus 17:5–6), and He commanded Moses to assemble the people and, in their presence, command the water to flow from the rock.

Not exactly following the Lord's instructions, Moses assembled the people, and chastised them, saying: "Hear now, ye rebels; must [Aaron and I] fetch you water out of this rock?" (Numbers 20:10). At that point, Moses smote the rock twice with his staff, rather than just commanding the water to flow as the Lord had instructed him to. The water flowed, but the Lord informed Moses and Aaron that they would not be entering the promised land because they "did not trust in [Him] enough to honor [Him] as holy in the sight of the Israelites" (NIV Numbers 20:12).

BACKGROUND

This is really a double miracle, in that it is performed twice. The first account of causing water to flow from a rock is recorded in Exodus 17:1–7, and the second in Numbers 20:1–13, though several elements of the miracles are different. The Exodus miracle takes place at the beginning of their forty-year sojourn, whereas the Numbers miracle takes place near the end of it. In the Exodus story, the Lord goes before Moses (implying that His glory was present and seen); but, in the Numbers account, Moses and Aaron see God's glory in the tabernacle, but then He does not visibly appear before them when the miracle is actually performed. In the Exodus narrative, Moses is commanded to smite the rock with his rod; but, in the Numbers miracle, Moses is simply instructed by the Lord to command water to flow from the rock. Exodus only mentions Moses during the miracle, whereas Numbers mentions Moses and Aaron. Thus, these are not two accounts of the same miracle, though they are remarkably similar miracles.[1]

The location of the first miracle was Rephidim, which means "resting place." God had led them there, and it would be the location where He would have them camp, or rest, for a time. But the incidents and attitudes there turned this time for resting into a time of strife, and their place for a miracle turned into a place of anger. Thus, after the miracle had taken place, Moses renamed the site from *Rephidim* (or "resting place") to *Massah* (i.e., "test") and *Meribah* (i.e., "contention," "strife," or "quarreling"), because there the Israelites tested the Lord and contended with Moses.

The location of the second miracle is Kadesh, just outside of Canaan. As in the first miracle, the place is renamed "Meribah" because of Israel's "quarreling" and "contentious" attitude.

SYMBOLIC ELEMENTS

Jesus is the rock depicted in both of these miracles; He is the source of the "living waters"(John 4) that saved Israel's life when it flowed forth from the stone. Regarding the rock in these two miracles, one text records:

> In some way Moses's rash action assaulted the holiness of the Lord (v.12; see also [Numbers] 27:14) [in the Numbers narrative], for Moses had not treated with sufficient deference the rock of God's presence. In some manner the rock speaks of God. This was a . . . symbol of his person, a gracious provision of his presence. In the [New Testament] we learn that the rock actually speaks of the person of the Lord Jesus Christ; it is called "Christ" by Paul in 1 Corinthians 10:4. Hence, unwittingly, Moses in his wrath had lashed out against the physical symbol of the embodiment of God's grace [in the Numbers 20 miracle].[2]

Jesus was the intended symbol behind the rock that saved Israel's life; and, thus, God's rebuke of Moses *may* have been, *in part*, because of his treatment of the rock.[3] In his book, *Types of Christ in the Old Testament*, Kenneth Trent notes numerous ways in which the rock of Exodus 17 and Numbers 20 typifies Christ. The following chart is a summary of Trent's teaching.[4]

THE ROCK	CHRIST
The ancient Israelite's lives were in danger because of want of physical water.	The lives of all of God's children are in danger because of their need for spiritual water.
The rock in Horeb was revealed to the people by God in answer to their great need.	Christ, the "Rock of Ages," was revealed to the people by God in answer to their great need as a fallen and sin-cursed people.

THE ROCK	CHRIST
In delivering its life-sustaining treasure, the rock served as a means of glorifying God.	Christ sought to glorify His Father in all that He said and did.
The rock in Horeb was filled with unrealized and hidden blessings that, to the causal passerby, were not evident.	Christ, our rock, was filled with unrealized and hidden blessings that, to the causal passerby, were not evident (see Isaiah 53:2).
The rock at Horeb had to be smitten before its treasures of life could be unleashed for the people.	It was not until Christ's blood flowed that the treasures of His redemption for us could be unleashed on our behalf.
The rock at Horeb was smitten but once.	"Christ was *once* offered to bear the sins of many" (Hebrews 9:28; emphasis added).
Paul tells us that the rock "followed" Israel until they reached the land flowing with "milk and honey" (1 Corinthians 10:4).	Jesus has promised us that he will be with us "even unto the end of the world" (Matthew 28:20).

Many aspects of these two miracles testify of Christ, our rock and our Redeemer.

The staff, or rod, of Moses is a common symbol of strength, authority, priesthood power, judgment, and divine guidance.[5] "The rod was in the hand of Moses, the power in the hand of God."[6] Even though Moses did not use his staff, or rod, in both of these miracles, he is commanded by God in each of the miracles to bring it with him (Exodus 17:5; Numbers 20:8), likely as a symbol that he is acting under God's delegated authority, rather than under his own power.

As noted elsewhere in this book, water traditionally carries two symbolic meanings—chaos and death,[7] or life and the Holy Spirit.[8] In the case of this miracle, the water is clearly a symbol of the Spirit, which saves and then sustains the lives of covenant Israel.

Application and Allegorization

Ada Haberson, one of the nineteenth century's most prolific typologists, saw what so many of the Church Fathers saw in these two miracles—namely, a foreshadowing of Jesus on the cross, where His smitten side produced water. She wrote:

> The *smitten rock* was the source of the rivers of water; just as the death of Christ must precede the decent of the Holy Spirit. In promising the outflowing rivers of water in John vii., the Lord evidently referred to this type. We read, "This spake He of the Spirit, which they that believe on Him should receive: for the Holy Ghost was not yet given; because that Jesus was not yet glorified." The Apostle Paul tells us that "that rock was Christ."[9]

As Habershon notes, millennia after the miracle, the Apostle Paul referred to this event with Christological application. He was quite clear that he understood the rock to have been a symbol of Christ (see 1 Corinthians 10:1, 4). Following Paul's lead, the Fathers of the Church took the symbolism one step further, and offered a twist that may be surprising to many readers. For example, Augustine wrote: "The rock was Christ in sign. . . . The rock was smitten twice with a rod; the double smiting signified the two wooden beams of the cross."[10] Elsewhere, Augustine penned this about the miracle recorded in Numbers 20:11,

> Blessed are they that hunger and thirst after righteousness, for they shall be filled." And our thirst is quenched from the rock in the wilderness: for "the Rock was Christ," and it was smitten with a rod that the water might flow. But that it might flow, the rock was smitten twice: because there are two beams of the cross. All these things, then, which were done in a figure, are made manifest to us.[11]

Like Augustine, Caesarius of Arles (circa 470–542 AD) also saw a foreshadowing of Jesus's crucifixion in Moses's double smiting of the rock. He wrote: "'Therefore Moses struck the rock twice with his staff.' What does this mean, brethren? . . . The rock was struck a second time because two trees were lifted up for the gibbet of the cross; the one stretched out Christ's sacred hands, the other spread out his sinless body from head to foot."[12] Though less specific, John of Damascus (circa 676–749 AD) clearly saw the same symbolic message in the Mosaic miracle. He wrote that "the rock [rent] and pouring forth streams of water" symbolized the "precious Cross" of Christ.[13] Around the same time that Augustine began serving as the bishop of Hippo, John Chrysostom (circa 349–407 AD) wrote: "Instead of water from a rock, [we have received the] blood from His side; instead of Moses' or Aaron's rod, the Cross."[14] Thus, for early Christians this second water-producing miracle serves to remind the believing biblical reader of the staff that pierced Christ's side, and the blood and water that flowed therefrom (see John 19:34). To the Fathers of the Church, the rock was more than just Christ as Paul explained it. Rather, it was "Jesus Christ, *and him crucified*" (1 Corinthians 2:2; emphasis added).[15] Though the water that came forth from the rock quenched Israel's physical thirst, in the mind of patristic exegetes, it foreshadowed the reality that Jesus's atoning sacrifice would quench covenant Israel's spiritual thirst. As Habershon noted: "The smitten rock was the source of the rivers of water; just as the death of Christ must precede the descent of the Holy Spirit."[16]

Because of its durability, unchangeability, solidity, and strength, a rock is a perfect symbol of Christ—the "Rock of Ages."[17] In the context of these two miracles, the rock not only highlights Christ's character, but also the nature of God's dependability. We need never doubt nor fear that He will neglect to provide. If we are but striving for worthiness, He will tend to our every need. Clearly, both of these water-from-a-rock miracles depicts Israel in less than perfect terms. So it is with you and I—we need not be perfect, but we must seek to be faithful and believing.

One commentator, drawing on the Church Fathers—who saw Atonement imagery in the smiting of the rock—acknowledged that the rock represents the crucified Christ of Calvary, whose blood flowed just as the water flowed.[18] But then noted:

> In the first instance [or miracle] God told Moses to strike the rock. That represents the stroke of God on Christ Jesus at Calvary (Exodus 17:6). In [the second miracle] God told him to speak to the rock. That rock is Christ (1 Cor. 10:4). Christ is not to be smitten again, once was sufficient. . . . The rock was to be spoken to the second time, which indicates that we are only to come to Him in prayer and praise with our petitions and receive again the abundance of forgiveness and the outpouring of the Holy Spirit.[19]

Thus, according to this aforementioned source, in the first miracle, we see Christ's sacrifice on our behalf. In the second, we see His post-martyrdom intercessions.[20]

The fact that God answered Israel's prayers through a rock has been seen as significant, not simply because the rock was a symbol of Christ, but also because of the unlikely source it was for water. In other words, if God had caused a desert spring to suddenly be discovered, such a resolve to their problem of thirst would be expected. But to use that which does not have water to produce water is a surprise. Hence, one text notes:

> God can bring good to His people from the most unlikely sources. Nothing seemed more unlikely to yield water than the barren rock of Horeb. So God often brings refreshing streams of comfort to His people out of hard circumstances. Paul and Silas could sing in the dungeon, and their imprisonment was made the means of adding to their converts in Philippi. The lot of John in Patmos seemed hard and dreary indeed, but at the bidding of Christ, streams of living water gushed forth there, which refreshed the soul of the apostle at the time, and have followed the church until the present. . . . Above all, out of the hard circumstances of the crucified Lord of glory, God has brought forth waters of everlasting life.[21]

How many times in your life has God brought answers or comfort from what appeared to be a trial or an unlikely source of relief? As the Lord reminded us through the Prophet Isaiah:

> My thoughts are not your thoughts, neither are your ways my ways, saith the Lord.
>
> For as the heavens are higher than the earth, so are my ways higher than your ways, and my thoughts than your thoughts. (Isaiah 55:8–9)

We need not worry about how the Lord will answer our prayers or meet our needs. All we need to do is trust that He will in His own way and in His own time.

In his two-volume work, *The Typology of Scripture*, Patrick Fairbairn suggests that, since the rock was Christ (see 1 Corinthians 10:4), and the passing through the Red Sea was baptism (see 1 Corinthians 10:1–2), and the manna was the body of Christ (John 6:31–33, 41), then the water that flowed from the rock might be seen as a symbol of Jesus's blood.[22] Thus, you have baptism and the sacrament (i.e., the bread and water) symbolized.

In the sixth century, Caesarius of Arles suggested a possible application of the symbolism behind Israel's thirst. He stated that most of us are "thirsty"—the righteous for God and the sinners for the fulfillment of their lusts.[23] The thirst of the righteous will always be quenched by God, but the wicked, no matter how much they "drink," will never quench their thirsts. Indeed, the more they drink of their sins, the thirstier they will become. Are you and I thirsting after the things that can be quenched—after the living waters? Or are we craving that which cannot satisfy?

Moses indicates that the children of Israel continually "tempted" or tested God (see Exodus 17:2). Their request for water, in Moses's estimation, showed a lack of faith, and implied their tendency to test or tempt the Lord. Of this, one commentator noted:

> Testing has to do with "putting God to the proof," that is, seeking a way in which God can be coerced to act or show himself. It is to . . . try to force God's hand in order thereby to determine concretely whether God is really present or not. Israel's testing of God consisted in this: if we are to believe that God is really present, then God must show us in a concrete way by making water materialize. It is to make one's belief in God contingent upon a demonstration. It is, in essence, an attempt to turn faith into sight. . . . This approach to God is often characteristic of believers. I will not take special precautions in the use of automobiles or guns or on dangerous ventures. God will take care of me. I will not take out insurance, God is my insurance policy. Such attitudes set God up for a test, holding God hostage, determining just how God is to show the divine power. It places God in the role of servant, at the beck and call of one in any difficulty.[24]

Does our approach to God suggest that we have faith in Him, or that we seek to test and tempt Him? While the line between these two may be subtle, it is, nevertheless, real. We read that the Israelites, because of their thirst, "murmured against Moses" their prophet (Exodus 17:3. See also Numbers 20:2). So many miracles of preservation had already been performed, but they still doubted and complained. One text offers the following application of these two manifestations of God's power in giving water from a rock.

> If we seek to criticize one of God's faithful leaders, we'd best beware. For God does not take such actions lightly. When we follow a leader who walks closely with God, it's better to appreciate him than grumble. Was God planning on letting His people die of thirst in the desert on their way to the Promised Land? That's unthinkable—except to those complaining Israelites. Had they trusted, they would have both received water and failed to malign Moses. Are we grumbling Israelites?[25]

Are you and I, as modern-day Israel, prone to grumble and complain about our leaders—both general and local? Do we speak critically of those whom the Lord has called to lead? If we do, we are as faithless as ancient Israel was on the occasions of these miracles. It must be remembered, and the Bible indicates, that by murmuring against Moses they were really murmuring against God, because He had called Moses. Thus, while you and I may believe that we can, with propriety, criticize an earthly leader of the Church or one of its congregations, to do so is to criticize the God who called them to that position. Finally, one commentator pointed out that one of the most praiseworthy traits of Moses was his consistent practice of taking his trials and difficulties to the Lord—which is evidenced by this miracle, and others.[26] (See, for example, Exodus 15:25; 16:4; 32:30; 33:8; Numbers 11:2, 11; 12:13; 14:13–19.)

NOTES

1. See Walter C. Kaiser Jr., "Exodus," in Frank E. Gaebelein, ed., *The Expositor's Bible Commentary* (Grand Rapids, MI: Zondervan, 1976–1992), 2:406.
2. Ronald B. Allen, "Numbers," in Frank E. Gaebelein, ed., *The Expositor's Bible Commentary* (Grand Rapids, MI: Zondervan, 1976–1992), 2:868.
3. See Gordon J. Wenham, *Numbers*, in *Tyndale Old Testament Commentaries* (Downers Grove, IL: InterVarsity Press, 1981), 149. It is worth noting that the book of Psalms highlights Moses's harsh words during the episode as playing some role in the penalty God had doled out. "Rash words came from Moses' lips" (NIV Psalm 106:33). Moses's rebuke of Israel, asking rhetorically "must we fetch you water?" could imply he was taking credit for the miracle, rather than giving God the credit (Numbers 20:10). See Dennis T. Olson, *Interpretation: A Bible Commentary for Teaching and Preaching—Numbers* (Louisville, KY: Westminster John Knox Press, 1996), 126–27; Louis Ginzberg, *The Legends of the Jews* (Philadelphia, PA: The Jewish Publication Society of America, 1912–1938), 6:91n490. See also Katharine Doob Sakenfeld, *Journeying with God: A Commentary on the Book of Numbers*, in *International Theological Commentary* (Grand Rapids, MI: Eerdmans, 1995), 114. Unfortunately, the passage is simply unclear on what exactly Moses and Aaron did wrong. One commentary offers the following explanation: "Some commentators find it difficult to see how Moses' action could be construed as unbelief. The key to the problem is to be found in a comparison of God's instructions to Moses with their execution. . . . There is a marked divergence between what was commanded and what was done. Moses was instructed to *take the rod, assemble the congregation* and speak to *the rock* ([V:]8), but in the event he *took the rod, gathered the assembly,* spoke to them instead of to the rock, and then *struck the rock* ([V:]9–11). Though this brought forth water, it was not produced in the divinely intended way, and counted as rebelling against God's command ([V:]24) and unbelief. . . . Thus, Moses' failure to carry out the Lord's instructions precisely was . . . an act of unbelief. . . . Moses' unbelief was compounded by his anger, expressed in his remarks to the people ([V:]10), 'he spoke words that were rash' (Ps. 106:33), and by striking the rock twice ([V:]11). DeVaulx suggests that there was an element of sacrilege in striking the rock, for it symbolized God. . . . Elsewhere God is often likened to a rock (e.g. Pss. 18:2; 31:3; 42:9, etc.). This understanding of the rock closely corresponds

to that of the targums, and of Paul, who says 'they drank from the supernatural Rock which followed them, and the Rock was Christ' (1 Cor. 10:4). In disobeying instructions and showing no respect for the symbol of God's presence, Moses failed to *sanctify* God." (Wenham, *Numbers*, in *Tyndale Old Testament Commentaries*, 150–51; emphasis in original.)

4.   See Kenneth E. Trent, *Types of Christ in the Old Testament: A Conservative Approach to Old Testament Typology* (Bloomington, IN: CrossBooks, 2010), 50–52.

5.   Kevin J. Conner, *Interpreting the Symbols and Types*, rev. ed. (Portland, OR: City Bible Publishing, 1992), 164 & 170; Leland Ryken, James C. Wilhoit, and Tremper Longman III, eds., *Dictionary of Biblical Imagery* (Downers Grove, IL: InterVarsity Press, 1998), 733–34; J. C. Cooper, *An Illustrated Encyclopaedia of Traditional Symbols* (London: Thames and Hudson, 1987), 140; Jack Tresidder, *Symbols and Their Meanings: The Illustrated Guide to More than 1,000 Symbols— Their Traditional and Contemporary Significance* (London: Duncan Baird Publishers, 2006), 139; Herbert Lockyer, *All the Miracles of the Bible: The Supernatural in Scripture—Its Scope and Significance* (Grand Rapids, MI: Zondervan, 1961), 76; Richard C. Trench, *Miracles and Parables of the Old Testament* (Grand Rapids, MI: Baker Book House, 1959), 64; Joseph Fielding McConkie, "Jesus Christ, Symbolism, and Salvation," in Robert L. Millet, ed., *Studies in Scripture: Acts to Revelation* (Salt Lake City, UT: Deseret Book, 1987), 6:204.

6.   Trench, *Miracles and Parables of the Old Testament*, 47.

7.   For example, Kselman and Barre, in Raymond E. Brown, Joseph A. Fitzmyer, and Roland E. Murphy, eds., *The New Jerome Biblical Commentary* (Englewood Cliffs, NJ: Prentice Hall, 1990), 541; Joseph A. Fitzmyer, *The Anchor Bible: The Gospel According to Luke I–IX* (New York: Doubleday, 1970), 739n31; C. S. Mann, *The Anchor Bible: Mark*, vol. 27 (New York: Doubleday, 1986), 278–79; Firmage, in David Noel Freedman, *The Anchor Bible Dictionary* (New York: Doubleday, 1992), 6:1132; Lamar Williamson Jr., *Interpretation: A Bible Commentary for Teaching and Preaching—Mark* (Atlanta, GA: John Knox Press, 1983), 104; Adam Clarke, *The Holy Bible, Containing the Old and New Testaments . . . with a Commentary and Critical Notes. . . .* (New York: T. Mason & G. Lane, 1837), 5:420; Sean Freyne, "The Sea of Galilee," in Freedman, *The Anchor Bible Dictionary*, 2:900; Leon L. Morris, *Revelation*, in *Tyndale New Testament Commentaries*, rev. ed. (Grand Rapids, MI: InterVarsity Press, 1987), 171; Walter L. Liefeld, "Luke," in Gaebelein, *The Expositor's Bible Commentary*, 8:913; J. C. Cooper, *An Illustrated Encyclopaedia of Traditional Symbols* (London: Thames and Hudson, 1987), 121. See also Walter L. Wilson, *A Dictionary of Bible Types* (Peabody, MA: Hendrickson, 1999), 361; Conner, *Interpreting the Symbols and Types*, 166.

8.   For example, see John 7:37–39; Numbers 8:7; Wilson, *A Dictionary of Bible Types*, 347 & 452; Ryken, Wilhoit, and Longman, *Dictionary of Biblical Imagery*, 931; Cooper, *An Illustrated Encyclopaedia of Traditional Symbols*, 189; Conner,

Interpreting the Symbols and Types, 163 & 179; Ada R. Habershon, *Hidden Pictures in the Old Testament* (Grand Rapids, MI: Kregel Publications, 1982), 237–38; James Hall, *Dictionary of Subjects & Symbols in Art*, rev. ed. (Boulder, CO: Westview Press, 1979), 128; Ada R. Habershon, *Study of the Types* (Grand Rapids, MI: Kregel Publications, 1974), 40, 143, 152; Herbert Lockyer, *All the Miracles of the Bible: The Supernatural in Scripture—Its Scope and Significance* (Grand Rapids, MI: Zondervan, 1961), 68.

9. Habershon, *Study of the Types*, 43; emphasis in original. See also 49.

10. Augustine, "On the Gospel of St. John," Tractate 26:12, in Philip Schaff, ed., *Nicene and Post-Nicene Fathers*, 1st series (Peabody, Massachusetts: Hendrickson Publishers, 1994), 7:172.

11. Augustine, "On The Gospel of St. John," Tractate 28:9, in Schaff, *Nicene and Post-Nicene Fathers*, 7:182.

12. Caesarius of Arles, "Sermon," 103.3, in Lienhard, *Exodus, Leviticus, Deuteronomy*, in *Ancient Christian Commentary on Scripture*, 239. Caesarius also wrote: "Behold, . . . unless this rock is struck, it does not have any water at all. But when it has been struck, it produces fountains and rivers, as we read in the Gospel: 'He who believes in me, from within him there shall flow rivers of living water.' When Christ was struck on the cross, he brought forth the fountains of the New Testament. Therefore, it was necessary for him to be pierced. If he had not been struck, so that water and blood flowed from his side, the whole world would have perished through suffering thirst for the word of God." (Ibid., 90.)

13. See John of Damascus, "Exposition of the Orthodox Faith," bk. IV, ch. XI, in Philip Schaff and Henry Wace, eds., *Nicene and Post-Nicene Fathers*, 2nd series (Peabody, MA: Hendrickson Publishers, 2004), 9:80–81.

14. John Chrysostom, "Homilies on Second Corinthians," Homily 11:18, in Schaff, *Nicene and Post-Nicene Fathers*, 2nd series, 12:333.

15. This is not to say that Paul missed the point of the "type" or its relationship to the cross. The only point I wish to make here is that Paul did not highlight the cross/Atonement symbolism, whereas the Church Fathers traditionally did.

16. Habershon, *Study of the Types*, 43.

17. Joseph Smith, *Teachings of the Prophet Joseph Smith*, Joseph Fielding Smith Jr., comp. (Salt Lake City, UT: Deseret Book, 1976), 41; "Rock of Ages," *Hymns*, 111.

18. See Wilson, *A Dictionary of Bible Types*, 346–47.

19. Ibid., 347.

20. Commentators have called the second miracle a "spoilt type," and have suggested the reason God was angry with Moses is because he ruined the typology of the miracle. (See Habershon, *The Study of the Miracles*, 60 & 143–44; Trent, *Types of Christ in the Old Testament*, 52.)

21. Trench, *Miracles and Parables of the Old Testament*, 47–48.

22. Patrick Fairbairn, *The Typology of Scripture*, 2nd ed. (Philadelphia, PA: Smith & English, 1989), 2:65.

23. See Caesarius of Arles, "Sermon," 103:2, in Lienhard, *Exodus, Leviticus, Deuteronomy,* in *Ancient Christian Commentary on Scripture*, 90. "When we come to the Lord as thirsty sinners, and are satisfied by Him, He gives us His Holy Spirit to dwell in our heart." (Habershon, *Hidden Pictures in the Old Testament*, 238.)

24. Terence E. Fretheim, *Interpretation: A Bible Commentary for Teaching for Preaching—Exodus* (Louisville, KY: John Knox Press, 1991), 189.

25. Pamela McQuade, *The Top 100 Miracles of the Bible: What They Are and What They Mean to You Today* (Uhrichsville, OH: Barbour Publishing, 2008), 54.

26. See Kaiser, "Exodus," in Gaebelein, *The Expositor's Bible Commentary*, 2:406.

MIRIAM *Gets* LEPROSY

NUMBERS 12:1–15

THE MIRACLE

Moses's sister, Miriam, had been speaking against her brother, the prophet, because he had taken a wife of the Cushites. The Lord was displeased with her murmuring and backbiting—particularly her declaration that God had spoken through she and Aaron as much as He had through Moses (see Numbers 12:2). In consequence, the Lord appeared to Miriam and Aaron in "a pillar of the cloud, and stood in the door of the tabernacle" (Numbers 12:5), and He chastised them for their sin. He also elevated Moses by saying he was a prophet's prophet. God told Miriam that typically he reveals Himself to prophets in visions or dreams, but with Moses He speaks face-to-face (see Numbers 12:6–8).

When God's glory withdrew, Miriam stood "leprous, white as snow" (Numbers 12:10). Moses begged the Lord to heal her. "In final clinching proof of Moses's special relationship to God, his prayer for his sister's healing is immediately answered."[1] However, the Lord still required that Miriam be sent to live outside of the camp for seven days, and to participate in the normal purification rites of others who had contracted this disease. So the Israelites continued to camp in the region while they waited for Miriam's purification by the Lord.[2]

BACKGROUND

Both Miriam and Aaron are said to be guilty in this story, but only Miriam is punished.[3] Scholars generally believe that this is because Miriam is the principal one in the attack against Moses. She is the one who speaks the criticisms. Aaron's chief sin appears to be that he did not stand up and rebuke her, but, rather, stood idly by as she criticized her brother, the prophet.[4]

The issue for which Miriam criticizes Moses is said to be his marriage to a Cushite wife (see Numbers 12:1). However, the more Miriam talks, the more it appears that her issue is one of sibling rivalry, and not a concern about her brother's choice of wives. Miriam had been a significant figure in the history of her brother and Israel. It was she that preserved his life as an infant (see Exodus 1). It was Miriam that arranged for Moses's birth mother to become his nurse when he was adopted into the family of Pharaoh (see Exodus 2). It was Moses's sister who led the singing in praise of God when Israel safely crossed the Red Sea (see Exodus 15).[5] Thus, she was no insignificant Saint. Nevertheless, as one commentator noted: "The marriage of Moses to a Cushite woman is not the central issue. This [is] only pretext; the real issue concerned Moses' special relationship with God."[6] Remember, it is Miriam who rhetorically asks: "Hath the Lord indeed spoken only by Moses? hath he not spoken also by us?" (Numbers 12:2).

Though it matters little, Miriam's condition was likely not what we would call leprosy, or "Hansen's disease," today. Indeed, it is believed that "true leprosy" (or Hansen's disease) was not present in the Middle East until New Testament times, if not later. Thus, this could not be "Hansen's disease" that Miriam was suffering from.[7] Rather, she likely was cursed with psoriasis, or possibly an extreme case of eczema.[8] Regardless, the curse carries the same symbolism for the reader.

SYMBOLIC ELEMENTS

The "cloud" was a symbol of God's presence: His glory. "The *withdrawal* of the cloud was the token of the withdrawal of the divine presence and direction"[9]—a consequence of Miriam's and Aaron's sin. "What happens to the rest of us when we are guilty of sin? The Spirit of God withdraws from us, the heavens turn to brass, and we are left alone to stew in our guilt until we repent."[10] Such was the case with Miriam, and such was represented by the withdrawal of God's glory.

As we noted in a previous chapter, leprosy is a common scriptural symbol for sin or spiritual sickness.[11] It is also a representation of the punishments of God.[12] Thus, in this miracle, Miriam learns both of God's displeasure with her behavior, but also of God's wrath and punishment upon those who reject the paths of the righteous. Miriam is a reminder to all that those who live arrogant lives, and those who place themselves above the Lord's appointed representatives, bring suffering upon themselves, and potentially ostracize themselves from the Church and the kingdom.

APPLICATION AND ALLEGORIZATION

One commentator noted, "Christ is that prophet of whom Moses was a shadow. In reference to Him, therefore, the lesson has tenfold weight."[13] As the Lord Himself has stated: "Whether by mine own voice or by the voice of my servants, it is the same" (D&C 1:38). This miracle reminds us that to criticize the Lord's prophet is to criticize God Himself. Whether we disagree with the direction or doctrine of one of the Lord's servants, or we—like Miriam—feel ourselves equally, if not more, qualified, it makes no difference. We are never justified in our criticisms. As to the issue of equality, one text states:

> Inequalities of position in the Church of God have their origin in the will of God. Vessels belonging to the same owner vary in the amount of cargo they carry because they vary in their capacity. . . . So there are intellectual inequalities among God's servants. "To one he gave five talents, to another two," etc. (Matt. xxv. 15). Why not give to each one the same number? . . . Because they are destined for different service, and this destiny must be [determined by] the will of their owners. Neither Miriam nor Aaron could grow into a Moses.[14]

God alone decides who presides over His kingdom. It is never left up to chance, luck, or coincidence. Those who have been called, like Moses, were appointed because of what they had, in spite of their human frailties or weaknesses. Owing to the fact that God seems entirely able to overlook the inadequacies of a man like Moses, you and I are covenant bound to do the same with our leaders today.

This miracle reminds us that jealousy *within* the Church hinders its progress just as much as a legion of devils *without*. The book of Numbers records that, because of the consequences of Miriam's jealousy, "the people journeyed not." (Numbers 12:15).[15] The Saints can have as much negative influence on the progress of the kingdom as any outside demonic force. In the book of Alma, we find this: "Alma saw the wickedness of the church, and he saw also that the example of the church began to lead those who were unbelievers on from one piece of iniquity to another, thus bringing on the destruction of the people" (Alma 4:11). Miriam's bad behavior harmed Israel's progress. We learn from her experience that our behavior has the same potential to harm the Church, and to harm our own spirituality.

One typologist drew a curious parallel between Miriam and the Jews who rejected Christ in the meridian of time.

> In answer to the prayer of Moses, Miriam was healed from her leprosy; and though she was treated as unclean, her defilement was regarded as far less than that which she had really contracted. It may be, therefore, that in answer to the prayer of the great Intercessor, of who Moses was a type, Israel as a nation, though cut off for a time, will be judged as unclean, not as though they were murderers, but as though they had merely been present at the death of their Messiah.[16]

In other words, just as Miriam was worthy of death, and would have received such a penalty were it not for Moses's intervention, so also were those who rejected Jesus in the first century; they would have been worthy of spiritual death were it not for Christ's intervention on their behalf: "Father, forgive them; for they know not what they do" (Luke 23:34).[17] We as Latter-day Israel too often act as Miriam did. Consequently, were it not for the Atonement of Christ, we too would be worthy of the spiritual death symbolized by the leprosy that Miriam brought upon herself.

NOTES

1. Gordon J. Wenham, *Numbers*, in *Tyndale Old Testament Commentaries* (Downers Grove, IL: InterVarsity Press, 1981), 113.
2. One commentator wrote: "The seven days . . . do not appear to be a period of quarantine or ritual purification . . . ; the seven-day banishment is a sign of the shame she has brought upon herself by rebelling against Moses and thus against God." (Dennis T. Olson, *Interpretation: A Bible Commentary for Teaching and Preaching—Numbers* [Louisville, KY: Westminster John Knox Press, 1996], 74.)
3. According to Jewish midrash both Aaron and Miriam were initially struck with leprosy. "Aaron's leprosy, however, lasted for a moment only, for his sin had not been as great as that of his sister who started the talk against Moses. His disease vanished as soon as he looked upon his leprosy. Not so with Miriam. Aaron in vain tried to direct his eyes upon her leprosy and in this way to heal her, for in her case the effect was the reverse; as soon as he looked upon her the leprosy increased, and nothing remained but to call for Moses' assistance." (Louis Ginzberg, *The Legends of the Jews* [Philadelphia, PA: The Jewish Publication Society of America, 1912–1938], 3:259.)
4. See, for example, Ronald B. Allen, "Numbers," in Frank E. Gaebelein, ed., *The Expositor's Bible Commentary* (Grand Rapids, MI: Zondervan, 1976–1992), 2:797 & 2:802; Herbert Lockyer, *All the Miracles of the Bible: The Supernatural in Scripture—Its Scope and Significance* (Grand Rapids, MI: Zondervan, 1961), 74.

5.   See Allen, "Numbers," in Gaebelein, *The Expositor's Bible Commentary,* 2:797; Olson, *Interpretation: A Bible Commentary for Teaching and Preaching—Numbers,* 69–70.

6.   Allen, "Numbers," in Gaebelein, *The Expositor's Bible Commentary,* 2:797. See also Wenham, *Numbers,* in *Tyndale Old Testament Commentaries,* 110–11; Olson, *Interpretation: A Bible Commentary for Teaching and Preaching—Numbers,* 71; Richard C. Trench, *Miracles and Parables of the Old Testament* (Grand Rapids, MI: Baker Book House, 1959), 57; Lockyer, *All the Miracles of the Bible,* 74.

7.   See Wenham, *Numbers,* in *Tyndale Old Testament Commentaries,* 113.

8.   See Allen, "Numbers," in Gaebelein, *The Expositor's Bible Commentary,* 2:803; Wenham, *Numbers,* in *Tyndale Old Testament Commentaries,* 113. See also Baruch A. Levine, *The Anchor Bible: Numbers 1–20,* vol. 4 (New York: Doubleday, 1993), 332.

9.   Lockyer, *All the Miracles of the Bible,* 74; emphasis in original.

10.   Stephen E. Robinson, *Believing Christ: The Parable of the Bicycle and Other Good News* (Salt Lake City, UT: Deseret Book, 1992), 118.

11.   See J. C. Cooper, *An Illustrated Encyclopaedia of Traditional Symbols* (London: Thames and Hudson, 1987), 96; Kevin J. Conner, *Interpreting the Symbols and Types,* rev. ed. (Portland, OR: City Bible Publishing, 1992), 152; Charles Haddon Spurgeon, *Spurgeon's Sermons* (Grand Rapids, MI: Baker Book Hosue, 1996), 7:311–27; Leland Ryken, James C. Wilhoit, and Tremper Longman III, eds., *Dictionary of Biblical Imagery* (Downers Grove, IL: InterVarsity Press, 1998), 507; Trench, *Miracles and Parables of the Old Testament,* 134–35. "The biblical word traditionally translated 'leprosy' does not (at least usually) refer to what we call leprosy (Hansen's disease) but rather covers a variety of skin diseases, including the different forms of psoriasis and vitiligo (both of which make the skin white, cf. 2 Kings 5:27). The leprosy in Leviticus that contaminates clothing or a house is mold or mildew (Lev 13:47–59; 14:33–57)." (Ryken, Wilhoit, and Longman, *Dictionary of Biblical Imagery,* 507. See also Douglas R. A. Hare, *Interpretation: A Bible Commentary for Teaching and Preaching—Matthew* [Louisville, KY: John Knox Press, 1993], 89.)

12.   Lockyer, *All the Miracles of the Bible,* 172; Trench, *Miracles and Parables of the Old Testament,* 135.

13.   Trench, *Miracles and Parables of the Old Testament,* 60.

14.   Ibid., 58.

15.   Ibid., 59.

16.   Ada R. Habershon, *Study of the Types* (Grand Rapids, MI: Kregel Publications, 1974), 77–78.

17.   One early Christian source also suggests a similar parallel. Origen wrote: "Now on careful consideration the narrative here seems to lack coherence. What has their saying 'Has the Lord spoken to Moses only? Has he not also spoken to

us?' to do with their indignation about the Ethiopian woman? If that was the trouble, they ought to have said, 'Moses, you should not have taken an Ethiopian wife and one of the seed of Ham. You should have married one of your own race and of the house of Levi.' They say not a word about this. They say instead, 'Has the Lord spoken to Moses only? Has he not also spoken to us?' Rather, it seems to be that in so saying they understood the thing Moses had done more in terms of the mystery [or symbolism]. They saw Moses—that is, the spiritual law—entering now into wedlock and union with the church that is gathered together from among the Gentiles. This is reason, apparently, why . . . Miriam, who typified the forsaken synagogue, . . . seeing [the] kingdom taken away . . . and given to a nation bringing forth the fruits thereof, [said], 'Has the Lord spoken to Moses only? Has he not also spoken to us?'" (Origen, "Commentary on the Song of Songs," 2:1, in Joseph T. Lienhard, ed., *Exodus, Leviticus, Deuteronomy,* in *Ancient Christian Commentary on Scripture* [Downers Grove, IL: InterVarsity Press, 2001], 220.)

THE EARTH OPENS and
SWALLOWS KORAH
and His ASSOCIATES

NUMBERS 16:29–34

THE MIRACLE

Korah, Dathan, Abiram, and On gathered some two hundred and fifty men to join them in a rebellion against Moses and Aaron. Their accusation against these two God-appointed brethren was that they were taking too much authority upon themselves. These rebels announced to their prophet that God had sanctified them just as much as Moses and Aaron, and that God was just as present in their midst as He was the prophets' lives (Numbers 16:1–3). As one text put it: "The complainants suggest that everyone is equal before God and that . . . no special prerogatives should belong to either [Moses] the prophetic or [Aaron] the priestly leader."[1]

In shock, Moses fell prostrate. He then told the rebels that in the morning the Lord would show them whom He considered holy, and who it was that truly belonged to God. The insurrectionists were instructed that on the morrow they should fill their incense burners with incense and hot coals, and then present themselves before the Lord at the tabernacle. In modern terminology, the prophet added as an epitaph: "You're the ones who have gone too far!" (see Numbers 16:4–7).

Moses told them that, because God had separated them from the rest of the Israelites, and had given them charge over the tabernacle, they should not be coveting the "high priesthood" (JST Numbers 16:10). He also informed them that, while they perceived themselves as rebelling against Moses, in reality they were rebelling against God (see Numbers 16:8–11).

When Moses summoned Dathan and Abiram to appear before him, they refused, saying that he had led them out of the "land of milk and honey" into a desert, and that he now might wish to gouge their eyes out.[2] At this accusation, Moses became angry, and asked the Lord to reject their offering, stating that he had never wronged them in any way (see Numbers 16:15).

When Moses, Aaron, and the rebels gathered the next day, the Lord appeared and said to His two prophets, "Separate yourselves from among this congregation, that I may consume them in a moment" (Numbers 16:21). Moses begged the Lord to only destroy the guilty. So God instructed him to tell the righteous, "Depart . . . from the tents of these wicked men, and touch nothing of theirs, lest ye be consumed in all their sins," which Moses did (Numbers 16:26. See also Numbers 16:16–27).

Moses then announced to all how Israel would know that the Lord had sent him, and that he was doing God's will rather than his own. He said, "If the rebel leadership die a natural death, then the Lord has not sent me. But if they die in an unusual way, like the earth opens up and swallows them and all of their possessions, you'll know that these men had rejected God" (see Numbers 16:28–30).

Instantly the earth opened, swallowed these ringleaders, their family members, their servants, and all of their possessions, and then the earth closed back up. The Israelites who witnessed this became frightened, thinking that they were going to be killed also. Finally, fire came down from heaven and killed the two hundred and fifty men who were supporters of Korah, Dathan, Abiram and On's rebellion (see Numbers 16:31–35).

BACKGROUND

Korah was a Levite. Consequently, he had a significant role in the maintenance of the tabernacle (see Numbers 4:1–20). Apparently, however, he felt that he was deserving or qualified for something better or higher.[3] The King James Version says that he and his associates wanted the priesthood—perhaps the Aaronic Priesthood that only Aaron and his descendants held (see Numbers 16:10). Of course, as a Levite, Korah may have already held the Levitical Priesthood, but, if he did, he would have been restricted in his duties, much like a deacon is limited in his authority, though he holds the Aaronic Priesthood. Levites aided the Aaronites; and Korah was not a descendant of Aaron. The Levites served to maintain the portable temple, but they were excluded from officiating in the sacrificial rites of the tabernacle.[4] Thus, Korah, if he held any priesthood, was very limited in how he could function.[5] As for Dathan, Abiram, and On, they were said to be Reubenites, and, therefore, would not have held any priesthood authority or office. The Joseph Smith Translation indicates that what Korah was seeking was not the priesthood, but the "high priesthood" (JST Numbers 16:10). Thus, apparently Korah wanted to hold the Melchizedek Priesthood, and lead the people as Moses did.[6] One commentator noted: "Their charge was that Moses had 'gone too far' in taking the role of spiritual leadership of the people; they asserted that the whole community is equally holy, hence Moses and Aaron had no special privilege with the Lord or special authority over them."[7]

The people who constituted this rebellion were not a collection of "rude, impudent ruffians."[8] On the contrary, Korah, Dathan, Abiram, and On were esteemed leaders among the Israelites, as were each of the two hundred and fifty officials or nobles who followed them. Thus, many of the Israelites would have listened to a rebellion of this size by men of such noteworthy rank. This is a significant challenge to Moses's authority and position over the Church. The relationship of Moses to those rebelling against him may be of interest. Korah was the first cousin to Aaron and Moses.[9] This would make his antagonism and organized rebellion all the more painful to the prophet and his brother. In addition, in the second chapter of Exodus, Moses took the life of an Egyptian guard who was beating an Israelite to death, Moses literally lost his position in Pharaoh's house over this act, and nearly lost his life because of it (see Exodus 2:11–15).[10] The Jewish midrash indicates that the Hebrew man that the Egyptian taskmaster was beating was Dathan, who, in our current miracle, is one of the main leaders in the rebellion against Moses.[11] Apparently Dathan's way of thanking Moses for saving his life years earlier was to rebel against him in the wilderness. This makes the act of Dathan and his counterparts all the more offensive and selfish.

Moses instructs Korah and his followers to each take incense burners (used for the rites of the tabernacle) and light them, and then appear at the tabernacle the very next day (Numbers 16:6–7). "This is remarkable since the [Levitical] priests alone were to hold censers. While Korah was of the house of Levi, . . . the others, as Reubenites, were not even remote possibilities. But Moses dared them to do as he demanded."[12] It is unclear what Moses's intention was. Certainly he would not authorize them to perform a rite, ritual, or ordinance if they were not authorized to perform it. Perhaps he was simply trying to highlight the impropriety of their desires. They wanted authority God had not given them, so they sought to take it.

Therefore, since they were not authorized by God to function in the temple as Aaronic priests, perhaps they thought that should just take that too. It is possible that Moses felt this request would wake them up to the ridiculous nature of their proposed coup.[13]

SYMBOLIC ELEMENTS

Incense and censers symbolize prayer or communion with God.[14] In the context of ancient temple worship, the offering of incense—originally a priestly rite—symbolically reminded all who it was that God had authorized to approach Him, or commune with Him, on behalf of Israel. The highlighting of censers in this miracle simply places our focus on what the controversy was; namely, who was authorized to hold and utilize the priesthood on behalf of God's covenant people.

The earth or ground is sometimes employed as a symbol for things which are worldly and temporal.[15] Thus, "Putting off shoes on entering a holy place represents leaving earthly contact outside . . . and [divesting] oneself of vice."[16] In this miracle, the ground or earth serves as a means of punishment, and also as a symbol of the sins of those consumed; they were filled with vices, including a love for the things of this world and the honors and respect of men, as found in rank and status.

As we noted previously, flames or fire can have a number of symbolic meanings. They can be associated with the glory of God or other celestial beings. But they can also represent God's judgment, as in this miracle, where the flames come out of heaven and consume the guilty.[17]

APPLICATION AND ALLEGORIZATION

Perhaps the most important message of this miracle is the dangers of aspiring to that which one has not been called to. In Doctrine and Covenants 88, the Lord commands modern Israel:

> Whatsoever ye ask the Father in my name it shall be given unto you, that is expedient for you;
>
> And if ye ask anything that is not expedient for you, it shall turn unto your condemnation. (D&C 88:64–65)

"Bloom where you're planted," as they say. Be satisfied with the calling the Lord has extended to you. Be faithful in whatever you've been called to do. "The issue is gratitude versus pride. A humble, grateful person thanks God for any task [or calling] and carries it out faithfully. A prideful person like Korah, selfishly desiring a bigger place, a larger slice of the action in God's kingdom, is in fact an enemy of God."[18] Too many men wish to be the bishop, but are not faithful as the home teacher.

On more than one occasion, Hugh Nibley noted that there are four things we must "never do under any circumstances."[19] (1) We must not accuse. The title "devil" means "accuser." Korah and his associates, under the inspiration of Satan, accused Moses and Aaron. When we accuse others we take upon ourselves the role of the "accuser," and we act the part of Korah. (2) We must never aspire. Satan aspired, and that was his undoing. Korah aspired, and he too was destroyed by it. (3) We must never contend. Remember, the Book of Mormon is quite clear that "that there should be no more contentions" among God's people (Mosiah 28:2). The Doctrine and Covenants informs us: "Satan doth stir up the hearts of the people to contention" (D&C 10:63). Korah and his cohorts were exceedingly contentious. (4) Finally, we must never coerce. That is the way Satan works. And this miracle is evidence that one cannot coerce God's prophet, and the coercion of God's people only adds their destruction to your own.[20] The miracle under discussion teaches us that those who are discontent with what God has called them to will surely experience spiritual death, and will likely take many down with them.

A second message in this miracle is the oft-repeated fact that, "Time vindicates the prophets." Moses and Aaron took a significant amount of criticism and suffered from some outright slander. And God allowed such to continue for a time. But, in the end, Moses and Aaron were still standing and their accusers had been destroyed. So it is with modern prophets. Joseph Smith and his successors have not always had it easy in the public eye. However, "God will, sooner or later, vindicate those of his servants who have been falsely accused."[21] Such is the promise of God![22]

In a proclamation from the Twelve Apostles to the world, dated April 6, 1845, the following bold interpretation of the miracle of Korah's destruction is given:

> Priests, bishops, and clergy, whether Catholic, Protestant, or Mahomedan, [upon Christ's return] will then have to yield their pretended claims to the priesthood, together with titles, honors, creeds and names; and reverence and obey the true and royal priesthood of the order of Melchisedech [*sic*], and of Aaron; restored to the rightful heirs, the nobility of Israel; or, the dearth and famine will consume them, and the plague sweep them quickly down to the pit, as in the case of Korah, Dathan and Abiram, Who pretended to the priesthood, and rebelled against God's chosen priests and prophets, in the days of Moses.[23]

The basic point of Brigham Young and the Twelve was that Korah, no matter how sincere he was, did not hold God's authority, and when told such by the prophet, he rejected God's message, so God rejected him. At Christ's return, the Twelve inform us, that there will be those in very similar situations. If they accept those whom God has authorized and ordained, they will be blessed. If they reject them, like Korah, Dathan, Abiram, and On did, they too will be held accountable. On a more general note, however, this caution of the Twelve may have application for all, including the Saints. One commentator noted: "Here, God gives us a concrete picture of what He thinks of rebellion against Him. For rebellion against His appointed, faithful leaders can also be rebellion against the Lord they serve. Have we been tempted to rebel against God by attacking His devoted followers, especially those leading in His name? Maybe we'd best watch the ground beneath us!"[24] We may not see ourselves as being like Korah (i.e., unauthorized, but seeking authority); however, when we reject, rebel against, or criticize God's appointed prophets, we may indeed be guilty of a similar sin.

The destruction of the masses by fire that came down from heaven seems an obvious type for the Second Coming of Christ, when the masses that constitute the wicked shall be destroyed by fire from heaven. Elder Bruce R. McConkie wrote: "Those who defied Moses and rebelled against his law were destroyed, like Korah and his band. . . . At our Lord's Second Coming all those who are in rebellion against Christ and his laws shall be cut off from among the people for they that come shall burn them up, leaving neither root nor branch."[25]

Significantly, in Numbers 16:26, God commanded Moses to tell faithful Israel: "Depart . . . from the tents of these wicked men, and touch nothing of theirs, lest ye be consumed in all their sins." If we wish to be among those who are preserved, both now and at the Second Coming, we must separate ourselves from those who love this wicked and fallen world. Saturating one's life with the sacred provides protection. But allowing significant doses of the world into our lives will certainly drag down the best of Christ's disciples.

Finally, there are curious parallels in the symbolism when one compares the sins and the means of killing the sinners. For example, one ancient source noted of the leaders of the rebellion: "They were swallowed up by the earth because they were steeped in earthly things, so that the nature of their punishment itself witnessed to their criminal deeds."[26] In other words, because their sin was loving the world and the honors of men, it was by the world that their lives were taken. Similarly, a modern commentator on the miracles said of the two hundred and fifty who were burned: "They were punished by the same element as that by which they had sinned."[27] In other words, they sinned by seeking to offer fire *before* the Lord when they were unauthorized. Now, by fire *from* the Lord, they were destroyed. As one text notes: "There were two sorts of traitors; the fire consumed the one, the earth swallowed up the other."[28] Perhaps there is a lesson in this for us.

NOTES

1.   Katharine Doob Sakenfeld, *Journeying with God: A Commentary on the Book of Numbers*, in *International Theological Commentary* (Grand Rapids, MI: Eerdmans, 1995), 98.

2.   "The expression 'to gouge out their eyes' (v.14) is a rhetorical exaggeration. The rebels charged Moses with blinding men to his true intentions. It is as though he were to gouge out their eyes so that they could not see the wicked things that he is alleged to have been doing to them." (Ronald B. Allen, "Numbers," in Frank E. Gaebelein, ed., *The Expositor's Bible Commentary* [Grand Rapids, MI: Zondervan, 1990], 2:838.) Another text states: "Gouging out the eyes was a known punishment imposed on runaway slaves, prisoners, and rebellious vassals." (Baruch A. Levine, *The Anchor Bible: Numbers 1–20* [New York: Doubleday, 1993], 414.) In other words, Moses would have perceived them as rebels, and, therefore, might have sought literally to blind them in one more attempt at controlling them.

3.   See Allen, "Numbers," in Gaebelein, *The Expositor's Bible Commentary*, 2:833.

4.   See Levine, *The Anchor Bible: Numbers 1–20*, 413. "Moses . . . points out that the Levites are greatly privileged. . . . They had the duty of doing *service in the tabernacle*, that is dismantling, carrying and erecting the tabernacle. . . . The Kohathites, of whom Korah was one, had the task of carrying the most sacred objects such as the ark [of the covenant] (4:1–20). They were next in rank to the priests." (Gordon J. Wenham, *Numbers*, in *Tyndale Old Testament Commentaries* [Downers Grove, IL: InterVarsity Press, 1981], 135; emphasis in original. See also Dennis T. Olson, *Interpretation: A Bible Commentary for Teaching and Preaching—Numbers* [Louisville, KY: Westminster John Knox Press, 1996], 102–3.)

5.   President J. Reuben Clark Jr. taught: "Israel, generally, did not have the Priesthood that Aaron had. Even the Levites, who had a secondary kind of officiating authority in taking care of the tabernacle, did not have the right to offer sacrifice, which belonged entirely to Aaron and his sons. (Num. 16.) . . . The Lord has always guarded his Priesthood with the utmost care, so that all during Israel's time, only a few held the Priesthood, and of that few only one family, seemingly, had the right to officiate. There evidently were individuals at various periods in Israel's history who held the Melchizedek Priesthood, but it was not generally possessed." (J. Reuben Clark Jr., in *Conference Report*, October 1956, 85–86.)

6. One commentator suggested: "Perhaps Korah's real desire was not only to demean Moses but to make himself [the high] priest instead of Aaron." (Allen, "Numbers," in Gaebelein, *The Expositor's Bible Commentary*, 2:835.) While the JST's "high priesthood" could possibly be taken this way, it seems unlikely that such is the meaning, since the term "high priesthood" is consistently used in scripture as a reference to the Melchizedek, not Aaronic, priesthood. (See, for example, Alma 4:20; 13:6–10; 14; 18; D&C 20:67; 78:1; 81:2; 84:29; 85:11; 107:9, 64–91.) Korah wanted to be the prophet, and this rebellion was his means of seeking that position, even though God had not called him, and his lack of authority and personal righteousness precluded him. Elder Orson Pratt taught that Korah and his comrades wanted to be "presidents." (See Orson Pratt, *Journal of Discourses* 3:297–98.) President J. Reuben Clark, Jr. argued that the controversy may have been that Korah, Dathan, Abiram, and On were not functioning as Levitical priests, but wanted to. He wrote: "When God sets up his Priesthood, and ordains and consecrates his priests, others not so commissioned may not pretend to priesthood powers. It was thus with Korah, Dathan, and Abiram, claiming equal authority with Aaron, and against these rebels God poured out speedy punishment for their sacrilege." (See J. Reuben Clark, Jr., *On the Way to Immortality and Eternal Life* [Salt Lake City, UT: Deseret Book, 1961], 138.) Korah was certainly the only decedent of Levi among the main four rebels, but, as one commentator noted, "He was not a member of the priestly family." (Allen, "Numbers," in Gaebelein, *The Expositor's Bible Commentary*, 2:837.) In other words, he may have been a Levite, but not of the lineage of Aaron. (See George A. Horton, Jr., "Insights into Exodus, Leviticus, Numbers, and Deuteronomy," in Monte S. Nyman and Robert L. Millet, eds., *The Joseph Smith Translation: The Restoration of Plain and Precious Things* [Provo, UT: BYU Religious Studies Center, 1985], 83.) But this still begs the question, how does this harmonize with the JST, which seems to clearly state that the Melchizedek Priesthood (or the highest office therein) was what Korah and his associates were after.

7. Allen, "Numbers," in Gaebelein, *The Expositor's Bible Commentary*, 2:833. While it is possible that the Reubenites wished to hold the common priesthood, that is clearly not what Korah wanted. And from the aforementioned quote and the miracle's narrative, it appears that leadership and its accompanying authority was really what Korah and his associates were seeking to usurp.

8. See Allen, "Numbers," in Gaebelein, *The Expositor's Bible Commentary*, 2:834. See also Levine, *The Anchor Bible: Numbers 1–20*, 411–12.

9. Sakenfeld, *Journeying with God: A Commentary on the Book of Numbers*, in *International Theological Commentary*, 98; Levine, *The Anchor Bible: Numbers 1–20*, 428.

10. One source indicates that, like Nephi, the Spirit of God urged Moses to kill the Egyptian, even though such was not Moses's will or intention. (See Louis

Ginzberg, *The Legends of the Jews* [Philadelphia: The Jewish Publication Society of America, 1967], 2:279.)

11. See Ginzberg, *The Legends of the Jews*, 2:279–80. See also Ginzberg, *The Legends of the Jews*, 3:239–40 & 5:405n75. According to the midrash, the reason the Egyptian taskmaster was beating Dathan was because the Egyptian had raped Dathan's wife, and Dathan had discovered this. Consequently, the taskmaster sought to take Dathan's life, but Moses intervened. (See Mark E. Petersen, *Moses: Man of Miracles* [Salt Lake City, UT: Deseret Book, 1977], 42, and Exodus Rabba i.33.)

12. Allen, "Numbers," in Gaebelein, *The Expositor's Bible Commentary*, 2:837.

13. One commentator wrote: "The dialogue between Moses and Korah is lively. Korah says *You have gone too far, . . . all . . . are holy. . . .* Moses proposes that all who claim such a holy status should demonstrate it by undertaking a priestly task, the offering of incense. Since two of Aaron's sons had died for offering fire which the Lord has not commanded (Lv. 10:1–2) Korah's alacrity in submitting to this test is striking." (Wenham, *Numbers*, in *Tyndale Old Testament Commentaries*, 135.)

14. Leland Ryken, James C. Wilhoit, and Tremper Longman III, eds., *Dictionary of Biblical Imagery* (Downers Grove, IL: InterVarsity Press, 1998), 419; Ada R. Habershon, *Study of the Types* (Grand Rapids, MI: Kregel Publications, 1974), 21; Kevin J. Conner, *Interpreting the Symbols and Types*, rev. ed. (Portland, OR: City Bible Publishing, 1992), 149; J. C. Cooper, *An Illustrated Encyclopaedia of Traditional Symbols* (London: Thames and Hudson, 1987), 87; Jack Tresidder, *Symbols and Their Meanings: The Illustrated Guide to More than 1,000 Symbols— Their Traditional and Contemporary Significance* (London: Duncan Baird Publishers, 2006), 38.

15. David Fontana, *The Secret Language of Symbolism: A Visual Key to Symbols and Their Meanings* (San Francisco, CA: Chronicle Books, 2000), 34; Kevin J. Todeschi, *The Encyclopedia of Symbols* (New York: Perigee Book, 1995), 289; Cassiodorus, "Exposition of the Psalms," 73:11, in Joseph T. Lienhard, ed., *Exodus, Leviticus, Numbers, Deuteronomy*, in *Ancient Christian Significance* (Grand Rapids, MI: Zondervan, 1961), 228; Wilson, *A Dictionary of Bible Types*, 128–29; Conner, *Interpreting the Symbols and Types*, 139.

16. Cooper, *An Illustrated Encyclopaedia of Traditional Symbols*, 152. Another source states, "Shoes are necessary only on the earth because of the filth of the ground. By removing them, we symbolically leave the world outside the Lord's sanctuary. Muslims and others remove their shoes when entering mosques and other holy places (in Islam, one may not pray with one's feet shod). The Japanese and some other peoples even remove their shoes upon entering a house." (John A. Tvedtness, "Priestly Clothing in Bible Times," in Donald W. Parry, ed., *Temples of the Ancient World: Ritual and Symbolism* [Salt Lake City, UT: Deseret Book, 1994], 671.)

17. See Wilson, *A Dictionary of Bible Types*, 158; Conner, *Interpreting the Symbols and Types*, (1992), 142; Ryken, Wilhoit, and Longman, *Dictionary of Biblical Imagery*, 288; Habershon, *Study of the Types*, 101; Ada R. Habershon, *The Study of the Miracles* (London: Morgan & Scott, 1911), 56.

18. Allen, "Numbers," in Gaebelein, *The Expositor's Bible Commentary*, 2:837.

19. Hugh Nibley, *Enoch the Prophet* (Salt Lake City, UT: Deseret Book, 1986), 4:274. See also 1:339.

20. Hugh Nibley, *Enoch the Prophet* (Salt Lake City, UT: Deseret Book, 1986), 4:274.

21. Richard C. Trench, *Miracles and Parables of the Old Testament* (Grand Rapids, MI: Baker Book House, 1959), 61.

22. Clark, *On the Way to Immortality and Eternal Life*, 139.

23. "Proclamation of the Twelve Apostles," April 6, 1845, in James R. Clark, comp., *Messages of the First Presidency* (Salt Lake City, UT: Bookcraft, 1965–1975), 1:259.

24. Pamela McQuade, *The Top 100 Miracles of the Bible: What They Are and What They Mean to You Today* (Uhrichsville, OH: Barbour Publishing, 2008), 56. Elsewhere we read: "Today those who rebel against the prophets—disobeying and openly defying their counsel and teachings—are not swallowed up in giant sinkholes or consumed by fire from heaven. Rather, they expose themselves to plagues and problems which, though not as visible, are more spiritually frightening and eternally deadly." (Brent L. Top, Larry E. Dahl, and Walter D. Bowen, *Follow the Living Prophets: Timely Reasons for Obeying Prophetic Counsel in the Last Days* [Salt Lake City, UT: Deseret Book, 1993], 179.)

25. Bruce R. McConkie, *The Promised Messiah: The First Coming of Christ* (Salt Lake City, UT: Deseret Book, 1978), 447–48n13.

26. Cassiodorus, "Exposition of the Psalms," 105:16–17, in Lienhard, *Exodus, Leviticus, Numbers, Deuteronomy*, in *Ancient Christian Significance*, 228.

27. Herbert Lockyer, *All the Miracles of the Bible: The Supernatural in Scripture—Its Scope and Significance* (Grand Rapids, MI: Zondervan, 1961), 75.

28. Trench, *Miracles and Parables of the Old Testament*, 63.

FIRE IS SENT DOWN *from* *the* LORD *to* DESTROY NADAB *and* ABIHU

LEVITICUS 10:1–2

THE MIRACLE

Aaron's sons had been ordained to the priesthood, and were commanded by God to serve alongside of their father in the tabernacle (see Exodus 28:40–43). As evidence of their onetime status and acceptance before the Lord, Nadab and Abihu (the two oldest sons of Aaron) had been blessed along with their father and their uncle, Moses, to see the face of God on Mount Sinai (see Exodus 24:9–11).

Unfortunately, knowingly, these two elder boys of the functioning chief priest decided to offer "strange fire" before the Lord—an act they had been commanded to not perform. God was displeased, and in response to their sin, He sent fire down from heaven, killing these two self-willed servants of the Lord.

BACKGROUND

What exactly is meant by "strange fire" is unknown.[1] There are multiple theories as to the exact sin of these two young men. Some hold that they entered the Holy of Holies when they were not authorized to do so, as that right was specifically reserved for their father, Aaron—who was the chief priest.[2] It has been suggested that they performed a rite or ritual that Aaron alone was authorized to perform.[3] One commentator believed that Nadab and Abihu had a right to offer incense, but they did it at a time other than during the "daily incense offering"—for which God rejected their offering.[4] Others have suggested that the two brothers might have used an incense other than what was authorized for that ordinance.[5] One text suggested that they may have not used the sacred censer associated with the Holy of Holies, but substituted, instead, one of their own.[6] Certainly they were casual in their obedience to the specifics of the rite, ignoring certain technical requirements, as though they weren't really important.[7] But the most common explanation as to the specific sin of Nadab and Abihu on this occasion is that they did not take the fire for the incense from the brazen altar in the court—where they should have gotten it—but, rather, obtained it elsewhere, or kindled it themselves.[8] In the end, we cannot say for certain what their sin was, and it matters little as it relates to the message of the miracle.

SYMBOLIC ELEMENTS

In scripture, fire can have a number of symbolic meanings. It is often associated with God's glory and the glory or brightness of the celestial kingdom and its inhabitants. It can be used as a symbol of the sanctifying power of the Holy Ghost, or any aspect of the Holy Ghost's mission. However, fire depicted as coming down from heaven to consume an item traditionally has one of two specific meanings;[9] it can represent acceptance (see Leviticus 9:24) or judgment (see Leviticus 10:2). So, for example, when Jesus returns, He will do so accompanied by fire from heaven. Those worthy of celestial glory will be embraced by the fire, but not harmed by it, suggesting that they have been accepted by God. Those who are unworthy will be consumed or destroyed by the fire, suggesting their judgment and rejection. It is clear that, in the miracle under examination, the fire that descended from heaven, taking the lives of Nadab and Abihu, symbolized their judgment. Elder Bruce R. McConkie put it this way: "The fire from heaven that devoured them was . . . a type and a shadow of the spiritual destruction awaiting all who pervert the right ways of the Lord with ordinances of their own. (Lev. 10:1–2.)"[10]

Incense is sometimes associated in scripture with our prayers ascending heavenward. However, it can also represent "true" or "everlasting worship" of God[11]—part of which is sincere, focused, and regular prayer. Because God's glory was frequently present with ancient Israel in the form of a cloud (see Exodus 13:21–22; Numbers 12:5; Deuteronomy 31:15), each time incense was burned in the tabernacle or temple it symbolically implied that God was present in that sacred edifice.[12] Thus, as a symbol of prayer, worship, and God's presence, incense always implied communion with the divine, which was the very thing Nadab and Abihu sought to have.

APPLICATION AND ALLEGORIZATION

Commentators on this miracle see a number of symbolic messages, all related to the idea that God, not man, is in charge of the rites, authorities, and ordinances of the gospel.

An obvious message of this story has to do with performing priesthood rites without authorization. Elder James E. Talmage (of the Twelve) and President Charles W. Penrose (of the First Presidency) both taught that performing a priesthood ordinance in the name of the Lord, when one has not been authorized by the Lord to do so, constitutes taking the name of God in vain.[13] Though Nadab and Abihu had the priesthood, they either did not have the keys or the authority to perform the ordinance that they did, or they determined they would alter that rite without God's permission. Either way, they were taking the name of God in vain because they acted or spoke in His name, but did not act the way He would have them act. This miracle cautions us to never forget that it is God who decides how things are to be done—not you or I. The prophet Isaiah lamented: "The earth also is defiled under the inhabitants thereof; because they have transgressed the laws, changed the ordinance, broken the everlasting covenant" (Isaiah 24:5). The actions of Nadab and Abihu exemplify what Isaiah was speaking of. In the third century, Cyprian of Carthage suggested that whenever someone replaces true doctrine with false doctrine, or acts with human authority rather than divine authority, they are following the examples of Nadab and Abihu.[14] Elsewhere, he noted: "The same penalty awaits those who bring strange water to a false baptism. The censure and vengeance of God overtakes heretics who do, against the church, what only the church is allowed [or authorized] to do."[15] We must leave the rites, rituals, and ordinances the way God that has revealed them. It is not for us to change, evolve, curtail, or alter what the Father has given. One typologist rhetorically asked: "Did they think to improve on God's plan? Or did they think that it did not matter what they did, as long as they were in earnest?"[16] It is not our place to try to improve what God has done, or what the Father has revealed. This miracle teaches us that, "If we worship God, we must worship Him in His way (John 4:24). . . . [Aaron's sons] performed their duty in an irregular manner. Worship is only acceptable to God when offered as He has directed (Exodus 30:9)."[17]

This brings up an additional point, that of the sincerity of the practitioner. Just because the man or woman performing the rite is sincere in what he or she is doing does not make the ordinance valid or authorized by God.

One commentator conjectured: "The two sons of Aaron . . . were earnest, they were zealous, they were apparently doing that which priests should do, but the fact that they used unlawful fire, strange fire, proved that their hearts were wrong. . . . God will not have as a substitute for His Word any of our schemes, plans and zealous efforts. When we substitute our judgment for God's judgment, we may expect only the wrath of God."[18] There are many sincere individuals in the world who, having taken authority unto or upon themselves, do things in the name of God that they have no authority to do. As this miracle teaches us, their sincerity does not authorize them.

Several authors have suggested that this miracle teaches us about the dangers of placing our trust in man—in ourselves—rather than in Christ. One text noted that, just as in Nadab and Abihu's day, a sinful man could not approach God carelessly and without a sacrifice to atone for his sins; so also, today we cannot approach God casually, or without the atoning blood of Christ who sacrificed Himself for us.[19] We need the Atonement in order to be accepted of God. To place ourselves, or our own works, above the Atonement is to ensure that we will receive what Nadab and Abihu did—eventual destruction. Our works cannot save us. Christ saves. But this miracle shows two men who seemed to think that they could be saved by performing a rite. They appear to have forgotten that the rite they were performing was only a symbol of their need to connect themselves to God—to have Him present in their lives through acts such as prayer. Said one theologian: "Strange incense is a figure of human activities and religious performances which are offered to God for His acceptance in competition with and instead of the life of the Lord Jesus. It is human merit substituted for Christ's merit."[20] We must keep commandments, and we must participate in the ordinances that the Lord has revealed to us in this last dispensation. But we must not forget that without Christ's Atonement our acts cannot save us. Thus, being connected to Him through personal righteousness is paramount. "Unfortunately men are feeble and frail, and no amount of oil outside will necessarily change the heart."[21] Ordinances without personal righteousness do not have the power to save—and the actions of Nadab and Abihu suggest that they did not have personal righteousness.

One last symbol has been highlighted as underlying this miracle. This miracle shows that priests and leaders are "beset by the same infirmities [that overtake] the laity."[22] There is nothing magic about being called as a bishop or Relief Society president that will now make one totally aloof from sin. On the contrary, it may be that those who are called to such positions are attacked by the adversary that much more, simply because of the calling in which they are serving. While the miracle associated with Nadab and Abihu sends a message that those who sin will be punished, we may also be able to draw a homily from the miracle about the human side of leaders. The Prophet Joseph once remarked: "I told them I was but a man, and they must not expect me to be perfect; if they expected perfection from me, I should expect it from them; but if they would bear with my infirmities and the infirmities of the brethren. I would likewise bear with their infirmities."[23] We should expect that those who are called to positions of leadership should be clean and worthy, and should strive to remain as such. We should believe that God inspires them beyond their native or natural abilities, and does so because He loves His children that they lead. But the miracle also suggests that we should be cautious about holding leaders to an unrealistic standard. One need only survey scripture to realize that most of the priesthood leaders depicted therein had a human side and made mistakes. We would do well to remember that, and to seek less to hold them to an unrealistic standard of perfection.

NOTES

1.   See Dennis T. Olson, *Interpretation: A Bible Commentary for Teaching and Preaching—Numbers* (Louisville, KY: Westminster John Knox Press, 1996), 26; Baruch A. Levine, *The Anchor Bible: Numbers 1–20*, vol. 4 (New York: Doubleday, 1993), 155; Ada R. Habershon, *Study of the Types* (Grand Rapids, MI: Kregel Publications, 1974), 158.

2.   "In Leviticus 8 Aaron, the high priest, is instructed to don distinctive vestments not worn by his sons. . . . The high priest is distinguished from other priests by virtue of his unique unction [or anointing]. . . . The Yom Kippur ritual of Leviticus 16 ordains a distinct role for Aaron, the chief priest, who alone enters the Holy of Holies to seek expiation for the community, and whose efforts in this regard are indispensable." (Levine, *The Anchor Bible: Numbers 1–20*, 155. See also R. Laird Harris, "Leviticus," in Frank E. Gaebelein, ed., *The Expositor's Bible Commentary* [Grand Rapids, MI: Zondervan, 1990], 2:566 & 589.)

3.   Herbert Lockyer, *All the Miracles of the Bible: The Supernatural in Scripture—Its Scope and Significance* (Grand Rapids, MI: Zondervan, 1961), 72. President J. Reuben Clark, Jr., said: "Nadab and Abihu . . . lacked the authority to make the offering they made." (J. Reuben Clark Jr., *On the Way to Immortality and Eternal Life* [Salt Lake City, UT: Deseret Book, 1961], 172.)

4.   See Levine, *The Anchor Bible: Numbers 1–20*, 155–56.

5.   See Habershon, *Study of the Types*, 158; Lockyer, *All the Miracles of the Bible*, 72.

6. See Lockyer, *All the Miracles of the Bible*, 72.

7. See Gordon J. Wenham, *Numbers*, in *Tyndale Old Testament Commentaries* (Downers Grove, IL: InterVarsity Press, 1981), 69.

8. "Since making a fire was rather a chore in former times, all fire was preserved carefully, and coals were carried about to start other fires. The fire on the incense altar, however, was not perpetual. It could hardly be, without constant attention, for the altar was only a foot and a half square in a confined place. The censers or firepans of Nadab and Abihu should have been lit from the great brazen altar in the court. The men carelessly took coals from a convenient hearth, laid incense on the coals, and went into the tabernacle heedlessly." (Harris, "Leviticus," in Gaebelein, *The Expositor's Bible Commentary*, 2:566. See also Olson, *Interpretation: A Bible Commentary for Teaching and Preaching—Numbers*, 26; Habershon, *Study of the Types*, 158; Lockyer, *All the Miracles of the Bible*, 72; Walter L. Wilson, *A Dictionary of Bible Types* [Peabody, MA: Hendrickson, 1999], 158.)

9. See Ada R. Habershon, *The Study of the Miracles* (London: Morgan & Scott, 1911), 55; Lockyer, *All the Miracles of the Bible*, 72; Leland Ryken, James C. Wilhoit, and Tremper Longman III, eds., *Dictionary of Biblical Imagery* (Downers Grove, IL: InterVarsity Press, 1998), 286–89; Kevin J. Conner, *Interpreting the Symbols and Types*, rev. ed. (Portland, OR: City Bible Publishing, 1992), 142; Wilson, *A Dictionary of Bible Types*, 157–64.

10. Bruce R. McConkie, *The Millennial Messiah: The Second Coming of the Son of Man* (Salt Lake City, UT: Deseret Book, 1982), 80. See also Bede the Venerable, "On the Tabernacle," 3:2 in Joseph T. Lienhard, ed., *Exodus, Leviticus, Numbers, Deuteronomy*, in *Ancient Christian Significance* (Grand Rapids, MI: Zondervan, 1961), 175, who said that the fire was a symbol of their "eternal damnation."

11. See Ryken, Wilhoit, and Longman, *Dictionary of Biblical Imagery*, 419.

12. See ibid.; Conner, *Interpreting the Symbols and Types*, 149.

13. See James E. Talmage, in *Conference Report*, October 1931, 51; Charles W. Penrose, discourse given November 4, 1882, in *Journal of Discourses*, 25:339; Charles W. Penrose, discourse given May 20, 1883, in *Journal of Discourses*, 25:45–46; Charles W. Penrose, discourse given July 26, 1884, in *Journal of Discourses*, 25:224 (25:223–25).

14. See Cyprian of Carthage, "The Unity of the Catholic Church," 18–19, in Lienhard, *Exodus, Leviticus, Numbers, Deuteronomy*, in *Ancient Christian Significance*, 174–75.

15. Cyprian of Carthage, "The Baptismal Controversy," 8, in Lienhard, *Exodus, Leviticus, Numbers, Deuteronomy*, in *Ancient Christian Significance*, 175.

16. Habershon, *Study of the Types*, 158.

17. Lockyer, *All the Miracles of the Bible*, 72.

18. Wilson, *A Dictionary of Bible Types*, 158.

19. See Harris, "Leviticus," in Gaebelein, *The Expositor's Bible Commentary*, 2:589.

20. Wilson, *A Dictionary of Bible Types*, 235–36.

21. Harris, "Leviticus," in Gaebelein, *The Expositor's Bible Commentary*, 2:566.

22. Lockyer, *All the Miracles of the Bible*, 72.

23. Joseph Smith, *Teachings of the Prophet Joseph Smith*, Joseph Fielding Smith, comp. (Salt Lake City, UT: Deseret Book, 1976), 268.

Aaron's Staff Buds

The Miracle

Questions about the right for Moses and Aaron to preside in their specific callings—Moses over the high priesthood and Aaron over the lesser priesthood—had been at the heart of the controversy that provoked the destruction of Korah, Dathan, Abiram, and On (see Numbers 16).

Now the Lord, seeking to clarify whom He has chosen to officiate in His temple, tells Moses to have each tribe of Israel bring forth the staff of one of the leaders of their tribe. Each staff should have the name of the man to whom it belongs written on it.

The labeled staffs were placed in front of the ark of the covenant overnight, with the promise that the staff of the tribe God had chosen to preside in the tabernacle would sprout or bud, thereby removing any doubt or justification for grumbling about which tribe was authorized in God's eyes.

In the morning when Moses retrieved the staffs, Aaron's staff had not only sprouted and budded, but had actually blossomed and produced almonds.[1] After the people were shown this miraculous occurrence, the staff of Aaron was taken back and placed with the ark of the covenant "to be kept as a sign to the rebellious" (NIV Numbers 17:10).

Background

The connection between this miracle and that in Numbers 16 is quite obvious. The Lord is vindicating His earlier act of destroying those who sought to usurp the offices of Aaron and Moses by showing, in a miraculous way, that His favor has fallen upon Aaron and his descendants rather than upon any of the other tribes of Israel.[2]

This miracle not only establishes Aaron's calling, but also serves to establish Moses's. The very first verse of this chapter and this miracle reads: "And the Lord spake unto Moses, saying" (Numbers 17:1). This same phrase, or its equivalent, comes up over 150 times in the book of Numbers alone. It is clear that the Lord is trying to establish for the reader that God speaks through Moses; and, therefore, Moses is called, authorized, and accepted of God.[3]

SYMBOLIC ELEMENTS

In this miracle, the staff or rod of Aaron was a symbol of strength, authority, and priesthood power.[4] By each tribe bringing forth a staff or rod, a test was being enacted to determine which tribe had been actually called of God to exercise His authority, or priesthood power, upon the earth—particularly in the tabernacle or temple of the Lord.

The number twelve is often a symbol for priesthood, including its power and right to govern.[5] Examples of this in scripture and in the temple are legion. Thus, the idea that twelve rods were brought forth is not coincidental. It highlights the fact that this miracle would determine who God had chosen to bear His holy priesthood.[6]

The ark of the covenant was a symbol of God's presence.[7] Of this miracle, one commentator noted: "The staffs would have been placed as near the ark as practical. The symbolism is that these staffs were right, as it were, in the 'lap' of God."[8]

Buds and blossoms symbolize renewal, rebirth, or life. We see them each spring as the earth resurrects from the long, hard winter wherein all things seem to die. The appearance of buds and blossoms on Aaron's dead staff symbolized the truth that, "The dead stick has come to life as a sign of God's special choosing of Aaron."[9] As to the almonds, one commentator conjectured:

> Why it bore almonds is not stated, but it is probably significant. Almond blooms early with white blossom and its fruits were highly prized (Gen. 43:11). White in Scripture symbolizes purity, holiness and God himself (*e.g.* Is. 1:18; Dn. 7:9; Rev. 20:11). Jeremiah associates the almond (*šāqēd*) with watching *šāqad*) (Je. 1:11–12). All these qualities were personified by Aaron and the tribe of Levi. They were the holy tribe par excellence, who represented Israel before God and God to Israel, and they were responsible for watching over the people by instructing them in the statues of the Lord (Lv. 10:11).[10]

Thus, the fruits of the staff remind us of the fruits of Aaron's labors in the tabernacle (on behalf of God's people). The type of fruit (i.e., almonds) represent the nature of Aaron's calling.

APPLICATION AND ALLEGORIZATION

It seems clear that a couple of symbolic messages are present in this miracle of Aaron's budding rod. The most obvious of those has to do with priesthood authorization. This miracle clearly teaches that it is God who chooses who holds His priesthood, and who is called to serve Him, not man. Aaron did not choose to be the head of the Levitical Priesthood, and the one in charge of the tabernacle. God appointed him to that calling, as this miracle shows. Hence, the book of Hebrews warns us: "No man taketh this honour unto himself, but he that is called of God, as was Aaron" (Hebrews 5:4). Aaron did not choose, and you and I have no authority to make such choices for ourselves. God calls the prophets and apostles; He calls the stake presidents and bishops. Our choice is to accept or deny a calling, but it is God who must always extend that calling; though some, like Aaron's cousin, Korah, seem to miss that.[11]

A less obvious, but perhaps more important type, has to do with Christ.[12] The blooming of the staff was for the purpose of designating which tribe would have the authority to officiate in the office of priest, serving the Lord in His tabernacle.[13] By establishing this in a miraculous way, there was to be no doubt in the minds of the people whom God had chosen, and who really had the power to save them by officiating on their behalf in the holy temple. In this miracle, we are told of twelve dead sticks, all of which were put forth before the Lord in His tabernacle.[14] Although there were twelve tribes that God was choosing from, the presence of the number twelve in this passage may well have a dual meaning, for, as noted above,[15] in antiquity, the number twelve was commonly associated with priesthood.[16] Its placement here may indicate, not simply that the Lord would extend a call to one of the twelve tribes, but more particularly that the call would be to officiate in the ordinances of the priesthood. Out of these twelve dead pieces of wood left in the temple, one of them came back to life and brought forth fruit.[17] Typologically speaking there is great significance in this. One commentator wrote:

> In Numbers 17 we have a beautiful type of the resurrection of the Lord Jesus Christ, in *the budding of Aaron's rod*. The twelve rods were laid up before the Lord. All were equally dead, and there was no sign of life in them; but when the morning came a wondrous miracle had taken place—one rod, that on which was inscribed the name of Aaron, had

become full of life: buds and blossom and fruit had all appeared. No eye saw the change take place; but when Moses came in the morning there was abundant evidence of life, reminding us of that morning when the women came to the sepulchre at the rising of the sun, and found that He whom they sought was not dead but was risen.[18]

After the rod came back to life, Moses brought it before the tribes of Israel and it was shown to the people. Having examined the budded rod, they then stood as witnesses of the miracle.

> And so we read in Acts that our risen Lord "showed Himself alive after His passion, by many infallible proofs." "Him God raised up the third day, and showed Him openly—not to all the people, but unto witnesses chosen before God." . . . Aaron's rod was caused to bud, to prove that he was God's chosen one; and Jesus Christ our Lord was "declared to be the son of God . . . by the resurrection from the dead" (Romans 1:4). There could be no doubt that He was accepted by God, since He raised Him from the dead. After the rod had been shown to the people, it was laid up in the presence of the Lord; and so when God had raised Christ from the dead, "He was seen many days of them which came up with Him from Galilee to Jerusalem," and then "sat down on the right hand of the majesty on high."[19]

The one sure sign that separates Jesus from all of the great moralists and thinkers of His day, or any other time in the history of the world, is that sacred event attested to by so many—His Resurrection from the dead. While all others who have claimed divinity are dead, He lives![20] Thus, as Paul states, it is "by the resurrection from the dead" that Jesus is "declared to be the Son of God" (Romans 1:4).

Related to the interpretations of this miracle as a message of authority, and as a symbol for Christ's Resurrection, is the symbolic reading of mankind as the dead sticks. Many commentators see fallen man as the rods or sticks that have lost their life. Said one author: "This [miracle] is an emblem of . . . the fact that He could take any old dead 'stick,' bring it into His presence, and change that person into a beautiful and fruitful Christian."[21] Elsewhere we read that, "God can bring life out of death and to cause that which is helpless to become prosperous."[22] We are all "dead by nature." But if we place ourselves before Him, just as Moses placed the rods before the ark, Christ can cause us to bud, blossom, and bring forth fruits.[23] The power of Christ to change us—to bring us back from the dead, not only physically, but also spiritually—can be seen in this miracle. And just as Aaron, a type for Christ, was the only one that God had authorized to do His saving work, so also is Jesus the only one we can trust or rely upon to revive, redeem, and resurrect us!

NOTES

1. "The staff of the tribe of Levi had to have Aaron's name written clearly on it. . . . The name of Aaron on the staff of Levi would limit the choice to him and his descendants; this was necessary to ward off attacks on his leadership similar to that of Korah by others of the Tribe of Levi but not of the family of Aaron." (Ronald B. Allen, "Numbers," in Frank E. Gaebelein, ed., *The Expositor's Bible Commentary* [Grand Rapids, MI: Zondervan, 1990], 2:846–47.)

2. See Allen, "Numbers," in Gaebelein, *The Expositor's Bible Commentary*, 2:845; Dennis T. Olson, *Interpretation: A Bible Commentary for Teaching and Preaching—Numbers* (Louisville, KY: Westminster John Knox Press, 1996), 110.

3. See Allen, "Numbers," in Gaebelein, *The Expositor's Bible Commentary*, 2:846.

4. Herbert Lockyer, *All the Miracles of the Bible: The Supernatural in Scripture—Its Scope and Significance* (Grand Rapids, MI: Zondervan, 1961), 76; Richard C. Trench, *Miracles and Parables of the Old Testament* (Grand Rapids, MI: Baker Book House, 1959), 64; Joseph Fielding McConkie, "Jesus Christ: Symbolism, and Salvation," in Robert L. Millet, ed., *Studies in Scripture: Acts to Revelation*, vol. 6 (Salt Lake City, UT: Deseret Book, 1987), 203; Kevin J. Conner, *Interpreting the Symbols and Types*, rev. ed. (Portland, OR: City Bible Publishing, 1992), 164 & 170; Leland Ryken, James C. Wilhoit, and Tremper Longman III, eds., *Dictionary of Biblical Imagery* (Downers Grove, IL: InterVarsity Press, 1998), 733–34; J. C. Cooper, *An Illustrated Encyclopaedia of Traditional Symbols* (London: Thames and Hudson, 1987), 140; Jack Tresidder, *Symbols and Their Meanings: The Illustrated Guide to More than 1,000 Symbols—Their Traditional and Contemporary Significance* (London: Duncan Baird Publishers, 2006), 139.

5. Richard D. Draper, *Opening the Seven Seals: The Visions of John the Revelator* (Salt Lake City, UT: Deseret Book, 1991), 24, 46, 56, 83; Jay A. Parry and Donald W. Parry, *Understanding the Book of Revelation* (Salt Lake City, UT: Deseret Book, 1998), 295; E. W. Bullinger, *Number in Scripture: Its Supernatural Design and Spiritual Significance* (Grand Rapids, MI: Kregel Publications, 1967), 2–3 & 107; Mick Smith, *The Book of Revelation: Plain, Pure, and Simple* (Salt Lake City, UT: Deseret Book, 1998), 288–89; Robert D. Johnston, *Numbers in the Bible: God's Design in Biblical Numerology* (Grand Rapids, MI: Kregel Publications, 1999), 39 & 83; John J. Davis, *Biblical Numerology: A Basic Study of the Use of Numbers in the Bible* (Grand Rapids, MI: Baker Book House, 1968), 122.

6. While the Hebrew is unclear, some think there may have been thirteen rods rather than twelve; one for Aaron, two for Joseph (i.e., Ephraim and Manasseh), and then one for each of the remaining tribes. (See Gordon J. Wenham, *Numbers*, in *Tyndale Old Testament Commentaries* [Downers Grove, IL: InterVarsity Press,

1981], 140; Baruch A. Levine, *The Anchor Bible: Numbers 1–20*, vol. 4 [New York: Doubleday, 1993], 421–22.) However, the typology of the passage strongly suggests only twelve.

7. Ada R. Habershon, *The Study of the Miracles* (London: Morgan & Scott, 1911), 151; Walter L. Wilson, *A Dictionary of Bible Types* (Peabody, MA: Hendrickson, 1999), 18; Kevin J. Conner, *Interpreting the Symbols and Types*, rev. ed. (Portland, OR: City Bible Publishing, 1992), 127; Leland Ryken, James C. Wilhoit, and Tremper Longman III, eds., *Dictionary of Biblical Imagery* (Downers Grove, IL: InterVarsity Press, 1998), 43; Kenneth E. Trent, *Types of Christ in the Old Testament: A Conservative Approach to Old Testament Typology* (Bloomington, IN: CrossBooks, 2010), 92–95.

8. Allen, "Numbers," in Gaebelein, *The Expositor's Bible Commentary*, 2:847.

9. Olson, *Interpretation: A Bible Commentary for Teaching and Preaching—Numbers*, 111.

10. Wenham, *Numbers*, in *Tyndale Old Testament Commentaries*, 140.

11. See Trench, *Miracles and Parables of the Old Testament*, 64–65.

12. The Christocentric reading of this miracle is the most common, and perhaps the most powerful reading of it. Note a few examples. One text states: "The story of Aaron's budding staff . . . [is] a type of the resurrected Christ who blossomed to life after being dead on the cross." (Olson, *Interpretation: A Bible Commentary for Teaching and Preaching—Numbers*, 112. See also Patrick Fairbairn, *The Typology of Scripture*, 2nd ed. [Philadelphia, PA: Smith & English, 1989], 2:331–32; Trench, *Miracles and Parables of the Old Testament*, 66.) Another source says: "Just as Aaron's rod sprouted among the Jewish people, so the cross of Christ flowered among the Gentiles." (Caesarius of Arles, "Sermon," 111:1–2, in Joseph T. Lienhard, ed., *Exodus, Leviticus, Numbers, Deuteronomy*, in *Ancient Christian Significance* [Grand Rapids, MI: Zondervan, 1961], 234.) Elsewhere we read: "The budding of Aaron's rod is a type of Christ in resurrection." (Lockyer, *All the Miracles of the Bible*, 76.) Finally, this: "Aaron's flowering staff was . . . joined [by the early Christians] with the image of the budding stump of Jesse, father of King David. Thus, Aaron's rod was a witness to the coming of God's Messiah in Isa. 11:1–2: 'A shoot shall come out of the stump of Jesse, and a branch shall grow out of his roots.'" (Olson, *Interpretation: A Bible Commentary for Teaching and Preaching—Numbers*, 112.)

13. Levine, *The Anchor Bible: Numbers 1–20*, 421; Ramban Nachmanides, *Commentary on the Torah*, vol. 1 (New York: Shilo Publishing House, 1971), 4:190; Katharine Doob Sakenfeld, *Journeying with God: A Commentary on the Book of Numbers*, in *International Theological Commentary* (Grand Rapids, MI: Eerdmans, 1995), 104.

14. "A sprout may arise from a living branch and even from the trunk of a tree that has been felled (see Isa 6:13). But it is clearly not possible for a wooden staff that is long dead to sprout again as though it were still part of a growing tree. . . . It is not normal . . . for a dead pole to sprout, flower, and produce its fruit—and all in the

process of a night. . . . This miracle is stunning!" (Allen, "Numbers," in Gaebelein, *The Expositor's Bible Commentary*, 2:847–48.)

15. See discussion of the number twelve in chapter six of this work.

16. Draper, *Opening the Seven Seals*, 46, 56, 83; Smith, *The Book of Revelation: Plain, Pure, and Simple*, 48, 267, 288.

17. Since the tribe of Levi is traditionally not counted as part of the twelve tribes, some commentators assume that there must have been thirteen, rather than twelve rods. (See, for example, Levine, *The Anchor Bible: Numbers 1–20*, 422.) However, this seems like an insufficient cause to call into question the text, which clearly states that there were twelve rods placed in the temple. It must be assumed that Ephraim and Manasseh were grouped under the tribe of Joseph in this particular episode.

18. Ada R. Habershon, *Study of the Types* (Grand Rapids, MI: Kregel Publications, 1974), 47–48; See also, "Constitution of the Holy Apostles" bk. 5, sec. 1, in Alexander Roberts and James Donaldson, eds., *Ante-Nicene Fathers* (Peabody, MA: Hendrickson Publishers, 1994), 7:442.

19. Habershon, *Study of the Types*, 47–48; See also Joseph Fielding McConkie, *Gospel Symbolism* (Salt Lake City, UT: Deseret Book, 1985), 46, 59n1, & 73; McConkie and Parry, *Understanding the Book of Revelation*, 94. Not only did the rod typify Christ's Resurrection, but Aaron himself—when serving in the tabernacle—functioned as a type for Christ. (Habershon, *Study of the Types*, 25 & 124; McConkie, *Gospel Symbolism*, 250; Trent, *Types of Christ in the Old Testament*, 57–58.)

20. See Lockyer, *All the Miracles of the Bible*, 76.

21. Wilson, *A Dictionary of Bible Types*, 349–50.

22. Ibid., 68.

23. See Trench, *Miracles and Parables of the Old Testament*, 66. Charles Spurgeon drew a similar analogy: "Suppose this morning you feel so dry and dead and barren, that you cannot serve God as you would, nor even pray for more grace, as you wish to do. Then you are something like these twelve rods. They are very dead and dry . . . Aaron's rod . . . is quite as dead and dry as any of the rest. . . . We see them next morning. Eleven are dry rods still; but see this rod of Aaron! What has happened? It was dry as death. See, it has budded! This is wonderful! But look, it has blossomed! There are almond flowers upon it. . . . This is marvelous! But look again, it has brought forth almonds! Here, you have them! . . . The heavenly power has come upon the dry stick, and it has budded and blossomed, and even brought forth almonds. Fruit-bearing is the proof of life and favour. Lord, take these poor sticks this morning, and make them bud. Lord, here we are, in a bundle, perform that ancient miracle in a thousand of us. Make us bud and blossom, and bear fruit! Come with divine power, and turn this congregation from a fagot into a grove. . . . Come Holy Spirit, produce fruit in us this day, through faith in Jesus Christ our Lord!" (Charles H. Spurgeon, "The Withered Fig Tree," sermon delivered September 29, 1889, accessed August 2, 2017, www.romans45.org /spurgeon/sermons/2107.htm.)

THE BRAZEN SERPENT *Is* LIFTED UP *by* MOSES

NUMBERS 21:4–9

THE MIRACLE

Because the Edomites would not allow the Israelites to pass through their land, the Israelites were traveling around Edom when this miracle took place. But, as usual, the Israelites became impatient (this time because of the inconvenience of having to backtrack), and so they began to murmur against God and Moses, saying, "Have you brought us here to die, without bread or water? We detest this monotonous manna!" (see Numbers 21:4–5).

As a consequence of their attitude, the Lord sent poisonous snakes that bit the Israelites, and many died. This provoked fear in and apologies from the Israelites, who begged Moses to have God take the snakes away. So Moses prayed to God on their behalf.

The Lord commanded Moses to make a snake out of brass, and place it atop a pole, and those who have been bitten but look upon the snake in faith will be healed. So Moses did as the Lord commanded.

BACKGROUND

While the Numbers account of this miracle tells us what Israel had to do to be saved from the poison of the snakes—namely, look with faith upon the brass serpent—what it does not tell us is whether the Israelites complied with Moses's instructions. In the book of Alma we are given a bit of additional information regarding this miracle—facts that are not recorded in the Pentateuch.

Behold, [Christ] was spoken of by Moses; yea, and behold a type was raised up in the wilderness, that whosoever would look upon it might live. And many did look and live.

But few understood the meaning of those things, and this because of the hardness of their hearts. But there were many who were so hardened that they would not look, therefore they perished. Now the reason they would not look is because they did not believe that it would heal them. (Alma 33:19–20)

Nephi confirms the words of Alma in his commentary on the miracle, and then adds an additional insight that neither Moses or Alma recorded. He tells us: "And the Lord . . . sent fiery flying serpents among them; and after they were bitten he prepared a way that they might be healed; and the labor which they had to perform was to look; and because of the simpleness of the way, or the easiness of it, there were many who perished" (1 Nephi 17:41). Thus, from the book of Numbers we learn what the Israelites needed to do in order to be saved, but from the books of Alma and from 1 Nephi we learn that many did not have the faith sufficient to obey the prophet's simple instructions, and, consequently, died. Nephi tells us that the Israelites thought that the way to be saved was "too simple."

Nephi also speaks of the serpents not just as "fiery serpents" (meaning snakes whose venom makes one's body burn[1]), but as "fiery *flying* serpents" (meaning snakes that could lunge quite a distance in order to strike their victims). This certainly implies that there would be no escaping their bites. Everyone was in danger.

An obvious incongruity appears in the miracle. One commentator noted: "The description of the plague seems to be of something that was spreading quickly; yet Moses had to take the time to fashion, or direct the fashioning of, a metal image of one of the poisonous snakes."[2] How long it would take to make such a statue or image one can only guess. But one would think hours, not minutes. Anyone bitten would surely die before such an image could be crafted. Jewish midrash offers a plausible explanation as to how Moses could come by a brass snake so quickly. It suggests that, just as Moses turned his staff into a serpent in Pharaoh's court, he likely turned it into a brass snake during this miracle.[3] Thus, the need could be almost instantaneously met.

The brass serpent did not disappear once this miracle was accomplished via it. Indeed, it was retained by Israel for some five hundred years, and eventually became an object of worship for them. When King Hezekiah saw that the Israelites were burning incense to it he broke it into pieces so as to end their idolatrous behavior (see 2 Kings 18:4).[4]

SYMBOLIC ELEMENTS

As noted previously, manna was a symbol of Christ.[5] As one text states: "The Lord Jesus speaks of the manna as a type of himself. . . (John 6:32–35, 48–51, 58). A rejection of the heavenly manna is tantamount to one spurning the grace of God in the Savior."[6] Thus, for the Israelites to say to Moses and to God, "We're sick of manna!" (see Numbers 21:4–5), was equivalent of saying, "We're sick of Christ, who, like this manna, sustains us from day to day, but not in the way we want Him to!"

As we noted in our discussion of Moses's rod (Exodus 4:1–9), the snake is a curious symbol. In contemporary Christian thinking, it is often associated with Satan and temptation. However, originally it symbolized healing, resurrection, and immortality.[7] Anciently, it was a symbol of Christ long before it was a representation of Satan![8] Thus, when the devil appeared to Adam and Eve in Eden in the form of, or through the use of, a serpent, he was actually seeking to appear as an "angel of light" (2 Nephi 9:9). In other words, he had chosen that symbol because he knew that the snake represented the Messiah, and that was what he wished to be viewed as.[9] Curiously, the Hebrew word for Messiah (*mashiyakh*) totals 358 in gematria.[10] Not coincidentally, the Hebrew word for serpent (*nakhash*) has the same numerical value: 358.[11] Thus, by the gematria employed in Numbers 21, it is confirmed that the serpent lifted up by Moses upon his staff was indeed a type for the Savior, Jesus Christ. Satan had attacked Israel by getting them to worship false gods, such as the cravings of the flesh. Now, the true Messiah appears, retaking His serpent symbol, and offers them healing—something only He had the power to give.

On a related note, the snake bites spoken of in this miracle were believed by the early Christian church to represent "evil actions, idolatries, and other sins."[12] One Church Father wrote:

The wounds caused by the fiery serpent [symbolize] the poisonous enticement of the vices, which afflict the soul and bring about its spiritual death. . . . The sins which drag down soul and body to destruction . . . are appropriately represented by the serpents, not only because they were fiery and poisonous and artful at bringing about death but also because our first parents were led into sin by a serpent.[13]

Just as every one of the Israelites was in danger,[14] so also are all of us bitten by sin (Romans 3:19, 23). Thus, we all need Christ and His healing power, as found in His Atonement.

Brass or copper are typically symbols of judgment.[15] Thus, when Moses raised the brazen serpent upon the pole in an attempt to destroy the effects of the fiery flying serpents, the employment of brass deepened the Christocentric typology because Christ will be the judge of all mankind (see John 5:22).[16] Similarly, in Daniel 10:6 and Revelation 1:15 (see also Revelation 2:18) Christ is described as having feet of brass. In both cases, it appears that the message is that beyond the image of strength, stability, and permanence, Christ's life was such that He could serve as the perfect judge because He lived the perfect life.[17]

APPLICATION AND ALLEGORIZATION

While there are a number of symbols present in this miracle, the most important is its representation of Christ's Atonement as necessary for the salvation of all of God's creations. Said one commentator: "In the cross is our only hope, since none of us have failed to bellyache when we have not liked the direction in which God has sent us. . . . None of us fails to be affected by moral and spiritual failure, so all of us need to look to the cross for our salvation. It will not stop sin from biting us, but it will bring us to the gracious Father, through the sacrifice of His only Son."[18] In Helaman 8:14–15 we find the following application of this miracle:

> Yea, did [Moses] not bear record that the Son of God should come? And as he lifted up the brazen serpent in the wilderness, even so shall he be lifted up who should come.
>
> And as many as should look upon that serpent should live, even so as many as should look upon the Son of God with faith, having a contrite spirit, might live, even unto that life which is eternal. (See also John 3:14–15)

Spurgeon wisely noted: "The healthiest way of living where serpents swarm is never to take your eye off the brazen serpent at all."[19] If we keep our eye on Christ, Satan will have no access to us.[20]

This miracle tells us what Israel needed to do to be saved; namely, "look to God and live" (Alma 37:47). But it also tells us a bit about what Christ needed to do to save us; namely, give His life. "The fashioning of the brazen serpent alone was not enough! It had to be lifted up! The coming of Jesus into the world alone was not enough. His deeds must have been lifted up!"[21]

Christ lived the perfect life, but He also needed to die the perfect death. This miracle highlights that fact, as well as the power resident in Christ's death to heal and to save!

One commentator has suggested that there is a message about proper repentance in this miracle. She wrote:

> It would have been no use for the bitten Israelites to bathe their wounds, or to put ointments or plasters on them, or to bandage them up; but there are many who try to get rid of their sins in this way. They bathe their wounds with tears of repentance; they put on the ointment of good words, or plasters of good resolutions, and bandage themselves with doing their best; but the bites of sin get no better with this sort of treatment; a look at the Crucified One is what they need.[22]

Though we must certainly do our part in the process of repentance, we must be cautious about relying more on our own merits than we do on Christ's. Indeed, those who refused to look with faith upon the brazen serpent were symbolic representations of those who are willing to work, but who are not willing to trust! We must do all that we can; but, in the end, we must also remember that it is Christ's Atonement, and not our feeble works, that save us from Satan, sin, and death. The Israelites, before they received God's intervention, had to repent first. Once they acknowledged their guilt, God could intervene (Numbers 21:7). "There can be no forgiveness of sin apart from personal repentance (Luke 13:33 and Acts 17:30)."[23] We must do our part, and then God can save us!

Finally, Elder A. Theodore Tuttle of the Seventy, offered this modern-day application of Moses's miracle of the fiery flying serpents.

> . . . When they came among the flying serpents, Moses fashioned a brazen serpent, raised it, and all they had to do was look at that serpent, and they would be healed. The account says that many perished because they wouldn't even look (see 1 Ne. 17:32, 41; see also Num. 21:8–9). He was trying to do what you and I as parents need to do with our families today—to develop faith in the Lord. And the way to do it is to recount the examples of faith that have happened in our history and in our heritage and with our people. That's the value of history. It contains accounts of faith of our own blood and ancestry and of our own people and our children. . . . We cannot go one generation without losing faith if we do not do this. And to rear a generation of faith for what we must do in these days, you and I simply must develop and increase faith in the Lord Jesus Christ.[24]

NOTES

1. The Hebrew can quite literally be translated into "the snakes that produce burning." (See Ronald B. Allen, "Numbers," in Frank E. Gaebelein, ed., *The Expositor's Bible Commentary* [Grand Rapids, MI: Zondervan, 1990], 2:876.) "The 'fiery serpents' spoken of in Numbers 21:6 is translated from the Hebrew *'seraphim,'* [which comes] from the Hebrew verb, *saraph,* meaning burn with flaming fire. Seraphim, or saraphim as it is sometimes spelled—[are] brilliant, shinning, flaming, fiery ones, as spoken of in Isaiah 6:2, and most likely those spoken of in Genesis 3:24—the 'cheruvim, and a flaming sword.' Any being that emits a brilliant, heavenly light is considered a saraph, be they the Father and Son in the Sacred Grove, or an angel who appears in glory, or yet *cheruvim*—heavenly creatures of various types appointed as guardians of sacred and holy things, as those described in Isaiah 6 and Revelation 4–5. Seraphim are also associated with various types of poisonous desert vipers of the Middle East whose venom causes a horrific internal burning, accompanied by an unquenchable thirst, before death mercifully takes the victim. The translation the 'fiery serpents' of Numbers 21:6 is 'seraphim.' The serpent of Eden (Genesis 3:1) comes from a different Hebrew term—*nakhash,* from a verb of the same spelling, meaning to hiss or whisper in a still, small voice; to whisper enchantments, divine; to watch and observe diligently, quietly; to share secret, forbidden things in dark whisperings. A number of pseudepigraphal sources suggest that Lucifer—a once premortal seraph—appeared in the guise of a seraph—an angel of light, and/or accompanied by or in the guise of a messianic symbol of the serpent speaking with a still, comforting voice, whispering forbidden things." (Kent J. Hunter, personal correspondence, May 26, 2017.)

2. Allen, "Numbers," in Gaebelein, *The Expositor's Bible Commentary,* 2:877.

3. Louis Ginzberg, *The Legends of the Jews* (Philadelphia: The Jewish Publication Society of America, 1967), 6:116n658.

4. One Protestant source states: "Hezekiah found it necessary to destroy the relic, that he might put an end to the idolatry. History repeats itself, and men would still worship, if they could, the sacred wood [of Christ's cross]; and, failing that, are obliged to be content with pictured or carved crosses and crucifixes." (Ada Habershon, *The Study of the Miracles* [London: Morgan & Scott, 1911], 143.)

5. See the miracle of "The Giving of Manna in the Wilderness" (Exodus 16:14–36; Numbers 11:7–9) discussed previously.

6. Allen, "Numbers," in Gaebelein, *The Expositor's Bible Commentary,* 2:876.

7. See Bruce Vawter, *On Genesis: A New Reading* (New York: Doubleday, 1977), 78.

8. See Andrew Skinner, "Savior, Satan, and Serpent: The Duality of a Symbol in the Scriptures," in Stephen D. Ricks, Donald W. Parry, and Andrew H. Hedges, eds., *The Disciple as Scholar: Essays on Scripture and the Ancient World in Honor of Richard Lloyd Anderson* (Provo, UT: Neal A. Maxwell Institute for Religious

Scholarship, 2000), 359–84; Walter L. Wilson, *A Dictionary of Bible Types* (Peabody, MA: Hendrickson, 1999), 363.

9. On a related note, the Hebrew word translated as "serpent" in the Genesis account of the Fall is related to the Hebrew word for "luminous" or "shining." Thus, some have suggested that the Genesis account should not read "serpent" but rather "angel of light." (See, for example, Victor P. Hamilton, *Handbook on the Pentateuch* [Grand Rapids, MI: Baker Academic, 1982], 42. See also "Revelation of Moses," in Alexander Roberts and James Donaldson, eds., *Ante-Nicene Fathers* [Peabody, MA: Hendrickson Publishers, 1994], 8:566.) Ginzberg records: "Satan assumed the appearance of an angel." (Louis Ginzberg, *The Legends of the Jews* [Philadelphia, PA: The Jewish Population Society of America, 1912–1938], 1:95; "Life of Adam and Eve," Latin version 9:1 and Greek version 17:1–2 and 29:15, in James H. Charlesworth, ed., *Old Testament Pseudepigrapha* [New York: Doubleday, 1983–1985], 2:260, 261, and 277; Robert Jamison, Andrew Robert Fausset, and David Brown, *Jamieson, Fausset and Brown's Commentary on the Whole Bible* [Grand Rapids, MI: Zondervan, 1999], Old Testament page 19; Adam Clarke, *The Holy Bible, Containing the Old and New Testaments . . . with a Commentary and Critical Notes. . . .* [New York: T. Mason & G. Lane, 1837], 1:48.) Some commentators on this miracle argue that the reason Moses is commanded to make a "brazen serpent" for Israel to exercise faith in is because Jesus, "who knew no sin," became sin for us, "that we might be made the righteousness of God in him" (2 Corinthians 5:21). While it is true the Jesus took upon Him flesh that He might help us to overcome the flesh, the symbolism of the serpent in this miracle is likely less about how Jesus took upon Himself the appearance of that which is human. Rather, it is more likely that the symbolism is centered on Jesus's role as healer and provider of Resurrection.

10. The word "gematria" means literally "to reckon by numbers." In most ancient societies, letters and numbers were used interchangeably. Each letter of an alphabet had a numerical value. Technically speaking, gematria is a mode of interpretation in which the numerical value is substituted for each letter in a word. By so doing, a word's numerical value could be determined and compared for potential relationships with other words possessing the same numerical value.

11. Alan F. Johnson, "Revelation," in Frank E. Gaebelein, ed., *The Expositor's Bible Commentary* (Grand Rapids, MI: Zondervan, 1990), 12:533; William Barclay, *Revelation of John* (Louisville, KY: Westminster John Knox Press, 2004), 2:295; David Fontana, *The Secret Language of Symbolism: A Visual Key to Symbols and Their Meanings* (San Francisco, CA: Chronicle Books, 2000), 152; John J. Davis, *Biblical Numerology: A Basic Study of the Use of Numbers in the Bible* (Grand Rapids, MI: Baker Book House, 1968), 143; Georges Ifrah, *The Universal History Numbers: From Prehistory to the Invention of the Computer* (New York: John Wiley & Sons, 2000), 253.

12. Justin Martyr, "Dialogue with Trypho," 94, Joseph T. Lienhard, ed., *Exodus, Leviticus, Numbers, Deuteronomy*, in *Ancient Christian Commentary on Scripture* (Downers Grove, IL: InterVarsity Press, 2001), 242.

13. Bede the Venerable, "Homilies on the Gospels," 2:18, in Lienhard, *Exodus, Leviticus, Numbers, Deuteronomy*, in *Ancient Christian Commentary on Scripture*, 241.

14. See Kenneth E. Trent, *Types of Christ in the Old Testament: A Conservative Approach to Old Testament Typology* (Bloomington, IN: CrossBooks, 2010), 107.

15. Ada R. Habershon, *Study of the Types* (Grand Rapids, MI: Kregel Publications, 1974), 97; Wilson, *A Dictionary of Bible Types*, 56–57; Trent, *Types of Christ in the Old Testament*, 107; Kevin J. Conner, *Interpreting the Symbols and Types*, rev. ed. (Portland, OR: City Bible Publishing, 1992), 131.

16. See our discussion of the "brass serpent" as a symbol for Christ (Numbers 21:4–9) above.

17. Leon L. Morris, *Revelation*, in *Tyndale New Testament Commentaries*, rev. ed. (Grand Rapids, MI: InterVarsity Press, 1987), 70; Wilson, *A Dictionary of Bible Types*, 58; J. Massyngberde Ford, *The Anchor Bible: Revelation*, vol. 38 (New York: Doubleday, 1975), 383.

18. Pamela McQuade, *The Top 100 Miracles of the Bible: What They Are and What They Mean to You Today* (Uhrichsville, OH: Barbour Publishing, 2008), 61.

19. Spurgeon, cited in Ada R. Habershon, *Hidden Pictures in the Old Testament* (Grand Rapids, MI: Kregel Publications, 1982), 93–94.

20. The Prophet Joseph is said to have taught: "The devil has no power over us only as we permit him. The moment we revolt at anything which comes from God, the devil takes power." (Joseph Smith, *Teachings of the Prophet Joseph Smith*, Joseph Fielding Smith, comp. [Salt Lake City, UT: Deseret Book, 1976], 181.)

21. Trent, *Types of Christ in the Old Testament*, 108. See also John 12:22–32.

22. Habershon, *Hidden Pictures in the Old Testament*, 90–91.

23. Trent, *Types of Christ in the Old Testament*, 108.

24. A. Theodore Tuttle, "Developing Faith," *Ensign*, November 1986.

Balaam's Ass

Numbers 22:21–33

The Miracle

King Balak of Moab feared the Israelites, both because of their numbers, and because of all that they had done to the Amorites (see Numbers 21:21–35; 22:1–4). So, he asks Balaam—a self-proclaimed prophet-mercenary who (for pay) goes about uttering curses on the enemies of those who hire him—if he will curse Israel on Balak's behalf.

Balaam is told by God, likely through the Spirit, that he should not curse Israel (Numbers 22:12), so Ballam tells Balak's messengers that God has told him that he cannot fulfill their request (Numbers 22:13–14).

In response, King Balak sends higher level officials to Balaam to offer him more money—"whatever he wants" (see Numbers 22:15–17). Balaam says that he will only do what God wants, no matter how much money they offer him. However, he goes with the king's emissaries this time, but with the intent of only doing what God tells him to (see Numbers 22:20). The fact that the angel of the Lord appears to Balaam to stop him on his way to Moab suggests that the Lord had not sent him in the first place. Most likely, Balaam was following his own directives—not the Lord's. It may be that the first refusal to go to Moab was in accordance with the dictates of the Spirit. However, when the king's men offer him more money, Balaam says that the Lord had changed His mind. More than likely, it was Balaam who changed his mind. Hence, the Lord stops him on his way.[1]

On the trip to Moab, the angel of the Lord appears to Balaam's donkey three times, but the false prophet apparently cannot see him until the third appearance. The first time, the angel appears on the road before them with a drawn sword. So, the animal swerves off the road, for which Balaam strikes her (see Numbers 22:23). The second encounter with the angel—again, only visible to the ass—is in a narrow path, like an alley. The donkey seeks to slide past the angel, and in the process, scrapes Balaam's foot on the wall. Again, her master strikes her violently (see Numbers 22:25). The third appearance of the angel is in a narrow place where the donkey has no way to get around it, or a way to turn herself around. So, she simply lies down on the ground, again provoking Balaam's anger (see Numbers 22:26–27).

After these three beatings, God gave the donkey utterance, and she chastisingly queried why Balaam kept beating her. Balaam rebukes the ass saying, "You're disobeying me, and if I had a sword right now I would kill you." The animal reminds Balaam of the years of service that she has provided him; at which point, Balaam's eyes were opened, and, for the first time, he too saw the angel with the drawn sword standing before them. Balaam, likely in fear, falls to the ground before the angel (Numbers 22:2–31).

The angel also chastised Balaam for beating the donkey, and explained that what Balaam was seeking to do in Moab was "perverse" and contrary to God's will (Numbers 22:32). He informs the pseudo prophet that the donkey, by disobeying Balaam's directives, had actually saved his life because, if he had gone to Moab, the Lord would have taken his life (see Numbers 22:33).

Balaam told the angel that he would repent and turn back for home. However, the angel informed him that such was not an option now. Balaam was to go to Moab and meet with King Balak, but Balaam was under strict orders to do the right thing this time (see Numbers 22:34–35).

BACKGROUND

Balaam is a controversial figure. LDS and non-LDS commentators alike struggle to know what to make of him, and to what degree one should believe that he was actually inspired of God. One text notes: "It is widely supposed that, since Balaam lived in northern Mesopotamia, he was a *bārû*, a priest-diviner, using the usual tricks of his trade such as dreams and omens to predict the future."[2] As suggested, this is a common take on Balaam. If such is true, then he would not be a legitimate prophet of Israel. He may be nothing more than a fortune-teller, who earnestly believed that he had divine powers, and sought promptings from the Light of Christ. The very fact that "he cannot see the angel of the Lord standing in his path, though his donkey can," seems proof enough that he is not a legitimate prophet, seer, and revelator.[3] In addition, he is almost universally condemned in scripture as a man filled with flaws: moral, ethical, and religious in nature.[4]

In Eden, God's plan unfolds through a serpent who seeks to entice Eve (see Genesis 3); now, on the road to Moab, God rebukes Balaam through a speaking ass. While the miracle sounds fanciful, causing an animal to speak is no more miraculous than causing the blind to see, the deaf to hear, or the lame to walk. Thus, this miracle should not be seen as too contrary to natural law to be possible.[5]

SYMBOLIC ELEMENTS

Anciently, the ass or donkey typified non-covenant peoples, perhaps even the apostate neighbors of Israel.[6] Using the donkey in this symbolic way, the Apostle Paul stated:

> Be ye not unequally yoked together with unbelievers: for what fellowship hath righteousness with unrighteousness? and what communion hath light with darkness?
>
> And what concord hath Christ with Belial? or what part hath he that believeth with an infidel?
>
> And what agreement hath the temple of God with idols? for ye are the temple of the living God; as God hath said, I will dwell in them, and walk in them; and I will be their God, and they shall be my people.
>
> Wherefore come out from among them, and be ye separate, saith the Lord, and touch not the unclean thing; and I will receive you. (2 Corinthians 6:14–17)[7]

Thus, the ass typically symbolized those outside of the covenant.

There is a potential dualism in Balaam and his beast of burden. One commentator wrote:

> The conduct of the ass prefigures that of Balaam. Just as Balaam drives on his ass until brought up short by the angel of the Lord, so Balak will push Balaam to curse Israel until he is stopped by his encounter with God. As God opens the ass's mouth, so he will put words in Balaam's to declare his will. This parallelism between Balaam and his ass suggests that the ability to declare God's word is not necessarily a sign of Balaam's holiness, only that God can use anyone to be his spokesman.[8]

Elsewhere, this same commentator noted: "The donkey's acts and words anticipate the problems Balaam is about to face. The ass was caught three times between the angel's sword and Balaam's stick. Soon Balaam will find himself trapped three times between Balak's demands and God's prohibitions."[9]

Application and Allegorization

While many messages may be drawn from this most peculiar miracle, one of the strongest, and most important, is the fact that God's will overrides any man's will, including any prophet's. When the Father selects a man as President of His Church, rest assured, He calls those who have turned their personal wills over to Him. No mortal man will ever be allowed to take the Church down a path that is contrary to God's will. As President Wilford Woodruff reminded the Saints: "The Lord will never permit me or any other man who stands as President of this Church to lead you astray. It is not in the programme. It is not in the mind of God. If I were to attempt that, the Lord would remove me out of my place, and so He will any other man who attempts to lead the children of men astray from the oracles of God and from their duty."[10] Regarding Balaam and his attempts to act contrary to God's will, one commentator wrote: "Balaam's own personal ability to steer the course of history . . . is minimal, less than the animal on which he rides. Lest Balaam have any thought that he can make an end run around God, the angel teaches Balaam that he must lay down his own initiative in cursing or blessing Israel and allow God to use him as God sees fit."[11] So it is with each of us. While we may thwart our own happiness and success by choosing to chart our own course through life, we will never be able to thwart God's work or will. We can seek, like Balaam, to go our own way. However, like Balaam, if that threatens (in any way) what God intends, He will block our path.

Another important lesson evident in this miracle is the reality that God can speak through whomever He needs to. One commentator wrote: "God is often pleased to use the most common and despised instruments to manifest his will."[12] So He did with Jesus; so He did with the Prophet Joseph; so He regularly does with the young missionaries that He sends out. The Apostle Paul taught: "God hath chosen the foolish things of the world to confound the wise; and God hath chosen the weak things of the world to confound the things which are mighty" (1 Corinthians 1:27). Jesus was but twelve years old when He confounded the doctors of the law in the temple. Joseph Smith was but fourteen when he contradicted the ministers of his day who were claiming that God no longer spoke to man. Young elders are but eighteen or nineteen years old when they are sent out to teach all classes—including the wise and educated. The Lord can speak through anyone who is willing to be His instrument. And in the miracle of Balaam's ass, it was the unlikely one that served as God's mouthpiece. As we've already noted, anciently, the donkey often symbolized non-covenant people. Sometimes it is those outside of our faith that occasionally provoke in us ideas and thoughts that inspire us to do God's will. Joseph Smith was provoked to utter the prayer that brought to pass the First Vision by a minister who did not believe as Joseph did. Saint Augustine had been reading the writings of the pagan Cicero, which got him interested in Christianity, to which he later converted. I myself have, on several occasions, read the theological writings of individuals outside of my faith, and in so doing, stumbled across gems that were clearly inspired. Thus, the miracle of Balaam's ass reminds us that God works through whomever He wants. Those who seek to be righteous and spirit-directed may find that He is moving them, simply because they are willing to be moved.

On a related note, one text states: "Balaam's story stands as a reminder that God does use improbable means to set people on improbable paths."[13] Often, God takes us down paths we did not intend to travel. In order to get us where He needs us—or where we need to be—God sometimes has to use unique means. The story of Balaam is a good example of that, and each of us can likely think of numerous personal examples of when God did the improbable because of where He needed to take us.

One commentator suggested that the lesson best drawn from this miracle is that obedience protects us from uncomfortable encounters. "In this experience Balaam begins to discover that . . . he will not be able to avoid a confrontation with Balak. He might never have had to deal with the tension between being paid and speaking truth if he had listened to God's first word to him and not asked again."[14] How often do we place ourselves in similar situations? We ignore God's word to us—given through priesthood leaders or the Spirit—and in so doing, bring upon ourselves the very negative experiences that God was trying to protect us from by giving us the counsel or advice in the first place. The Prophet Joseph certainly learned this lesson when he pressed the Lord for a "Yes" answer to Martin Harris's request to take the first 116 pages of the Book of Mormon home to show to family and friends. We should learn from Balaam's experience that many uncomfortable encounters can be avoided if we will but obey God's commands.

One Protestant scholar, in commenting on the symbolism of Balaam in this miracle, offered the following modern-day equivalents to Balaam's sins.

> This man is typical of one who claims to be a servant of God and is sometimes used of God, but for the sake of prominence and prosperity is willing to lead his flock astray and to invite worldliness to come in among

the members. . . . Balaam was willing to go wrong and to do wrong so long as he received ample payment for his services. This is typical of modern-day preachers who will promote and permit wicked, worldly things and who will teach error because of the pay they receive from those who like to hear them.[15]

NOTES

1. "Balaam may secretly have been hoping that God's mind had changed. . . . Of course, God's mind has not changed. Thus God must get Balaam's attention through the angel to reemphasize Balaam's duty to speak only God's word." (Katharine Doob Sakenfeld, *Journeying with God: A Commentary on the Book of Numbers*, in *International Theological Commentary* [Grand Rapids, MI: Eerdmans, 1995], 126.)

2. Gordon J. Wenham, *Numbers*, in *Tyndale Old Testament Commentaries* (Downers Grove, IL: InterVarsity Press, 1981), 170. One text suggests: "Rather than see Balaam as a true believer caught up in greed, it is better to understand that he was a sorcerer, more specifically, a *bārû* diviner . . . for whom the God of Israel was just another deity he might manipulate. . . . Balaam is not a good prophet who went bad or a bad prophet trying to be good. He is altogether outside Israel's prophetic tradition. . . . He believed that he had a way with the gods, a hold on them. To him Yahweh was not the Lord of heaven but just another deity whom he might manipulate. He was in for the surprise of his life." (Ronald B. Allen, "Numbers," in Frank E. Gaebelein, ed., *The Expositor's Bible Commentary* [Grand Rapids, MI: Zondervan, 1990], 2:888.)

3. See Wenham, *Numbers*, in *Tyndale Old Testament Commentaries*, 170.

4. See, for example, Numbers 31:8, 16; Deuteronomy 23:3–6; Joshua 13:22; 24:9–10; Judges 11:23–25; Nehemiah 13:1–3; Micah 6:5; 2 Peter 2:15–16; Jude 1:11; Revelation 2:14.

5. See Herbert Lockyer, *All the Miracles of the Bible: The Supernatural in Scripture—Its Scope and Significance* (Grand Rapids, MI: Zondervan, 1961), 78–79; Richard C. Trench, *Miracles and Parables of the Old Testament* (Grand Rapids, MI: Baker Book House, 1959), 71.

6. Howard Eilberg-Schwartz, *The Savage in Judaism: An Anthropology of Israelite Religion and Ancient Judaism* (Bloomington, IN: Indiana University Press, 1990), 126–28. Eilberg-Schwartz shows that the ass is a common symbol in the East for "resident aliens," or those who are not of the covenant race, but live among them. Moses Maimonides drew this same parallel in the twelfth century when he indicated that the ox and ass in this verse were calculated to conjure up in the mind of readers, kosher issues. (See Ian Cairns, *Word and Presence: A Commentary on the Book of Deuteronomy*, in *International Theological Commentary* [Grand Rapids,

MI: Eerdmans, 1992], 196. See also J. C. Cooper, *An Illustrated Encyclopaedia of Traditional Symbols* [London: Thames and Hudson, 1987], 16.)

7. Paul employs the Greek word *akathartos* which can imply ceremonial or moral impurity, as the Hebrew word *taw-may'* does.

8. Gordon J. Wenham, *Numbers*, in *Tyndale Old Testament Commentaries* (Downers Grove, IL: InterVarsity Press, 1981), 167–68.

9. Ibid., 171.

10. Wilford Woodruff, discourse given October 6, 1890, in Brian H. Stuy, comp., *Collected Discourses* (Burbank, CA: B. H. S. Publishing, 1987–1992), 2:137. See also "Excerpts from Three Addresses by President Wilford Woodruff Regarding the Manifesto," in Official Declaration 1.

11. Dennis T. Olson, *Interpretation: A Bible Commentary for Teaching and Preaching—Numbers* (Louisville, KY: Westminster John Knox Press, 1996), 145.

12. Trench, *Miracles and Parables of the Old Testament*, 71.

13. Sakenfeld, *Journeying with God: A Commentary on the Book of Numbers*, in *International Theological Commentary*, 128.

14. Ibid., 126–27.

15. Walter L. Wilson, *A Dictionary of Bible Types* (Peabody, MA: Hendrickson, 1999), 27. See also 2 Peter 2:15; Jude 1:11; Revelation 2:14.

GOD WRITES *on* TABLETS *of* STONE *with* HIS FINGER

EXODUS 24:12; 29:12

DEUTERONOMY 9:10; 10:1–4

THE MIRACLE

In Moses's initial encounter with God upon Mount Sinai, he received from the Lord, "The words of the everlasting covenant of the holy priesthood" (JST Deuteronomy 10:2). These words, or "laws," were written by God's own finger upon tablets of stone.

The prophet, in anger over the sins of the people, broke those first tablets—containing the higher law. But God again carved His word into tablets of stone; this time, offering Israel only that which has come to be known as the "lower law," or the "law of Moses."

Moses delivered these commandments "set in stone" to the people, and charged them to live in obedience to God's words.

BACKGROUND

When God placed Adam upon the earth, He gave him the fulness of the gospel. Included in that "fulness" were the truths, Melchizedek Priesthood, and saving ordinances that we enjoy in this—the dispensation of the fulness of times.

Ultimately, the Israelites found themselves in bondage to the Egyptians—living as slaves to a Pharaoh who treated them like subhumans. During their captivity, their understanding of the truth was lost, and their power to obey the true and living God waned. Many of the Egyptian beliefs and practices became common among some of the Israelites. Some even gravitated toward Egypt's gods.

The giving of the true law upon Sinai—both the Mosaic law and the higher law—was an effort by the God of Israel to turn His people from the false teachings and practices of the Egyptians to the eternal laws and ways of the everlasting God.

SYMBOLIC ELEMENTS

The finger symbolically represents the being who wields it. In the case of this passage, it helps us to understand that the words written are God's words and will—not Moses's. The finger is also a symbol for authority or power.[1] What comes from it is authorized of God and written under the authority and power of God. It also suggests that the words written can provide power to those who heed them.

Scripturally, stone carries two connotations: hardness and permanence.[2] The symbol of hardness implies pride or a lack of receptivity—a refusal to absorb something. Thus, just as stones generally do not "soak up" liquid, someone symbolically represented by a "rock" will not "soak up" what is being taught to them. The symbol of permanence implies the eternal nature of something. Thus, a house of wood rots away with time. A house of stone, however, has a permanence to it.

APPLICATION AND ALLEGORIZATION

Regardless of which application of stone one selects, the fact that both the higher law and the lesser law were written by the finger of God informs the reader that what Moses brought down from Sinai stood in opposition to the laws and practices of the Egyptians. This new law that Moses proffered was divine in its origin, given by God Himself, whereas the Egyptian beliefs were created by a man who had sought to deify himself, calling himself god—something the Ten Commandments would specifically forbid!

The most common interpretation of this miracle has to do with the "hardness" symbol sometimes associated with stone. One text notes:

> When Moses received the Ten Commandments, they were written on tablets of stone, a fact that seemed to prophets of a later generation symbolic of hard, unresponsive hearts: "I will remove from your body the heart of stone and give you a heart of flesh" (Ezek 36:26 NRSV; cf. Jer 31:33). Paul took up the contrast between "the ministry of death, chiseled

in letters on stone tablets," and the greater glory of the ministry of the Spirit (2 Cor 3:7 NRSV . . .), which transformed lives.[3]

In other words, Israel—having spent several years in bondage in a land filled with pagan beliefs and practices—received God's laws (higher and lower) on stone tablets as a symbolic representation that they, the Israelites, were spiritually hardened by the world in which they had been living. They were not, according to the symbol, as receptive as God would have hoped. We must not allow our hearts to lose their receptivity to the things of the Spirit because of the fallen world in which we dwell. Unlike the ancient Israelites, we have a degree of control over our environment. However, like them, through disobedience, we can find ourselves in bondage to the world and its enticements, thereby losing our ability to feel and know those things that only come through the Spirit of the Lord.

Paul's comments to the Saints at Corinth about needing to allow God's words to be written "in fleshy tables of the heart" (2 Corinthians 3:3) is also a reminder that there is a distinction to be made between having a testimony and being truly converted to the gospel of Jesus Christ. As Elder David A. Bednar recently pointed out:

> A testimony is spiritual knowledge of truth obtained by the power of the Holy Ghost. Continuing conversion is constant devotion to the revealed truth we have received—with a heart that is willing [to obey] and for righteous reasons. Knowing that the gospel is true is the essence of a testimony. Consequently being true to the gospel is the essence of conversion.[4]

To have a testimony may imply that one believes; however, to be converted enables one to live as Christ wishes us to live. When we are converted, the commandments are written "in fleshy tables of the heart." Rather than being as "stone," we are susceptible to absorption—taking in, and making a part of our natures, those things which can make us like Christ.

Finally, the fact that the words of Jehovah were written in stone, rather than dictated (as revelations typically are), may be symbolically suggestive of their permanence or eternal consequence. As Ambroasiaster (flourished AD 366–384) noted: "The things which are promised [on Sinai] are eternal and . . . unlike temporal things written in ink, which fades and loses its power."[5] The tablets of stone in this miracle inform the reader that God's laws are not fleeting or changing. They are binding and eternal! Even the law of Moses was binding on ancient Israel, if they hoped to gain salvation. It became, because of their weaknesses, the law by which God would judge them—the law for their day and time. So it is with the divinely given laws that we live by in our day. They are "set in stone"—eternal, everlasting, and unchanging!

The miracle of God writing the commandments upon stone tablets with His own hand is an invitation to you and I to soften our hearts, acknowledge the source of the commands, and embrace and live those eternal covenants and commandments without which there can be no salvation!

NOTES

1. Leland Ryken, James C. Wilhoit, and Tremper Longman III, eds., *Dictionary of Biblical Imagery* (Downers Grove, IL: InterVarsity Press, 1998), 286.

2. Ibid., 815.

3. Ibid.

4. David A. Bednar, "Converted to the Lord," *Ensign*, November 2012.

5. Ambrosiaster, "Commentary on Paul's Epistles," in Gerald Bray, *1–2 Corinthians*, in *Ancient Christian Commentary on Scripture* (Downers Grove, IL: InterVarsity Press, 1999), 212.

THE PARTING *of* *the* JORDAN RIVER

JOSHUA 3–4

THE MIRACLE

Joshua and the people of Israel were camped for three days on the banks of the Jordan River. During that encampment, the Lord informed Joshua: "This day will I begin to magnify thee in the sight of all Israel, that they may know that, as I was with Moses, so I will be with thee" (Joshua 3:7). The miracle that followed was the fulfillment of this promise to the new prophet.

In anticipation of the miracle that was about to happen, Joshua instructed the people of Israel to sanctify themselves so that the Lord could "do wonders" among them (Joshua 3:5). By way of instruction, the people were told that, when they saw the priests bearing the ark of the covenant, they should, "Go after it. . . . that ye may know the way by which ye must go" (Joshua 3:3, 4).

And so, the priests bearing the ark took it, and waded into the shallow of the water, so that their feet were covered by the Jordan River. As they did so, the waters parted, "and all the Israelites passed over on dry ground, until all the people were passed clean over Jordan" (Joshua 3:17).

Then, in accordance with the command of the Lord, one man was chosen from each tribe—as a representative of his tribe. Those twelve men each took a large stone from the bottom of the Jordan River and carried it to the shore. The stones were placed on the shore at the spot of the miracle, to serve as a perpetual memorial of what had happened there, so that it would not be forgotten by them, or their children (see Joshua 4:5–9).

BACKGROUND

The crossing of the Jordan River marks the completion of God's redemptive act that began with Israel's exodus from Egypt. This is evidenced by the various parallels between those two events. In addition, Psalm 114 speaks of these two events—the exodus and Israel's entrance into the promised land—as crucial events through which God made Israel His covenant people.[1] Thus, one commentary states: "The crossings of the Red Sea and the Jordan were mighty miracles that were to be celebrated by Israel forever (cf. Ps. 114). They marked Israel's exodus from the land of bondage and entrance into the Land of Promise. They were a sign of Israel's transition from slavery to freedom."[2]

The place of encampment after Israel passed over the Jordan River was named "Gilgal," which is traditionally translated as "rolling" or "to roll."[3] In Joshua 5:9, the Lord states: "This day have I rolled away the reproach of Egypt from off you. Wherefore the name of the place is called Gilgal unto this day." In other words, the reproach of their slavery in Egypt had formally been "rolled away" because God had fulfilled His promise to Israel's ancestors to bring them to a "promised land" where they could live their religion unmolested.[4]

Though there are sites that some speculate to have been the ancient Gilgal, the exact location of this ancient encampment remains enigmatic.[5]

As in this miracle, the creating of stone memorials was commonplace in the Hebrew Bible (e.g., Genesis 28:18–22; 31:45–47; Joshua 4:2–9; 24:26–27; 1 Samuel 7:12). Some sources see in Joshua 4:8–9 evidence that two sets of stones were collected; one for a memorial and one for the priests to stand on while they held the ark in the water.[6] However, some commentators see this as a misreading of the text, arguing instead that there was only one set—the one placed in Gilgal for a memorial.[7]

While it appears nonthreatening, the swiftness of the Jordan River—in addition to its muddy bed and zigzag currents—can easily sweep one off one's feet.[8] Commentators on the miracle often point out that the significance of the miracle was heightened by the time of year in which it took place. During its flood stage, the Jordan was wider than its normal ninety to one hundred feet, and deeper than its typical three to ten feet.[9] "What a time to try moving hundreds of thousands of people and their baggage across a river!"[10] Accordingly, the miracle would have seemed much more stupendous to the onlookers because of the greatly swollen river.[11]

A number of commentators have pointed out that the Jordan River has a history of earthquakes that have temporarily dammed the river from time to time. Commentators conjecture that this is how the miracle took place.[12] Perhaps. Certainly God often works through natural means, though it is important to emphasize that the text is silent on exactly how God brought to pass the "heaping up" of the waters so that Israel could pass on dry ground. One commentator wisely noted: "If an earthquake was responsible for stopping the Jordan River, it was still a miracle. The discovery of secondary causes only serves to explain how God did what he did, and only God's intervention can account for the miraculous timing."[13]

It has been assumed by scholars that Joshua's command for the people to "sanctify" or "consecrate" themselves likely included a physical washing of themselves and their clothing, and also an abstaining of sexual relations for a time.[14] One source renders the command to "sanctify" as follows:

> Literally, "Make yourselves holy." That is, prepare to be in the presence of The Holy One; see [Joshua] 7:13 and Deuteronomy 23:13–15. Neither of the translations, "Sanctify" (RSV [and KJV]) and "Hallow" (NEB), does justice to the range of prescriptions, which includes abstinence from sexual activity and from certain foods as well as participation in purification rites (Exod 19:10–15; Num 11:18; and the story of Uriah in 2 Samuel 11). "Because the war was sacral, a sphere of activity in which Israel's God was present, the camp and warriors had to be ritually purified."[15]

Six times in Joshua 1–6, we are told that God spoke to Joshua (see Joshua 1:1; 3:7; 4:1, 15; 5:9; 6:2). It is evident that not only is Joshua not acting solely on his own initiative, but, rather, upon God's command. It is also evident that Joshua is the "new Moses"—Israel's new prophet, seer, and revelator.[16] The repeated mention of God speaking to and through Joshua establishes him as Moses's prophetic successor (see Joshua 3:7). Similarly, like Peter—who imitates the miracles of Christ (Acts 3:1–11)[17]—Joshua now imitates the miracles of his predecessor. In so doing, Joshua's first public miracle convinces the people that God was with Joshua as He had been with Moses (see Joshua 4:14).

SYMBOLIC ELEMENTS

Joshua is a standard symbol of Jesus—and was seen as such very early in Christian history. For example, in the fourth century, Cyril of Jerusalem wrote, Joshua "was in many things a type" of Jesus the Christ. Cyril explained that, just as Joshua began to "rule" Israel starting at the Jordan River, so also Jesus began His ministerial "reign" after being baptized in the Jordan. Likewise, just as Joshua selected twelve men to carry the stones and set up a memorial for the miracle, Jesus called twelve apostles to hold up the "stone of Israel"—the "rock of our salvation"—and to memorialize the miracle of His life and teachings. Just as Joshua saved Rahab, the harlot, Jesus seeks to save each of us sinners, whose spiritual lives mirror the harlot because of our unfaithfulness to our God.[18] Moreover, just as Joshua brought down the walls of Jericho, Jesus foretold of the temple at Jerusalem: "There shall not be left here one stone upon another, that shall not be thrown down" (Matthew 24:2).[19] Joshua's name mirrors Jesus. Joshua's name was initially "Oshea" (Numbers 13:16), which means "salvation." The name Joshua, which means, "Jehovah is salvation," is the Hebrew equivalent of the Greek name "Jesus."[20] Thus, in all things, Joshua can be seen as a type for Christ.

The ark of the covenant is highlighted in this miracle, and it becomes the focus. Indeed, because of it's symbolic significance, it is depicted as the source of the miracle. One commentary notes:

> The ark was a portable shrine built as a rectangular box, twenty-seven inches wide by twenty-seven inches high by forty-five inches long. It was overlaid with gold. The cover of the ark has a golden cherub on each end facing toward the middle. It was between these two cherubs that God met with Israel (Exod 25:10–22). The ark symbolized God's presence among his people.[21]

The ark of the covenant was "the visible sign of the Divine Presence, as the pillar of cloud and fire had hitherto been."[22] It "symbolized [Israel's] belief that Yahweh went with them, guiding them to places of rest (Num. 10:33)."[23] It contained the tablets on which the Ten Commandments had been written, and, thus, symbolized the reality that Judaism was a revealed religion with living prophets. It contained a pot of manna (see Exodus 16:33–34), which was a symbolic reminder of God's grace and mercy upon the Israelites during their time in the wilderness. The manna also reminded God's people that they were dependent upon Him for physical and spiritual food.[24] Consequently, the ark was a composite symbol of God's presence, His revelatory voice, and His constant acts of grace on behalf of those who love and follow Him.

The Jordan River in this miracle has been seen as a symbol for barriers associated with the mortal experience. On one hand, it reminds us of the trials of life that beset each of us—trials that we seek to overcome.[25] The geography of the Jordan Valley is instructive; it is largely a deep cleft.

There are three levels which must be crossed. The upper level, called the Ghor in Arabic, is possible to cultivate and, especially at Jericho, is fertile and green. The middle level is desolate, with gray soil of clay, unfit for habitation or cultivation. The lowest level, called the Zor, is thick jungle (Jer. 12:5). In ancient times wild animals lurked here (Jer. 50:44). The crossing would mean going down from the cultivated land, passing through the desert area, penetrating the jungle, going through water, then coming up out of the jungle, crossing the desert, and entering the green and fertile area "on the other side."[26]

Just as the Jordan Valley requires that you leave the comfortable, traverse the barren, and then even make your way through the dangerous before you can inherit the promised land; so also, the mortal experience seems ever to take us from our places of comfort into patches of barrenness, and even into the dangerous, before we reach the comforts that we seek.

On a separate note, the Jordan River suggests the boundary that separates the profane world from the "holy land," or land of promise.[27] Crossing the Jordan can, therefore, point to overcoming one's trials; but can also point to the establishment of Zion. An additional typological symbol traditionally seen in the crossing of the Jordan is the eschatological passing through the veil to inherit one's eternal reward.

The twelve men whom Joshua singles out in the miracle certainly have some symbolic significance. The number twelve is often associated with priesthood.[28] However, owing to the fact that he draws one man from each of the twelve tribes, it is more likely that—in this miracle—the emphasis is on how these events affect or are germane to all of God's covenant people.[29] Of course, the placing of the twelve stones in this miracle may remind the reader of the twelve pillars set up by Moses (in Exodus 24:4), and the twelve stones that Elijah used to build an altar to God on Mount Carmel (see 1 Kings 18:31–35).[30]

> The present narrative places the instructions of Joshua to "take *twelve men*" ([Joshua] 3:12) immediately after the statement that God himself will take the power away from (not drive out . . .) the *seven* nations (v. 10). In this way the seven and the twelve are placed in relationship to each other. The twelve symbolize the new covenant society of freedom and justice that was God's intention for the land. The seven symbolize the entire number of the oppressive and corrupt authorities presently ruling the land. . . . When the "Lord of all the earth" had taken power away from the seven and given it to the twelve, the people who had been under the oppressive rule of the seven would be free to join the new society of

the twelve. In fact, this is what happened in the course of the struggle for the land.[31]

Thus, the numbers herein do not seem coincidental.

One commentary posed this question, "Why use stones?" The same source explains: "They are plentiful and long-lasting, certainly. But they also represented the 'stone of Israel,' the Lord who was preparing the way for Israel (Genesis 49:24)."[32] Thus, the stones are symbols for the need to remember—remember spiritual experiences, remember covenants, remember God!

APPLICATION AND ALLEGORIZATION

Joshua commanded Israel to sanctify themselves before the miracle took place. It is true that, with only rare exceptions, if we wish to brush shoulders with God through a miraculous experience, we must first be seekers of personal holiness.[33] The degree to which we encounter God in our mortal lives is directly related to the degree to which we seek to sanctify ourselves. If we are holy, God will reveal holy things to us. If we are not, we have no promise. Indeed, believers should be warned; if they do not live lives of personal holiness, Satan will take from them the very testimonies they once bore.

Just as Paul spoke of Israel's passing through the Red Sea as a symbol of baptism (see 1 Corinthians 10:1–5), the early Church Christians saw Israel's being led by Joshua to the Jordan River to cross over into the promised land as a symbol of Christ leading us to baptism that we might return to God's presence.[34] When we *truly* seek to follow Christ, we will *always* be led to make and keep sacred covenants. On a related note, the Israelites were told to "go after" the ark "that ye may know the way by which ye must go" (Joshua 3:3, 4). By implication, we today are invited to follow the Lord and His authorized messengers. "Then follow the ark of God; His written Word and unerring Spirit will give you . . . right judgment, and lead you to a right decision in all things."[35]

It has previously been mentioned that the ark is a symbol of God's presence. In Joshua 3:10, the prophet informs the people that the ark will go before them into the land of Canaan—the "promised land"—and "hereby ye shall know that the living God is among you, and that he will without fail drive out from before you the Canaanites." Of this promise, one commentator explained: "God assures Israel that he will certainly drive out the inhabitants of the land. . . . The ark will go ahead of Israel into Canaan. . . . Although its inhabitants do not yet acknowledge it, they will do so as the symbol [i.e., the ark] which represents God's presence and power enters their land."[36] The presence of the ark, going before the covenant people, will chase their enemies from the promised land and from their presence. In a like manner, if God's covenant people in the latter days keep the Lord's Spirit with them, they will be intolerable to their enemies and protected by their God. In Doctrine and Covenants 45 we read: "And it shall be said among the wicked: Let us not go up to battle against Zion, for the inhabitants of Zion are terrible; wherefore we cannot stand" (D&C 45:70).

In this miracle, we are told that Joshua received inspired direction from God, which he then conveyed to his "officers" or representatives (see Joshua 1:1–10). They, in turn, conveyed that divine counsel to the laity of covenant Israel (see Joshua 3:2–5). This passing of revelation through channels of authority sets a pattern for the Church in subsequent dispensations, and it supports the truth articulated in Doctrine and Covenants 1:38, "whether by mine own voice or by the voice of my servants, it is the same."

The parting of the Jordan River serves as a symbol of God's willingness to intervene when His faithful followers run up against seemingly insurmountable challenges. As one commentary on the miracle pointed out, "Hindrances beset us to the very last in our passage to the promised land. But the same hand that hath made the way hard, hath made the way sure."[37] This same source points out, "No sooner did the feet of the priests touch the water, than they were divided. So the circumstances of most hopeless difficulty in which God's servants often find themselves, are sent that the interference of the Most High may be most effectually exhibited in their deliverance."[38] This promise is not only applicable to the general membership of the Church, but it seems to have specific application to leaders in the Church because it was the priests who entered the waters and saw them part on their behalf. As leaders in the Church today seek to "part the waters" of adversity and sin for those whom they serve, this miracle offers special promise of God's divine aid.

God commanded Joshua to have twelve men—one from each tribe—take stones and create a memorial by which they and their posterity would remember the miracle that God performed on behalf of His people on that spot. One commentary on this miracle asked, "Do we have memorials to the work God has done in our lives? Do we remain mindful of His blessings and power?"[39] Elsewhere we read, "This crossing of the Jordan by all the Israelites is not just an experience of the present generation. Future generations of Israelites will also acknowledge it. They will 'participate' in it through observing the sign and through hearing the explanation."[40] The divine command to build something that would remind future generations of God's dealing with past generations is also an invitation to you and I today to make sure that our own posterity knows of the miracles that God has performed in our own lives. Our memorial may be a journal, but it will certainly also be verbal retellings of those miracles to our children and grandchildren.

Speaking of the application of this miracle, Kenneth L. Barker noted: "The priests were commanded to take up the ark and cross over, but they were not told how they would be enabled to cross the river, which was overflowing its banks ([Joshua] v.15). In a similar way the Lord led Israel to the Red Sea without indicating how they would get across. Very often God waits for us to set out in faith before he opens the way for us."[41] Metaphorically speaking, often we must get our feet wet before God will open the way.[42] If we cannot muster the faith to take a step into the dark, we limit the potential miracles and blessings in our lives. This narrative attests to the reality that you and I must initiate many of the miracles available to us. They are there for the having, but we first must act.

As already noted, Joshua is a perfect symbol of Christ. Thus, one typologist explained: "Here again we have a beautiful type of Him who went down into the waters of judgment, and thus caused the river of death to dry up before the feet of His people. He conquered death. The ark was the last to leave the Jordan, for God was their 'rearward.' He is 'the Alpha and the Omega.'"[43] Just as the priests were the first to enter Jordan and the last to leave it, Christ leads the way and stands behind His faithful Saints. One commentator suggested that this serves as an example to leaders today, who must exhibit more courage and consecration than do those whom they lead. They must be the first to serve and the last to leave.[44]

One commentator saw in the temporary parting of the Jordan River a divine reminder that there are limitations to God's grace (e.g., Mormon 2:15) and, thus, we should not procrastinate our repentance (see Alma 13:27). He wrote, "the check" on the waters of the Jordan "was not meant to be perpetual. We are reminded that the suspension of the power of death has its limits. When the day of grace is over the waters will 'return unto their place and flow over all the banks as before' (see Isaiah 28:16–20)."[45] Thus, while God works with us as we seek to overcome our carnal and fallen state (see Mosiah 27:25), there will come a time when we must account for our lives. When that day arrives, the time for repentance will have passed. Now is the time to prepare to meet God (see Alma 13:21).

The driving back of the Jordan was a "token of its Creator's presence."[46] Thus, one commentator explained:

> We have sometimes, in our streets [in England], seen the stream of ordinary traffic suspended, for a time, to give way to the passing by of the [queen] and her attendants. The people are crowded together in masses on each side of the way, waiting respectfully until their sovereign has passed by. Then the crowds disperse, each man resumes his onward way, and the stream flows on in its wonted course. So it was when Jordan's king came, by the ark of His presence, to the waters. "The water stood on an heap," while the ark stood in its bed, and when the soles of the priests' feet were lifted up unto the dry land, the waters returned unto their place, and flowed over all his banks, as they did before. . . . Nature had acknowledged her Master and King, and had given way for the passage of His chosen people.[47]

As we acknowledge and reverence our earthly leaders—or at least we should—this miracle can remind us of an even more important reverence that we should have for our divine leader and His representatives. If nature can faithfully acknowledge its God (and the symbols of that same divine being), we too should seek to develop such reverence. Too many feel no need to sing hymns, which are, an act of worship. Too many comfortably keep their eyes open during corporate prayer. Too many take lightly that which makes fun of the sacred. Like the water of the Jordan River, you and I should drive back our humanity so that we can be worthy to entertain the divine.

One text sees in this miracle the promise that God can make death less fearful for the faithful. The author wrote: "Death is a way which no [living] man has yet gone, even as the path through [the] Jordan had been hitherto untrodden. But as they would feel it less dreadful, when they followed the ark, so the Christian may walk fearlessly through the valley of death if God be with him."[48] If we have faith in Christ, and if we seek to faithfully follow Him, we can walk "through the valley of the shadow of death" with no fear (Psalm 23:4). Christ will lead the way, and our spirits will be at peace.

In Joshua 4:10, it tells us that, "the people hasted," or hurried, "and passed over" the Jordan River. In the third century, Origen of Alexandria drew this application from the miracle:

> It seems to me the words "the people hastened to cross" were not added idly by the Holy Spirit. For this reason, I also think that when we come to baptism for salvation and receive the sacraments of the Word of God,

we should not do it idly or negligently, but we should hurriedly press on all the way until we cross over everything.

For to cross over everything is to accomplish all the things that are commanded. Therefore let us hasten to cross, that is, to fulfill at the beginning, what is written: "Blessed are the poor in spirit." Then, when we have set aside all arrogance and taken up the humility of Christ, we may deserve to attain the blessed promise.[49]

May we each "hasten" to do the will of the Lord so that His promised blessings might speedily flow into our lives each and every day.

NOTES

1. See Kenneth L. Barker, "Joshua," in Frank E. Gaebelein, ed., *The Expositor's Bible Commentary* (Grand Rapids, MI: Zondervan, 1994), 3:265. See also E. John Hamlin, *Inheriting the Land: A Commentary on the Book of Joshua*, in *International Theological Commentary* (Grand Rapids, MI: Eerdmans, 1983), 22.

2. Barker, "Joshua," in Gaebelein, *The Expositor's Bible Commentary*, 3:272.

3. See G. Johannes Botterweck and Helmer Ringgren, eds., *Theological Dictionary of the Old Testament*, vol. 3 (Grand Rapids, MI: Eerdmans, 1978), 20–23. Some Hebraists have interpreted *Gilgal* to mean "(sacred) circle of stones" or "a circle of stones." See Francis Brown, S. R. Driver, and Charles A. Briggs, *The Brown-Driver-Briggs Hebrew and English Lexicon* (Peabody, MA: Hendrickson Publishers, 1999), 166, s.v. #1537; Wade R. Kotter, "Gilgal," in David Noel Freedman, ed., *The Anchor Bible Dictionary* (New York: Doubleday, 1992), 2:1022; Robert G. Boling and G. Ernest Wright, *The Anchor Bible: Joshua*, David Noel Freedman, ed. (New York: Doubleday, 1982), 186. However, Botterweck and Ringgren reject the translation of *Gilgal* as "sacred circle of stones." See Botterweck and Ringgren, *Theological Dictionary of the Old Testament*, 22. The *Anchor Bible Commentary* on Joshua seems to make a connection between the Hebrew word "Gilgal" (rendered in that commentary as "The Circle") and the organizing of the stones in an apparent circle, stating that the formation of the stones gave Gilgal its name. "Unlike many other stone circles . . . it is claimed that this one at least did not have a pagan origin." (See Boling and Wright, *The Anchor Bible: Joshua*, 186.)Elsewhere we read: "Joshua may have piled the stones in a heap, as in 7:26, or he may have placed them in a circle. (Gilgal sounds like the Hebrew word for circle)." (Barker, "Joshua," in Gaebelein, *The Expositor's Bible Commentary*, 3:271.)

4. See Botterweck and Ringgren, *Theological Dictionary of the Old Testament*, 22.

5. See Kotter, "Gilgal," in Freedman, *The Anchor Bible Dictionary*, 2:1023; Richard S. Hess, *Joshua*, in *Tyndale Old Testament Commentaries* (Downers Grove, IL: InterVarsity Press, 1996), 115; Boling and Wright, *The Anchor Bible: Joshua*, 192.

6. See Hess, *Joshua*, in *Tyndale Old Testament Commentaries*, 104; Herbert Lockyer, *All the Miracles of the Bible: The Supernatural in Scripture—Its Scope and Significance* (Grand Rapids, MI: Zondervan, 1961), 82; Boling and Wright, *The Anchor Bible: Joshua*, 155 & 174; Hamlin, *Inheriting the Land: A Commentary on the Book of Joshua*, in *International Theological Commentary*, 27.

7. Richard Hess reasoned: "Joshua sets up twelve stones in the middle of the Jordan River. The text seems to suggest that this is a second memorial, in addition to the twelve stones mentioned already. The absence of purpose for this action, as well as its omission in any previous instructions and in all later accounts, raises questions. Why is it in the text? Perhaps . . . it may refer to a platform for the priests to stand on, or a literary device to emphasize Joshua's excess of zealous obedience. However, the best solution is to recognize the following features: (1) the style of repetition and review already begun in verse 8 and continued in verse 10; (2) the similarity in language to the erection of the first set of stones referred to in verses 8 and 20; (3) the use of grammatical repetition to focus on a key feature; and (4) the unique and unlikely feature (in Hebrew grammar) of introducing a completely new topic in midstream with only a single reference to it. Thus, a translation relating these stones to the first set is preferred: Joshua set up the twelve stones that had been in the middle of the Jordan." (Hess, *Joshua*, in *Tyndale Old Testament Commentaries*, 109.) Boling and Wright noted: "An invisible underwater stone platform could scarcely have attained much symbolic value." (Boling and Wright, *The Anchor Bible: Joshua*, 174.) On the other hand, one commenter suggested, "Some commentators assume that only one memorial was set up and argue that two variant accounts have been combined here. . . . The NIV translators have opted for one memorial. The Hebrew text, however, states that Joshua erected two memorials, one of which was in the middle of the river where it could be seen whenever the river was low." (Barker, "Joshua," in Gaebelein, *The Expositor's Bible Commentary*, 3:270.)

8. See Boling and Wright, *The Anchor Bible: Joshua*, 178.

9. See Hess, *Joshua*, in *Tyndale Old Testament Commentaries*, 109; Boling and Wright, *The Anchor Bible: Joshua*, 178; Barker, "Joshua," in Gaebelein, *The Expositor's Bible Commentary*, 3:270.

10. D. Kelly Ogden and Andrew C. Skinner, *Verse By Verse—The Old Testament Volume One: Genesis through 2 Samuel, Psalms* (Salt Lake City, UT: Deseret Book, 2013), 331.

11. See Hess, *Joshua*, in *Tyndale Old Testament Commentaries*, 115; Boling and Wright, *The Anchor Bible: Joshua*, 168; Lockyer, *All the Miracles of the Bible*, 81; Richard C. Trench, *Miracles and Parables of the Old Testament* (Grand Rapids, MI: Baker Book House, 1959), 75.

12. For example, *The Anchor Bible Commentary* on Joshua states: "The collapse of very soft limestone banks temporarily damming this meandering stream is

recorded for 7 December 1267 and again in 1906. Preceded by an earthquake, it was observed again on 11 July 1927. . . . There is one long geological fault line which has created a valley of the northern lakes, the Jordan River, the Dead Sea, the Arabah, and Gulf of Aqabah in the south. It is in fact not hard to understand how some have taken the present form of the story to reflect a temporary damming of the Jordan." (Boling and Wright, *The Anchor Bible: Joshua*, 168–69.) *The Expositor's Bible Commentary* similarly states that "'the vicinity . . . was famous for the occasional landslides which dammed the floods of the Jordan.' . . . the water stopped too far upstream for the Israelites to have seen it, and the timing had to be perfect for the waters to be exhausted at the precise moment that the priests stepped into the river. . . . With the water from upstream 'completely cut off,' the water flowing downstream was soon emptied into the Dead Sea." (Barker, "Joshua," in Gaebelein, *The Expositor's Bible Commentary*, 3:268. See also 3:272; Hamlin, *Inheriting the Land: A Commentary on the Book of Joshua*, in *International Theological Commentary*, 26; Ogden and Skinner, *Verse By Verse—The Old Testament Volume One: Genesis through 2 Samuel, Psalms*, 331–32; Leland Ryken, James C. Wilhoit, and Tremper Longman III, eds., *Dictionary of Biblical Imagery* [Downers Grove, IL: InterVarsity Press, 1998], 461.) This same source states: "The Hebrew term for 'dry ground'. . . does not require that the riverbed be powdery dry but simply means that it was no longer covered with water." (Barker, "Joshua," in Gaebelein, *The Expositor's Bible Commentary*, 3:268.)

13. Barker, "Joshua," in Gaebelein, *The Expositor's Bible Commentary*, 3:272.

14. See Hess, *Joshua*, in *Tyndale Old Testament Commentaries*, 100; Barker, "Joshua," in Gaebelein, *The Expositor's Bible Commentary*, 3:266.

15. Boling and Wright, *The Anchor Bible: Joshua*, 163.

16. See ibid.; Barker, "Joshua," in Gaebelein, *The Expositor's Bible Commentary*, 3:269.

17. See Alonzo L. Gaskill, *Miracles of the New Testament: A Guide to the Symbolic Messages* (Springville, UT: CFI, 2014), 268–69.

18. See Cyril of Jerusalem, "Catechetical Lectures," in Philip Schaff and Henry Wace, eds., *Nicene and Post-Nicene Fathers*, 2nd series (Peabody, MA: Hendrickson Publishers, 2004), 10:11, in 7:60.

19. Ibid. See also Gregory of Nyssa, "On the Baptism of Christ," in Schaff and Wace, *Nicene and Post-Nicene Fathers*, 5:522; Prudentius, "Hymns for Every Day," 177–80, in John R. Franke, ed., *Joshua, Judges, Ruth, 1–2 Samuel*, in *Ancient Christian Commentary on Scripture* (Downers Grove, IL: InterVarsity Press, 2005), 20.

20. See Gerhard Kittel, ed., *Theological Dictionary of the New Testament* (Grand Rapids, MI: Eerdmans, 1984), 3:284; Brown, Driver, and Briggs, *The Brown-Driver-Briggs Hebrew and English Lexicon*, 448, s.v. #1954 and 221, s.v. #3091. Ogden and Skinner wrote: "Joshua who led the people to a newness of life, bore

the name by which the Messiah would be known while he sojourned in mortality. The name *Jesus* is the Anglicized Greek from of the Hebrew name *Joshua* (or, more particularly, *Yeshua*). The Hebrew name *Yehoshua* literally means 'Jehovah is salvation.' Just as Christ is the salvation of all people in an eternal sense, so Joshua, son of Nun, was the salvation of his people in a temporal sense."(Ogden and Skinner, *Verse By Verse—The Old Testament Volume One: Genesis through 2 Samuel, Psalms*, 333.)

21. Barker, "Joshua," in Gaebelein, *The Expositor's Bible Commentary*, 3:265.

22. Trench, *Miracles and Parables of the Old Testament*, 74. See also Ryken, Wilhoit, and Tremper, *Dictionary of Biblical Imagery*, 43 & 461.

23. Hamlin, *Inheriting the Land: A Commentary on the Book of Joshua*, in *International Theological Commentary*, 24.

24. See ibid.

25. See Trench, *Miracles and Parables of the Old Testament*, 75–76.

26. Hamlin, *Inheriting the Land: A Commentary on the Book of Joshua*, in *International Theological Commentary*, 30.

27. See Hess, *Joshua*, in *Tyndale Old Testament Commentaries*, 98.

28. See Richard D. Draper, *Opening the Seven Seals: The Visions of John the Revelator* (Salt Lake City, UT: Deseret Book, 1991), 24, 46, 56, 83; Mick Smith, *The Book of Revelation: Plain, Pure, and Simple* (Salt Lake City, UT: Deseret Book, 1998), 48, 53, 267, 288. See also Jay A. Parry and Donald W. Parry, *Understanding the Book of Revelation* (Salt Lake City, UT: Deseret Book, 1998), 295; Matthew B. Brown and Paul Thomas Smith, *Symbols in Stone: Symbolism on the Early Temples of the Restoration* (American Fork, UT: Covenant, 1997), 146. Non-LDS commentators often also associate this number with the equivalent of the priesthood, referring to it as a symbol for "ruling" power, church "governance," "apostolic government" or "divine governance"—which are equivalent to priesthood. (See Kevin J. Conner, *Interpreting the Symbols and Types*, rev. ed. [Portland, OR: City Bible Publishing, 1992], 176; Robert D. Johnston, *Numbers in the Bible: God's Design in Biblical Numerology* [Grand Rapids, MI: Kregel Publications, 1999], 83–84; John J. Davis, *Biblical Numerology: A Basic Study of the Use of Numbers in the Bible* [Grand Rapids, MI: Baker Book House, 1968], 122; E. W. Bullinger, *Number in Scripture: Its Supernatural Design and Spiritual Significance* [Grand Rapids, MI: Kregel Publications, 1967], 253.) Non-LDS commentators have also described multiples of twelve as a "symbol of priesthood courses and order." (See, for example, Conner, *Interpreting the Symbols and Types*, 176; J. Massyngberde Ford, *The Anchor Bible: Revelation*, vol. 38 [New York: Doubleday, 1975], 72–73.)

29. See Boling and Wright, *The Anchor Bible: Joshua*, 172.

30. See ibid., 185; Hamlin, *Inheriting the Land: A Commentary on the Book of Joshua*, in *International Theological Commentary*, 27.

31. Hamlin, *Inheriting the Land: A Commentary on the Book of Joshua*, in *International Theological Commentary*, 28; emphasis in original.

32. Ogden and Skinner, *Verse By Verse—The Old Testament Volume One: Genesis through 2 Samuel, Psalms*, 334.

33. See Trench, *Miracles and Parables of the Old Testament*, 76.

34. See, for example, Origen, "Homilies on Joshua" 4:2, in Franke, *Joshua, Judges, Ruth, 1–2 Samuel*, in *Ancient Christian Commentary on Scripture*, 17–18.

35. Trench, *Miracles and Parables of the Old Testament*, 75.

36. Hess, *Joshua*, in *Tyndale Old Testament Commentaries*, 112–13.

37. Trench, *Miracles and Parables of the Old Testament*, 77.

38. Ibid., 75–76.

39. Pamela McQuade, *The Top 100 Miracles of the Bible: What They Are and What They Mean to You Today* (Uhrichsville, OH: Barbour Publishing, 2008), 62.

40. Hess, *Joshua*, in *Tyndale Old Testament Commentaries*, 108.

41. Barker, "Joshua," in Gaebelein, *The Expositor's Bible Commentary*, 3:266.

42. Elder Neal A. Maxwell put it this way: "We sometimes must do the hard things we have been asked to do before we will be blessed. Joshua and his priests, in a little-read replication of the parting and crossing of the Red Sea, crossed the flooded Jordan River in another miracle. But the miracle did not begin for ancient Israel until after Joshua and his priests got the soles of their feet wet. (Joshua 3:15–17.)" (Neal A. Maxwell, *All These Things Shall Give Thee Experience* [Salt Lake City, UT: Deseret Book, 1979], 44–45.)

43. Ada Habershon, *The Study of the Miracles* (London: Morgan & Scott, 1911), 152.

44. See Trench, *Miracles and Parables of the Old Testament*, 75.

45. Lockyer, *All the Miracles of the Bible*, 82.

46. Trench, *Miracles and Parables of the Old Testament*, 74.

47. Ibid.

48. Ibid., 76.

49. Origen, "Homilies on Joshua" 5:1, in Franke, *Joshua, Judges, Ruth, 1–2 Samuel*, in *Ancient Christian Commentary on Scripture*, 22.

THE CESSATION *of the* GIVING *of the* MANNA

JOSHUA 5:12

THE MIRACLE

After the miraculous crossing of the Jordan River, the children of Israel camped at Gilgal and celebrated the Passover. Once in Canaan, they ate unleavened bread and grain from that land.[1] Upon eating the grain, the manna—that God had provided them daily for forty years—immediately ceased, never to be provided by God again. From that day forward, they relied upon the fruits of the land of Canaan for their sustenance.

BACKGROUND

The reference to eating unleavened cakes "on the morrow after the passover" (Joshua 5:11) is traditionally understood to be a reference to the "feast of unleavened bread," which "was originally separate from and as sequel to [the] Passover (Exod 12:15–20)."[2]

The book of Joshua emphasizes the fact that Israel was celebrating their first Passover in the promised land on the anniversary of the very first Passover when they were fleeing Egypt. One commentator pointed out: "The words 'on that very day' [as found in the Hebrew] (Josh. 5:11; cf. Exod. 12:17) link this feast with the actual beginning of the journey out of Egypt, which is also said to have happened on the 15th day of the first month (Exod. 12:51; Num. 33:3)."[3] Thus, God began and ended their forty-year journey with the same commemoration of His divine deliverance of His covenant people. Hence, on this first day in Canaan, they would have been reminded of the bitterness of their bondage in Egypt and of the fulfillment of God's miraculous promises as He brought them into the land of promise.

SYMBOLIC ELEMENTS

Manna is a commonly employed symbol in scripture.[4] It is referenced in the book of Exodus, and also in the Psalms. In addition, mention is made of it in the books of Deuteronomy, Numbers, Nehemiah, Joshua, John, Hebrews, and Revelation. Even the Book of Mormon speaks of this miraculous food from heaven. As noted earlier in this text, one dictionary of symbols states of this prominent symbol that it, "Invites all to taste and touch and smell and see that the Lord is good, his gifts delicious, nutritious, abundant and free, unearned and undeserved." It is a symbol for "God's ability—and willingness—to provide for his children (even complaining ones)."[5] Thus, manna symbolizes God's grace, and His gifts freely given and entirely undeserved.

In this miracle, the grain or corn can symbolize things that we need to sustain us: both temporal and spiritual things. Some commentators see it as a continuation of the divine sustenance imagery (found in the manna), while others see it as standing in contrast to the manna.

APPLICATION AND ALLEGORIZATION

Manna was called the "bread from heaven" (Exodus 16:4. See also Psalm 105:40), and Jesus compared Himself with the bread that came down from heaven (see John 6:31–65). Commentators generally see a prefiguring of Jesus's miraculous feeding of bread to the thousands (see Mark 6:30–44; 8:1–10) in the miracle of the manna.[6] Jesus is the bread of life, and you and I need a relationship with Him if we are to be sustained during this very difficult mortal experience. Because Jesus is the "Word of God" (see John 1:1–4), the manna is often seen as a symbol for God's word. With that in mind—and in light of the miracle under examination—one Jewish source represents God as declaring, "If I bring Israel to their land right away, every man will be taking possession of his field and vineyard and they will neglect the Torah. Therefore I will send them around the desert for forty years so that they will eat manna and . . . thus the Torah will be incorporated into their bodies."[7] By way of application, the manna of God's word is something we need in daily doses as we try to make our way to the promised land of God's celestial kingdom. However, once we are there, we will not need the scriptures and those earthly vehicles designed to aid us in our fallen state. Thus, one commentator pointed out, "The manna that fell daily . . . suddenly ceased when the need was over." This "is an illustration of His providence."[8] This miracle attests to the fact that "extraordinary means are only temporary."[9] God gives us what we need in the season that we need it, but we must embrace and use the daily manna that He offers us or we will not have the tools necessary to reach the promised land.

While the Exodus account describes manna as tasting like "wafers made with honey" (see Exodus 16:31), one commentator noted, "There is a legend among the Jews that the flavor of the Manna was just what each person liked best."[10] Indeed, in one Jewish midrash on the book of Exodus, we read: "The manna that God has given us, we can taste in it the taste of bread, the taste of meat, the taste of fish, the taste of locusts, the taste of all the delicacies in the world."[11] This same source adds, "Anyone who wanted to eat something baked would taste in [the manna] all the baked goods of the world, and anyone who wanted to eat something boiled would taste in it all the boiled dishes in the world."[12] Similarly, in the Apocrypha we read,

> [God], "you spoonfed your people with angel food, and unwearyingly furnished them from heaven bread . . . suited to every taste. For your sustenance displayed your sweetness toward your children, and serving the desire of him that tasted it, changed its nature in accordance with what anyone wished." (Wisdom of Solomon 16:20–21)[13]

By way of application, the gospel offers each of us exactly what we need; and, for each of us, it can be delicious to our spiritual tastes. The Apostle Paul wrote, "I am made all things to all men, that I might by all means save some" (1 Corinthians 9:22). The Spirit tends to operate in this same way. How the Spirit speaks to me is not necessarily how the Spirit will speak to you, because my needs (spiritually speaking) are not necessarily the same as your needs. God feeds the righteous spiritually, but He gives them the things that are spiritually palatable to them, so that they will love the divine manna He offers.

Origen of Alexandria, in his commentary on the Gospel of John, explained that the Israelites—once they entered the promised land—"'ate unleavened bread and fresh from the grain of the holy land,' *a food better than the manna*. For God does not feed them on lesser foods when they have received the land according to promise."[14] Symbolically speaking, Origen suggests that the great and miraculous blessings we enjoy in this life will be nothing compared to what God has in store for us in the celestial kingdom. As blessed as many of our lives are here—and as miraculous as many of our experiences are—God holds in reserve even greater things for those who will be exalted. For, "Eye hath not seen, nor ear heard, neither have entered into the heart of man, the things which God hath prepared for them that love him" (1 Corinthians 2:9).

From this miracle, Origen drew another related analogy. He noted that the Israelites left Egypt with "dough in their clothes," and that sustained them for a time. Then, when that had run out, God "rained manna on them" to meet their daily needs and to sustain them as they journeyed. Finally, when He brought them into the promised land, He allowed them to eat freely of "the fruit of the palms." Of this, Origen suggested a metaphor. The food that Israel brought with them on their sojourn in the wilderness represents the meager knowledge, or "little learning," we have without the gospel in our lives. The manna symbolizes the "divine law" that God gives to help us traverse the wilderness of mortality. Finally, the "fruit of the palms" is the higher and desirous knowledge that is reserved for those who enter the promised land—meaning those who merit a place in the heaven of our God.[15] "For by my Spirit will I enlighten them, and by my power will I make known unto them the secrets of my will—yea, even those things which eye has not seen, nor ear heard, nor yet entered into the heart of man" (D&C 76:10).

As a completely different application of the miracle, the Hebrew of Joshua 5:12 reads, "And the manna ceased on the morrow, *when they ate of the produce of the land*; and the people of Israel had manna no more, but ate of the fruit of the land of Canaan that year."[16] Manna was called the "the grain" (Hebrew) or "corn of heaven" (Psalm 78:24). Metaphorically speaking, one could say that the story depicts the children of Israel choosing to eat the "corn" or "grain" of the land, and, so, the "grain of heaven" ceased to be provided. While certainly the story is not illustrating this, as an application, if we choose the things of this world over the things of God, those sacred things will go away and all we will be left with are the things of this fallen world—those things which surely "cannot satisfy" (2 Nephi 9:51).

NOTES

1. There are a variety of views on the origin of the grain eaten in the miracle: (1) The Israelites brought it into Canaan, having originally gathered it in Shittim; (2) They gathered grain from the fields in Jericho when they arrived there; (3) Friendly Canaanites gave it to them when they entered the land. (See E. John Hamlin, *Inheriting the Land: A Commentary on the Book of Joshua*, in *International Theological Commentary* [Grand Rapids, MI: Eerdmans, 1983], 39.) The footnote in the LDS edition of the KJV suggests that it was grain "from the previous year" (Joshua 5:11, footnote *c*). Whether that was Canaanite grain or grain from Shittim is not stated in the text—though the vast majority of commentators see this as grain from the land of Canaan.

2.   Robert G. Boling and G. Ernest Wright, *The Anchor Bible: Joshua*, David Noel Freedman, ed. (New York: Doubleday, 1982), 191. See also Richard S. Hess, *Joshua*, in *Tyndale Old Testament Commentaries* (Downers Grove, IL: InterVarsity Press, 1996), 124; E. John Hamlin, *Inheriting the Land: A Commentary on the Book of Joshua*, in *International Theological Commentary* (Grand Rapids, MI: Eerdmans, 1983), 38.

3.   Hamlin, *Inheriting the Land: A Commentary on the Book of Joshua*, in *International Theological Commentary*, 38. See also Ellis T. Rasmussen, *A Latter-day Saint Commentary on the Old Testament* (Salt Lake City, UT: Deseret Book, 1994), 197.

4.   For a more detailed discussion of the symbolic meaning of manna, see our previous discussion in the chapter titled, "The Giving of Manna in the Wilderness" (Exodus 16:14–36 & Numbers 11:7–9).

5.   Leland Ryken, James C. Wilhoit, and Tremper Longman III, eds., *Dictionary of Biblical Imagery* (Downers Grove, IL: InterVarsity Press, 1998), 534.

6.   See Kenneth L. Barker, "Joshua," in Frank E. Gaebelein, ed., *The Expositor's Bible Commentary* (Grand Rapids, MI: Zondervan, 1994), 3:275; Kenneth L. Woodward, *The Book of Miracles: The Meaning of the Miracle Stories in Christianity, Judaism, Buddhism, Islam* (New York: Simon & Schuster, 2000), 114.

7.   Mekhilta of Rabbi Ishmael, Wayhi 1, cited in James L. Kugel, *Traditions of the Bible: A Guide to the Bible As It Was at the Start of the Common Era* (Cambridge, MA: Harvard University Press, 1998), 620.

8.   Ada R. Habershon, *The Study of the Miracles* (London: Morgan & Scott, 1911), 206.

9.   Barker, "Joshua," in Gaebelein, *The Expositor's Bible Commentary*, 3:275.

10.   Ada R. Habershon, *Types in the Old Testament* (Grand Rapids, MI: Kregel Publications, 1988), 81.

11.   "Mekhilta of Rabbi Ishmael," Amaleq 1, cited in Kugel, *Traditions of the Bible*, 618.

12.   "Mekhilta of Rabbi Ishmael," Shirtah 4, cited in Kugel, *Traditions of the Bible*, 619.

13.   David Winston, *The Anchor Bible: The Wisdom of Solomon*, David Noel Freedman, ed. (New York: Doubleday, 1979), 297.

14.   Origen, "Commentary on the Gospel of John," 6:233–35, in Franke, *Joshua, Judges, Ruth, 1–2 Samuel*, in *Ancient Christian Commentary on Scripture*, emphasis added.

15.   See Origen, "Homilies on Joshua" 6.1, in Franke, *Joshua, Judges, Ruth, 1–2 Samuel*, in *Ancient Christian Commentary on Scripture*, 29.

16.   See also RSV Joshua 5:12.

THE FALLING *of the* WALLS *of* JERICHO

JOSHUA 6:1–25

THE MIRACLE

Because the Israelites were residing nearby, the city of Jericho had been secured. Its gates were locked, and no one was allowed to enter or leave the city. The inhabitants of the city were "paralyzed by fear" of the Israelites and their God[1] (see Joshua 2:9–11; 5:1).

Joshua received a revelation from the Lord, informing him that God would give Jericho into their hands. As part of that revelation, the Lord revealed how the sons of Israel were to take the city. "Only 'the armed men' were involved. The women, children, and livestock remained in the camp."[2] The priests would bear the ark of the covenant. In front of them would be seven priests, each bearing a trumpet made out of a ram's horn. In front of the trumpeters would be armed men. Behind the ark would be the company of Israelites, and behind them would be more armed men. In accordance with the Lord's instructions, Joshua so organized the people.

Also, in accordance with his revelation, Joshua informed the sons of Israel that they were to circle the city of Jericho once each day for seven days; and, on the seventh day, they were to march around it seven times. Each day, as they paraded around the city, the priests would blow their trumpets but the people would keep silent. On the seventh day, as the priests made a "long blast" with their trumpets, all the men would "shout with a great shout," and—according to the promises of the Lord—the walls of the city would fall down (Joshua 6:5).

Joshua instructed the sons of Israel that, when the walls fell, they were to save no one—except Rahab and her household. They were to be spared because she had hid and protected the two spies that Joshua had sent into the city (see Joshua 2). Also, Joshua informed the people that they were not to take for themselves anything that God had banned, for, in so doing, they would bring a curse upon the "camp of Israel" (Joshua 6:18). They were to gather the silver, gold, and vessels of brass and iron because those would be placed in the treasury of God's house. But the other spoils should not be gathered.

The people did as Joshua instructed, and, as the Lord had promised, the walls of Jericho came tumbling down. The armed Israelites immediately entered the city and destroyed by the sword everything and everyone the Lord had condemned: man, woman, child, ox, sheep, and ass (see Joshua 6:21). However, the two spies that Rahab had protected (see Joshua 2:1–6) went to her home and—true to the oath of protection they had sworn to her (see Joshua 2:12–14)—took her and her family and all those who dwelt in her house and escorted them out of the camp. Then the city—and all that was in it—was burned, but Rahab dwelt with the Israelites from that time forward.

BACKGROUND

Jericho was a small town just northwest of the Dead Sea—potentially a "center of idol worship."[3] This first victory of Jehovah's covenant people west of the Jordan River is of symbolic importance.[4] It establishes that God is with them, and that He keeps His promises to those who faithfully obey His dictates. However, the size of Jericho should not be overestimated. One scholarly source suggested that it was a city most likely not much larger than eight or eight and a half acres; whereas, a large city during that era would have covered closer to twenty acres, and would have had some three thousand inhabitants.[5] Another source suggested that it, "Occupied only about five or six acres."[6] Elsewhere we read, "Jericho was a tiny walled city with a circumference of less than a mile."[7] Thus, the conquering of Jericho was important, but not a huge enterprise.[8] The very fact that they were able to march around the entire city seven times in one day suggests that it would not have been very large.[9] It *may* be that only 1,200 to 1,300 people lived in Jericho, perhaps significantly fewer than that. In addition, one commentary pointed out that, "The bulk of the population of an ancient town lived outside the walls."[10] Thus, the fact that the Israelites could freely make their way around the city each day for a week and "Not be encumbered with defensive towers, houses, and the various outbuildings such as surrounded the typical city [suggests] that Jericho is mostly ruins at the outset" of the Israelite attack on it.[11] Elsewhere we find this: "Fear had caused the thousands living outside the walled city to flee inside it for protection."[12]

In the narrative, the falling of the walls is depicted as a miracle. Some have assumed that this miracle took place through natural means, such as an earthquake. Such is feasible, owing to the fact that the city of Jericho is believed to have sat on part of a long and very unstable fault line.[13]

Joshua 2:15 informs us that Rahab's "house was upon the town wall, and she dwelt upon the wall." Thus, it is assumed by scholars that the part of the wall where she lived did not collapse, but instead, was miraculously preserved.[14] It may be the case that Rahab's house was part of a casemate wall or corner turret, which would reduce the likelihood of collapse when the rest of the wall came down.[15]

For many, the complete destruction of the inhabitants of Jericho is "one of the most perplexing moral problems in the Bible."[16] However, one scholarly source suggested that the reason the Israelites were commanded by God to conquer and destroy an entire city and its inhabitants, but then not inhabit the land, might have been because Jericho was most likely ridden with disease.

> Schistosomiasis is [a potentially deadly disease[17]] caused by a blood fluke parasite whose intermediate host, a species of snail (*Bulinus truncates*), has been found in excavations at Tell es-Sultan [the proposed site of biblical Jericho]. This host organism is known to thrive best in water that is contaminated during usage by human beings, a process for which the single Jericho spring at the foot of the tell is unusually well situated. Moreover, genito-urinary schistosomiasis causes dramatic external signs. . . . [The disease's] debilitating effects in attitudes of defeatism and despair (leaving "fortifications" in dilapidated disrepair?) and especially reduced fertility follow quite naturally.
>
> If the reason for the [divine] prohibition [against] . . . settlement there was in fact knowledge of high infant mortality, the terms of the poetic "curse" [in V:26] suddenly make sense, as do the remarks made to Elisha at Jericho in 2 Kgs 2:19, "Behold, the situation of this city is pleasant, as my lord sees, but the water is bad and the land is unfruitful" (RSV). Is it mere coincidence that there is a four-hundred-year gap in settlement at Jericho, just where geography, historical movements, and climatological conditions in the Middle Bronze and Late Bronze ages might have all converged for the flourishing of this disease whose etiology is clear?[18]

It may well be that Jehovah, in His omniscience, commanded the Israelites to destroy the city and everything in it so as to protect His covenant people from contracting a disease they themselves did not understand.[19]

Ram's horn trumpets (or *shofar*) were commonly used among the military in Bible times to rally the troops (see Judges 3:27; 6:34), to end fighting (see 2 Samuel 2:28; 18:16; 20:22), and to signal a victory (see 1 Samuel 13:3).[20]

The story speaks of putting the confiscated gold, silver, brass, and iron in "the house of the Lord" (Joshua 6:24). This *may* have been a sanctuary at Gilgal, or the portable tabernacle, but it is hard to imagine that this has reference to the Jerusalem temple because it would not be built for nearly two hundred years.[21]

SYMBOLIC ELEMENTS

Like all prophets before and after him, Joshua's life typifies Christ's.[22] Joshua was Israel's leader in battle (see Exodus 17:9–10), whereas Jesus leads us in battle against Satan and sin (see Revelation 3:21). Joshua's name was changed from Oshea to Joshua (see Numbers 13:16), which means "Jehovah saves"; whereas the Savior's premortal name (Jehovah) was changed to His mortal name and title—Jesus the Christ. Joshua (a Hebrew name) is the equivalent of the Greek name Jesus; thus, the Savior—as a mortal—would have been known as Joshua or Yeshua. Joshua showed Israel the way to the promised land, and Jesus guides us to our eternal promised land—the celestial kingdom. From very early in Christian history, Moses was seen as a typological symbol of the First Coming of Christ, and Joshua was seen as a type of His Second Coming.[23] At His First Coming, Jesus was crucified with His arms outstretched; and Moses held his arms outstretched as he looked over covenant Israel (see Exodus 17:11–12). At His Second Coming, Jesus will destroy the enemies of God; and Joshua, as a type for Christ, was the great leader in the battle sent to destroy those who fought against covenant Israel in his day (see Joshua 6–12). In the second century, Justin Martyr wrote:

> It was declared by symbol, even in the time of Moses, that there would be two advents of this Christ. . . . By what Moses and Joshua did, the same thing was symbolically announced and told beforehand. For the one of them [Moses], stretching out his hands, remained till evening on the hill, his hands being supported; and this reveals a type of no other thing than of the cross: and the other [prophet], whose name was altered to Jesus (Joshua), led the fight, and Israel conquered.[24]

Thus, while Joshua is a type for Christ—as all prophets are—he is also uniquely a type of Christ's Second Coming, and this symbolism sets him apart from the vast majority of other prophets. As Joshua conquered the enemies of God, so also shall Jesus return and battle God's enemies.

One source suggested that Rahab's conversion made her a symbol of the "primordial chaos mastered by God in the beginning of time."[25] Regarding the harlot, and her symbolic place in scripture, the *Dictionary of Biblical Imagery* states,

> The antihero is a familiar archetype in modern literature—the protagonist characterized by an absence of the traits or roles that conventionally qualify a person to be considered heroic. It is no surprise that we find antiheroes in a book that subverts worldly standards of success as often as the Bible does. The key text is 1 Corinthians 1:26–31, where Paul asserts regarding those who came to faith in Christ that "not many of you were wise according to worldly standards, not many were powerful, not many were of noble birth" (RSV). Biblical narrative gives us numerous examples of the pattern. . . .
>
> Even a prostitute (Rahab) makes it into the roll call of faith (Heb 11:31). The antihero motif also finds its way in latent form into the hero stories of the Bible, where the list of wholly idealized characters is exceedingly brief and where even the most heroic characters are usually portrayed as having flaws.[26]

Jericho, as a city, appears to be an archetype. It presents a model that so many other cities after it will follow. "Jericho's fate strikes fear into other kings and cities ([Joshua] 9:3; 10:1), and is a pattern to be followed in the treatment of other cities ([Joshua] 10:28, 30). Its name heads the list of conquered cities in Canaan ([Joshua] 12:9–24). Thus, Jericho appears as 'the city,' representative of other cities in Canaan."[27] With God's help, the Israelites destroyed many enemy cities. While the Israelites were the instrument, God was behind the demise of each city. Of course, there were precursors also—other doomed cities that came before Jericho that God chose to destroy. For example, Cain's city (see Genesis 4:17), Nimrod's city (see Genesis 10:9–10), Babel (see Genesis 11:4), and Sodom (see Genesis 19:4–29). The destruction of the enemies of God and His people is a recurring theme in the Hebrew Bible, and Jericho is a doomed city that stands as "a paradigm of a society which can no longer survive as it is."[28]

Walls are mentioned frequently in scripture. They can carry positive and negative connotations that are contingent upon the context.[29] As a positive symbol, they usually represent protection and security.[30] When used as a negative symbol, they commonly serve as a representation of an obstacle that must be overcome.[31] Additionally, walls are also symbolic of vulnerability or misplaced trust (e.g., trusting in the 'arm of flesh' over the 'arm of God'). Broken walls are symbols of defeat.[32] One source explained:

> City walls "up to heaven" (Deut. 1:28; cf. 3:5; Num. 13:28) are symbols not only of impregnability, but of collective pride against which God's judgment must come (Deut. 28:52). The collapsed walls of Jericho anticipate the day of judgment "against every fortified wall" (Isa. 2:15), the "high wall, bulging out, about to collapse" because of the iniquity of Judah (30:13), or "the high fortifications of his walls [which] he will bring down, lay low, and cast to the ground, even to the dust (25:12). Ezekiel seems to have used the fallen walls of Jericho as a paradigm for all the cities of the world in the final struggle, when "every wall shall tumble to the ground" (Ezek. 38:20).[33]

Thus, as is evident in this particular miracle, the walls stand as a negative symbol to be overcome or destroyed in order for God's will to move forward.

While horns were sometimes associated with music (e.g., 2 Chronicles 5:12), rams' horns were typically used to announce war or to warn the people.[34] Regarding their use in this narrative, one text noted, "Marching around the city with trumpets, or *shofars* (rams' horns), signified a declaration of war."[35] The ark of the covenant—here, as elsewhere—symbolized the Lord's presence and His participation in the action about to take place.[36] The point of highlighting the ark in this miracle is to remind the reader that God was behind what was happening, and that He was the ultimate cause of Israel's success. He was with them, and it was by His power that they believed they would conquer.

The number seven is the most common of symbolic scriptural numbers. One source notes, "Seven is the number of divine perfection or completeness."[37] Elsewhere, we are informed, "The preponderance of the number seven—seven priests, seven trumpets, seven days, seven circumlocutions—emphasized the completeness of the Lord's battle."[38] Throughout this miracle, the number seven is employed to inform the reader of God's power, and of the decisiveness of His victories.

APPLICATION AND ALLEGORIZATION

In Joshua 6:1, we are informed that the gates of Jericho were tightly "shut up," preventing any of the residents of that locale from interacting with covenant Israel. Of the symbolic import of this portion of the narrative, one source states:

> If the mission of these spies had been, at least in part, to seek out those who believed in Israel's God, then the act of shutting the gates in Joshua 2 signified the official rejection of this opportunity. The shut gates in 6:1 serve the same purpose. Jericho has refused to hear the message of Israel, proclaimed in the great deeds of the exodus, in the crossing of the Red Sea and of the Jordan, and in the military victories that had already occurred. The act of shutting forms a physical barrier to Israel's divinely ordained movement. . . . As with the natural barrier of the Jordan, it must be overcome. If Israel is to realize the promises of God, Jericho's gates must be opened. In this sense, the exception of Rahab is symbolically paralleled by her window, the one opening to Jericho which is not "shut" against the Israelites. . . . Jericho is *tightly shut up*. This may symbolize the attitude of the citizens of Jericho, also "shut up" in their refusal to hear the message of Israel.[39]

To what extent do you and I "tightly shut up" our hearts and minds to the counsel of the Lord? Are we openly and fully receptive to His words, as given in scripture and the teachings of the living prophets? Do we shut the doors of our hearts or minds to counsel given to us by our local leaders who hold priesthood keys? Are we like the inhabitants of Jericho who forfeited the opportunity for blessings because they thought they knew better than God's representatives did? Or are we instead willing to let the Lord in? Are we willing to allow Him to pull down the walls we've created in our hearts and minds? "The walls He destroys today may not be physical ones, but He still removes dangers that lure believers from truth and keep them from fulfilling His mission. What wall has tumbled down before you?"[40]

God requires punishment for the wicked and unrepentant as this miracle suggests. However, this miracle also highlights God's desire to send mercy, even to those whose wickedness is nearing the point of no return, if they will repent and turn to Him (see 2 Chronicles 7:14; Jeremiah 18:8). God did not will the destruction of Jericho, nor the destruction of Rahab—one of its residents. But Jericho was unrepentant, whereas Rahab changed her life and conformed to God's will (see Hebrews 11:31). Consequently, the former was destroyed and the latter was saved. As the proverb states, "Pride goeth before destruction, and an haughty spirit before a fall" (Proverbs 16:18). Are we sufficiently humble that God does not need to humble us? If humility and submissiveness is what we need, God will send us the experiences that will provoke it. But, as this miracle suggests, it is much less painful to simply choose a life of submissiveness, rather than have that submission forced upon us.

The blowing of the trumpets and the resulting destruction of the wicked in this miracle appears to foreshadow the events of the last days. Paul speaks of the sounding of the "trump" in this way: "For the Lord himself shall descend from heaven with a shout, with the voice of the archangel, and with the trump of God: and the dead in Christ shall rise first" (1 Thessalonians 4:16).[41] Note how both the shout and the trump precede the Resurrection of the dead. In the book of Revelation, John speaks of seven trumps heralding the events of the last days. Six trumpets blast, one after another (Revelation 8:7–8, 10, 12, 9:1, 13). However, when the seventh trump finally sounds, a voice from heaven declares, "The kingdoms of this world are become the kingdoms of our Lord, and of his Christ; and he shall reign for ever and ever" (Revelation 11:15). In other words, the sounding of the trump is a herald that the telestial world in which we now live in is about to fall. Satan is about to lose his power over humankind, and God is about to take control of the earth and all things upon the face thereof.[42]

Over the years, as I have sat on the rostrum at church and looked out over the congregation, I have been disappointed at the number of Latter-day Saints who do not sing the sacred hymns. Cassiodorus, a sixth-century father of the church, saw in this miracle a message for those who choose to not join in the singing of hymns to God: "The divine reading attests that the walls of Jericho at once collapsed at the din of trumpets. So there is no doubt that the sounds of music, at the Lord's command or with his permission, have unleashed great forces."[43] The sacred hymns of the Church are absolutely the source of "great forces." As we sing their lyrics, we can be filled with the Spirit and also with God's love. Those who choose to not sing both reject an opportunity to worship their God (see D&C 25:12), but also reject an opportunity to feel the Holy Ghost—and to be sanctified thereby.

Many readers of this narrative see little in it that can help followers of Christ in the latter days draw closer to Him who brought down the walls of Jericho. However, one commentary on this miracle suggested three applications that can be drawn from this story.

> As we look for the message of this part of the Joshua story for our own time, we should think along these lines: (1) The battle is not ours, but God's; we must subject our wills and our methods to him (Josh. 5:13–15 . . .). (2) We must try to discern the social, political, and religious points at which radical discontinuity is called for, i.e., at what points we

must separate ourselves from the "abominable practices" of the society around us. (3) God's purpose in calling his people and giving them living space is that all families of the earth should be blessed (Gen. 12:3). This stands behind and above all conflicts and struggles in which we may be engaged.[44]

These are valid applications. We *do* need to submit our wills to God, and realize that we cannot succeed without Him. We *do* need to be more willing to set aside the attractive things of this world that hinder the Spirit from being our constant companion. And we *do* need to embrace our mission to bless the world with the truths of the gospel. We must do so with love and a measure of tolerance, but we *must* proclaim the truths of the restored gospel "boldly, [and] nobly, . . . till it has penetrated every continent, visited every clime, swept every country, and sounded in every ear, till the purposes of God shall be accomplished, and the Great Jehovah shall say the work is done."[45] To some, it will seem as though we are declaring war on their world and their way of life. To others, our work and witness will be a welcomed respite from the world, and an invitation to partake of the abundance of life (see John 10:10).

In this miracle, Rahab is mentioned almost in passing—though she is an important part of it. Her appearance here establishes that God keeps His promises because she had been promised that she and her family would be protected (see Joshua 2); and, in this narrative, we see that they are. Her mention here seems designed to testify of the Atonement of Christ; so many people were destroyed, but a prostitute was saved. We know that she later married Salmon—an Israelite—and became the ancestress of King David and thereby of Christ (see Matthew 1:5). Consequently, a sinful Gentile woman of the accursed race of Canaan became forgiven and numbered among God's covenant people. One commentary suggested of Rahab that "she was a trophy of God's grace."[46] The people of Jericho did not repent, and were destroyed, but the prostitute Rahab did repent, and was saved. As one source put it, "For the Christian, the story of Rahab is the story of the shepherd's search for the one lost sheep (Mt. 18:12–14; Lk. 15:4–7). It is the concern of Jesus for the despised of the world (Mt. 15:21–28; Jn. 8:1–11). It is the transformation of values to which Christianity calls disciples. Those rejected by the world are precious to God (1 Cor. 1:18–31; Jas. 2:5)."[47]

One text on miracles said of the falling of the walls, "The miracle was wrought independently of any conflict on Israel's part."[48] Indeed it was. Among its many messages, this story is also a call to humility. The Israelites could not, with propriety, take any credit for the falling of Jericho's walls. They may have marched and shouted and blasted their horns, but none of these things could bring the walls down. It was God, and God alone, who deserves the credit. And so this miracle invites you and I to remember that, when we play some small role in God's mighty miracles, we should give credit where credit is due—and all credit belongs to God.

If any of us had been given the assignment that Joshua was—namely, to bring down the walls of a city—most of us would probably come up with some very similar solutions to the challenge. However, this miracle is instructive, in that it highlights God's tendency to do things differently than men would. President Howard W. Hunter once taught:

> When Joshua led the children of Israel over the Jordan River, the first city they confronted was Jericho. Spies were sent out, and a council of war was held. Joshua's generals undoubtedly set forth arguments as to the kind of weapons, armaments, and tactics that would be needed if they were to breach the wall successfully and destroy the city. Traditionally, it would have meant a lengthy siege. In the meantime, the reputation of the Israelites had preceded them, for the gates of walled Jericho were already closed. The biblical account reads: "Now Jericho was straitly shut up because of the children of Israel: none went out, and none came in." (Josh. 6:1)
>
> In fact, the military planning was so far advanced that according to Joshua, "about forty thousand prepared for war passed over before the Lord unto battle, to the plains of Jericho." (Josh. 4:13)
>
> But the Lord had a better way: "And the Lord said unto Joshua, See, I have given into thine hand Jericho, and the king thereof, and the mighty men of valour." (Josh. 6:2)
>
> Yes, Jehovah has a better plan. Jericho would fall, but in the Lord's way. Instead of being armed with swords and spears, they were armed with rams' horns. Instead of taking a battering ram, they were to take the sacred ark. They were led not by generals, but by priests; they wore not armor, but priestly garments. And in place of a battle cry, there was perhaps a hosanna shout. Instead of setting them to a long, devastating military siege, the Lord promised that after only seven days "the wall of the city shall fall down flat, and the people shall ascend up every man straight before him."[49]

God's ways are seldom our ways (see Isaiah 55:8–9). His ways are higher, better, holier, and kinder than our "natural man" will lead us to be (see Mosiah 3:19). We would do well to follow the admonition of Alma,

"Counsel with the Lord in all thy doings, and he will direct thee for good" (Alma 37:37).[50] To paraphrase Robert Burns, "The best laid schemes of mice and men often go awry!"[51] But God we may always trust![52]

In a similar vein, Elder Neil L. Andersen suggested that this particular miracle calls us to trust in the counsel and teachings of living prophets. He said:

> Thirty-five hundred years ago as Joshua spoke, it meant leaving behind false gods, going to battle against the Canaanites, and following with sharp attention the words of the Prophet. We can almost hear the whining of the skeptics as Joshua announced his battle plans for taking the city of Jericho. First, he said, they would quietly, without any speaking, circle the city one time for each of six days. Then on the seventh day they would compass the city seven times. Following, the priests would blow the trumpets, and at that time all the people would shout with a great shout. Then, Joshua assured them, the walls would come down (see Josh. 6). When the walls came down, the skeptics were quiet.[53]

There will always be skeptics—some from outside the Church, but many within. We have each heard them decrying the counsel of the prophets, saying that it is uninformed, antiquated, or hateful. But as with those who heeded Joshua's unconventional advice, those of us who will follow the teachings of the living prophets will, in the end, see the inspiration behind their often unpopular, but always true teachings.

Regarding Joshua's command that the Israelites not take of the spoils of Jericho, Origen of Alexandria explained: "This is what is indicated by these words: Take heed that you have nothing worldly in you, that you bring down with you to the church neither worldly customs nor faults nor equivocations of the age. But let all worldly ways be anathema to you. Do not mix mundane things with divine; do not introduce worldly matters into . . . the church."[54] In other words, Origen felt that the command for the covenant people to not partake of the spoils of the pagan people of Jericho was a symbolic invitation for you and I to be cautious that we do not make the things of the world a part of God's church. The gospel and LDS culture are sometimes hard to differentiate between. And while cultural things have their place, we must never put those ahead of or in the place of the things that have actually been revealed from heaven.

Finally, as noted in the "Symbolic Elements" section above, this miracle reminds us of the dangers of trusting in the arm of flesh. "That which the sinner trusts in as a means of security may be his destruction. The men of

Jericho, doubtless, looked to their walls as a means of defense, and they became instrumental in their destruction. They prevented their escape before the final catastrophe; they must have crushed many in their fall, and they formed a pavement upon which their conquerors could enter their city."[55] There are so many wonderful things in the world in which we live. But the "things" of morality must only become supplements to our lives, not the focus of our faith or security. We must never place our trust in that which cannot save. The citizens of Jericho did, and they were met with disastrous consequences.

NOTES

1. Kenneth L. Barker, "Joshua," in Frank E. Gaebelein, ed., *The Expositor's Bible Commentary* (Grand Rapids, MI: Zondervan, 1994), 3:277; Richard S. Hess, *Joshua*, in *Tyndale Old Testament Commentaries* (Downers Grove, IL: InterVarsity Press, 1996), 129.
2. Barker, "Joshua," in Gaebelein, *The Expositor's Bible Commentary*, 3:278.
3. D. Kelly Ogden and Andrew C. Skinner, *Verse By Verse—The Old Testament Volume One: Genesis through 2 Samuel, Psalms* (Salt Lake City, UT: Deseret Book, 2013), 335.
4. Some scholars question whether the concurring of Jericho by the Israelites ever actually took place. See, for example, Robert G. Boling and G. Ernest Wright, *The Anchor Bible: Joshua*, David Noel Freedman, ed. (New York: Doubleday, 1982), 211–14; E. John Hamlin, *Inheriting the Land: A Commentary on the Book of Joshua*, in *International Theological Commentary* (Grand Rapids, MI: Eerdmans, 1983), 45; Kenneth L. Woodward, *The Book of Miracles: The Meaning of the Miracle Stories in Christianity, Judaism, Buddhism, Islam* (New York: Simon & Schuster, 2000), 59.
5. Boling and Wright, *The Anchor Bible: Joshua*, 205.
6. Barker, "Joshua," in Gaebelein, *The Expositor's Bible Commentary*, 3:280.
7. Ellis T. Rasmussen, *A Latter-day Saint Commentary on the Old Testament* (Salt Lake City, UT: Deseret Book, 1994), 198. See also Ogden and Skinner, *Verse By Verse—The Old Testament Volume One: Genesis through 2 Samuel, Psalms*, 336.
8. See Boling and Wright, *The Anchor Bible: Joshua*, 204–5.
9. Ellis Rasmussen suggested that the "Israelite army could probably have walked seven times around Jericho in half a day on the seventh day of the siege." (Rasmussen, *A Latter-day Saint Commentary on the Old Testament*, 198. See also Ogden and Skinner, *Verse By Verse—The Old Testament Volume One: Genesis through 2 Samuel, Psalms*, 336.)
10. Boling and Wright, *The Anchor Bible: Joshua*, 206.
11. Ibid., 205–6.
12. Ogden and Skinner, *Verse By Verse—The Old Testament Volume One: Genesis through 2 Samuel, Psalms*, 336.

13. See Boling and Wright, *The Anchor Bible: Joshua*, 208; Barker, "Joshua," in Gaebelein, *The Expositor's Bible Commentary*, 3:281; Lockyer, *All the Miracles of the Bible*, 83; Ada Habershon, *The Study of the Miracles* (London: Morgan & Scott, 1911), 19–20. Ogden and Skinner pointed out, "An earthquake possibly brought the walls down in order for the Israelites to quickly overrun the place. Seismic activity is frequent at that site in the Rift Valley: the epicenter of the strongest earthquake in the land during the twentieth century was near Jericho." (Ogden and Skinner, *Verse By Verse—The Old Testament Volume One: Genesis through 2 Samuel, Psalms*, 336.)

14. See, for example, Barker, "Joshua," in Gaebelein, *The Expositor's Bible Commentary*, 3:282; Hess, *Joshua*, in *Tyndale Old Testament Commentaries*, 133.

15. See Hess, *Joshua*, in *Tyndale Old Testament Commentaries*, 133n1.

16. Barker, "Joshua," in Gaebelein, *The Expositor's Bible Commentary*, 3:280. See also Hamlin, *Inheriting the Land: A Commentary on the Book of Joshua*, in *International Theological Commentary*, 45–46; Hamlin, *Inheriting the Land: A Commentary on the Book of Joshua*, in *International Theological Commentary*, 52.

17. Estimates regarding the number of deaths annually from this disease vary. In 2014, the World Health Organization estimated that twelve thousand people die from this disease each year. In addition, each year approximately twenty million more suffer severe consequences from the disease. Schistosomiasis is the most deadly of the neglected tropical diseases. (See "Schistosomiasis," *World Health Organization*, January 2017, accessed August 3, 2017, www.who.int/mediacentre/factsheets/fs115/en/.)

18. Boling and Wright, *The Anchor Bible: Joshua*, 214.

19. Of course, people or things that threatened to "pollute" the religion of God's people were considered *herem* in Hebrew—meaning, they were banned from use or contact. If you took a "banned thing" into your home, you would pollute the house and be personally "unclean" as a result. A city that had turned from God (Deut. 13:12–14) became *herem*, and would have to be "*heremized*" (or "utterly destroyed"). Jericho is certainly depicted in this miracle as *herem*. While the text does not focus as much on the whys, this may have been because of the disease referenced already, or the idolatry presupposed, or because of a combination of factors associated with the beliefs and practices of Jericho. (See Hamlin, *Inheriting the Land: A Commentary on the Book of Joshua*, in *International Theological Commentary*, 52–53.) This same source states: "We know . . . from a study of the history of the time that there was no mass 'genocide' committed by the Israelites." (Hamlin, *Inheriting the Land: A Commentary on the Book of Joshua*, in *International Theological Commentary*, 54.)

20. See Boling and Wright, *The Anchor Bible: Joshua*, 206. See also Hess, *Joshua*, in *Tyndale Old Testament Commentaries*, 129.

21. See Boling and Wright, *The Anchor Bible: Joshua*, 209; Barker, "Joshua," in Gaebelein, *The Expositor's Bible Commentary*, 3:282.

22. See our discussion in an earlier chapter of Joshua as a type for Christ ("The Parting of the Jordan River"). See also Kenneth E. Trent, *Types of Christ in the Old Testament: A Conservative Approach to Old Testament Typology* (Bloomington, IN: CrossBooks, 2010), 112–13.

23. See, for example, Irenaeus, "Against Heresies" bk. 4, ch. 33:1, in Alexander Roberts and James Donaldson, eds., *Ante-Nicene Fathers* [Peabody, MA: Hendrickson Publishers, 1994], 1:506; Tertullian, "Against Marcion," bk. 3, ch. 28, in Roberts and Donaldson, *Ante-Nicene Fathers*, 3:337; Cyprian of Carthage, "The Treatises of Cyprian," Treatise 11:8, in Roberts and Donaldson, *Ante-Nicene Fathers*, 5:501; Archelaus, "The Acts of the Disputation with the Heresiarch Manes," sec. 44, in Roberts and Donaldson, *Ante-Nicene Fathers*, 6:220; "Sibylline Oracles," 8:251, in James H. Charlesworth, ed., *Old Testament Pseudepigrapha* (New York: Doubleday, 1983–1985), 1:424; Origen, "Homilies on Joshua" 7.3, in John R. Franke, ed., *Joshua, Judges, Ruth, 1–2 Samuel*, in *Ancient Christian Commentary on Scripture* (Downers Grove, IL: InterVarsity Press, 2005), 38. See also Trent, Trent, *Types of Christ in the Old Testament: A Conservative Approach to Old Testament Typology*, 112–13.

24. Justin Martyr, "Dialogue with Trypho" 111, in Roberts and Donaldson, *Ante-Nicene Fathers*, 1:254.

25. J. E. Cirlot, *A Dictionary of Symbols*, 2nd ed. (New York: Routledge & Kegan Paul, 1971), 271.

26. Leland Ryken, James C. Wilhoit, and Tremper Longman III, eds., *Dictionary of Biblical Imagery* (Downers Grove, IL: InterVarsity Press, 1998), 34.

27. Hamlin, *Inheriting the Land: A Commentary on the Book of Joshua*, in *International Theological Commentary*, 47. Similarly, Origen wrote: "We frequently find Jericho to be placed in Scripture as a future of this world. . . . Consequently, this Jericho (that is, the world) is about to fall." (Origen, "Homilies on Joshua" 6.4, in Franke, *Joshua, Judges, Ruth, 1–2 Samuel*, in *Ancient Christian Commentary on Scripture*, 39.)

28. Hamlin, *Inheriting the Land: A Commentary on the Book of Joshua*, in *International Theological Commentary*, 48. This same source states, "We may see the king and the military aristocracy of feudal Jericho as symbols of the historical powers of evil entrenched in social systems, oppressive structures, and destructive relationships." (Ibid., 48–49.)

29. Cirlot, *A Dictionary of Symbols*, 362.

30. Ryken, Wilhoit, and Longman, *Dictionary of Biblical Imagery*, 924; J. C. Cooper, *An Illustrated Encyclopaedia of Traditional Symbols* (London: Thames and Hudson, 1987), 187; Kevin J. Todeschi, *The Encyclopedia of Symbols* (New York: Perigee Book, 1995), 280; Cirlot, *A Dictionary of Symbols*, 362.

31. Todeschi, *The Encyclopedia of Symbols*, 280. See also Cirlot, *A Dictionary of Symbols*, 362.

32. Ryken, Wilhoit, and Longman, *Dictionary of Biblical Imagery*, 924–25; Todeschi, *The Encyclopedia of Symbols*, 280.

33. Hamlin, *Inheriting the Land: A Commentary on the Book of Joshua*, in *International Theological Commentary*, 49.

34. See Ryken, Wilhoit, and Longman, *Dictionary of Biblical Imagery*, 900.

35. Ogden and Skinner, *Verse By Verse—The Old Testament Volume One: Genesis through 2 Samuel, Psalms*, 336.

36. Ibid.; Barker, "Joshua," in Gaebelein, *The Expositor's Bible Commentary*, 3:279; Woodward, *The Book of Miracles*, 59.

37. Barker, "Joshua," in Gaebelein, *The Expositor's Bible Commentary*, 3:278.

38. Ogden and Skinner, *Verse By Verse—The Old Testament Volume One: Genesis through 2 Samuel, Psalms*, 336. Another source pointed out: "The stratagem of waiting seven days" before attacking Jericho "has a number of parallels: Moses waited on Mount Sinai until the seventh day before God spoke to him (Exod. 24:16). At one time the armies of Syria and Israel camped opposite each other for seven days before engaging in battle (1 Kings 20:29). On another occasion the army of Israel took a roundabout journey of seven days on the way to attack Moab (2 Kings 3:9). Job's friends sat with him for seven days before they began to speak (Job 2:11–13). When transported to the exiled Israelites, Ezekiel also sat in silence for seven days (Exek. 3:15)." (Barker, "Joshua," in Gaebelein, *The Expositor's Bible Commentary*, 3:278.) It is also worth noting that this battle is connected in the text with the Passover, and here serves as a memorial of their first victory over their enemies during the Passover in Egypt. (See Hess, *Joshua*, in *Tyndale Old Testament Commentaries*, 130.)

39. Hess, *Joshua*, in *Tyndale Old Testament Commentaries*, 128.

40. Pamela McQuade, *The Top 100 Miracles of the Bible: What They Are and What They Mean to You Today* (Uhrichsville, OH: Barbour Publishing, 2008), 65. Paulinus of Nola said, "For the person without Christ, a wall will become a web." ("Poem" 16:129, in Franke, *Joshua, Judges, Ruth, 1–2 Samuel*, in *Ancient Christian Commentary on Scripture*, 37.)

41. Similarly, in 1 Corinthians, the Apostle Paul wrote, "In a moment, in the twinkling of an eye, at the last trump: for the trumpet shall sound, and the dead shall be raised incorruptible, and we shall be changed" (1 Corinthians 15:52).

42. See Hamlin, *Inheriting the Land: A Commentary on the Book of Joshua*, in *International Theological Commentary*, 51.

43. Cassidorus, "Exposition on the Psalms" 80:4, in Franke, *Joshua, Judges, Ruth, 1–2 Samuel*, in *Ancient Christian Commentary on Scripture*, 38.

44. Hamlin, *Inheriting the Land: A Commentary on the Book of Joshua*, in *International Theological Commentary*, 54–55.

45. Joseph Smith, in *History of the Church*, B. H. Roberts, ed., (Salt Lake City, UT: Deseret Book, 1978), 4:540.

46. Barker, "Joshua," in Gaebelein, *The Expositor's Bible Commentary*, 3:280.

47. Hess, *Joshua*, in *Tyndale Old Testament Commentaries*, 134–35.

48. Lockyer, *All the Miracles of the Bible*, 83.

49. Howard W. Hunter, "Walls of the Mind," *Ensign*, September 1990.

50. The Apostle Paul, commenting on the rather unusual procedure employed to bring down the walls of Jericho, explained it in one simple sentence: "By faith the walls of Jericho fell down" (Hebrews 11:30). Elder James E. Talmage concurred when he wrote, "With full confidence in the instructions and promises of God, Joshua and his intrepid followers laid [spiritual] siege to Jericho; and the walls of that city of sin fell before the faith of the besiegers without the use of battering rams or other engines of war." (James E. Talmage, *Articles of Faith* [Salt Lake City: Deseret Book Co., 1984], 93–94.)

51. Robert Burns, "To A Mouse," (1785), st. 7.

52. I like the comment of Ada Habershon, "We are not commanded to fight against the world, but to carry Christ with us against the temptations, and we shall then gain the victory as the children of Israel did when they carried the Ark around Jericho." (Ada R. Habershon, *Types in the Old Testament* [Grand Rapids, MI: Kregel Publications, 1988], 127.)

53. Neil A. Andersen, "Prophets and Spiritual Mole Crickets," *Ensign*, November 1999.

54. Origen, "Homilies on Joshua" 7:4, in Franke, *Joshua, Judges, Ruth, 1–2 Samuel*, in *Ancient Christian Commentary on Scripture*, 37.

55. Richard C. Trench, *Miracles and Parables of the Old Testament* (Grand Rapids, MI: Baker Book House, 1959), 78.

THE SLAYING *of* ISRAEL'S ENEMIES *with* HAILSTONES *from* HEAVEN

JOSHUA 10:10–11

THE MIRACLE

The king of Jerusalem, Adoni-zedek, heard that Joshua had taken the city of Ai and destroyed it as he had Jericho. Upon conquering Ai, the people of Gibeon struck a peace treaty with the Israelites, becoming their allies. This concerned the king of Jerusalem, so he approached the kings of Hebron, Jarmuth, Lachish, and Eglon, and asked them to join forces with him to attack the city of Gibeon (see Joshua 10:1–4).

When the five kings attacked Gibeon, the Gibeonites sent word to Joshua, begging him to come quickly to help them fight off their attackers. Joshua and his army marched from Gilgal to Gibeon (see Joshua 10: 6–7). As they made their way, the Lord spoke to Joshua, saying, "Fear them not: for I have delivered them into thine hand; there shall not a man of them stand before thee" (Joshua 10:8).

The Israelites surprised the Gibeonites' attackers, throwing them into confusion; and Israel defeated them soundly (see Joshua 10:9–10). As the enemies of Israel and Gibeon fled, God sent "great stones from heaven upon them"—killing even more than had been slain by the sword of the Israelites (Joshua 10:11).

BACKGROUND

The name Adoni-zedek means "my Lord is righteous"[1] or "Lord of Righteousness."[2] This most likely was a title, rather than his given name.[3]

The Hebrew can imply that the king worshipped a deity named Zadqu, or that his deity (whoever it may be) was righteous.[4]

One source on miracles described the unlikely allegiance between the Gibeonites and Israelites in these terms:

> Having neglected to consult his heavenly Captiain, Joshua made the treaty without inquiring of the Lord ([Joshua] 9:14).
>
> Disguised as ambassadors in old clothes with worn-out waterskins and moldy bread, the Gibeonites appeared to have come from a very far country to make a league with victorious Israel. Having had no experience of worn garments and stale provisions (Deuteronomy 29:5, 6), the Israelites, seeing the impoverished garb of the Gibeonites, fell for the ruse and secured their safety by deceit. When Joshua saw that they had been taken in, he reduced the Gibeonites to servitude. Having given his word, honorable Joshua kept his oath (Psalm 15:4; Ecclesiastes 5:2; see II Samuel 21:2–6).[5]

The fear of Adoni-zedek and his allies, which ultimately lead to war, was natural. Joshua and his people had won over the realm of the Hivites, who had controlled the strategic area north and west of Jerusalem. This posed a direct threat to the other kingdoms surrounding Gibeon. Thus, the march against the newly conquered land and its inhabitants was predictable.[6]

The nighttime march from Gilgal to Gibeon was about twenty miles; it would have taken about eight to ten hours, and required an ascent of 3,300 feet.[7] Thus, Joshua and his men would have been taxed by the time they reached the battlefield, which makes their victory all the more miraculous.

This is the first time in the Bible that we encounter the name "Jerusalem." One commentator suggested that, in Joshua's day, this was likely a fortified city confined to the eastern hill—south of today's "Old City." At this point in Jerusalem's history, the population was quite mixed, perhaps explaining Ezekiel's words, "Thy father was an Amorite, and thy mother an Hittite" (Ezekiel 16:3).[8]

SYMBOLIC ELEMENTS

One of the gods of the Canaanites was Baal Hadad (aka Baalshamin). He was a storm god, and would naturally be thought of as the source of hailstorms. "In second-millennium BC Hittite and first-millennium BC Assyrian sources, 'stones from heaven' are used by deities in similar contexts of battling with the enemy."[9] Consequently, when the heavens rained down large hailstorms, the Canaanites most likely perceived this as a sign that Baal was working against them and was in favor of the Israelites.[10]

Hail in scripture is frequently employed as a symbol of God's wrath or power—expressed in an act of judgment (e.g., Haggai 2:17; Exodus 9:13–35; Psalm 78:47).[11] One text suggests:

> Ignorant of the meteorological forces that produce hail, the ancients postulated heavenly storehouses stocked with water, snow and ice (Job 38:22). These weapons stockpiles were reserved for the day of battle and war (Job 38:23). For the Hebrew poet, God as Divine Warrior brandishes these weapons so that "out of the brightness of his presence clouds advanced, with hailstones and bolts of lightning" (Ps 18:12 NIV).[12]

In this miracle, the hailstones are employed in this symbolic way. They were symbols of God's wrath and also of His concern for His people. To the Israelites, these were the weapons of Jehovah. To the Canaanites, perhaps they were the armaments of Baal who had turned on his own.

APPLICATION AND ALLEGORIZATION

Joshua 10:10–11 informs us that,

> The Lord discomfited them before Israel, and [the Lord] slew them with a great slaughter at Gibeon, and [the Lord] chased them along the way that goeth up to Beth-horon, and [the Lord] smote them to Azekah, and unto Makkedah.
>
> And it came to pass . . . that the Lord cast down great stones from heaven upon them.

Clearly, God was the source of this miracle—as He is the source of *all* miracles. By making a nighttime march, Joshua and his men took their enemies by surprise, and the Lord used this to create disorder. Of this, one commentator wrote: "This is another instance where human efforts and divine intervention worked hand in hand."[13] The divine hailstones are described as more effective than the swords of Joshua's army, which, again, shows how our small our efforts are in comparison to God's part in the miracles of our lives. God expects us to participate fully in His work, but He is always the primary contributing partner. In the words of the psalmist, "In God we boast all the day long, and praise thy name for ever" (Psalm 44:8).

As with the preceding miracles, Joshua can be seen as a type for Christ. In this context, Origen of Alexandria saw in this miracle the truth that friendship with Jesus brings hostility from the people and powers around you. He wrote:

> There is no doubt that when a human soul associates itself with the Word of God, it is immediately going to have enemies, and that those it once

considered friends will be changed into adversaries. The soul should not only expect to suffer this from humans, but it should also know that such will likewise be forthcoming from opposing powers and spiritual iniquities. Thus it happens that whoever longs for friendship with Jesus knows he must tolerate the hostilities of many. . . .

Even now, therefore, the Gibeonites, such as they are, are assaulted because of friendship with Jesus [Joshua], even though they are "hewers of wood and carriers of water." That is, although you are the least worthy in the Church, nevertheless, because you belong to Jesus, you will be assailed by five kings.

The Gibeonites, however, are not abandoned or scorned by Jesus [Joshua] or by the leaders and elders of the Israelites; instead they offer help for their weakness.[14]

How true this is. Perhaps it was for this reason that Jesus warned:

If the world hate you, ye know that it hated me before it hated you.

If ye were of the world, the world would love his own: but because ye are not of the world, but I have chosen you out of the world, therefore the world hateth you.

Remember the word that I said unto you, The servant is not greater than his lord. If they have persecuted me, they will also persecute you. (John 15:18–20)

When we join the ranks of those who follow Christ, we should expect there to be challenges, persecution, and the like. But, as with the Apostle Paul, may we boldly proclaim—even amid the persecution—"I am not ashamed of the gospel of Christ" (Romans 1:16).

NOTES

1. Francis Brown, S. R. Driver, and Charles A. Briggs, *The Brown-Driver-Briggs Hebrew and English Lexicon* (Peabody, MA: Hendrickson Publishers, 1999), 11.

2. See Kenneth L. Barker, "Joshua," in Frank E. Gaebelein, ed., *The Expositor's Bible Commentary* (Grand Rapids, MI: Zondervan, 1994), 3:301.

3. See Robert G. Boling, *The Anchor Bible: Judges*, vol. 6 (New York: Doubleday, 1975), 275.

4. See Richard S. Hess, *Joshua*, in *Tyndale Old Testament Commentaries* (Downers Grove, IL: InterVarsity Press, 1996), 29.

5. Herbert Lockyer, *All the Miracles of the Bible: The Supernatural in Scripture—Its Scope and Significance* (Grand Rapids, MI: Zondervan, 1961), 85.

6. See E. John Hamlin, *Inheriting the Land: A Commentary on the Book of Joshua*, in *International Theological Commentary* (Grand Rapids, MI: Eerdmans, 1983), 86.

7.　See Barker, "Joshua," in Gaebelein, *The Expositor's Bible Commentary*, 3:302; Boling, *The Anchor Bible: Judges*, 281; Hamlin, *Inheriting the Land: A Commentary on the Book of Joshua*, in *International Theological Commentary*, 86.

8.　See Boling, *The Anchor Bible: Judges*, 278.

9.　Hess, *Joshua*, in *Tyndale Old Testament Commentaries*, 196.

10.　See Barker, "Joshua," in Gaebelein, *The Expositor's Bible Commentary*, 3:302.

11.　See Walter L. Wilson, *A Dictionary of Bible Types* (Peabody, MA: Hendrickson, 1999), 207; Leland Ryken, James C. Wilhoit, and Tremper Longman III, eds., *Dictionary of Biblical Imagery* (Downers Grove, IL: InterVarsity Press, 1998), 359; Ada R. Habershon, *The Study of the Miracles* (London: Morgan & Scott, 1911), 51.

12.　Ryken, Wilhoit, and Longman, *Dictionary of Biblical Imagery*, 359.

13.　Barker, "Joshua," in Gaebelein, *The Expositor's Bible Commentary*, 3:302; See also Boling, *The Anchor Bible: Judges*, 278.

14.　Origen, "Homilies on Joshua" 11.2, in John R. Franke, ed., *Joshua, Judges, Ruth, 1–2 Samuel*, in *Ancient Christian Commentary on Scripture* (Downers Grove, IL: InterVarsity Press, 2005), 56–57.

JOSHUA COMMANDS *the* SUN *to* STAND STILL

JOSHUA 10:12–14

THE MIRACLE

On the day that the children of Israel were to fight the Amorites (in order to chase them out of Gibeon), Joshua prayed to God for help. In the presence of all his people, the King James Version says Joshua commanded the sun to stand still so that it would remain shining over Gibeon as they fought. And, just as he had commanded, the KJV narrative records that the sun continued to shine down on that land the "whole day" (Joshua 10:13). This enabled the children of Israel to avenge the Amorites for attacking Gibeon; and this miracle stood as a testament to the people that God was indeed fighting on their behalf.

BACKGROUND

While the King James Version of this miracle states that, in answer to Joshua's prayer, the sun stood still in the sky—not setting until the battle was won—not all commentators interpret the Hebrew in this passage that same way.[1] For example, some understand the Hebrew to be saying that Joshua prayed that the dawn would not come too soon, as the Amorites might see them approaching. Others see it as saying that Joshua prayed that the clouds would hold so that the heat of the sun would not beat down on the Israelites, who were already wearied from their twenty-mile night hike. Others interpret the Hebrew to be saying that Joshua requested that God not allow the mist of the valley to be evaporated by the sun so that the Israelites could surprise the Amorites under the cover of the morning mist or fog. Many suggest that Joshua might have been calling for an eclipse of the sun as a means of striking fear in the hearts of the Amorites. Some interpret the passage to be saying that God radically altered the orbit of the planet Venus so as to make it appear that the sun stood still—and so as to provide a prolonging of the light. And some commentators have even gone so far as to interpret that "sun" in this passage as a pagan deity which Joshua was commanding to "stay out" of the battle and not fight on behalf of the Amorites.[2] While the text is simply unclear, what seems to be certain is the declaration at the end of the miracle: "And there was no day like that before it or after it, that the Lord hearkened unto the voice of a man: for the Lord fought for Israel" (Joshua 10:14). A miracle happened. However, we cannot be exactly certain what that miracle was.

If we accept the King James Version's reading of this miracle, the "the extension of light may have been performed so the combined Amorite resistance could be broken in a single siege to leave no time for armies to regroup and prolong the carnage (Josh. 10:12*a*; Hel. 2:15)."[3]

One commentary interpreted the miracle as follows: "The pass of Beth Horon descends westward into the Valley of Aijalon. There the battle raged as Joshua called out for the sun to stand still (Heb. *dôm*) at Gibeon in the east and the moon at the Valley of Aijalon to the west. The locations of these heavenly bodies suggest that the time of the occurrence was early enough in the morning for both the sun and moon to be visible."[4] The consequence would be that the enemy facing Israel would be looking directly into the blinding sun as they sought to defeat God's covenant people.[5]

Though we cannot be dogmatic about what exactly happened on that day, one commentator pointed out that, "It is natural that people of ancient times would think of the sun 'going down' in its supposed orbit around the earth. They did not know that the apparent movements of the sun and moon are caused by the revolutions of the earth on its axis."[6] In other words, the biblical account may or may not be scientifically accurate because the text is simply recording what the observers perceived as happening. Such a fact does *not* call into question the value of the Bible. It only points to the fact that the Bible is offering a narrative, not a scientific treatise, and that the narrative is offered as a teaching device, not as a statement about the science behind the event being examined.

In support of this reading, the following statement was published in the *New Era*: "The accounts of the Creation in the scriptures are not meant to provide a literal, scientific explanation of the specific processes, time periods, or events involved."[7] The science is not the point of scriptural stories—the application is. Joshua's commanding of the sun and moon to stand still "is the Biblical miracle that particularly offended Thomas Jefferson because scientifically we know the havoc that such a phenomenon would cause. But Jefferson was a literalist and missed the story's point."[8] When we read scripture, we should read it for the doctrine and morals it teaches, not for its potential challenges to scientific laws. Indeed, owing to the fact that miracles almost always *appear* to contradict *known* scientific laws, one should be careful about assuming that the scriptures are trying to teach us anything about science. In addition, Isaiah 55:8–9 reminds us that we don't understand God's ways and workings. Thus, we should also be cautious about assuming that God is limited in His ability to do whatever He needs to do simply because you and I see His ability as contradictory with the laws of science that we believe we know. While the sun *may* have literally stopped—or simply *appeared* to have stopped—what matters is that God is truly omnipotent and did what He omnisciently knew needed to be done to preserve His people. Beyond that, little else matters.

In Joshua 10:13, we are informed that the prophet's prayer is recorded in the book of Jasher. This lost text, referred to at least twice in the Hebrew Bible (see Joshua 10:13; 2 Samuel 1:18), has been described as a "lost source book of early Israelite poetry."[9] This same source states, "It seems to have been a collection of ancient national songs, the antiquity of which is suggested by the relatively poor state of preservation of the Hebrew texts in each case. The book must have contained a variety of songs, for each of the 3 citations is quite different."[10]

SYMBOLIC ELEMENTS

The sun and moon are the most prominent symbolic features in this miracle. Generally speaking, these two celestial objects can symbolize a number of things. However, in this miracle, many commentators see them as symbols of deities worshiped by the Amorites. One text notes, "In most traditions the Sun is the universal Father, with the Moon as Mother. . . . The sun and rain are the primary fertilizing forces, hence the bridegroom as sun and bride as moon goddess."[11] Elsewhere we read, "The idea that [the sun] may have been the pagan deity worshiped at Gibeon is worth keeping in mind."[12] With that in mind—and knowing that we cannot know for certain—one source suggested that Joshua knew the hailstones would be sufficient to slaughter the Amorites, "But he desired that it might be known that the sun and moon, their gods, were servants to the God whom they should serve."[13] If that was the case, the Amorites would have seen in this miracle (and the miracle of the hailstones) as a complete attack upon them by their own deities. The symbolic message would have been that the gods of the Amorites were fighting on behalf of the children of Israel.

It is generally supposed that the worship of the sun and moon and stars was the first form which idolatry assumed, and we may therefore suppose it was the one most difficult to eradicate. By no conceivable miracle could the inhabitants of Canaan have been taught their folly in this matter so impressively as in that in which the very gods in whom they confided stood still and left them to perish.[14]

APPLICATION AND ALLEGORIZATION

As for the potential application of this miracle, one text suggested, "For the Christian, the repeated mention of God's miraculous intervention in Israel's wars recalls the spiritual warfare with sin that forms a daily struggle. This too involves spiritual forces. Although they may not always manifest themselves in the overtly miraculous, they are no less real."[15] Thus, the Apostle Paul wrote:

> For we wrestle not against flesh and blood, but against principalities, against powers, against the rulers of the darkness of this world, against spiritual wickedness in high places.
>
> Wherefore take unto you the whole armour of God, that ye may be able to withstand in the evil day, and having done all, to stand. (Ephesians 6:12–13)

Mortality is a spiritual battle. However, for those who seek to be faithful, God will help fight their fight as He did time and again on behalf of His ancient covenant people. In each of these recorded battles, the key seemed to always be to faithfully follow the guidance of the prophet. Those who did, not only survived, but also prospered. Traditionally, those who thought they knew better died.

This miracle is a testament to the truth taught in the book of James, "The effectual fervent prayer of a righteous man availeth much" (James 5:16). And so it does! Joshua's faith-filled prayer invoked a miracle. One commentator saw in this narrative a message about the importance of prayer. She wrote, "God does not often stop the sun and moon in their courses. But He does listen to prayer *every day*. So if we face attackers . . . , we need not fear. God answers prayer—sometimes in amazing ways. But *we do need to pray*."[16] In this same spirit, the LDS Bible Dictionary entry on "Prayer" states, "Blessings require some work or effort on our part before we can obtain them. Prayer is a form of work and is an appointed means for obtaining the highest of all blessings."[17] If we wish to receive the blessings of Joshua, too we must do the works of Joshua. May our prayers be as faith-filled, and our blessings as timely.

One text on the miracles offered this application of the motionless moon and sun:

> Material blessings serve God in a higher region when they are used to attain moral ends. The fig-tree mentioned in Mark xi. came into a higher service when it was smitten by Christ that it would have stood in if it had merely produced figs for ages. It was promoted into a mortal teacher, and so became a co-worker with God. The bread and wine used in the Lord's supper are raised to a higher platform than that which bread and wine ordinarily occupies, because they then speak to that part of man which does not live by material bread. The sun and moon had not hitherto been called to this honour, but now these signs, which had in the past been merely physical blessings, were put to a higher use.
>
> Material blessings which are the common property of all men become the special servants of those who live a life of faith upon the Giver. The servant of God uses His common gifts to sustain life in which he may form a character for the society of His Master. Therefore he has a higher claim to the service of the world of matter around him. Therefore "all things are yours" (1 Cor. iii. 21). Joshua had a common interest in the physical blessings of the sunlight, but, as one on the side of Jehovah against idolaters, he could enlist its help for the attainment of moral ends.[18]

God can take simple things and turn them into miracles. He does this daily in our own lives, and with our meager gifts. Simple things become sacred because God uses them to bless us and others. The trick is to train ourselves to be aware of these daily manifestations of God's power.

If the sun and moon really were Amorite gods, then this miracle reminds us that *any* false god we place our trust in will, in the most crucial hour, fail us. The true and living God can always be appealed to, but the gods of this world will never be there to support their supplicants when their faith and fate hang in the balance. As one commentator wrote, "God still continues to deal so with men when they place their trust in any object below Himself. He shows them how little [these false gods] can do in the time of trial or how they may be turned into a source of suffering."[19]

Origen of Alexandria saw an interesting application of this miracle. Just as Joshua commanded it to remain light until he was able to get his work of destroying the enemy done, Origen suggested that Jesus ("Joshua" in Hebrew) prolongs the light so that you and I—soldiers in His army—can fight the battle against the enemy of all righteousness. He wrote:

> Therefore, until the promise of the Father is fulfilled and the churches spring forth in the various nations and "the whole fullness of the nations"

ether so that then "all Israel may be saved," the day is lengthened and the setting is deferred and the sun never sinks down but always rises as long as "the sun of righteousness" pours the light of truth into the hearts of believers. But when the measure of believers is complete and the already weaker and depraved age of the final generation arrives, when "the love of many persons will grow cold by increasing iniquity" and very few persons remain in whom faith is found, then "the days will be shortened."

In the same way, therefore, the Lord knows to extend the day when it is time for salvation and to shorten the day when it is time for tribulation and destruction. We, however, while we have the day and the extent of light is lengthened for us, "let us walk becomingly as in the day" and let us perform the works of light.[20]

Though not part of the miracle proper, at the end of this narrative we learn that the five kings that unitedly attacked the people of Gibeon and fought the children of Israel fled and hid in a cave at Makkedah. Eventually, they were tracked down and Joshua smote each of them (see Joshua 10:15–26). Jerome saw this as having symbolic significance. He wrote,

We may see in [this] a type of the overthrow of the world by the preaching of the gospel. . . . Five kings who previously reigned in the land of promise, and opposed the Gospel army were overcome in battle with Joshua. I think it is clearly to be understood that before the Lord led his people . . . , sight, smell, taste, hearing, and touch had dominion, and that to these, as to five princes, everything was subject. And when they took refuge in the cave of the body and in a place of darkness, Jesus entered the body itself and slew them.[21]

This perspective was a fairly common one among the ancient Christians. Thus, Origen similarly taught:

But let us also see what it means when it says there were five kings and they fled into caves. We have often said the battle of Christians is twofold. Indeed, for those who are perfect, such as Paul and the Ephesians, it was not, as the apostle himself says, "a battle against flesh and blood but against principalities and authorities, against the rulers of darkness in this world and spiritual forces of iniquity in the heavens." But for the [spiritually] weaker ones and those not yet mature, the battle is still waged against flesh and blood, for those are still assaulted by carnal faults and frailties.

I think this is indicated even in this passage; for we said that a war was declared by five kings against the Gibeonites, whose figure I maintained was of those who are [spiritually] immature. These, therefore, are assaulted by five kings. Now these five kings indicate the five corporeal senses: sight, hearing, taste, touch and smell; for it must be through one of these that each person falls away into sin. These five senses are compared to those five kings who fight the Gibeonites, that is, carnal persons.

That they are said to have fled into caves can be indicated, perhaps, because a cave is a place buried in the depths of the earth. Therefore, those senses that we mentioned above are said to have fled into caves when, after being placed in the body, they immerse themselves in earthly impulses and do nothing for the work of God but all for the service of the body.[22]

From the perspective of Jerome and Origen, the natural man is constantly at war with God's children (see Mosiah 3:19; 1 Corinthians 2:14). Just as the soldiers of the Amorites in Joshua's day united to attack, so also our senses can seemingly attack us as Satan uses them to entice us to sin. But, if Christ is allowed to reign in our lives, He will slay the sources of temptation, that we might be freed from the influence of the adversary. We must let Him into the "cave of our body" so that He can subdue our enemies. And we must remember that we cannot win the battle alone. If Christ is not our general, the "five princes," whom the adversary constantly seeks to employ, will take our spiritual lives. But if Christ reigns, they too will become subject to the Master.

NOTES

1. According to one commentary, in the Hebrew Joshua spoke of the moon as "standing still" or "stopping." (The Hebrew word used here regarding the moon is 'āmad, which has been interpreted to mean "stop" or "stand still"). However, the Hebrew word associated with Joshua's command of the sun (in this passage) is dāmam, which is commonly translated "be silent"—and can imply that something not speak or act or perform its traditional duty. (See Kenneth L. Barker, "Joshua," in Frank E. Gaebelein, ed., *The Expositor's Bible Commentary* [Grand Rapids, MI: Zondervan, 1994], 3:303; Francis Brown, S. R. Driver, and Charles A. Briggs, *The Brown-Driver-Briggs Hebrew and English Lexicon* [Peabody, MA: Hendrickson Publishers, 1999], 198 & 763; E. John Hamlin, *Inheriting the Land: A Commentary on the Book of Joshua*, in *International Theological Commentary* [Grand Rapids, MI: Eerdmans, 1983], 87–88; Herbert Lockyer, *All the Miracles of the Bible: The Supernatural in Scripture—Its Scope and Significance* [Grand Rapids, MI: Zondervan, 1961], 85.) For this reason, various commentators and translators render the verse and its meaning differently.

2. See Barker, "Joshua," in Gaebelein, *The Expositor's Bible Commentary*, 3:303; Robert G. Boling, *The Anchor Bible: Judges*, vol. 6 (New York: Doubleday, 1975), 283; Richard S. Hess, *Joshua*, in *Tyndale Old Testament Commentaries* (Downers Grove, IL: InterVarsity Press, 1996), 197–98; Hamlin, *Inheriting the Land: A Commentary on the Book of Joshua*, in *International Theological Commentary*, 87.

3. Ellis T. Rasmussen, *A Latter-day Saint Commentary on the Old Testament* (Salt Lake City, UT: Deseret Book, 1994), 200. See also D. Kelly Ogden and Andrew C. Skinner, *Verse By Verse—The Old Testament Volume One: Genesis through 2 Samuel, Psalms* (Salt Lake City, UT: Deseret Book, 2013), 340.

4. Hess, *Joshua*, in *Tyndale Old Testament Commentaries*, 196. See also Boling, *The Anchor Bible: Judges*, 288.

5. See Boling, *The Anchor Bible: Judges*, 283.

6. Hamlin, *Inheriting the Land: A Commentary on the Book of Joshua*, in *International Theological Commentary*, 88.

7. "What does the Church believe about dinosaurs?," in "To the Point," *New Era*, February 2016.

8. Kenneth L. Woodward, *The Book of Miracles: The Meaning of the Miracle Stories in Christianity, Judaism, Buddhism, Islam* (New York: Simon & Schuster, 2000), 60. "The objection raised [is] that if the earth had stopped in its orbit, it would have fallen into the sun." (Lockyer, *All the Miracles of the Bible*, 85.)

9. See Duane L. Christensen, "Jashar, Book Of," in David Noel Freedman, *The Anchor Bible Dictionary* (New York: Doubleday, 1992), 3:646.

10. Ibid. Christensen refers to "3 citations" because it is his opinion that 1 Kings 8:12–13 is actually quoting from a song in the Book of Jasher, erroneously referred to as the "Book of the Song."

11. J. C. Cooper, *An Illustrated Encyclopaedia of Traditional Symbols* (London: Thames and Hudson, 1987), 162.

12. Boling, *The Anchor Bible: Judges*, 283. See also J. Glen Taylor, *Yahweh and the Sun: Biblical and Archaeological Evidence for Sun Worship in Ancient Israel* (Sheffield, England: JSOT Press, 1993), 114–18.

13. Richard C. Trench, *Miracles and Parables of the Old Testament* (Grand Rapids, MI: Baker Book House, 1959), 86.

14. Ibid., 87.

15. Hess, *Joshua*, in *Tyndale Old Testament Commentaries*, 199.

16. Pamela McQuade, *The Top 100 Miracles of the Bible: What They Are and What They Mean to You Today* (Uhrichsville, OH: Barbour Publishing, 2008), 68; emphasis added.

17. Bible Dictionary, "Prayer," 707.

18. Trench, *Miracles and Parables of the Old Testament*, 85–86.

19. Ibid., 87.

20. Origen, "Homilies on Joshua," 11.2–3, in John R. Franke, ed., *Joshua, Judges, Ruth, 1–2 Samuel*, in *Ancient Christian Commentary on Scripture* (Downers Grove, IL: InterVarsity Press, 2005), 59.

21. Jerome, "Against Jovinianus" 1.21, in Franke, *Joshua, Judges, Ruth, 1–2 Samuel*, in *Ancient Christian Commentary on Scripture*, 60.

22. Origen, "Homilies on Joshua" 11.4, in Franke, *Joshua, Judges, Ruth, 1–2 Samuel*, in *Ancient Christian Commentary on Scripture*, 60.

DEW *on* GIDEON'S FLEECE

JUDGES 6:36-40

THE MIRACLE

The Midianites were about to attack the Israelites, but God had promised that He would intervene and save His people by the hand of Gideon.[1] However, Gideon had his doubts. So, he prayed, asking God if He was really going to save Israel as He had promised. In an effort to receive a confirmation, Gideon asked for a sign. He told God that he would lay a piece of fleece on the ground and leave it out overnight. If God would allow the dew to fall on the fleece only, but not on the other parts of the ground, then he would know that God would keep His promise to Gideon. God did so and, in the morning, the ground was dry, but the fleece had sufficient water on it to fill a bowl with water (see Judges 6:38). While this was the sign that Gideon had requested, he still felt uncertain. He worried that he would offend God by asking for an additional miraculous sign. Nevertheless, begging that God "not be angry" with him (see Judges 6:39), Gideon prayed one more time; this time requesting that, on the morrow, the ground would be damp but the fleece he had laid out would be completely dry. God did as he asked, and Gideon knew that God would keep His word.

BACKGROUND

The logic of Gideon's double request is often missed by the Western reader. One commentary on this passage pointed out that, "Fishermen living on one of the streamless and springless Desert Islands have obtained sufficient water for their livelihood by spreading out fleece in the evening and wringing dew from them in the morning."[2] Such was not an uncommon practice. "With the physical properties of fleece lying exposed overnight on [warm] bare rock, the differentials of condensation and evaporation necessary to give rise to the story are entirely understandable."³ It may be that Gideon realized that only after the first miracle had taken place. Thus, his request for the second miracle may have been provoked by the late recognition that the first could happen quite naturally, and may not have actually been a response by God.⁴ However, the second request—a damp ground but dry fleece—could only happen if indeed God had caused it. Thus, Gideon's additional request may not have been evidence of his lack of faith, only evidence that he had not really thought his first request through prior to making it.

SYMBOLIC ELEMENTS

Regarding the symbolic meaning of dew, one text suggested that dew represents, "Spiritual refreshment" or "blessings." This same source states, "Sweet dew is peace and prosperity."⁵ Elsewhere we read, "Dew is a symbol of plenty given (Gen. 27:28) or withheld (v. 39), of security, prosperity, salvation, and victory—in short, of *shalom* (Deut. 33:28–29). God's blessing on Israel is like the gentle descent of dew (Hos. 14:5–6). The test was this: Could Yahweh give or withhold this blessing? . . . Gideon received his answer and was ready to lead his people."⁶ The *Dictionary of Biblical Imagery* offers this explanation:

> Dew is a multifaceted image and symbol whose usage in the Bible is firmly rooted in the climatic conditions of a region where dew serves a vital function relatively foreign to the experiences of the Western world. . . .
> The symbolic meanings of dew flow from its physical properties. Because dew is a source of the very water on which life depends, it symbolizes blessing, favor or prosperity. . . .
> The physical properties of dew also yield a kaleidoscope of individual symbols.⁷

One encyclopedia of symbolism says that fleece is symbolically, "Regarded as the life-force of the sheep and, by implication, all life-sustaining produce, such as cattle, corn, etc., also progeny and longevity."⁸ One commentary on the book of Judges notes: "Jews have seen [Gideon's fleece] as a symbol of their people, chosen (wet) or rejected (dry)."⁹

APPLICATION AND ALLEGORIZATION

One commentary on the book of Judges offers the following application of this miracle: "The patience of the Lord is remarkably shown in this section, in which Gideon twice sought confirmation of the challenge presented to him. The Lord very graciously accommodated himself to Gideon's request, understanding fully the frailty of human nature. . . . The Lord deals more tenderly and graciously with His children than any earthly father."[10] Indeed, as the psalmist said, "[God] knoweth our frame; he remembereth that we are dust" (Psalm 103:14). President J. Reuben Clark, Jr., taught: "I do not think [our Heavenly Father] intends to shut any of us off because of some slight transgression, some slight failure to observe some rule or regulation. There are the great elementals that we must observe, but he is not going to be captious about the lesser things."[11] Perhaps Gideon's humanity is some-what observable in this miracle, but so is God's graciousness. "Those who dread lest the Divine anger should visit them because they ask for tokens of Divine guidance, will never feel the wrath which they fear. . . . Could a parent be displeased with a child whose only desire was to know certainly his father's will?"[12]

From a completely different angle, one might draw from this miracle a lesson about prayer. Praying for personal revelation to guide one's steps is appropriate, and even encouraged by God (see Matthew 7:7). However, doubting God's revelations is another matter. Of Gideon's manifest disbe-lief in God's word, one commentator noted:

> Like Gideon, many a modern-day believer whose faith needs bolstering has "put out the fleece" to help him find the Lord's will. If this "fleece" consists of a careful observation and interpretation of God's leading through circumstances, the procedure can be a healthy one. But Gideon's method was to make purely arbitrary demands of God and insist on immediate guidance. Such an approach can hardly be recommended for Christians today. In Luke 1:18 Zechariah, the father of John the Baptist, doubted the words of Gabriel and was struck dumb (v. 20). Despite Gideon's lack of faith and insistence on a second sign, God in mercy not only chose to withhold punishment but condescended to answer him.[13]

In other words, it is fine for you and I to seek revelation on what we do not know; and it is fine for us to request clarification on revelations already given (in scripture or even in our personal lives). However, it is never our place to tell God how to reveal or when to reveal. Nor should we be so faithless as to ask for a revelation, and then doubt the very revelation we requested and received. Our faith in God must include faith in His will, timing, and method of revealing His will to us.

In a similar vein, R. C. Trench suggested that this miracle highlights the weakness common to almost all humans: "Although the first sign was miraculous, it failed to satisfy Gideon. . . . Christian men are sometimes visited, often in answer to prayer, by some special providence which, at the moment, they feel is a direct interposition in their favour. But how soon after suggestions enter the mind that, after all, what has happened can be explained by the laws of ordinary providence."[14] One of the great weaknesses of man is to question the voice of God when it comes. We petition in faith, but then commonly doubt when the answer comes. Gideon's story reminds us of this weakness and our need to be more faith-filled when we ask for God's intervention.

One commentary on the miracles suggests that this story teaches humility. Gideon was a great warrior. Perhaps he had reason to trust in his own strength in fighting the Midianites. However, rather than believing that he was sufficient, Gideon evidenced his sense that "human strength alone" was not enough. Without the help and intervention of the Lord, this great warrior felt "utterly helpless."[15] Perhaps this miracle is a subtle reminder to each of us that we must never become arrogant or prideful; we must never get to the point that—because of our gifts—we feel self-sufficient; for surely, if we do, we will fall.

In his commentary, *All the Miracles of the Bible*, Herbert Lockyer suggested that this miracle prophetically points to the Jews' eventual rejection of Christ. He wrote:

> Many commentators point out that the dew is not only a mark of divine blessing and a symbol of his reviving grace but prophetic of His dealings with Israel as a nation. "Israel heretofore was the dry fleece, while the nations around were flourishing," says Fausset. "Now she is to become filled with the Lord's vigor, whilst the nations around lose it. The fleece becoming afterwards dry whilst the ground around was wet symbolizes Israel's rejection of the Gospel whilst the Gentile world is receiving the gracious dew. Afterwards Israel in its turn shall be as the dew to the Gentile world" (Micah 5:7).[16]

One author suggested that this miracle reminds us that God is in charge of the laws of nature and, if we have faith, He can use those for our benefit and in our behalf.[17]

This same commentary stated of this miracle, "Gideon and his men were going to engage the Midianites; could God distinguish between the small fleece of Israel and the vast floor of Midian? Yes, by this [Gideon] is made to know that He can."[18] In other words, we can see in this miracle evidence that God is aware of us individually. Amid the massive throng, our

Heavenly Father knows and cares about the one. In the words of the Lord, "Even the very hairs of your head are all numbered. Fear not therefore: ye are of more value than many sparrows" (Luke 12:7).

In the spirit of the aforementioned comment that the "Jews have seen [Gideon's fleece] as a symbol of their people, chosen (wet) or rejected (dry),"[19] Origen of Alexandria explained,

> The people of Israel [are] as a "fleece," with the surrounding ground being the Gentiles, while the dew that fell "upon the fleece" was the word of God written for this people alone. For only to Israel did the dew of the divine law arrive, whereas all the surrounding nations remained dry, none of them being infused with the moisture of divine locution. In the second sign, however, where he asked that the dew fall on the ground and that the fleece remain dry, a completely different rationale can be observed. We should see this entire people, who were gathered together from nations around the world, now having within themselves the divine dew; see them infused with the dew of Moses, irrigated by the word of the prophets; see them green from evangelical and apostolic water. The fleece, however, that is, the Jewish people, suffers aridity and dryness in the word of God, according to which it is written: "The children of Israel will be for a long time without king, without prince, without prophet; they will have no altar, no victim, no sacrifice" [Hosea 3:4].[20]

NOTES

1. The Israelites had fallen into bondage under the hands of the Midianites and, so, God sent an angel to Gideon, informing him that he had been called to be Israel's deliverer (Judges 6:11–24). In response to God's command, that night Gideon—accompanied by ten other men—went into his father's house and destroyed Joash's pagan altar, and set up an altar to Jehovah on that same spot. Then, on the newly constructed altar, they sacrificed a bull to Israel's God (Judges 6:25–32). This provoked the pending attack by the Midianites.

2. Robert G. Boling, *The Anchor Bible: Judges*, vol. 6 (New York: Doubleday, 1975), 141.

3. Ibid.

4. "The reason for the chance in the detail of the sign was probably Gideon's realization that the fleece would absorb a heavy dew much more readily than the rock of the threshing-floor and would therefore dry much less quickly when the sun arose." "Judges: An Introduction and Commentary," in Arthur E. Cundall and Leon Morris, *Judges and Ruth*, in *Tyndale Old Testament Commentaries* (Downers Grove, IL: InterVarsity Press, 1968), 109. See also Herbert Lockyer, *All the Miracles*

of the Bible: The Supernatural in Scripture—Its Scope and Significance (Grand Rapids, MI: Zondervan, 1961), 88.

5.   J. C. Cooper, *An Illustrated Encyclopaedia of Traditional Symbols* (London: Thames and Hudson, 1995), 50.

6.   E. John Hamlin, *Inheriting the Land: A Commentary on the Book of Joshua*, in *International Theological Commentary* (Grand Rapids, MI: Eerdmans, 1983), 96.

7.   Leland Ryken, James C. Wilhoit, and Tremper Longman III, eds., *Dictionary of Biblical Imagery* (Downers Grove, IL: InterVarsity Press, 1998), 207. See also Walter L. Wilson, *A Dictionary of Bible Types* (Peabody, MA: Hendrickson, 1999), 115.

8.   Cooper, *An Illustrated Encyclopaedia of Traditional Symbols*, 69.

9.   Hamlin, *Inheriting the Land: A Commentary on the Book of Joshua*, in *International Theological Commentary*, 104.

10.   "Judges: An Introduction and Commentary," in Cundall and Morris, *Judges and Ruth*, in *Tyndale Old Testament Commentaries*, 109.

11.   J. Reuben Clark Jr., in *Conference Report*, October 1953, 84.

12.   Richard C. Trench, *Miracles and Parables of the Old Testament* (Grand Rapids, MI: Baker Book House, 1959), 89.

13.   Herbert Wolf, "Judges," in Frank E. Gaebelein, ed., *The Expositor's Bible Commentary* (Grand Rapids, MI: Zondervan, 1994), 3:424.

14.   Trench, *Miracles and Parables of the Old Testament*, 88.

15.   See Lockyer, *All the Miracles of the Bible*, 88.

16.   Ibid.

17.   See Trench, *Miracles and Parables of the Old Testament*, 89.

18.   Ibid., 90.

19.   Hamlin, *Inheriting the Land: A Commentary on the Book of Joshua*, in *International Theological Commentary*, 104.

20.   Origen, "Homilies on Judges" 8.4, in John R. Franke, ed., *Joshua, Judges, Ruth, 1–2 Samuel*, in *Ancient Christian Commentary on Scripture* (Downers Grove, IL: InterVarsity Press, 2005), 157.

THE DEFEAT *of the* PHILISTINES *and* WATER *for* SAMSON

JUDGES 15:15–19

THE MIRACLE

In Lehi, Samson slew a thousand Philistine men, wielding only the jawbone of an ass.[1] Once he had done so, he renamed the place Ramath-lehi.

After this great feat of strength, Samson found that he was "sore athirst" (Judges 15:18); and so he prayed to God, saying, "You gave me this great victory, shall I now die of thirst and fall into the hands of my uncircumcised enemies?" (see Judges 15:18).

In response to Samson's prayer, God caused a spring to suddenly open up in a hallow, and water flowed out, quenching Samson's thirst and returning his strength. So, Samson named the spring En-hakkore—"the spring of him who calls" (Judges 15:19, footnote *a*).

BACKGROUND

Lehi is an unknown location situated somewhere along the Philistine frontier.[2] The name "Lehi" means "jaw" (or "cheek"); and, thus, it appears that the city was named "Lehi" after Samson slew a thousand Philistine men in that location, using the "jawbone" of an ass as his weapon.[3]

The name Ramath-lehi means "height of a jawbone" or "jawbone hill."[4] In antiquity, military incursions often took place on or at an elevated location.[5] Samson apparently names this location "jawbone's height" or "hill" because it was on that hill in Lehi that he slew the Philistines.

En-hakkore means "spring of one calling" or "spring of the caller"—meaning the spring of water for the one who called upon God.[6] Samson names the spring that miraculously appears, "En-hakkore," to commemorate the fact that there he prayed, and there God answered that prayer with divinely sent water.

The Hebrew word translated "hallow" (see KJV Judges 15:19) means a place where you "pound" something into dust, or where you "break in pieces" something you're grinding. In other words, the term basically implies a "mortar," as in a mortar and pestle.[7]

Regarding Samson's remarkable feat of slaying a thousand men single-handedly, one commentary suggests a possible alternate reading of the Hebrew term translated (in the KJV) as "thousand" (see Judges 15:15). The term may have originally meant "contingents," and, thus, implied a smaller number. The Hebrew word used here is ᵇ*lāpīm*, and is often translated as, "thousands, but also reflects,

> A complex semantic history. The word is etymologically connected with "head of cattle," like the letter aleph, implying that the term was originally applied to the village or population unit in a pastoral-agricultural society. From that it came to mean the quota supplied by one village or "clan" . . . for the military muster. "Originally the contingent was quite small, five to fourteen men [are mentioned] in the quota lists of Num 1 and 26. . . . Finally, the word became a technical term for a military unity of considerable size, which together with the use of the same word for the number "1,000" has obscured its semantic range.[8]

One commentator suggested that the recovery of this "old military usage" of the word, later obscured by the common use of the term for the number one thousand, "brings a popular story into the realm of probability."[9]

SYMBOLIC ELEMENTS

Samson is the central character of this miracle—though, perhaps God *should be.* Those who know his story know it to be an enigmatic one.

> No biblical character is more paradoxical than Samson (Judg 13–16). A figure of heroic physical strength, he is also a morally and emotionally weak person whose frailty is highlighted by the tragic pattern of the O[ld] T[estament] story. A Nazarite from birth, set apart to a holy lifestyle, Samson nonetheless specializes in liaisons with Philistine women of questionable repute. Though a national deliverer, Samson is a lone ranger who is never seen in the company of supportive companions. Strong of

body and weak of will, Samson is like the self-indulgent athlete who thrills on the field and appalls off it. In our imagination he is both prime specimen of physical strength (the biblical counterpart of Hercules) and helpless blind man. . . . Yet somewhere inside this flawed man was a passion for God. God noticed and used him. So did the author of [the book of] Judges, who gave Samson more space [in his book] than any other judge to send the implied message "if God could use this person, he can use anyone."[10]

While Samson's slaying of a large group of men is miraculous, the miracle described herein places its emphasis on the water that miraculously appeared from the rocky ground, and not on Samson's superhuman strength. Water is often associated with the Holy Spirit, and its sanctifying influence.[11]

Bands that bind (see Judges 15:13–14) are often symbols of hindrances or limitations that keep the wearer from succeeding at some mission or duty.[12]

The ass, from whence came Samson's weapon, may itself carry some potential symbolism. As noted previously, the donkey was a traditional symbol in antiquity for Israel's non-covenant, perhaps even apostate neighbors.[13]

APPLICATION AND ALLEGORIZATION

One of the obvious applications of this miracle is the truth that God intervenes on our behalf so very often in order to meet our every need. In this narrative, He intervened—giving Samson strength beyond his own to defeat his mortal enemies. Then He intervened a second time to provide water for Samson when his physical body was about to expire. As mortals, we're prone to see all of the events or times in our lives where we feel like God hasn't intervened. However, He intervenes on our behalf much more than we realize. It may be unwise to say in our prayers that we are "grateful for all of the blessings" God gives us. We certainly are not! Indeed, we don't notice most of them. We can be grateful that we are so richly blessed, but to say that we are grateful for all of them implies that we've noticed all of them, and the vast majority of what God does for you and me goes unnoticed. Even in the times when it appears that He has let us down, He may actually be intervening. Did my car break down because He had abandoned me? Or did it break down because God was caring for me and my family by keeping me off of the road and away from an otherwise inevitable fatal accident?

This miracle testifies that God was aware of Samson's various needs, and He met them. He is certainly aware of our needs, and meets them too.

As already noted, Samson is a paradoxical figure. He is so great, and yet so flawed. He believes strongly, but fails God miserably; and yet, God uses him in spite of his imperfections. In many ways, this story is a testament to God's willingness to use weak people to do great things. No bishop is perfect; no Relief Society president is perfect. But God is, and He can get His work done through imperfect vessels such as Samson, and you and me!

God gave water to Samson to quench his desperate thirst. Water often represents God's Spirit. When you and I are desperate for the things of God's Spirit, He will provide. Often those spiritual experiences come through very miraculous circumstances—just as the water came miraculously to Samson. He thirsted and pled for the water; and you and I must "hunger and thirst after righteousness" and plea for His divine aid, and we too "shall be filled with the Holy Ghost" (3 Nephi 12:6).

Leading up to this miracle, the men of Judah bound Samson with strong cords and took him to his enemies, the Philistines (see Judges 15:13). However, in an experience akin to that of Nephi of old (see 1 Nephi 7:17–18), "The Spirit of the Lord came mightily upon [Samson], and the cords that were upon his arms became as flax that was burnt with fire, and his bands loosed from off his hands" (Judges 15:14). It is evident from the text that Samson didn't burst the bands himself. Rather, God's Spirit came upon him, making the bands weak. Just as our Father in Heaven made weak that which bound Samson, He can make weak—and surmountable—the things that bind us. We can never remove these things on our own. However, if we will get and keep His Spirit with us, He will make it possible for us to overcome all things.

While Samson acknowledged God's hand in the miracle (see Judges 15:18), when the slaughter took place, he largely took credit, chanting, "With the jawbone of an ass, heaps upon heaps, with the jaw of an ass have I slain a thousand men" (Judges 15:16). The Moffatt translation of the Bible seems to offer a clearer sense of what Samson was saying:

> With the jaw-bone of an ass
> I have piled them in a mass!
> With the jaw-bone of an ass
> I have assailed assailants!

Thus we see that Samson initially bragged about his great accomplishment, and then, when he thought he was about to die of thirst, he gave God credit, saying, "*Thou* hast given this great deliverance" (Judges 15:18; emphasis added). One text on the miracle explained:

> Water was sent in a strange manner and to a strange place when Samson was nearly dying of thirst. He had just cast from him the jaw-bone of the ass with which God had given him a great deliverance, for with it he had slain a thousand men. He prided himself on his achievement, but soon learned his helplessness; and, as he cried to God, a little well of water sprang up . . . , and the great champion was refreshed.[14]

The author's point is that, though Samson felt a measure of pride in his great victory, God helped him to see that he was nothing more than a mortal man. Through the Lord's tutoring, Samson was reminded that—no matter how many feats of strength he made manifest, and no matter how many great things he had accomplished—he was yet mortal, and God could take his life at any point. This is a subtle reminder to you and me of our own need to manifest humility, and to recognize that even our greatest accomplishments are really the accomplishments of the Lord. If we are not humble, God may remind us of who is really in charge. And yet, with all of that said, God's grace and mercy are exhibited when He takes this boastful man, teaches him a lesson, and then pours out His mercy upon Samson by meeting his needs.[15]

When the armies of the Philistines approached the men of Judah, Samson's own people were—without hesitation—willing to turn him over to his enemies (see Judges 15:10–13). Their reaction brings to mind the lament of Job, "My kinsfolk have failed, and my familiar friends have forgotten me" (Job 19:14). The backstory of this miracle testifies to the fact that we can rely upon our God, but our friends and associates will often fail us.

With the understanding that the ass can be a symbol of non-covenant people, Caesarius of Arles explained:

> Now when Samson destroyed a thousand men with a jawbone from the body of an ass, the Gentiles were prefigured in the ass; for thus Scripture speaks concerning both Jews and Gentiles: "An ox knows its owner, and an ass its master's manger." [Isaiah 1:3] Before the [first] coming of Christ all the Gentiles were torn to pieces by the devil and lay scattered like dry bones from the ass's body, but when Christ the true Samson came [into mortality], he seized them all in his holy hands. He restored them by the hands of his power, and with them overcame his and our adversaries. Thus, we who had given our members to the devil before so that he might

kill us, were seized by Christ and became instruments of justice unto God.[16]

Caesarius argues that the ass is a symbol for the Gentiles who, prior to Christ's birth, were non-covenant people manipulated by the hand of the devil. However, after Christ came and established the gospel upon the earth, it was the Gentiles who fully embraced it and carried it to the world's greatest religion that it has become. Thus, they who were once the tools of Satan now take God's message to the world, as His instruments of justice.

NOTES

1.   Samson had angered the Philistines and, for this reason, they had "come up" against the men of Judah. Rather than defending Samson, his own people bound him and carried him to the Philistines. (See Judges 15:9–13.)

2.   Meir Lubetski, "Lehi," in David Noel Freedman, *The Anchor Bible Dictionary* (New York: Doubleday, 1992), 4:274. Robert Boling conjectures that it might be in the vicinity of Beth-shemesh. (See Robert G. Boling, *The Anchor Bible: Judges*, vol. 6 [New York: Doubleday, 1975], 238.)

3.   See Herbert Wolf, "Judges," in Frank E. Gaebelein, ed., *The Expositor's Bible Commentary* (Grand Rapids, MI: Zondervan, 1994), 3:472. See also Francis Brown, S. R. Driver, and Charles A. Briggs, *The Brown-Driver-Briggs Hebrew and English Lexicon* (Peabody, MA: Hendrickson Publishers, 1999), 534; Arthur E. Cundall and Leon Morris, *Judges and Ruth*, in *Tyndale Old Testament Commentaries* (Downers Grove, IL: InterVarsity Press, 1968), 171; Ellis T. Rasmussen, *A Latter-day Saint Commentary on the Old Testament* (Salt Lake City, UT: Deseret Book, 1994), 221; D. Kelly Ogden and Andrew C. Skinner, *Verse By Verse—The Old Testament Volume One: Genesis through 2 Samuel, Psalms* (Salt Lake City, UT: Deseret Book, 2013), 368.

4.   See Wolf, "Judges," in Gaebelein, *The Expositor's Bible Commentary*, 3:472; Brown, Driver, and Briggs, *The Brown-Driver-Briggs Hebrew and English Lexicon*, 928; Cundall and Morris, *Judges and Ruth*, in *Tyndale Old Testament Commentaries*, 172.

5.   See Boling, *The Anchor Bible: Judges*, 239.

6.   See Brown, Driver, and Briggs, *The Brown-Driver-Briggs Hebrew and English Lexicon*, 745 & 894; Boling, *The Anchor Bible: Judges*, 240; Cundall and Morris, *Judges and Ruth*, in *Tyndale Old Testament Commentaries*, 173.

7.   See Brown, Driver, and Briggs, *The Brown-Driver-Briggs Hebrew and English Lexicon*, 509; Cundall and Morris, *Judges and Ruth*, in *Tyndale Old Testament Commentaries*, 173. Boling thinks the Hebrew refers to a "rocky spring." (See Boling, *The Anchor Bible: Judges*, 239–40.)

8.   Ibid., 54–55. See also Cundall and Morris, *Judges and Ruth*, in *Tyndale Old Testament Commentaries*, 171.

9. See Boling, *The Anchor Bible: Judges*, 238.

10. Leland Ryken, James C. Wilhoit, and Tremper Longman III, eds., *Dictionary of Biblical Imagery* (Downers Grove, IL: InterVarsity Press, 1998), 756–57. See also Ogden and Skinner, *Verse By Verse—The Old Testament Volume One: Genesis through 2 Samuel, Psalms*, 368.

11. See Walter L. Wilson, *A Dictionary of Bible Types* (Peabody, MA: Hendrickson, 1999), 452–53; Ada R. Habershon, *Study of the Types* (Grand Rapids, MI: Kregel Publications, 1974), 143; Kevin J. Conner, *Interpreting the Symbols and Types*, rev. ed. (Portland, OR: City Bible Publishing, 1992), 23, 26, 179.

12. See Wilson, *A Dictionary of Bible Types*, 29.

13. Howard Eilberg-Schwartz, *The Savage in Judaism: An Anthropology of Israelite Religion and Ancient Judaism* (Bloomington, IN: Indiana University Press, 1990), 126–28; Ian Cairns, *Word and Presence: A Commentary on the Book of Deuteronomy*, in *International Theological Commentary* (Grand Rapids, MI: Eerdmans, 1992), 196.

14. Ada R. Habershon, *The Study of the Miracles* (London: Morgan & Scott, 1911), 61.

15. As one sixth-century source stated, "Although we had been dried up because of lack of the dew of God's grace, we merited to be changed into fountains and rivers. At that time Samson prayed and a fountain issued from the jawbone. This fact is clearly fulfilled in us, for the Lord himself said, 'He who believes in me, from within him there shall flow rivers of living water.'" (Caesarius of Arles, "Sermon" 119.4, in John R. Franke, ed., *Joshua, Judges, Ruth, 1–2 Samuel*, in *Ancient Christian Commentary on Scripture* [Downers Grove, IL: InterVarsity Press, 2005], 157.)

16. Caesarius of Arles, "Sermon" 119.4, in Franke, *Joshua, Judges, Ruth, 1–2 Samuel*, in *Ancient Christian Commentary on Scripture*, 156.

THE STATUE *of* DAGON
the FISH-GOD FALLS

THE MIRACLE

The Philistines captured the ark of the covenant and placed it in their temple, before the idol of their god, Dagon (see 1 Samuel 5:2). The next day, when the people arose and entered the temple, they found that the statue of Dagon had fallen upon its face; it lay prostrate before the ark. They picked up the statue, and put it back in its place (see 1 Samuel 5:3). However, the next day, when they entered the temple, they once again found the god prostrate before the ark of the covenant, but this time the head and hands of Dagon had been broken off and were lying on the threshold of the temple (see 1 Samuel 5:4). Because of this, when the priests or people enter the temple of Dagon, they step over the threshold instead of stepping on it (see 1 Samuel 5:5).

BACKGROUND

Dagon was a popular deity in Mesopotamia and Syria. A cult to him even appears in Palestine during the last half of the second millennium before Christ. In Ugaritic literature, Dagon is the father of Baal—the storm god.[1] No text from antiquity clearly identifies what kind of a god Dagon was, or what he presided over. Some have assumed that his name comes from the Semitic root for "fish," and, thus, he could have been a god of the maritime peoples. Others believe that his name was derived from a Semitic root for "grain," suggesting that he was a god of fertility—namely, the fertility of the land. It has also been suggested that his name comes from an Arabic root for "cloudy" or "raining," making him a storm-god, like his son,

Baal. It the end, although we can establish his popularity, we know nothing solid about his identity.[2]

Though Dagon would not traditionally be placed in the threshold of the temple—since that location represented the line between the sacred and the profane[3]—nevertheless, the fact that his head landed there made it sacred to his followers.[4] It is for this reason that they refused to step there after the statue had been destroyed.[5]

SYMBOLIC ELEMENTS

The ark represented the God of the Israelites. To place it in the temple of Dagon, before the statue of that deity, suggested that the Philistine god had ascendancy over the Israelite deity.[6]

The prostrate position is a symbol for subservience, adoration, and worship.[7] One prostrates one's self before God and kings.

Heads and hands often represent the thinking and doing of a being. To sever those implies that the power of the being to think and to act have been removed.[8] The removal of these parts of the body symbolizes the "decisive defeat of the enemy."[9]

APPLICATION AND ALLEGORIZATION

As noted before, the ark was a symbol for the presence of God. It was an outward sign of Jehovah. That being said, John Chrysostom noted,

> If you believe the place is holy because the law and the books of prophets are there, then it is time for you to believe that idols and the temples of idols are holy. Once, when the Jews were at war, the people of Ashdod conquered them, took their ark, and brought it into their own [Philistine] temple. Did the fact that it contained the ark make their temple a holy place? By no means! It continued to be profane and unclean, as the events straightway proved.[10]

In other words, the thing that makes the church or temple holy is the beliefs and behaviors of the people. If we do not live our religion, we negate the potential Spirit in each of those sacred domains. If we are members of the Lord's Church, but are pagan in our thoughts or deeds, we should not expect that we will feel God's Spirit as we attend church or the temple. Just as the ark couldn't make the temple of Dagon a holy place, the truths, ordinances, and priesthood keys of Mormonism can't make its meetings and sacred space powerful, except if those who worship therein have lives that match the message.

The narrative seems designed to teach a doctrinal truth about Israel's God; namely, that He is the only true and living God.

> The purpose of the initial episode (vv2–5) is to illustrate Yahweh's superiority to Dagon, a circumstance the preceding events [i.e., the Philistine capturing of the ark] have left in some doubt. It was the chief boast of Israel that her god was greater than the gods of other names, and here he is pitted against the god of her ancient rival. This is a contest of national deities: Yahweh the god of Israel against Dagon the god of Philistia and, insofar as the Philistines were the quintessential enemy, of every hostile nation. The showdown itself—for this is in fact a test of strength—takes place off stage, and we may not ask what wonders occur in the darkened temple. But the result is clear: the god of Israel has triumphed. His rival is humbled.[11]

Dagon lost his head and hands. His power was gone. He was in subjection to the one true God—Jehovah. Indeed, he appeared to worship, adore, and submit to Jehovah. As one commentator put it, by prostrating himself before the ark, "Dagon acknowledges the lordship of Yahweh."[12] The Philistines are left feeling humiliated because they brought their god a trophy of Jehovah, and he bows in humble adoration before it.[13] The severing of Dagon's head and hands not only highlights his loss of power, but implies that Jehovah has slain the Philistine god.

By way of application, one source pointed out that Jehovah appeared to have lost the battle with Dagon and the Philistines, owing to the fact that the ark had been captured by Israel's enemies. However, "Extraordinary as it may seem, it is Yahweh himself who has been guiding these events for purposes of his own."[14] In other words, seeming setbacks in the life of the Church—in days past or days present—may not be what they seem to be. Because God is in charge, and because He has a plan that is much larger than any of us can see, seeming reversals in the fate and life of the Church may actually be evidence that Jehovah is working to bring to pass His will in ways that we would not predict. Jesus was crucified, but that brought about the Atonement. The Three Witnesses—Oliver Cowdery, David Whitmer, and Martin Harris—were, for a time, disaffected, but that bolstered the credibility of their witness when they did not deny it during those years outside of the Church. What appears to you and I as potential failure may only be God setting things up for His next divine victory. As one text reminds us, "God works in silence and in secret against false systems of religion to give men a public and sudden proof of their folly."[15]

One source explained the message of this miracle in this way: "The destruction of *Dagon*, the heathen deity of the Philistines, proves God's power over all kinds of inanimate objects and shows that the supernatural can pervade all particles of matter."[16] In other words, you and I should believe that God's miracles are not simply limited to the spiritual realm. He has the ability to remove physical obstacles as well as spiritual ones. When there is a need, and when it is in accordance with God's will, we can expect that prayers for physical things will be answered just as readily as our prayers for spiritual things.

One commentary on the miracles suggested that the cutting off of the head and hands of Dagon was a prophetic foreshadowing of the cutting off of all idols at the coming of the Lord (see Isaiah 2:11–22). When the Lord returns, all false gods will be overturned, and all those who have worshipped idols will, like Dagon, be brought low.

As an indictment against the faithlessness of even the best of us, one text on the miracles suggested that this story testifies to the fact that *even a miracle* is often insufficient evidence to get people to acknowledge their God.

> Dagon testified by his first fall that "an idol is nothing in the world" (1 Cor. viii. 4). But the Philistines set him up again. His fall upon the threshold seemed to tell them that he was only fit to be *trodden under foot*, yet they venerated even the spot on which he fell. Israel, as a nation, was formed and sustained by miracle for forty years, and were delivered by miracle over and over again, yet God's testimony concerning them is, "Ephraim is joined unto idols (Hosea iv. 17). A delusion *proved* is not a delusion *abandoned*. Why? Because "men *love* darkness rather than light, because their *deeds* are evil" (John iii. 19).[17]

Regarding how this miracle relates to Christ's Atonement, Ada R. Habershon—in one of her many works on scriptural typology—penned this:

> It is remarkable that the Ark was three days in the temple of Dagon (1 Sam. v. 2–4). On two succeeding "morrows" we read that the idol lay on the ground before it, and on the second occasion it was broken in pieces. It is not likely that the Philistines allowed it to remain longer in the temple. . . . We cannot doubt that as Jonah's "three days and three nights in the whale's belly" were a type of the "three days and three nights" spent by the Lord Himself "in the heart of the earth" (Matt. xii. 40), so also were the three days spent by the Ark in the house of the fish-god.[18]

Notes

1. See Lowell K. Handy, "Dagon," in David Noel Freedman, *The Anchor Bible Dictionary* (New York: Doubleday, 1992), 2:2; Ronald F. Youngblood, "1 and 2 Samuel," in Frank E. Gaebelein, ed., *The Expositor's Bible Commentary* (Grand Rapids, MI: Zondervan, 1994), 3:601; P. Kyle McCarter, *The Anchor Bible: 1 Samuel*, vol. 8 (New York: Doubleday, 1980), 122.

2. See Handy, "Dagon," in Freedman, *The Anchor Bible Dictionary*, 2; McCarter, *The Anchor Bible: 1 Samuel*, 121–22; Youngblood, "1 and 2 Samuel," in Gaebelein, *The Expositor's Bible Commentary*, 3:601–2.

3. See J. C. Cooper, *An Illustrated Encyclopaedia of Traditional Symbols* (London: Thames and Hudson, 1995), 171.

4. See Gnana Robinson, *Let Us Be Like the Nations: A Commentary on the Books of 1 and 2 Samuel*, in *International Theological Commentary* (Grand Rapids, MI: Eerdmans, 1993), 35.

5. See Youngblood, "1 and 2 Samuel," in Gaebelein, *The Expositor's Bible Commentary*, 3:600. McCarter argues that, "The sacred character of the threshold of the house of Dagon is traced fancifully to holy contamination resulting from contact with the broken extremities of the cultic image." McCarter, *The Anchor Bible: 1 Samuel*, 122.

6. See McCarter, *The Anchor Bible: 1 Samuel*, 124.

7. See Leland Ryken, James C. Wilhoit, and Tremper Longman III, eds., *Dictionary of Biblical Imagery* (Downers Grove, IL: InterVarsity Press, 1998), 522; Youngblood, "1 and 2 Samuel," in Gaebelein, *The Expositor's Bible Commentary*, 3:600; McCarter, *The Anchor Bible: 1 Samuel*, 124; Kevin J. Todeschi, *The Encyclopedia of Symbols* (New York: Perigee Book, 1995), 47.

8. See Ryken, Wilhoit, and Longman, *Dictionary of Biblical Imagery*, 367; Merrill F. Unger, *Unger's Bible Dictionary* (Chicago: Moody Press, 1966), 461; Todeschi, *The Encyclopedia of Symbols*, 81.

9. Ryken, Wilhoit, and Longman, *Dictionary of Biblical Imagery*, 367.

10. John Chrysostom, "Discourses Against Judaizing Christians," 6.7.1, in John R. Franke, ed., *Joshua, Judges, Ruth, 1–2 Samuel*, in *Ancient Christian Commentary on Scripture* (Downers Grove, IL: InterVarsity Press, 2005), 215.

11. McCarter, *The Anchor Bible: 1 Samuel*, 124–25.

12. Ryken, Wilhoit, and Longman, *Dictionary of Biblical Imagery*, 339.

13. "Yahweh . . . has been brought there as a trophy of war. . . . It was the custom of the peoples of the ancient Near East to carry off the 'gods' of a conquered enemy and deposit them in place of worship at home. . . . Clearly a captured god was the final proof of the subjugation of a victim. . . . The god was the cohesive center of a fighting force and indeed of a people at large. Furthermore a captured god ensconced in the temple of a rival, insofar as earthly events were believed to mirror decisions made in heaven, might be regarded as palpable evidence of the

subordination of one divine being to another." (McCarter, *The Anchor Bible: 1 Samuel*, 125. See also Robinson, *Let Us Be Like the Nations*, 34.)

14. McCarter, *The Anchor Bible: 1 Samuel*, 125. See also Ada R. Habershon, *The Study of the Miracles* (London: Morgan & Scott, 1911), 152–53.

15. Richard C. Trench, *Miracles and Parables of the Old Testament* (Grand Rapids, MI: Baker Book House, 1959), 93.

16. Herbert Lockyer, *All the Miracles of the Bible: The Supernatural in Scripture—Its Scope and Significance* (Grand Rapids, MI: Zondervan, 1961), 96.

17. Trench, *Miracles and Parables of the Old Testament*, 94; emphasis in original.

18. Ada R. Habershon, *Types in the Old Testament* (Grand Rapids, MI: Kregel Publications, 1988), 129.

GOD SENDS THUNDER DOWN *upon the* PHILISTINES

1 SAMUEL 7:2–10

THE MIRACLE

It had been twenty years since the Israelites had regained the ark of the covenant from the Philistines. Samuel had told the people that, if they would fully turn their hearts to the true and living God and reject all "foreign gods," that He would deliver them out of the hands of the Philistines. The people trusted his word, and ceased all idolatry among them. Therefore, all Israel assembled themselves at Mizpeh, where Samuel interceded on their behalf with the Lord.

When the Philistines heard that the Israelites had assembled, they prepared to attack them. The Israelites began to fear, and said to Samuel, "Do not cease to pray to God on our behalf, that He might protect us from our enemies" (see 1 Samuel 7:8). In response, Samuel offered a young lamb as a sacrifice to God, on behalf of the people. As he did so, the Philistines drew near to attack. However, as they approached, God sent down incredibly loud thunder that frightened the Philistines so much that it threw them into a state of confused chaos and a full retreat, allowing the Israelites to pursue and smite them.

BACKGROUND

In 1 Samuel 7:3, Samuel commands the Israelites to "put away the strange gods and Ashtaroth from among you." In response, verse 4 says, "The children of Israel *did* put away Baalim and Ashtaroth" (emphasis added). Baal and Ashtaroth were the chief god and goddess in the Canaanite pantheon during that era of Israelite history.[1] They were each associated with pagan fertility rites. One scholar wrote that their association "with fertility, particularly as expressed in depraved sexual ritual at Canaanite shrines, made them especially abominable in the Lord's eyes."[2] It has been suggested that, in this passage, they may be representative not only of themselves, but of pagan deities generally.[3] One text states, "The nomadic Israelites who learned agriculture from the native Canaanites were tempted to ascribe agricultural fertility to Baal and Ashtaroth (cf. Hos. 2:5, 8) and to worship Yahweh with the cultic rituals of Baal (cf. Hos. 4:12–14; Amos 4:4–5; 5:5). The prophets of the [Old Testament] had to warn the Israelites against such negative syncretism."[4] If this is the case, these Israelites may well have been engaging it some very immoral practices in the name of God.[5]

Mizpeh means "watchtower," and was apparently a center of worship for the Israelites after they no longer had the tabernacle—prior to building Solomon's temple.[6] To this day, its exact location is in dispute.[7]

It is not clear exactly what the rite of pouring out water (described in 1 Samuel 7:6) is. It certainly has strong parallels to a similar rite performed in the temple during the Feast of Tabernacles (or Feast of Booths)—wherein the priest would take water from the pool of Siloam and pour it out on the great altar. (There, the water is a symbol of the outpouring of God's Spirit.) However, there are not enough details in the 1 Samuel narrative to say for certain what this rite is.[8] Based on the evidence, one commentator offered the following conjecture.

> What we have, then, is almost certainly a ritual of community purification. Its form may reflect pre-Exilic practice at Mizpeh, and some connection with the observance of the Feast of Booths and the Day of Atonement (or its antecedents) may be taken for granted. The details of the ceremony suggest a need for purification. . . . Probably the water libation . . . was supposed also to wash away guilt.[9]

Where the King James Version says, "The Lord thundered with a great thunder" (1 Samuel 7:10), the Hebrew reads more along the lines that He "thundered in a loud voice."[10]

The Jewish historian, Josephus, added a layer to the story not found in the biblical account. He wrote:

> God disturbed their enemies with an earthquake, and moved the ground under them to such a degree, that he caused it to tremble, and made them to shake, insomuch that by its trembling, he made some unable to keep their feet, and made them fall down, and, by opening its chasms, he caused that others should be hurried down into them; after which he

caused such a noise of thunder to come among them, and made fiery lightning shine so terribly round about them, that it was ready to burn their faces; and he so suddenly shook their weapons out of their hands, that he made them fly and return home naked.[11]

Josephus does not give a source for his additional details. It may be that a tradition had developed over time in Judaism, adding these additional layers to the story.

SYMBOLIC ELEMENTS

Baal and Ashtaroth are standard symbols for pagan deities, and also for immorality in its various forms.[12]

Water here seems to function as a symbol for the outpouring of God's Spirit, and its sanctifying and cleansing influence.[13]

As with any lamb that is sacrificed to Jehovah, in this passage, the "suckling" or young lamb appears to be a type for Christ and His atoning sacrifice on behalf of God's children.[14]

Thunder is regularly employed in scripture as a symbol of God's power and wrath.[15]

APPLICATION AND ALLEGORIZATION

In 1 Samuel 7:6, we learn that the Israelites fasted, as part of their repentance. The Church teaches fasting as one of its tenets. However, not many of us fast (outside of the first Sunday of the month) for our fallen and sinful natures. Leo the Great remarked:

> At one time the Hebrew people . . . , because of the offensiveness of their sins, were held under the heavy domination of the Philistines. In order to be able to overcome their enemies, . . . they restored strength of soul and body with a self-imposed fast. They . . . deserved that hard and wretched subjection because of neglect of God's commandments and the corruption of their lives, and . . . in vain did they fight with weapons unless they had first made war on their sins. By abstaining, therefore, from food and drink they imposed the penalty of severe punishment on themselves, and to conquer their enemies, they first conquered the enticement of gluttony in themselves. . . .
>
> We too, dearly beloved, situated as we are among many struggles and battles, if we wish to overcome our enemies in the same way, . . . may be healed by the same practice. Indeed, our situation is the same as theirs, seeing that they were attacked by bodily adversaries, we by spiritual enemies. If our spiritual enemies may be overcome by the correction of

our lives . . . , even . . . our bodily enemies will also give way to us. They will be weakened by our correction, since not their merits but our own sins made them onerous to us.

Therefore, dearly beloved, in order that we may be able to overcome our enemies, let us seek divine help by observing the commands of heaven, knowing that in no other way can we prevail over our foes except by prevailing over ourselves as well.[16]

We sin because we do not have self-mastery; we are controlled by our thoughts and our appetites. Fasting, properly done, can help us to put our bodies in subjection to our spirits. Thus, like the Israelites in this miracle, many of us would be benefited by fasting more often than once a month—and all of us could probably improve our fast-Sunday fast. Leo is correct; we are in a battle, and the enemy uses our bodies against us. Fasting is a gift from God, because it is one of the great tools for placing the body in subjection to the Spirit, and salvation can only come to those who master the flesh.

Idolatry is hardly a thing of the past. Our types of idols have changed, but the worship of false gods is alive and well. One commentary on this miracle states that, "[People of the twenty-first century] are no longer tempted to worship these fertility gods, Baal and Ashtaroth. But these 'fertility' gods are today replaced by the gods of 'consumerism,' . . . the gods of power, wealth, and consumer goods. Repentance in today's context would then mean putting away these Mammons, the gods of consumerism, and in serving only the LORD."[17] We are certainly a society that loves its false gods. While the commentator is correct that we do not worship Baal and Ashtaroth—it cannot be denied that the immorality of Canaanite worship seems alive and well in our hedonistic society of today. It may have a different meaning, but the worship of appetites, passions, and the human body are everywhere around us.

Commentators frequently point out that, though the Philistines were approaching, the Israelites did not stop their worship in order to address their pending concern. Rather, the prayers and sacrifice continued, as the Israelites desperately sought to keep their focus on the Lord. This may be a subtle invitation to you and I. When we are faced with our most difficult challenges in life, we cannot allow ourselves to become distracted. Rather, we should turn to the Lord and keep our focus on Him. Too often, when life gets difficult, people turn to outlets and vices to ease their pain and to distract themselves from the struggles at hand. However, this miracle reminds us that the wise and safe thing to do is to focus on the Lord, and let His thundering voice drown out the sound of our enemy—regardless of the form it takes.

In his work *Miracles and Parables of the Old Testament*, Richard Trench highlights the faith exhibited by Samuel:

> It is to be remarked that Samuel spoke confidently as to the issue of his prayer, "the Lord *shall* send," etc. Our prayers are [often] conditioned with "May be," or "May it please the Lord;" but this is not the form here used by the prophet. He arises to the same confidence as Moses expressed when he said, "I will spread abroad my hands unto the Lord, and the thunder shall cease." (Exodus 9:29)[18]

Prayers require faith. They require that the person who utters them truly believes in God's power and willingness to reveal or intervene. Samuel had that kind of faith, and the Lord heard his prayer. If we are to expect the miracles of Samuel in our lives, then we need to muster the faith of Samuel in our prayers.

Israel had sinned mightily before their God. They had not kept their covenants. In an effort to repent and return to full communion with their God, they did several things: they prayed, they washed, and they made sacrifice. Prayer is a symbol of their earnest pleas for forgiveness. The water poured out reminds us of ordinances that the Lord has revealed (e.g., baptism, the sacrament, the temple initiatory ordinances) that allow us to access His atoning blood, and, thereby, be cleansed from our sins. And the sacrificed lamb reminds us that it is in and through Christ's atoning blood—and in no other way—that you and I can be redeemed and regain communion with God (see Mosiah 3:17; Alma 38:9).

One early Christian source saw Samuel, in this miracle, as a symbol for Christ instructing Christians to do the works of God that they might gain salvation. He wrote,

> He said, "and prepare your hearts for the Lord and serve him alone, and he will deliver you from the hand of the Philistines." The Lord, the author of a new priesthood which is manifested in the flesh according to the order of Melchizedek, teaches the whole house of Israel, that is, the church made up of those desiring to see God, to remove from themselves the traditions of the Pharisees. He teaches them not only to prepare works (a thing that the law also taught) but also to prepare their very hearts for serving the Lord alone. He said, "You have heard that it was said by the fathers . . . I however, say to you," for in this way they would be able to be freed from all their enemies in the life to come.[19]

Samuel knew that his people had loved and followed other gods, and that this had harmed them spiritually. Jesus is certainly aware of our hearts, and our tendency to also follow after false gods, thereby harming our personal spirituality, and even the spirituality of the Church as a whole. When you and I allow ourselves to place the gods of this world before the true and living God, we rob ourselves and our posterity of significant blessings. Indeed, we make it harder for them and us to achieve salvation in the next life, and peace and joy in this one. In addition, when we as a people allow false gods to be part of our day-to-day lives, the Church is weakened. Outside observers are less impressed by the Church—less drawn to it. Conversions don't happen as they should. And the kingdom of God simply does not grow at the rate the Lord intended. Like ancient Israel, we must put away our false gods. On its most basic level, this miracle testifies to the reality that God protects the repentant from their enemies. If we sincerely sorrow for our sins, and earnestly desire to change, then His thunderous voice will be heard and felt in our lives—fighting off each of our enemies. When we wallow in our sins, we *are* enemies to God and ourselves. However, if we will turn to God in fasting, prayer, and personal sacrifice, the heavens will be opened and His hand will fight off the spiritual enemies that attack us and seek to keep us unworthy to commune with God.

NOTES

1. See Ronald F. Youngblood, "1 and 2 Samuel," in Frank E. Gaebelein, ed., *The Expositor's Bible Commentary* (Grand Rapids, MI: Zondervan, 1994), 3:608.
2. Ibid.
3. Youngblood, "1 and 2 Samuel," in Gaebelein, *The Expositor's Bible Commentary*, 3:608; P. Kyle McCarter, *The Anchor Bible: 1 Samuel*, vol. 8 (New York: Doubleday, 1980), 143.
4. Gnana Robinson, *Let Us Be Like the Nations: A Commentary on the Books of 1 and 2 Samuel*, in *International Theological Commentary* (Grand Rapids, MI: Eerdmans, 1993), 44.
5. Baldwin likewise notes, "This depraved cult had become widespread at this period, involving Israel in breaking the first and second commandments, and resulting in loathsome sexual indulgence. The Canaanite way of life was totally opposed to everything Israel should have stood for as the people of God, and therefore repentance, if it was to be credible, had to entail renunciation of this foreign worship." (Joyce G. Baldwin, *1 and 2 Samuel*, in *Tyndale Old Testament Commentaries* [Downers Grove, IL: InterVarsity Press, 1988], 78.)
6. McCarter, *The Anchor Bible: 1 Samuel*, 143.

7. See McCarter, *The Anchor Bible*, 144; Patrick M. Arnold, "Mizpeh," in David Noel Freedman, *The Anchor Bible Dictionary* (New York: Doubleday, 1992), 4:879–81.

8. See McCarter, *The Anchor Bible*, 144.

9. McCarter, *The Anchor Bible*, 144. See also Baldwin, *1 and 2 Samuel*, in *Tyndale Old Testament Commentaries*, 79. Robinson argues for a totally different meaning of this rite: "As a ritual act the people 'drew water and poured it out before the Lord' (1 Sam. 7:6). This was not a common act of sacrifice in Israel. The only other place where a similar instance occurs is 2 Sam. 23:16–17, where David pours out to the Lord the water which his men drew from the well of Bethlehem before capturing that city. Perhaps that was a ritual act to claim David's right over Bethlehem. The fact that the Philistines saw in Israel's gathering at Mizpeh a political act decided to attack perhaps suggests that Mizpeh was under Philistine occupation. Thus the Israelite gathering there and the Israelites' performance of this 'water-pouring ritual' were meant to assert Israel's claim over the land." (Robinson, *Let Us Be Like the Nations*, 45.)

10. See McCarter, *The Anchor Bible*, 145; Youngblood, "1 and 2 Samuel," in Gaebelein, *The Expositor's Bible Commentary*, 3:609; Robinson, *Let Us Be Like the Nations*, 46.

11. Josephus, "Antiquities of the Jews," bk. 6, ch. 2:2, in *The Complete Works of Josephus*, William Whiston, trans. (Grand Rapids, MI: Kregel Publications, 1981), 125.

12. See Leland Ryken, James C. Wilhoit, and Tremper Longman III, eds., *Dictionary of Biblical Imagery* (Downers Grove, IL: InterVarsity Press, 1998), 339.

13. See Ryken, Wilhoit, and Longman, *Dictionary of Biblical Imagery*, 931; J. C. Cooper, *An Illustrated Encyclopaedia of Traditional Symbols* (London: Thames and Hudson, 1995), 189.

14. See Ryken, Wilhoit, and Longman, *Dictionary of Biblical Imagery*, 484; J. C. Cooper, *An Illustrated Encyclopaedia of Traditional Symbols* (London: Thames and Hudson, 1995), 94.

15. See Ryken, Wilhoit, and Longman, *Dictionary of Biblical Imagery*, 339, 869; J. C. Cooper, *An Illustrated Encyclopaedia of Traditional Symbols* (London: Thames and Hudson, 1995), 172.

16. Leo the Great, "Sermon" 39:1–2, in John R. Franke, ed., *Joshua, Judges, Ruth, 1–2 Samuel*, in *Ancient Christian Commentary on Scripture* (Downers Grove, IL: InterVarsity Press, 2005), 222.

17. Robinson, *Let Us Be Like the Nations*, 44.

18. Richard C. Trench, *Miracles and Parables of the Old Testament* (Grand Rapids, MI: Baker Book House, 1959), 95; emphasis added.

19. Bede the Venerable, "Four Books on 1 Samuel," 1.7, in Franke, *Joshua, Judges, Ruth, 1–2 Samuel*, in *Ancient Christian Commentary on Scripture*, 221–22.

JEROBOAM'S HAND
Is WITHERED

1 KINGS 13:1–6

THE MIRACLE

Jeroboam stood by the altar to make an offering when a man of God, who had come to Bethel from Judah, uttered a prophecy. He predicted that Josiah would offer human sacrifice on that very altar—sacrificing the lives of the priests of Beth-el upon the altar. As a sign that this would indeed happen, the man of God predicted that the altar that Jeroboam had set up would split in half, and the ashes from the sacrifices that had been offered thereon would fall to the ground (see 1 Kings 13:1–3).

When King Jeroboam heard this, he cried out against the prediction, and stretched forth his hand toward the man of God, saying, "Seize him!" At that very moment, Jeroboam's hand shriveled up so that he could not move it, and the altar split in two (see 1 Kings 13:4–5).

Jeroboam begged the man of God, "Pray for me that my hand may be restored." So the man of God "besought the Lord" on the king's behalf, and his hand was restored to its normal form and function (see 1 Kings 13:6).

BACKGROUND

Jeroboam was not simply the king, but the leader of a false sacrificial cult that had defiled the altar at Beth-el, and that challenged God's approved system of offerings and sacrifices.[1] It was a mere shadow of the truth, and a mockery of it. The Jewish historian Josephus wrote of him, "He built an altar before the heifer, and undertook to be high priest himself." He added, "[Jeroboam] went up to the altar, with his own priests about him."[2]

The "man of God" (or prophet) in this miracle is left unnamed in the biblical account. However, Josephus suggested that his name was Jadon or Yadon.[3] Various commentators connect Jadon (Yadon) with the prophet Iddo in the book of 2 Chronicles (see 2 Chronicles 13:22).[4] Contrary to what one might expect, the miraculous punishment of King Jeroboam, followed by his equally miraculous healing, did not cause him to turn from his evil ways (see 1 Kings 13:4–10, 33). Which only goes to show that miracles do not have converting power (see D&C 63:9). Jeroboam was anxious to have his hand restored, but wasn't the least bit concerned about the "withering up of his moral nature."[5] Tragic! And, unfortunately, not rare!

SYMBOLIC ELEMENTS

According to the law of Moses, ashes of sacrifices were to be carried off to a clean and authorized place for their proper disposal (see Leviticus 1:16; 4:12; 6:10–11). The fact that here they were "poured out" from the altar onto the ground—along with the fact that the altar was destroyed—symbolically suggests that the sacrificial cult of Jeroboam was rejected by God. It was invalid, and God was highlighting that by this unexpected miracle.[6]

Altars are often symbols for God and Christ.[7] In this case, the altar is used for false religious worship. Thus, one text suggested, "Here we may think of a false altar which is a type of the religious plans and schemes of men wherein they hope to appease the god of their imagination, and to obtain his favor even though what they are doing is not Scriptural."[8]

The hand is a traditional symbol for what one does or pursues.[9] Thus, one commentator suggested, "The shriveled hand (Heb[rew] . . . 'dried up') would be taken as a sign of divine disfavor (Z[echariah] 11:17), just as the healing was a sign that the man of God was an authentic messenger."[10]

APPLICATION AND ALLEGORIZATION

Jeroboam performs unauthorized acts at an altar. Thus, his hand—symbolic of his works—is withered. One of the miracle's messages seems to be that when you and I do things that are unauthorized in God's sight, they will ultimately wither or dry up. God may allow us to function falsely for a time—as He did Jeroboam—but, like the corrupt king, we too will see a day when our power and works will be brought to an end. God will only tolerate sin for so long before He cuts the sinner off from the powers that he uses to accomplish his evil works. "All human power and skill engaged against God will wither."[11]

On a similar note, it may be pointed out that just as Jeroboam stretched forth his hand to stop the man of God, there are others who seek to thwart the work of His kingdom. "Jeroboam's outstretched hand was the type of all human opposition to God's rule, especially the opposition of the rulers of the world. Its withering was the exposition of 'No weapon formed against thee shall prosper' (Isa. Liv. 17); 'He that sitteth in the heavens shall laugh' (Psa. Ii. 4, &c.)."[12]

One commentary on this miracle suggested that Jeroboam's curse should be a warning to each of us. "This sudden affliction proves that the God who made the body can suspend the use of any of its members when He deems fit."[13] Admittedly, God seldom responds in this way in our day—though perhaps it would be good if He did. Certainly some deserve such a rebuke!

Of this miracle, one source states, "The prophet foretells, 350 years before the occurrence took place, the very name of the king who should terribly avenge the calf worship of Bethel."[14] In other words, this miracle is a testament to the prophetic mantle. It witnesses that God's prophets can and do see the future. While they may be circumspect in what they share with us today, as it was in times past, God's mantle and their priesthood keys allow them to see as seers see, and know what prophets know.

Seeing this miracle as an indictment against the false religious practices that have crept into Christianity, one commentator wrote, "How we should bless Him that we live in an age of grace, and that He does not deal with us in supernatural judgment when we add our own inventions to His worship!"[15] It is true that much of what God has given has been corrupted, and much of His appropriate religious practice has been supplanted by the rites and rituals of men. Ada Habershon explained,

> God can only be worshipped in His own appointed way. In His grace He does not now strike men with paralysis or leprosy, when they add their inventions to His worship, or when they strive to come into His presence presumptuously; but it may be that there is a spiritual counterpart, and that those who now transgress are paralyzed and thrust forth from His service. Judgment *does* fall upon the house of God, as the Apostle Paul shows in another connection: "For this cause many are weak and sickly among you, and many sleep."[16]

Those in the "true Church" can be purged, if needs be, just as readily as those in some false religion. God expects the Saints to be saintly. And if they are not, He will take away their power and authority, and "Amen to the priesthood or the authority of that man" (D&C 121:37).

Jeroboam's response to his divinely crippled hand is instructive. One text suggested, "We should pray for deliverance, not only from our present calamity, but from the sin which brought it on. Jeroboam prayed that his hand might be cured. It was cured—and yet he went on offending God till he had sealed the ruin of his family."[17] When seeming tragedy strikes—as a result of our sinful choices—rather than praying for God to remove the devastating circumstance we find ourselves in, we should pray that He helps us to overcome the character flaw that has led us down that road. We are ever concerned about the pain and consequences of our sins, but too many are *not* concerned about the *cause* of them.

Ambrose of Milan saw in this miracle a sign and symbol of God's grace—of His earnest desire to forgive us when He sees the smallest sign of repentance in our heart.

> But when in the temple of our God, that wicked king Jeroboam took away the gifts that his father had laid up and offered them to idols on the holy altar, did not his right hand, which he stretched, wither, and his idols, which he called on, were not able to help him? Then, turning to the Lord, he asked for pardon, and at once his hand, which had withered by sacrilege, was healed by true religion. So complete an example was there set forth in one person, both of divine mercy and wrath, when he who was sacrificing suddenly lost his right hand but when penitent received forgiveness.[18]

Ambrose's suggestion is that God wants to forgive, and does so readily. We know the rest of the story; namely, that Jeroboam ultimately backslid, and turned back to his sins. However, we also know that God knew that he would do that, but, nevertheless, forgave him anyway when he did show some sign of repentance. Thus, by way of application, God seeks to forgive you and I when He sees even a sliver of repentance. He certainly knows that we will struggle in the future, but forgives us anyway—and quickly—when we try to repent of our weaknesses and sins. Thus, this miracle can be seen as a testament to the fact that God is indeed grace-filled and loving. As the Qur'an says time and again, "God is oft-forgiving [and] most merciful" (see Surah 2:173; 24:22; 39:53). This miracle can be seen as a testament to that fact.

NOTES

1.   Richard D. Patterson and Hermann J. Austel, "1 and 2 Kings," in Frank E. Gaebelein, ed., *The Expositor's Bible Commentary* (Grand Rapids, MI: Zondervan, 1994), 4:118.

2. Josephus, "Antiquities of the Jews," bk. 8, ch. 8:5, in *The Complete Works of Josephus*, William Whiston, trans. (Grand Rapids, MI: Kregel Publications, 1981), 35.

3. Ibid.

4. See Patterson and Austel, in "1 and 2 Kings," in Gaebelein, *The Expositor's Bible Commentary*, 4:120; Donald J. Wiseman, *1 and 2 Kings*, in *Tyndale Old Testament Commentaries* (Downers Grove, IL: InterVarsity Press, 1988), 146.

5. Richard C. Trench, *Miracles and Parables of the Old Testament* (Grand Rapids, MI: Baker Book House, 1959), 104.

6. See Israel Wolf Slotki, *Kings*, in *Soncino Books of the Bible* (London: The Soncino Press, 1978), 98; Patterson and Austel, "1 and 2 Kings," in Gaebelein, *The Expositor's Bible Commentary*, 4:118–19; Mordechai Cogan, *The Anchor Bible: 1 Kings*, vol. 10 (New York: Doubleday, 2001), 368; Wiseman, *1 and 2 Kings*, in *Tyndale Old Testament Commentaries*, 146.

7. See Walter L. Wilson, *A Dictionary of Bible Types* (Peabody, MA: Hendrickson, 1999), 9–11; Hugh T. Henry, *Catholic Customs and Symbols* (Cincinnati, OH: Benziger Brothers, 1925), 45; J. C. Cooper, *An Illustrated Encyclopaedia of Traditional Symbols* (London: Thames and Hudson, 1995), 11; Leland Ryken, James C. Wilhoit, and Tremper Longman III, eds., *Dictionary of Biblical Imagery* (Downers Grove, IL: InterVarsity Press, 1998), 21.

8. Wilson, *A Dictionary of Bible Types*, 10.

9. See Alonzo L. Gaskill, *The Lost Language of Symbolism: An Essential Guide for Recognizing and Interpreting Symbols of the Gospel* (Salt Lake City, UT: Deseret Book, 2003), 43–45; Ryken, Wilhoit, and Longman, *Dictionary of Biblical Imagery*, 362; Patterson and Austel, "1 and 2 Kings," in Gaebelein, *The Expositor's Bible Commentary*, 4:121.

10. Wiseman, *1 and 2 Kings*, in *Tyndale Old Testament Commentaries*, 146.

11. Trench, *Miracles and Parables of the Old Testament*, 104.

12. Ibid.

13. Herbert Lockyer, *All the Miracles of the Bible: The Supernatural in Scripture— Its Scope and Significance* (Grand Rapids, MI: Zondervan, 1961), 107.

14. Trench, *Miracles and Parables of the Old Testament*, 103.

15. Lockyer, *All the Miracles of the Bible*, 107.

16. Ada R. Habershon, *The Study of the Miracles* (London: Morgan & Scott, 1911), 179; emphasis added.

17. Trench, *Miracles and Parables of the Old Testament*, 105.

18. Ambrose, "Concerning Virgins," 2.5.38, in Marco Conti, ed., *1–2 Kings, 1–2 Chronicles, Ezra, Nehemiah, Esther*, in *Ancient Christian Commentary on Scripture*: (Downers Grove, IL: InterVarsity Press, 2008), 84.

ELIJAH IS FED *by* RAVENS

1 KINGS 17:4–6

THE MIRACLE

Elijah, the Tishbite prophesied to Ahab that there would be neither rain nor dew in Gilead, except if he (the prophet) commanded it (see 1 Kings 17:1).

Then Elijah received a revelation from God, telling him to go to the brook Cherith, which was east of the Jordan River. Elijah was to "hide" there for a period of time. There, God promised, He would send ravens to feed Elijah bread and meat, morning and evening. And the prophet would also have the brook to drink from (see 1 Kings 17:2–4).

Elijah did as God commanded, and God was true to His word, providing (via the ravens) meat and bread twice daily, and water from the brook (see 1 Kings 5–6).

BACKGROUND

While the biblical account does not offer any background on Elijah's sudden impression to bring a multiyear drought upon Ahab, the Talmud offers the following explanation:

> Elijah's first appearance in the period of the Kings was his meeting with Ahab in the house of Hiel, the Beth-elite, the commander-in-chief of the Israelitish army, whom he was visiting to condole with him for the loss of his sons. God Himself had charged the prophet to offer sympathy to Hiel, whose position demanded that honor be paid him. Elijah at first refused to seek out the sinner who had violated the Divine injunction against rebuilding Jericho, for he said that the blasphemous talk of such evil-doers always called forth his rage. . . . As the prophet entered the general's house, . . . Hiel . . . acknowledged that he had been justly afflicted with Joshua's curse against him who should rebuild Jericho.

Ahab mockingly asked him: "Was not Moses greater than Joshua, and did he not say that God would let no rain descend upon the earth, if Israel served and worshipped idols? There is not an idol known to which I do not pay homage, yet [I and all those who follow me] enjoy all that is goodly and desirable. Dost thou believe that if the words of Moses remain unfulfilled, the words of Joshua will come true?" Elijah rejoined: "Be it as thou sayest: 'As the Lord, the God of Israel liveth, before whom I stand, there shall not be dew nor rain these years, but according to my word.'"[1]

According to the Jewish tradition, Ahab gloated that he was a man who had broken all of the commandments against idolatry, and yet nothing bad had happened to him. Elijah, hearing this, ensures that such is no longer the case.

Calling Elijah a "Tishbite" simply designates that he was from a place called Tishbe. The texts suggests that Tishbe is in Gilead. However, "no town of Tishbe in Gilead is attested in ancient sources."[2] Thus, it is not exactly certain where he hailed from.

King Ahab was the son of Omri, and thus, his successor. He reigned in northern Israel during the ninth century, and is singled out in scripture as one of the worst kings of the northern kingdom (see 1 Kings 16:33; 2 Kings 21:3, 13; Micah 6:16).[3] In 1 Kings 16:29–17:1, it suggests that the drought spoken of in this miracle was a direct result of Ahab's idolatry. "Elijah emerges from the wilderness to denounce Ahab for polluting the monotheism of Israel."[4]

In the King James Version, Elijah swears, "As the Lord God of Israel liveth" (1 Kings 17:1). The Hebrew phrases this, "By the life of Jehovah."[5] Swearing by the life of God suggests that this cannot be fulfilled. In other words, God can't die and, thus, this prophecy cannot fail. "The invocation of the deity sanctions the oath, asserting the truth of the words spoken."[6]

This miracle speaks of a severe drought in Gilead during the days of Ahab and Elijah. Drought would not be an infrequent occurrence in Israel. However, dewfall would be known year-round and would be particularly abundant on the coastal plain, helping to sustain crops during the summer months. So, the total cessation of all moisture—including dew—would be seen as evidence of "divine visitation" upon Ahab and his people.[7] Similarly, drinking from the *wadi*, or brook, also suggests a miracle, as desert wadis are typically dry most of the year, and certainly would be during a drought.[8] 1 Kings 18:1 suggests that the drought Elijah brought lasted around three years.[9]

The wisdom of Ahab's worship of storm gods, such as Baal, is directly challenged by the drought. Baal is the pagan deity that can provide rain. Here, Elijah shows that Baal is nothing; he can't lift this plague sent down by Jehovah. Thus, Jehovah is proven to be the true and living God, and Baal is shown to be powerless and incapable of intervening on behalf of those who foolishly worship him.[10]

In the narrative, God tells Elijah that He is sending him to the brook or *wadi* of Cherith to "hide" (1 Kings 17:3).[11] However, the story at hand doesn't explain what he is hiding from. Yet Obadiah's statement (in 1 Kings 18:10, 17) suggests that King Ahab sought out Elijah to take his life because he perceived the prophet as the source of Israel's troubles. "Instead of blaming the disease, their rebellion against God, [Ahab and Jezebel] burned with hate against the physician."[12] While Ahab and Elijah do not appear to be enemies at the beginning of the drought, it appears that God—in His foreknowledge—sent Elijah away (once the drought started) because He knew that Ahab and his wife would be angered by it and would eventually seek out the prophet in order to slay him, as a means of ending the drought and Israel's woes.[13]

SYMBOLIC ELEMENTS

As with all prophets of God, Elijah's life and ministry typify Christ's life and ministry. For example, we are told that the elements obeyed Elijah's every word (see 1 Kings 17:1). We learn that he multiplied a meager amount of food in order to feed the faithful (see 1 Kings 17:9–16). Elijah also raised the dead (see 1 Kings 17:17–24). He fasted for forty days and nights (see 1 Kings 19:8). The prophet passed his authority on to his appointed successor (see 1 Kings 19:19–21). At the conclusion of his earthly ministry, he ascended miraculously into heaven in the sight of his followers (see 2 Kings 2:11). In addition, Elijah was promised to return in the latter-days (see Malachi 4:5–6). Each of these elements of the prophet's life have a parallel in the life of Christ.[14] It is no wonder that the theophoric name, "Elijah," means "My God is Jehovah."[15]

Traditionally, the raven is a negative symbol. "In ancient Mesopotamia, ravens were considered ominous creatures."[16] Ravens are scavengers that often symbolize evil, mortification, corruption, sin, wandering, unrest, uncleanliness, carrion, impurity, destruction, deceit, and death.[17] It isn't evident why, in this narrative, they are employed.[18] Could it suggest that, in the end, the wicked will serve the righteous? Or could it imply that even in such dark and ominous times (such as a deathly famine), that God still overrides the wicked and evil on behalf of the holy? Biblical typologist, Walter

Wilson, suggested this of the raven (in 1 Kings 17:4): "This is a type of . . . an unsaved person, who naturally is compelled to minister to God's servant against his own nature."[19]

Metaphorically, rain (or dew) is frequently associated with outpourings of the Holy Ghost, revelations, blessings, heavenly influences, as well as sanctification, God's grace, etc. (see Deuteronomy 11:11; 32:2; Ezekiel 36:25–26; John 3:5; 7:37–39; 1 John 5:6–8).[20]

As noted above, this drought lasted somewhere between three and three and a half years. The number three is a commonly employed symbolic number in scripture. Indeed, next to the number seven, "three" is the most common symbolic number in holy writ.[21] When the number three appears in scripture, it frequently serves to emphasize divine involvement, backing, or influence.[22] Thus, a drought of three years would be a drought sent by God.[23]

APPLICATION AND ALLEGORIZATION

As an application of this miracle, one commentary suggested that this is really a message—not about drought—but about how God takes care of His own. "Note how the Lord intervenes to provide food and comfort for his messenger to enable him to continue his work. For this he uses humans ([1 Kings 17] v. 15), nature (birds, [1 Kings 17] v. 6) and messengers or angels ([1 Kings] 19:4–8). God similarly intervened for his people at creation (Ge. 1:29–30; 9:3), in their desert wanderings (Ex. 16:31–35) and for Jesus Christ himself (Mt. 4:11)."[24] God cares for us physically as well as spiritually and, if we "seek . . . first the kingdom of God, and his righteousness," He will make sure all other necessary things are "added unto" us (Mathew 6:33).[25] Time and again, God provides for His covenant people. That help is most readily available when they are faithful to him.

A drought struck the land, divinely sent as it was. Ahab and his people suffered, but so did God's prophet. In this, there is a subtle reminder: "It is no unusual thing with God to suffer His own children to be enwrapped in the common calamities of offenders."[26] We should not assume that, just because we are faithful members of the Church, we will be spared the trials sent upon the wicked. Even the covenant people are called to bear *some* of what this fallen world brings. Certainly Elijah's experience was less painful than that of the idolatrous Israelites. But, nonetheless, he suffered too. The gospel doesn't take away *all* of the trials, but it does tend to make them bearable.

One popular text on the miracles offers this application: "Over and over, God uses His control of this world to show forth His power. Are we open to the message? Or will it take a three-year drought to get our attention?"[27] There are signs of the times, and evidences of God's existence, all around us. Does our love for the world prevent us from seeing those signs and evidences? Does God need to bring us to our knees—as He did Ahab—before we will earnestly turn to Him? Even if you consider yourself a faithful Latter-day Saint, are there idols you continue to cling to? Are there small things that you are holding back from the Lord? If we do not wish to live our lives in a spiritually drought-stricken state, we must turn our lives and hearts fully over to the Lord.

Famine or draught is a common symbol for apostasy (see Deuteronomy 11:16–17; Revelation 12:6). Hence, one text suggested that this miracle highlights how you and I—even if there is apostasy all around us—can be protected and spiritually nourished by God. Apostasy is an individual, personal matter. Even in cases of mass apostasy (such as in the Kirtland era), each person had to choose for themselves to leave the faith. Thus, just as apostasy was rampant in Israel in Elijah's day, but the prophet remained faithful and spiritually nourished, you and I can keep our covenants and have the Spirit of the Lord, no matter what those around us (family or friends) are doing.[28]

At first, the command to go into the wilderness and be fed by ravens seems quite miraculous, even dramatic. But then, as one thinks about what the Lord is commanding, it actually seems quite revolting. Birds acquiring carrion, clearly from other dead animals, and then dropping that off from their mouths to your feet.

> The proverb says, "Trust in the Lord with all thine heart; and lean not unto thine own understanding. In all thy ways acknowledge him, and he shall direct thy paths" (Proverbs 3:5–6). As seekers after the face of Christ, if instead of trusting the Lord to provide for us, we allow our minds to be preoccupied with worry and vain and frantic maneuvering concerning our temporal needs, then we only prolong the trials and difficulties of our wilderness journey. . . . God is not only capable but also willing and anxious to assist in providing us with exactly what we need in order to survive His wilderness. But in the Lord's wilderness school the key is sufficiency, not excess. While Elijah was in the wilderness the Lord commanded him, "Thou shalt drink of the brook; and I have commanded the ravens to feed thee there. So [Elijah] went and did according unto the word of the Lord. . . ." (1 Kings 17:4–6).
>
> These were not the kinds of meals Elijah might have chosen, yet they seem to have been sufficient, and they were granted in a miraculous manner.[29]

As an application, this miracle reminds us that we need to trust God and His plan for us. That includes being willing to make the sacrifices He calls upon us to make. At times, in most of our lives, He will call us into the wilderness. He will ask us to do hard and even undesirable things. However, if we'll trust in Him—His will and His ways—He will make it possible for us to accomplish what He is asking, and endure what He is calling us to endure. There is purpose in all that God requires of us. And the distasteful requests—such as the one that Elijah was required to engage in—are sanctifying and ultimately empowering.

On a related note, the miracle highlights that Elijah was forced to eat food from the mouth of birds, and drink water from a hole in the ground. While this sounds like filthy fodder, it is to be remembered that those in Ahab's kingdom are suffering for want of food and water.[30] Thus, perhaps this miracle can also be seen as a call to be grateful even in your trials. When you have less than you want, there are always others who have even less. When you have something different than what you want, there are always others who have nothing.

One commentator saw in this miracle a statement about the divine purpose of animal and plant life. Thus, in Genesis 1:28, we read that man was created to, "Have dominion over the fish of the sea, and over the fowl of the air, and over every living thing that moveth upon the earth." And in the Psalms we are told that God has "Put all things under [the] feet" of man (Psalm 8:6). The divine command for the ravens to serve Elijah has been seen as a symbol for the reality that God has given all these things to His children to be their servants. We must be wise stewards of them, and not abuse them. But they are given of God for the fulfillment of our righteous needs. It has been said, "They were intended to be [man's] servants, and although he has forfeited his right to rule *them* by refusing to acknowledge God's right to rule *him*, yet, when he returns to his allegiance, he may expect in some degree, to return to his position as king of the creatures beneath him, and to be ministered to by them."[31]

As an additional application, one text drew from the miracle of the ravens feeding Elijah, "Our inferiors may, in the hands of God, be greater blessings than our equals or superiors. Ravens were better friends to Elijah at this time than the king of Israel or any of his subjects."[32] Ironically, whom do men treat the worst? Those they deem to be their inferiors. And who do they treat with the most regard? Those they *perceive* as being their equals. Perhaps there is a lesson in this miracle as to who really deserves our respect, and who it is that is most inclined to serve us in our hour of need.

NOTES

1. Louis Ginzberg, *The Legends of the Jews* (Philadelphia: The Jewish Publication Society of America, 1967), 4:195–96. Ginzberg is summarizing the Talmudic tractate Sanhedrin 113a.

2. Mordechai Cogan, *The Anchor Bible: 1 Kings*, vol. 10 (New York: Doubleday, 2001), 425. See also Jerome T. Walsh, "Tishbe," in David Noel Freedman, *The Anchor Bible Dictionary* (New York: Doubleday, 1992), 6:578; Ellis T. Rasmussen, *A Latter-day Saint Commentary on the Old Testament* (Salt Lake City, UT: Deseret Book, 1994), 292.

3. See Winfried Thiel, "Ahab," in Freedman, *The Anchor Bible Dictionary*, 1:100.

4. Kenneth L. Woodward, *The Book of Miracles: The Meaning of the Miracle Stories in Christianity, Judaism, Buddhism, Islam* (New York: Simon & Schuster, 2000), 61.

5. See Cogan, *The Anchor Bible: 1 Kings*, 425.

6. Ibid.

7. See Cogan, *The Anchor Bible: 1 Kings*, 425–26; Donald J. Wiseman, *1 and 2 Kings*, in *Tyndale Old Testament Commentaries* (Downers Grove, IL: InterVarsity Press, 1988), 164.

8. See Cogan, *The Anchor Bible: 1 Kings*, 426.

9. Luke 4:25 suggests that the drought was about three and one half years long.

10. See Richard D. Patterson and Hermann J. Austel, "1 and 2 Kings," in Frank E. Gaebelein, ed., *The Expositor's Bible Commentary* (Grand Rapids, MI: Zondervan, 1994), 4:138. See also Herbert Lockyer, *All the Miracles of the Bible: The Supernatural in Scripture—Its Scope and Significance* (Grand Rapids, MI: Zondervan, 1961), 109.

11. The *wadi*, or brook, of Cherith, east of Jordan, has yet to be identified. See Cogan, *The Anchor Bible: 1 Kings*, 426; Israel Wolf Slotki, *Kings*, in *Soncino Books of the Bible*, 123; D. Kelly Ogden and Andrew C. Skinner, *Verse By Verse—The Old Testament Volume One: Genesis through 2 Samuel, Psalms* (Salt Lake City, UT: Deseret Book, 2013), 2:33–34.

12. Clovis Gillham Chappell, *The Cross Before Calvary* (New York: Abingdon Press, 1960), 47.

13. See Cogan, *The Anchor Bible: 1 Kings*, 426; Patterson and Austel, "1 and 2 Kings," in Gaebelein, *The Expositor's Bible Commentary*, 4:138; Israel Wolf Slotki, *Kings*, in *Soncino Books of the Bible*, 123.

14. See James L. Ferrell, *The Hidden Christ: Beneath the Surface of the Old Testament* (Salt Lake City, UT: Deseret Book, 2009), 254–55. Augustine wrote, "Blessed Elijah typified our Lord and Savior. Just as Elijah suffered persecution by the Jews, so our Lord, the true Elijah, was condemned and despised by the Jews. Elijah left his own people, and Christ deserted the synagogue; Elijah departed into the wilderness, and Christ came into the world. Elijah was fed in the desert

by ministering ravens, while Christ was refreshed in the desert of this world by the faith of the Gentiles." (Augustine, "Sermons," 124.1, in Marco Conti, ed., *1–2 Kings, 1–2 Chronicles, Ezra, Nehemiah, Esther*, in *Ancient Christian Commentary on Scripture* [Downers Grove, IL: InterVarsity Press, 2008], 101.)

15. See Cogan, *The Anchor Bible: 1 Kings*, 425.

16. Ibid., 426.

17. See Alonzo L. Gaskill, *The Lost Language of Symbolism: An Essential Guide for Recognizing and Interpreting Symbols of the Gospel* (Salt Lake City, UT: Deseret Book, 2003), 311. See also Maurice H. Farbridge, *Studies in Biblical and Semitic Symbolism* (London: Routledge, 1923), 80.

18. The ninth-century Nestorian bishop, Isho'dad of Merv, wrote: "When the priests, [Elijah's] brothers, saw that he had escaped the anger of Ahab, they saved for him a part of the food and bread reserved to them, and a raven brought it to him through divine intervention." "Books of Sessions 1 Kings," 17.6, in Conti, *1–2 Kings, 1–2 Chronicles, Ezra, Nehemiah, Esther*, in *Ancient Christian Commentary on Scripture*, 100. "Hebrew—'oreb, from 'arab, meaning to grow dusky or darkened; also related to another verb of the same spelling—'arab, denoting one who gives or takes on pledge; to make a bargain, traffic, barter; to intermingle, intermix or associate with others. It has been suggested by some researchers that Elijah was under the care of a nearby clan of Arabs who were seen as dark, mysterious, and nomadic, belonging to very tight-knit family and clan associations. Also, their reputation as barterers, traders and merchants was well deserved—a tradition that carries on to our day. If I had to put money on either actual ravens or a local clan of Arabs supplying Elijah with bread, the Hebrew favors the Arab hypothesis." (Kent J. Hunter, personal correspondence, May 26, 2017.)

19. Walter L. Wilson, *A Dictionary of Bible Types* (Peabody, MA: Hendrickson, 1999), 355. The ravens may not be symbolic at all. Perhaps God selected ravens simply because they are birds of prey and would, therefore, be inclined to scavenge for meat. (See Richard C. Trench, *Miracles and Parables of the Old Testament* [Grand Rapids, MI: Baker Book House, 1959], 109.)

20. Joseph Fielding McConkie, *Gospel Symbolism* (Salt Lake City, UT: Deseret Book, 1985), 268; J. C. Cooper, *An Illustrated Encyclopaedia of Traditional Symbols* (London: Thames and Hudson, 1995), 136, 188–89; Leland Ryken, James C. Wilhoit, and Tremper Longman III, eds., *Dictionary of Biblical Imagery* (Downers Grove, IL: InterVarsity Press, 1998), 694; Wilson, *A Dictionary of Bible Types*, 332–33; Nadia Julien, *The Mammoth Dictionary of Symbols: Understanding the Hidden Language of Symbols* (New York: Carroll & Graf Publishers, Inc., 1996), 343–45; Kevin J. Todeschi, *The Encyclopedia of Symbols* (New York: Perigee Book, 1995), 214, 281–82; David Fontana, *The Secret Language of Symbolism: A Visual Key to Symbols and Their Meanings* (San Francisco, CA: Chronicle Books, 2000), 113.

21. Robert D. Johnston, *Numbers in the Bible: God's Design in Biblical Numerology* (Grand Rapids, MI: Kregel Publications, 1999), 55.

22. E. W. Bullinger, *Number in Scripture: Its Supernatural Design and Spiritual Significance* (Grand Rapids, MI: Kregel Publications, 1967), 107; John J. Davis, *Biblical Numerology: A Basic Study of the Use of Numbers in the Bible* (Grand Rapids, MI: Baker Book House, 1968), 123; J. E. Cirlot, *A Dictionary of Symbols*, 2nd ed. (New York: Routledge & Kegan Paul, 1971), 232; Johnston, *Numbers in the Bible*, 55.

23. As noted, Luke says the drought lasted three and one half years (rather than just three). Three and one half is a symbolic number often used in apocalyptic literature to represent a "period of distress." (See Cogan, *The Anchor Bible: 1 Kings*, 426.]) It sometimes symbolizes that which is "arrested midway in its normal course." (See Richard D. Draper, *Opening the Seven Seals: The Visions of John the Revelator* [Salt Lake City, UT: Deseret Book, 1991], 121, 138. See also Jay A. Parry and Donald W. Parry, *Understanding the Book of Revelation* [Salt Lake City, UT: Deseret Book, 1998], 138.) If Luke's account is accurate, then the three and one half year drought could be an obvious symbol of God sending "distress" for a period upon Ahab and his people because of their idolatry. Moreover, just as the drought began suddenly, it would be arrested midcourse when God abruptly sent rain upon drought-stricken Gilead. That being said, it seems that the account in 1 Kings would be more trusted than Luke's, simply because the 1 Kings account is written not so long after the events transpired. Luke, on the other hand, is describing the drought approximately one thousand years after it happened.

24. Donald J. Wiseman, *1 and 2 Kings*, in *Tyndale Old Testament Commentaries* (Downers Grove, IL: InterVarsity Press, 1988), 164.

25. See Trench, *Miracles and Parables of the Old Testament*, 111.

26. Ibid., 110.

27. Pamela McQuade, *The Top 100 Miracles of the Bible: What They Are and What They Mean to You Today* (Uhrichsville, OH: Barbour Publishing, 2008), 72.

28. See Lockyer, *All the Miracles of the Bible*, 109.

29. Blaine M. Yorgason, *I Need Thee Every Hour: The Joy of Coming to Christ* (Salt Lake City, UT: Deseret Book, 2004), 268–69.

30. See Trench, *Miracles and Parables of the Old Testament*, 110.

31. Ibid., 109; emphasis in original.

32. Ibid., 110. Trench also noted, "How unlikely were *ravens* to feed the prophet. Birds whose instincts would have prompted them rather to snatch his food away. So how unexpectedly at times do even the enemies of godliness promote the interests of the godly. The ravens of the world, its cruel, covetous, rapacious men, have often, one way or other, been purveyors to His church. The brethren of Joseph contributed to Joseph's exaltation, and Haman had to hold the bridle for the man whose life he had aimed at." (Trench, *Miracles and Parables of the Old Testament*, 111.)

THE BARREL *of* MEAL *and* *the* CRUSE OF OIL ARE MIRACULOUSLY EXTENDED

1 KINGS 17:8–16

THE MIRACLE

Having dwelt in hiding (at the brook of Cherith) for quite some time, God caused the water of the *wadi* to dry up, and commanded Elijah to, "Get thee to Zarephath" where, He informed Elijah, there was a woman whom God had commanded to "sustain" the prophet (see 1 Kings 17:7–9).

So Elijah made his way to Zarephath, and when he arrived at the gate of the city, a widow was there gathering sticks for fuel. Elijah approached her and requested a drink of water. As she turned to get him a drink, he called out to her to also bring him "a morsel of bread." In sorrow, the woman lamented that she had no bread baked; instead, she had but a handful of flour and a miniscule amount of oil to her name. She informed Elijah that she had been gathering sticks to make a fire so as to cook her meager provisions so that she and her son could have one last small meal before they both died of starvation (see 1 Kings 17:10–12).

Elijah said to the widow, "Don't fear, but do as I have asked you. Make me a little cake first, and then make something for you and your son. If you will do so," he promised in the name of the Lord, "Your flour will not run out and your container of oil will remain full until the day that the Lord sends rain again upon the eart" (see 1 Kings 17:13–14).

In an act of faith, the widowed mother did as he had asked; and she and her son did eat many days, and the flour did not run out, nor did the container of oil run dry. The promise of the Lord, as delivered by Elijah, was fulfilled (see 1 Kings 17:15–16).

BACKGROUND

Zarephath of Sidon was a town on the Mediterranean coast, just miles south of Sidon. It was Jezebel's homeland; and it was among the Phoenician cities taken by Sennacherib in 710 BC.[1] Zarephath was Gentile territory, and it was the home of Baal. It was situated outside of the borders of Israel; and, thus, in the minds of some, it was, "Outside of YHWH's territory."[2] The widow, in this narrative, would have been a "simple, godly non-Jewish woman."[3] Consequently, her statement, "As the Lord *thy* God liveth," or "In the name of YHWH" (1 Kings 17:12) is rather surprising. She clearly recognized Elijah as an Israelite, perhaps by his speech; or, perhaps, because the Spirit was inspiring her to recognize this holy man whom God had foreordained her to serve.[4] In the King James Version, God says He had "commanded" a certain widow of Zarephath to sustain the prophet. While the Hebrew can appropriately be translated "commanded," it can also be rendered as, "laid a charge upon," "appointed," or "ordained."[5] It seems evident from the narrative that the woman was not expecting Elijah. Thus, God likely had not informed her (through His Spirit) that she would be receiving a man of God. Instead, it appears that God is saying to Elijah that there is a widow in Zarephath that I have prepared and foreordained to help you.

While it seems likely that the Spirit would have revealed to Elijah that the woman gathering sticks was she whom God had foreordained to help him, nevertheless, one commentator suggested that, "Elijah is likely to have recognized her by 'her widow's garb' (Gen 38:14), dress typically worn long after the mourning period (cf. [Judith] 8:5; 10:3; 16:8)."[6]

Whereas the King James Version says that the woman had a "son" (in the singular), in the Septuagint (i.e., the Greek version of the Old Testament), the woman speaks of she and her "sons" (in the plural). This would explain why, in the King James Version (1 Kings 17:15), it says that she "and her house, did eat many days" after Elijah's miracle. The implication being that she may have had several sons, rather than just the one.[7]

SYMBOLIC ELEMENTS

The woman of Zarephath is described as a widow. "Widowhood was a mark of dependency, since such women often lacked the means to support themselves, even more so in times of famine."[8] The word widow appears nearly one hundred times in the Bible. "The widow is an archetypal image of affliction and desolation."[9]

In scripture, the act of eating is an important symbol. Among other things, eating "is a prime evidence of God's providence, sometimes the result of miraculous provision."[10]

APPLICATION AND ALLEGORIZATION

It was the drying up of the brook that forced Elijah to move from the wilderness to Zarephath (see 1 Kings 17:7–9). In this there may be a lesson for you and me. God caused ravens to feed Elijah; He certainly could have provided additional water, if He so desired to. But He didn't! How often does God send us a trial in order to bless us, and in order to get us where He needs us? Elijah may have been content in his desert abode, but by that becoming intolerable, his circumstance was bettered—as was the circumstance of the widow and her family. God sometimes motivates us to change by making our present circumstances intolerable or undesirable. On occasion, He does so to improve our situation. At other times, He does so to get us where He needs us most. Regardless, God uses trials (such as the motivating one in this miracle) to accomplish His work in the world, and in our own lives.

"The episode . . . stands impressed in the pages of history as a lasting memorial to the availability of God's full provision to all who believe, whether Jew or Gentile (Matt 10:41–42; Luke 4:25–26)."[11] While the children of Israel suffered under the conditions of the drought, God provided for this Gentile woman and her family. "Surely she must have thought about the power of a God who did this. Perhaps she even came to know Him because of it."[12] God loves His children; but He does not limit His blessings to those who are members of His Church. If the members turn their backs on Him, they may place themselves beyond the reach of His blessings. If others outside the faith trust in Him and reach out to Him, He will readily bless them, as He did the Gentile widow of Zarephath.[13]

On a related note, one commentator suggested that the message of the miracle is that, "The most unlikely people may be used by God to help our need."[14] How true this is. The widow of Zarephath was a Gentile, but God worked through her to feed the hungry and thirsty prophet. Cyrus, king of Persia (a pagan) was God's instrument in rebuilding His holy temple. Alexander Doniphan, a non–Latter-day Saint, intervened during the 1838 Mormon War to prevent the execution of the Prophet Joseph Smith. Stephen H. Webb, the Roman Catholic scholar, wrote glowingly about LDS theology and the Book of Mormon, including what other Christians could learn from Latter-day Saints.[15] Good, moral men and women have been used by God throughout the history of the world to accomplish His work. While the Father consistently works through His covenant people, He also employs those not of the faith to move forth the cause of Zion. May God exalt each of these "friends of the faith" in the highest of heavens!

One commentator spoke of Elijah's request of the woman as "inconsiderate."[16] If you look at this as something other than a spiritual exercise, that would seem to be true.[17] However, we know that more is happening here than would have been evident to the woman. "The prophet put a severe test before her."[18] Yet, the "faith of the woman is noteworthy."[19] As is often said, "Faith precedes the miracle"—and this was a woman who, though a Gentile, was capable of manifesting great faith. "The widow gave her all, . . . without asking where the next meal would come from, and found that in making God's will her *first* concern, He made her need *His* first concern."[20] Do we have such faith? Would we, given similar circumstances, trust our feelings as faithfully as she trusted hers? If we desire the blessings of this widow, we must have the faith—and do the works—that she did.[21]

In describing this encounter, one commentary on the miracles suggested a possible application. "God does not see people the way we do. To us, well-to-do, powerful, or highly spiritual people seem important. We can imagine God doing wonderful things for them. But so often, God chooses to bless the quietly faithful or totally unworldly person we'd pass by in a minute."[22] We reverence General Authorities and General Auxiliary officers in the Church for their faith and faithfulness. We esteem our bishops and stake presidents. Yet how many of the humble, faithful followers are looked over or not noticed. How many, working in the "trenches" of the ward or stake, are missed as they quietly, faithfully do what is asked of them? The humble widow in this story is a reminder that much good is done by ordinary members of the Church. Perhaps here and there we could take note of them, and lovingly acknowledge them for their faithfulness and contributions to the kingdom.

Rather than multiplying the meal and oil instantly and dramatically, so that there was sufficient meal and oil for the remainder of the famine, God multiplied it in small increments—day by day, bit by bit. And so He does in our lives. The miracles we experience are typically small; many are imperceptible if we do not look for them. But they *are* there.[23] However, to not notice the multitude of small daily miracles is an act of ingratitude. Perhaps God doesn't multiply the "flour and oil" in our personal lives in dramatic ways so that we'll need to develop greater, more sustained faith. If sufficient "flour and oil" are always on hand, for what do we need to exercise faith? If there are no reasons to doubt, then our faith quickly atrophies. However, we too must pray that He "give[s] us this day our daily bread" (Matthew 6:11). This is an act of mercy on the part of the Father, because it offers us the opportunity to develop spiritual strength. The Father of us all seeks to develop His children into faith-filled disciples; and the best way to accomplish that is to keep us seeking and trusting every day that He will provide. And He does!

Richard Trench suggested that this miracle reminds us that, "Self-denial springing from faith in God, will bring Divine interposition and an increase of blessing."[24] Archbishop Trench goes on to say,

> The widow of Zarephath denied herself the gratification of appetite when she was doubtless suffering from want of food; more than that, she delayed to appease the hunger of her *son* and made a cake *first* for God's prophet. . . . She was willing to make her child's life of secondary consideration when God so commanded, and . . . she received a most abundant reward. God will be under obligation to no man. "A cup of cold water only in the name of a disciple" (Matt. x. 42) shall in "no wise lose its reward." If we give unto Him, He will give us back "good measure and running over."[25]

God invites to us pay tithing, not because He needs our money, but because we need the personal development that comes from it, and the blessings associated with it. God invites us to fast, not because He wants hungry Saints, but because we need the development that comes from it, and the blessings associated with it. Any sacrifice that God calls us to make, any self-denial we engage in, ultimately spiritually strengthens us, and also richly blesses us. Self-sacrifice was the pattern of Christ's life. It must be the pattern of the lives of His truest disciples.

Augustine allegorized this story, suggesting that the widow was a symbol for the Church of Christ, which would be established many years after Elijah's ministry. He wrote, "That widow to whom the prophet was sent typified the church, just as the ravens that ministered to Elijah prefigured the Gentiles. Thus, Elijah came to the widow because Christ was to come to the church."[26] Augustine went on to say:

> Let us now consider what the water and the wood signify. We know that both are very pleasing and necessary for the church, as it is written: "He is like a tree planted near running water." [2 Kings 4:4[27]] In the wood is shown the mystery of the cross, in the water the sacrament of baptism. Therefore, she had gone out to gather two sticks of wood, for thus she

replied to blessed Elijah when he asked her for food: "As the Lord lives, I have nothing but a handful of meal and a little oil in a cruse; and behold, I am going out to gather two sticks that I may make food for me and my son . . . and we will eat it and die." The widow typified the church, as I said above; the widow's son prefigured the Christian people. Thus, when Elijah came, the widow went out to gather two sticks of wood. Notice . . . that she did not say three or four, nor only one stick; but she wanted to gather two sticks. She was gathering two sticks of wood because she received Christ in the type of Elijah; she wanted to pick up those two pieces because she desired to recognize the mystery of the cross. Truly, the cross of our Lord and Savior was prepared from two pieces of wood, and so that widow was gathering two sticks because the church would believe in him who hung on two pieces of wood. For this reason that widow said, "I am gathering two sticks that I may make food for me and my son, and we will eat it and die." It is true, beloved; no one will merit to believe in Christ crucified unless he dies to this world. For if a person wishes to eat the body of Christ worthily, he must die to the past and live for the future.[28]

Again, Augustine is merely allegorizing. Nevertheless, his insight is both interesting and instructive.

As a simple but meaningful application, one source states, "Giving, not getting, not saving, is the way to abundance."[29] Or, as the hymn states, "Because I have been given much, I too must give."[30] Wealth is not found in hoarding our temporal blessings, but in blessing others with them. The widow exemplified this. Importantly, she was not a wealthy woman who gave freely, but, rather, an impoverished woman who freely shared. (To give when you are wealthy is, in ways, much easier than to give when you have almost nothing.) Thus, this miracle suggests that the poor are also called upon to share what they have with others. That may be money, food, talents, or time, but we *must* give. May we, with the widow, say within ourselves, "I cannot see another's lack and I not share."[31]

NOTES

1. See Mordechai Cogan, *The Anchor Bible: 1 Kings*, vol. 10 (New York: Doubleday, 2001), 427.

2. See ibid., 432.

3. See Richard D. Patterson and Hermann J. Austel, "1 and 2 Kings," in Frank E. Gaebelein, ed., *The Expositor's Bible Commentary* (Grand Rapids, MI: Zondervan, 1994), 124.

4. See Cogan, *The Anchor Bible: 1 Kings*, 428.

5. See Francis Brown, S. R. Driver, and Charles A. Briggs, *The Brown-Driver-Briggs Hebrew and English Lexicon* (Peabody, MA: Hendrickson Publishers, 1999), 845.

6. Cogan, *The Anchor Bible: 1 Kings*, 427. See also Israel Wolf Slotki, *Kings*, in *Soncino Books of the Bible* (London: The Soncino Press, 1978), 124. Judith is one of the books of the Apocrypha.

7. See Cogan, *The Anchor Bible: 1 Kings*, 428.

8. Ibid., 427.

9. Leland Ryken, James C. Wilhoit, and Tremper Longman III, eds., *Dictionary of Biblical Imagery* (Downers Grove, IL: InterVarsity Press, 1998), 946.

10. Ibid., 226.

11. Patterson and Austel, "1 and 2 Kings," in Gaebelein, *The Expositor's Bible Commentary*, 4:140.

12. Pamela McQuade, *The Top 100 Miracles of the Bible: What They Are and What They Mean to You Today* (Uhrichsville, OH: Barbour Publishing, 2008), 74.

13. McQuade added, "Sometimes we stand amazed when good things happen to unbelievers and wonder why the faithful Christian is passed over. We need to understand that God has His own purposes. He is working out a wider plan that may bring salvation to a hurting soul. Let's not judge too quickly. Instead, let's trust in the Lord who rules this earth and can touch any heart in it." (McQuade, *The Top 100 Miracles of the Bible*, 75.)

14. Richard C. Trench, *Miracles and Parables of the Old Testament* (Grand Rapids, MI: Baker Book House, 1959), 113.

15. See, for example, Stephen H. Webb, *Mormon Christianity: What Other Christians Can Learn From the Latter-day Saints* (New York: Oxford University Press, 2013; Stephen H. Webb and Alonzo L. Gaskill, *Catholic and Mormon: A Theological Conversation* (New York: Oxford University Press, 2015); Stephen H. Webb, "Mormonism Obsessed with Christ," *First Things Magazine*, February 2012, www.firstthings.com/article/2012/02/mormonism-obsessed-with-christ.

16. Israel Wolf Slotki, *Kings*, in *Soncino Books of the Bible*, 125. Ephrem the Syrian suggested, "When he found her barefoot and dressed in rags in the act of gathering some wood, wasted by starvation and made miserably thin, he . . . himself was ashamed of asking for her bread so that he first asked her for water." ("On the First Book of Kings," 17.2, in Conti, *1–2 Kings, 1–2 Chronicles, Ezra, Nehemiah, Esther*, in *Ancient Christian Commentary on Scripture*, [2008], 104.)

17. "In the wisdom of our day, the prophet's request may seem unfair and selfish. In the wisdom of our day, the widow's response may appear foolish and unwise. That is largely because we often learn to make decisions based upon what we see. We make decisions based on the evidence before us and what appears to be in our immediate best interest. 'Faith,' on the other hand, 'is the substance of things hoped for, the evidence of things not seen.' Faith has eyes that penetrate the

darkness, seeing into the light beyond. 'Your faith should not stand in the wisdom of men, but in the power of God.'" (Joseph B. Wirthlin, "Shall He Find Faith on the Earth?," *Ensign*, November 2002.)

18. Patterson and Austel, "1 and 2 Kings," in Gaebelein, *The Expositor's Bible Commentary*, 4:139.

19. D. Kelly Ogden and Andrew C. Skinner, *Verse By Verse—The Old Testament Volume One: Genesis through 2 Samuel, Psalms* (Salt Lake City, UT: Deseret Book, 2013), 2:34.

20. Herbert Lockyer, *All the Miracles of the Bible: The Supernatural in Scripture—Its Scope and Significance* (Grand Rapids, MI: Zondervan, 1961), 110; emphasis in original.

21. Elder Theodore M. Burton said this of the miracle's application: "I have tried to compare her spirit of obedience with our willingness to obey the word of God as spoken by modern prophets. These prophets hold the same fullness of authority given to Elijah. They have told us to keep at least a year's supply of food on hand for any future emergency. We have only their word of prophecy to rely on, just as the widow relied on that of Elijah. We should obey as she did. By so doing, we will be able to save ourselves and our families from want." (Theodore M. Burton, "The Power of Elijah," *Ensign*, May 1974.) Another text states, "If God had not meant the widow's preservation He would not have required of her to see her last morsels go down another's throat. In all achievements the difficulty of the enterprise makes way for the glory of the actor." (Trench, *Miracles and Parables of the Old Testament*, 114.)

22. McQuade, *The Top 100 Miracles of the Bible*, 75.

23. For example, "We are astonished at the little miracle [which happened to the widow] at Sarepta [or Zarephath], but we pass over with indifference the large miracle which is repeated year by year for the whole world." (Trench, *Miracles and Parables of the Old Testament*, 114.)

24. Trench, *Miracles and Parables of the Old Testament*, 112.

25. Ibid., 112–13.

26. Augustine, "Sermon" 124.2, in Conti, *1–2 Kings, 1–2 Chronicles, Ezra, Nehemiah, Esther*, in *Ancient Christian Commentary on Scripture*, 103–4.

27. Augustine is quoting from the Peshitta, which is the standard version of the Bible in the Syriac Christian tradition.

28. Augustine, "Sermon," 124.3, in Conti, *1–2 Kings, 1–2 Chronicles, Ezra, Nehemiah, Esther*, in *Ancient Christian Commentary on Scripture*, 104.

29. Trench, *Miracles and Parables of the Old Testament*, 114.

30. "Because I Have Been Given Much," *Hymns*, no. 219.

31. Ibid.

ELIJAH RAISES *the* SON OF *the* WIDOW *of* ZAREPHATH *from* THE DEAD

1 KINGS 17:17–24

THE MIRACLE

Sometime after the miracle of the multiplied flour and oil, and while Elijah was still residing with the widow and her son, the boy fell ill and died. Distraught as she was, the woman said to Elijah, "Did you come here to call attention to my sins and to kill my son?" (see 1 Kings 17:17–18).

Elijah took the boy from his mother's arms and carried him up to the roof chamber, where the prophet had been staying. Once Elijah had laid the boy upon the bed, he prayed to God, saying, "O Lord my God, hast thou also brought evil upon the widow with whom I sojourn, by slaying her son?" (1 Kings 17:20).

Elijah then three times stretched himself out upon the child, and cried out to God, "O Lord my God, I pray thee, let this child's soul come into him again" (1 Kings 17:21). God heard Elijah's prayer, and the boy came back to life (see 1 Kings 17:22).

The prophet then led the young man down to where the anxious widow was, and presented him to his mother, saying "See, thy son liveth" (1 Kings 17:23); to which the widow replied, "Now by this I know that thou art a man of God, and that the word of the Lord in thy mouth is truth" (1 Kings 17:24).

BACKGROUND

This is the first time in the Bible that we hear of someone being brought back to life. While this is a more common miracle in the New Testament than the Old, in neither of those sacred books is bringing the dead back to life a common occurrence.[1] Of course, one must distinguish between bringing a person back to life and resurrecting someone. Many commentators confuse the two and wrongly assume that the boy in this story was resurrected rather than resuscitated.

In Judaism, there is a "widespread view" that the son of this widow eventually became a prophet—namely, the prophet Jonah.[2] The presumption by some is that, after repeated miracles at Elijah's hand, the widow converts and then raises her son in the faith, leading to his prophetic call in adulthood.[3]

The woman's question ("Art thou come unto me to call my sin to remembrance, and to slay my son?") suggests that she felt like God was unaware of her. However, when Elijah came to dwell with her, then God (who watched over His prophet) became aware of her sins; and, consequently, took out His wrath upon her by killing her son.[4]

When the King James Version says that the prophet "stretched himself upon the child three times," the Hebrew is literally, he "measured" himself, but can be translated as "stretched" or "extended."[5] One commentary explains, "The prophet positioned himself directly upon the child, mouth to mouth, eyes to eyes, palms to palms, symbolically transferring his life force to the deceased."[6]

The "upper room" that Elijah stayed in would most likely have been a temporary shelter on the roof of the house—one only accessible from the outside of the home. This would have guaranteed that the widow had privacy, and also would have safeguarded her reputation.[7]

After the healing of her son, the woman says, "I know that thou art a man of God" (1 Kings 17:24). One commentator on the Hebrew suggested that a better rendering of the line would be, "Now I know beyond all doubt."[8] She had already "believed," but now she was absolutely certain.[9]

Ogden and Skinner conjecture that Elijah brought the boy back to life by "using some form of artificial resuscitation."[10]

SYMBOLIC ELEMENTS

Breath is a common scriptural symbol for life.[11] It is sometimes used as a synonym for "spirit" or "wind."[12] One dictionary of symbolism notes,

"Human breath, equated with the divine breath, is an allotment of life, a portion of the divine spark and a gift (Job 27:3). The necessity of breathing becomes an image for total dependence upon God. Referring to all creation, the psalmist writes, 'When you take away their breath, they die and return to the dust' (Ps 104:29 NIV; cf. Job 34:14–15)."[13] Breath is a symbol for life; thus, its absence represents death.

As already noted, three is the number in scripture that typically represents the Godhead. Doing something three times suggests who it is that one is seeking intervention from. Thus, when Elijah thrice stretches himself out upon the boy, this shows us that the prophet is calling upon God to perform this miracle. It shows that he is aware that God is the only one who has the power to bring the boy back to life.[14]

The parallels between this miracle and the miracle of Elisha raising the son of the Shunamite woman (see 2 Kings 4:8–27) are undeniable, and clearly intentional. In both miracles, the mothers show hospitality to the holy man who comes to visit—by giving them a room to stay in (see 1 Kings 17:19; 2 Kings 4:9–10). In both cases, there is a son who falls sick and dies unexpectedly (see 1 Kings 17:17; 2 Kings 4:18–20). In both stories, the prophet is verbally attacked because he is seen as the cause of the boy's passing (see 1 Kings 17:18; 2 Kings 4:28). In both miracles, the prophet prays to God to intervene (1 Kings 17:20–21; 2 Kings 4:33). And in each narrative, some unique act is performed in order to facilitate the reviving of the deceased child (see 1 Kings 17:21; 2 Kings 4:34–35).[15] While the stories are not identical, it is evident that the person who penned them saw the parallels, and wished for his reader to pick up on them also.

APPLICATION AND ALLEGORIZATION

It seems evident from the narrative that the widow believed that some forgotten sin in her past was the reason that her son had died.[16] However, we know that such is not doctrinally accurate. This episode brings to mind Jesus's conversation with the disciples in John 9, where they ask if a man born blind was so afflicted because his parents had sinned. Jesus responded, "Neither hath this man sinned, nor his parents: but [he was born blind] that the works of God should be made manifest in him" (John 9:3). And so it is here. The woman's sins were not the cause, but "the testing had come in order that her newly found faith might be brought to settled maturity."[17]

Trench saw evidence in this miracle that certain people have gifts not generally held by humankind. He wrote, "Special blessings are connected with special persons. There was no other man in Israel at this time whose prayer would have brought the dead to life. God has, in all ages of the world, connected special blessings with special individuals."[18] And who are those special individuals today? Not simply living prophets and apostles—though they are too. But all who bear the holy priesthood, are worthy of it, and have sufficient faith to pronounce the promises that God whispers into their ears and hearts as they administer to those in need. Praised be God for allowing you and me to live in this—the greatest dispensation in the history of the world! Praised be God for allowing you and me to have access to the restored gospel and its priesthood power!

I'm struck by the following quotation from the book, *Miracles and Parables of the Old Testament*, "The widow was a person of real piety; but then as it would seem, . . . she was acquainted with God in a partial and superficial manner. Probably her religious feelings were more natural than spiritual. Two invisible guests break in upon her; the Lord and the Spirit. The one inflicts the blow, the other expounds it. The one slays her son, the other makes her sensible of the reason why."[19] God's acts in our lives are purposeful; they are always designed to be instructive. And so, in an effort to make a more spiritual woman out of the widow, Jesus sends her a curveball—an unexpected jolt. Then the Holy Ghost steps in and quietly says, "Let me help you to make sense of all that has happened in your life." God does this exact same thing in each of our lives. Jesus sends us experiences to increase our spirituality and our connection to Him. Then the Spirit—if we have it with us—helps us to make sense of those experiences. The key is to remember that, if we're not living in such a way as to have the Spirit active in our personal lives, then these experiences are going to be very painful and very confusing. The Holy Ghost is called "the Comforter" for a reason. Let us never place ourselves in a situation where we have to navigate the vicissitudes of life without inspired perspective and gracious comfort from the Holy Ghost.

As their application of this miracle, Ogden and Skinner simply ask, "The widow sacrificed all she had for the Lord's prophet and, by extension, the Lord's kingdom. Are we willing to do the same?"[20]

Another commentator suggested that the simple message of this miracle is that prayer works! "What miracle is impossible to faithful prayers?"[21] Doubtless, Elijah's prayer was powerful because, when there was no emergency, he still prayed powerfully. If you and I wish to see miracles through our prayers, we must become "powerful pray-ers" long before the miracle is needed. Do our daily prayers evidence that kind of faith and closeness to God? If not, now is the time to improve upon our communications with the divine. The day will come when each of us will desperately need God's intervention. Have we developed that direct connection to Him wherein we can call down the powers of heaven in the very hour that we need them?

In the fourth century, Ephrem the Syrian drew an allegory from this miracle, suggesting that it testified of Christ, the Resurrection, and the ordinance of baptism. He wrote:

> "He stretched himself on the child three times and cried out to the Lord, 'O Lord my God, let this child's life come into him again.'" These words contain many symbols. The Scripture shows us immediately that through the invocation of the three names [meaning, the name of the Father, Son, and Holy Spirit] a human being will come back to life. If he kills the ancient Adam [or fallen man within himself] with the help of the Messiah in the holy baptism. The divine [Apostle] Paul says, "If we have died with the Messiah, we believe that we will also live with him." [Romans 6:8] And what follows [in this miracle] agrees precisely with this meaning: "He stretched himself on the child," because in this [new] life, which he will give us after we are dead to that ancient Adam [or natural main within us], "he will transform the body of our humiliation [and sin] that it may be conformed to the body of his glory." And here you can also see a symbol of the triple descent of the Son of God to the dead: the first symbol consists here in the fact that he was made flesh and included his infinite nature into the womb of the Virgin; the second, that he stretched his body on the wood [of the cross] and was crucified; the third, that whoever accepts death lies in the grave and goes down to Sheol, so that, in order to vivify humankind, God consented to stretch his majesty on our smallness.[22]

In the spirit of Moses 6:63, where the pre-mortal Christ testifies, "And behold, all things have their likeness, and all things are created and made to bear record of me, both things which are temporal, and things which are spiritual; things which are in the heavens above, and things which are on the earth, and things which are in the earth, and things which are under the earth, both above and beneath: all things bear record of me." Ephrem the Syrian sees Jesus in every element of this miracle. Augustine saw this same symbolism, when he wrote:

> The son of the widow lay dead because the son of the church, that is, the Gentiles, was dead because of many sins and offenses. At the prayer of Elijah, the widow's son was revived; at the coming of Christ, the church's

son or the Christian people were brought back from the prison of death. Elijah bent down in prayer, and the widow's son was revived; Christ sank down in his passion, and the Christian people were brought back to life. . . . In the fact that he bowed three times is shown the mystery of the Trinity [or Godhead]. . . . The whole Trinity restored the widow's son or the Gentiles to life. Moreover, this is further demonstrated in the sacrament of baptism, for the old person is plunged in the water three times, in order that the new person may merit to rise.[23]

NOTES

1. See Ellis T. Rasmussen, *A Latter-day Saint Commentary on the Old Testament* (Salt Lake City, UT: Deseret Book, 1994), 293.

2. See the Talmudic tractate, *Yerushalmi Sukkah*, ch. 5:55a; Louis Ginzberg, *The Legends of the Jews* (Philadelphia: The Jewish Publication Society of America, 1967), 4:197; 6:318n9; 6:351n38; Ada R. Habershon, *The Study of the Miracles* (London: Morgan & Scott, 1911), 274; Herbert Lockyer, *All the Miracles of the Bible: The Supernatural in Scripture—Its Scope and Significance* (Grand Rapids, MI: Zondervan, 1961), 111.

3. *The Expositor's Bible Commentary* states, "The Syriac translation, followed by Jerome [in the Vulgate Bible], that the lad was the prophet Jonah is totally unsatisfactory and historically impossible (cf. 2 Kings 14:25)." (Richard D. Patterson and Hermann J. Austel, "1 and 2 Kings," in Frank E. Gaebelein, ed., *The Expositor's Bible Commentary* [Grand Rapids, MI: Zondervan, 1994], 4:141.)

4. See Mordechai Cogan, *The Anchor Bible: 1 Kings*, vol. 10 (New York: Doubleday, 2001), 428; Patterson and Austel, "1 and 2 Kings," in Gaebelein, *The Expositor's Bible Commentary*, 4:140; Israel Wolf Slotki, *Kings*, in *Soncino Books of the Bible* (London: The Soncino Press, 1978), 126; Donald J. Wiseman, *1 and 2 Kings*, in *Tyndale Old Testament Commentaries* (Downers Grove, IL: InterVarsity Press, 1988), 166; Lockyer, *All the Miracles of the Bible*, 111.

5. See Francis Brown, S. R. Driver, and Charles A. Briggs, *The Brown-Driver-Briggs Hebrew and English Lexicon* (Peabody, MA: Hendrickson Publishers, 1999), 551; Cogan, *The Anchor Bible: 1 Kings*, 429; Wiseman, *1 and 2 Kings*, in *Tyndale Old Testament Commentaries*, 166–67.

6. Cogan, *The Anchor Bible: 1 Kings*, 429.

7. See Patterson and Austel, "1 and 2 Kings," in Gaebelein, *The Expositor's Bible Commentary*, 4:141.

8. Israel Wolf Slotki, *Kings*, in *Soncino Books of the Bible*, 126.

9. McQuade asks, "Can one doubt that by this point she had come to faith?" (Pamela McQuade, *The Top 100 Miracles of the Bible: What They Are and What They Mean to You Today* [Uhrichsville, OH: Barbour Publishing, 2008], 77.)

10. D. Kelly Ogden and Andrew C. Skinner, *Verse By Verse—The Old Testament Volume One: Genesis through 2 Samuel, Psalms* (Salt Lake City, UT: Deseret Book, 2013), 2:34.

11. See Cogan, *The Anchor Bible: 1 Kings*, 428.

12. See Leland Ryken, James C. Wilhoit, and Tremper Longman III, eds., *Dictionary of Biblical Imagery* (Downers Grove, IL: InterVarsity Press, 1998), 119.

13. Ibid.

14. See Patterson and Austel, "1 and 2 Kings," in Gaebelein, *The Expositor's Bible Commentary*, 4:141.

15. See Cogan, *The Anchor Bible: 1 Kings*, 432.

16. See Patterson and Austel, "1 and 2 Kings," in Gaebelein, *The Expositor's Bible Commentary*, 4:140.

17. Ibid.

18. Richard C. Trench, *Miracles and Parables of the Old Testament* (Grand Rapids, MI: Baker Book House, 1959), 116.

19. Ibid., 117.

20. Ogden and Skinner, *Verse By Verse—The Old Testament Volume One: Genesis through 2 Samuel, Psalms*, 2:34.

21. Trench, *Miracles and Parables of the Old Testament*, 116.

22. Ephrem the Syrian, "On the First Book of Kings," 17:2, in Conti, *1–2 Kings, 1–2 Chronicles, Ezra, Nehemiah, Esther*, in *Ancient Christian Commentary on Scripture*, (2008), 105.

23. Augustine, "Sermon" 124.4, in Conti, *1–2 Kings, 1–2 Chronicles, Ezra, Nehemiah, Esther*, in *Ancient Christian Commentary on Scripture*, 105.

ELIJAH COMMANDS FIRE *to* COME DOWN *from* HEAVEN

1 KINGS 18:17–40

THE MIRACLE

Ahab accused Elijah of "troubling" Israel. However, the prophet pushed back on the king's accusation, asserting that Israel's troubles were the direct result of the king and his family forsaking the commandments and worshiping Baal (see 1 Kings 18:17–18).

Thus, Elijah told the king to gather the Israelites and all of the 450 "prophets of Baal" and the 400 "prophets of the groves" (or "prophets of Asherah," who eat at Jezebel's table) to Mount Carmel. So the king did as Elijah had asked (see 1 Kings 18:19–20).

Once the people and false prophets had gathered, Elijah reprovingly asked of them, "How long halt ye between two opinions? if [Jehovah] be God, follow him: but if Baal, then follow him." The people stood by silently as Elijah rebuked them (1 Kings 18:21).

The prophet of Jehovah then informed them that he was but one man— and the sole prophet of the Lord—and yet Baal's false prophets totaled 450. Nevertheless, he was about to issue a challenge to those idolatrous priests. Elijah had them bring forth two bullocks. He let the priests of Baal choose which of the two they wanted. After, they would sacrifice their bull, cutting it in pieces and placing it on the wood upon their altar. Elijah would do the same with the remaining bull. Then he instructed the priests of Baal to call upon their gods and ask them to send down fire from heaven to consume the sacrifice that lay upon the altar. Elijah indicated that he would ask Jehovah to do the same thing with the sacrifice that he had placed upon his altar. The God that actually consumed the sacrifice would be recognized as the true and living God. All the people agreed that this would be a fair and acceptable test (1 Kings 18:22–24).

The priests of Baal called upon their god from morning until noon, saying "O Baal, hear us," but there was no answer. And so they hopped about the altar they had built, hoping Baal would respond (1 Kings 18:26). But Elijah mocked them, saying "Call loudly. For he is a god. Maybe he is in a conversation [and can't hear you], or he is occupied,[1] or may be on the way, or perhaps he is asleep and will wake up," if you call upon him more loudly (ABT, 1 Kings 18:27).[2] So the false prophets of Baal prayed more loudly, and cut themselves with knives and swords until blood gushed from their wounds. From midday until the time of the evening sacrifice, the priests of Baal "prophesied"; but nothing happened in response. Their god did not hear them (see 1 Kings 18:27–29).

Then Elijah said to the people, "Come near" (1 Kings 18:30). Elijah then repaired an old damaged altar of Jehovah by taking twelve stones—one for each of the tribes of Israel—and using them to reerect the fallen altar on which he would offer his sacrifice.[3] Then he dug a trench around the altar. He placed wood upon the altar, then the pieces of the sacrificed bull. Then he had them pour twelve barrels of water over the bull and the wood so that all were completely soaked, and the trench was filled with water (see 1 Kings 18:30–36). Then Elijah prayed, saying, "Lord God of Abraham, Isaac, and of Israel, let it be known this day that thou art God in Israel, and that I am thy servant, and that I have done all these things at thy word" (1 Kings 18:36). At that moment, fire came down from heaven and consumed the bull, the wood, the stones, the water, and even the dust (see 1 Kings 18:38).

When the people saw the miracle, they fell on their faces, and cried out that Jehovah, "Is the God" (1 Kings 18:39). The priests of Baal were then rounded up and taken to the brook Kishon, and there they were slain for corrupting the people (see 1 Kings 18:40).

BACKGROUND

Mount Carmel is actually a range of Mediterranean hills and mountains which run southeast from modern-day Haifa.[4] The Hebrew word, *Carmel*, actually means "garden," "vineyard," or "orchard."[5] One author pointed out that the mountain became "symbolic of majesty and fertility."[6] The association with fertility is appropriate, since some of what took place on Mount Carmel had to do with pagan fertility rites performed in the "groves" upon the mountain.

The title *ba'al* (Baal) did not originally refer to a specific deity, but, rather, was an appellation that meant "lord" or "possessor." Thus, the God of Israel could originally appropriately be called Baal and, at times, was.[7] However, beginning in the ninth century BC, the term increasingly became associated with the Canaanite god, and could no longer—with propriety—be used by Israelites for Jehovah.[8] In 1 Kings 18:18, Elijah says that the Israelites had begun to worship "Baalim," which is the plural for Baal. One commentator suggested that the "Baalim" or "Baals," "May reflect the perception that the Canaanite god Baal had many manifestations." This same source indicated that "The Baal referred to [in this miracle] is Baal-Shamem, a storm god who was revered under other names: Baal Hadad and Hadad-Rimmon. . . . This god continued to be worshiped on Mount Carmel as late as the third century CE in the form of 'Heliopolitan Zeus, god of Carmel.' . . . Elijah's challenge to this particular Baal was most apt, because the underlying issue of the contest . . . was the ability of the true god to bring fire, and ultimately rain."[9] Elijah (and his God) had brought a drought. Could Baal (and his priests) end that?

Elijah famously asked the apostate Israelites, "How long halt ye between two opinions?" (1 Kings 18:21). The Hebrew of this verse has been translated as, "How long will you keep hopping between the two boughs?"[10] In other words, the imagery of the original analogy was of a bird indecisively jumping from branch to branch in a tree, just as the Israelites indecisively jumped from god to god.

In 1 Kings 18:40, we're told that the 450 "prophets of Baal" were put to death for their sins. However, we're not told what happened to the 400 "prophets of the groves" (or "prophets of Asherah") who ate at Jezebel's table. Mordechai Cogan suggested that they too were put to death, but that "a scribal oversight might explain its absence in the concluding scene."[11]

King Ahab's obedience to Elijah's request to bring the people together was not because he respected the prophet or his words. Rather, he most likely obeyed because he thought doing as Elijah had asked might get the prophet to end the drought.[12]

The narrative tells us that, at one point, the priests of Baal "leaped upon the altar" (1 Kings 18:26) as they tried to get Baal to consume their sacrifice with fire. Of this, one text suggests, "A ritual dance of some sort is implied by the hopping, limping step . . . of the Baal prophets. . . . In the present instance, the rite, which might have included music and song, was meant to attract the god's attention to his attendants' request."[13] Perhaps the dance partially explains Elijah's choice (in the very next verse) to mock the priests of Baal.

Elijah's choice to pour twelve barrels (or "jars"[14]) of water on the wood, the bull, the altar, and into the trough, was to ensure that each was so soaked that there was little way for any of it to catch fire. This would increase the impressiveness of the miracle.[15]

It is interesting that the "prophets" of Baal and the prophet of Jehovah use the same language in petitioning God's intervention: "O Baal, hear us" (1 Kings 18:26) versus "O Lord, hear me" (1 Kings 18:37). Thus, the priests of Baal could not argue that they had simply used the wrong formula and thereby received no response.

The slaughter of the priests after the miracle often offends twenty-first-century religious and moral sensitivities. However, one commentator rightly pointed out that, "The slaughter at the Kishon is no different than the one over which Moses presided at Mount Sinai (cf. Exod 32:26–28 . . .)."[16] We should not judge their laws and manner of dealing with apostates who destroy the faith of others by twenty-first-century standards. Such simply did not apply in Elijah's day. In the days of our ancient prophet, what the priests of Baal did was "high treason against God, the King of the national theocracy (Deuteronomy 13:9–11, 15; 18:20)."[17]

SYMBOLIC ELEMENTS

John A. Tvedtnes explained, "The name *Carmel* comes from Hebrew/Canaanite *karm-El*, meaning 'vineyard of El,' and was probably considered by the Canaanites to be sacred to the old Canaanite God [El], as well as to Baal and to the Canaanites' two chief goddesses."[18] Thus, when Elijah challenges the priests of Baal to a dual of the gods, he does so on Carmel because of what it would imply: "Baal is defeated by Yahweh on Baal's own ground."[19] Indeed, this entire miracle is saturated in symbols of Canaanite gods and their defeat by Jehovah.

> The Canaanite pantheon comprised a large number of nature deities, each one responsible for his or her segment of the universe.
>
> According to Canaanite mythology, the king of the gods was *El* (meaning "god" or "strong one"). . . . His wife was *Asherah*, a fertility goddess whose name means "grove."[20] The groves (generally of oak or terebinth trees) condemned so frequently in the Bible were dedicated to her worship.
>
> Myths concerning four of the children of El and Asherah are also important to our understanding of the story of Elijah:

Baal is a title meaning "lord," but also "husband." He also bore the name Hadad, "thunderer," for he was the weather God, responsible for lightning, thunder, wind, and rain.

Anath is sometimes called "the virgin," but as the "mother of nations" she is often depicted as the wife of her brother Baal. Her name means "surface (of the earth)," and as such she received the rains sent down by Baal to produce vegetation. She is therefore a fertility goddess, like her mother, Asherah. . . .

Yamm ("sea") was the god of the waters on and under the earth. Many natural phenomena were interpreted in terms of his struggle with Baal for power. . . .

Mot ("death") was the god of the underworld, where the spirits of the dead were sent. He was the antithesis of Baal, . . . and though brothers, they were enemies.

. . . The divine lightning [that came down and consumed Elijah's offering] had an even greater significance [than would be evident to the reader if he or she missed the Canaanite symbolism in the story]. It destroyed the bullock, symbol of El, as well as the wood, symbol of El's wife Asherah, thus making Jehovah more powerful than any of the Canaanite deities. The fire also destroyed the water, symbol of Yamm, who . . . was more powerful than Baal. More powerful even than Yamm, however, was Anath. . . . Jehovah's lightning bolt consumed not only the stones of the altar, but also the dust—both elements sacred to this earth goddess. There could be no doubt in the minds of those who observed this great miracle: Jehovah was *the God!*[21]

Just as the original drought symbolized Baal's death or, at the very least, his impotence, in this miracle, Elijah included symbol after symbol for various Canaanite gods whom Jehovah would be shown to defeat or utterly destroy.

The narrative informs us that, when their prayers for Baal's intervention weren't readily answered, the priests of Baal cut themselves and bled profusely. One commentary on miracle notes, "The shedding of blood is associated in biblical sources with rites of mourning, probably an expression of extreme grief, and was outlawed for Israelites [See Leviticus 19:27–28; 21:4–5; Deuteronomy 14:1]. . . . By analogy, the Baal prophets in a moment of great distress resorted to a bloody rite in the hope that it would move Baal to action, thus extricating them from their predicament."[22] Another source tells of a Canaanite myth where Baal is slain by his brother Yamm, and their father El then mourns the death of his son by making cuts in his skin with a sharpened stone. Thus, the cutting in this miracle could possibly suggest that the priests of Baal worried that—after three years of drought and no response to their current prayer—Baal had actually died.[23]

The twelve stones of the altar that Elijah built can symbolize the fact that a valid rite has to be performed by proper priesthood authority, since the number twelve is often associated with priesthood or priesthood power.[24] However, the twelve stones can also symbolize, "The participation of 'all Israel' in the proceedings being commemorated."[25]

Fire is a common symbol for the glory or presence of God (e.g., Exodus 3:2; 19:18; 24:17). As one source notes, "Although fire cannot be transformed, it can and does transform all that comes within its influence. So can the Divine Being. Hence fire has ever been regarded as a type of the pure and Holy God."[26] Fire is also associated in scripture with divine approval or God's acceptance of an act or offering (e.g., 1 Chronicles 21:26).[27] In this miracle, both may be implied.

In antiquity, bulls were often employed as symbols of deities.[28] In the case of this particular narrative, the bull most likely symbolized El—the king of the Canaanite deities—"whose full title in the Ugaritic literature is 'Father Bull El.'"[29] Therefore, the complete destruction of the bull upon the altar of Jehovah implied that Israel's God had obliterated the most powerful of all Canaanite deities.

APPLICATION AND ALLEGORIZATION

When Ahab—as directed by Elijah—had gathered the people and priests of Baal on Mount Carmel, their choice was the same as Joshua's choice: "Choose you this day whom ye will serve" (Joshua 24:15). Unfortunately, unlike Joshua's people, the Israelites of Elijah's day did not choose Jehovah.[30] They stood silent, hoping the fertility gods that they worshipped would somehow defeat the very God that brought their ancestors out of Egypt, provided manna and quail in the wilderness, gave them the law on Sinai, and blessed them with their inheritance in the promised land. So many blessings were ignored because of the temptations offered by a false god. We too, so often, pursue our false gods—ignoring all the while the tremendous blessings that we have received in our own lives at the hand of the true and living God. And, like the Israelites in this miracle, our false gods will also let us down.[31]

On a similar note, Ogden and Skinner wrote, "A powerful lesson can be drawn for us in our day: you can't hedge your bets when it comes to the kingdom of God; you can't keep one foot in the kingdom and the other in the world; you can't please the world and expect God to approve."[32]

When Elijah and Ahab meet, just before this miracle takes place, Ahab's first words to the prophet are "You're a troublemaker!" (see 1 Kings 18:17). In a way, this is surprising. Israel had suffered for three years under a drought that Jehovah had brought because of the idolatry of the people. One would expect that this would have softened Ahab's heart or provoked some degree of humility and penitence. Clearly, such was not the case! When our hearts are hard, God will sometimes send us trials to bring us to our knees, in order to provoke repentance. For some, this is effective. For others, the heart only gets harder (as it did with King Ahab).[33]

As a rather sobering application of the miracle, Kenneth Woodward suggested that this narrative reminds us of the consequences of our faithlessness for our opportunity to experience miracles.

> This is a sweeping, powerful miracle—on a par . . . with those worked by Moses and Aaron in their contest with Pharaoh's magicians. But it is also the last of the *public* miracles in the Hebrew Bible. Hereafter, no more miracles will be witnessed by a sizable portion of the Israelite people. And this privatization of the miraculous, we will now see, coincides with the increasing diminishment of the palpable presence of God Himself in the Biblical narrative.[34]

How does this apply to the Saints of the latter days? While I do not think one can say that the less public nature of miracles in the Church (since the death of the Prophet Joseph) is evidence that God has rejected His earthly organization, because part of that is a direct result of the leadership seeking to keep the sacred sacrosanct. Nevertheless, I do think the aforementioned application invites you and me to ask ourselves about the frequency of miracles in our personal lives. If they are happening less and less often, perhaps—like the Israelites of old—it is because God is less a part of our day-to-day lives. If we wish to experience the divine on a personal and powerful level, we must do the things that provoke the miraculous. Living a terrestrial life does not provoke miracles. But daily attempts at celestial living always lead to that "palpable presence of God" that should be part of the lives of His covenant people.

John Chrysostom suggested the following application of Elijah's boldness toward King Ahab: "Elijah said to Ahab with boldness: 'It is not that I trouble Israel, but you and your father's house.' You see that this poverty [of the prophet] especially produces boldness? For while the rich person is a slave, being subject and in the power of every one wishing to do him [harm], one who has nothing fears no confiscation or fine."[35] When we have nothing to lose, often we can be the most true to our conscience. As the Psalmist said, "In God I have put my trust; I will not fear what flesh can do unto me" (Psalm 56:4); or, as the Lord commanded, "Fear not what man can do, for God shall be with you forever and ever" (D&C 122:9).

Ambrose and Origen each saw the ordinances of baptism symbolized in what Elijah did.[36] The bull was a symbol for El, one of the gods of the Canaanites, and, thus, for one who was not a member of the Church. It was thoroughly doused in water, as a symbol of baptism. Indeed, water was poured over it three times, symbolizing the three members of the Godhead. And twelve containers of water were poured out, symbolizing the need for the ordinance to be performed by proper priesthood authority. After the bull was doused with water, fire came down from heaven, consuming the old bull—reminding us of how the baptism of fire must follow the baptism of water; thereby, destroying the old or natural man within us.

Richard Trench suggested that the contest between Elijah and the priests of Baal was a foreshadowing of the "contest which is still going on [today] between light and darkness, and which will be decided by fire in the future (2 Thess. i.8)."[37] Indeed, there are a number of things about this miracle that remind us of the last days and Christ's ultimate return. There is the tension between good and evil that is so prevalent in our world today. There is the "inequality of numbers" in the story—i.e., one prophet versus 450 priests of Baal. Today, those who are for revealed religion and modern prophets are greatly outnumbered by those who are against such things.)[38] There is the symbolism present in the fact that one man ultimately defeated the masses, just as Jesus will defeat the evil masses upon His return.[39] Thus, the symbol for the wicked (the bull) was utterly consumed by fire, just as, at Jesus's return, all the wicked shall be completely destroyed by God's glory. Finally, the narrative seems symbolic because "Praying and working will bring the 'restitution of all things.' As Elijah restored the altar and continued in prayer before it till the decisive hour came, so God's minority labour and pray, and, in the evening of the present dispensation, heaven will yield the answer."[40]

When Ahab accuses Elijah of being a troublemaker, the prophet turns that back on the king and says "No! You and your family are the troublemakers because you have caused Israel—God's covenant people—to sin" (see 1 Kings 18:17–18). Clovis Chappell noted, "That is the secret of all the real trouble. All our woes come fundamentally from the refusal to do the will of God."[41] Chappell added, "Sad to say, the final scene [in this miracle] is not the falling of the divine fire but the falling of the sword upon the necks of the false prophets. It is one of bloody violence. . . . If we preach unbrotherliness by our lips and our lives, sooner or later we shall reap a harvest of violence."[42] The king sinned, and the consequence was that his people sinned. A parent chooses to live a sinful life and, more often than not, their children become partakers of those same sins. Our choices affect others, and they certainly affect us. In the words of the hymn, "Keep the commandments! In this there is safety; in this there is peace."[43]

NOTES

1.   One commentary on the Hebrew suggested that the phrase "He is occupied" or "He is pursuing" (as the King James renders it) means that Baal was attending to the "call of nature" (i.e., using the bathroom). This same source suggests that Elijah was offering "a piece of biting sarcasm." (See Israel Wolf Slotki, *Kings*, in *Soncino Books of the Bible* [London: The Soncino Press, 1978], 132. See also Donald J. Wiseman, *1 and 2 Kings*, in *Tyndale Old Testament Commentaries* [Downers Grove, IL: InterVarsity Press, 1988), 169.)]

2.   See Mordechai Cogan, *The Anchor Bible: 1 Kings*, vol. 10 (New York: Doubleday, 2001), 435.

3.   *The Anchor Bible Dictionary* suggests that this was not the same altar used by the priests of Baal but, instead, an old altar that had previously been used on that mountain when the true priests of Jehovah used to worship upon it prior to when Jezebel "slew the prophets of the Lord" (1 Kings 18:13). (See Henry O. Thompson, "Carmel, Mount," in David Noel Freedman, *The Anchor Bible Dictionary* [New York: Doubleday, 1992], 1:875. See also Herbert Lockyer, *All the Miracles of the Bible: The Supernatural in Scripture—Its Scope and Significance* [Grand Rapids, MI: Zondervan, 1961], 111; Richard D. Patterson and Hermann J. Austel, "1 and 2 Kings," in Frank E. Gaebelein, ed., *The Expositor's Bible Commentary* [Grand Rapids, MI: Zondervan, 1994], 4:146, where it is suggested that "the availability of a fallen altar to Yahweh here may have provided an additional reason for selecting Mount Carmel as the contest place.") Mordechai Cogan indicated, "Activity at the YHWH cult site on the mountain was suspended during Jezebel's purge" of the true Israelite prophets. (See Cogan, *The Anchor Bible: 1 Kings*, 439. See also 440.) Jewish commentators have suggested that the altar used by Elijah was the very same one built by Saul. (See Israel Wolf Slotki, *Kings*, in *Soncino Books of the Bible*, 133.)

4.   See Thompson, "Carmel, Mount," in Freedman, *The Anchor Bible Dictionary*, 1:874.

5.   See Francis Brown, S. R. Driver, and Charles A. Briggs, *The Brown-Driver-Briggs Hebrew and English Lexicon* (Peabody, MA: Hendrickson Publishers, 1999),

502; Thompson, "Carmel, Mount," in Freedman, *The Anchor Bible Dictionary*, 1:874.

6. See Cogan, *The Anchor Bible: 1 Kings*, 439.

7. For example, Saul named one of his sons "Ishbaal," meaning "man of the lord." However, Saul was not reverencing a foreign deity when he named his son this. Rather, he meant his son's name to imply "man of Jehovah."

8. See Martin Rose, "Name of God in the Old Testament," in Freedman, *The Anchor Bible Dictionary*, 4:1007–8.

9. Cogan, *The Anchor Bible: 1 Kings*, 439–40. See also Israel Wolf Slotki, *Kings*, in *Soncino Books of the Bible*, 130.

10. Cogan, *The Anchor Bible: 1 Kings*, 435.

11. Ibid., 439.

12. See Pamela McQuade, *The Top 100 Miracles of the Bible: What They Are and What They Mean to You Today* (Uhrichsville, OH: Barbour Publishing, 2008), 78.

13. Cogan, *The Anchor Bible: 1 Kings*, 440. See also Patterson and Austel, in "1 and 2 Kings," in Gaebelein, *The Expositor's Bible Commentary*, 4:144; Israel Wolf Slotki, *Kings*, in *Soncino Books of the Bible*, 131. The Tyndale commentary on the passage indicates that the Hebrew of this verse "denotes a circumambulation [ritualistic circling] of the altar [on foot]." Wiseman, *1 and 2 Kings*, in *Tyndale Old Testament Commentaries*, 169.

14. This would be the type of "jar" a woman would carry on her shoulder. See Brown, Driver, and Briggs, *The Brown-Driver-Briggs Hebrew and English Lexicon*, 461; Cogan, *The Anchor Bible: 1 Kings*, 443.

15. See Cogan, *The Anchor Bible: 1 Kings*, 443; Patterson and Austel, in "1 and 2 Kings," in Gaebelein, *The Expositor's Bible Commentary*, 4:144.

16. Cogan, *The Anchor Bible: 1 Kings*, 444. See also Wiseman, *1 and 2 Kings*, in *Tyndale Old Testament Commentaries*, 170.

17. Lockyer, *All the Miracles of the Bible*, 112.

18. John A. Tvedtnes, "Elijah: Champion of Israel's God," *Ensign*, July 1990. See also D. Kelly Ogden and Andrew C. Skinner, *Verse By Verse—The Old Testament Volume One: Genesis through 2 Samuel, Psalms* (Salt Lake City, UT: Deseret Book, 2013), 2:35.

19. Henry O. Thompson, "Carmel, Mount," in Freedman, *The Anchor Bible Dictionary*, 1:875.

20. Maurice Farbridge suggested that, "In the earliest times the altars stood under trees" and "the sacred tree or its substitute, the pole, came to be looked upon as a symbol of the deity." (Maurice H. Farbridge, *Studies in Biblical and Semitic Symbolism* [London: Routledge, 1923], 34.)

21. Tvedtnes, "Elijah: Champion of Israel's God." Tvedtnes added, "Atop the mount there still exists today one of the largest forests of oak trees in Israel, these being the symbol of Asherah. As the most prominent piece of land in the area, it was considered part of the body of Anath, the earth goddess. Furthermore, because

it is the highest mountain in the region, during thunderstorms it receives more lightning strikes than other points; probably this was thought to indicate Baal's presence. The mountain also receives more rainfall than any other spot in Israel, making it an even more suitable representation of Anath, on whom Baal sends his rain." (Tvedtnes, "Elijah: Champion of Israel's God.")

22. Cogan, *The Anchor Bible: 1 Kings*, 441.

23. Tvedtnes, "Elijah: Champion of Israel's God."

24. See Richard D. Draper, *Opening the Seven Seals: The Visions of John the Revelator* (Salt Lake City, UT: Deseret Book, 1991), 24, 46, 56, 83; Jay A. Parry and Donald W. Parry, *Understanding the Book of Revelation* (Salt Lake City, UT: Deseret Book, 1998), 295; E. W. Bullinger, *Number in Scripture: Its Supernatural Design and Spiritual Significance* (Grand Rapids, MI: Kregel Publications, 1967), 2–3, 107; Mick Smith, *The Book of Revelation: Plain, Pure, and Simple* (Salt Lake City, UT: Deseret Book, 1998), 288–89; Robert D. Johnston, *Numbers in the Bible: God's Design in Biblical Numerology* (Grand Rapids, MI: Kregel Publications, 1999), 39 & 83; John J. Davis, *Biblical Numerology: A Basic Study of the Use of Numbers in the Bible* (Grand Rapids, MI: Baker Book House, 1968), 122.

25. Cogan, *The Anchor Bible: 1 Kings*, 442.

26. Richard C. Trench, *Miracles and Parables of the Old Testament* (Grand Rapids, MI: Baker Book House, 1959), 118.

27. See Cogan, *The Anchor Bible: 1 Kings*, 443; Patterson and Austel, in "1 and 2 Kings," in Gaebelein, *The Expositor's Bible Commentary*, 4:147; Trench, *Miracles and Parables of the Old Testament*, 118.

28. See J. C. Cooper, *An Illustrated Encyclopaedia of Traditional Symbols* (London: Thames and Hudson, 1995), 26–27; E. Cirlot, *A Dictionary of Symbols*, 2nd ed. (New York: Routledge & Kegan Paul, 1971), 34–35.

29. Tvedtnes, "Elijah: Champion of Israel's God."

30. See Patterson and Austel, in "1 and 2 Kings," in Gaebelein, *The Expositor's Bible Commentary*, 4:144.

31. One commentary noted, "The prophets of Baal had kept up their wailing and wild ritual for the better part of a day and met with dead silence. Elijah's petition had lasted less than a minute but produced spectacular results. The difference lay in the One addressed." (Patterson and Austel, in "1 and 2 Kings," in Gaebelein, *The Expositor's Bible Commentary*, 4:145.)

32. Ogden and Skinner, *Verse By Verse—The Old Testament Volume One: Genesis through 2 Samuel, Psalms*, 2:35.

33. See McQuade, *The Top 100 Miracles of the Bible*, 78.

34. Kenneth L. Woodward, *The Book of Miracles: The Meaning of the Miracle Stories in Christianity, Judaism, Buddhism, Islam* (New York: Simon & Schuster, 2000), 64.

35. John Chrysostom, "On the Epistle to the Hebrews" 18:4, in Marco Conti, ed., *1–2 Kings, 1–2 Chronicles, Ezra, Nehemiah, Esther*, in *Ancient Christian Commentary on Scripture* (Downers Grove, IL: InterVarsity Press, 2008), 107.

36. See Ambrose, "On Elijah and Fasting," 22.83, and Origen, "Commentary on the Gospel of John," 6.125, in Conti, *1–2 Kings, 1–2 Chronicles, Ezra, Nehemiah, Esther*, in *Ancient Christian Commentary on Scripture*, 110.

37. Trench, *Miracles and Parables of the Old Testament*, 118.

38. See ibid., 118–19.

39. See ibid., 119.

40. Ibid.

41. Clovis Gillham Chappell, *The Cross Before Calvary* (New York: Abingdon Press, 1960), 47.

42. Ibid., 49.

43. "Keep the Commandments," *Hymns*, no. 303.

ELIJAH IS SUSTAINED *for* FORTY DAYS *as* HE TREKS *to* MOUNT HOREB

1 KINGS 19:1–8

THE MIRACLE

After Elijah had slain Ahab and Jezebel's false prophets, the queen was wroth with him. So she sent a message to Jehovah's prophet saying in effect, "May the gods take my life if I do not kill you by this time tomorrow" (see 1 Kings 19:1–2).

Knowing that his life was in grave danger, Elijah took his servant to Beer-sheba, and then went about a day's journey into the wilderness where he could hide (see 1 Kings 19:3).

There the prophet found a juniper tree, and prayed to God that he might die there, saying: "O Lord, take away my life; for I am not better than my fathers" (1 Kings 19:4).

After he had fallen asleep under the tree, an angel awoke him, and said "Arise and eat." Elijah looked and, there before him, was a fire of coals, and on those coals was a freshly baked cake. In addition, there was a flask of water—all miraculously provided. So Elijah ate, and then slept again (see 1 Kings 19:5–6).

A second time, the angel again woke him and told him to eat,; but this time the angel commanded him to journey to Horeb—to the "mount of God" (1 Kings 19:7–8). So Elijah arose and ate, and the food he consumed gave him the strength to make the forty-day journey to Horeb.

BACKGROUND

Though King Ahab had just witnessed an unexplainable miracle—the consuming of the water-soaked bull, wood, altar, and ground at the hands of Elijah's God—his heart was not softened by it. He returns to his wife, complaining that Jehovah's prophet is causing more problems. This rebelliousness in the face of undeniable facts is evidence of how very hard Ahab's heart was.

If Jezebel had really wanted Elijah dead, she would have sent mercenaries to take care of him without warning him. Thus, her threat may have simply been designed to scare him into leaving the region. "Without a leader revolutionary movements usually stumble and fall away."[1] Jezebel may have felt that, if she could get rid of Elijah, his followers who pushed back on her Baalism might fade away also.

The text states that Elijah went to Beer-sheba, and from there, a day's journey into the wilderness. This lets us know that he was no longer within the realm of King Ahab and Queen Jezebel. Presumably, being outside of their political jurisdiction made him feel less worried for his personal safety.[2]

In Jewish tradition, the "servant" that Elijah leaves in Beer-sheba was the son of the widow of Zarephath whom Elijah had miraculously raised from the dead.[3]

The King James Version says that Elijah went into the "wilderness" (1 Kings 19:4). However, the Hebrew suggests it was less a "wilderness" or "desert," and more the "steppe"—where nomads would take their sheep and goats to graze.[4]

The tree under which Elijah takes refuge—described as a "juniper" tree (in the King James Version)—is a broom shrub typically used by nomads for fuel (see Psalm 120:4), and, when desperate, for food (see Job 30:4).[5] The Septuagint—the Greek version of the Hebrew Bible—refers to it as a "bush"; though this "bush" may grow as high as ten feet.[6]

We're told that Elijah fled for his life. However, by the time he reaches the broom tree in the steppe, he speaks of wanting to die. This isn't necessarily a contradiction in the text. It may be that by the time he has made his arduous journey, he is physically tired and also conscious that Ahab and Jezebel are not going to repent and are not likely going to leave him alone. This may explain the seeming change in the prophet's desires.

In the King James Version of the narrative, we are first told that an "angel" appears to Elijah (1 Kings 19:5), then we are told that it was "the angel of the Lord" (1 Kings 19:7). Drawing on the fact that the Hebrew word for "angel" can also appropriately be translated as "messenger," the Septuagint (in 1 Kings 19:7) simply says "someone" touches the prophet.[7]

SYMBOLIC ELEMENTS

In this narrative of Elijah being sustained for forty days in the wilderness—and in the verses that follow the actual miracle—there is a clear attempt by the author to highlight how Elijah is the new Moses. Parallel after parallel exists between their two lives and ministries.

> Among the prominent themes of 1 Kgs 19 is the return of Elijah "on Israel's tracks to the mountain of revelation, and there he receives the revelation."[8] . . . Throughout, the narrator has creatively used motifs associated with Moses, enriching his tale with literary allusions that, at times, attain verbal resemblance to their earlier tradition. Elijah journeyed forty days into the desert in order to reach the mountain of God (v. 8), where Moses had spent "forty days and forty nights" receiving the Law (Exod 24:18); during his second stay on the mountain, Moses did not take bread or water (cf. 34:28), while Elijah made his long trek to Horeb sustained only by the food he had consumed in the wilderness near Beersheba (1 Kgs 19:8). Elijah came to a cave on Horeb (v. 8) and was bidden to take his place on the mountain as YHWH passed by, just as Moses had stood in "the crevice of a rock" for a similar theophany (Exod 33:22). When YHWH "was passing by" (1 Kgs 19:11), Elijah "covered his face with his cloak" (v. 13); Moses was privileged with having YHWH "cover" him with his hand (Exod 33:23; at the burning bush, Moses himself hid his face [3:6]). YHWH's appearance to Israel at Sinai in fire and thunder (Exod 19:18; cf. 3:2) is reenacted for Elijah (1 Kgs 19:11–12). . . . And like Moses, who was not permitted to enter the Promised Land but only to see it from afar, Elijah was not to attain the final triumph over Baal but only to know that it would be accomplished by his successors. In sum, Elijah is depicted as having reached the pinnacle of his career, privileged with a personal revelation of Moses-like dimensions.[9]

Elijah travels some forty days to Horeb. The number forty is a fairly common scriptural symbol. Some commentators interpret this number as simply meaning "a lengthy period of time."[10] Because this instance is applied to years, it certainly can mean that. However, the symbolism in the number goes beyond this simple definition. In scripture, the number represents a period of trial, testing, probation, or mourning.[11] This certainly seems descriptive of what Elijah experienced as he trekked through the wilderness toward Horeb—emotionally heavy because his repeated miracles had not brought a softening of the heart of the king and queen of Israel.

APPLICATION AND ALLEGORIZATION

Elijah had performed a series of rather remarkable miracles. He had brought upon the unrepentant people of Israel a three-year drought (see 1 Kings 17:1). He had lived off food provided to him by ravens (see 1 Kings 17:2–7). He had multiplied the meal and oil of a widow so that her and her household were provided for, for an extended period of time (see 1 Kings 17:8–16). He had raised a young man from the dead (see 1 Kings 17:17–24). And he had brought down fire from heaven (see 1 Kings 18:1–39). He may well have expected that his priesthood power would also soften the hearts of the king and queen who so loathed him. However, it did not, and the prophet seemed quite shattered by that reality. One commentary on this miracle suggested that the story of Elijah reminds us of the reality that, "God does not always move in the realm of the extraordinary. To live always seeking one 'high experience' after another is to have a misdirected zeal. The majority of life's service is in quiet, routine, humble obedience to God's will."[12] There is no question that God performs miracles in our lives and in the life of the Church. Some of those are quite remarkable, even dramatic. However, major spiritual experiences are the exception, not the rule. Our day-to-day lives are more often about the "still small voice" (see 1 Kings 19:12; 1 Nephi 17:45; D&C 85:6) guiding and directing us as we seek to live in harmony with its subtle promptings.

Most commentaries on this passage speak of the weakness of Elijah that are evidenced in this section of 1 Kings. Ogden and Skinner noted, "Here we catch a glimpse of . . . the truth that even prophets get discouraged."[13] Yet, in a rather unexpected insight, one commentary on the miracle suggested, "Elijah exhibited symptoms of manic depression, wishing for death, together with loss of appetite, an inability to manage and with excessive self-pity. He was unmoved by visitors, even by a visit from God and vision, but was restored when given a new and demanding task to fulfil."[14] The point being that God did great things through a man who may have struggled with a significant handicap. God's instruments don't need to be perfect. Indeed, often He chooses those who are not perfect or polished, because—aware of their weaknesses—they usually are humble, and, thus, are capable of being used by Him.

On this same note, observe how God didn't simply provide Elijah food; He also provided one who did not want to live anymore with companionship. In the past, He fed him in the wilderness by having ravens drop food off to the prophet. However, now that Elijah was in a rather bad place, God did more than drop of the proverbial casserole; He sent His angel to encourage and instruct Elijah—motivating him to eat when, in a state of depression, he most likely would not have without such encouragement. As one text noted, "The *sympathy* of his angelic visitor was no doubt part of the meal in whose strength he afterwards went 'forty days.'"[15]

The fact that the series of dramatic miracles Elijah performed had no effect on the hearts of Jezebel and Ahab is a reminder of the truth thatmiracles don't convert people. They are intriguing, no doubt. But the notion that someone will develop true, lasting faith based on some miraculous experience has been proven false time and again. The Spirit converts. Exercising faith by taking a step into the unknown, and then recognizing the hand of God afterwards converts. Living the commandments and keeping covenants converts. But miracles are as readily dismissed as the messengers who testify of them. If we wish to be converted, the best thing we can do is to forget about seeking signs, and, instead, follow Christ's counsel: "If any man will do [God's] will, he shall know of the doctrine, whether it be of God, or whether I speak of myself" (John 7:17).

Of the bread and water highlighted in this miracle, one Latter-day Saint author wrote, "It is hard to miss the symbolism that points to the modern sacramental emblems with their attendant promise of eternal life."[16] Indeed, the bread and water provided Elijah by the "angel of the Lord" preserved his life as he made his arduous journey to see the face of God at Horeb. In like manner, the bread and water of the sacrament preserve our spiritual lives as we make the grueling trek through mortality—seeking to return to the Father where we shall also see His face. Elijah was told that he could not possibly successfully make his journey without the nourishment that the bread and water would provide him (see 1 Kings 19:7). Similarly, you and I cannot successfully make it back to God without the spiritual nourishment that the sacrament provides us. For this very reason, Latter-day Saints should take the ordinance of the sacrament more seriously. We should be more repentant when we partake—having in mind specific sins that we will fight in the upcoming week to overcome. We should be more focused when we partake—setting aside distractions, such as our cell phones. We should be more sorrowful when we partake—genuinely sorry about the pain we have caused ourselves, others, and Christ.

One commentary offered this application of the miracle: "Our Lord's command to His disciples was, 'If they persecute you in one city, flee to another' (Matt. x. 23), and He Himself 'would not walk in Jewry because the Jews sought to kill him' (John vii. I)."[17] Those who seek to do God's will, and who stand up for the faith, should expect to be persecuted and rejected. Elijah was. Joseph Smith was. Jesus was! We too may be called to endure persecution for Christ's name.

NOTES

1. Richard D. Patterson and Hermann J. Austel, "1 and 2 Kings," in Frank E. Gaebelein, ed., *The Expositor's Bible Commentary* (Grand Rapids, MI: Zondervan, 1994), 4:148; Israel Wolf Slotki, *Kings*, in *Soncino Books of the Bible* (London: The Soncino Press, 1978), 136–37.

2. See Mordechai Cogan, *The Anchor Bible: 1 Kings*, vol. 10 (New York: Doubleday, 2001), 451; Israel Wolf Slotki, *Kings*, in *Soncino Books of the Bible*, 137; Donald J. Wiseman, *1 and 2 Kings*, in *Tyndale Old Testament Commentaries* (Downers Grove, IL InterVarsity Press, 1988), 172.

3. See Israel Wolf Slotki, *Kings*, in *Soncino Books of the Bible*, 137.

4. See Cogan, *The Anchor Bible: 1 Kings*, 451.

5. See Francis Brown, S. R. Driver, and Charles A. Briggs, *The Brown-Driver-Briggs Hebrew and English Lexicon* (Peabody, MA: Hendrickson Publishers, 1999), 958; Cogan, *The Anchor Bible: 1 Kings*, 451.

6. See Patterson and Austel, "1 and 2 Kings," in Gaebelein, *The Expositor's Bible Commentary*, 4:149; Wiseman, *1 and 2 Kings*, in *Tyndale Old Testament Commentaries*, 172.

7. See Cogan, *The Anchor Bible: 1 Kings*, 451.

8. The mountain of Jehovah is called both Horeb (e.g., Exodus 3:1; Deut. 1:6; 4:10; cf. 1 Kings 8:9) and also Sinai (Exodus 19:11; Lev. 25:1).

9. Cogan, *The Anchor Bible: 1 Kings*, 456–57. See also Patterson and Austel, "1 and 2 Kings," in Gaebelein, *The Expositor's Bible Commentary*, 4:149; Wiseman, *1 and 2 Kings*, in *Tyndale Old Testament Commentaries*, 172.

10. See Joel F. Drinkard, "Numbers," in Paul J. Achtemeier, ed., *Harper's Bible Dictionary* (New York: Harper & Row, 1985), 712; Mick Smith, *The Book of Revelation: Plain, Pure, and Simple* (Salt Lake City, UT: Deseret Book, 1998), 289.

11. John J. Davis, *Biblical Numerology: A Basic Study of the Use of Numbers in the Bible* (Grand Rapids, MI: Baker Book House, 1968), 121n79, 122; J. C. Cooper, *An Illustrated Encyclopaedia of Traditional Symbols* (London: Thames and Hudson, 1995), 120; E. W. Bullinger, *Number in Scripture: Its Supernatural Design and Spiritual Significance* (Grand Rapids, MI: Kregel Publications, 1967), 266; Robert D. Johnston, *Numbers in the Bible: God's Design in Biblical Numerology* (Grand Rapids, MI: Kregel Publications, 1999), 85; Maurice H. Farbridge, *Studies in*

Biblical and Semitic Symbolism (London: Routledge, 1923), 144, 155–56; Kevin J. Todeschi, *The Encyclopedia of Symbols* (New York: Perigee Book, 1995), 187.

12. Patterson and Austel, "1 and 2 Kings," in Gaebelein, *The Expositor's Bible Commentary*, 4:148.

13. D. Kelly Ogden and Andrew C. Skinner, *Verse By Verse—The Old Testament Volume One: Genesis through 2 Samuel, Psalms* (Salt Lake City, UT: Deseret Book, 2013), 2:36.

14. Wiseman, *1 and 2 Kings*, in *Tyndale Old Testament Commentaries*, 171. Byron Merrill also suggested that Elijah was suffering from "depression." Byron R. Merrill, *Elijah: Yesterday, Today, and Tomorrow* (Salt Lake City, UT: Deseret Book, 1997), 53. Lockyer similarly suggested, "The events of Carmel had been a great strain, mentally and physically, and the lion-hearted prophet gave way . . . to feelings of despair and despondency." (Herbert Lockyer, *All the Miracles of the Bible: The Supernatural in Scripture—Its Scope and Significance* [Grand Rapids, MI: Zondervan, 1961], 113. See also Richard C. Trench, *Miracles and Parables of the Old Testament* [Grand Rapids, MI: Baker Book House, 1959], 121.)

15. Trench, *Miracles and Parables of the Old Testament*, 121; emphasis in original.

16. Merrill, *Elijah: Yesterday, Today, and Tomorrow*, 54.

17. Trench, *Miracles and Parables of the Old Testament*, 120.

FIRE COMES DOWN *from* HEAVEN *to* CONSUME THE MESSENGERS *of the* KING OF SAMARIA

2 KINGS 1:2–17

THE MIRACLE

Ahaziah, the king of Israel (and son of Ahab), had fallen through the lattice in his upper chamber, and had injured himself. So he sent his representatives to inquire of Baal-zebub—the god of Ekron—as to whether he would recover from his severe injury. God inspired Elijah to go out to meet them on their way to inquire regarding the king's recovery. He asked them, "Is it because there is no God in Israel that you are going off to consult Baal-zebub?" (see 2 Kings 1:3). Then Elijah informed them that the king would never leave his bed, but would certainly die (see 2 Kings 1:2–4).

When the king's representatives learned this, they returned to the king and informed him that they had met a man who had said the king would die. The king inquired as to what the man looked like. They informed him that the man was hairy and wore a leather belt around his waist. The king then realized that it was Elijah that they had been speaking of (see 2 Kings 1:5–9).

So King Ahaziah sent an officer, accompanied by fifty soldiers, to speak to Elijah, who was sitting atop a hill. They said to the prophet, "Thou man of God, the king hath said, Come down" (2 Kings 1:9). Elijah's only response was, "If I be a man of God, then let fire come down from heaven, and consume thee and thy fifty." At that instant, fire came down from heaven, and all fifty-one of the king's men were consumed by it (2 Kings 1:10).

When the king learned what happened, he sent another captain and his fifty men to speak to Elijah. They also told Elijah that he needed to. "Come down quickly" from the hill and speak to the king. Again, Elijah simply replied, "If I be a man of God, then let fire come down from heaven, and consume thee and thy fifty" (2 Kings 1:12). And it did! All fifty-one men were destroyed (see 2 Kings 1:11–12).

A third time the king sent an officer and his fifty soldiers to Elijah. However, this third officer—as he drew near to Elijah—fell upon his knees and plead with the prophet, saying, "O man of God, I pray thee, let my life, and the life of these fifty [of] thy servants, be precious in thy sight" (2 Kings 1:13). As the captain said these words, the angel of the Lord told Elijah he should go with the king's captain—and that he should not be afraid to do so. So Elijah descended the hill and went before the king (see 2 Kings 1:14–15).

Elijah's message to Ahaziah, king of Israel, was this: "Thus saith the Lord, since you sent your messengers to inquire of Baal-zebub—as though there were no God in Israel—you will not get well, but will certainly die" (see 2 Kings 1:16). And true to the prophecy of Elijah, the king died (see 2 Kings 1:17).

BACKGROUND

While it can't be stated for certain, it appears that the king fell through a "screenlike structure over a window or the open area of the roof" and fell some distance to the ground, severely injuring himself.[1]

The name Baal-zebub means literally "Baal-of-the-flies" (or "Lord of the flies").[2] Lexicons traditionally connect "Baal-zebub" with the New Testament name, "Beelzebub" (see Matthew 10:25; Mark 3:22; Luke 11:15), whom Jews of the first century perceived as "the prince of the devils" (Matthew 12:24).[3] Ekron, where Baal-zebub was being worshipped, was a Philistine city on the border of the territory settled by the Israelite tribes.[4]

The exact meaning of the description of Elijah as a "hairy man" (2 Kings 1:8) is disputed. Some believe that it means that he had an inordinate amount of body hair.[5] Others argue that it means he wore a garment of hair tied with a belt around his waist.[6]

The number of men sent to Elijah, at any given time, simply to request that he come meet with the king seems unnecessarily large. One commentary on the episode noted, "The morality of the act has often been misunderstood as the 'inhumanity of the destruction of the innocent captains and fifties.' . . ."[7] In response, Israel Wolf Slotki suggested, "The large number of soldiers sent indicates the king's intention to capture and execute him. This explains Elijah's drastic treatment of the contingents (verses 10 and 12)."[8] Owing to all of the revelation that Elijah had been receiving throughout his ministry—and in response to the behaviors of the kings of Israel—it seems unlikely that the Lord would leave him ignorant of the king's intentions in this matter.

SYMBOLIC ELEMENTS

We are told that, in order to commune with Elijah, the hosts of the king had to ascend the hill upon which he sat. In scripture, hills and mountains are often symbols for the temple.[9] Elijah's presence there suggests his closeness to God. It implies that he was close to the divine, while those in the valley below were distant from deity.

As noted previously, fire is a standard symbol for the glory or presence of God. It can represent His power to sanctify, but also His wrath upon the unrepentant—as in this miracle's narrative. Here it also reminds us that it was *not* Elijah that condemned these men to death; but God.[10] The quintessential symbol of the divine destroyed them—not the hairy man of Tishbe.

APPLICATION AND ALLEGORIZATION

In his trial, King Ahaziah turns to a false god instead of to Jehovah—as though Jehovah didn't exist at all; or as though He could not be trusted to fix the king's injuries. Ahaziah was

> Seeking help where it was not to be found in direct violation of the law of God. If a member of a family were to break his arm, and instead of applying to the family surgeon who had in the past given full proof of his skill, were to seek the advice of a quack, he would be sinning against himself, and insulting the man who was able and willing to cure him. This was the conduct of Ahaziah towards the God of his nation, when, having met with an accident, he sent to the god of Ekron, and thereby slighted and despised Him who alone could help him.[11]

Pamela McQuade pointed out, "Sometimes we ignore the tenderheartedness of God. Do we know that we can hurt Him when we go elsewhere with our troubles?"[12] In our own trials, do we turn to God? Or do we turn to false gods (e.g., pornography, drugs, shopping, Netflix, etc.) as though God didn't exist at all—or as though He isn't capable or interested in helping us at all? By turning to a false god, Ahaziah died. If you and I (in our trials) turn to the gods of this world, we will surely die spiritually because the gods of this world have no power to save nor to heal.

It is curious that the men who ordered (or commanded) Elijah did not get what they wanted from him. But the man who humbly approached him and pled his cooperation was met with compliance. While completely foreign to this story, one could draw from this a message about how we interact with others. Do we *order* or *command* those from who we desire a particular behavior (e.g., our children or employees), as though they owe us exact obedience? In the narrative at hand, that kind of approach actually brought God's wrath. Perhaps God is not pleased when we treat our children or others that we have stewardship for in this manner.

Ahaziah sent fifty-one of his men to Elijah to take him into custody. However, they were all slain in a miraculous manner—by fire from heaven—leaving nothing but scorched earth and smoldering corpses. Yet, in what can only be described as a self-destructive act of pride, Ahaziah sent another fifty-one men to accost the prophet, and to lose their lives in the exact same manner. Still entrenched, he sent a third batch—knowing that they most likely would suffer the same fate. (Were it not for the humility of the captain of the third contingent, such likely would have been their end.) Even when the prophet finally came to speak with the king, there is no evidence in the story that Ahaziah's heart had softened. The dramatic miracles of Elijah could not humble him. The death of 102 of his men could not humble him. The threat of his own death could not humble him. Of this extreme obstinacy, one source noted, "When an ox is being driven to the slaughter, he seems to be conscious of his coming doom, and tries to avoid being driven to the place of death. But men rush on to their own destruction even when God sends messengers to drive them *from* the way of ruin."[13] Pride is one of the most self-destructive of vices. How many of God's children have fallen because of this "universal sin"?[14] How many have lost their faith or membership in the Church because of their pride? How many have destroyed a marriage or other relationships because of pride? President Ezra Taft Benson said pride is "the cause for discontent, divorce, teenage rebellion, family indebtedness, and most other problems we face."[15] Like Ahaziah, if we allow ourselves to become prideful beings, we will surely lose our souls.

One source points out, "Ahaziah's captains died, not for his sin, but for their participation in his defiance of God. The escape of the third captain proves this."[16] Guilt by association is real; and it can be deadly. I knew of a young man, for example, who was reared in a faithful LDS family. In high school, he began to "hang out" with those who were not keeping the commandments—largely because he felt that he could be a good influence upon them. In the end, they wielded more influence upon him than he did upon them. In time, addictions developed, faith was lost, and the formerly faithful young man found himself completely unaffiliated with the Church. Like Ahaziah's soldiers, who died because of their support of a wicked man, those who wish to retain their faith and standing with God must keep themselves aloof from sin. While we should not cut ourselves off from all who believe or live differently than ourselves, we must not place ourselves in situations where our spirituality might be killed by our association with others. Just as Ahaziah's men died though their affiliation with him, we too may lose our spiritual lives if we are not cautious about our associations.

NOTES

1.   Mordechai Cogan and Hayim Tadmor, *The Anchor Bible: II Kings*, vol. 11 (New York: Doubleday, 1988), 24. See also Richard D. Patterson and Hermann J. Austel, "1 and 2 Kings," in Frank E. Gaebelein, ed., *The Expositor's Bible Commentary* (Grand Rapids, MI: Zondervan, 1994), 4:170; Israel Wolf Slotki, *Kings*, in *Soncino Books of the Bible* (London: The Soncino Press, 1978), 166; Donald J. Wiseman, *1 and 2 Kings*, in *Tyndale Old Testament Commentaries* (Downers Grove, IL: InterVarsity Press, 1988), 192. "The typical Syrian upper balcony was enclosed with a jointed wood lattice-work that, while suitable for privacy, could easily be broken. Patterson and Austel, "1 and 2 Kings," in Gaebelein, *The Expositor's Bible Commentary*, 4:172.

2.   Francis Brown, S. R. Driver, and Charles A. Briggs, *The Brown-Driver-Briggs Hebrew and English Lexicon* (Peabody, MA: Hendrickson Publishers, 1999), 127; Cogan and Tadmor, *The Anchor Bible: II Kings*, 25; Wiseman, *1 and 2 Kings*, in *Tyndale Old Testament Commentaries*, 192; Ellis T. Rasmussen, *A Latter-day Saint Commentary on the Old Testament* (Salt Lake City, UT: Deseret Book, 1994), 300. Slotki suggested that Baal-zebub was "a Philistine god believed to control the movements of flies to and from a locality. In a hot country like Palestine flies may be the cause of serious epidemic." (Israel Wolf Slotki, *Kings*, in *Soncino Books of the Bible*, 166.) Rasmussen argued that Baal-zebub was "the Philistine god of both disease and healing." (Rasmussen, *A Latter-day Saint Commentary on the Old Testament*, 300. See also D. Kelly Ogden and Andrew C. Skinner, *Verse By Verse— The Old Testament Volume One: Genesis through 2 Samuel, Psalms* [Salt Lake City, UT: Deseret Book, 2013], 2:43.) Patterson and Austel render Baal-zebub "Baal is prince." (See Patterson and Austel, "1 and 2 Kings," in Gaebelein, *The Expositor's Bible Commentary*, 4:172.) Wiseman challenges this translation. (See Wiseman, *1 and 2 Kings*, in *Tyndale Old Testament Commentaries*, 192.)

3. See Gerhard Kittel, ed., *Theological Dictionary of the New Testament* (Grand Rapids, MI: Eerdmans, 1984), 1:605–6; Brown, Driver, and Briggs, *The Brown-Driver-Briggs Hebrew and English Lexicon*, 127. See also *1 and 2 Kings*, in *Tyndale Old Testament Commentaries*, 192; Rasmussen, *A Latter-day Saint Commentary on the Old Testament*, 300; Ogden and Skinner, *Verse By Verse—The Old Testament Volume One: Genesis through 2 Samuel, Psalms*, 2:43.

4. See Cogan and Tadmor, *The Anchor Bible: II Kings*, 25; Israel Wolf Slotki, *Kings*, in *Soncino Books of the Bible*, 166.

5. Cogan and Tadmor, for example, argue that the Hebrew can only be translated as "hairy man," and not "hairy coat/hair-shirt" (as it is rendered in the New English Bible and the New American Bible translations). (See Cogan and Tadmor, *The Anchor Bible: II Kings*, 26.) Slotki rendered the Hebrew literally as "master (or, possessor) of hair," and suggested that it meant "one with a long beard and unshorn hair on his head." (Israel Wolf Slotki, *Kings*, in *Soncino Books of the Bible*, 167.)

6. Patterson and Austel, for example, argue that the syntax in addition to Zechariah 13:4 suggests that it had to be a garment of hair or hair-shirt. (See Patterson and Austel, "1 and 2 Kings," in Gaebelein, *The Expositor's Bible Commentary*, 4:172.) Cogan and Tadmor suggest that it wasn't until the intertestamental period that the "hairy coat became associated with Elijah." (See Cogan and Tadmor, *The Anchor Bible: II Kings*, 26.)

7. Wiseman, *1 and 2 Kings*, in *Tyndale Old Testament Commentaries*, 193.

8. Israel Wolf Slotki, *Kings*, in *Soncino Books of the Bible*, 168. See also Richard C. Trench, *Miracles and Parables of the Old Testament* (Grand Rapids, MI: Baker Book House, 1959), 130.

9. See Hugh Nibley, *Enoch the Prophet* (Salt Lake City, UT: Deseret Book, 1986), 224; Leland Ryken, James C. Wilhoit, and Tremper Longman III, eds., *Dictionary of Biblical Imagery* (Downers Grove, IL: InterVarsity Press, 1998), 573; J. C. Cooper, *An Illustrated Encyclopaedia of Traditional Symbols* (London: Thames and Hudson, 1995), 110; Jack Tresidder, *Symbols and Their Meanings: The Illustrated Guide to More than 1,000 Symbols—Their Traditional and Contemporary Significance* (London: Duncan Baird Publishers, 2006), 116.

10. See Herbert Lockyer, *All the Miracles of the Bible: The Supernatural in Scripture—Its Scope and Significance* (Grand Rapids, MI: Zondervan, 1961), 115.

11. Trench, *Miracles and Parables of the Old Testament*, 128.

12. Pamela McQuade, *The Top 100 Miracles of the Bible: What They Are and What They Mean to You Today* (Uhrichsville, OH: Barbour Publishing, 2008), 81.

13. Trench, *Miracles and Parables of the Old Testament*, 128.

14. Ezra Taft Benson, *The Teachings of Ezra Taft Benson* (Salt Lake City, UT: Bookcraft, 1988), 435.

15. Ibid.

16. Trench, *Miracles and Parables of the Old Testament*, 129.

ELIJAH PARTS *the* JORDAN

2 KINGS 2:7–8

THE MIRACLE

Just before Elijah's translation, he and Elisha were headed to Jordan (at the command of Jehovah). When they came to the water's edge, Elijah took off his cloak, rolled it up, and smote the waters of the Jordan River with it. The river parted, and Elijah and Elisha crossed over on dry ground. As the miracle was performed, fifty "sons of the prophets" observed from a distance (see 2 Kings 2:6–8).

BACKGROUND

In the verses leading up to this miracle, Elijah thrice tells Elisha to wait for him in a particular location while the prophet does his work. In each case, Elisha responds, "As the Lord liveth, and as thy soul liveth, I will not leave thee" (see 2 Kings 2:2, 4, 6). Of Elisha's commitment to his predecessor and mentor, one source suggests, "God gave [Elijah] a friend, Elisha by name. This was the first friend he had ever had. It was in this man's companionship that Elijah did that last heroic mile."[1]

Nine times in the books of Kings, you find reference to the "sons of the prophets" (see 1 Kings 20:35; 2 Kings 2:3, 5, 7, 15; 4:1, 38; 5:22; 6:1). This phrase comes up nowhere else in the standard works of the Church. (In the verses leading up to this miracle, we find these "sons of the prophets" referenced—and at least fifty of them observe the miracle of Elijah parting the Jordan [see 2 Kings 2:7].) Of them, Ogden and Skinner wrote, "The 'sons of the prophets' are seen in a somewhat subordinate relation to Elijah and Elisha, but their nature and function as an institution in Israel are not clear."[2] President Joseph Fielding Smith perceived these "sons" to be the equivalent of an Old Testament dispensation "School of the Prophets."[3]

Herbert Lockyer wrote, "Elijah, the acknowledged head of the prophetic schools, received divine intimation of his approaching end and under divine guidance, visited Gilgal, Bethel, Jericho, and Jordan successively. Doubtless the renowned prophet gave parting counsels to the prophetic students in these places, who also had received the divine announcement of their leader's immediate translation."[4]

Elijah's use of his rolled-up cloak to perform this miracle has caused many commentators to link this imagery to Moses's use of his staff to smite and part the waters of the Red Sea (see Exodus 14:21–31).[5] The staff and cloak each appear to be utilized as "the symbol of [their] office."[6]

SYMBOLIC ELEMENTS

The crossing of the Jordan River in this miracle is significant, particularly because most of the crossings of the Jordan described for us in scripture have people crossing it in order to *enter* Canaan (the promised land). However, Elijah crossed in the opposite direction—*out* of Canaan.

> Whereas Israel had crossed into Canaan to take possession of its God-appointed earthly heritage . . . , Elijah passed out of Canaan through the boundary waters of Jordan to his heavenly service, there to await his future renewed earthly appearance (cf. Mal 4:5; Matt 17:4; Mark 9:5; Luke 9:33; Rev 11:6 [D&C 2]). In this regard, his ministry anticipated that of his Messiah who came incarnately to an earthly service (John 1:12) and subsequently as resurrected Savior ascended again into heaven, there to await his triumphant, glorious second advent (cf. Zech 14:3, 9; Matt 24:30; Acts 1:9–11; 1 Tim 3:16; Rev 19:11–17).[7]

Thus, in crossing the river, Elijah mirrors Christ, whom he typifies.

Elijah's "mantle"—cloak or outer robe—is central to this miracle. One source states, "In priestly tradition, special outerwear depicted power."[8] The British typologist, J. C. Cooper, indicated that robes or mantles are standard symbols for "the power of heaven" or priesthood, and the wearer is to be viewed as the "earthly representative" of God.[9] One expert in biblical clothing wrote, "Some traditions," both in the Old and New Testaments, "portray the outer garment of special persons as conveying power."[10] Thus, the implication of the mantle that Elijah used to perform this miracle is that the prophet held priesthood power.

APPLICATION AND ALLEGORIZATION

The crossing of the Jordan River in this miracle well represents any obstacle overcome through God's aid and intervention. We each run up against impediments and complications in our lives; and, as in this miracle, God can remove them. However, it will be noted that God did not do *all* of the work; Elijah had to do *his* part. He made the trek to the Jordan River and he actively performed the actions (that he could) to part the river. So also, you and I must confront our obstacles—moving toward them just as Elijah moved toward the river. In addition, we must do our part, just as Elijah did his (by smiting the river with his mantle). While God did the bulk of the work in this story, you and I must do all that we can to remove the obstacles that come our way—just as the prophet did all that he could.

Bede the Venerable—an early eighth-century Northumbrian monastic—saw the following symbolism in the miracle at hand:

> Elijah came to the river Jordan, and having laid aside his cloak, he struck the waters and divided them. The Lord came to the stream of death, in which the human race ordinarily was immersed, and laying aside from himself for a time the clothing of flesh that he had assumed, struck down death by dying and opened up for us the way to life by rising. The change and decline of our mortal life is properly represented by the river Jordan, since the meaning of Jordan in Latin is "their descent," and since as the river flows into the Dead Sea, it loses its praiseworthy waters.[11]

Bede would have resonated with the Book of Mormon's declaration that, "all things which have been given of God from the beginning of the world, unto man, are the typifying of him" (2 Nephi 11:4).

By way of application, one commentator on this miracle asked, "Want to know if people are what they claim? Look at their lives. What they do proves who they are, just as [Elijah's] miracle showed others that God had given him His power."[12] Similarly, Jesus taught,

> Ye shall know them by their fruits. Do men gather grapes of thorns, or figs of thistles?
> Even so every good tree bringeth forth good fruit; but a corrupt tree bringeth forth evil fruit.
> A good tree cannot bring forth evil fruit, neither can a corrupt tree bring forth good fruit.
> Every tree that bringeth not forth good fruit is hewn down, and cast into the fire.
> Wherefore by their fruits ye shall know them. (Matthew 7:16–20)

The lives of prophets and apostles—ancient and modern—evidence this truth; you must bring forth fruits commensurate with your calling and covenants. The way the General Authorities have lived their lives is a testament to their lives of holiness, and their commitment to God and Christ. As a disciple of Christ, does *your* life testify to those who observe it that you are committed to Jesus and the covenants you have made with Him? Does God perform miracles (that bless others) though you?

It is curious that Elisha was so doggedly committed to being by Elijah's side until the very end. There are obvious explanations for this—both in Elisha's character and also in his position as successor. However, perhaps an allegorized application can also be drawn from this part of the narrative. As an undergrad in college, I worked in a nursing home. I was surprised and disheartened by the number of residents who had family members living in the area, but who received no visits from family or friends. They were left to age and then die *alone*. Yet, being with someone when they pass is often a profoundly spiritual experience. It was sad to see family not care enough to visit their aging mother, father, or grandparent; but it was also sad to see them miss this most sacred of all transitions—passing from mortal life to eternal life. Elisha stayed with Elijah until the very end of his mortal ministry, and, in so doing, was blessed to witness a miracle that he would have otherwise missed. As you and I walk hand in hand with the elderly, until they have concluded their mortal journeys, we too may be privy to the profoundly spiritual experiences often associated with the last moments of a person's mortal life.

As a final application, the love and camaraderie between Elijah and Elisha—as depicted in this miracle—highlights the brotherhood that certainly exists between members of the First Presidency and the Quorum of the Twelve Apostles. It reminds us of the bond that *can* develop in any presidency, as we serve and sacrifice alongside of each other. Indeed, perhaps one of the signs that our presidency has been successful is to be found in the bond we feel, one toward another.

NOTES

1.   Clovis Gillham Chappell, *The Cross Before Calvary* (New York: Abingdon Press, 1960), 52. Similarly, Lockyer wrote, "How good of God it was to give Elisha to Elijah as an intimate companion in the closing period of his work. His life and lot has been a very lonely one and he needed companionship; so God gave him Elisha, just as he gave young Timothy to the aged Paul." (Herbert Lockyer, *All*

the Miracles of the Bible: The Supernatural in Scripture—Its Scope and Significance [Grand Rapids, MI: Zondervan, 1961], 115.)

2.   D. Kelly Ogden and Andrew C. Skinner, Verse By Verse—The Old Testament Volume One: Genesis through 2 Samuel, Psalms (Salt Lake City, UT: Deseret Book, 2013), 2:44. See also Ellis T. Rasmussen, A Latter-day Saint Commentary on the Old Testament (Salt Lake City, UT: Deseret Book, 1994), 301. Ogden and Skinner go on to suggest that they may have been "disciples who followed the prophets, preserved their words, and spread their messages. . . . The sons of the prophets were spiritually mature and perceptive." (Ogden and Skinner, Verse By Verse—The Old Testament Volume One: Genesis through 2 Samuel, Psalms, 2:46.)

3.   See Joseph Fielding Smith, Church History and Modern Revelation, (Salt Lake City, UT: Deseret News, 1953), 1:373.

4.   Lockyer, All the Miracles of the Bible, 115.

5.   See, for example, Richard D. Patterson and Hermann J. Austel, "1 and 2 Kings," in Frank E. Gaebelein, ed., The Expositor's Bible Commentary (Grand Rapids, MI: Zondervan, 1994), 4:175; Lockyer, All the Miracles of the Bible, 116; Donald J. Wiseman, 1 and 2 Kings, in Tyndale Old Testament Commentaries (Downers Grove, IL: InterVarsity Press, 1988), 195. See also Pamela McQuade, The Top 100 Miracles of the Bible: What They Are and What They Mean to You Today (Uhrichsville, OH: Barbour Publishing, 2008), 82; Kenneth L. Woodward, The Book of Miracles: The Meaning of the Miracle Stories in Christianity, Judaism, Buddhism, Islam (New York: Simon & Schuster, 2000), 61–62.

6.   Wiseman, 1 and 2 Kings, in Tyndale Old Testament Commentaries, 195.

7.   Patterson and Austel, "1 and 2 Kings," in Gaebelein, The Expositor's Bible Commentary, 4:175–76.

8.   Douglas R. Edwards, "Dress and Ornamentation," in David Noel Freedman, The Anchor Bible Dictionary (New York: Doubleday, 1992), 2:233. See also, Geoffrey W. Bromiley, ed., The International Standard Bible Encyclopedia, rev. ed. (Grand Rapids, MI: Eerdmans, 1989), 4:204.

9.   J. C. Cooper, An Illustrated Encyclopaedia of Traditional Symbols (London: Thames and Hudson, 1995), 140.

10. Edwards, "Dress and Ornamentation," in Freedman, The Anchor Bible Dictionary, 2:233, 236.

11. Bede the Venerable, "Homilies on the Gospels," 2.15, in Marco Conti, ed., 1–2 Kings, 1–2 Chronicles, Ezra, Nehemiah, Esther, in Ancient Christian Commentary on Scripture (Downers Grove, IL: InterVarsity Press, 2008), 144.

12. McQuade, The Top 100 Miracles of the Bible, 82.

Elijah *Is* Taken Up *into* Heaven

2 Kings 2:9–12

The Miracle

As they were crossing over the Jordan River together, Elijah turned to Elisha and asked, "What can I do for you before I am taken out of your midst?" (see 2 Kings 2:9). Elisha responded, "Let a double portion of thy spirit be upon me" (2 Kings 2:19). The prophet indicated that what Elisha had asked was a difficult thing to promise. "But," said Elijah, "if—when I am taken up—you can see me ascending, then your request will be granted. However, if my translation happens in a way that you are not able to view it, then you will not receive a double-portion of the Spirit" (see 2 Kings 2:10).

As the two were speaking, "a chariot of fire, and horses of fire" appeared, resting between the two of them. Then Elijah ascended into heaven in "a whirlwind" (2 Kings 2:11). And Elisha, looking on—and witnessing the miracle—cried out, "My father, my father, the chariot of Israel, and the horsemen thereof" (2 Kings 2:12). Elisha had witnessed the translation of Elijah, and so testified by his cries. But, from that time forward, he saw Elijah no more. And, as a sign of his sorrow, he made a tear in his garment (see 2 Kings 2:12).

Background

Elisha's request for a "double portion" (or "double share") of the Spirit mirrors the language of Deuteronomy 21:17, wherein we learn that the first-born in a family receives a "double share" of the father's inheritance, implying his chosen status as heir apparent.[1] It does not appear that Elisha is begging to be successor. Indeed, 1 Kings 19:16–21 suggests that Elisha's succession was already decided. It appears Elisha's request is simply that he will have the spiritual endowments necessary to complete the task that is about to fall to him.[2]

While the King James Version has Elisha asking for a double portion of "thy [Elijah's] spirit" (2 Kings 2:9), some commentators interpret the "spirit" Elisha is seeking as the Holy Spirit—not "some inherent personal quality" of Elijah.[3] Others interpret it as a request for "spiritual gifts" *like unto* Elijah's—gifts that can only be had through the Holy Spirit.[4]

Elijah's statement that promising a double portion of God's Spirit is "a hard thing" (2 Kings 2:10) simply implies that Elijah knew it was not his to promise who would have strong spiritual endowments and who would not. Only God can make such promises.[5] Jesus made a very similar statement in the twentieth chapter of the gospel of Matthew.

> Then came to him the mother of Zebedee's children with her sons, worshipping him, and desiring a certain thing of him.
>
> And he said unto her, What wilt thou? She saith unto him, Grant that these my two sons may sit, the one on thy right hand, and the other on the left, in thy kingdom.
>
> But Jesus answered and said, . . . *it is not mine to give*, but it shall be given to them for whom it is prepared of my Father. (Matthew 20:20–23; emphasis added)

Commentators often point out that "Elijah was taken up to heaven in the *whirlwind*, not in the *chariot of fire and horses of fire* which merely 'came between the two of them' (Heb.) and cut him off from human sight."[6] The suggestion being that the chariot and fire allowed Elijah to be transfigured privately—not in full view of onlookers. Elisha was apparently the only one to view the transfiguration. The Hebrew of this verse doesn't say that Elijah was taken up in "a whirlwind" (KJV), but in "*the* whirlwind" (or "*the* storm"). This was not just any storm or wind—this was God's whirlwind![7]

As Elijah departed, Elisha cried out, "My father, my father, the chariot of Israel, and the horsemen thereof" (2 Kings 2: 12). This declaration is commonly explained as follows: "Elisha calls his master 'the chariot of Israel and the horsemen thereof,' meaning thereby doubtless that Elijah was a more real defense to Israel than the horsemen and chariots of her warriors."[8]

SYMBOLIC ELEMENTS

Elijah and Elisha witness the miraculous (and unexplained) appearance of a fiery chariot pulled by fiery horses. "Fire is a regular feature of divine manifestation (e.g. Exod 3:2, 13:21, 19:18) and is of the divine essence (cf. Deut 4:24); thus the vehicles beheld by Elisha were those of the Lord (cf. Hab 3:8)."[9] Elsewhere, we are told that the fiery chariot and horses represent "the glory that surrounds [God's] presence."[10] Another source states, "Horses and chariots . . . came to be used . . . as a means of representing Divine power (Ps. lxviii, 17; civ, 3)."[11] In Isaiah 66:15, we read, "For, behold, the Lord will come with fire, and with his chariots like a whirlwind, to render his anger with fury, and his rebuke with flames of fire." This imagery parallels that of Elijah's departure, and seems designed to paint the prophet as a typological symbol of Christ.[12]

Rending one's clothes is a traditional visible symbol of grief or mourning (see Genesis 37:34; 2 Samuel 1:11; 13:31; Job 1:20). Elisha's act here thus shows his sadness and pain at the loss of his mentor, whom he loved.[13]

APPLICATION AND ALLEGORIZATION

Elijah's last act, prior to translation, is instructive, as it relates to applications we might draw. "Elijah, sensing the imminency of his departure, asked what further thing he could do for his successor. To the very end he remained concerned for others and for the continuance of God's work."[14] How often, in Church callings, do members peter out at the end—losing commitment to or interest in the thing God has called them to do? When we are commanded to "endure to the end" (2 Nephi 31:16; D&C 14:7), that doesn't just mean to the end of mortality. It also means to the end of any assignment we receive. Can a person truly say that they have "endured to the end" of this mortal experience if they have been less than faithful in serving in callings?

A related application is to be found in these words: "During the time we spend here we find ourselves called to do certain work and find ourselves possessed of faculties adapted to perform it. Reasoning from analogy we may be sure that in another part of God's universe we shall find ourselves in possession of the powers needed to do God's work under other circumstances."[15] God *did* give Elisha what he needed in order to succeed Elijah. And so He will for us in our callings. And, as weak and inadequate as we are here, He will also endow us with what we will need (when we get to the other side) to do what He does there, which we shall all one day be called to do ourselves.

Elisha worries that he will not have the gifts of his predecessor in the prophetic office. Ultimately, he would manifest many of the same gifts— though not exactly the same ones. One commentator explained, "Elijah's miracles were those of judgment, while Elisha's were those of mercy."[16] Yet, it is best that Elisha not have the exact gifts of Elijah because with the passing of the previous prophet there comes the closing of an era. God calls new men to wear the prophetic mantle because the Church needs to move into its next phase. The Prophet Joseph's gifts were decidedly different from those of Brother Brigham. And President Joseph Fielding Smith was significantly different in his focus and approach from President Harold B. Lee. Certain gifts come with the office. However, prophets each have their unique talents and specific vision of the work; and that reality prevents the work from stagnating. By way of application, you and I need not worry if our skills seem different or less than the man or woman who held the calling before us. If God calls you or me to a position of responsibility in the Church, it is because you or I are the one He needs in that position at this time in the Church's history.

Elder Boyd K. Packer saw in Elisha's request for a "double portion" of Elijah's spirit a statement about temple and family history work. "That request for a double portion of the spirit of Elijah provokes me to deep thought, for the spirit of Elijah, as we still may learn, is something so moving and so powerful, and something tied so closely to the most sacred authority of the priesthood, that obviously it would be glorious to be under the constant influence of even a part of that spirit, let alone a double portion."[17] Elder Packer's thought is that you and I too should be seeking a "double portion" of the "spirit of Elijah," that our hearts might be consumed with the work of redeeming the dead. I have found in my own life that that spirit comes as we immerse ourselves in researching our kindred dead, and in taking their names to the temple. If we'll find ourselves in the house of the Lord as often as we're able—and, where possible, with family names—then we will enjoy a "double portion" of the "spirit of Elijah" in our lives.

Elder Bruce C. Hafen of the Seventy suggested that this particular miracle is a testament to the reality that angels minister to individuals upon the earth today.

> After all, the angels are there. And someday, perhaps not so far away in time or space, we might be prepared enough and have reason enough at last to see the angels of Kirtland once more. The conditions on which our vision may pierce the veil are not fully known to us. Those conditions are not always known even to the prophets. When Elijah was about to be taken from the earth, his successor as prophet to Israel, Elisha, asked that a double portion of Elijah's spirit might remain with him. Elijah said this was "a hard thing; nevertheless, if thou see me when I am taken from thee, it shall be so unto thee; but if not, it shall not be so." Suddenly, flaming

horses and a chariot of fire appeared and took Elijah by a whirlwind into heaven. And the Lord granted the desire of Elisha's heart, for his eyesight pierced the veil: "And Elisha saw [the angels], and he cried, My father, my father, the chariot of Israel and the horsemen thereof." (2 Kings 2:9–12.)

Who are those horsemen? When do they come, and where do they go?

They must not be far away, for they have come again in the modern age. Not long before the dedication of the Kirtland Temple, Joseph Smith's scribe saw "In a vision, the armies of heaven protecting the Saints in their return to Zion." The next day, after Joseph and the Twelve had sealed holy anointings on the heads of one another, "The heavens were opened unto Elder Sylvester Smith, and he, leaping up, exclaimed: 'The horsemen of Israel and the chariots thereof!'"

Whoever they are, in their chariots of fire, the horsemen of Israel watch over the Saints with such care and power that we know of a surety: "They that be with us are more than they that be with them." (2 Kings 6:16.)

From . . . [President] J. Reuben Clark, Jr., I learn that angels can be very near at the blessing of a sick child or at a baby's birth. From the history of Kirtland, I learn that they come to celebrate and bear unforgettable witness in the formation of faith, even if we must wait for more complete witnesses until our faith has been tried by fire. From the scriptures, I learn that God's angels can ever bear us up, whether we see them or not. Knowing this, I suppose that the angels come in our hours of greatest personal need. A moment of high spiritual significance in one person's life may not seem to have cosmic or historic meaning, but such moments can have acute personal consequences that matter very much to those who are sent to strengthen us from beyond the veil.[18]

NOTES

1. See Israel Wolf Slotki, *Kings*, in *Soncino Books of the Bible* (London: The Soncino Press, 1978), 172; Richard D. Patterson and Hermann J. Austel, "1 and 2 Kings," in Frank E. Gaebelein, ed., *The Expositor's Bible Commentary* (Grand Rapids, MI: Zondervan, 1994), 4:176; Mordechai Cogan and Hayim Tadmor, *The Anchor Bible: II Kings*, vol. 11 (New York: Doubleday, 1988), 32.

2. See Patterson and Austel, "1 and 2 Kings," in Gaebelein, *The Expositor's Bible Commentary*, 4:176.

3. Cogan and Tadmor, *The Anchor Bible: II Kings*, 32; Patterson and Austel, "1 and 2 Kings," in Gaebelein, *The Expositor's Bible Commentary*, 4:178.

4. See Ellis T. Rasmussen, *A Latter-day Saint Commentary on the Old Testament* (Salt Lake City, UT: Deseret Book, 1994), 300.

5. See Israel Wolf Slotki, *Kings*, in *Soncino Books of the Bible*, 172; Herbert Lockyer, *All the Miracles of the Bible: The Supernatural in Scripture—Its Scope and Significance* (Grand Rapids, MI: Zondervan, 1961), 116; Boyd K. Packer, *The Holy Temple* (Salt Lake City, UT: Deseret Book, 1999), 108–9.

6. Donald J. Wiseman, *1 and 2 Kings*, in *Tyndale Old Testament Commentaries* (Downers Grove, IL InterVarsity Press, 1988), 195. See also Israel Wolf Slotki, *Kings*, in *Soncino Books of the Bible*, 172; Patterson and Austel, in "1 and 2 Kings," in Gaebelein, *The Expositor's Bible Commentary*, 4:176–178; Lockyer, *All the Miracles of the Bible: The Supernatural in Scripture—Its Scope and Significance*, 116; Richard C. Trench, *Miracles and Parables of the Old Testament* (Grand Rapids, MI: Baker Book House, 1959), 133; Ada R. Habershon, *The Study of the Miracles* (London: Morgan & Scott, 1911), 147n26. God spoke to Job out of a whirlwind (Job 38:1), and Ezekiel described God's whirlwind as a great fiery cloud (see Ezekiel 1:4).

7. See Patterson and Austel, "1 and 2 Kings," in Gaebelein, *The Expositor's Bible Commentary*, 4:177.

8. Trench, *Miracles and Parables of the Old Testament*, 133. See also Cogan and Tadmor, *The Anchor Bible: II Kings* (1988), 32; Wiseman, *1 and 2 Kings*, in *Tyndale Old Testament Commentaries*, 196; Israel Wolf Slotki, *Kings*, in *Soncino Books of the Bible*, 173.

9. Cogan and Tadmor, *The Anchor Bible: II Kings*, 32. See also Wiseman, *1 and 2 Kings*, in *Tyndale Old Testament Commentaries*, 195–96; Patterson and Austel, "1 and 2 Kings," in Gaebelein, *The Expositor's Bible Commentary*, 4:178.

10. D. Kelly Ogden and Andrew C. Skinner, *Verse By Verse—The Old Testament Volume One: Genesis through 2 Samuel, Psalms* (Salt Lake City, UT: Deseret Book, 2013), 2:44.

11. Maurice H. Farbridge, *Studies in Biblical and Semitic Symbolism* (London: Routledge, 1923), 77–78.

12. See Ogden and Skinner, *Verse By Verse—The Old Testament Volume One: Genesis through 2 Samuel, Psalms*, 2:44.

13. See Cogan and Tadmor, *The Anchor Bible: II Kings*, 32; Patterson and Austel, "1 and 2 Kings," in Gaebelein, *The Expositor's Bible Commentary*, 4:178; Byron R. Merrill, *Elijah: Yesterday, Today, and Tomorrow* (Salt Lake City, UT: Deseret Book, 1997), 85.

14. Patterson and Austel, "1 and 2 Kings," in Gaebelein, *The Expositor's Bible Commentary*, 4:176.

15. Trench, *Miracles and Parables of the Old Testament*, 134.

16. Lockyer, *All the Miracles of the Bible*, 117.

17. Packer, *The Holy Temple*, 108.

18. Bruce C. Hafen, *The Believing Heart: Nourishing the Seed of Faith*, 2nd ed. (Salt Lake City, UT: Deseret Book, 1990), 115–16.

ELISHA PARTS *the* JORDAN

2 KINGS 2:13–15

THE MIRACLE

After Elijah ascended to heaven in the whirlwind, Elisha picked up the translated prophet's mantle and walked back to the shore of the Jordan River. With Elijah's cloak, Elisha smote the river (as Elijah had done) and said, "Where is the Lord God of Elijah?" (2 Kings 2:14). As he did so, the waters parted and Elisha crossed back over (see 2 Kings 2:13–14).

When he arrived on the other side of the river, the fifty sons of prophets (who had been waiting there, witnessing the miracle) said to each other, "The spirit of Elijah doth rest on Elisha." Then they came to him and bowed down before him (2 Kings 2:15).

BACKGROUND

One source suggested that here we see depicted "the succession of Elisha to the 'fathership' over the Sons of the Prophets."[1] In other words, while there are others in the narrative referred to as "prophets," Elisha is now the "presiding prophet."

As Elisha smote the waters with Elijah's mantle, he said, "Where is the Lord God of Elijah?" (2 Kings 2:14). One commentary on the Hebrew states, "This is not a question seeking information, but a solemn invocation. Elisha, who had just witnessed the miraculous ascent of Elijah, would not be likely to doubt the power of the *God of Elijah*."[2] In other words, the new prophet is invoking the name of the God of his predecessor, as a means of having his power as he performs the needed miracle.

SYMBOLIC ELEMENTS

As noted above, the cloak represented power or authority. After Elijah had disappeared, Elisha "took up" or "picked up" the mantle that Elijah had left behind. While this was a physical act, it has significant symbolic connotations. It implied that he was accepting his call as the new prophetic leader of God's people. Lockyer put it this way: "As Elijah ascended, his mantle fell off, indicating his work on earth was done. Now Elisha takes it up, as the symbol or badge that the prophetic office has been divinely transferred to him."[3] In addition, using that mantle to repeat the miracle just performed by Elijah established for those who had witnessed it that Elisha was *absolutely* Elijah's successor.[4]

Like all prophets, Elisha can be seen as a type for Christ. Both had control over the elements (see 2 Kings 3:17; Mark 4:41). Both fed the multitude when they had almost nothing on hand (see 2 Kings 4:42–44; Mark 6:33–44). Both healed the sick (see 2 Kings 5; Matthew 8). Both had the gift of prophecy. And both suffered at the hands of wicked men.[5]

APPLICATION AND ALLEGORIZATION

This miracle is largely about succession in leadership within God's Church. Frequently told in Mormonism is the story of how, upon Joseph's death, Brigham Young was transfigured to look and even sound like the prophet.[6] What is less well known is the transfiguration of President Heber J. Grant upon the death of his predecessor, President Joseph F. Smith. Historian Ronald L. Walker wrote: "From the announcement of his apostolic call, there were whispers and innuendos about his selection. While his closest associates welcomed his appointment, Elder Grant was painfully aware that it had taken President Taylor's written revelation to convince others that he was apostolic timber. No one doubted his integrity—only his preparation for the calling and what some saw as his preoccupation with business."[7] Over time, President Grant rose through the ranks of leadership in the Church, eventually becoming president of the Quorum of the Twelve. Upon the death of President Joseph F. Smith, President Grant was set apart as the Church's seventh president.

> At first some Latter-day Saints seemed uncertain about their new leader. His brisk and informal ways were in marked contrast to President Smith's conservative style. "Some of our wisest and most faithful and diligent Latter-day Saints . . . felt that it was almost a calamity when I came to the Presidency," he ruefully remarked many years later.

Some doubters received an immediate reassurance. Reminiscent of one of the Church's most cherished traditions surrounding President Brigham Young's succession to leadership, many Saints testified that as they first saw President Grant address them, his face seemed to be transformed into President Joseph F. Smith's visage. Others claimed that they viewed President Smith's figure standing next to their new president.[8]

In order to help doubting members know that God had indeed passed the mantle of authority from Joseph F. Smith to Heber J. Grant, God gave a miraculous manifestation. And so it was with Elijah and Elisha. In the latter, the "sons of the prophets" saw the former. The mantle of Elijah had fallen upon Elisha, both figuratively and literally; and Elijah's former disciples began to follow the new prophet.

This miracle is also a testament to God's immutable character. In scripture, He is repeatedly said to be "the same yesterday, today, and forever" (1 Nephi 10:18. See also Hebrews 13:8; D&C 20:12). "He has always been, and always will be, the same to men of like character."[9] Repeating the same miracle He performed through Moses (see Exodus 14), Joshua (see Joshua 3), and Elijah (see 2 Kings 2), the Lord gives Elisha—and each of us—confidence in His unchanging nature. "Those that walk in the spirit and steps of their godly, faithful predecessors, shall certainly experience the same grace that they experienced."[10]

NOTES

1.   Mordechai Cogan and Hayim Tadmor, *The Anchor Bible: II Kings*, vol. 11 (New York: Doubleday, 1988), 34.

2.   Israel Wolf Slotki, *Kings*, in *Soncino Books of the Bible* (London: The Soncino Press, 1978), 173.

3.   Herbert Lockyer, *All the Miracles of the Bible: The Supernatural in Scripture—Its Scope and Significance* (Grand Rapids, MI: Zondervan, 1961), 117.

4.   See Pamela McQuade, *The Top 100 Miracles of the Bible: What They Are and What They Mean to You Today* (Uhrichsville, OH: Barbour Publishing, 2008), 82; Lockyer, *All the Miracles of the Bible*, 116.

5.   See D. Kelly Ogden and Andrew C. Skinner, *Verse By Verse—The Old Testament Volume One: Genesis through 2 Samuel, Psalms* (Salt Lake City, UT: Deseret Book, 2013), 2:48–49.

6.   See, for example, Claire Koltko, Natalie Ross, Brittany McEwen, and Jennifer Johnson, comps., *The Eyewitness History of the Church: Journey to Zion's Hill*, vol. 3 (Springville, UT: Cedar Fort, 2006), 17–22.

7.   Ronald L. Walker, "Heber J. Grant," in Leonard J. Arrington, ed, *The Presidents of the Church: Biographical Essays* (Salt Lake City, UT: Desert Book, 1986), 232.

8.   Walker, "Heber J. Grant," in Arrington, *The Presidents of the Church*, 242–43.
9.   Richard C. Trench, *Miracles and Parables of the Old Testament* (Grand Rapids, MI: Baker Book House, 1959), 138.
10.   Ibid.

ELISHA HEALS *the* WATERS *of the* JORDAN

2 KINGS 2:19–22

THE MIRACLE

The men of the city of Jericho approached Elisha and said to him, "This city's location is a good one, but the water is bad; and, thus, the ground is barren." So Elisha said to them, "Bring me a new container, and put salt in it" (see 2 Kings 2:19–20).

The men did as Elisha asked, and he then took the container and the salt, and he went out to the spring and threw the salt in. Elisha then declared, "Thus saith the Lord, I have healed these waters; there shall not be from thence any more death or barren land" (2 Kings 2:21). And the waters were healed, and remained healed, in accordance with the words Elisha had spoken (see 2 Kings 2:21–22).

BACKGROUND

Though the city of Jericho had been rebuilt during Ahab's reign (see 1 Kings 16:34), the land had apparently remained unproductive—presumably because the waters still suffered from the curse issued upon the land by Joshua (see Joshua 6:26).[1]

Commentaries on these verses suggest that the "men of the city" (2 Kings 2:19) in this miracle are individuals who "had learned from the sons of the prophets of the supernatural powers bestowed upon Elisha."[2]

Whereas the King James Version says, "The ground [is] barren" (2 Kings 2:19), the Hebrew says "the land miscarrieth," or the "country suffers miscarriages."[3] Of this, Israel Slotki wrote, "On account of the bad water which man and beast drank and trees absorbed, women miscarried, cattle cast their young prematurely and trees shed their fruits before they were ripe."[4]

The *Ain es-Sultan*—a fountain of sweet water rising to the surface near the ruins of ancient Jericho—is sometimes referred to as the "Fountain of Elisha," and is traditionally believed to be the spring at the center of this miracle.[5]

SYMBOLIC ELEMENTS

Ogden and Skinner wrote, "Salt is such a significant element and symbol that it is mentioned in the Old and New Testaments, the Book of Mormon, and the Doctrine and Covenants."[6] As noted previously, salt was an ancient symbol of preservation and covenant making.[7] It was a required component of the meal offering and burnt offering under the law of Moses (see Leviticus 2:13; Numbers 18:19; Ezekiel 43:24). McQuade wrote, "[Salt was] a sign of God's covenant with His people."[8] Anciently, those who were Christ's covenant people were called to make covenants that would preserve themselves and those to whom they took the gospel. For this reason, Christ commissioned His followers to be the "salt of the earth" (see Matthew 5:13; 3 Nephi 12:13; D&C 101:39–40), and to have "salt in themselves" (Mark 9:49–50). Thus, salt is a symbol of covenants and also of permanence. In antiquity, salt was often associated with life, incorruptibility, fidelity, wisdom, the elect, purity, discretion, and strength.[9]

As one reads the story of this miracle, one is reminded of a similar miracle in the ministry of Moses.

> When faced with the crisis of the harmful waters at Jericho, Elisha, as YHWH's messenger, effects a cure which makes them potable, thus restoring life to the townspeople. Tales such as this, of miraculous, sustaining acts by holy men of God, are part of the traditional lore— *legenda*—of prophetic circles; thus, it is told of Moses that he sweetened the waters at Marah (Exod. 15:23–25). . . . An unmistakable literary affinity exists between the tale of Moses and that of Elisha; in both, the prophet acts after hearing a complaint and casts (. . . Exod 15:25 and 2 Kgs 2:21) a healing agent (. . . Exod 15:26; 2 Kgs 2:21, 22) into the bitter source.[10]

As is so common in scripture, the lives of the prophets often parallel each other.[11] Elisha and Moses are no exception.

APPLICATION AND ALLEGORIZATION

One commentary suggested, "Knowledge of the symbolism of salt and its curative powers seems to have prompted Elisha to use it to purify the spring at Jericho."[12] With salt as an ancient symbol of covenants, Elisha's use of salt (in this miracle) to heal the waters and, consequently, the land, reminds us of the truth that covenants—faithfully kept—have the power to heal. If we will allow covenants into our lives, they will purify us, strengthen us, and heal the very things that spiritually ail us. Of course, it isn't the covenants that have the power to heal; rather, it is the faithful keeping of those covenants. If you and I enter into covenants, but do not keep and live them, they will have no real, lasting effect in our lives or upon our posterity. Hence, one commentator rhetorically asked, "When God does good things for us, do we recognize that He's keeping [His] covenant with us? Are we keeping our part of the covenant too?"[13]

Of Elisha's work in this miracle, one commentary points out, "The miraculous powers [exhibited in this healing were] performed not for his own glorification but to help others."[14] When Elisha announces, "I have healed these waters" (2 Kings 2:21), it should be noted that the prophet prefaces these words with "Thus saith the Lord." In other words, Elisha gives God *all* credit for what has just happened; the prophet takes none for himself.[15] This is a reminder to any priesthood holder who is privileged to participate in a miracle; God must *always* be acknowledged as the source of the miraculous. The priesthood holder is only a conduit—and an imperfect conduit at that. And though a man may be living his life worthily so as to serve as that conduit, he still can take no credit for the miracle because God has gifted him with the priesthood (by which the miracle took place)—something the man does not deserve to hold, but has been blessed with the privilege to receive in spite of his personal weaknesses.

One commentator explained the application of this miracle in this way, "Elisha wrought the cure [of the waters] through means supplied by the people of Jericho so that their faith might be strengthened through submission and active participation in God's cleansing work."[16] In other words, wise leaders understand the importance of involving those they lead in the work of the Lord. In so doing, they provide opportunities for their flocks to witness for themselves the miracles that God performs through His anointed leaders, and they can feel personally the power that comes from participating in the miraculous work of the Lord. Elisha could have completed this miracle entirely on his own and could have been praised mightily for so doing. But he saw the teaching opportunity this dilemma offered, and he used it to strengthen the faith of his flock. As much as is possible, leaders in the modern Church look for opportunities to involve and teach those whom they lead. If the laity can participate in the day-to-day miracles of the kingdom, their faith that God is in the details will increase, and their own leadership skills will develop.

Donald Wiseman suggested this simple application of the miracle: "Elisha's act was one of showing God's mercy to a community in time of stress."[17] Another commentator wrote, "Elisha worked much as Jesus later worked—with compassion to help people in need."[18] God is indeed so very good to us, and grateful disciples will *always* be able to see many examples of God's merciful intervention in the history of their state or nation. Just as God saw the people of Jericho in dire straits and intervened, He frequently blesses the community, state, or nation who turns to Him. The reverse is also true. The nation that rejects their God will lose His blessings, and will be "wanderers among the nations" (Hosea 9:17).

In the early fifth century, Maximus of Turin offered an interesting application of Elisha's healing of the barren waters of Jericho.

> Since the holy apostle Paul says that "these things happened to them as a figure," [1 Corinthians 10:6] let us see what the true meaning is of this figure—that is to say, what that city is that suffers sterility and what the vessel means and also why sprinkled salt should confer health. In the same apostle [i.e., Paul] we read that this is said of the church: "Rejoice, you sterile ones who do not bear; break forth and shout, you who do not beget." [Galatians 4:27; Isaiah 54:1] The church, then, is that sterile city that, because of the bad condition of the waters before the coming of Christ (that is to say, because of the sacrilege of the Gentile peoples), was unable to conceive children for God in its sterility. But when Christ came, taking on a human body like a clay vessel, he cleansed the bad condition of the waters; that is to say, "He cut off the sacrileges of the peoples," and immediately the church, which used to be sterile, began to be fruitful.[19]

When Jesus came upon the earth, Maximus suggests, Judaism was in apostasy, and could not bear fruits (in God's name) because of it. But Christ's coming, ministry, and Atonement healed the covenant people—and healed God's Church—so that it could be fruitful again. And Jesus can do the same for each of us in our personal lives if we will let Him in. "O God, if Thou cast into the fountain of our hearts but one cruseful of the salt of Thy Spirit, we are whole."[20]

The *Dictionary of Biblical Imagery* suggests, "When Elisha treated a bad water supply at Jericho with salt, it may have symbolized a new beginning in terms of removing the curse Joshua had leveled on it."[21] That would explain why the prophet requested a "new cruse" or container (2 Kings 2:20), adding to the symbolism of a new beginning. If this is indeed at the heart of the symbolism, then it is a reminder of the Lord's promise, "Behold, he who has repented of his sins, the same is forgiven, and I, the Lord, remember them no more" (D&C 58:42).

NOTES

1. See Donald J. Wiseman, *1 and 2 Kings*, in *Tyndale Old Testament Commentaries* (Downers Grove, IL: InterVarsity Press, 1988), 197; Richard D. Patterson and Hermann J. Austel, "1 and 2 Kings," in Frank E. Gaebelein, ed., *The Expositor's Bible Commentary* (Grand Rapids, MI: Zondervan, 1994), 4:177; Richard C. Trench, *Miracles and Parables of the Old Testament* (Grand Rapids, MI: Baker Book House, 1959), 140.

2. Israel Wolf Slotki, *Kings*, in *Soncino Books of the Bible* (London: The Soncino Press, 1978), 174. See also Herbert Lockyer, *All the Miracles of the Bible: The Supernatural in Scripture—Its Scope and Significance* (Grand Rapids, MI: Zondervan, 1961), 118; Maximus of Turin, "Sermon" 84.3–4, in Marco Conti, ed., *1–2 Kings, 1–2 Chronicles, Ezra, Nehemiah, Esther*, in *Ancient Christian Commentary on Scripture* (Downers Grove, IL: InterVarsity Press, 2008), 147.

3. See Wiseman, *1 and 2 Kings*, in *Tyndale Old Testament Commentaries*, 197; Israel Wolf Slotki, *Kings*, in *Soncino Books of the Bible*, 174.

4. Israel Wolf Slotki, *Kings*, in *Soncino Books of the Bible*, 174. See also D. Kelly Ogden and Andrew C. Skinner, *Verse By Verse—The Old Testament Volume One: Genesis through 2 Samuel, Psalms* (Salt Lake City, UT: Deseret Book, 2013), 2:47; Lockyer, *All the Miracles of the Bible*, 118.

5. See Cogan and Tadmor, *The Anchor Bible: II Kings*, 36; Israel Wolf Slotki, *Kings*, in *Soncino Books of the Bible*, 175; Wiseman, *1 and 2 Kings*, in *Tyndale Old Testament Commentaries*, 197.

6. Ogden and Skinner, *Verse By Verse—The Old Testament Volume One: Genesis through 2 Samuel, Psalms*, 2:47.

7. Patrick Fairbairn, *The Typology of Scripture*, 2nd ed. (Philadelphia, PA: Smith & English, 1989), 2:313; Kevin J. Conner, *Interpreting the Symbols and Types*, rev. ed. (Portland, OR: City Bible Publishing, 1992), 165; Patterson and Austel, "1 and 2 Kings," in Gaebelein, *The Expositor's Bible Commentary*, 4:178; Israel Wolf Slotki, *Kings*, in *Soncino Books of the Bible*, 174; Maurice H. Farbridge, *Studies in Biblical and Semitic Symbolism* (London: Routledge, 1923), 272.

8. Pamela McQuade, *The Top 100 Miracles of the Bible: What They Are and What They Mean to You Today* (Uhrichsville, OH: Barbour Publishing, 2008), 83.

9. J. C. Cooper, *An Illustrated Encyclopaedia of Traditional Symbols* (London: Thames and Hudson, 1995), 144; Farbridge, *Studies in Biblical and Semitic Symbolism*, 272; Lockyer, *All the Miracles of the Bible*, 118.

10. Cogan and Tadmor, *The Anchor Bible: II Kings*, 37. See also Lockyer, *All the Miracles of the Bible*, 118.

11. See Alonzo L. Gaskill, *The Lost Language of Symbolism: An Essential Guide for Recognizing and Interpreting Symbols of the Gospel* (Salt Lake City, UT: Deseret Book, 2003), 199–217.

12. Ogden and Skinner, *Verse By Verse—The Old Testament Volume One: Genesis through 2 Samuel, Psalms*, 2:47.

13. McQuade, *The Top 100 Miracles of the Bible*, 83.

14. Wiseman, *1 and 2 Kings*, in *Tyndale Old Testament Commentaries*, 197. See also Lockyer, *All the Miracles of the Bible*, 118.

15. Trench wrote, "How careful is the man of God that no part of God's glory should stick to his own fingers." (Trench, *Miracles and Parables of the Old Testament*, 141.)

16. Patterson and Austel, "1 and 2 Kings," in Gaebelein, *The Expositor's Bible Commentary*, 4:177.

17. Wiseman, *1 and 2 Kings*, in *Tyndale Old Testament Commentaries*, 197. See also Lockyer, *All the Miracles of the Bible*, 118.

18. Ellis T. Rasmussen, *A Latter-day Saint Commentary on the Old Testament* (Salt Lake City, UT: Deseret Book, 1994), 301.

19. Maximus of Turin, "Sermon" 84.3–4, in Marco Conti, ed., *1–2 Kings, 1–2 Chronicles, Ezra, Nehemiah, Esther*, in *Ancient Christian Commentary on Scripture* (Downers Grove, IL: InterVarsity Press, 2008), 148.

20. Trench, *Miracles and Parables of the Old Testament*, 141.

21. Leland Ryken, James C. Wilhoit, and Tremper Longman III, eds., *Dictionary of Biblical Imagery* (Downers Grove, IL: InterVarsity Press, 1998), 752.

God Miraculously
Provides Water *and* Makes
It Look like Blood

2 Kings 3:16–23

The Miracle

Ahab's son, Jehoram, had succeeded his father as king of Israel, and Jehoshaphat was king of Judah at the time. Jehoram was evil like his father and mother—though he did get rid of the image of Baal that his father had made. Nevertheless, he did cling to the sins of Jeroboam.[1]

Mesha, the king of Moab, had (in times past) paid tribute to the king of Israel. However, when Ahab died, Mesha was no longer willing to pay. So Jehoram determined that he would force Mesha to pay, and so he reached out to Jehoshaphat, asking, "Will you go with me to battle against Moab?" Jehoshaphat indicated that he would (see 2 Kings 3:7). They determined to pass through Edom on their way to Moab, so they enlisted the king of Edom to help them in their war (see 2 Kings 3:8).

By the end of their seven-day journey, they were out of water. They could not quench their own thirst, nor the thirst of their animals (see 2 Kings 3:9). In frustration, Jehoram cried out, "Has the Lord called the three of us together simply to hand us over to the Moabites?" Jehoshaphat asked, "Isn't there a prophet of Jehovah here that we can get some direction from?" And so the three kings went down to Elisha to get some advice (see 2 Kings 3:10–11).

When Elisha learned of Jehoram's request, he said to him, "What do the two of us have to do with each other? Go to the prophets of Baal whom your mother and father put their trust in." But Jehoram said, "No! For it was Jehovah who called we three kings together—perhaps to hand us

___

over to the Moabites." Elisha responded, saying, "I swear, if I didn't respect Jehoshaphat, I wouldn't even look at you, Jehoram" (see 2 Kings 3:13–14).

Elisha then said, "Bring me a musician." And while the harpist played his stringed instrument for Elisha, the Spirit of the Lord came upon him, and Elisha told the three kings, "Dig ditches throughout the valley. Though there will be neither wind nor rain, the ditches will fill with water and you will have what you need to drink—both for you and your animals." And then Elisha added, "God will hand Moab over to you." Indeed, the prophet continued, "You will destroy every fortified city, you will cut down every good tree, you'll stop up all of the springs, and you'll ruin every fertile field by filling it with stones" (see 2 Kings 3:15–19).

The very next morning, water flowed from the direction of Edom, filling the ditches with water as Elisha had promised (see 2 Kings 3:30). But that same day, the people of Moab had heard that the combined armies of the Israelites, Judahites, and Edomites were about to attack, so the Moabites called up every able-bodied man—young or old—to prepare to defend their nation (see 2 Kings 3:21).

When the Moabites arose the next morning, the sun was shining on the water and it appeared as though it was blood. The Moabites assumed that the three armies had turned on each other and had slaughtered each other—and that the threat to Moab was no more. So the Moabites went to gather the spoils. However, when they came to the Israelite camp, the Israelite soldiers sprung up and attacked the Moabites, who turned and fled. The Israelites entered Moab and slew the people. As Elisha had predicted, they destroyed the towns, threw stones into the fields, chopped down the trees, and blocked up the springs (see 2 Kings 3:22–25).

When the king of Moab saw that he had lost the fight against the Israelites, he turned to attack the armies of Edom, but failed. Therefore, Mesha (the king of Moab) took his firstborn son and offered him as a sacrifice upon the wall; and his fury against Israel, who had returned to their own land, was great (see 2 Kings 3:26–27).

BACKGROUND

The language used by Jehoshaphat—"I will go up: I am as thou art, my people as thy people, and my horses as thy horses" (2 Kings 3:7)—suggests that theirs is more than a casual relationship between the two nations.[2] The language implies treaty relations between Israel and Judah. The willingness of the Edomites to quickly jump into the battle was likely due to the fact that Edom—at this time—did not have an independent king, but rather, a "deputy of Jehoshaphat" presiding over the land as "king."[3]

One commentary, criticizing Jehoram and extolling Jehoshaphat, noted, "The king of Israel was terrified, seeing only certain doom (v. 10). Jehoshaphat, whatever his shortcomings, was concerned with spiritual things (cf. . . . 1 Kings 22:41–53); and, as on another occasion (1 Kings 22:7), he asked for a true prophet of the Lord (v. 11)."[4] In the end, Jehoram was saved by his more spiritual sidekick.

The consulting of Elisha during their battle against the Moabites has struck some as strange. However, one commentator explained:

> That diviners were consulted prior to going to war or in the course of a battle is not itself novel. In early Israel, this practice was wholly a priestly function related to the Urim and Thummim oracle entrusted to their care (fc. Num 27:21; Judg 1:1–2; 1 Sam 30:7–8). Not until the mid-ninth century B.C.E., during the height of the Aramaean wars, do we note the transfer of mantic, divinatory functions from the priesthood to popular prophets. It is nevertheless striking that in no other biblical story is a prophet found among the troops in the army camp.[5]

Some translations (such as the KJV) have Elisha commanding Israel and her allies to dig trenches throughout the land so that they can capture the water that will miraculously come. Others, however, suggest that the Hebrew would better be rendered "the natural depressions" upon the face of the land will "fill up."[6] Owing to the fact that the water came the very next day—not giving sufficient time for the digging of trenches—it is most likely that Elisha was referring to the miraculous filling of natural depressions upon the face of the land which already existed.

Elisha called for a "minstrel" or "musician" (2 Kings 3:15). The Hebrew word, translated as "minstrel" in the King James Version, means someone who plays a stringed instrument.[7] While it is uncertain exactly what the string instrument was that the musician played, some sources interpret it as a harp.[8] The prophet's call for a musician has caused some to assume that Elisha was an ecstatic or mystic. However, responding to such claims, one source suggested, "It is more likely amid these calamitous circumstances [that] Elisha simply wanted soothing music played so that he might be quieted before God and thus . . . be brought to a mood conducive for God to reveal to him his will."[9]

Elisha's prophecy about what Israel (and her allies) will do to the land—overthrowing cities, destroying fields and trees, and damming up water supplies (2 Kings 3:19)—had been seen by some as a command, not just a prediction.[10] Certainly the despoiling of fruit trees, the ruining of fields of crops, and the blocking of water sources for irrigation suggests that they were doing all that they could to cripple their enemy. It may well be that Elisha was advising Israel and her allies on how to thoroughly disable the Moabites so that there would not be fear of a retaliatory attack.[11]

One of the reasons that the Moabites had not considered that the water on the ground could indeed be simply water instead of blood, was the fact that there had been no rain in Moab for some time. Commentators generally think that God caused it to rain in Edom, and that water flowed along the slope of the mountains into the indentations on the ground in the land between Edom and Moab. Since this happened unannounced to the inhabitants of Moab, they didn't stop to think that the liquid that appeared bloodlike could be water caused to look reddish by the morning sun reflecting off it.[12]

The surprising human sacrifice of the son of the king of Moab (and heir to the throne) has been explained in this way. "Mesha's sacrifice, performed on the city wall being assaulted by Israelite troops, is best taken as a propitiatory act offered to the angry Moabite deity Chemosh *in extremis*, not as a regular cultic offering."[13] Ephrem the Syrian, on the other hand, believed that Mesha offered his son to Jehovah, thinking that such might appease the God of the Israelites, and spare him and the Moabite people from what seemed like certain destruction.[14]

SYMBOLIC ELEMENTS

In the scriptures, water is a dualistic symbol. Sometimes it represents the Holy Ghost and its influence (i.e., cleansing, sanctification, renewal, refreshing, etc.), and, at other times, it symbolizes the opposite (chaos, instability, or death).[15] Curiously, in this miracle, it appears to be used in both ways. The Israelites (and their allies) were refreshed and saved by it, but the Moabites were thrown into chaos and ultimate death because of it.

While harps do not seem like obvious symbols, they do have subtle connotations in art and scripture. For example, in religious art, harps are commonly featured "among the instruments played by concerts of angels."[16] Elsewhere we read, harps "may be associated with becoming involved in spiritual activities [and the] need to listen to spiritual information or insight."[17] One dictionary of religious imagery points out that "the playing of harps . . . seems to have accompanied the prophetic function (1 Sam 10:5; 2 Kings 3:15). Harps are, therefore, instruments that accompany both worship and divine speech."[18] This same source adds, "Harps lend an other-worldly atmosphere to the picture of heavinly realms (Rev 5:8; 14:2; 15:2)."[19]

APPLICATION AND ALLEGORIZATION

One commentary on this miracle stated, "We cannot understand why the prophet had need to call for a minstrel to soothe his disturbed and ruffled spirit so that he could be in an equable and placid frame of mind to receive a divine communication."[20] Those familiar with the "still small voice" (see 1 Kings 19:12; 1 Nephi 17:45) of the Spirit know exactly why Elisha needed to create a peaceful and Spirit-conducive environment. Trench wrote,

> The soul that has to bear the message of God to others needs to rise into some degree of harmony with the mind of God, to partake in some measure of the holy calm which belongs to Him. Music prepares the heart of the good man to receive, and hence to be the bearer of special help from the Divine Spirit. The gentle playing of the brook over a very rugged rock will in time render it smooth as the water itself. So will the waves of music passing over a sanctified soul.[21]

Music has an undeniable power. President J. Reuben Clark, Jr. taught, "We get nearer to the Lord through music than perhaps through any other thing except prayer."[22] President Boyd K. Packer wrote, "Music can set an atmosphere of worship which invites [the] spirit of revelation."[23] Elisha understood this principle. Latter-day Saints need to apprehend it and apply it in their own lives. Over the years, I have been disappointed as I have looked out on various congregations and noted an increasing number of Saints who choose to not sing the sacred hymns of the Church. For Elisha, music provoked personal revelation. For you and I, sacred sounds can also open the windows of heaven and allow us to feel God's Spirit and hear His voice.

One commentary on this miracle suggested that the same element—water—was a blessing to one group and a curse to another.[24] And so it is with so many things in this world. The Internet can take us instantly into the world of the prophets, or it can deliver us into the den of demons. Prescription medications can deliver us from pain, or doom us to a life of agony and addiction. A desire to be led by God in life's decisions can make us more Spirit-directed, or can debilitate us when we feel we need a revelation on the smallest of decisions. Elder Dallin H. Oaks taught, "Satan uses every possible device to degrade and enslave every soul. He attempts to distort and corrupt everything created for the good of man, sometimes by diluting that which is good, sometimes by camouflaging that which is evil."[25] God has created so many things for our blessing and benefit. If used in the way that God intended, they will be exactly that in our lives—a blessing and benefit. If, on the other hand, we follow the adversary's advice, things designed to aid us may destroy us. Satan will ever seek to keep you and me from seeing things "as they really are" (Jacob 4:13). We must be vigilant to that fact. If we keep our lives right, we will have "eyes to see, and ears to hear" (Deuteronomy 29:4). However, like the Moabites in this narrative, if we follow the false gods of this fallen world, we will "have eyes to see, and see not" and "have ears to hear, and hear not" (Ezekiel 12:2)—and the very things that God intended to bless us will serve to destroy.

The narrative of this miracle makes it quite clear that were it not for Jehoshaphat's willingness to exercise faith in Jehovah and His prophet, Jehoram and his people would have been destroyed. Thus, a lesson has been drawn from this miracle: "That God, sometimes, for the sake of one man's character, helps those with whose character He has not sympathy."[26] If ever there was a reason to surround ourselves with those who have believing blood, perhaps it is this.

In the King James Version of this miracle, it appears to tell the Israelites and their allies to dig ditches so that the much-needed water can be miraculously provided and collected.[27] In this miracle, God does not tell them *how* he will perform the miracle, only that He *will*. It was the duty of the Israelites to exercise faith in what they could not see, and to believe in a promise that seemed impossible. The nineteenth-century British author and pastor, Charles Spurgeon, offered this application: "Have we this day grace enough to make trenches into which the divine blessing may flow? Alas! we too often fail in the exhibition of true and practical faith. Let us this day be on the lookout for answers to prayer. As the child who went to a meeting to pray for rain took an umbrella with her; so let us truly and practically expect the Lord to bless us. Let us make the valley full of ditches and expect to see them all filled."[28]

NOTES

1. Jeroboam was the first king of the northern kingdom of Israel. He became king at the death of Solomon, when the kingdom split and the ten tribes broke off.

2. "Jehoshaphat remained a relative of Jehoram of Israel; for his son (and coregent), also named Jehoram, was married to the Jehoram of Israel's aunt, Athaliah." Richard D. Patterson and Hermann J. Austel, "1 and 2 Kings," in Frank E. Gaebelein, ed., *The Expositor's Bible Commentary* (Grand Rapids, MI: Zondervan, 1994), 4:180.

3.   See Mordechai Cogan and Hayim Tadmor, *The Anchor Bible: II Kings*, vol. 11 (New York: Doubleday, 1988), 44. See also Patterson and Austel, "1 and 2 Kings," in Frank E. Gaebelein, ed., *The Expositor's Bible Commentary*, 4:180; Israel Wolf Slotki, *Kings*, in *Soncino Books of the Bible* (London: The Soncino Press, 1978), 177; Donald J. Wiseman, *1 and 2 Kings*, in *Tyndale Old Testament Commentaries* (Downers Grove, IL: InterVarsity Press, 1988), 200.

4.   Patterson and Austel, "1 and 2 Kings," in Gaebelein, *The Expositor's Bible Commentary*, 4:180. See also Israel Wolf Slotki, *Kings*, in *Soncino Books of the Bible*, 178. Wiseman writes, "Jehoram despairs while Jehoshaphat looks to God." (Wiseman, *1 and 2 Kings*, in *Tyndale Old Testament Commentaries*, 200.)

5.   Cogan and Tadmor, *The Anchor Bible: II Kings*, 49. See also Patterson and Austel, "1 and 2 Kings," in Gaebelein, *The Expositor's Bible Commentary*, 4:181; Wiseman, *1 and 2 Kings*, in *Tyndale Old Testament Commentaries*, 200.

6.   See Patterson and Austel, "1 and 2 Kings," in Gaebelein, *The Expositor's Bible Commentary*, 4:179–80; Cogan and Tadmor, *The Anchor Bible: II Kings*, 45.

7.   See Francis Brown, S. R. Driver, and Charles A. Briggs, *The Brown-Driver-Briggs Hebrew and English Lexicon* (Peabody, MA: Hendrickson Publishers, 1999), 618.

8.   See Patterson and Austel, "1 and 2 Kings," in Gaebelein, *The Expositor's Bible Commentary*, 4:179–80; Wiseman, *1 and 2 Kings*, in *Tyndale Old Testament Commentaries*, 200; Ephrem the Syrian, "On the Second Book of Kings," 3.16, in Conti, *1–2 Kings, 1–2 Chronicles, Ezra, Nehemiah, Esther*, in *Ancient Christian Commentary on Scripture*, 152.

9.   Leon J. Wood, *The Holy Spirit in the Old Testament* (Grand Rapids, MI: Zondervan, 1976), 118. See also Israel Wolf Slotki, *Kings*, in *Soncino Books of the Bible*, 179; Wiseman, *1 and 2 Kings*, in *Tyndale Old Testament Commentaries*, 200; Ellis T. Rasmussen, *A Latter-day Saint Commentary on the Old Testament* (Salt Lake City, UT: Deseret Book, 1994), 302.

10.   See Cogan and Tadmor, *The Anchor Bible: II Kings*, 45; Ephrem the Syrian, "On the Second Book of Kings," 3.23, in Conti, *1–2 Kings, 1–2 Chronicles, Ezra, Nehemiah, Esther*, in *Ancient Christian Commentary on Scripture*, 153. Wiseman challenges the view that this could be a command, noting that cutting down fruit-bearing trees of one's enemy is banned in Deuteronomy 20:19. (See Wiseman, *1 and 2 Kings*, in *Tyndale Old Testament Commentaries*, 201.)

11.   See Israel Wolf Slotki, *Kings*, in *Soncino Books of the Bible*, 179; Patterson and Austel, "1 and 2 Kings," in Gaebelein, *The Expositor's Bible Commentary*, 4:182.

12.   See Israel Wolf Slotki, *Kings*, in *Soncino Books of the Bible*, 180; Ephrem the Syrian, "On the Second Book of Kings," 3.25, in Conti, *1–2 Kings, 1–2 Chronicles, Ezra, Nehemiah, Esther*, in *Ancient Christian Commentary on Scripture*, 153; Patterson and Austel, "1 and 2 Kings," in Gaebelein, *The Expositor's Bible Commentary*, 4:180.

13. Cogan and Tadmor, *The Anchor Bible: II Kings*, 47. See also Wiseman, *1 and 2 Kings*, in *Tyndale Old Testament Commentaries*, 201–2; Patterson and Austel, "1 and 2 Kings," in Gaebelein, *The Expositor's Bible Commentary*, 4:181; Israel Wolf Slotki, *Kings*, in *Soncino Books of the Bible*, 181.

14. See Ephrem the Syrian, "On the Second Book of Kings," 3.25–27, in Conti, *1–2 Kings, 1–2 Chronicles, Ezra, Nehemiah, Esther*, in *Ancient Christian Commentary on Scripture*, 153–54.

15. See Alonzo L. Gaskill, *The Lost Language of Symbolism: An Essential Guide for Recognizing and Interpreting Symbols of the Gospel* (Salt Lake City, UT: Deseret Book, 2003), 20, 160–61, 265, 360n75, 400n42, 401.

16. James Hall, *Dictionary of Subjects & Symbols in Art*, rev. ed. (New York: Harper & Row, 1979), 145.

17. Kevin J. Todeschi, *The Encyclopedia of Symbols* (New York: Perigee Book, 1995), 129.

18. Leland Ryken, James C. Wilhoit, and Tremper Longman III, eds., *Dictionary of Biblical Imagery* (Downers Grove, IL: InterVarsity Press, 1998), 364

19. Ibid., 578. See also Todeschi, *The Encyclopedia of Symbols*, 129.

20. Herbert Lockyer, *All the Miracles of the Bible*, 119.

21. Richard C. Trench, *Miracles and Parables of the Old Testament* (Grand Rapids, MI: Baker Book House, 1959), 146.

22. J. Reuben Clark Jr., in *Conference Report*, October 1936, 111.

23. Boyd K. Packer, *Mine Errand From the Lord: Selections from the Sermons and Writings of Boyd K. Packer*, Clyde J. Williams, comp. (Salt Lake City, UT: Deseret Book, 2008), 555.

24. Lockyer, *All the Miracles of the Bible*, 119. Elsewhere we read, "It was the occasion of life to one army and of death to the other. The one was brought about by the supernatural interposition, the other by a natural, though mistaken, inference. The cloud that was the help of Israel at the Red Sea, became the destruction of the Egyptians." (Trench, *Miracles and Parables of the Old Testament*, 147.)

25. Dallin H. Oaks, "Our Strengths Can Become Our Downfall," *Ensign*, October 1994.

26. Trench, *Miracles and Parables of the Old Testament*, 147.

27. As noted above, the Hebrew is not clear on whether the men were to dig their own trenches or use ditches that already existed.

28. Charles Haddon Spurgeon, "Faith's Checkbook," cited in *Daily Devotion: January to December with Jesus* (Editora Dracaena: Santa Catarina, Brazil, 2015), s.v. "November 4."

ELISHA MIRACULOUSLY MULTIPLIES *the* OIL *of a* WIDOW

2 KINGS 4:1–7

THE MIRACLE

One of the sons of the prophets—a disciple of Elijah and Elisha—had died, and his wife approached the prophet and said, "My husband was a believer in Jehovah, and your servant; but he has died, and creditors are now coming to take my two children away to work as slaves to pay off our debts" (see 2 Kings 4:1). Elisha asked her, "What shall I do for thee? tell me, what hast thou in the house?" (2 Kings 4:2). The widow replied, "I don't really have anything other than a single pot of oil." Elisha instructed her to go and borrow empty containers from her neighbors—and not just a few—and then go home, and, in privacy, pour oil into each of the borrowed containers until each is full (see 2 Kings 4:2–4). So, the woman did as Elisha had instructed, and filled container after container with oil. At one point, she asked one of her sons to bring her another container, but he indicated that they had no more (see 2 Kings 4:5–6).

Therefore, the widow went to Elisha and explained that, via her one container of oil, she had been able to fill many borrowed containers with oil. The prophet then instructed her, "Now go and sell all of the oil that you have on hand, and pay off your debt. Then you and your sons can live off of whatever proceeds remain" (see 2 Kings 4:7).

BACKGROUND

This widow of one of the "sons of the prophets" is believed, in ancient Jewish and early Christian tradition, to have been the wife of Obadiah—the steward of King Ahab (see 1 Kings 18:3, 12). According to lore dating back to antiquity, Obadiah had used his own fortune, and had even gone into debt, in order to support "prophets who were in hiding" because of the threats by Jezebel—the king's "iniquitous spouse." The widow carried on this work, even after her husband's passing. At some point after the death of Obadiah, "The king sought to hold the children responsible for the debt of the father."[1]

The threat of placing children, or even a wife, into indentured servitude was real. Biblical law regulated how this was to occur (see Exodus 21:7; cf. Amos 2:6; Isaiah 50:1). Leviticus 25:39–42 suggests that those sold into servitude were to be released in the jubilee year, but they could also be released by special decree (see Nehemiah 5). The Code of Hammurabi (§117) indicates that the period of service for an indentured slave in Babylon was three years.[2] So the widow's voiced concerns are not hyperbole.[3]

The prophet's question, "What can I do for you?" suggests that he knows the law and sees little he can do to override that.[4] He had no power to overturn the temporal laws. However, like Jesus (see Matthew 17:24–27), the Spirit would direct Elisha to answer a temporal problem in a spiritual manner.

The amount of oil the woman had on hand is a point of uncertainty. Several sources suggest that it was only as much as one would use in a "single application," or "hardly sufficient to anoint the little finger."[5] Elsewhere we read that it would have only been as much as would fit in "a small anointing flask."[6] Thus, the magnitude of the miracle is increased by the limited amount of oil used to produce it.

SYMBOLIC ELEMENTS

Of the symbolism behind the oil in this miracle, symbologist Walter Wilson wrote, "[It] represents the blessings of God which He pours out upon the man or the woman of faith in order that the needs of their life may be met."[7] Elsewhere we read, "Within a biblical understanding, all of life is evidence of God's provision, inasmuch as all existence is dependent on God."[8]

APPLICATION AND ALLEGORIZATION

One source suggested that the oil in this episode is to remind us of the Holy Spirit, and its conveyance of God's grace and mercy.[9] The unending outpouring of oil here draws our minds to the Lord's promise in the Gospel of John, "Whosoever drinketh of the water that I shall give him shall never thirst; but the water that I shall give him shall be in him a well of water springing up into everlasting life" (John 4:14; cf. John 7:37–39). Jesus promises those who believe in and follow Him that they will have a well—a well of the Spirit and of God's grace—spring up in them, and that it will never run dry. In the narrative under consideration, the woman also has a well of oil that—so long as there are pots to receive it—does not run dry. This never-ending "well" allows her to pay her debts to her creditor. The spiritual "well" that Jesus offers us will allow us to pay our eternal debt to our satanic creditor through Christ's spilt blood (see D&C 38:4). As one early Christian source stated,

> We assert with confidence and assurance that holy Elisha was an image of our Savior. . . . This widow typified the church. . . . This widow, that is, the church, had contracted a heavy debt of sins, not of material substance. She had a debt, and she endured a most cruel creditor, because she had made herself subject to the devil by many sins. She was captive because the Redeemer had not yet come, but after Christ our Lord the true Redeemer visited the widow, he freed her from all debts. Now let us see how that widow was freed—how, except by an increase of oil? In the oil we understand mercy. Notice, brothers: the oil failed, and the debt increased; the oil was increased, and the debt disappeared. . . . Then, at the coming of the true Elisha, Christ our Lord, the widow or the church was freed from the debt of sin by an increase of oil, that is, by the gift of grace and mercy.[10]

If, like the woman, we continue to do the works that Christ and His prophets have commanded of us, the blessings of sanctification and mercy will never run out. The "well" of forgiveness and blessings will never run dry for those who are obedient to the dictates and directives of God's anointed. "Devout obedience can produce brimful spiritual blessings!"[11]

One source pointed out that the woman's husband had "feared the Lord" (2 Kings 4:1) while alive, but now (in death) his widow and children suffered. He had been a servant to his nation, yet, upon his death, his children and wife are threatened with imprisonment by one of his fellow citizens—perhaps even one of the government.[12] By way of application, faithfulness to God or country does not guarantee protection from trials. Some of the most holy have been called to suffer—Jesus being chief among them. Rather than asking, "Why me?" you and I should ask, "Why not me?" God promises blessings for our sacrifices on behalf of the kingdom. However, there is no promise that we will be void of suffering. "Sometimes the adverse surroundings of God's children seem to triumph over them for a while, but a time comes when goodness is seen to assert its superior value. There was a period in Joseph's history [in Egypt] which seemed to say that uprightness of life was not of much account in the eyes of the Ruler of the World, but bye-and-bye [*sic*] the reward came."[13] Many of the blessings that will come are postponed until we have "endure[d] all things" (2 Timothy 2:10).

On a related note, Elisha's counsel, "Shut the door upon thee and upon thy sons" (2 Kings 4:4), is a reminder of the truth that God's work to meet our needs is often performed in secret. Next year's needs for food will be met as a result of secret work going on right now beneath the soil. Nature, while the metaphorical door is shut, works miracles that will be manifest in due time. So also, the human soul is taken care of by God's unseen works, as we secretly wait upon Him.[14] "The command to fill the jars behind closed doors delivers the miracle from a mere spectacle; it was a private need, privately met by a sovereign and loving God (cf. Matt 6:6)."[15]

President Ezra Taft Benson saw in this miracle a rather interesting and timely application. He taught,

> By a miracle Elisha enabled her to acquire a goodly supply of oil. Then he said to her: "Go, sell the oil, and pay thy debt, and live thou and thy children of the rest." (See 2 Kings 4:1–7.)
>
> "Pay thy debt, and live." How fruitful these words have ever been! What counsel they are for us today! . . .
>
> The Lord desires His Saints to be free and independent in the critical days ahead. But no man is truly free who is in financial bondage. "Think what you do when you run in debt," said Benjamin Franklin; "you give to another power over your liberty." "Pay thy debt, and live," said Elisha (2 Kings 4:7). And in the Doctrine and Covenants the Lord says, "It is my will that you shall pay all your debts" (D&C 104:78). . . .
>
> Get out of debt if it is at all humanly possible. . . . Even in times of economic stability it is sound practice to live within one's income and avoid unnecessary debt.[16]

One source suggested that "this [miracle] shows the prophet's moral concern for a serious social problem. . . . One lesson implied . . . here is that God does not fail as the God of the widow and fatherless (Dt. 10:18; Ja. 1:27) as do some earthly rulers" and governments.[17] Part of being a Christian is to be socially conscious. Thus, on every tithing slip there is a line for "humanitarian aid." God expects His true disciples to be concerned for the welfare of each other, but also for those outside the faith. What better way to share the gospel than to live it by loving and serving others, including those not of our faith. The world has a number of serious social problems, and you and I can be part of the solution. Elisha saw a woman who was unemployed and in financial difficulty. He didn't give her money, but he taught her how to get out of debt and how to provide for her family. As disciples of Christ, we should be conscious of needs and use our gifts (as the prophet used his) to bless and teach and help others.

NOTES

1. See Louis Ginzberg, *The Legends of the Jews* (Philadelphia: The Jewish Publication Society of America, 1967), 4:240–42; Josephus, "Antiquities of the Jews," bk. 9, ch. 4, in *The Complete Works of Josephus*, William Whiston, trans. (Grand Rapids, MI: Kregel Publications, 1981), 198–99; Ephrem the Syrian, "On the Second Book of Kings," 4.1, in Marco Conti, ed., *1–2 Kings, 1–2 Chronicles, Ezra, Nehemiah, Esther*, in *Ancient Christian Commentary on Scripture* (Downers Grove, IL: InterVarsity Press, 2008), 155. Whiston notes, "That this woman was no other than the widow of Obadiah, is confirmed by the Chaldee paraphrast, and by the Rabbins and others. Nor is it unlikely that these debts were contracted by her husband for the support of those 'hundred of the Lord's prophets, whom he maintained by fifty in a cave,' in the days of Ahab and Jezebel, (1 Kings xviii.4)." (Whiston, *The Complete Works of Josephus*, 198n†. See also Israel Wolf Slotki, *Kings*, in *Soncino Books of the Bible* [London: The Soncino Press, 1978], 182; Mordechai Cogan and Hayim Tadmor, *The Anchor Bible: II Kings*, vol. 11 [New York: Doubleday, 1988], 55; Richard D. Patterson and Hermann J. Austel, "1 and 2 Kings," in Frank E. Gaebelein, ed., *The Expositor's Bible Commentary* [Grand Rapids, MI: Zondervan, 1994], 4:183; Donald J. Wiseman, *1 and 2 Kings*, in *Tyndale Old Testament Commentaries* [Downers Grove, IL: InterVarsity Press, 1988], 202; Herbert Lockyer, *All the Miracles of the Bible: The Supernatural in Scripture—Its Scope and Significance* [Grand Rapids, MI: Zondervan, 1961], 119.)

2. See Patterson and Austel, "1 and 2 Kings," in Gaebelein, *The Expositor's Bible Commentary*, 4:183; Cogan and Tadmor, *The Anchor Bible: II Kings*, 55; Israel Wolf Slotki, *Kings*, in *Soncino Books of the Bible*, 182; Lockyer, *All the Miracles of the Bible*, 119.

3. While some ancient Jewish sources make the king the "creditor" who sought to imprison the widow's sons, other Jewish sources refer to the "creditor" as Jehoram (the King's son). See Israel Wolf Slotki, *Kings*, in *Soncino Books of the Bible*, 182.

4. See Cogan and Tadmor, *The Anchor Bible: II Kings*, 55.

5. Ibid.; Ginzberg, *The Legends of the Jews*, 6:345n8. See also Pamela McQuade, *The Top 100 Miracles of the Bible: What They Are and What They Mean to You Today* (Uhrichsville, OH: Barbour Publishing, 2008), 85; Lockyer, *All the Miracles of the Bible*, 119.

6. Wiseman, *1 and 2 Kings*, in *Tyndale Old Testament Commentaries*, 202.

7. Walter L. Wilson, *A Dictionary of Bible Types* (Peabody, MA: Hendrickson, 1999), 301.

8. Leland Ryken, James C. Wilhoit, and Tremper Longman III, eds., *Dictionary of Biblical Imagery* (Downers Grove, IL: InterVarsity Press, 1998), 683.

9. Lockyer, *All the Miracles of the Bible*, 120.

10. Caesarius of Arles, "Sermon" 128.1, in Marco Conti, ed., *1–2 Kings, 1–2 Chronicles, Ezra, Nehemiah, Esther*, in *Ancient Christian Commentary on Scripture* (Downers Grove, IL: InterVarsity Press, 2008), 155–56. See also Ephrem the Syrian, "On the Second Book of Kings," 4.3, in Conti, *1–2 Kings, 1–2 Chronicles, Ezra, Nehemiah, Esther*, in *Ancient Christian Commentary on Scripture*, 156.

11. Patterson and Austel, "1 and 2 Kings," in Gaebelein, *The Expositor's Bible Commentary*, 4:183. Lockyer records the following application of this miracle: "Only when there was no vessel left to fill was the miraculous supply of oil stayed." This, he continues, is "a type of [or symbol for] prayer, with 'shut doors' (Matthew 6:6), which brings down supplies of grace so long as we and ours have hearts open to receive it (Psalm 81:10; Ephesians 3:20)." (Lockyer, *All the Miracles of the Bible*, 120.)

12. See Richard C. Trench, *Miracles and Parables of the Old Testament* (Grand Rapids, MI: Baker Book House, 1959), 149.

13. Ibid., 149.

14. See ibid., 150.

15. Patterson and Austel, "1 and 2 Kings," in Gaebelein, *The Expositor's Bible Commentary*, 4:183. See also Lockyer, *All the Miracles of the Bible*, 119.

16. Ezra Taft Benson, *The Teachings of Ezra Taft Benson* (Salt Lake City, UT: Bookcraft, 1988), 288. See also Thomas S. Monson, "Goal beyond Victory," *Ensign*, November 1988.

17. See Wiseman, *1 and 2 Kings*, in *Tyndale Old Testament Commentaries*, 202–3.

THE SON *of the* SHUNAMMITE COUPLE IS RAISED *from the* DEAD

2 KINGS 4:18–37

THE MIRACLE

Elisha often passed through Shunem, where there dwelt a couple who had no children. The husband was older, and any hope for a child at this point in their lives seemed unrealistic. Under the influence of the Spirit, Elisha promised the woman that, within a year, she would give birth to a son; and she did (see 2 Kings 4:8, 16–17).

The boy grew into a young lad. One day, the youth approached his father, who was laboring in the field, and said that his head was hurting him. The boy's father had one of the servants carry the child in to his mother. The young man sat on his mother's lap until noon, when he died. His mother carried him up to the room that Elisha always stayed in when he passed through Shunem; she laid him on the prophet's bed, and then she shut the door (see 2 Kings 4:19–21).

The deceased boy's mother then asked her husband to get one of the servants to take her (on a donkey) to Elisha (see 2 Kings 4:22). Her husband asked, "[Why] go to him to day? it is neither [a] new moon, nor [the] sabbath." She simply replied, "It shall be well" (2 Kings 4:23). Then she saddled the donkey and told her servant, "Don't slow down unless if I ask you to." So they set out to find Elisha near Mount Carmel (see 2 Kings 4:24–25).

As she neared where the prophet was, he saw her in the distance, and sent his servant (Gehazi) to meet her and to ask, "Is it well with thee? is it well with thy husband? is it well with the child?" But when Gehazi asked the Shunammite woman these things, she simply said, "It is well" (2 Kings 4:26).

However, when the woman approached Elisha, she fell at his feet. Gehazi tried to push her away, but the prophet said, "Let her alone"—indicating that she was in distress, though the Spirit had not revealed to Elisha why (see 2 Kings 4:27).

The woman said to the man of God, "Did I ask you for a son? Didn't I tell you, *don't raise my hopes?*" Realizing her concern, Elisha told Gehazi to take the prophet's staff and quickly go to the boy—not stopping to talk to anyone. The servant was to lay the staff on the face of the boy. So, while the woman stayed with Elisha, Gehazi went quickly to her home, and did as Elisha had counseled, but nothing happened. Therefore, the prophet's servant went back to meet Elisha (who, along with the boy's mother, was on his way), and informed him that it had not worked (see 2 Kings 4:28–31).

When Elisha arrived at the house, he went into the room where the boy lay, and shut the door. The prophet then prayed for God's help, after which he laid atop of the boy—mouth to mouth, eyes to eyes, and hands to hands, until the boy's body warmed up. Then Elisha arose and paced about the floor for a time, and then again stretched himself out on top of the boy. Suddenly, the child sneezed seven times and opened his eyes. Elisha summoned his servant, and told him to call the child's mother. When she came in and saw that her son was alive, she fell at Elisha's feet, and then took her son and left the room (see 2 Kings 4:32–37).

BACKGROUND

This miracle takes place in Shunem, a town in the hill territory of Issachar, approximately twenty miles from Mount Carmel, where Elisha was at the time of the boy's death.[1] According to Jewish tradition, the "Shunammite woman" (i.e., the boy's mother) was the sister of the "fair damsel," Abishag, the Shunammite—who ministered to King David (1 Kings 1:3, 15).[2]

The text states that the boy's father was out "reaping" (see 2 Kings 4:18), and "reaping is done at a time of the year when the sun is very hot."[3] It has been suggested that the boy's ailment, from which he ultimately dies, was a sunstroke—perhaps caused by being out in the field for a prolonged period without a head covering.[4]

When the husband tells his wife to *not* go looking for the prophet unless it is a "new moon" or "the Sabbath" (see 2 Kings 4:23), his thinking is likely that Elisha would not be available on a workday (i.e., a day other than a

Sabbath or feast day). He would be attending to the affairs of life, like one's bishop might be on an ordinary workday. Additionally, the fact that the father suggested that his wife wait has been taken as a sign that perhaps the woman. who had put the boy in the prophet's room and closed the door (see 2 Kings 4:21), may not have told her husband that their son had died. Indeed, when he asked why she was going on a non-Sabbath and non-holiday, her response was, "It shall be well" (KJV 2 Kings 4:23), or "It's alright" (NIV), suggesting that perhaps the father did not know that the boy was dead.[5]

In this miracle, the Shunammite woman appears somewhat dismissive of Gehazi. For example, when he asks her if something is wrong, she inaccurately says, "It is well" (2 Kings 4:26). When he heads to her home in an attempt to heal her son, she chooses to stay behind with Elisha, rather than travel home with Gehazi (see 2 Kings 4:30). Judaism has a tradition that Gehazi had acted inappropriately toward the woman—even lustfully—and, consequently, she did not trust him.[6] Certainly, Gehazi's weakness as a disciple would become evident later in the book of 2 Kings, where his greed and deceitfulness ultimately brings upon him the wrath of God in the form of leprosy (see 2 Kings 5:1–27).[7] Perhaps this explains the Shunammite woman's avoidance of Elisha's servant. Additionally, when the boy's mother says to Elisha, "As the Lord liveth, and as thy soul liveth, I will not leave thee" (2 Kings 4:30), that has been taken to suggest that she "force[d] Elisha to return with her to the side of the lad. . . . Action by proxy will not do."[8] Again, perhaps her declaration was spawned by her distrust of Gehazi.

One commentary suggested that the point of Gehazi going to the deceased boy before Elisha was twofold. First, the prophet was elderly and could not get there quickly, but his servant could arrive much faster. Second, the placing of the staff upon the body (see 2 Kings 4:29, 31) "would stay further physical degeneration until [the prophet] could come."[9]

Rather than Elisha lying on top of the boy, as the King James Version suggests that he did (see 2 Kings 4:34), the Hebrew suggests that he simply crouched over him—most likely because the small frame of the child might have been harmed by having a full-grown man resting his entire body weight upon him.[10]

SYMBOLIC ELEMENTS

The staff in this miracle has been seen as a symbol of "God-given prophetic power" (see Exodus 4:1–4; 17:8–13).[11] Hence, Elisha sent it with Gehazi to place it upon the deceased boy.

Early Christians often saw the wooden staff in this miracle as a symbol of the cross of Jesus, but without Christ crucified to it. Consequently, several early Christian sources say that the reason it didn't heal the boy was to remind us that the law of Moses—without Christ crucified—did not have the power to save.[12]

APPLICATION AND ALLEGORIZATION

The Shunammite woman had every reason to doubt. Her faith in God and His prophets could very well wane in such a circumstance, as might yours or mine. However, she mustered all the belief she could—hoping that God's prophet might once again do the seemingly impossible in her life. "He had previously announced life for her who had no hope of producing life; perhaps he could once more give life to her son."[13] Her choice to believe when she had reason to doubt is instructive. The modern era is a time that tries people's souls. Where faith was once commonplace—and doubters were the exception to the rule—disbelief and doubt seem to be the norm today, and faith the exception. But the Shunammite woman, when she had a seemingly valid reason to doubt, reminded herself of the reasons that she had to believe; and she put her trust in those faith-promoting experiences of the past, rather than allowing the doubts of the present to destroy her faith. For those who find themselves struggling with their faith today, following the example of the Shunammite woman may help. When you run across little things that cause you to question your testimony, do not throw the baby out with the bath water. Think about all of the things you *do know*, and the various spiritual experiences you've had *in the past*. Remind yourself of encounters you've had with the Holy Ghost, miracles you've experienced in priesthood blessings or prayers, evidences you've read about or heard, and keep those at the forefront of your thoughts as you try to resolve the things that have recently caused you to doubt. In the end, you may have to place some things on the shelf, since we do not have answers to all of life's questions. However, if you can remember the many times you've felt the Spirit telling you, "This is right," "This is good," or "This is true," those memories can serve to help you exercise faith during those times when you are struggling with something you don't know or understand. In the end, the Shunammite woman's faith was confirmed because she didn't give up hope, and she didn't throw out the miracles of the past because of the trials and doubts of the present. If we follow her lead, we too will have our faith confirmed.

Throughout this narrative, Elisha uses his "servant" (Gehazi) to contact the woman, and also to try to raise the boy from the dead. One source suggested that this was "to involve Gehazi in the ministry so that he might have opportunity to mature in the faith."[14] Speaking of how Alma used Amulek in the work of the Lord, President Deiter F. Uchtdorf taught,

> When Alma went out . . . to teach among the people of Ammonihah, he had a second witness at his side—Amulek, one of their own. . . .
> Alma found Amulek and asked him for help.
> And Alma received help.
> For whatever reason, sometimes we as leaders are reluctant to find and ask our Amuleks. Perhaps we think that we can do the work better by ourselves, or we are reluctant to inconvenience others, or we assume that others would not want to participate. Too often we hesitate to invite people to use their God-given talents and engage in the great work of salvation. . . .
> In whatever position you currently serve—whether you are a deacons quorum president, a stake president, or an Area President—to be successful, you must find your Amuleks.
> It may be someone who is unassuming or even invisible within your congregation. It may be someone who *seems* unwilling or unable to serve. Your Amuleks may be young or old, men or women, inexperienced, tired, or not active in the Church. But what may not be seen at first sight is that they are hoping to hear from you the words "The Lord needs you! I need you!"
> Deep down, many want to serve their God. They want to be an instrument in His hands. They want to thrust in their sickle and strive with their might to prepare the earth for the return of our Savior. They want to build His Church. But they are reluctant to begin. Often they wait to be asked.
> I invite you to think of those in your branches and wards, in your missions and stakes, who need to hear a call to action. The Lord has been working with them—preparing them, softening their hearts. Find them by seeing with your heart.
> Reach out to them. Teach them. Inspire them. Ask them.[15]

Elisha used Gehazi, and Alma used Amulek. Perhaps this miracle serves as a pattern for you and me. Are there those around us that the Lord would have us tutor and train? We should follow the example of the Lord's prophet—Elisha and Alma—and bless others with opportunities to be part of God's work.

It has been pointed out that, prior to performing the miracle, Elisha prayed (see 2 Kings 4:33–37).[16] The Lord has commanded, "Ye must not perform any thing unto the Lord save in the first place ye shall pray unto the

Father in the name of Christ" (2 Nephi 32:9). To not pray before giving a priesthood blessing or performing a ministering visit suggests that we think we are sufficient without God's help. However, the Lord's command is that we not knock on the door or lay hands on one in need before we invoke His name and ask for His aid.

Trench offered this application of the miracle: Elisha "prayed, he stretched himself upon the child, [and then] he *waited*—the most difficult part of all."[17] Elder Neal A. Maxwell suggested the importance of being willing to say not only, "Thy will be done, O Lord," but "Thy timing be done" as well.[18] This miracle can remind us of the importance of "wait[ing] upon the Lord" (Psalm 37:9). Miracles happen, but often not on our time frame. We must not be hasty to judge God's dispensation of His providence, nor should we be so backward as to think that we can improve upon it.[19] A significant part of having faith is having faith in God's timing.

The King James Version of this miracle calls the Shunammite mother, "A great woman" (2 Kings 4:8). However, the Hebrew suggests that she was, "Great with wealth" or "Well-to-do."[20] Of her, one source states,

> The wealthy Shunammite woman was one of those people for whom good works is a way of life. She surely knew how to use her money wisely and began by feeding Elisha whenever he came to town. Then she suggested to her husband that they build a little room on their roof for the man. Just to make it more convenient, you know. Now Elisha had a place to spend the night too.[21]

Surely there is a lesson in this for you and me. First, it is an invitation to be generous with our personal wealth. What God blesses us with we should use to bless and help others. Second, it reminds us of the counsel of the book of Hebrews, "Be not forgetful to entertain strangers: for thereby some have entertained angels unawares" (Hebrews 13:2). While she may have been impressed with Elisha when she first met him, there was certainly no way for this woman to know of the blessing he would be in the life of their family. Finally, the woman gave to this acquaintance without any expectation of a blessing in return. However, in the end, he was the miraculous means of her becoming a mother, and then he was the means of her remaining a mother, after her son unexpectedly died. God certainly pays us back for any sacrifices we make in His name. And, like the Shunammite woman, there are hidden blessings awaiting those who proffer Christlike service to those in need.

In a rather curious application, Augustine wrote, "Elisha, who had sent his staff with his servant, was to follow later himself and bring the child to life. After hearing that the child had not revived, Elisha came in person; he was a type of our Lord, who had sent his servant ahead of him with a staff that represents the law [of Moses]. . . . The Lord accomplished what the staff had failed to do; grace achieved what the law could not."[22]

According to Jewish tradition, Gehazi's inability to raise the boy from the dead was a direct result of his own doubts about Elisha's power to restore life. "His skepticism rendered him unworthy of being the agent through whom a miracle was performed."[23] Miracles are wrought by faith. Disbelief disables the holder of the priesthood. If we wish to see God's hand manifest, we must believe that it is possible for Him to act in our lives, and in the lives of those to whom we minister. However, if we doubt such to be possible or even probable, that lack of faith may prevent the very miracle we seek.

NOTES

1. See Elizabeth F. Huwiler, "Shunem," in David Noel Freedman, *The Anchor Bible Dictionary* (New York: Doubleday, 1992), 5:1228; Israel Wolf Slotki, *Kings*, in *Soncino Books of the Bible* (London: The Soncino Press, 1978), 186.
2. Israel Wolf Slotki, *Kings*, in *Soncino Books of the Bible*, 183.
3. Ibid., 185.
4. See Mordechai Cogan and Hayim Tadmor, *The Anchor Bible: II Kings*, vol. 11 (New York: Doubleday, 1988), 57; Israel Wolf Slotki, *Kings*, in *Soncino Books of the Bible*, 185 & 188; Herbert Lockyer, *All the Miracles of the Bible: The Supernatural in Scripture—Its Scope and Significance* (Grand Rapids, MI: Zondervan, 1961), 120. See also Donald J. Wiseman, *1 and 2 Kings*, in *Tyndale Old Testament Commentaries* (Downers Grove, IL: InterVarsity Press, 1988), 204.
5. See Richard D. Patterson and Hermann J. Austel, "1 and 2 Kings," in Frank E. Gaebelein, ed., *The Expositor's Bible Commentary* (Grand Rapids, MI: Zondervan, 1994), 4:186. See also Israel Wolf Slotki, *Kings*, in *Soncino Books of the Bible*, 186; Cogan and Tadmor, *The Anchor Bible: II Kings*, 57; Wiseman, *1 and 2 Kings*, in *Tyndale Old Testament Commentaries*, 204; Pamela McQuade, *The Top 100 Miracles of the Bible: What They Are and What They Mean to You Today* (Uhrichsville, OH: Barbour Publishing, 2008), 87.
6. See Louis Ginzberg, *The Legends of the Jews* (Philadelphia: The Jewish Publication Society of America, 1967), 6:242–45. See also Patterson and Austel, "1 and 2 Kings," in Gaebelein, *The Expositor's Bible Commentary*, 4:185.
7. *The Anchor Bible Dictionary* states of him, "The dominant picture of Gehazi within the biblical narrative . . . is that of avarice." (Duane L. Christensen, "Gehazi," in Freedman, *The Anchor Bible Dictionary*, 2:926.)

8. Cogan and Tadmor, *The Anchor Bible: II Kings*, 58. See also Israel Wolf Slotki, *Kings*, in *Soncino Books of the Bible*, 187.

9. Patterson and Austel, "1 and 2 Kings," in Gaebelein, *The Expositor's Bible Commentary*, 4:186.

10. See Israel Wolf Slotki, *Kings*, in *Soncino Books of the Bible*, 188; Cogan and Tadmor, *The Anchor Bible: II Kings*, 58.

11. See Patterson and Austel, "1 and 2 Kings," in Gaebelein, *The Expositor's Bible Commentary*, 4:186. See also Walter L. Wilson, *A Dictionary of Bible Types* (Peabody, MA: Hendrickson, 1999), 349–51; Leland Ryken, James C. Wilhoit, and Tremper Longman III, eds., *Dictionary of Biblical Imagery* (Downers Grove, IL: InterVarsity Press, 1998), 733–34; Wiseman, *1 and 2 Kings*, in *Tyndale Old Testament Commentaries*, 205.

12. See, for example, Caesarius of Arles, "Exposition 1 of Psalm 70.19," in Marco Conti, ed., *1–2 Kings, 1–2 Chronicles, Ezra, Nehemiah, Esther*, in *Ancient Christian Commentary on Scripture* (Downers Grove, IL: InterVarsity Press, 2008), 161; Ephrem the Syrian, "On the Second Book of Kings," 4.30–5, in Conti, *1–2 Kings, 1–2 Chronicles, Ezra, Nehemiah, Esther*, in *Ancient Christian Commentary on Scripture*, 161; Gregory the Great, "Morals on the Book of Job," 9.40.63, in Conti, *1–2 Kings, 1–2 Chronicles, Ezra, Nehemiah, Esther*, in *Ancient Christian Commentary on Scripture*, 162.

13. Patterson and Austel, "1 and 2 Kings," in Gaebelein, *The Expositor's Bible Commentary*, 4:185.

14. Ibid., 4:187.

15. Dieter F. Uchtdorf, "Learn from Alma and Amulek, *Ensign*, November 2016; emphasis in original.

16. Ellis T. Rasmussen, *A Latter-day Saint Commentary on the Old Testament* (Salt Lake City, UT: Deseret Book, 1994), 302.

17. Richard C. Trench, *Miracles and Parables of the Old Testament* (Grand Rapids, MI: Baker Book House, 1974), 153.

18. Neal A. Maxwell, "Plow in Hope," *Ensign*, May 2001.

19. Trench, *Miracles and Parables of the Old Testament*, 155.

20. See Patterson and Austel, "1 and 2 Kings," in Gaebelein, *The Expositor's Bible Commentary*, 4:186; Cogan and Tadmor, *The Anchor Bible: II Kings*, 56; Lockyer, *All the Miracles of the Bible*, 120.

21. McQuade, *The Top 100 Miracles of the Bible*, 86.

22. Augustine, "Exposition on the Psalm," 70.19, in Conti, *1–2 Kings, 1–2 Chronicles, Ezra, Nehemiah, Esther*, in *Ancient Christian Commentary on Scripture*, 160–61. See also Caesarius of Arles, "Exposition 1 of Psalm 70.19," in Conti, Conti, *1–2 Kings, 1–2 Chronicles, Ezra, Nehemiah, Esther*, in *Ancient Christian Commentary on Scripture*, 161.

23. Israel Wolf Slotki, *Kings*, in *Soncino Books of the Bible*, 187. See also Ginzberg, *The Legends of the Jews*, 6:243.

A POT *of* POTTAGE IS
HEALED *by* ELISHA

2 KINGS 4:38–41

THE MIRACLE

Elisha returned to Gilgal from Shunem. At that time, there was a famine in the land. He and the "sons of the prophets" were assembled in a meeting, and Elisha instructed his servant to take a large pot and cook some stew for those gathered (see 2 Kings 4:38).

One of those gathered—perhaps the prophet's servant, or one of the "sons of the prophets"—went out into the field and collected herbs for the meal, and, in so doing, found some unknown wild gourds to cut up and put in the stew (see 2 Kings 4:39).

As the men ate the prepared meal, the taste was so bad—because of the gourds—that they cried out to Elisha, "O thou man of God, there is death in the pot," and they could not eat it because of the terrible taste (2 Kings 4:40).

In response, Elisha told his servant to bring him some flour, which he mixed into the stew, and then served it to his guests. It no longer tasted bad, nor was it harmful to them (see 2 Kings 4:41).

BACKGROUND

The Gilgal mentioned here is most likely the one located approximately eight miles north of Bethel, in the hill country on the way to Shiloh—and not the more famous Gilgal of Joshua's day. This Gilgal has been identified with the modern city of Jiljulieh, which occupies the summit of a hill north of Bethel.[1]

One commentator on the miracle indicated, "This *meeting* is thought to be a 'school' session," wherein Elisha taught his underlings in their duties in the prophetic office.[2]

The gourds in this miracle have been identified as *citrullus colocynthis* (i.e., the "apple of Sodom"), which is a small, yellow-colored melon that has been known to be fatal. When the fruit is ripe, the pulp inside dries, forming a bitter-tasting powder—which would have aroused the suspicion of those eating the stew that they had been poisoned.[3] One commentator explained that this particular gourd, still known to this day, "Can be used in small amounts as a laxative, but in large quantity . . . can cause death."[4] It has been suggested that the "sons of the prophets" tasted the stew and immediately "suffered its violent, purgative effect"—thereby sensing that "there [was] death in the pot" (2 Kings 4:40).[5]

SYMBOLIC ELEMENTS

Elisha, presiding over this meal, has been seen as a type for Christ who would come and abundantly provide fodder for His disciples—as He too sat as a presiding figure over the "sons of the prophets" in His day[6] (see Matthew 15:29–39; Mark 14:12–25; Luke 24:28–31; John 6:1–13; 21:9–13; 1 Corinthians 11:23–25).

The gourds, melons, or "apples of Sodom" (in this miracle) seem to represent anything bad that we introduce into our lives—allowing our hearts or minds to become corrupted, and risking spiritual death if we do not purge ourselves of it.

Flour or meal is often seen as a symbol for Christ.[7] One source states, "This is no doubt a type of the beautiful white, smooth life of Christ in which there was no sin, nor evil. His life was pure grace, pure love, pure holiness and pure beauty."[8] Just as Christ's Atonement can heal you and I—even resurrecting us from death—the flour (which typified Him) healed the stew, resurrecting the dead dinner that it might meet the needs of those who were to partake of it. One source states, "There are many death-dealing pots which Christ, as the Meal, can alone rid of their disastrous effects."[9]

APPLICATION AND ALLEGORIZATION

In the fourth century, Ephrem the Syrian interpreted this miracle as a symbol for the plan of salvation. You and I, because of the Fall of Adam, gather that which is harmful to us because—like the servant of Elijah—we "kn[o]w them not" (2 Kings 4:39). In other words, so often we don't see the dangers of the things that we take into our hearts and minds. We ingest that which can make us spiritually sick, even if it doesn't actually spiritually kill us. If we mix Christ into our lives (in heavy doses), it can reverse the effects of the telestial poisons we ingest. Just as the bitterness of the stew was removed, He can remove the bitterness of sin from our lives. In addition, just as the stew was no longer harmful to those who had partaken of it, Jesus can heal us and take away those things that have harmed us spiritually. But, we *must* incorporate Him into our lives if this curative effect is to be achieved. Believing isn't sufficient; we must live a life in which Christ is fully present each day. Having flour on the shelf couldn't heal the stew; and having a belief in Jesus, but not incorporating Him into our day-to-day lives, will similarly allow the poisons of mortality to take their full effect.[10]

In his commentary on the *Miracles and Parables of the Old Testament*, Richard Trench offered this explanation of this miracle's applicability to our lives.

> Man's extremity is often reached before God interposes. The wine was quite exhausted at Cana before the Saviour made more. Abraham's knife was lifted to slay his son, when the angel of Jehovah called to him (Gen. xxii. II). Israel came to the very border of the Red Sea before the waters were divided. So here the hungry men tasted the pottage before the miracle was wrought.[11]

God is in the business of building faith, and if He always intervened the moment things appeared to be going south, you and I would never develop the faith necessary to produce faith unto salvation. God must stretch us, and test our trust in Him. His tendency to hold back, so that we can faithfully hold on, is one means of developing in each of us the type of faith we will need if we are ever to become like Him.

One commentary on this miracle points out that Elisha most likely could have simply blessed the stew and healed it. Instead, he had flour brought forth and he physically mixed it in. Supernatural intervention often requires some measure of human effort. When Jesus was about to raise Lazarus from the dead, He first commanded that the stone over the mouth of his tomb be taken away (see John 11:39). When He determined to make more wine at the wedding at Cana, Jesus commanded that the pots first be filled with water (see John 2:7). If there are to be miracles, "Human effort must do what it can" first.[12] As we do all that we *can*, we free God to do all that He *must*. Miracles don't come to the lazy, but to those who are willing to do all in their power to lay hold on God's gracious gifts.

One text suggested that this miracle reminds us to stick to our areas of expertise, and let others do that which they are more qualified to do than are we.

> We ought to seek to know for what work we are qualified. The man who volunteered to gather herbs for the pottage might have been well fitted for other work; but his undertaking that for which ignorance of the nature of herbs disqualified him, had well nigh been the death of all the sons of the prophets. As the eagle is adapted for the air and the lion to roam the forest, so there is a sphere of labour in the world for which each man is adapted. When this law is not heeded, injury to the individual and to society is the result.[13]

By way of application, a bishop might find himself in a counseling situation where the issue is *not* sin, but mental health. He might do well to pass such work onto the trained counselor who has sufficient expertise in the field to meet the needs of the member. Similarly, a Relief Society president might discover a family who needs some financial training, and it might be outside of her personal expertise. In such a circumstance, she would do well to draw on the resources of those with training in this area so that the struggling family might receive the help that will enable them to get themselves permanently out of debt. Each of us should recognize where we have strengths, and where we do not; and we should allow those who are more qualified to deal with the things we know we cannot—or should not.

Several commentators on this miracle have suggested, by way of application, that this narrative reminds us of those who teach false doctrine—but are unaware of it. They gather false notions and interject those in their sermons or teachings, not realizing such will spiritually poison their hearers. "What is to be done?" one asks. "There is only one remedy. The meal must be added, the pure Word of God. This is the great antidote for the poison of evil doctrine. If we detect the poison flavor of error in anything that is set before us, 'then bring the meal,' and there will be 'no harm, no evil thing in the pot.'"[14] Christ and His word hold the key. The word "canon," which we typically use in reference to the authorized scriptural books of the Church, means "measuring rod" or "ruler." The canon is the thing that we can measure all doctrine by. If a teaching measures up to the content of scripture—ancient and modern—then it should be embraced. If it doesn't measure up, we know to cast it out and, thereby, avoid being poisoned by false teachings.

NOTES

1. See Wade R. Kotter, "Gilgal," in David Noel Freedman, *The Anchor Bible Dictionary* (New York: Doubleday, 1992), 2:1023; Richard D. Patterson and Hermann J. Austel, "1 and 2 Kings," in Frank E. Gaebelein, ed., *The Expositor's Bible Commentary* (Grand Rapids, MI: Zondervan, 1994), 4:174; Donald J. Wiseman, *1 and 2 Kings*, in *Tyndale Old Testament Commentaries* (Downers Grove, IL InterVarsity Press, 1988), 205.

2. See Wiseman, *1 and 2 Kings*, in *Tyndale Old Testament Commentaries*, 205. Another suggested they were listening to Elisha "teaching and [sharing] his memories of Elijah." (Ada R. Habershon, *Types in the Old Testament* [Grand Rapids, MI: Kregel Publications, 1988], 231.)

3. See Mordechai Cogan and Hayim Tadmor, *The Anchor Bible: II Kings*, vol. 11 (New York: Doubleday, 1988), 58; Israel Wolf Slotki, *Kings*, in *Soncino Books of the Bible* (London: The Soncino Press, 1978), 189; Wiseman, *1 and 2 Kings*, in *Tyndale Old Testament Commentaries*, 205.

4. Ellis T. Rasmussen, *A Latter-day Saint Commentary on the Old Testament* (Salt Lake City, UT: Deseret Book, 1994), 303. See also Ephrem the Syrian, "On the Second Book of Kings" 4.39, in Marco Conti, ed., *1–2 Kings, 1–2 Chronicles, Ezra, Nehemiah, Esther*, in *Ancient Christian Commentary on Scripture* (Downers Grove, IL: InterVarsity Press, 2008), 164.

5. Herbert Lockyer, *All the Miracles of the Bible: The Supernatural in Scripture—Its Scope and Significance* (Grand Rapids, MI: Zondervan, 1961), 121.

6. See Patterson and Austel, "1 and 2 Kings," in Gaebelein, *The Expositor's Bible Commentary*, 4:188.

7. See, for example, Ada R. Habershon, *Study of the Types* (Grand Rapids, MI: Kregel Publications, 1974), 29–30; Kevin J. Conner, *Interpreting the Symbols and Types*, rev. ed. (Portland, OR: City Bible Publishing, 1992), 143; Joseph Fielding McConkie, *Gospel Symbolism* (Salt Lake City, UT: Deseret Book, 1985), 88; Ada R. Habershon, *The Study of the Miracles* (London: Morgan & Scott, 1911), 175.

8. Walter L. Wilson, *A Dictionary of Bible Types* (Peabody, MA: Hendrickson, 1999), 171.

9. Lockyer, *All the Miracles of the Bible*, 121.

10. See also Ephrem the Syrian, "On the Second Book of Kings" 4.41, in Conti, *1–2 Kings, 1–2 Chronicles, Ezra, Nehemiah, Esther*, in *Ancient Christian Commentary on Scripture*, 164–65.

11. Richard C. Trench, *Miracles and Parables of the Old Testament* (Grand Rapids, MI: Baker Book House, 1974), 156.

12. Ibid.

13. Ibid., 157.

14. Habershon, *Types in the Old Testament*, 232–33. See also Trench, *Miracles and Parables of the Old Testament*, 156–57.

ELISHA MIRACULOUSLY MULTIPLIES FOOD

2 KINGS 4:42–44

THE MIRACLE

A man, from Baal-shalisha, approached Elisha with twenty loaves of barley bread (baked from the first ripe grain), along with some heads of new grain. The prophet said to him, "Give it to the people that they might eat" (see 2 Kings 4:42).

The man asked Elisha, "What, should I set this [meager amount of food] before an hundred men?" (2 Kings 4:43). The prophet responded, indicating that it would not only be sufficient to feed them, but that there would be extra left over. And so the man did as Elisha had instructed, and the people ate; and there was food to spare—just as the Lord had promised there would be (see 2 Kings 4:43–44).

BACKGROUND

The exact site of Baal-shalisha is in dispute. Commentators simply do not agree, in part because of early statements about its location by sources, such as Eusebius.[1] Baal-shalisha means literally "thrice-great lord," and is *possibly* located somewhere in the northern part of the central hill country, near Gilgal, and most likely north of Bethel.[2]

Though the text is silent on the subject, it has often been suggested that the "servitor" who brought Elisha this bread and grain was most likely his servant, Gehazi.[3]

The narrative under examination says that the man brought to Elisha "the firstfruits" (2 Kings 4:42). One commentary pointed out, "Normally these portions were reserved for God (Lev 23:20) and the Levitical priests (Num 18:13; Deut 18:4–5). Because the religion in the northern kingdom was apostate, the loaves had been brought by their owner to one whom he considered to be the true repository of godly religion in Israel."[4]

SYMBOLIC ELEMENTS

Elisha's name means, "God is the Savior,"[5] thus, it will be no surprise to the reader that his miracles are often connected with similar miracles performed by Jesus. One source notes, "The wonders performed by prophetic figures in the O[ld] T[estament] foreshadow the miracles of Jesus in the Gospels."[6] Elsewhere we read, "The multiplication of the loaves in accordance with the word of the Lord through his prophet anticipates the messianic ministry of the Living Word himself (cf. Matt 14:16–20; 15:36–37; John 6:11–13)."[7]

> There is an analogy: 1. in the small quantity of the food and the large number to be fed. 2. In both cases the miracle was wrought to meet a pressing need (Mark viii. 3). 3. In both cases exception was taken to the smallness of the quantity to afford food for so many. Elisha's servitor said, "What! should I set this before a hundred men?" Andrew asked, "What are they among so many?" (John vi. 9). 4. In both meals, out of the insufficiency came more than enough. "They did eat and left" (Verse 44; John vi. 13).[8]

Wiseman suggests, "The acceptance by Elisha of the first fruits . . . may indicate recognition of him as the Lord's representative."[9] It is symbolic evidence that he was the acknowledged presiding figure over the Old Testament Church.

Bread in scripture is often seen as a "gift"—a "gift of hospitality," and, even more, "a divine gift." "That God is quite literally the giver of bread appears in several remarkable miracles stories."[10] Miracles in which God multiplies bread symbolize His "compassion and provision extended to the needy who are devoid of resources."[11]

APPLICATION AND ALLEGORIZATION

The selflessness of the prophet is seen in this miracle. "Famine had struck Gilgal. So, when a man came to Elisha with his firstfruits offering, it was a momentous occasion. 'Give the holy offering to the hungry people,' Elisha commanded."[12] Prophets and apostles—and those who serve with them in the hierarchy of the Church—are, by nature, selfless; and so they *must be.* They give their lives to teach and lead. They travel every weekend to some far-flung part of the globe to minister to Saints and sinners alike.

Elisha could have taken the bread for himself—as he too was surely famished from the dearth that had hit the land. But instead, he commanded his servant to give to the people. Prophets give, never thinking of themselves; and their families give freely of their husbands and fathers, so that we might be blessed by their ministries. We owe a great debt of gratitude to these sacrificial souls for their lives of service and sacrifice on our behalf.

Lockyer, another commenter, suggested that "feeding the hungry . . . symbolizes Christ, the Bread of heaven as being sufficient for all."[13] Jesus *is* sufficient for all! And as the mortal experience is (by nature) a drought of spiritual things, we must always remember that the only way we can gain *true nourishment* is by turning to Christ. It is the tendency of almost all people to turn to the things of this world when they feel emotionally, temporally, or otherwise malnourished. However, looking for strength or solace in the temporal things of life will always leave us feeling unnourished and unsatisfied. Christ is the Bread of Life who can meet all our needs!

It has been suggested that there is a reminder in this miracle that we should use our sustenance—as the servant of Elisha did—to ensure that the missionaries, prophets, and apostles have sufficient to do their work; so that they can focus on spreading the gospel, and not on earning a living. Just as the man from Baal-shalisha gave freely of what he had to support Elisha and his associates, we too should give freely and generously of what God has blessed us with, so the poor might serve missions, and that those called of God might preside over this work.[14]

The servant's doubts about the bread being sufficient highlight a weakness in some of us. Do we ever doubt the prophetic wisdom or insight of the prophets? Are we prone to call into question their decisions or policies—as though they are operating under the same influence and with the same knowledge and vision that you and I labor under and with? If they are indeed prophets—*and I testify that they are*—do they not have the gift of "seeing"? Are they not "revelators" who reveal? We must not be like the servant of Elisha who assumes that he sees better than the prophet, and wishes to correct his command.[15]

One source suggests that "while Elisha did not *perform* the miracle, he did *predict* it."[16] Another stated, "There is a contrast [between Elisha and Jesus], inasmuch as Christ multiplied the loaves by a power resident in Himself, whereas the prophet did but foretell what should take place."[17] This is a reminder that we should never take credit for God's workings. We may be instruments in His hands, but we are *never* the cause. Whether we have pronounced a priesthood blessing that results in a cure, given a talk or lesson that was powerfully Spirit-filled, or offered inspired counsel under the influence of the Holy Ghost to one desperately in need, God is the source of all that is good—and you and I should ever give Him credit. In the words of the scripture, "He must increase, but I must decrease" (John 3:30).

NOTES

1. See Mordechai Cogan and Hayim Tadmor, *The Anchor Bible: II Kings*, vol. 11 (New York: Doubleday, 1988), 59.

2. See Gary A. Herion, "Baal-Shalishah," in David Noel Freedman, *The Anchor Bible Dictionary* (New York: Doubleday, 1992), 1:553. See also Israel Wolf Slotki, *Kings*, in *Soncino Books of the Bible* (London: The Soncino Press, 1978), 190.

3. See Pamela McQuade, *The Top 100 Miracles of the Bible: What They Are and What They Mean to You Today* (Uhrichsville, OH: Barbour Publishing, 2008), 89; Donald J. Wiseman, *1 and 2 Kings*, in *Tyndale Old Testament Commentaries* (Downers Grove, IL: InterVarsity Press, 1988), 206; Richard D. Patterson and Hermann J. Austel, "1 and 2 Kings," in Frank E. Gaebelein, ed., *The Expositor's Bible Commentary* (Grand Rapids, MI: Zondervan, 1994), 4:187; Richard C. Trench, *Miracles and Parables of the Old Testament* (Grand Rapids, MI: Baker Book House, 1974), 160.

4. Patterson and Austel, "1 and 2 Kings," in Gaebelein, *The Expositor's Bible Commentary*, 4:187. See also Wiseman, *1 and 2 Kings*, in *Tyndale Old Testament Commentaries*, 205–6.

5. Walter L. Wilson, *A Dictionary of Bible Types* (Peabody, MA: Hendrickson, 1999), 137.

6. Leland Ryken, James C. Wilhoit, and Tremper Longman III, eds., *Dictionary of Biblical Imagery* (Downers Grove, IL: InterVarsity Press, 1998), 525.

7. Patterson and Austel, "1 and 2 Kings," in Gaebelein, *The Expositor's Bible Commentary*, 4:188. See also Ellis T. Rasmussen, *A Latter-day Saint Commentary on the Old Testament* (Salt Lake City, UT: Deseret Book, 1994), 303; D. Kelly Ogden and Andrew C. Skinner, *Verse By Verse—The Old Testament Volume Two: 1 Kings Through Malachi* (Salt Lake City, UT: Deseret Book, 2013), 52; Wiseman, *1 and 2 Kings*, in *Tyndale Old Testament Commentaries*, 206; Ryken, Wilhoit, and Longman, *Dictionary of Biblical Imagery*, 449.

8. Trench, *Miracles and Parables of the Old Testament*, 159.

9. Wiseman, *1 and 2 Kings*, in *Tyndale Old Testament Commentaries*, 205–6.

10. Ryken, Wilhoit, and Longman, *Dictionary of Biblical Imagery*, 117.

11. Ryken, Wilhoit, and Longman, *Dictionary of Biblical Imagery*, 420.

12. McQuade, *The Top 100 Miracles of the Bible*, 89.

13. Herbert Lockyer, *All the Miracles of the Bible: The Supernatural in Scripture—Its Scope and Significance* (Grand Rapids, MI: Zondervan, 1961), 121.

14. See Trench, *Miracles and Parables of the Old Testament*, 158.
15. See Trench, *Miracles and Parables of the Old Testament*, 160.
16. Lockyer, *All the Miracles of the Bible*, 121.
17. Trench, *Miracles and Parables of the Old Testament*, 159.

NAAMAN THE LEPER *Is*
HEALED *by* ELISHA

2 KINGS 5:1–15

THE MIRACLE

Naaman was a commander of the army of Ben-Hadad II, king of Syria (or Aram), and he was highly regarded because, through him, God had given the king's armies victory. Nevertheless, Naaman was plagued with leprosy.[1]

Aware of the captain's condition, the Israelite servant of Naaman's wife said to her mistress, "I wish he would go to see the prophet who is in Samaria. He could cure him" (see 2 Kings 5:3).

So, Naaman went to the king and asked for permission to go to Samaria to visit Elisha, and the king granted it. Indeed, the king gave Naaman many gifts to present to the king of Israel (see 2 Kings 5:5), and a letter addressed to the king, stating, "I have . . . sent Naaman my servant to thee, that thou mayest recover him of his leprosy" (2 Kings 5:6).

When the king of Israel read the letter, he was angry and tore his clothes, saying, "Am I God, [who has power] to kill and to make alive, that this man doth send unto me to recover a man of his leprosy?" Does the king of Syria seek "a quarrel against me"? (2 Kings 5:7).

When Elisha heard what had happened, and how upset the king of Israel was, he sent him a message saying, "Let him come now to me, and he shall know that there is a prophet in Israel" (2 Kings 5:8). So Naaman went to where Elisha was staying, and stood at the door of the prophet's house. Elisha sent out a messenger to tell him to go to the Jordan River and wash in it seven times promising that, after so doing, Naaman's skin would be healed (see 2 Kings 5:9–10).

At this, the renowned commander of the Syrian army was angered, and went away, saying, "I thought, He will surely come out to me, and stand, and call on the name of the Lord his God, and strike his hand over the place, and recover the leper. Are not . . . [the] rivers of Damascus, better than all the waters of Israel? may I not wash in them, and be clean?" (2 Kings 5:11–12). With this, Naaman left Elisha's residence enraged.

Feeling that their captain had nothing to lose, Naaman's servants approached and said, "If the prophet had bid thee do some great thing, wouldest thou not have done it? how much rather then, when he saith to thee, Wash, and be clean?" (2 Kings 5:13). Naaman was touched by this, and so he went down into the Jordan River and immersed himself seven times. When he came out of the water, his skin was whole again, clear as the flesh of a little child (see 2 Kings 5:14–15).

So Naaman returned to Elisha, accompanied by his entire entourage, and said, "Behold, now I know that there is no God in all the earth, but in Israel" (2 Kings 5:15).

BACKGROUND

Though the King James Version (following older translations, like the Latin Vulgate) speaks of Naaman having "leprosy" (or "Hansen's disease"), his status as "captain of the host" (2 Kings 5:1) and his consequent social standing make it doubtful that he would have had leprosy.[2] Whatever his skin condition was, it was almost certainly not the same disease we call "leprosy" today. Indeed, there is some question as to whether leprosy (as we know it today) was even known during this early period.[3]

While Elisha sent his messenger to Naaman, instead of coming himself, this should not necessarily be taken as a slight toward the king's commanding officer.[4] Certainly, Naaman took this as an offense by one "both ethnically and socially inferior to himself."[5] However, there is no evidence that Elisha was seeking to be offensive by what he did. One commentary on the Hebrew suggested that "by keeping his personality in the background, he indicates that the miracle to be performed is not of his doing, but an act of God."[6]

Sending the letter of introduction and appeal to the king of Israel served to confuse the king. One commentary suggested a possible explanation as to why the king of Syria sent it to King Jehoram instead of to the prophet. "The King of Aram [or Syria] assumes that a prophet would be a member of the royal entourage."[7] Were such the case, sending the letter to the king—rather than to one of his subjects—would make sense.

The clean, clear rivers of Damascus had as their source the snow-covered mountains of the region, whereas Elisha had instructed Naaman to wash in "the muddy ditch called Jordan."[8] Perhaps this had some influence on Naaman's initial refusal to obey the prophet.

Symbolic Elements

One source suggested of Naaman that he is a symbol of all sinners who are confused and lost in their disease of the soul. They travel to and fro, looking for this and that, hoping to find a cure for their misery, but often avoiding the very cure when it is presented to them.

> [Naaman] may be taken as a type of a lost sinner who realizes his need [for help] but [who] goes to the wrong place and the wrong person for the remedy. . . . After learning his mistake, he then went to God's man, the prophet, who gave him God's remedy. At first, he rejected God's remedy because it did not agree with his own ideas. Through the persuasion of his servant, he decided to obey the man of God, and when he followed those instructions he received the cleansing he desired.[9]

As noted earlier in this text, leprosy is a common scriptural symbol for sin or spiritual sickness.[10] It serves as such because of "its corruption, its defilement, its contagion, and its fatal results."[11] It was also commonly perceived as a sign of God's punishment—hence it was often called by the Jews "the finger of God."[12] "Washing in [the] Jordan can typify the spiritual healing of the leprosy of sin through washing in the 'fountain opened for uncleanness' (Job 33:25; Zechariah 13:1; John 3:5)."[13]

Jehoram, king of Israel, tore his clothes upon reading the letter from the king of Syria. While the rending of a garment is often a sign of grief or mourning, it is also a symbol of nervous irritation, agitation, or fear—as in this narrative.[14]

The number seven is the Hebrew number that means "whole" or "complete." Thus, the fact that Naaman immersed himself seven times in the Jordan River "signified total obedience to the divine word and so 'rebirth.' *Seven times* is a symbolic perfect number."[15] Elsewhere, we read that the number seven was associated with the "divine covenant" and, thus, "the cure depended on that covenant."[16] Similarly, one early Christian source suggested, "Sin is the leprosy of the soul. . . . and human nature must be delivered from this disease by Christ's power which is hidden in baptism."[17]

APPLICATION AND ALLEGORIZATION

"Naaman not only needed that his flesh should become like the flesh of a little child, but that his heart should become like the heart of a little child."[18] In this vein, D. Kelly Ogden and Andrew C. Skinner offered the following application of the miracle.

> Naaman's pride almost prevented him from receiving the Lord's blessings, because he was thinking, in a sense, "I am too great a man to be treated this way." Do we sometimes deprive ourselves of experiences because of pride, experiences that could otherwise be great blessings in our lives? We also need to remember Mosiah 3:19: "For the natural man is an enemy to God, and has been from the fall of Adam, and will be, forever and ever, unless he yields to the enticings of the Holy Spirit, and putteth off the natural man and becometh a saint through the atonement of Christ the Lord, and becometh as a child, submissive, meek, humble, patient, full of love, willing to submit to all things which the Lord seeth fit to inflict upon him, even as a child doth submit to his father."[19]

Pride is a debilitating vice that robs us of the Spirit of the Lord, and can steal from us the blessings that the Lord has in store for humble and submissive souls.

On a similar note, Caesarius of Arles wrote, "Naaman believed he would recover his health as the result of his *own* rivers."[20] He doubted the validity of what Elisha had asked of him. How many of our Christian brothers and sisters similarly reject the restored gospel, and its baptism by immersion through proper priesthood authority? They suppose, as did Naaman, that *their* fonts are as valid and as spiritually cleansing as the Latter-day Saint's fonts. They suppose that our invitation that they be rebaptized by proper authority is a silly and nonsensical request. Like Naaman, many stomp off, doubting that what we offer will give them what they want. Yet, as the miracle shows, God's prophet and Church do hold the keys of spiritual cleansing. Like Naaman, we can exercise our agency and manifest our pride, but to do so will only rob us of blessings and of full access to God's Spirit.

Naaman is depicted as this great, accomplished, and honored man (see 2 Kings 5:1); and yet we are informed that he has a terrible disease. "Despite all of his skill and bravery, position and prestige, Naaman was a leper."[21] No one is immune from the vicissitudes and trials of life. Fame, rank, and wealth make no difference in the eyes of God.[22] Temptations come to us all, as do very difficult and often painful trials. Naaman's experience reminds us that "all are alike unto God" (2 Nephi 26:33).

The Israelite girl who worked as the servant of Naaman's wife—and who had been brought to Syria when captured in a raid—may easily be overlooked in this miracle (see 2 Kings 5:2). However, her actions offer an important application for the reader. It was her courage to bear testimony to nonbelievers that she knew that there were living prophets upon the earth that ultimately brought about the healing of Naaman, but also facilitated his conversion to the Gospel (see 2 Kings 5:17–18). Because of her lowly position, she had reason to be hesitant to share her faith. Nevertheless, she exemplified the counsel found in Doctrine and Covenants 30:11, "Yea, you shall ever open your mouth in my cause, not fearing what man can do, for I am with you." In so doing, she provoked a miracle. May we have the faith of this unnamed member of the Church, and likewise open our mouths to testify of the truths of the restored gospel.

One commentary on the miracles spoke of King Jehoram's knee-jerk reaction to the letter from King Ben-Hadad—where the king of Israel becomes angry and stressed about what he perceived *might* happen. "Nothing like assuming the worst in any situation."[23] Perhaps there is a lesson in this. What seemed like a bad thing turned out to be a good thing. How often in our own lives do we assume the worst—or allow ourselves to become stressed about what *might* happen—only to learn later that there was really nothing to get worried about? Worry and stress seldom help, and can often hurt the situation at hand. Reacting as King Jehoram did will seldom help us to better handle the circumstances at hand.

Having Naaman wash in the muddy waters of the Jordan, instead of the pristine rivers of Damascus, was a reminder to him—*and to each of us*—that healing does *not* come through water or consecrated oil, *but through faith.*[24] The most eloquent blessing cannot heal a faithless person; and the most clumsily pronounced words—if faith is present—will convey the power and blessings of God. Too often we get caught up in the forms, and forget the faith that is necessary for any healing to be achieved.

One text noted, "A great man may expect *some great thing* . . . while God often tests us with small things."[25] I suppose we all wonder how we will fare when the great tests of life come our way. Nevertheless, a more telling sign of our devotion to God may be found in how we face the day-to-day challenges that come our way. If we are faithful in the little things, the big ones will be fairly easy to handle. If, on the other hand, we struggle with the small stuff, then that "great thing" that will surely come will also surely overwhelm us!

Richard Trench offered an interesting warning that might be drawn from this miracle. "A mortal malady does not necessarily subdue the heart. Naaman, the subject of a most loathsome disease, is just as haughty as the same Naaman in perfect health. Men may pass though God's hottest furnaces, and come out of its fires, like the potter's vessel, harder than they entered them."[26] Trials will come to all of us, but what we do with those trials is up to the individual. We may allow them to change and develop us, or we may allow them to make us bitter and cynical. The choice is entirely ours. If we love God, and trust in Him, we will find the will to submit and allow Him to change us. If, on the other hand, our true love is ourselves, then such trials will traditionally be our undoing.

NOTES

1. Wiseman suggests that the king is Ben-Hadad III, rather than Ben-Hadad II. (See Donald J. Wiseman, *1 and 2 Kings*, in *Tyndale Old Testament Commentaries* [Downers Grove, IL: InterVarsity Press, 1988], 206.)

2. See Richard D. Patterson and Hermann J. Austel, "1 and 2 Kings," in Frank E. Gaebelein, ed., *The Expositor's Bible Commentary* (Grand Rapids, MI: Zondervan, 1994), 4:191; Leland Ryken, James C. Wilhoit, and Tremper Longman III, eds., *Dictionary of Biblical Imagery* (Downers Grove, IL: InterVarsity Press, 1998), 507; Douglas R. A. Hare, *Interpretation: A Bible Commentary for Teaching and Preaching—Matthew* (Louisville, KY: John Knox Press, 1993), 89; Pamela McQuade, *The Top 100 Miracles of the Bible: What They Are and What They Mean to You Today* (Uhrichsville, OH: Barbour Publishing, 2008), 90.

3. See Mordechai Cogan and Hayim Tadmor, *The Anchor Bible: II Kings*, vol. 11 (New York: Doubleday, 1988), 63; David P. Wright and Richard N. Jones, "Leprosy," in David Noel Freedman, *The Anchor Bible Dictionary* (New York: Doubleday, 1992), 4:277–79; Wiseman, *1 and 2 Kings*, in *Tyndale Old Testament Commentaries*, 207. Naaman most likely had skin lesions and other defects of the skin, such as swelling, scabs, flaking or scaly skin, and perhaps patchy skin tones.

4. See Herbert Lockyer, *All the Miracles of the Bible: The Supernatural in Scripture—Its Scope and Significance* (Grand Rapids, MI: Zondervan, 1961), 122.

5. Patterson and Austel, "1 and 2 Kings," in Gaebelein, *The Expositor's Bible Commentary*, 4:191.

6. Israel Wolf Slotki, *Kings*, in *Soncino Books of the Bible* (London: The Soncino Press, 1978), 192.

7. Wiseman, *1 and 2 Kings*, in *Tyndale Old Testament Commentaries*, 207.

8. See Wiseman, *1 and 2 Kings*, in *Tyndale Old Testament Commentaries*, 207; Kelly Ogden and Andrew C. Skinner, *Verse By Verse—The Old Testament Volume One: Genesis through 2 Samuel, Psalms* (Salt Lake City, UT: Deseret Book, 2013),

2:53; McQuade, *The Top 100 Miracles of the Bible*, 91; Lockyer, *All the Miracles of the Bible*, 122.

9.   Walter L. Wilson, *A Dictionary of Bible Types* (Peabody, MA: Hendrickson, 1999), 288.

10.   See McQuade, *The Top 100 Miracles of the Bible*, 90; J. C. Cooper, *An Illustrated Encyclopaedia of Traditional Symbols* (London: Thames and Hudson, 1995), 96; Kevin J. Conner, *Interpreting the Symbols and Types*, rev. ed. (Portland, OR: City Bible Publishing, 1992), 152; Charles Haddon Spurgeon, *Spurgeon's Sermons* (Grand Rapids, MI: Baker Book House, 1996), 7:311–27; Ryken, Wilhoit, and Longman, *Dictionary of Biblical Imagery*, 507; Richard C. Trench, *Miracles and Parables of the Old Testament* (Grand Rapids, MI: Baker Book House, 1974), 134–35.

11.   Ada R. Habershon, *Types in the Old Testament* (Grand Rapids, MI: Kregel Publications, 1988), 221.

12.   Lockyer, *All the Miracles of the Bible*, 172; Trench, *Miracles and Parables of the Old Testament*, 135.

13.   Lockyer, *All the Miracles of the Bible*, 122.

14.   See Maurice H. Farbridge, *Studies in Biblical and Semitic Symbolism* (London: Routledge, 1923), 213; Patterson and Austel, "1 and 2 Kings," in Gaebelein, *The Expositor's Bible Commentary*, 4:191; Israel Wolf Slotki, *Kings*, in *Soncino Books of the Bible*, 191; Ellis T. Rasmussen, *A Latter-day Saint Commentary on the Old Testament* (Salt Lake City, UT: Deseret Book, 1994), 303.

15.   Wiseman, *1 and 2 Kings*, in *Tyndale Old Testament Commentaries*, 207–8.

16.   See Lockyer, *All the Miracles of the Bible*, 122.

17.   Ephrem the Syrian, "On the Second Book of Kings," 5.10–11, in Marco Conti, ed., *1–2 Kings, 1–2 Chronicles, Ezra, Nehemiah, Esther*, in *Ancient Christian Commentary on Scripture* (Downers Grove, IL: InterVarsity Press, 2008), 167.

18.   Habershon, *Types in the Old Testament*, 218.

19.   Ogden and Skinner, *Verse By Verse—The Old Testament Volume One: Genesis through 2 Samuel, Psalms*, 2:53.

20.   Caesarius of Arles, "Sermon," 129.4–5, in Conti, *1–2 Kings, 1–2 Chronicles, Ezra, Nehemiah, Esther*, in *Ancient Christian Commentary on Scripture*, 169; emphasis added.

21.   Lockyer, *All the Miracles of the Bible*, 122.

22.   See ibid.

23.   McQuade, Lockyer, *All the Miracles of the Bible*, 91.

24.   See Lockyer, *All the Miracles of the Bible*, 122.

25.   Wiseman, *1 and 2 Kings*, in *Tyndale Old Testament Commentaries*, 207.

26.   Trench, *Miracles and Parables of the Old Testament*, 163.

GEHAZI *Is* SMITTEN *with* LEPROSY

2 KINGS 5:15–27

THE MIRACLE

After Elisha had healed Naaman of his leprosy, the grateful captain of the host of Syria offered the prophet a gift for his miraculous intervention. Of course, Elisha declined, though Naaman urged him to reconsider (2 Kings 5:15–16).

When the prophet continued to refuse Naaman's gifts, the captain requested that he be allowed to carry some of the soil of Israel back to his homeland, for he was committed to never again offer burnt offerings to any god other than Jehovah. That being said, Naaman asked for forgiveness for the fact that he would be required by the king of Syria to accompany him to the temple of Rimmon, where the king would bow before his pagan god—and where Naaman would be expected to bow next to his king (see 2 Kings 5:17–18). Naaman pled, "[Jehovah], pardon thy servant in this thing" (2 Kings 5:18). To which Elisha responded, "Go in peace" (2 Kings 5:19).

After Naaman had departed, Gehazi (Elisha's servant)—seeing that the prophet had refused the gifts the captain had offered him—hurried to catch up to Naaman. When he did, Gehazi lied, saying, "My master hath sent me, saying, Behold, even now there be come to me from mount Ephraim two young men of the sons of the prophets: give them, I pray thee, a talent of silver, and two changes of garments" (2 Kings 5:22). Naaman gladly gave Gehazi what he had asked for and had two of his servants carry the goods for Gehazi. The prophet's servant dismissed Naaman's aids as they neared the city of Jerusalem, taking and then concealing the goods given prior to returning to Elisha (see 2 Kings 5:20–24).

When Gehazi had returned, the prophet asked him where he had been. The servant lied, saying he hadn't been anywhere. However, Elisha informed him that he knew what he had done. And, as a consequence of his dishonest and sinful behavior, the prophet said to Gehazi, "The leprosy . . . of Naaman shall cleave unto thee, and unto thy seed for ever" (2 Kings 5:27). And Gehazi was immediately smitten with the disease (see 2 Kings 5: 25–27).

BACKGROUND

Naaman's request to take soil back to his homeland was based on his concern that the king of Syria would surely require that he kneel before the pagan god, Rimmon. Thus, if he were to take the soil of Israel with him, "Whenever circumstances forced him to bow ceremonially to the Aramean gods with his king, he might in reality be placing his knees in the soil of the true God of Israel (vv. 17–18). Thus he might be a true though secret believer."[1] It has been noted that the transporting of soil was a widespread custom in antiquity.[2] With Naaman's duty to "follow publically the state cults" of Syria, "Elisha may have felt that available Israelite soil" could help Naaman by affording him "some tangible reminder of his cleansing and new relationship to God."[3]

Rimmon was a Syrian storm god whose name means "pomegranate," but who was often referred to as the "thunderer." Anciently, he was often equated with other gods, such as Addad (or Hadad), Adonis, Teshub, and the Canaanite Baal.[4]

Elisha rhetorically asked Gehazi, "Is it a time to receive money, and to receive garments, and oliveyards, and vineyards, and sheep, and oxen, and menservants, and maidservants?" (2 Kings 5:26). While his servant had received from Naaman money and garments, he had not actually received land, livestock, or servants. However, Elisha has already indicated that he was able to know, through revelation, Gehazi's actions and heart (see 2 Kings 5:25–26). Thus his comments here, to his servant, suggest that Elisha believed Gehazi *planned* on using the money acquired from Naaman to purchase land, livestock, and servants for himself.[5]

It is commonly suggested that the sins of Gehazi in this episode would have ended his tenure as the prophet's "servant" or "secretary." The reference in 2 Kings 8:4 to Gehazi has been taken as evidence that the prophet's servant either repented and was forgiven, or that the story told there is given out of its proper chronological sequence.[6]

SYMBOLIC ELEMENTS

Gehazi and Naaman are juxtaposed in this narrative. They represent an ironic twist of fate for both. We're told that, when Gehazi approached Naaman's chariot, the captain stopped and got out, to see what he could do for the prophet's servant (see 2 Kings 5:21).

> Naaman's descent from his chariot to meet Elisha's servant is a mark of his being a changed man. No longer a proud, arrogant person (vv. 9–13), the grateful (v. 15), reverent (v. 17), and humble (v. 18) Aramean came down from his honored place to meet a prophet's servant. He who had been a fallen, hopeless sinner displayed the true believer's grace. Contrariwise Gehazi, who had enjoyed all the privileges of his master's grace, was about to abuse them and fall from that favor.[7]

As noted previously, leprosy is often used in the scriptures to symbolize God's wrath upon an unrepentant sinner.[8] Elisha gave Gehazi a chance to repent—to come clean—when he asked him, "Where have you been?" (see 2 Kings 5:25). However, Gehazi simply lied on top of the sin of greed that he had already committed. Thus, the leprosy in this episode represents God's wrath and Gehazi's unrepentant heart.

APPLICATION AND ALLEGORIZATION

"Gehazi needed to learn that the ministry has no place for those who would make merchandise of it."[9] Elisha did all that he could to make sure Naaman—in his interactions with God's prophet—understood that men of God *never* serve or bless for money. However, Gehazi sent the exact opposite message by his dishonest and greedy behavior. One source notes, "The prophet would on no account take a gift for Naaman's cure, since the recovery was effected by God and not by him. He was merely the instrument or agent who must claim neither credit nor reward. By so doing, Elisha demonstrated the difference between a servant of the true God and the idolatrous priests who performed no rite without material reward."[10] One would think that someone present to witness the raising of the dead would also have the presence of mind to shun sin. However, Gehazi did not; and he was cursed as a consequence. While greed won't make us leprous—at least, not on the surface—it will, nevertheless, damage our hearts and minds just as certainly as leprosy damaged Gehazi's skin.[11] Paul warns us that "the love of money is the root of all evil" (1 Timothy 6:10). Gehazi is the poster child for this truth. So many spiritual blessings had been his; however, greed allowed evil to take root in his heart, and his blessings were lost. And so they can be for us, if we give in to the sins of greed or priestcraft.

As he prepared to deceitfully approach Naaman, Gehazi swore, "*As the LORD liveth*, I will run after him, and take [some of that which he offered to Elisha]" (2 Kings 5:20; emphasis added). Gehazi swore an oath *in the name of the Lord* prior to his sin. In God's name, he committed his evil act. *Unconscionable!* One source noted, "To stamp base metal with the image and name of the king [in an act of counterfeiting] is regarded as a great crime against country and monarch. How much greater the crime of stamping upon our evil actions the name of God. Yet some of the most diabolical acts that stain the page of history have been wrought in the name of the Sinless Redeemer."[12] May we never be as callous as Gehazi was. And yet, having taken upon ourselves the name of Christ, are not our bad behaviors (as members of the Church) also evidence of a callousness that disregards God's blessings and our own covenants? If we, as members of the Lord's Church, act in cold, greedy, unkind, or unchristian ways, how are we different or better than Elisha's servant?

It has been said that those who lie in order to deceive, must then lie in order to conceal their deceit.[13] Lies do not typically stand independent. They often must be supported by the crutches of other lies. Thus, one should think carefully before putting their foot into the trap which is dishonesty, for it is certain—at some point—to snap shut. When it does, the pain will be significant, and the damage may be permanent, as Gehazi's curse suggests.

Similarly, the punishment that came to Gehazi reminds us of the truth that those who grossly sin, and who seek to conceal those sins, will eventually have to face the consequences. While humans are not omniscient, God is; and there will come a day of recompense when each of us will have to pay for that which we sought to conceal from God and His authorized servants. The repeated promise of scripture comes to mind: "Therefore whatsoever ye have spoken in darkness shall be heard in the light; and that which ye have spoken in the ear in closets shall be proclaimed upon the housetops" (Luke 12:3). And this: "There is nothing covered, that shall not be revealed; and hid, that shall not be known" (Matthew 10:26). And also this: "The Lord [when He comes] . . . will bring to light the hidden things of darkness, and will make manifest the counsels of the hearts" (1 Corinthians 4:5). "Let no man indulge in sin under the imagination of secrecy. Many sins take their rise from this single source, that men say in their hearts: 'Thou God seest not.'"[14]

Gehazi's leprosy being passed down to his descendants (see 2 Kings 5:27) reminds us of the truth that, when we sin, our posterity suffers also. It is not that God curses *them* for *our* failings. Rather, it is that our failings and sins influence the spiritual lives of our families. If, for example, a person leaves the Church, their posterity will be raised without the influence of the gospel, and that family's absence from the faith can last for generations. Thus, in all our sin, let us think selflessly about the fact that the evils we choose to embrace will not simply harm ourselves, but our posterity also.

NOTES

1. Richard D. Patterson and Hermann J. Austel, "1 and 2 Kings," in Frank E. Gaebelein, ed., *The Expositor's Bible Commentary* (Grand Rapids, MI: Zondervan, 1994), 4:190. It has been argued, "Naaman's intention was to erect an altar out of the earth he was taking back with him." (Israel Wolf Slotki, *Kings*, in *Soncino Books of the Bible* [London: The Soncino Press, 197], 194. See also Donald J. Wiseman, *1 and 2 Kings*, in *Tyndale Old Testament Commentaries* [Downers Grove, IL: InterVarsity Press, 1988], 208.)

2. Patterson and Austel, "1 and 2 Kings," in Gaebelein, *The Expositor's Bible Commentary*, 4:192.

3. Ibid.

4. See Richard Carlyon, *A Guide to the Gods* (New York: Quill, 1982), 331; Mordechai Cogan and Hayim Tadmor, *The Anchor Bible: II Kings*, vol. 11 (New York: Doubleday, 1988), 65; Patterson and Austel, "1 and 2 Kings," in Gaebelein, *The Expositor's Bible Commentary*, 4:192; Israel Wolf Slotki, *Kings*, in *Soncino Books of the Bible*, 194.

5. See Cogan and Tadmor, *The Anchor Bible: II Kings*, 66; Israel Wolf Slotki, *Kings*, in *Soncino Books of the Bible*, 196.

6. See Ellis T. Rasmussen, *A Latter-day Saint Commentary on the Old Testament* (Salt Lake City, UT: Deseret Book, 1994), 303–4: Kelly Ogden and Andrew C. Skinner, *Verse By Verse—The Old Testament Volume One: Genesis through 2 Samuel, Psalms* (Salt Lake City, UT: Deseret Book, 2013), 2:54.

7. Patterson and Austel, "1 and 2 Kings," in Gaebelein, *The Expositor's Bible Commentary*, 4:190. See also Cogan and Tadmor, *The Anchor Bible: II Kings*, (1988), 67.

8. Herbert Lockyer, *All the Miracles of the Bible: The Supernatural in Scripture—Its Scope and Significance* (Grand Rapids, MI: Zondervan, 1961), 172; Richard C. Trench, *Miracles and Parables of the Old Testament* (Grand Rapids, MI: Baker Book House, 1974), 135.

9.   Patterson and Austel, "1 and 2 Kings," in Gaebelein, *The Expositor's Bible Commentary*, 4:190.

10. Israel Wolf Slotki, *Kings*, in *Soncino Books of the Bible*, 193.

11. See Pamela McQuade, *The Top 100 Miracles of the Bible: What They Are and What They Mean to You Today* (Uhrichsville, OH: Barbour Publishing, 2008), 93–94.

12. Trench, *Miracles and Parables of the Old Testament*, 164.

13. Ibid., 165.

14. Ibid., 166.

ELISHA MAKES *an*
AX-HEAD FLOAT *in* WATER

2 KINGS 6:1–7

THE MIRACLE

Elisha and the sons of the prophets had been meeting together in Jericho, near the Jordan River. However, the place where they met was inadequate in its size. So, the sons of the prophets approached Elisha and requested that they all go to the Jordan River and build a place where they could live and meet. Elisha agreed, and they all went (see 2 Kings 6:1–4).

As they were cutting down trees for the new building, the iron ax-head came off of the handle of one of the axes being employed, and the heavy ax-head fell into the water—sinking to the bottom. The brother who was using the ax was distraught, indicating that it was a borrowed ax. Elisha asked him where it had fallen into the water. When he saw where, the prophet cut a stick and threw it in that same spot, and the ax-head floated to the surface. Elisha said to the man who had lost it, "Take it up to thee," and the man reached out and took it (see 2 Kings 6:4–7).

BACKGROUND

One source suggested that "Elisha was in the habit of gathering the Sons of the Prophets for instruction and guidance."[1] This regular gathering may have had a function similar to the gathering of General Authorities, Area Seventies, General Auxiliary, and General Officers the week prior to the spring general conference.

One commentator explained that the reason they didn't build the new home of the prophets in Jericho, but instead relocated to Jordan was because "there was an abundance of timber" near the Jordan River.[2]

The distress over the lost ax-head was explained by Ogden and Skinner in this way: "At that time an iron ax-head was a valuable and costly tool which one of the sons of the prophets probably could not afford to purchase anew."[3]

SYMBOLIC ELEMENTS

Regarding its symbolic merit in this miracle, commenters Ryken, Wilhoit, and Longman noted, "Wood participates in an image of salvation when . . . Elisha throws a branch into the Jordan and a lost axhead [*sic*] floats to the surface (2 Kings 6:1–7)."[4]

Iron is often seen as a symbol of God's strength, power, judgment, and destruction.[5] One source suggested that iron, "As the hardest metal known at that time," was a symbol of "great power and persistence," in addition to "unconquerable strength."[6] In this miracle, iron certainly seems to have connection to Christ and His power to restore and even raise up.

APPLICATION AND ALLEGORIZATION

As the most obvious application of this miracle, the volume *Miracles and Parables of the Old Testament* offers this insight:

There is no such thing as a trifle in nature where honor and probity are concerned. Here we have the lamentation of an honest man, not because he had lost a most valuable utensil, but because he had lost what belonged to another person. . . . A lesson of social honesty is forcibly inculcated by this miracle. The duty of the debtor is founded on the eternal laws of justice and charity.[7]

One commentator on this miracle implied that it shows the love of the prophets for the individual, as "Elisha relieved the distress of *one*."[8] Too often we're attentive to the ninety-nine, but we forget the one. In his book, *The Power of Everyday Missionaries*, Clayton M. Christensen wrote,

Attendance numbers are important, but I can't help wonder if we are sometimes collecting the right answer to the wrong question as it relates to building the kingdom of God. The right question was framed by the Savior in His parable of the good shepherd: "How think ye? If a man have an hundred sheep, and one of them be gone astray, doth he not leave the ninety and nine, and goeth into the mountains, and seeketh that which is gone astray?" (Matthew 18:12). In other words, the Savior suggested that the right question is, "Who *didn't* come today?" . . .

I've always wondered why the Savior preceded the telling of His parable of the good shepherd with the question, "What think ye?" . . . Perhaps, in our parlance, this would be phrased as, "What in the world are you *thinking* when all you do is count the number of my sheep that came into the fold every Sunday and then go home? The ones that *I'm* most worried about are those that didn't come!"[9]

Christiansen concludes his discussion by suggesting that, as shepherds in a ward, each week we should be asking ourselves, "Who could have been here today that didn't come?"[10] Indeed, as Christians—even if we don't have a leadership calling in the ward or stake—it is our duty to try to think what Jesus would think, say what He would say, and do what He would do "in every situation."[11] Jesus was (and is) constantly concerned about the "one." Are you?

I like a statement offered by Archbishop Richard Trench, which seems related to the previous application of the miracle. Trench wrote, "God does not esteem the omnipotence, which formed the universe, dishonored by being placed at the service of His children. These men [building their building], though . . . laborers, are all kings and priests before the Lord."[12] Oh, how God cares about each of us. And how He holds us—His children—in the highest regard, in spite of our fallen and lowly condition.

The Buddha taught, "Life is pain."[13] A person need not live long before they become aware of the truthfulness of that declaration. Our pain and suffering are caused by a number of things—some of which are our own making, while others may be the result of the choices of other people or the natural consequence of mortality. However, sin is certainly a major source of the pain we experience, and the pain we cause others. But there is help available to you and I as we battle our pain-causing sins and addictions. Herbert Lockyer wrote, "God can . . . easily make our hard, heavy hearts, sunk down in the world's mud, to float upon life's stream and see heaven again."[14] Similarly, President Henry B. Eyring recently wrote, "I testify that with the help of God the Father, the Savior of the world, and the Holy Ghost, we can be assured that we will be given more than enough power to withstand whatever evil forces we face."[15] Just as the ax-head in this miracle sunk and was lost because of the neglectfulness of its user, we are often sunk and lost in this "lone and dreary world." And yet, God is willing to help us regain what we've lost through our own neglectfulness or sin. Just as God's prophets provided the answer anciently, so also today, they stand ready to direct us to the relief we need from the problems we have. "Not one concern of ours is small—If we belong to Him: To teach us this, the Lord of all, once made the iron to swim."[16]

On a related note, one source pointed out that "the man who lost" the ax-head "appealed to the prophet, and to him alone."[17] Let this be a lesson to you and me. When trials and temptations come, it is to the Lord's prophets—ancient and modern—that we should turn for our solutions. Too often we turn to the world and what it offers. However, its "solutions" are almost *always* contrary to God's will and ways. May we have the faith to trust in the words and wisdom of the Lord's anointed, and, in so doing, reap the aid and blessings that the Lord has prepared for His faithful followers.

Emphasizing the words of two of Lehi's sons, we are reminded that "all things . . . are the typifying of [Christ]" (2 Nephi 11:4), and that "none of the prophets have written, nor prophesied, save they have spoken concerning this Christ" (Jacob 7:10–11). Therefore, note this application, which stands as a testament to those declarations. First of all, the Hebrew translation, "it was borrowed," is acknowledged by scholars to also mean that it was "begged [for] or prayed for."[18] Therefore, the issue may not have been so much that something that didn't belong to the man had been lost. Rather, it is probable that the concern was that something he had prayed for, longed for, and finally received, appeared to have just been lost. Certainly, the loss of the ax-head in the water is significant. As noted previously, water has two standard symbolic meanings in scripture. At times it represents the Holy Ghost, cleansing, and life (for example, see John 7:37–39; Numbers 8:7; Exodus 17:6); and, other times, it symbolizes chaos, death, and the grave (Genesis 7; Mark 5:13; Revelation 8:10–11; 11:6).[19] From a Christocentric typological perspective, note the following elements of this curious story:

- For much of his life, a certain man had prayed for and sought for something that he deemed precious, even sacred.

- The man finally obtained that which he had been so earnestly seeking.

- In the midst of working to build a new house (to replace the one the prophets and priesthood had outgrown), that thing so valued to the man—and necessary that the house might be completed—was lost.

- The cherished item fell into the water, and the man knew exactly where, although he could no longer see it.

- By an act of the priesthood, the valued item (ax-head) was raised up and restored to the builders of the house.

Unfortunately, the potential typological meaning of this miracle escapes most. However, in this story, it appears that we have an illustration of what Christ did by going down into the proverbial "waters of death," and then rising again. As one commentator put it, "That which was lost and sunken was raised and restored."[20]

- Jesus came to rebuild God's house (Church), which was at that time in apostasy.

- Many, like Simeon in the temple, had sought the coming of the Messiah for many years—including through personal fervent prayer (see Luke 2:25–35).

- Numerous individuals, including some of the disciples of Jesus, saw the Messiah's death as a loss of that which they had so earnestly sought.

- Some felt that the house they had begun to build, namely the restored gospel in the meridian of times, would never be completed because Christ had died.

- However, by an act of the priesthood, Jesus was raised from His grave.[21]

- And much like Christ's statement to His disciples shortly after His Resurrection, "Handle me, and see; for a spirit hath not flesh and bones, as ye see me have" (Luke 24:39), so also the man who thought the ax-head was lost is told, "Take it up to thee. And he put out his hand, and took it" (2 Kings 6:7).

Could there be an application in this miracle, reminding us of Christ—His death and Resurrection? Could the distress of the man who lost the ax-head mirror the distress of the early disciples of Jesus at His Crucifixion? Could the restoration of the ax-head to those who had once had it remind us of the return of Christ to His faithful disciples after His Resurrection—and His eventual return to each of us upon His Second Coming? Truly, all things testify of Christ!

Herbert Lockyer, also seeing the Christocentric symbolism in the miracle, suggested a slightly different—but related—application: "Do we not have here another type of Christ? Was he not the 'Branch' (Zechariah 3:8;

6:12) who was cut down and who, because He descended into the waters of death for us, is not able to raise us up into the air of heaven and restore us to our Owner for His use?"[22] Jesus was temporarily lost because of His death, and you and I are temporarily lost because of our sins. But Jesus can and will save the repentant soul from sin and death. May we praise His name always! (see Psalm 150:1–6).

NOTES

1.   Mordechai Cogan and Hayim Tadmor, *The Anchor Bible: II Kings*, vol. 11 (New York: Doubleday, 1988), 69.

2.   Israel Wolf Slotki, *Kings*, in *Soncino Books of the Bible* (London: The Soncino Press, 1978), 196. See also Herbert Lockyer, *All the Miracles of the Bible: The Supernatural in Scripture—Its Scope and Significance* (Grand Rapids, MI: Zondervan, 1961), 123.

3.   Kelly Ogden and Andrew C. Skinner, *Verse By Verse—The Old Testament Volume One: Genesis through 2 Samuel, Psalms* (Salt Lake City, UT: Deseret Book, 2013), 2:55. See also Pamela McQuade, *The Top 100 Miracles of the Bible: What They Are and What They Mean to You Today* (Uhrichsville, OH: Barbour Publishing, 2008), 94.

4.   Leland Ryken, James C. Wilhoit, and Tremper Longman III, eds., *Dictionary of Biblical Imagery* (Downers Grove, IL: InterVarsity Press, 1998), 965.

5.   See J. C. Cooper, *An Illustrated Encyclopaedia of Traditional Symbols* (London: Thames and Hudson, 1995), 88; Walter L. Wilson, *A Dictionary of Bible Types* (Peabody, MA: Hendrickson, 1999), 236–37; Ryken, Wilhoit, and Longman, *Dictionary of Biblical Imagery*, 427; Kevin J. Todeschi, *The Encyclopedia of Symbols* (New York: Perigee Book, 1995), 144.

6.   Ryken, Wilhoit, and Longman, *Dictionary of Biblical Imagery*, 426–27.

7.   Richard C. Trench, *Miracles and Parables of the Old Testament* (Grand Rapids, MI: Baker Book House, 1974), 169.

8.   See Ellis T. Rasmussen, *A Latter-day Saint Commentary on the Old Testament* (Salt Lake City, UT: Deseret Book, 1994), 304; emphasis added.

9.   Clayton M. Christensen, *The Power of Everyday Missionaries: The What and How of Sharing the Gospel* (Salt Lake City, UT: Deseret Book, 2013), 126–27, 129.

10.   Ibid., 148.

11.   Bruce R. McConkie, *Doctrinal New Testament Commentary: Acts–Philippians*, vol. 2 (Salt Lake City, UT: Bookcraft, 1987), 322.

12.   Trench, *Miracles and Parables of the Old Testament*, 170.

13.   See David Kherdian, *The Buddha: The Story of an Awakened Life* (Ashland, OR: White Cloud Press, 2004), 55–56; Bhikkhu Ñāṇamoli, *The Life of the Buddha* (Onalaska, WA: BPS Pariyatti Editions, 1992), 24; Richard A. Gard, ed., *Buddhism: The Way of Buddhism* (New Jersey: Prentice Hall Press, 1962), 109.

14. Lockyer, *All the Miracles of the Bible*, 124.

15. Henry B. Eyring, "Armed with Righteousness," *Ensign*, March 2017.

16. Lockyer, *All the Miracles of the Bible*, 124.

17. Trench, *Miracles and Parables of the Old Testament*, 167.

18. See, for example, Donald J. Wiseman, *1 and 2 Kings*, in *Tyndale Old Testament Commentaries* (Downers Grove, IL: InterVarsity Press, 1988), 209 Francis Brown, S. R. Driver, and Charles A. Briggs, *The Brown-Driver-Briggs Hebrew and English Lexicon* (Peabody, MA: Hendrickson Publishers, 1999), 981.

19. "The sea is a common symbol for chaos and death." (John S. Keslman and Michael L. Barre, "Psalms," in Raymond E. Brown, Joseph A. Fitzmyer, and Roland E. Murphy, *The New Jerome Biblical Commentary* [Englewood Cliffs, NJ: Prentice Hall, 1990)] 541.) Water can "denote the abode of the dead (see Psalm 107:26; Romans 10:7) or the final prison of Satan and the demons (Revelation 20:3). It is used often in the LXX [as] . . . the symbol of chaos and disorder." (Joseph A. Fitzmyer, *The Anchor Bible: The Gospel According to Luke I–IX* [New York: Doubleday, 1970], 739n31.) It is the "place of final punishment for demons," according to C. S. Mann. (*The Anchor Bible: Mark*, vol. 27 [New York: Doubleday, 1986], 278–79. See also, "Firmage," in David Noel Freedman, ed., *The Anchor Bible Dictionary* [New York: Doubleday, 1992], 6:1132; Lamar Williamson Jr., *Interpretation: A Bible Commentary for Teaching and Preaching—Mark* [Atlanta, GA: John Knox Press, 1983], 104; Adam Clarke, *The Holy Bible, Containing the Old and New Testaments . . . with a Commentary and Critical Notes. . . .* [New York: T. Mason & G. Lane, 1837], 5:420; Freyne, in Freedman, *The Anchor Bible Dictionary* [New York: Doubleday, 1992], 2:900; Leon L. Morris, *Revelation*, in *Tyndale New Testament Commentaries*, rev. ed. [Grand Rapids, MI: InterVarsity Press, 1987], 171; Walter L. Liefeld, "Luke," in Frank E. Gaebelein, ed., *The Expositor's Bible Commentary* [Grand Rapids, MI: Zondervan, 1994], 8:913.)

20. Ada R. Habershon, *Study of the Types* (Grand Rapids, MI: Kregel Publications, 1974), 42. See also, John 12:23–24.

21. Both President Brigham Young and President Spencer W. Kimball taught that Resurrection is a priesthood ordinance. (See Brigham Young, August 24, 1872, in *Journal of Discourses* 15:137–39; Spencer W. Kimball, in *The Church News, Conference Issues*, 1970–1987.)

22. Lockyer, *All the Miracles of the Bible*, 123–24.

ELISHA KNOWS *the* WORDS *of the* KING THAT HE HAD SPOKEN *in* PRIVATE

2 KINGS 6:8–12

THE MIRACLE

The king of Syria (or Aram) had gone to war with Israel. In the process of the ongoing war, he would inform his servants where he planned to camp and attack in his battle with the Israelites. However, Elisha would send messages to the king of Israel, telling him not to send his troops to the places that the king of Syria was secretly occupying—thereby enabling the Israelites to avoid being attacked and defeated by the Syrians. Thus, the Israelites were saved on numerous occasions by Elisha's inspired directions (see 2 Kings 6:8–10).

The king of Syria was enraged by the fact that somehow the Israelites were constantly in the know regarding Syria's battle plans. Thus, the Syrian king summoned his officers and demanded of them that they tell him who was leaking this information: "Will ye not shew me which of us is for the king of Israel?" (2 Kings 6:11). One of his officers replied, "None, my lord, O king: but Elisha, the prophet . . . telleth the king of Israel the words that thou speakest in thy bedchamber" (see 2 Kings 6:12).

BACKGROUND

Not all commentators see this as a miracle. Representative of this sentiment is the following comment. "Elisha . . . provided an efficient intelligence service. His knowledge was probably gained from informants . . . rather than [from] second sight" or revelation.[1]

Whereas the King James Version has the king of Syria being "sore troubled" (2 Kings 6:11) about the fact that the king of Israel always seems to know his plans, the Hebrew suggests that the king was "storming about" as he yelled at his officers over the apparent leaking of Syria's battle plans.[2]

SYMBOLIC ELEMENTS

Knowing the unknowable—as in this narrative—serves as a potential symbol of the gift of discernment associated with a priesthood mantle or priesthood keys (see D&C 46:27).[3]

APPLICATION AND ALLEGORIZATION

Prophets are called "seers" because of their divine gift to "see." Acting on behalf of God—who is the ultimate seer—these divinely appointed revelators can and do know more than any human could, in and of themselves. This same gift also applies to leaders holding priesthood keys on a local level. "Truly the innermost secrets of men lie open to the omniscient God (cf. Dan 2:22)."[4] In some cases, such as in this miracle, He reveals those to His living representatives. In other situations, He simply holds on to such secrets until the Judgment Day. Nevertheless, God knows, and we—if unrepentant—will be held to account.

Elisha knows what could not be known, and he uses that knowledge to protect one group and thwart another. He is not acting based on his own will or whims. Rather, he is responding to the whisperings of the Spirit that have directed his revelations.

> The supernatural knowledge of the prophet . . . , when it does not lead to reverence, arouses hatred in the human souls who are the subjects of it. Joseph's knowledge of the future destiny of his family gave rise to the jealously of his brethren (Gen. xxxvii. 5–11). The knowledge of human hearts possessed by the Son of God, generated hatred in those hearts which were unwilling to submit to His rule. So in the case of Elisha and the King of Syria, the prophet's supernatural insight interfered with his plans, and therefore led him to take action against him. . . . This action was the immediate occasion of the miracle. It was obviously as foolish as it was wicked. Reflection would have showed the king that if Elisha really was in possession of state secrets, they must be revealed to him by a superhuman power, for the exercise of which the prophet was not responsible. God therefore was the Being against whom to direct opposition. But in this matter the Syrian king was only an example of the folly of all who, in any age, "take counsel together against the Lord and against His anointed" (Psa. ii. 2).[5]

NOTES

1.   Donald J. Wiseman, *1 and 2 Kings*, in *Tyndale Old Testament Commentaries* (Downers Grove, IL: InterVarsity Press, 1988), 209.

2.   See Mordechai Cogan and Hayim Tadmor, *The Anchor Bible: II Kings*, vol. 11 (New York: Doubleday, 1988), 72.

3.   See Leon R. Hartshorn, "Discernment, Gift Of," in Daniel H. Ludlow, ed., *Encyclopedia of Mormonism* (New York: Macmillan, 1992), 1:384.

4.   Richard D. Patterson and Hermann J. Austel, "1 and 2 Kings," in Frank E. Gaebelein, ed., *The Expositor's Bible Commentary* (Grand Rapids, MI: Zondervan, 1994), 4:194.

5.   Richard C. Trench, *Miracles and Parables of the Old Testament* (Grand Rapids, MI: Baker Book House, 1974), 170–71.

ANGELIC HORSES *and* CHARIOTS APPEAR *to* ELISHA *and* HIS FRIGHTENED SERVANT

2 KINGS 6:13–17

THE MIRACLE

The king of Syria was so angry about the fact that Elisha knew (by revelation) his battle plans, and that Elisha used that knowledge to help the Israelites, that he sent his men to spy out where the prophet was, that he might be captured (see 2 Kings 6:13).

The Syrian king's men found Elisha in Dothan, and reported this to the king, who then sent a great army by night to surround the city (see 2 Kings 6:13–14).

When Elisha's servant awoke the next morning, and saw the army that encircled them, he alerted the prophet, and exclaimed, "What shall we do?" (see 2 Kings 6:15).

Elisha encouraged his servant, "Fear not: for they that be with us are more than they that be with them" (2 Kings 6:16). Concerned that the young man's faith would not hold out, the prophet prayed to God, and asked him to open the servant's eyes so that he could "see." The Lord did, and the boy saw that the hills were "full of horses and chariots of fire round about Elisha" (see 2 Kings 6:17).

BACKGROUND

The servant in this passage is unnamed. Previously, we were told that the name of Elisha's servant was Gehazi. However, his receipt of leprosy for using his office to dishonestly acquire monetary gain (see 2 Kings 5) suggests that the servant here must be someone else.[1]

The text states that the location of this miracle is Dothan (see 2 Kings 6:13), which is believed to lay at the mouth of the valley leading to the plain of Jezreel, approximately eight and a half miles north of Samaria.[2]

SYMBOLIC ELEMENTS

Encyclopedias of symbolism often note that, among other things, horses are sometimes symbols for "courage."[3] They can also represent "power" (associated with war)[4]—but also "Divine power."[5] One text states that "in the East, [the horse] stands for fire and the heavens"[6]—which is distinctly represented here (see 2 Kings 6:17).

One commentary suggests that chariots, in some of the Abrahamic traditions, can carry the symbolic meaning of "the Church."[7] They also represent "battle,"[8] and sometimes "divinity."[9]

APPLICATION AND ALLEGORIZATION

The focus of this miracle is the unseen hosts—literally "armies"—who protected Elisha and those who aligned themselves with the prophet, and, thus, with God. By way of application, it has been said, "For everyone today who tries to keep his covenants, it may be said spiritually, if not physically, that the hosts of heaven that be with us are more than they that are against us."[10] When we sin, we walk the danger-strewn path of mortality alone. When, on the other hand, we align ourselves with the living prophets, we have the aid and support of millions—on both sides of the veil.

In this same spirit, one early Christian source drew from this miracle the idea that "he errs who thinks that when he has waged a war successfully, he has overcome by his own power. For he ought to know that adversaries are conquered more by merits than by strength and are overcome not so much by power as by holiness, just as holy Elisha overcame his foes not by arms but by prayer."[11] Two lessons can be drawn from this statement. First, we should remember that any success we have in our lives is most likely being augmented by forces from the other side of the veil. May we not, in arrogance, take credit for that which God instead deserves credit. Second, this application of the miracle also reminds us that virtue and holiness are the greatest powers we can exhibit in our lives—even when we are confronted by our enemies. Rather than turning to fists or verbal fights, may we instead turn to the virtues of the Lord. Holiness has a power to soften the hearts of even the meanest of men.

There may be a message in this miracle about the broad and expansive vision of prophets in comparison to the limited vision of humankind.

> In proportion to the elevation of our mortal nature, the unseen will be revealed. Elisha saw more than his servant. A man on the lower deck of a vessel can see something of the ocean, one standing on the upper deck can see much more, but the man at the mast-head has the widest view. So with soul-elevation and the ordinary unperceived realities of the spiritual world.[12]

This is an important point. Prophets see what you and I do not. Why? First of all, they have a divinely given calling and ordination that provides them with priesthood keys by which they can accomplish what God has called them to do. Second, and perhaps, more importantly, for much of their lives they have chosen to suppress their fallen nature while elevating their spiritual nature. Thus, the veil has thinned for them, and they see what you and I do not. Nevertheless, as you and I elevate our spirituality and suppress our carnal side, God will thin the veil for us too—as He ultimately did for Elisha's servant. As we slowly work toward that important and universal goal, may we, in the interim, trust in the view and vision of the living prophets.

If the chariot can be seen as a symbol for the Church, then this miracle is a reminder that each of us have a duty to support and sustain the prophet. Elisha knew that there were unseen forces around him. He did not need to call upon their aid. They sustained him without being asked to.[13] Are you and I constantly standing alongside the living prophet? Does he have to ask us to engage before we do, or are we anxiously engaged because we already know what he would have us do? May we make the living prophet as grateful for us as Elisha surely felt for those who surrounded and supported him. The best way we can do this is by consecrating our lives, living our covenants, and faithfully serving each and every day.

Drawing on this miracle, Maximus of Turin offered this insight: "How much more do spiritual eyes discern than fleshy ones! The one perceives a throng of warriors, and the other catches sight of a sign of protection."[14] Maximus seems to be inviting you and me to see others, not with the fleshy, judgmental eyes of the natural man—eyes that do not perceive others as God sees them—but, instead, with the divine eyes of charity, forgiveness, and love. He also appears to be reminding us that we need to see our own trials and experiences with the eye of faith—believing that we have the help we need to do anything that comes our way.

Elder Bruce C. Hafen of the Seventy offered an application of this miracle that relates to the receipt of a challenging Church calling. He wrote,

> Sometimes Church leaders may ask us to accept callings or to assume obligations that strike us as inconvenient or distasteful—or worse. At such times we may feel like saying to ourselves in a tone of irritation, "The Lord *will not* leave me alone." But at other times, when we, like the young servant, feel overwhelmed and surrounded by enemies and troubles, there comes the comforting assurance: The Lord will not leave me alone.[15]

May we ever trust that He will never abandon us, and may we always be grateful that He chooses to call upon us!

In his book *We Will Prove Them Herewith*, Elder Neal A. Maxwell also saw a modern message in this ancient miracle. Elder Maxwell wrote,

> As described by Zephaniah, Church members in the last days live, though blessed with the light of the gospel, in a day of gloominess. (Zephaniah 1:15.) In these times of widespread commotion, disorder, unrest, agitation, and insurrection, the hearts of many will fail. (D&C 45:26; 88:91.) Others will be sorely tried but will, in their extremities, seek succor from seers as did the anxious young man who approached the prophet Elijah as ancient Israel was surrounded: "Alas, my master! how shall we do?" The answer of today's prophets will be the same: "Fear not: for they that be with us are more than they that be with them." Only when we are settled spiritually can we understand that kind of arithmetic. Only then will our eyes, like the young man's be opened. (2 Kings 6:15–17.)[16]

The first "official" Christian crusade (AD 1096–1099)[17] was said to have been made up of some five thousand knights, mostly from France, Germany, and southern Italy.[18] In addition, if the record is true, thousands of other combatants participated—accompanied by a variety of family members who wished to settle in Jerusalem once it was conquered.[19] The crusaders engaged in several battles along the way to Jerusalem, and they apparently won most of them.[20] During one battle in Antioch—where the Christians were losing terribly—a miracle akin to the one under examination happened. Peter Bartholomew—a man described as "a disreputable and unreliable character"[21]—claimed that Andrew (the brother of the Apostle Peter) appeared to him.[22] According to tradition, Andrew told him where the very spear that Jesus was stabbed with while on the cross was buried (see John 19:34).[23] Andrew claimed that if the Christians could find the sacred lance associated with the Crucifixion—and carry it into battle with them—with its help, they would be able to destroy their Muslim foes. "All day long workmen dug into the floor [of St. Peter's Cathedral] and found nothing. . . . At last, Peter himself, clad only in a shirt, leapt into the trench. Bidding all present to pray, he triumphantly produced a piece of iron" that was believed to be the head of the spear that pierced the Savior's side.[24] With the spear in their possession, they began a multiday fast. Then the miracle happened. One commentator wrote:

> They have no mortal chance to survive. They have only a hundred remaining horses, and no strength. They are haggard and weak. [They are led by] a funny looking peasant holding up a small spear. Behind the soldiers come priests in white robes chanting prayers and holding up crosses. . . . As [the crusaders] approach the great Turkish army, there appears from the heavens "a countless number of men on white horses," whose banners are gleaming white. . . . The crusaders call upon the name of God and [then] charge. . . . By the end of the morning, the incredible battle is over. . . . Against all odds, the crusaders have withstood. . . . They've put to flight the most powerful army that a Moslem ruler could assemble.[25]

The crusaders were fearful, but they saw with their spiritual eyes that "they that be with [them were] more than they that be [against] them" (2 Kings 6:16). In the year AD 1098, God repeated the miracle he had performed thousands of years earlier for Elisha; and the outcome was the same. Let us never forget the promise of modern-day scripture, that the Lord has "given the heavenly hosts and . . . angels charge concerning [us]" (D&C 84:42).

NOTES

1. Patterson and Austel wrote, "If the events of the chapter follow chronologically after those of ch. 5, Elisha's servant cannot be Gehazi." (Richard D. Patterson and Hermann J. Austel, "1 and 2 Kings," in Frank E. Gaebelein, ed., *The Expositor's Bible Commentary* [Grand Rapids, MI: Zondervan, 1994], 4:194. See also Herbert Lockyer, *All the Miracles of the Bible: The Supernatural in Scripture—Its Scope and Significance* [Grand Rapids, MI: Zondervan, 1961], 124.)

2. See Donald J. Wiseman, *1 and 2 Kings*, in *Tyndale Old Testament Commentaries* (Downers Grove, IL: InterVarsity Press, 1988), 210.

3. See J. C. Cooper, *An Illustrated Encyclopaedia of Traditional Symbols* (London: Thames and Hudson, 1995), 85; David Fontana, *The Secret Language of Symbolism: A Visual Key to Symbols and Their Meanings* (San Francisco, CA: Chronicle Books, 2000), 83.

4. See Fontana, *The Secret Language of Symbolism: A Visual Key to Symbols and Their Meanings*, 83. See also Leland Ryken, James C. Wilhoit, and Tremper

Longman III, eds., *Dictionary of Biblical Imagery* (Downers Grove, IL: InterVarsity Press, 1998), 400; Maurice H. Farbridge, *Studies in Biblical and Semitic Symbolism* (London: Routledge, 1923), 77.

5. See Farbridge, *Studies in Biblical and Semitic Symbolism*, 77–78.

6. See Fontana, *The Secret Language of Symbolism: A Visual Key to Symbols and Their Meanings*, 83.

7. See Cooper, *An Illustrated Encyclopaedia of Traditional Symbols*, 33.

8. See Fontana, *The Secret Language of Symbolism: A Visual Key to Symbols and Their Meanings*, 72.

9. See Jack Tresidder, *Symbols and Their Meanings: The Illustrated Guide to More than 1,000 Symbols—Their Traditional and Contemporary Significance* (London: Duncan Baird Publishers, 2006), 133; Farbridge, *Studies in Biblical and Semitic Symbolism*, 77–78; Ryken, Wilhoit, and Longman, *Dictionary of Biblical Imagery*, 139.

10. Kelly Ogden and Andrew C. Skinner, *Verse By Verse—The Old Testament Volume One: Genesis through 2 Samuel, Psalms* (Salt Lake City, UT: Deseret Book, 2013), 2:55. See also Richard C. Trench, *Miracles and Parables of the Old Testament* (Grand Rapids, MI: Baker Book House, 1974), 173.

11. Maximus of Turin, "Sermon" 83.2–3, in Marco Conti, ed., *1–2 Kings, 1–2 Chronicles, Ezra, Nehemiah, Esther*, in *Ancient Christian Commentary on Scripture* (Downers Grove, IL: InterVarsity Press, 2008), 174–75.

12. Trench, *Miracles and Parables of the Old Testament*, 173.

13. See ibid.

14. Maximus of Turin, "Sermon" 83.2–3, in Conti, *1–2 Kings, 1–2 Chronicles, Ezra, Nehemiah, Esther*, in *Ancient Christian Commentary on Scripture*, 174.

15. Bruce C. Hafen, *The Believing Heart: Nourishing the Seed of Faith*, 2nd ed. (Salt Lake City, UT: Deseret Book, 1990), 103; emphasis added.

16. Neal A. Maxwell, *We Will Prove Them Herewith* (Salt Lake City, UT: Deseret Book, 1982), 19.

17. See William J. Dohar, "Crusades," in Richard P. McBrien, ed., *The Harper Collins Encyclopedia of Catholicism* (New York: HarperCollins, 1995), 384; Bob O'Gorman and Mary Faulkner, *The Complete Idiot's Guide to Understanding Catholicism*, 2nd ed. (New York: Alpha Books, 2003), 310; Seán Lang, *European History for Dummies* (West Sussex, England: John Wiley and Sons, 2011), 103.

18. See Bruce L. Shelley, *Church History In Plain Language*, 2nd ed. (Nashville, TN: Thomas Nelson Publishers, 1995), 188.

19. See Paul L. Williams, *The Complete Idiot's Guide to the Crusades* (Indianapolis, IN: Alpha Books, 2002), 61.

20. See Williams, *The Complete Idiot's Guide to the Crusades*, 61–69.

21. See Steven Runciman, *A History of the Crusades* (New York: Cambridge University Press, 1988), 243.

22. See ibid., 241–46.

23. See Runciman, *A History of the Crusades*, 242; Lang, *European History for Dummies*, 103.

24. Runciman, *A History of the Crusades*, 245.

25. See Williams, *The Complete Idiot's Guide to the Crusades*, 75. See also Runciman, *A History of the Crusades*, 248.

ELISHA PRAYS THAT *the* SYRIANS BE SMITTEN *with* BLINDNESS *and* THEN THEY ARE HEALED *at* HIS REQUEST

2 KINGS 6:18–23

THE MIRACLE

Elisha was dwelling in Dothan, when the king of Syria and his armies surrounded the prophet by night, intending to take him into custody. As the king's men approached the prophet, Elisha prayed to the Lord, requesting that God smite the Syrians who had come to arrest him with blindness—and the Lord heeded Elisha's request (see 2 Kings 6:13–14, 18).

Elisha then approached the blinded Syrians and said, in essence, "You're in the wrong city and the person you're seeking isn't here. Follow me and I'll lead you to the man you're seeking." Unable to see, the Syrians trusted Elisha and followed him, and he led them to Samaria (see 2 Kings 6:19).

Once the Syrians were far from Dothan, Elisha asked God to restore their sight again, and the Lord did. Suddenly, Elisha's would-be captors realized that they were in Samaria (see 2 Kings 6:20).

When the king of Israel realized that his sworn enemies—the Syrians—were in his land, he asked Elisha, "Shall I smite them?" Elisha encouraged the king not to kill them, but to feed them and then send them back to their king in Syria. So the king did so, and, after the Syrians had eaten and drunk, they were sent back to their land and their king (see 2 Kings 6:21–23). As a consequence of the king of Israel's mercy upon them, "The bands of Syria came no more into the land of Israel" to fight them (2 Kings 6:23).

BACKGROUND

One source suggested that, just as Elisha knew that there were unseen forces with him and his people, so also he most likely knew that the Syrians were coming to try to capture him. "Doubtless . . . [Elisha] allowed himself to be trapped so that the subsequent entrapment of the Arameans [or Syrians] might work to God's glory and for his good."[1]

One commentator rendered the Hebrew in this verse as suggesting that the armies of Syria didn't just go blind, but, instead, were robbed of their sight by a "blinding light"[2]—an unexplained flash of brightness that temporarily[3] took their vision. Another commentary on the Hebrew suggested that their blindness consisted of "confused vision," resulting in "seeing an object that is not there and not seeing one that is."[4] Similarly, Lockyer wrote,

> Elisha prayed that his enemies might be struck with mental blindness so that they could not recognize him as the man they wanted, nor realize that they were being led astray (Luke 24:16). The Syrians were dazed, bewildered. They had a confusion of mind amounting to illusion. "They saw, but knew not what they saw" (Genesis 19:11). Because of their confused state they were led off on a wrong way and marched into Samaria and found themselves at the mercy of the Israelites.[5]

Samaria, to which Elisha slyly led the Syrian army, was about ten miles from Dothan, where Elisha had been residing.[6] It was "the middle of Israelite headquarters."[7]

Some are bothered by the prophet's seeming dishonesty in this narrative. As a means of explaining it away, it has been suggested that, though Elisha "tricked" the Syrians, "In a sense his words are true; the city where Elisha would ultimately be found would be Samaria, not Dothan."[8] Perhaps, but it may be more accurate to say that the prophet simply sought to preserve his own life—as one man against an entire army. His choice here to deceive those who threatened his life does not seem significantly different than the patriarch Abraham's, when he told those he feared that Sarah was his "sister" (see Abraham 2:22–23; Genesis 12:10–12; 20:1–7).

SYMBOLIC ELEMENTS

Whereas sight implies knowledge and perspective, blindness is often seen as a symbol for divine punishment upon the disbelieving.[9] *The Dictionary of Biblical Imagery* states:

> Blinding is a punishment for wrongdoing in neighboring nations (2 Kings 25:7), but never in Israel. On occasion, in order to promote his

own purposes, God temporarily blinds individuals or groups of people, either totally or in regard to something they attempt to see (Gen 19:11; 2 Kings 6:18; Acts 9:9; 13:11). . . .

Figuratively, blindness refers to an inability to recognize truth, usually a culpable condition. . . . Such blindness to the truth and mental confusion could actually be the result of God's judgment on those who did not *want* to admit the truth and who therefore forfeit the ability to perceive it at their cost."[10]

Elisha's would-be captors are blind to the reality that he is a prophet of God. After receiving the hospitality recommended by Elisha and provided by the king of Israel, the Syrians are able to "see" and, thus, attack no more (see 2 Kings 6:23).

APPLICATION AND ALLEGORIZATION

Elisha's counsel to treat Israel's enemies with kindness and hospitality "proved ultimately to be the divine remedy for the momentary ills of Israel: the Arameans [or Syrians] reported Israel's kindness [to their king], and their guerrilla raids ceased."[11] One commentator noted, "Clemency often leads to peace."[12] Such was certainly the case in this narrative. Here, Elisha lives what Christ would later command, "I say unto you, Love your enemies, bless them that curse you, do good to them that hate you, and pray for them which despitefully use you, and persecute you" (Matthew 5:44). In this spirit, Truman Madsen wrote of the Prophet Joseph, "When mistreated, he was inclined to 'get even' by offering the hospitality of his home."[13] And, regarding those who rejected his prophetic mantle, Joseph once said, "If ye will not embrace our religion[,] embrace our hospitalities."[14] Pamela McQuade wrote, "When we face enemies, or even just troublesome people, are we constantly set on battle? Or are we open to a firm but gentler solution? Sometimes kindness has a powerful impact on others, when warfare would only antagonize and destroy. God provides the wisdom that will help us know when to use each. Are we listening to Him?"[15] We really should be more inclined than we naturally are to use hospitality and kindness toward those who are enemies. Charity has a power to soften hearts like little else; and "in doing good to our enemies, we do most good to ourselves."[16]

On a related note, how Elisha blinded these men is uncertain, and perhaps unimportant. Nevertheless, there may by an application in the reality that God can blind us physically or spiritually. He allows us to see what He wills that we see. Of Jesus's approach to teaching, Matthew recorded that

He spake unto "them in parables: because they seeing see not; and hearing they hear not, neither do they understand" (Matthew 13:13). Just as the Syrians could not see what was clearly right before them, we can wonder how often the Lord withholds from you and me what we might otherwise see, were we not faithless, disobedient, or simply focused on the things of the world instead of the things of God. Fortunately, as the miracle attests, the "blindness" only need be temporary. God will allow us to "see" when we are no longer willing to rebel.

Of this miracle, one text suggested the following application: "Sometimes the healing-power of the physician can only be felt by first subjecting the patient to suffering. The infliction of blindness upon these heathen men was the first step to revealing to them the benevolent character of the God of Israel, through the kindness of His prophet."[17] It is certainly true that, at times, God uses suffering as a means of getting our attention—as a way to turn us toward Him. This is not to imply that all of life's difficulties are the doing of God—nor evidence that we are sinners. However, it is to suggest that, when necessary, the Father of us all may employ such measures if we simply refuse to conform to His will.

It has been pointed out that the king of Israel acknowledged the prophet's "superior authority" over his own political power (see 2 Kings 6:21).[18] Such a relationship may foreshadow the condition that will exist during the Millennium, when a theocracy is established and the laws of men are swallowed up by the laws of God. Elder Bruce R. McConkie wrote, "For the present we are subject to the laws of the land; when the true and perfect millennial order prevails, all rule and government, both civil and ecclesiastical, will come from our Eternal Head."[19]

NOTES

1. Richard D. Patterson and Hermann J. Austel, "1 and 2 Kings," in Frank E. Gaebelein, ed., *The Expositor's Bible Commentary* (Grand Rapids, MI: Zondervan, 1994), 4:194.

2. See Mordechai Cogan and Hayim Tadmor, *The Anchor Bible: II Kings*, vol. 11 (New York: Doubleday, 1988), 74.

3. See Francis Brown, S. R. Driver, and Charles A. Briggs, *The Brown-Driver-Briggs Hebrew and English Lexicon* (Peabody, MA: Hendrickson Publishers, 1999), 703.

4. Israel Wolf Slotki, *Kings*, in *Soncino Books of the Bible* (London: The Soncino Press, 1978), 199.

5. Herbert Lockyer, *All the Miracles of the Bible: The Supernatural in Scripture—Its Scope and Significance* (Grand Rapids, MI: Zondervan, 1961), 125.

6. Patterson and Austel, "1 and 2 Kings," in Gaebelein, *The Expositor's Bible Commentary*, 4:194.

7. Ellis T. Rasmussen, *A Latter-day Saint Commentary on the Old Testament* (Salt Lake City, UT: Deseret Book, 1994), 304. One commentator wrote, "Elisha slipped into the ranks of the blind men and told them to follow him. He led them to his fortress hometown." (Pamela McQuade, *The Top 100 Miracles of the Bible: What They Are and What They Mean to You Today* [Uhrichsville, OH: Barbour Publishing, 2008], 96.)

8. Patterson and Austel, "1 and 2 Kings," in Gaebelein, *The Expositor's Bible Commentary*, 4:194.

9. See Donald J. Wiseman, *1 and 2 Kings*, in *Tyndale Old Testament Commentaries* (Downers Grove, IL: InterVarsity Press, 1988), 210; Walter L. Wilson, *A Dictionary of Bible Types* (Peabody, MA: Hendrickson, 1999), 43–44; Ada R. Habershon, *The Study of the Miracles* (London: Morgan & Scott, 1911), 178.

10. Leland Ryken, James C. Wilhoit, and Tremper Longman III, eds., *Dictionary of Biblical Imagery* (Downers Grove, IL: InterVarsity Press, 1998), 99; emphasis added.

11. Patterson and Austel, "1 and 2 Kings," in Gaebelein, *The Expositor's Bible Commentary*, 4:194.

12. Wiseman, *1 and 2 Kings*, in *Tyndale Old Testament Commentaries*, 210.

13. Truman G. Madsen, *Joseph Smith the Prophet* (Salt Lake City, UT: Bookcraft, 1989), 31.

14. Journal entry, January 29, 1843, in Andrew H. Hedges, Alex D. Smith, and Richard Lloyd Anderson, eds., *The Joseph Smith Papers, Journals Volume 2: December 1841–April 1843* (Salt Lake City, UT: The Church Historian's Press, 2011), 253.

15. McQuade, *The Top 100 Miracles of the Bible*, 96.

16. Richard C. Trench, *Miracles and Parables of the Old Testament* (Grand Rapids, MI: Baker Book House, 1974), 176.

17. Ibid., 172.

18. See, for example, Wiseman, *1 and 2 Kings*, in *Tyndale Old Testament Commentaries*, 210.

19. Bruce R. McConkie, *The Millennial Messiah: The Second Coming of the Son of Man* (Salt Lake City, UT: Deseret Book, 1982), 598.

THE SYRIANS ARE SCARED AWAY *by the* SOUND *of* CHARIOTS *and* HORSES THAT DO NOT EXIST

2 KINGS 7:6–7

THE MIRACLE

Ben-hadad,[1] king of Syria, had taken Samaria. His siege of the city lasted so long that it evoked a severe famine which, in turn, brought about severe inflation. Things had gotten so bad that the Israelites had resorted to cannibalism—eating their young in order to survive (see 2 Kings 6:24–29).

Jehoram, king of Israel, went to Elisha—frustrated by how bad things had become. Elisha prophesied to the king that, by the very next day, conditions would improve and goods would be available. The king's chief aide scoffed, finding such a promise preposterous (see 2 Kings 6:31–7:2). Elisha responded to his skepticism by saying, "Behold, thou shalt see it with thine eyes, but shalt not eat thereof" (2 Kings 7:2). In other words, it will definitely happen but, because you have not believed, you will miss out on partaking of the blessing.

During that night, the Syrian army, who were encamped with their plethora of supplies, thought that they heard chariots and horses and the marching of a huge army. In their terror, they presumed that the king of Israel had hired the Hittites and Egyptians to join him in an attack on the army of the Syrians. Fearing what they assumed to be certain death, every one of Ben-hadad's soldiers fled their camp, leaving behind all of their supplies and possessions. On the morrow, the Israelites confiscated all that had been left, and Elisha's prophecy was fulfilled (see 2 Kings 7:6–7).

BACKGROUND

The "famine" described in this narrative may be the same one depicted in 2 Kings 8:1. If it was this same famine, it would be important to note that "the siege which stopped the importation of foodstuffs intensified the scarcity" of commodities beyond what would have been the case if only the drought were in play.[2]

Regarding the cannibalism that was said to have been taking place among the Jews of this time (see 2 Kings 6:28–29), one commentary explained, "Cannibalism in time of siege was the prophetic threat for Israel's disobedience (Lev 26:29; Deut 28:53, 57; Ezek 5:10). It was to befall Jerusalem both in [Old Testament] times (Lam 2:20; 4:10) and in [New Testament] times (cf. Jos. *War*, VI, 201–13 [iii.4])."[3]

Elisha promises food to the siege-weary and famine-stricken residents of Samaria. However, he doesn't promise normal prices for that food (see 2 Kings 7:1). In this miracle, the cost of the flour Elisha miraculously provides is still many times its normal price (see 2 Kings 7:16). However, in the midst of their pain, this still felt like a remarkable blessing.

The narrative states of the Syrian army that they, "Left their tents, and their horses, and their asses, even the camp as it was, and fled for their life" (2 Kings 7:7). Of this, one commentator wrote, "Instead of using the animals to help their escape the Syrians left them behind, an indication of the extreme panic which seized hold of them."[4]

SYMBOLIC ELEMENTS

One text on scriptural symbolism notes, "Food shows the abundant providence of God. People in Scripture do not *find* food as a random good but receive it as a gift from God's hand. . . . Especially in the [Old Testament], physical food clearly pictures providence, pleasure and God's intended order. . . .[5] Part of God's ultimate blessing for Israel would be a land untroubled by famine (Ezek 34:29; 36:29–30)."[6] On the other hand,

[Famine] was regarded as one of a number of divinely ordained scourges that God uses to punish both his people and others for their sins (Deut 32:24; 2 Sam 21:1; 1 Kings 17:1; Ps 105:16; Is 14:30; 51:19; Jer 11:22; 14:1–18; 24:10; 42:13–17). For Israel it is a curse particularly associated with breaking God's covenant (Deut 28). The conditions for relief are consequently tied in with the willingness of the people to repent and to seek the Lord (1 Kings 8:32–40; 2 Chron 20:8–9).[7]

In this particular miracle, the famine seems to foreshadow the waning faith of God's people. For example, the king[8] says to Elisha, "Behold, this evil [famine and besiegement] is of the Lord; what, should I wait for the Lord any longer?" (2 Kings 6:33). In effect, the king is asking the prophet, should I even bother to pray anymore? Similarly, when Elisha predicts that the very next day supplies would be available, Jehoram's chief aide scoffs at the suggestion (see 2 Kings 7:2). Thus, the behavior of those who should have believed fits well into the standard motif of famine as a symbol of scourging for disbelief.

APPLICATION AND ALLEGORIZATION

There are those who, in the midst of their trials, can only see the proverbial "glass" as half-empty. The Israelites certainly could have done the same. However, rather than complaining that God's miracle still left them paying more than they should for their fodder,[9] they instead rejoiced that they had any food at all. I have known too many who profess to be "Saints," but who struggle to see the blessings amid their trials. The popular phrase "first-world problems" comes to mind. How often are we disenchanted with our circumstances, forgetting that we are among the most blessed people on the face of the planet? The worst day for most of us would be considered the envy of nearly any soul living in a third-world country. Don't have enough money to purchase the home of your dreams? Imagine living in a mud and straw hut. Not enough cash to get that third car for the kids to drive? Imagine having no car, and walking *everywhere* you go. Not enough savings to send your son or daughter to the Ivy League College of their dreams? Imagine your children growing up with no hope for even a grade-school education. While it may be true that not all of our blessings come in the exact package that we want, selfishness and ingratitude cause us to not be able to see how tremendously blessed we each are.

Similarly, one source on the miracles pointed out that this story is a testament to the fact that "God's mercies far exceed man's deserts. The King of Israel received the promise of deliverance when he was plotting against the life of the best subject in his kingdom" (2 Kings 6:31).[10] We should never feel deserving of our blessings. Grateful? Yes! But deserving? No! God gives us so much when we are so unworthy of His divine regard. Undeserving as we are, may we ever be in awe of His unfailing blessings upon us.

In times past, Elisha had provided food for the hungry in a decidedly miraculous manner—in a way that would be hard to describe as anything other than a miracle (see 2 Kings 4:38–44). However, here his approach is quite different. He predicts something miraculous will happen, but he doesn't explain how. The recipients never see the miracle take place, and we only know how it was accomplished because the narrator informs us. By way of application, the miraculous is not always evidentially such. By that I mean, some things are obviously miracles (e.g., the priesthood blessing that instantly heals a person who is sick). However, miraculous things often take place in our lives that we are simply unaware of. Things happen "behind the scenes," *per se*. They are no less miraculous than the ones we see at the hands of the priesthood, but often, we miss their miraculous nature because God has brought them to pass by seemingly natural means. "Extraordinary means are not used by God where ordinary means will answer the purpose."[11] The risk, of course, is that when such seemingly "unmiraculous" miracles happen in our lives—and I personally believe they take place on most days—we don't notice them as blessings, and we don't feel the gratitude we should for them because they're shrouded in normalcy. Shame on us, as followers of Christ, if we do not see His hand as evident in our day-to-day experiences.

It will be noted that the king of Israel became angry with Elisha because the prophet had not removed the famine *and* the Syrian army (see 2 Kings 6:26–31); something that the king perceived that Elisha had the power to do.[12] Ultimately, at the king's pleading with the prophet, the Lord takes *part* of the trial away, but not *all* of it. By way of application, we should remember that God does not always remove our burdens when we are righteous. Even those who faithfully live the covenants and keep God's commandments still suffer. In Mosiah 24:14–15, God states,

> I will . . . ease the burdens which are put upon your shoulders, that even you cannot feel them upon your backs, even while you are in bondage; and this will I do that ye may . . . know of a surety that I, the Lord God, do visit my people in their afflictions.
>
> And now it came to pass that that the burdens which were laid upon Alma and his brethren were made light; yea, the Lord did strengthen them that they could bear up their burdens with ease, and they did submit cheerfully and with patience to all the will of the Lord.

This miracle is a testament to the reality that God expects His covenant people to endure their trials. When the famine was on, and the city was besieged, Elisha was just as hungry as the other Israelites. He was righteous—and surely the Lord enabled him to "submit cheerfully and with patience" to all that God saw fit to inflict upon him. We too must embrace what God sends. We would do well to follow the counsel of Mother Teresa, who said, "Take whatever [God] gives and give whatever He takes with a big smile." And then she added, be willing "to be used by Him as it pleases *Him*."[13]

Allegorizing this miracle, one early Christian saw in this famine a metaphor about spiritual starvation. For example, the conditions which prevailed caused the Israelites to turn to eating their young—*to cannibalism*! The aforementioned source suggested that this represents how we wrongfully turn to things other than God's word to meet our needs in times of trouble; and often, what we turn to is abominable in the eyes of the Lord. (Oh, how we see this today in the rampant use of pornography and in the commonality of substance abuse.) This same early Christian source suggested that "[the] famine in Samaria became so great that a donkey's head was sold for eighty shekels of silver. The donkey's head . . . signifies the teaching coming from the ravings of the philosophers and the scientists of the world."[14] In other words, some among the early Christians worried that members of the Church would put more emphasis on worldly philosophies and earthly substitutes than they would on the remedies that God has provided for what ails us spiritually. In the words of Elder Bruce R. McConkie, "The philosophies of men, mingled with scripture, soon replace the pure word [of God] written in the holy record."[15] Where do you turn for peace? Is it to the world you turn for answers? Or do you turn to God? In our miracle, those who turned to the things of the world found themselves on the brink of spiritual starvation. Can we expect anything different in our own lives?

NOTES

1. Because of the events described in this narrative, it has been suggested that the Syrian king referenced here is Ben-hadad III. (See Mordechai Cogan and Hayim Tadmor, *The Anchor Bible: II Kings*, vol. 11 [New York: Doubleday, 1988], 79 & 85; Donald J. Wiseman, *1 and 2 Kings*, in *Tyndale Old Testament Commentaries* [Downers Grove, IL: InterVarsity Press, 1988], 210.)
2. See Israel Wolf Slotki, *Kings*, in *Soncino Books of the Bible* (London: The Soncino Press, 1978), 200. See also Ogden and Skinner (2013), 2:55.
3. Richard D. Patterson and Hermann J. Austel, "1 and 2 Kings," in Frank E. Gaebelein, ed., *The Expositor's Bible Commentary* (Grand Rapids, MI: Zondervan, 1994), 4:198. See also Israel Wolf Slotki, *Kings*, in *Soncino Books of the Bible*, 201.
4. Israel Wolf Slotki, *Kings*, in *Soncino Books of the Bible*, 204.

5.   Leland Ryken, James C. Wilhoit, and Tremper Longman III, eds., *Dictionary of Biblical Imagery* (Downers Grove, IL: InterVarsity Press, 1998), 297–98; emphasis added.

6.   Ibid., 267.

7.   Ibid.

8.   It is argued that, where the KJV translates the Hebrew into "messenger," a better rendering would be "king." (See Patterson and Austel, 1 and 2 Kings," in Gaebelein, *The Expositor's Bible Commentary*, 4:196; Cogan and Tadmor, *The Anchor Bible: II Kings*, 81.)

9.   Cogan and Tadmor argue that "Elisha's prediction of abundance was only relative; the cost of choice flour was still many times its normal price." (See Cogan and Tadmor, *The Anchor Bible: II Kings*, 81.)

10.   Richard C. Trench, *Miracles and Parables of the Old Testament* (Grand Rapids, MI: Baker Book House, 1974), 177.

11.   Ibid.

12.   See Israel Wolf Slotki, *Kings*, in *Soncino Books of the Bible*, 202.

13.   Mother Teresa, *Where There Is Love, There Is God: Her Path to Closer Union with God and Greater Love for Others* (New York: Doubleday Religion, 2010), 299; emphasis added.

14.   See Ephrem the Syrian, "On the Second Book of Kings," 6.24–25, in Marco Conti, ed., *1–2 Kings, 1–2 Chronicles, Ezra, Nehemiah, Esther*, in *Ancient Christian Commentary on Scripture* (Downers Grove, IL: InterVarsity Press, 2008), 177.

15.   Bruce R. McConkie, *The Millennial Messiah: The Second Coming of the Son of Man* (Salt Lake City, UT: Deseret Book, 1982), 163.

A MAN WHOSE CORPSE
TOUCHES ELISHA'S
DEAD BODY IS RAISED
from the DEAD

2 KINGS 13:20–21

THE MIRACLE

Elisha the prophet had fallen sick with an unnamed illness and ultimately died from it. Thereafter, his remains were interred in a sepulcher at the local place of burial (see 2 Kings 13:14, 20).

Each spring, Moabite raiders would enter the country and raid the land. On one occasion, some Israelites were burying a man when they spotted such a band, and so they quickly threw the corpse in Elisha's tomb, and then fled the graveyard—seeking protection. However, when the body of the recently deceased man landed on the bones of Elisha, the man came back to life and stood upon his feet (see 2 Kings 13:20–21).

BACKGROUND

It has been estimated that, by the time Elisha passed away, he had held the prophetic office for some fifty plus years.[1]

The fact that Elisha's entombed corpse had decayed to the point of being nothing more than bones suggests that the prophet had died quite some time before this miracle took place.

One source rightly suggests that this miracle has been taken by some as evidence that the relics of the deceased "saints" should be venerated and used as a source for miracles. "By some it has been . . . supposed that there was an inherent virtue, or life-giving power, in the bones of Elisha, and that the same power exists in the bones of all men of extraordinary goodness." This same source goes on to remind the reader that "it was not the prophet's bones which brought the dead to life, but the Living God."[2]

Louis Ginzberg notes a very common Talmudic legend that the man whose corpse was revived by contact with Elisha's bones died a second time shortly after his brief resuscitation.[3] His brief restoration to life was a testament to Elisha's divine call, and also provoked those who had hastily buried him to finish their job of giving the man a proper burial in a grave of his own.

SYMBOLIC ELEMENTS

The power of Elisha's bones to raise a dead man has been seen as symbolic. One source notes that the Hebrew word for "bone" means "essence" or "self." This same source states,

> In keeping with this . . . , individuals refer to their bones when describing the deepest aspects of their lives, the core of their being, their very selves. . . .
>
> That a lifeless body, upon touching Elisha's bones, should receive its spirit again and stand upright underscores the importance and power associated with the bones (2 Kings 13:21; cf. 1 Kings 13:31). As the last part of the human body to decay, the bones enshrined and preserved the essence of an individual. The bones are the remains (Amos 6:10; Gen 50:25; Ex 13:19) and symbolize the fate of the individual. The bones of the wicked lie "strewn at the mouth of Sheol" (Ps 141:7). . . .
>
> As the last surviving part of an individual, bones were to be treated with respect (Sir 49:15; 1 Macc 13:25).[4]

Thus, not only did Elisha have the power to raise the dead during his life (see 2 Kings 4:8–37), but clearly this power remained with him beyond death and into the grave.[5] In this miracle, we have "a post-mortem corroboration of his undying influence."[6]

APPLICATION AND ALLEGORIZATION

It has been suggested that the restorative power of Elisha's dead body is a type for "the vivifying power of Christ's death (Isaiah 26:19)."[7] Just as Elisha's dead body brought life to the dead, so also Christ's lifeless body would bring life to all humanity.[8] "In this miraculous act, God held up to view a mighty image of the future—of the regenerating, life-giving power which should be shed abroad in the world by the death of Elisha's great Master, Jesus Christ."[9]

Origen of Alexandria saw in this miracle evidence of the law of Moses's inferiority to the law of Christ. He explained that the law of Moses says,

> "Whatever soul touches anything unclean, or the carcass of unclean beasts, and conceals it and is defiled, or if he touches the uncleanness of a person or anything unclean by which he is defiled," [Leviticus 5:2–3] and so forth. These, to be sure, are observed by the Jews indecently and uselessly enough. And why should one who, for example, touches a dead animal or the body of a dead person be held to be impure? What if it is the body of a prophet? What if it is the body of a patriarch or even the body of Abraham himself? What if he touches the bones, will he be unclean? What if he should touch the bones of Elisha, which raised a dead person? Will that one be unclean who touches the bones of the prophets and likewise do they make that one himself unclean whom they raise from the dead? See how unsuitable the Jewish interpretation is.[10]

Origen's point was that the law and its prescriptions are useless if they are not seen as symbols of Christ and His power over sin and death.

Richard Trench explained why this miracle was important for those in Israel who had survived the prophet.

> It was probably intended to revive, in the mind of Israel, hope in God as to the future of the nation. Elisha, on his dying bed, had foretold the deliverance of Israel from the yoke of Syria: their present sufferings from the Moabites would naturally discourage the heart of the people and lead them to forget the promise, which was not yet, it may be presumed, completely fulfilled. This [reviving] by means of Elisha's dead body would be the means of a resurrection of hope in Elisha's God.[11]

In some way, perhaps this miracle is a reminder of the need for "authentic spiritual experiences" in our lives; the kind that, when we hit patches of mortal difficulty, we can look back on and exercise faith in. Certainly, this *last* miracle of Elisha reminded all those who witnessed it of his *many* miracles and promises of the past. Those whose faith may have been waning since the prophet's death were, by this miracle, reminded of all of the "authentic spiritual experiences" that they had received via this man of God. Those would then carry them through the trials of the present. In so many ways, we in the latter days need such experiences, so that we have something bright and hopeful to rely upon in our darkest of days.

In this same vein, it seems evident that "God would have the dust of departed saints remind us of their holy lives. He would have the child, when he stands by the grave of a sainted mother, call to mind her holy words and deeds; and the church or nation which has been blest [*sic*] with a godly and gifted teacher remember and follow the teachings which He gave them while in the flesh (Heb. xiii. 7)."[12] The graves of loved ones—influential ones—are sacred, because they remind us of their faithfulness and virtue; they remind us of who they were and what their lives call each of us to be. Elisha's bones called up the miracle of the healing of a man; but, more importantly, they called up the miracle of the recollection of a life well lived and a God faithfully served. May we remember, with intent, the lives and legacy of those who have gone before us.

NOTES

1. Richard D. Patterson and Hermann J. Austel, "1 and 2 Kings," in Frank E. Gaebelein, ed., *The Expositor's Bible Commentary* (Grand Rapids, MI: Zondervan, 1994), 4:226; Mordechai Cogan and Hayim Tadmor, *The Anchor Bible: II Kings*, vol. 11 (New York: Doubleday, 1988), 149.

2. Richard C. Trench, *Miracles and Parables of the Old Testament* (Grand Rapids, MI: Baker Book House, 1974), 179–80.

3. Louis Ginzberg, *The Legends of the Jews* (Philadelphia: The Jewish Publication Society of America, 1967), 6:347n1. See also Herbert Lockyer, *All the Miracles of the Bible: The Supernatural in Scripture—Its Scope and Significance* (Grand Rapids, MI: Zondervan, 1961), 126.

4. Leland Ryken, James C. Wilhoit, and Tremper Longman III, eds., *Dictionary of Biblical Imagery* (Downers Grove, IL: InterVarsity Press, 1998), 113–14.

5. See Cogan and Tadmor, *The Anchor Bible: II Kings*, 150.

6. Lockyer, *All the Miracles of the Bible*, 126.

7. Ibid.

8. See Ephrem the Syrian, "On the Second Book of Kings," 13.21, in Marco Conti, ed., *1–2 Kings, 1–2 Chronicles, Ezra, Nehemiah, Esther*, in *Ancient Christian Commentary on Scripture* (Downers Grove, IL: InterVarsity Press, 2008), 199.

9. Trench, *Miracles and Parables of the Old Testament*, 183–84.

10. Origen, "Homilies on Leviticus," 3.3.1, Conti, *1–2 Kings, 1–2 Chronicles, Ezra, Nehemiah, Esther*, in *Ancient Christian Commentary on Scripture*, 200.

11. Trench, *Miracles and Parables of the Old Testament*, 180–81.

12. Ibid., 181.

SENNACHERIB'S HOSTS
Are DESTROYED

2 KINGS 19:35

2 CHRONICLES 32:21

ISAIAH 37:36

THE MIRACLE

The Assyrian king, Sennacherib, had captured and despoiled some forty-six Judean cities; and it was his intent to do the same to Jerusalem (see 2 Kings 18:13).

Distraught by the pending threat, King Hezekiah went to the temple to know God's will regarding what he and his people should do. In addition, Hezekiah sent several of his men and priests to the prophet, Isaiah, in an effort to receive counsel from the prophet. Hezekiah asked Isaiah to join with him in prayer for God's people (see 2 Kings 19:14–20).

Isaiah assured Hezekiah that he need not fear: "Thus saith the Lord concerning the king of Assyria, [Sennacherib] shall not come into this city, nor shoot an arrow there, nor come before it with shield, nor cast a bank against it (2 Kings 19:32). . . . Behold, I will send a blast upon him, and he shall . . . return to his own land; and I will cause him to fall by the sword in his own land (2 Kings 19:7). . . . For I will defend this city" (2 Kings 19:34).

That very night, as Sennacherib and his armies encamped outside the city, ready to attack, "The angel of the Lord went out, and smote in the camp of the Assyrians" 185,000 soldiers (2 Kings 19:35). When the king of Assyria awoke the next morning, he and his few remaining men found a veritable graveyard, with nearly two hundred thousand bodies covering the ground.

With his army decisively defeated by the God of Israel, Sennacherib broke camp and returned to Nineveh; never again to return to Judah (see 2 Kings 19:36).

One day, while worshipping the god Nisroch, Sennacherib was stabbed to death by two of his sons; thus fulfilling the prophecy of Isaiah regarding him (see 2 Kings 19:37).

BACKGROUND

One Jewish source says of the sudden and miraculous death of Sennacherib's army, "According to tradition, the disaster occurred during the first night of the Passover festival."[1] While it appears from evidence in the text that this miracle *did* happen around the same time as the Jewish Passover, there is nothing specific in the text to confirm this tradition.

Sennacherib's death took place approximately twenty years after he returned from Jerusalem (circa 681 BC). According to the biblical narrative, his sons, Adrammelech and Sharezer, stabbed him and then fled to Urartu (modern-day Armenia), leaving their brother (Esarhaddon) to reign in their father's stead (681–686 BC).[2] As for their motive for slaying their father, one commentary provides the following insight.

> In . . . ancient sources, a single son and not two, as in v. 37, is mentioned. . . . New evidence [has shown] that Sennacherib's murderer was Arad-Ninlil (pronounced "Arda-milissu"), who was bypassed in the line of succession in favor of Esarhaddon, a younger son. The form [of the name] in [the third-century BC writings of] Berossos (in an excerpt by [the Greek historian] Abydenos) is Adramelos, virtually identical with the Assyrian name. Accordingly the biblical Adrammelech would be a slight corruption of the original name [of Sennacherib's murderer].
>
> A son named Sharezer is not attested in any other source [other than the Bible], but there is no reason to doubt that he was Adrammelech's accomplice.[3]

It is curious that, at the time of his death, Sennacherib is said to have been worshipping Nisroch—whose name means "the great eagle". What seems strange is that the Bible mentions this when no Assyrian sources attest to such a god in Assyria. Some commentators have suggested that perhaps he was actually worshipping Ninurta, the Assyrian god of war; or, perhaps Ashur, the chief god of Assyria; or even Nuska, the sun god.[4]

SYMBOLIC ELEMENTS

While the word "protect," and its cognates, only come up a few dozen times in the standard works, the concept of divine "protection" is a very common symbol in scripture. "The images and stories of protection in the Bible reinforce two dominant themes of Scripture: the weakness and vulnerability of people and God's sovereign power and inclination to be compassionate toward the human plight."[5]

Fear of dark and what lurks therein is a common symbolic element in literature and life. The *Dictionary of Biblical Imagery* notes,

> Darkness has no existence by itself, being definable simply as an absence of light. It is a physical and spiritual reality as well as an apt symbol for some of the profoundest human experiences. . . .
>
> Considered in itself, darkness [is] thus a strongly negative image in human experience. It is physically oppressive; it is the natural environment for a host of evil happenings; and it is associated with death . . . and ultimate evil.[6]

With this in mind, another source suggested, "The dangers of night which pass with morning light was a popular image associated with divine salvation—e.g., in prayers: Ps 46:4, 90:14, 143:8; Lam 3:22f.; and in historical accounts: Exod 11:4, 2 Kgs 3:20, 2 Chr 20:20; cf. Isa 17:14."[7] Darkness reminds us of the absence of God and His blessings; light is a symbol of their return. To not survive the darkness is a symbol of ultimate surrender to evil and its associated powers.

There has been a great deal of conjecture as to what disease took the lives of 185,000 Assyrian soldiers in one night (e.g., bubonic plague, dysentery).[8] Regardless, "The ancients attributed disease to the 'hand of God'."[9] While the text states, "the angel," or "messenger" in Hebrew, "of the Lord . . . smote" the soldiers (2 Kings 19:35), God often uses natural means to bring to pass His will.[10] Thus, it *could have* been a disease that served as the symbolic agent of God's wrath.

APPLICATION AND ALLEGORIZATION

The most obvious application of this miracle is its message about prayer. The Lord said to Hezekiah, "That which thou hast prayed to me against Sennacherib king of Assyria I have heard" (2 Kings 19:20). By implication, our prayers *are* heard by God, and they *do* matter in the eternal scheme of things. We do not have the power to change God's will, but, if our wills are aligned with His, He will bring to pass our righteous desires—as laid out before Him in solemn, faith-filled prayer.

Sennacherib spoke of the God of Israel—or any god, for that matter—as unable to defeat him. He saw himself as unconquerable (see 2 Kings 19:10–13) While we don't see many people in our day that make such bold and blasphemous statements, certainly many—including some who have fallen into inactivity—live in such a way as to defy God. They live their lives as though their covenants do not matter—as though God has not the power to punish or correct them. For those who have taken such a path, the example and the ultimate end of Sennacherib is worth taking note of.

The complete fulfillment of Isaiah's prophecy (described herein) took some twenty years to be accomplished. The Lord's prophet made it clear that the king of Assyria would die, but that did not happen overnight—though his army certainly was slain almost immediately. God's word is fulfilled on God's timetable. Of this fact, one commentary noted, "While God's program may seem to tarry (cf. 2 Peter 3:4–9), it *will* be accomplished. The mills of God grind slowly but exceedingly fine."[11]

As another related application of this miracle, D. Kelly Ogden and Andrew C. Skinner explained:

> The Lord can protect those who have faith and trust in him. During the American Revolutionary War, for example, it is amazing how often the Lord helped by freezing the ground so American revolutionaries could transport cannons or providing clouds to hide the soldiers' escape. Consider also the protection given to Zion's Camp led by Joseph Smith in 1834. The Lord sent a fierce storm wind, rain, thunder, lightning, and hail to protect them from their enemies (Smith, *History of the Church*, 2:104–5).[12]

The Lord is in charge. He will prevail! If we align ourselves with Him—and with His will—we will also prevail. God will "pull the strings" necessary to preserve and protect His covenant people, *if* they keep their covenants. This does not mean that their lives will be stress-free or trial-free; certainly those in Jerusalem had stress and trials in the midst of Sennacherib's threats. However, as they endured those in faith, God came to their aid. And so He will for each of us as we faithfully live our lives and keep our covenants. As noted previously, "The mills of God grind slowly," but they do grind, bringing to pass God's ultimate will.

This miracle offers a warning about misplacing our trust. In the narrative, we learn that the Assyrians sought to intimidate Hezekiah and his people.

> Before the battle for Jerusalem began, the Assyrian king Sennacherib sent his supreme commander, his chief officer, and his field commander to Israel to intimidate the small nation. Hadn't they seen what he'd done to the nations around them? the field commander, their spokesman, asked. How could Israel hold out? Why not give up now, make a bargain with Sennacherib, and join Assyria. . . . The commander made certain the people of Jerusalem heard these words, as he spoke to Hezekiah's representatives. "Hezekiah and the Lord cannot protect you," was the gist of his message.[13]

Hezekiah and his people had reason to fear. They had reason to give in to the pressures of Sennacherib and his army. But our source continues,

> Hezekiah was an admirable man who stood firm for his Lord. Even . . . [an] attempt to scare him into compromise did not work—he turned . . . to God in worship instead of wasting his time in fear.
>
> The God we trust in is as reliable today as He was in Hezekiah's time. He will fight our battle for us, and often, when we trust Him in remarkable circumstances, He will respond in an unexpected way. The problem we expected may never come to pass. The difficult issue will be resolved with no action on our part. Or the enemy will simply return home, never to bother us again.
>
> Hezekiah's trust was not misplaced. Neither will ours be.[14]

The challenge is to muster the faith to believe—to not be intimidated by life's daunting circumstances, or the pressures of those who wish to control or harm us. May we, when faced with seemingly insurmountable challenges, respond as King Hezekiah did, and simply turn from our foes and face our God.

In this same vein, the narrative tells us that Sennacherib's servant—a zealous, reckless, and blasphemous man—had sent Hezekiah a letter taunting him, and insulting his faith and his God. Hezekiah, we are told, "Went up into the house of the Lord, and spread [the taunting and blasphemous letter] before the Lord" (2 Kings 19:14). As one commentator put it, "[The king] left the matter with Him."[15] It seems that there is a message in this for you and me. When there are trials, and when we are buffeted by some enemy, let us make our way to the temple, and then "leave the matter before the Lord." Some things we simply can't change, but God *can*! May we have the wisdom to know what battles we can and should fight, and which ones we should leave to the Lord.

In speaking of this miracle, Athanasius of Alexandria made an interesting point about Satan—and those who follow him. He wrote,

> Since the evil spirits have no power, they play as on a stage, changing their shapes and frightening children by the apparition of crowds and by their changed forms. This is why they are to be despised the more for their powerlessness. The true angel sent by the Lord against the Assyrians had no need of crowds or apparitions from without, or loud noises or clappings, but he used his power quietly and destroyed 185,000 at one time. Powerless demons such as these, however, try to frighten, if only by empty phantoms.[16]

God constantly does things worthy of fanfare, but does not seek it. Lucifer, on the other hand, is all about the credit, the tinsel, and the applause. What was his request in the grand council in heaven? To the Father, he said, "Give me thine honor" (Moses 4:1). Jesus, who is in all things in the image and pattern of the Father, said, "The glory be thine forever" (Moses 4:2). Just as God, in this miracle, goes about doing what He needs to do to further the divine plan, perhaps you and I can draw from this a lesson on how we should do our work: quietly, contentedly, and without any desire for credit, fanfare, or applause.

NOTES

1. Israel Wolf Slotki, *Kings*, in *Soncino Books of the Bible* (London: The Soncino Press, 1978), 287.

2. See Richard D. Patterson and Hermann J. Austel, "1 and 2 Kings," in Frank E. Gaebelein, ed., *The Expositor's Bible Commentary* (Grand Rapids, MI: Zondervan, 1994), 4:268; Donald J. Wiseman, *1 and 2 Kings*, in *Tyndale Old Testament Commentaries* (Downers Grove, IL: InterVarsity Press, 1988), 280.

3. Mordechai Cogan and Hayim Tadmor, *The Anchor Bible: II Kings*, vol. 11 (New York: Doubleday, 1988), 240. See also Israel Wolf Slotki, *Kings*, in *Soncino Books of the Bible*, 288; Wiseman, *1 and 2 Kings*, in *Tyndale Old Testament Commentaries*, 284–85. In the biblical rendering of the name, *r* and *d* have been interchanged by metathesis, and *k* may have entered the text as a late scribal error for *s*.

4. See A. Kirk Grayson, "Nisroch," in David Noel Freedman, ed., *The Anchor Bible Dictionary* (New York: Doubleday, 1992), 4:1122; Israel Wolf Slotki, *Kings*, in *Soncino Books of the Bible*, 287. Others have suggested he was worshipping Marduk. (See Patterson and Austel, "1 and 2 Kings," in Gaebelein, *The Expositor's Bible Commentary*, 4:271; Cogan and Tadmor, *The Anchor Bible: II Kings*, 239.)

Farbridge suggested that "Nisroch" was the lengthened Hebrew form of "Nesher." (See Maurice H. Farbridge, *Studies in Biblical and Semitic Symbolism* [London: Routledge, 1923], 83.)

5.   Leland Ryken, James C. Wilhoit, and Tremper Longman III, eds., *Dictionary of Biblical Imagery* (Downers Grove, IL: InterVarsity Press, 1998), 679.

6.   Ibid., 191–92.

7.   Cogan and Tadmor, *The Anchor Bible: II Kings*, 239.

8.   One commentary on the passage records this: "The hypothesis that the 'angel of the Lord,' which wiped out 185,000 Assyrians in their sleep, was actually a plague is certainly credible. But a more potent pathogen than *Yersinia pestis*, the causative agent of bubonic plague, could account for such rapid morality. The bacteria *Clostridia botulinum* grows in alkaline foods, such as vegetables, and releases a toxin that causes paralysis when it is ingested. The victim will die in less than twenty-four hours from an inability to breathe. Small amounts of the toxin are lethal, and its effects can be widespread if many among a given population, such as an army, eat the same infected food. On the other hand, plague is transmitted more slowly by fleas on rats and may not be fatal for a few days. The description the Old Testament gives is not conclusive, but it may be that the 'angel of the Lord' who 'went forth' did so by conveying botulism food poisoning." (Kelly Ogden and Andrew C. Skinner, *Verse By Verse—The Old Testament Volume One: Genesis through 2 Samuel, Psalms* [Salt Lake City, UT: Deseret Book, 2013], 2:80.)

9.   Wiseman, *1 and 2 Kings*, in *Tyndale Old Testament Commentaries*, 284.

10.   Trench wrote, "True it is that all death is from God, but He uses disease or accident as the means by which to bring about the dissolution of the...body in almost every instance." (Richard C. Trench, *Miracles and Parables of the Old Testament* [Grand Rapids, MI: Baker Book House, 1974], 183.)

11.   Patterson and Austel, in "1 and 2 Kings," in Gaebelein, *The Expositor's Bible Commentary*, 4:268; emphasis added.

12.   Ogden and Skinner, *Verse By Verse—The Old Testament Volume One: Genesis through 2 Samuel, Psalms*, 2:82.

13.   Pamela McQuade, *The Top 100 Miracles of the Bible: What They Are and What They Mean to You Today* (Uhrichsville, OH: Barbour Publishing, 2008), 98.

14.   Ibid., 100.

15.   Herbert Lockyer, *All the Miracles of the Bible: The Supernatural in Scripture—Its Scope and Significance* (Grand Rapids, MI: Zondervan, 1961), 127.

16.   Athanasius, "Life of St. Anthony," 28.9–10, in Marco Conti, ed., *1–2 Kings, 1–2 Chronicles, Ezra, Nehemiah, Esther*, in *Ancient Christian Commentary on Scripture* (Downers Grove, IL: InterVarsity Press, 2008), 221.

THE SHADOW *Is* REVERSED TEN DEGREES

2 KINGS 20:9–11

2 CHRONICLES 32:24

ISAIAH 38:8

THE MIRACLE

Hezekiah had become deathly ill. Upon learning of this, Isaiah came to his bedside and informed him that the Lord had revealed that he would indeed die, and, thus, the king should set his house in order (see 2 Kings 20:1).

Hezekiah wept bitterly, and prayed to God—detailing his faithfulness and wholehearted devotion over the years. The king pled that his life might be spared (see 2 Kings 20:2–3). While the king was praying, Isaiah was on his way out of the grounds of the palace, when suddenly a revelation came to the prophet (see 2 Kings 20:4), saying, "Turn again, and tell Hezekiah the captain of my people, Thus saith the Lord, the God of David thy father, I have heard thy prayer, I have seen thy tears: behold, I will heal thee" (2 Kings 20:5).

So, Isaiah returned to Hezekiah's bedside, and informed him that God was going to give the king fifteen additional years of life, and He would also defend Hezekiah and his people from the Assyrians (see 2 Kings 20:6).

Hezekiah asked Isaiah what sign there was that God would heal him, and that he would be able to go up to the temple three days hence. The prophet told him that God would make the shadow of the sun move forward or backward to evidence God's promise to the king. Hezekiah reasoned that making the shadow retreat would be a greater miracle than making the sun go down more quickly, and so he asked that such be the sign. Hearing the king's request, Isaiah prayed that it might be so, and God made the shadow of the setting sun retreat—evidencing that He would indeed keep his promise to Hezekiah to extend his life fifteen more years (see 2 Kings 20:8–11).

Isaiah instructed those of Hezekiah's house to prepare a poultice of figs and apply it to the king's ulcerated sore. They did so, and the king was healed (see 2 Kings 20:7).

BACKGROUND

Hezekiah is believed by some commentators to have been approximately thirty-nine years old at the time he contracted his deathly illness.[1] It has been conjectured that he suffered from the autoimmune disease *pemphigus vulgaris*, a condition that causes blisters and sores on the skin, mucus membranes, in the mouth, and on the genitals.[2] The condition can be fatal—particularly in ancient times, where there was no effective treatment—as the sufferer is subject to infection in the sundry and numerous lesions that it causes.

While a casual reading of the text leaves one with the impression that Hezekiah's desire to have his life extended was entirely about his personal wants and needs, there appears to be something more going on in these verses. *The Expositor's Bible Commentary* explains,

> Hezekiah's concerns were deeper than any personal desire for added years. This is clear from the Lord's answer to Hezekiah's prayer (vv.5–6). What would become of that nation? His reforms were barely yet in progress. What would become of Judah? There was so much more to be done. Deeper still, he would die without a male heir, for no son had yet been born to him. What, then, would become of the house of David? The program and person of God were at stake, and Hezekiah believed that somehow he was vitally involved in them. How could it end like this?[3]

In 2 Kings 20:6, the Lord promises Hezekiah, "I will add unto thy days fifteen years; and *I will deliver thee and this city out of the hand of the king of Assyria.*" Of this last clause, one commentary states,

> The promise of rescue does not make sense in the present context, for both Hezekiah and Jerusalem had been rescued in the preceding chapter. . . . It is probable, therefore, that the story of Hezekiah's illness originally preceded the narrative of Sennacherib's campaign and that it contained a prophecy of personal as well as national salvation. Later the story [was most likely] removed to its present position in chapter 20.[4]

The statement (in the King James Version) that God would make the shadow of the sun "go down ten degrees," or "return backward ten degrees"

(2 Kings 20:9–10) has confused some. The King James Version sounds as though it is referring to the shadow cast on a sundial (see 2 Kings 20:11). While that is possible, there is some question as to whether the sundial had yet to be invented.[5] In addition, ten degrees on a sundial would be such a small amount as to be difficult to actually detect—hardly a miraculous sign. The Hebrew word translated as "degrees" in the King James Version is typically rendered "steps."[6] Edward Young suggested the following:

> It is thought that the device consisted of two sets of steps each facing a wall whose shadow fell upon steps. As the sun arose, the eastern steps would be in the wall's shadow, which, as the day advanced, would grow shorter. On the other hand, during the afternoon, the steps facing west would more and more be in the shadow. . . . Possibly it was mid-day when Isaiah spoke. The shadow had just descended the eastern steps and now was ready to ascend the western steps. Instead, however, the shadow again ascended the eastern steps.[7]

While it doesn't matter whether literal steps or a sundial were used to measure this miracle, the steps (referenced in the Hebrew, and commonly accepted by scholars) make more sense, and would effect a much greater visible miracle.

In the King James Version of this miracle, the Lord says to Hezekiah (through Isaiah), "On the third day thou shalt go up unto the house of the Lord" (2 Kings 20:5). Patterson and Austel explained, "The mention of Hezekiah's going to the temple on the third day is both a recognition of his godly habit of life and a reminder of his obligation to render thanks to the Lord for his healing."[8]

SYMBOLIC ELEMENTS

As noted previously, darkness is often associated with ignorance, death, sin, and the influence of the adversary.[9] Therefore, the withdrawal of darkness—as in this miracle—is a perfect symbol for the retreat of death and the return of life.[10]

The three days leading up to healing (in this miracle) has been taken by some as an intentional symbol. The fact that the king was in a state of decay or corruption, but on the third day would be healed, has been seen by some as a type for Christ—the heavenly King whose body, for three days was in the tomb in a state of corruption, but on the third day, was healed from death and corruption by the Resurrection from the dead.[11]

Allegorizing this passage, one early Christian source explained the symbolism of the figs in this miracle in this way, "The fig [refers] to the

Holy Spirit. . . . And therefore Hezekiah is commanded first to make a plaster with a lump of figs—that is, the fruit of the Spirit—that he may be healed."[12] In support of the doctrine implied by this interpretation, Elder Bruce R. McConkie wrote, "The miracle of healing comes by the power of the Holy Ghost."[13]

APPLICATION AND ALLEGORIZATION

It is worth noting that in this miracle, the prophet was not only the source for spiritual news to be delivered to Hezekiah, but he was also the source for advice on the king's health.[14] Ezra Taft Benson once noted, "The prophet can receive revelation on any matter—temporal or spiritual."[15] Through His living prophets and apostles, the Lord may give us guidance on commandments, finance, health, education, or a host of other subjects. God's prophets are not limited regarding the areas in which they can receive revelation for the Church over which they preside.

Significantly, though the Lord heals Hezekiah, he did so through what would have been considered (in those days) standard medical practice.[16] The point being, God inspires science as well as religion, and many of those trained in medical science have been divinely guided by God to discover treatments and cures to curtail the pain and extend the life of God's children. How many prophets have been able to extend the number of years they were able to serve because of faithful doctors and nurses who—through their training—could fight off aging, defeat disease, and promote wellness? This miracle reminds us that the medical sciences are a gift from God, and we should use them as the inspired resource that they are.

One might also draw from this miracle a doctrinal truth about healing; namely, that "it is God who determines the length of life. Sickness and health are in His hand."[17] We can do all that is in our power to lengthen our lives, but when God determines that our time has come, there is nothing we can do to change that. President Spencer W. Kimball taught, "I am positive in my mind that the Lord has planned our destiny. We can shorten our lives [by living recklessly], but I think we cannot lengthen them very much."[18]

On a related note, some might see in this miracle a statement about the power of personal prayer to change the mind and will of God. Such an interpretation, however, would be erroneous. The LDS Bible Dictionary's entry on "Prayer" offers the following oft-quoted statement about the purpose of prayer. "The object of prayer is *not* to change the will of God but to secure for ourselves and for others blessings that God is already willing to grant but that are made conditional on our asking for them. Blessings require some work or effort on our part before we can obtain them. Prayer is a form of work and is an appointed means for obtaining the highest of all blessings."[19] This being the case, perhaps God intended all the while to heal Hezekiah, if he would but ask.[20]

Robert Trench offers an important application of this miracle, as it relates to sickness and health.

> That bodily health is no indication of God's favor, nor sickness any proof of His displeasure. If we were to make the temporal condition of men a rule by which to judge of their relations to God and His law, we should repeat the mistake of bygone ages which He has Himself sternly rebuked (Job xlii. 7, 9). The king of Judah was one of the best men of his time; he was so great a favorite with God that he could venture to ask favor after favor, yet he is [still] smitten with sickness.[21]

Sometimes we get sick because God is trying to mold and develop us. Sometimes illness is a result of sinful behavior. However, there are also times when bad health is simply a consequence of the mortal condition. We cannot, nor should we, judge someone for their trials. To suggest that we know that there is somehow a cause and effect (as it relates to sin and sickness—or with regard to *any* trial) is to pretend that we have the omniscient mind of God.

NOTES

1. See Edward J. Young, *The Book of Isaiah: A Commentary* (Grand Rapids, MI: Eerdmans, 1992), 2:510. See also Franz Delitzsch, *Biblical Commentary on the Prophecies of Isaiah* (London: Forgotten Books, 2012), 2:112.
2. See Mordechai Cogan and Hayim Tadmor, *The Anchor Bible: II Kings*, vol. 11 (New York: Doubleday, 1988), 255. One source suggested that perhaps the king had contracted the very disease that killed the 185,000 members of the Assyrian army. (See Herbert Lockyer, *All the Miracles of the Bible: The Supernatural in Scripture—Its Scope and Significance* [Grand Rapids, MI: Zondervan, 1961], 128.)
3. Richard D. Patterson and Hermann J. Austel, "1 and 2 Kings," in Frank E. Gaebelein, ed., *The Expositor's Bible Commentary* (Grand Rapids, MI: Zondervan, 1994), 4:272. See also Israel Wolf Slotki, *Kings*, in *Soncino Books of the Bible* (London: The Soncino Press, 1978), 289.
4. Cogan and Tadmor, *The Anchor Bible: II Kings*, 255. See also Israel Wolf Slotki, *Kings*, in *Soncino Books of the Bible*, 288.
5. Young, *The Book of Isaiah: A Commentary*, 2:514.
6. Francis Brown, S. R. Driver, and Charles A. Briggs, *The Brown-Driver-Briggs Hebrew and English Lexicon* (Peabody, MA: Hendrickson Publishers, 1999), 752:

Victor L. Ludlow, *Isaiah: Prophet, Seer, and Poet* (Salt Lake City, UT: Deseret Book, 1982), 331; Israel Wolf Slotki, *Kings*, in *Soncino Books of the Bible*, 290.

7.   Young, *The Book of Isaiah: A Commentary*, 2:515n12. See also Ludlow, *Isaiah: Prophet, Seer, and Poet*, 331; Cogan and Tadmor, *The Anchor Bible: II Kings*, 256.

8.   Patterson and Austel, "1 and 2 Kings," in Gaebelein, *The Expositor's Bible Commentary*, 4:273. See also Donald J. Wiseman, *1 and 2 Kings*, in *Tyndale Old Testament Commentaries* (Downers Grove, IL InterVarsity Press, 1988), 286–87.

9.   See Leland Ryken, James C. Wilhoit, and Tremper Longman III, eds., *Dictionary of Biblical Imagery* (Downers Grove, IL: InterVarsity Press, 1998), 191–93; Walter L. Wilson, *A Dictionary of Bible Types* (Peabody, MA: Hendrickson, 1999), 108–9.

10.   Spiritually speaking, when Satan's darkening influence is chased away, the revelatory light of the gospel is allowed to reign.

11.   See Wiseman, *1 and 2 Kings*, in *Tyndale Old Testament Commentaries*, 286.

12.   Methodius, "Symposium or Banquet of the Ten Virgins," 10.5, in Marco Conti, ed., *1–2 Kings, 1–2 Chronicles, Ezra, Nehemiah, Esther*, in *Ancient Christian Commentary on Scripture* (Downers Grove, IL: InterVarsity Press, 2008), 224.

13.   Bruce R. McConkie, *The Mortal Messiah* (Salt Lake City, UT: Deseret Book, 1979–1981), 3:41n1.

14.   See Patterson and Austel, "1 and 2 Kings," in Gaebelein, *The Expositor's Bible Commentary*, 4:273.

15.   Ezra Taft Benson, *The Teachings of Ezra Taft Benson* (Salt Lake City, UT: Bookcraft, 1988), 136.

16.   See Patterson and Austel, "1 and 2 Kings," in Gaebelein, *The Expositor's Bible Commentary*, 4:273.

17.   Lockyer, *All the Miracles of the Bible*, 129.

18.   Spencer W. Kimball, *Faith Precedes the Miracle* (Salt Lake City, UT: Deseret Book, 1971), 37. President Kimball continued, "Just as Ecclesiastes (3:2) says, I am confident there is a time to die, but I believe also that many people die before 'their time' because they are careless, abuse their bodies, take unnecessary chances, or expose themselves to hazards. . . . I believe we may die prematurely [through unrighteous living], but seldom exceed our time very much. . . . God controls our lives . . . but gives us our agency. We may . . . foolishly shorten or terminate [our lives]." But, if we are living righteously, when our time comes the Lord *will* take us. (Kimball, *Faith Proceeds the Miracle*, 103–5.)

19.   Bible Dictionary, "Prayer," 707.

20.   Edward Young wrote, "By revealing to the king only a part of what was to occur, God causes Hezekiah to turn to Him completely, seeking aid only from Him and so acknowledging that only in Yahweh, the God of David, are deliverance and help to be found." (Young, *The Book of Isaiah: A Commentary*, 2:512.)

21.   Richard C. Trench, *Miracles and Parables of the Old Testament* (Grand Rapids, MI: Baker Book House, 1974), 189.

Shadrach, Meshach, and Abed-nego Survive the Fiery Furnace

Daniel 3

The Miracle

King Nebuchadnezzar commissioned the creation of a ninety-foot-tall idol, and summoned the various provincial officials to come to the dedication of the image—which they did. During the dedication, some Chaldean nobles approached the king, informing him that—though he had issued a decree that all should worship the image or be burned in the fire— Shadrach, Meshach, and Abed-nego had refused to worship the idol (see Daniel 3:1–12).

Upon hearing this news, the king was furious and ordered that Shadrach, Meshach, and Abed-nego be brought before him. When they arrived, he threatened them, saying that he would throw them in the furnace if they did not worship his idol (see Daniel 3:13–15). Rhetorically, he asked, "And who is that God that shall deliver you out of my hands [if you're burning in an oven]?" (Daniel 3:15).

Shadrach, Meshach, and Abed-nego informed the king that they didn't have to defend their choice to not worship an idol. And if the king were to throw them into the furnace, their God would save them; and even if He didn't, they would still not bow to Nebuchadnezzar's false god (see Daniel 3:16–18).

Enraged by their insolence, Nebuchadnezzar had the furnace heated to seven times its normal temperature, and commanded that the three of them be bound and thrown into the flames. The furnace was so hot that

Nebuchadnezzar's men—who tossed Shadrach, Meshach, and Abed-nego in—were killed by the heat (see Daniel 3:19–22).

As the king looked into the furnace, he was shocked, and asked his advisors, "Did not we cast [only] three men bound into the midst of the fire? . . . Lo, I see four men loose, walking in the midst of the fire, and they have no hurt; and the form of the fourth is like the Son of God" (Daniel 3:24–25).

Therefore, the king called out to Shadrach, Meshach, and Abed-nego, and beckoned them to come out of the fire, which they did. None of them were harmed, nor was the hair on their heads singed. Their clothing was not scorched, nor did they smell of smoke (see Daniel 3:26–27).

The king instantly knew that they had been preserved by God and cried out, "Blessed be the God of Shadrach, Meshach, and Abed-nego, who hath sent his angel, and delivered his servants that trusted in him!" (Daniel 3:28). Nebuchadnezzar issued a new decree, stating that any who spoke against the God of Shadrach, Meshach, and Abed-nego would be cut into pieces, and their house would be turned into a pile of rubble. Then the king promoted Shadrach, Meshach, and Abed-nego in the province of Babylon (see Daniel 3:29–30).

BACKGROUND

In Daniel 2:47, King Nebuchadnezzar had declared to Daniel, "Your God is a God of gods, and a Lord of kings." However, his behavior here—forcing all, including the Jews, to worship the patron god of the Chaldean government—might suggest that his confession of Jehovah was more superficial than real.

> He may have felt, like many pagans, that multiple loyalties were permissible in worshiping the gods. He may have seen no more conflict between worshiping several different deities than between serving a local government and the central [or national] government. In any event, he laid down no requirement for his subjects to renounce or to cease private worship of their own personal gods; he simply demanded complete loyalty to the state, as represented by this public ceremony of prostration before his patron god (presumably Nabu). Failure to do this would not only amount to impiety and irreligion, it would also be treason.[1]

In support of the idea that Nebuchadnezzar doesn't ever seem to be *fully* converted to the God of Israel, notice how—when he makes his new decree that no one speak a word against the God of Shadrach, Meshach, and Abed-nego (see Daniel 3:29)—he doesn't order people to worship Jehovah; only that they not speak badly regarding Him. One commentator wrote, "The edict [of Nebuchadnezzar] does no more than declare legal in the empire the religion of the Jews."[2] Just as the king forced the worship of Nabu's image upon his people, one would think (if he was *truly* converted to Jehovah) that he would now force the worship of Him; but he does not.[3]

Nebuchadnezzar's name actually contains the name of the god Nabu (nabu-kudurri-usur), and means literally "O god Nabu, protect my frontier-markers."[4]

Shadrach, Meshach, and Abed-nego are Babylonian names. The Hebrew names of these three faithful souls were Hananiah, Mishael, and Azariah (see Daniel 1:6). Like King Nebuchadnezzar, Abed-nego also has a Babylonian theophoric name, meaning "servant of Nebo" or "Nabu."[5]

The men who brought to the attention of Nebuchadnezzar that Shadrach, Meshach, and Abed-nego had not prostrated themselves before the idol of the state are called, in the King James Version, "Chaldeans" (see Daniel 3:8). Of their identity, one commentary suggested the following:

> This term [Chaldeans] designated originally an Aramaic-speaking people who infiltrated into Babylonia in the first half of the first millennium B.C. and gradually gained ascendancy there. But in Hellenistic times, when itinerant astrologers and fortune-tellers from Babylonia were well-known throughout the Mediterranean world, the term "Chaldean" was often used, not in its original, political sense (as in Dan 5:30; Ezra 5:12), but in the derived sense of "astrologers, fortune-tellers" (as certainly in Dan 2:2–5, 10; 4:4; 5:7, 11, and probably also in 3:8).[6]

It is commonly suggested that the reason these Chaldean fortune-tellers accuse Shadrach, Meshach, and Abed-nego was because they resented the king's promotion of foreigners to political office, and, thus, they sought to get back at the three of them.[7]

It is traditionally understood that the furnace in this episode was the equivalent of a limekiln, which would have a vertical shaft with an opening at the top, and then an opening at the bottom for extracting the fused lime. Thus, Shadrach, Meshach, and Abed-nego were thrown in from the top of the furnace (Daniel 3:20–22), but the king saw them through the opening on the lower part of the kiln (Daniel 3:24–26).[8]

While the narrative does not give the identity of the fourth person in the oven, the Talmud suggests that it was the angel Gabriel.[9] On the other hand, D. Kelly Ogden and Andrew Skinner, among others, have suggested that the fourth person was actually none other than Jehovah.[10] Ellis T. Rasmussen pointed out,

> The phrase "the Son of God" is used to translate the Aramaic *bar 'elahin*, which means, literally, "a son of the gods." Naturally the king had no acquaintance with the Son of God whom we worship, and he would certainly not have been qualified to see Him. . . . The Aramaic word means "a divine being"; later the king called him an "angel" of the God of the Hebrews (Dan. 3:13–28).[11]

It has been suggested that the reason Shadrach, Meshach, and Abed-nego were not harmed in the fire was that God transfigured them. (Cf. Helaman 5:23; 3 Nephi 28:19–22)[12]

In the Septuagint (or Greek version) of this narrative, there is an additional lengthy twenty-two verse section (not found in the Hebrew version) in which Abed-nego (aka Azariah) offers a prayer to the Lord. In that additional portion (present today in the Apocrypha and translations like the Latin Vulgate), we learn that Shadrach, Meshach, and Abed-nego "walked about in the heart of the flames, singing hymns to God and blessing the Lord."[13]

SYMBOLIC ELEMENTS

The number seven appears once again, still carrying its traditional connotation of "full" or "complete." Thus, Nebuchadnezzar's order that the furnace be heated up "'seven times' hotter than ordinarily" has been seen as "an idiomatic way of saying 'as hot as possible.'"[14]

Fire has a number of symbolic meanings, potentially applicable here, including the glory of God, sanctification, judgment, God's eschatological fire, etc.[15]

The cords with which Shadrach, Meshach, and Abed-nego were bound are standard symbols for anything that places us in bondage. Thus, freedom from those bindings symbolizes emancipation, escape, redemption, and the like.[16]

APPLICATION AND ALLEGORIZATION

Shadrach, Meshach, and Abed-nego said to King Nebuchadnezzar,

> If we are thrown into the blazing furnace, the God we serve is able to deliver us from it. . . .
> But even if he does not, . . . we will not serve your gods or worship the image of gold. (NIV Daniel 3:17–18)

Of this, one commentator wrote, "Scripture contains few more heroic words than 'But even if he does not.'"[17] Similarly, John Chrysostom wrote, "It is the greatest punishment to commit sin, though we may remain unpunished; it is the greatest honor and repose to live virtuously, though we may be punished."[18]

Those who sign up as disciples are expected to be faithful, *even if* the odds are not in their favor. A person can hardly be considered a true disciple if they are only faithful when things look like they are going to turn out their way. Shadrach, Meshach, and Abed-nego's example of faith under daunting circumstances is remarkable and inspiring. In some ways, their trial is every person's trial. Robert Anderson explained, "We may assume that the point of this part of the story is that if the faithful Jew is to demonstrate his loyalty to the one true God he must be prepared to see it through step by step with ever increasing risk to his own life. From the initial act of confession . . . there is an ascending scare of temptations, of opportunities to recant."[19] And so it is. The more faithful we are, the more trials and temptations we can expect, as God seeks to develop us. Thus, the prophet Joseph taught, "When the Lord has thoroughly proved him, and finds that the man is determined to serve Him *at all hazards*, then the man will find his calling and his election made sure."[20] Tried and developed we must be! Shadrach, Meshach, and Abed-nego appear to have passed the test.

The narrative speaks of a fourth figure in the fire—a divine being. One commentator suggested, "The point of the story is that the man of faith, who holds fast to what God requires of him, will not be left alone [in his trials]."[21] Similarly, Elder Neal A. Maxwell wrote, "When we have that kind of courage, neither will we walk alone in our own 'fiery furnace,' for, as is recorded in Daniel, there was a fourth Form in that fiery furnace with the valiant threesome, and the Form was 'like the Son of God'! (Daniel 3:25.)"[22]

One commentary on this miracle suggested, "The persecution of the three Jews because of their religious convictions . . . was written to show that martyrdom is to be preferred to apostasy."[23] While this may sound like a bold assertion, commitment to God *is* more important than physical preservation. Why? Well, as Jesus rhetorically asked, "For what shall it profit a man, if he shall gain the whole world, and lose his own soul?" (Mark 8:36). Clinging to the gospel, even over our own lives, is important because the gospel of Jesus Christ *is* the thing which offers us *eternal* life. Though it is unlikely that we will ever have to choose between God and our mortal lives; nevertheless, if we were ever confronted with this devastating dichotomy, may we—in that very hour—remember the choice and the faithfulness of Shadrach, Meshach, and Abed-nego.

Of Nebuchadnezzar's role in this narrative, one commentator wrote, "In the story he is representative of ungodly power, of a human pride that cannot tolerate the exclusive claim of a monotheistic faith. . . . The attraction of polytheism is that it widens every choice; it imposes no limitation."[24] Like Nebuchadnezzar, so much of the world today moves more and more toward relativism. Just as polytheism requires less commitment and imposes no limitations, in a world that argues that everything is relative (e.g., morals, truth, right and wrong, etc.), what possible limitations could there be? However, when we insist on no limitations in earth life, God must then insist on limitations in eternal life; not because He is punitive, but because those who have rejected His invitation to curtail sin and worldliness will not have become like Him—and thus will not be prepared to do what He does and to live as He lives. "Choose ye this day, whom ye will serve" (Alma 30:8). The creature? Or the Creator?

If it was His intent to save them—*which it clearly was*—God could have prevented Shadrach, Meshach, and Abed-nego from being cast into the furnace.[25] However, He chose instead to take them down that fear-filled road in order to fulfill His higher purposes—and in order to develop in them the faith required for all who would become like God. There is a lesson in this for you and me. God will ask us to do hard things. One cannot develop faith in any other way. If the way is always easy and the path is always obvious, what need is there for faith in God and Christ? As in the story of Shadrach, Meshach, and Abed-nego, God will save those who exercise full faith in Him. Yet, we must be given that opportunity to trust and believe when there is reason to doubt and lose faith. As Chrysostom put it, "If they had foreknown" that God would definitely save them, "there would have been nothing wonderful in their doing what they did. For what marvel is it if, when they had a guarantee of safety, they defied all terror?"[26] Again, we must be given that opportunity to trust and believe when there is reason to doubt and lose faith. If we endure *those* experiences in faith, then God will exalt us on high (see D&C 121:8).

It may well be that Shadrach, Meshach, and Abed-nego's endurance of the flames in the oven is a typological foreshadowing of the Second Coming of Christ. Just as they were transfigured, God will transfigure all the righteous at His Second Coming, allowing them to endure the fire of His presence just as Shadrach, Meshach, and Abed-nego endured the fire of the furnace.[27] And just as the wicked servants of Nebuchadnezzar were consumed by the fire (while the righteous were preserved), so also, at Christ's Coming the wicked shall be consumed while the faithful are protected. Elder Orson Hyde taught,

> We are to be operated upon by the Holy Ghost, and undergo such a material change by its power that we can abide the day of burning in which the Son of God will be revealed with the same comfort that Shadrach, Meshach, and Abed-nego did in the fiery furnace. They were cast into that devouring element and moved as pleasantly and as agreeably as the fish moves in the sea, its native element. When that day comes, it will be made [clear] who is pure; for it will bear upon every individual; and those who are not right and pure will be devoured and destroyed. If we are faithful, we can abide that day and feel that we are wrapped in nothing more than in a blaze of glory, because we shall be prepared for it. But if we do not live our religion, we shall be consumed in that day; and it will be a day that no creature can dodge. Hypocrisy and deceit will then be no shield. Pure and unadulterated goodness alone will enable us to stand in that day. We shall then know who possesses the qualifications of Saints, and who does not.[28]

One early Christian source suggested that this miracle reminds us of our need to be obedient to our earthly rulers, but only to the degree that such obedience does not require us to turn our backs on God. There we must draw the line.[29] Richard Trench likewise stated, "There is a limit to the obedience which God requires us to render to the civil magistrate."[30] This is not to suggest that we should act as anarchists; only that "no human authority can be allowed to come in competition with the authority of God."[31] In the millennial day, this truth with be proven when God establishes His theocracy, and all earthly governments are done away with.[32]

It has been suggested that, in this miracle, we have a symbol for the Atonement of Christ. "The salvation of God wrought therein is typified; the Son of God walking in the furnace of God's wrath [caused] by our sins; . . . yet bringing us forth without so much as 'the smell of fire' passing on us."[33] In other words, you and I—through our sinfulness—deserve the fire, but Christ walks with us through the afflictions caused by our sins, and brings us out unscathed, and without a hint of evidence that we have sinned. How marvelous is God's plan! How gracious is Christ's unfailing love!

ALONZO L. GASKILL

NOTES

1. See Andrew E. Hill, "Daniel," in Frank E. Gaebelein, ed., *The Expositor's Bible Commentary*, vol. 8 (Downers Grove, IL: InterVarsity Press, 1988), 7:50. See also Ellis T. Rasmussen, *A Latter-day Saint Commentary on the Old Testament* (Salt Lake City, UT: Deseret Book, 1994), 619. Joyce Baldwin suggested that the statue was "intended to unite his kingdom under one religion." (See Joyce G. Baldwin, "Daniel," in *Tyndale Old Testament Commentaries* [Downers Grove, IL: InterVarsity Press, 1978], 99.)

2. Baldwin, "Daniel," in *Tyndale Old Testament Commentaries*, 106.

3. See Judah J. Slotki, *Daniel, Ezra, Nehemiah*, in *Soncino Books of the Bible* (London: Soncino Press, 1978), 29.

4. See Richard Carlyon, *A Guide to the Gods* (New York: Quill, 1982), 328; Kelly Ogden and Andrew C. Skinner, *Verse By Verse—The Old Testament Volume One: Genesis through 2 Samuel, Psalms* (Salt Lake City, UT: Deseret Book, 2013), 2:403.

5. Abednego's Hebrew name means "Jehovah has helped." The Babylonian name "Shadrach" means "royal" or "great scribe," and his Hebrew name (Hananiah) means "God has favored" or "God has been gracious." The Babylonian name "Meshach" means "guest of the king," and his Hebrew name means "Who is what God is?"

6. Louis F. Hartman and Alexander A. Di Lella, *The Anchor Bible: The Book of Daniel*, vol. 23 (New York: Doubleday, 1978), 129. See also pages 157 & 161; Robert A. Anderson, *Signs and Wonders: A Commentary on the Book of Daniel*, in *International Theological Commentary* (Grand Rapids, MI: Eerdmans, 1984), 31.

7. See, for example, Baldwin, "Daniel," in *Tyndale Old Testament Commentaries*, 103–4; Hill, "Daniel," in Gaebelein, *The Expositor's Bible Commentary*, 7:53.

8. See Judah J. Slotki, *Daniel, Ezra, Nehemiah*, in *Soncino Books of the Bible*, 23; Hartman and Di Lella, *The Anchor Bible: The Book of Daniel*, 161; Hill, "Daniel," in Gaebelein, *The Expositor's Bible Commentary*, 7:56.

9. Judah J. Slotki, *Daniel, Ezra, Nehemiah*, in *Soncino Books of the Bible*, 27.

10. See Ogden and Skinner, *Verse By Verse—The Old Testament Volume One: Genesis through 2 Samuel, Psalms*, 2:404. See also Victor L. Ludlow, *Isaiah: Prophet, Seer, and Poet* (Salt Lake City, UT: Deseret Book, 1982), 350; Neal A. Maxwell, *All These Things Shall Give Thee Experience* (Salt Lake City, UT: Deseret Book, 1979), 48–49; Herbert Lockyer, *All the Miracles of the Bible: The Supernatural in Scripture—Its Scope and Significance* (Grand Rapids, MI: Zondervan, 1961), 137; Irenaeus, "Against Heresies," 4.20.11, in Kenneth Stevenson and Michael Glerup, eds., *Ezekiel, Daniel*, in *Ancient Christian Commentary on Scripture* (Downers Grove, IL: InterVarsity Press, 2008), 182; Hippolytus, "Scholia on Daniel," 3.92 [25], in Stevenson and Glerup, *Ezekiel, Daniel*, in *Ancient Christian Commentary on Scripture*, 182; Richard C. Trench, *Miracles and Parables of the Old Testament* (Grand Rapids, MI: Baker Book House, 1974), 198.

11. Rasmussen, *A Latter-day Saint Commentary on the Old Testament*, 620. See also Ogden and Skinner, *A Latter-day Saint Commentary on the Old Testament*, 2:404.

12. Ogden and Skinner, *A Latter-day Saint Commentary on the Old Testament*, 2:404.

13. See "The Prayer of Azariah" V:1 (or the Septuagint version of Daniel 3:24), in Carey A. Moore, *The Anchor Bible: Daniel, Esther, and Jeremiah—the Additions*, vol. 44 (New York: Doubleday, 1977), 54. For the entire Prayer of Azariah (or Abednego), see Moore, *The Anchor Bible: Daniel, Esther, and Jeremiah—the Additions*, 54–56.

14. Hartman and Di Lella, *The Anchor Bible: The Book of Daniel*, 162.

15. See Leland Ryken, James C. Wilhoit, and Tremper Longman III, eds., *Dictionary of Biblical Imagery* (Downers Grove, IL: InterVarsity Press, 1998), 286–89.

16. See ibid., 112–14.

17. Hill, "Daniel," in Gaebelein, *The Expositor's Bible Commentary*, 7:55. Speaking of Shadrach, Meshach, and Abednego, President Spencer W. Kimball stated, "Integrity! The promises of eternal life from God supersede all promises of men to greatness, comfort, immunities. These men of courage and integrity were saying, 'We do not have to live, but we must be true to ourselves and God.' . . . No virtues in the perfection we strive for are more important than integrity and honesty. Let us then be complete, unbroken, pure, and sincere, to develop in ourselves that quality of soul we prize so highly in others." (Spencer W. Kimball, *Teachings of Presidents of the Church: Spencer W. Kimball* [Salt Lake City, UT: The Church of Jesus Christ of Latter-day Saints, 2006], 133.)

18. John Chrysostom, "Homilies Concerning the Statues," 6.14, in Stevenson and Glerup, "Ezekiel, Daniel," in *Ancient Christian Commentary on Scripture*, 178.

19. Anderson, "Signs and Wonders: A Commentary on the Book of Daniel," in *International Theological Commentary*, 33.

20. Joseph Smith, discourse given 27 June, 1839, in Andrew F. Ehat and Lyndon W. Cook, comps., *The Words of Joseph Smith* (Provo, UT: Religious Studies Center, Brigham Young University, 1980), 5; emphasis added.

21. Anderson, "Signs and Wonders: A Commentary on the Book of Daniel," in *International Theological Commentary*, 37.

22. Maxwell, "All These Things Shall Give Thee Experience," 48–49.

23. Hartman and Di Lella, *The Anchor Bible: The Book of Daniel*, 159–60.

24. Anderson, "Signs and Wonders: A Commentary on the Book of Daniel," in *International Theological Commentary*, 33.

25. See Lockyer, *All the Miracles of the Bible*, 137.

26. John Chrysostom, "Homilies on 1 Corinthians," 28.6, in Stevenson and Glerup, "Ezekiel, Daniel," in *Ancient Christian Commentary on Scripture*, 178.

27. Ogden and Skinner, *A Latter-day Saint Commentary on the Old Testament,* 2:404. Elder Bruce R. McConkie wrote, "So shall it be at the Second Coming when the same literal fire burns over all the earth. The wicked shall be consumed and the righteous shall be as though they walked in the furnace of Nebuchadnezzar." (Bruce R. McConkie, *The Millennial Messiah: The Second Coming of the Son of Man* [Salt Lake City, UT: Deseret Book, 1982], 525.)

28. Orson Hyde, in *Journal of Discourses,* 5:355.

29. Lockyer, *All the Miracles of the Bible,* 137.

30. See Tertullian, "On Idolatry," 15, in Stevenson and Glerup, "Ezekiel, Daniel," in *Ancient Christian Commentary on Scripture,* 178.

31. Trench, *Miracles and Parables of the Old Testament,* 197.

32. Ibid.

33. Elder Bruce R. McConkie wrote of the millennial day, "Both church and state, as the world knows them, will soon cease to be. When the Lord comes again, he will set up anew the political kingdom of God on earth. It will be joined with the ecclesiastical kingdom; church and state will unite; and God will govern in all things. But even then, as we suppose, administrative affairs will be departmentalized, for the law will go forth from Zion (in Jackson County), and the word of the Lord from Jerusalem (in Palestine). But, nonetheless, once again the government of the earth will be theocratic. God will govern. This time he will do it personally as he reigns over all the earth. And all of this presupposes the fall of Babylon, and the death of false religions, and the fall of all earthly governments and nations. And these things, as we are aware, shall surely come to pass." (McConkie, *The Millennial Messiah: The Second Coming of the Son of Man,* 596.)

A HAND MIRACULOUSLY
APPEARS *and* WRITES
on the KING'S WALL

DANIEL 5:1–9

THE MIRACLE

King Belshazzar held a great feast for a thousand nobles. He ordered that the gold and silver goblets that King Nebuchadnezzar had taken from the temple at Jerusalem be brought in so that the king, his wives and concubines, and his nobles could drink from them. As they did, they praised the gods of gold, silver, bronze, iron, wood, and stone (see Daniel 5:1–4).

Suddenly, the fingers of a human hand appeared, and began to write a message on the plastered wall. As the king watched this miracle unfold, his face turned pale and he was so frightened that his knees began to knock and his legs gave way (see Daniel 5:5–6).

The king called for the astrologers and diviners in his kingdom and promised them that whoever could tell him the meaning of the writing would be clothed in purple, have a gold chain placed around their neck, and be made the third-highest ruler in the kingdom (see Daniel 5:7).

The various wise men of the kingdom tried, but none could interpret the meaning of the writing on the wall. Thus, the king became even more distraught, and his face grew paler. His nobles were all baffled (see Daniel 5:8–9).

BACKGROUND

The Aramaic name "Belshazzar" is a corruption of a theophoric Akkadian name, which means "O Bel, protect the king!"[1] Technically speaking,

Belshazzar was never king of Babylon. Rather, he was crown prince, and in the third year of his father's seventeen-year reign, he was appointed co-regent with his father. One commentary points out that "during the many long periods when his father was absent from the capital, Belshazzar was, for all practical purposes, ruler of the Neo-Babylonian empire."[2]

The book of Daniel calls Belshazzar the son of Nebuchadnezzar (see Daniel 5:2). However, he was actually the son of Nabonidus, not Nebuchadnezzar. *The Anchor Bible Dictionary* points out that Nabonidus "ruled as king of Babylon for seventeen years (556–539 BC), and . . . was on the throne when Cyrus took Babylon in 539 BC. Nabonidus, the father of Belshazzar, appears only in the book of Daniel, but was confused with the infamous Babylonian king Nebuchadnezzar."[3] At best, Belshazzar may have been a descendant of Nebuchadnezzar on his mother's side; but Nabonidus was not a descendant of Nebuchadnezzar, and was simply a usurper of his throne.[4]

In explaining the setting and motivations behind Belshazzar's behavior, *The Expositor's Bible Commentary* offers this description:

> Belshazzar the king was presiding over the state banquet for a thousand of his nobles (v. 1). The time had come for offering toasts and pouring out libations to the gods of Babylon. In his drunken bravado he thought of a novel way of entertaining his guests. What about those beautiful golden goblets and bowls from Solomon's temple (v. 2)? Why not use them? After all, they had been fashioned for a defeated god named Yahweh, worshiped by the captive people of Judah. No sooner said than it was done (v. 3). The sacred vessels, laid away for forty-seven years, were brought to the banquet hall. Belshazzar began to regale his guests by taunting Yahweh, whose reputation Nebuchadnezzar's decrees had established a few decades before, and by praising Marduk, Bel, Nebo, Ishtar, and other gods (v. 4). He drank from the holy vessels and his guests followed suit. Once again an arrogant Babylonian monarch defied the Lord God of Israel. . . . The stage was set for the one true God to intervene.[5]

Though we will not be discussing in detail Daniel's interpretation of the handwriting upon the wall, verses 25–28 offer Daniel's interpretation of what the finger wrote:

> And this is the writing that was written, MENE, MENE, TEKEL, UPHARSIN.
>
> This is the interpretation of the thing: MENE; God hath numbered thy kingdom, and finished it.

TEKEL; Thou art weighed in the balances, and art found wanting.

PERES; Thy kingdom is divided, and given to the Medes and Persians.

Belshazzar's fate was sealed, and the end of the Babylonian kingdom assured.

One commentary on this miracle points out that "Sheshbazzar[6] was given custody of the vessels [from Solomon's temple], which according to Ezra 1:10 included 'thirty bowls of gold, two thousand four hundred and ten bowls of silver'. If this were so, then each of Belshazzar's guests, his thousand lords plus his wives and concubines, had no difficulty in acquiring a handsome vessel with which to continue the bacchanalian festival."[7]

The Aramaic word translated as "hand," here carries the connotation of "palm of the hand," and "designates the hand from the wrist to the tips of the fingers." In other words, no part of the body of the being doing the writing was present other than the hand.[8]

It doesn't appear that the characters in which the message was written were of an unknown script. As one commentator pointed out, "Daniel read them off as Aramaic, the *lingua franca* of the capital."[9] Rather, it appears that the four words were recognized, but their meaning was too cryptic for those present to decipher.[10] Literally translated, the phrase on the wall would have potentially been rendered by those trying to interpret it as, "Counted, counted, shekel [to] divide"[11]—or, as one commentary on the Hebrew rendered it, "A maneh, a maneh, a shekel and half shekels."[12] For obvious reasons, the "wise men" of Belshazzar's court were stumped by this stunted sentence.

Belshazzar was offering the interpreter of the cryptic phrase the third-highest position in the government. He could not offer anything else higher than this, as he was viceroy under his father, Nabonidus.[13]

SYMBOLIC ELEMENTS

Belshazzar offers the interpreter of the four-word phrase to "Be clothed with scarlet, and have a chain of gold about his neck" (Daniel 5:7). "The royal purple (really crimson) and the gold torque or collar (of solid metal, rather than in the form of a chain) were symbols of high nobility."[14]

The king sees a divine finger write upon the wall. "A finger can often be an image that brings with it mercy/grace [as in the case of the brother of Jared—Ether 3] or judgment [as in the case of King Belshazzar]."[15] In the Bible, fingers are often associated with the concepts of "power and influence." The phrase "the finger of God" is often used to symbolize the authority of God (see Exodus 31:18), His trademark or signature (see Exodus 8:19), God's work (see Psalm 8:3), or the power of God (see Exodus 8:19).[16] In this miracle, the divine finger represents—at the very least—God revealing the acts He is about to bring to pass. Thus, the *Dictionary of Biblical Imagery* states, "The most customary way God reveals his presence and purpose is through appearances to human beings. We can scarcely think of the OT without remembering a host of such appearance scenes—divine appearances [to men like] . . . Belshazzar in the form of a hand writing a message of judgment on the wall (Dan 5:5–9)."[17]

APPLICATION AND ALLEGORIZATION

One important theme in this narrative is God's displeasure with sacrilege. The king mocks the true and living God and defiles the things of the temple.[18] God's displeasure is depicted in stripping from Belshazzar the kingdom he hoped to one day be king over—just as He will strip from those who do not keep their temple covenants the kingdom they hope to one day be kings or queens over—namely the celestial kingdom.

Elder Jeffrey R. Holland once rhetorically asked, "Can't you buy anything in this world for money?"[19] Belshazzar certainly believed that one could; and thus, acting on the principle that wealth will buy *anything*, he offers his reward of royal fame, golden baubles, and power (see Daniel 5:7). However, contrary to Satan's seductive promises, Belshazzar learns that revelation cannot be bought with money. Divinely sought answers require a divinely ordered life. He would *eventually* get his answer, but it would be to his utter condemnation.

Another prominent theme in this miracle story is the superiority of the wisdom of the servants of Jehovah, when compared to the thinking and "wisdom" of the "wise men" of this fallen world.[20] With the added companionship of the Holy Ghost—and if we live lives in harmony with God's commandments and our covenants—we can expect to have wisdom and direction beyond our own native capabilities. In this story, the approximately eighty-one-year-old[21] Daniel has intellectual (spiritually discerning) gifts far superior to his younger Babylonian counterparts—because righteous Daniel has the added help of God's Spirit.[22]

On a related note, God's hand is often manifest and yet it goes unnoticed. Too often He intervenes in our lives, but out of a spirit of ingratitude or inattentiveness, we don't notice God's day-to-day dealings. In the case of this narrative, the king saw God's hand manifest in his life, but couldn't understand the meaning of it. Whereas ingratitude may cause us to miss God's activity in our lives, sinfulness can make us incapable of understanding the meaning of the divine encounters we have. Living a Spirit-filled life allows us to discern both God's presence, but also His meaning.

NOTES

1. See Louis F. Hartman and Alexander A. Di Lella, *The Anchor Bible: The Book of Daniel*, vol. 23 (New York: Doubleday, 1978), 183; Judah J. Slotki, *Daniel, Ezra, Nehemiah*, in *Soncino Books of the Bible* (London: Soncino Press, 1978), 39.

2. Hartman and Di Lella, *The Anchor Bible: The Book of Daniel*, 186.

3. Ronald H. Sack, "Nabonidus," in David Noel Freedman, ed., *The Anchor Bible Dictionary* (New York: Doubleday, 1992), 4:973. See also Robert A. Anderson, *Signs and Wonders: A Commentary on the Book of Daniel*, in *International Theological Commentary* (Grand Rapids, MI: Eerdmans, 1984), 52–53; Kelly Ogden and Andrew C. Skinner, *Verse By Verse—The Old Testament Volume One: Genesis through 2 Samuel, Psalms* (Salt Lake City, UT: Deseret Book, 2013), 2:405.

4. See Hartman and Di Lella, *The Anchor Bible: The Book of Daniel*, 185–86. See also Ogden and Skinner, *Verse By Verse—The Old Testament Volume One: Genesis through 2 Samuel, Psalms*, 2:405.

5. Andrew E. Hill, "Daniel," in Frank E. Gaebelein, ed., *The Expositor's Bible Commentary*, vol. 8 (Downers Grove, IL: InterVarsity Press, 1988), 7:70.

6. Sheshbazzar is the Babylonian name for Zerubbabel.

7. Anderson, *Signs and Wonders: A Commentary on the Book of Daniel*, in *International Theological Commentary*, 54.

8. Hartman and Di Lella, *The Anchor Bible: The Book of Daniel*, 184. See also Judah J. Slotki, *Daniel, Ezra, Nehemiah*, in *Soncino Books of the Bible*, 40.

9. Hill, "Daniel," in Gaebelein, *The Expositor's Bible Commentary*, 7.71.

10. See Hartman and Di Lella, *The Anchor Bible: The Book of Daniel*, 188; Ellis T. Rasmussen, *A Latter-day Saint Commentary on the Old Testament* (Salt Lake City, UT: Deseret Book, 1994), 621–22; Ogden and Skinner, *Verse By Verse—The Old Testament Volume One: Genesis through 2 Samuel, Psalms*, 2:405.

11. See Hill, "Daniel," in Gaebelein, *The Expositor's Bible Commentary*, 7:73. See also 7:74–75.

12. Judah J. Slotki, *Daniel, Ezra, Nehemiah*, in *Soncino Books of the Bible*, 45. "The names of the three coins or weights . . . each . . . had a double meaning." (Judah J. Slotki, *Daniel, Ezra, Nehemiah*, in *Soncino Books of the Bible*, 45.)

13. See Hill, "Daniel," in Gaebelein, *The Expositor's Bible Commentary*, 7:73.

14. Hartman and Di Lella, *The Anchor Bible: The Book of Daniel*, 184. See also Judah J. Slotki, *Daniel, Ezra, Nehemiah*, in *Soncino Books of the Bible*, 41.

15. Leland Ryken, James C. Wilhoit, and Tremper Longman III, eds., *Dictionary of Biblical Imagery* (Downers Grove, IL: InterVarsity Press, 1998), 286.

16. See ibid.

17. Ibid., 716.

18. See Hartman and Di Lella, *The Anchor Bible: The Book of Daniel*, 186. "Belshazzar . . . had the vessels brought from [Solomon's] temple to his palace, where he not only put them to profane use as mere drinking cups, but also added sacrilege to profanation by 'praising' his pagan gods in a quasi-cultic act as the wine was drunk from the sacred vessels. This sacrilege called for . . . punishment from Yahweh." (Hartman and Di Lella, *The Anchor Bible: The Book of Daniel*, 187.) Slotki similarly pointed out, "It cannot be supposed that the palace was deficient in drinking vessels. His deliberate purpose must have been to display his contempt of Israel's God." (Judah J. Slotki, *Daniel, Ezra, Nehemiah*, in *Soncino Books of the Bible*, 39.)

19. Jeffrey R. Holland and Patricia T. Holland, "The Inconvenient Messiah," *BYU Speeches*, February 27, 1982, speeches.byu.edu/talks/jeffrey-r-and-patricia-t -holland_inconvenient-messiah/.

20. See Hartman and Di Lella, *The Anchor Bible: The Book of Daniel*, 186.

21. See Hill, "Daniel," in Gaebelein, *The Expositor's Bible Commentary*, 7:71; Rasmussen, *A Latter-day Saint Commentary on the Old Testament*, 621.

22. It has been suggested by some that the Holy Ghost was not operative prior to the day of Pentecost (Acts 2). However, the LDS Bible Dictionary pointed out that "the Holy Ghost has been manifest in every dispensation of the gospel since the beginning, being first made known to Adam (1 Ne. 10:17–22; Moses 6:51–68). . . . It is abundantly clear that the Holy Ghost was operative in earlier dispensations." (See Bible Dictionary, "Holy Ghost," 660–61)

DANIEL IS PRESERVED
in the LIONS' DEN

DANIEL 6:1-24

THE MIRACLE

Darius, king of Babylon, positioned 120 local leaders to rule throughout his kingdom—and over them he placed three administrators, one of which was Daniel. To these three all of the local leaders were accountable (see Daniel 6:1).

Daniel so distinguished himself that the king sought to place him over the whole kingdom. However, this angered the local leaders and the other two national administrators. They were so angry at Daniel's pending promotion that they tried to find grounds for charges against him for his conduct in government affairs. Because of Daniel's trustworthiness, they were unable to do so. Consequently, they sought to find fault with him regarding his religion (see Daniel 6:2–5).

The 122 local and national leaders went as a group to King Darius, and, having praised him, said that he should issue an edict that anyone who prays (during the next thirty days) to any god or man—other than the king—will be thrown into the lions' den. They urged the king to put the decree in writing, so that, in accordance with the laws of the Medes and Persians, it could not be repealed. Heeding their advice, the king did so (see Daniel 6:6–9).

When Daniel learned of the decree, he did not change his prayer habits. Three times each day, he went into the upper room of his home—where the windows opened toward Jerusalem—and he prayed on his knees to the God of Israel, giving Him thanks. The 122 leaders then spied on Daniel; and, finding him praying, they went as a group to the king and told him that Daniel was praying to the God of Israel. Then they pushed the king, reminding him that such was against the law, and pointed out to him that his decree was not retractable (see Daniel 6:10–13).

Loving Daniel as he did, the king was overwhelmed by the news. He sought to do all that he could to save his friend; however, the various leaders would not allow Darius to negate his own law, and so the king gave the order that Daniel be thrown into the lions' den (see Daniel 6:14–16). Before the den was sealed, the king said to Daniel, "Thy God whom thou servest continually, he will deliver thee" (see Daniel 6:16). Then the stone was place over the mouth of the den, and the king sealed it with his signet—as did the other nobles—to ensure that no one allowed Daniel to escape (see Daniel 6:17).

The king returned to his palace, and spent a sleepless night, not eating or drinking, nor being entertained; but worrying continually about Daniel. At the first light of dawn, the king hurried to the lions' den and called out to Daniel in an anguished voice, "O Daniel, servant of the living God, [was] thy God, whom thou servest continually, able to deliver thee from the lions?" (Daniel 6:20). Daniel shouted back, "O king, live forever. My God hath sent his angel, and hath shut the lions' mouths, that they have not hurt me" (Daniel 6:21–22). Daniel indicated to the king that the God of Israel had found him innocent, and, therefore, protected him through the night. Daniel also proclaimed his faithfulness toward the king, in spite of the things the other leaders had claimed (see Daniel 6:18–22).

The king was overwhelmed with joy, and ordered that Daniel be lifted out of the den. Upon inspection, it was evident that Daniel—because of his trust in God—had not a wound upon him (see Daniel 6:23).

Darius then commanded that the men who had falsely accused Daniel be thrown into the lions' den, along with their wives and children: "And the lions had the mastery of them, and brake all their bones in pieces" (Daniel 6:24).

BACKGROUND

One source calculates that Daniel would have been about eighty-three years of age at the time of this miracle.[1]

Elsewhere we are told that "Darius the Mede [is] none other than Cyrus the Persian, using what may well have been his enthronement name."[2] Though the theory is definitely not widely embraced, if it is true, it would explain Darius's love for Daniel and his trust in the God of Israel who had mentioned Cyrus by name years before the monarch's birth (see Isaiah 44:28–45:1)

Though neither a Mede nor a Persian, Daniel's long experience with Babylonian government made him an obvious choice as one of the three "commissioners" or "presidents" to preside (under the king) over the 120 "princes" or "satraps."[3] "But after he had assumed office and turned in a record of exceptional performance, it became obvious that he had superhuman knowledge and skill; and he became a likely choice for prime minister."[4]

Daniel is described as "[going] into his house; and his windows being open in his chamber toward Jerusalem, he kneeled upon his knees three times a day, and prayed, and gave thanks before his God" (Daniel 6:10). Of this, one commentary suggests,

> The Jewish custom of facing, while at prayer, toward the Temple of Jerusalem or its ruined site began during the Babylonian exile (cf. I Kings 8:44, 48 . . .) and continued thereafter throughout the Diaspora (cf. 1 Ezd 4:58). The first Muslims, following Jewish custom, faced Jerusalem in prayer; but the direction (*qiblah*) was soon changed toward the Kaaba in Mecca. When a Jew prayed in a room, he did so at an open window (cf. Tobit 3:11) facing Jerusalem. Daniel prayed three times a day, at dawn, at midday, and toward evening—a custom already referred to in Ps 60:18 and later prescribed in the Talmud.[5]

The king knew that Daniel was a Jew; and, thus, one wonders why Darius would have passed a law that would potentially harm one whom he was so fond of. One commentator explained,

> As an official delegation, they presented their proposal, falsely implying that Daniel had concurred in their legislation. "The royal administrators [of whom Daniel was chief], prefects, satraps, advisers and governors have all agreed" (v. 7)—i.e., in drawing up the decree. Darius should have noticed that Daniel was not there to speak for himself. Yet Darius had no reason to suspect that the other two royal administrators would misrepresent Daniel's position in this matter, and certainly the reported unanimity of all the lower echelons of government must have stilled any doubts Darius had about the decree. The suggested mode of compelling every subject in the former Babylonian domain to acknowledge the authority of Persia seemed a statesmanlike measure that would contribute to the unification of the Middle and Near East. The time limit of one month [also] seemed reasonable.[6]

The statement that Darius "laboured till the going down of the sun to deliver" (Daniel 6:14) has been interpreted to mean that the king "thought of ways of protecting him from the lions, perhaps by overfeeding them or by covering Daniel with armor."[7] Elsewhere we read, "Behind the informative note in v. 14 . . . we are invited to imagine the fevered activity of the court lawyers looking for that never-to-be-found loophole."[8] In other words, the king did what he could to come up with an ingenious plan to save his dear friend, though to no avail.

The placement of the seal of the king and the lords upon the rock covering the mouth of the pit, in which Daniel had been thrown, was to ensure that neither party—independent of the other—had the ability to surreptitiously intervene in the terrible process that was about to take place.[9] The king would have reason to rescue Daniel, and the lords would have reason to hasten his death.[10] With the double seal, the next morning, each could attest that no mortal had played a role in the events of the night.

SYMBOLIC ELEMENTS

One scholar offered the following assessment of the overarching symbolism in this passage. "In the present story, Daniel is really a figure of the Jewish people; and the pagan king, therefore, is a symbol of paganism."[11] Another text suggested that Daniel is an ideal type for Christ—as are all prophets.[12] As a typological symbol for the Savior, there are a number of parallels between Daniel's experience and Jesus's. Here are a few commonly noted ones.

DANIEL	CHRIST
He was a child of no blemish (Daniel 1:4).	Jesus was the "lamb without blemish" (1 Peter 1:19).
He had more wisdom than all the wise at a young age (Daniel 1:20).	"And all that heard [Jesus] were astonished at his understanding and answers" (Luke 2:47).
He was preferred above all because an excellent spirit was in him (Daniel 6:3).	"And the Lord said unto me: These two facts do exist, that there are two spirits, one being more intelligent than the other; there shall be another more intelligent than they; I am the Lord thy God, I am more intelligent than they all" (Abraham 3:19).

DANIEL	CHRIST
No error or fault was found in him (Daniel 6:4).	Jesus "did no sin, neither was guile found in his mouth" (1 Peter 2:22).
Those jealous of his power sought occasion under the law against him, but could find none (Daniel 6:4).	Those jealous of Jesus's power sought occasion under the law to convict him, but could find no legitimate crime (John 18:28–38; Matthew 27:18).
Leaders sought to entrap him (Daniel 6:5–9).	"Then went the Pharisees, and took counsel how they might entangle him in his talk" (Matthew 22:15).
He continued in righteousness, notwithstanding the threat (Daniel 6:10–11).	Because of unfailing obedience and faithfulness, the scriptures refer to the Savior as "Jesus Christ the righteous" (1 John 2:1).
He was condemned to death (Daniel 6:12–13).	"And they were instant with loud voices, requiring that he might be crucified. . . . And Pilate gave sentence that it should be as they required. And he . . . delivered Jesus to their will" (Luke 23:23–25).
The ruler sought to have him released (Daniel 6:14).	"And from thenceforth Pilate sought to release him" (John 19:12).
The people would not allow his release (Daniel 6:15).	"The Jews cried out, saying, If thou let this man go, thou art not Caesar's friend: whosoever maketh himself a king speaketh against Caesar" (John 19:12).
The den of death was sealed with a stone (Daniel 6:17).	"And [Joseph of Arimathea] rolled a great stone to the door of the sepulchre" (Matthew 27:60).

DANIEL	CHRIST
Rising early in the morning, believer(s) came to the place to see him (Daniel 6:19).	"The first day of the week cometh Mary Magdalene early, when it was yet dark, unto the sepulchre" (John 20:1).
Those who believed in him assumed he was dead (Daniel 6:20).	After Jesus's death, and not understanding that Jesus would rise from the dead, His disciples when back to their former trades (John 21).
Being delivered from death, his message to those who sought him is "live for ever" (Daniel 6:21).	Jesus taught His disciples that by partaking of the symbols of His death they could "live for ever" (John 6:51).
He was delivered from death because "before [God] innocency was found in [him]" (Daniel 6:22).	"For the Messiah also suffered for sins once for all, an innocent person for the guilty, so that he could bring you to God" (ISV 1 Peter 3:18).
He came forth in perfect condition (Daniel 6:23).	"And they shall see me in the clouds of heaven, clothed with power and great glory" (D&C 45:44).
Those who fight against him shall die (Daniel 6:24).	"Behold, all they that were incensed against thee shall be ashamed and confounded: they shall be as nothing; and they that strive with thee shall perish" (Isaiah 41:11).
As a result of his miraculous deliverance, the gospel of the Lord's deliverance was published throughout all the earth (Daniel 6:25–27).	"Go ye into all the world, and preach the gospel to every creature" (Mark 16:15).

For ancient Israelites, lions were vicious, almost unstoppable killers who would take from their flocks at will. Lions, in the Hebrew Bible, evoke images of "ferocity, destructive power, and irresistible strength." The symbolic "mouth of the lion is a predicament from which escape seems hopeless (Dan 6:22; 2 Tim 4:17; cf. Ps 22:21; Heb 11:33)."[13] This standard symbolic meaning seems to apply well to the setting and situation described in this miracle.

Pits are common symbols for "prison"—the metaphor being drawn from actual use, where a dry cistern often functioned as a jail (see Zechariah 9:11). They also symbolize an "inescapable predicament" and the "grave"—death being inescapable.[14] Daniel's incarceration in the pit-like den of the lions seems to capture each of these images; he is imprisoned, it seems inescapable, and death seems certain.

APPLICATION AND ALLEGORIZATION

Daniel's choice to continue to pray to the God of Israel, rather than holding off for a month (as commanded), was not an act of belligerence toward the king or the laws of the land.[15] Certainly, his regular prayers to God had "safeguarded" him from the "corrupting influences of Babylonian culture."[16] However, he may also have felt that to hold off for a month was to offend the very Being who had placed him in—and sustained him in—his position of power in the government. Dare he try to succeed in his government post alone? "Daniel could not compromise. For him the issue was whether he was going to please man or obey God. Daniel had to choose between loyalty to his Lord and obedience to a sinful government commanding him to perform idolatry. So he was willing to risk his life for the Lord, trusting him for deliverance even as Shadrach, Meshach, and Abednego had been delivered years before."[17] As a modern example of this same approach to faith, leadership, and the risks posed, consider the experience of President Ronald Reagan. As governor of California, Reagan had a spiritual experience in which he believed he was told by God that he would become President of the United States.[18] Consequently, Reagan felt like his election was a calling from God; and, thus, he felt he had a duty to testify of God in his position. For example, after securing his party's nomination on July 17, 1980, Reagan said to those gathered in the convention center, "I'll confess that I've been a little afraid to suggest what I'm going to suggest—*I'm more afraid not to*: that we begin our crusade joined together in a moment of silent prayer."[19] Reagan lamented, "Not enough of us use our talents and our positions in testimony of God's goodness." He added, "My own prayer is that I can . . . perform the duties of this position so as to serve God."[20] Because he believed that he had been called to the presidency by God, Reagan frequently and openly spoke of God when he gave speeches. One source noted that "The Presidential Handwriting File at the

Reagan Library . . . is filled with examples of religious phrases and verses handwritten into speechwriters' texts by Reagan."[21] When he would review drafts of speeches that his speechwriters had composed, the president was known to heavily edit them—inserting statements about God and Christ.[22] Reagan was frequently and aggressively criticized for his openness about his belief in God. For example, one Soviet news analyst condescendingly noted, "Whenever Mr. Reagan delivers a speech, he always mentions his religious feelings."[23] The *New York Times* and the *Washington Post* were particularly critical of the president's tendency to use "religious statements [in] his public discourse."[24] For instance, the *Times* said that the "only appropriate venue for [the types of remarks that Reagan regularly made was] in church." "You don't have to be a secular humanist to take offense at [the] display of what, in America, should be *private* piety. It is an offense to Americans . . . when a President speaks that way."[25] Similarly, on February 13, 1984, a reporter from *Knight Ridder* (the second-largest newspaper publisher at the time) took Reagan to task for his outspoken Christianity, and his "divisive" preaching of "the Gospel of Christ" from the Oval Office. To this, Reagan responded that he felt, "There is a responsibility in this position . . . to do those things."[26] Reagan wore the criticisms by the press as "a badge of honor."[27] There is a lesson to be learned from men like Daniel and Reagan; both knew that God had blessed them and positioned them, and both felt a duty to live faithful to the God who had—that they might receive the divine support they knew they needed. Both faced serious risks for their choices; Daniel thrown into the lions' den, and Reagan into the den of media lions. Both felt that God blessed and sustained them for their efforts to stand up for their God—and for openly living their faith. Are we as committed to Christ? Do we live our religion openly and faithfully? Are we missing the blessings that God has in store for us—*or our families*—because we are ashamed of the gospel of Jesus Christ? (see Romans 1:16).

We read that "Daniel was taken up out of the den, and no manner of hurt was found upon him, because he believed in his God" (Daniel 6:23). By way of application, it is worth noting that we have no promise that we will *always* be spared from the hurt our enemies seek to bring upon us. However, *in the end*, we—like Daniel—shall be elevated out of the hands of our enemies, without mar or scar. Similarly, like Daniel's enemies, those who fight against God and His anointed servants shall ultimately be destroyed. Thus, there may be difficult days when we face the lions. However, the end result of the faithful will ever be the same; they shall be raised up and all earthly scars—whether they be physical, emotional, or spiritual—will be removed. What a glorious promise!

One commentator on this story offers an interesting insight regarding the prayers of the pagan king, Darius, on behalf of Daniel—a member of the household of faith. "It is this prayer above all that makes this chapter different from all that has gone before, because an 'outsider,' a king of the nations, is exercising faith, however dimly, in Daniel's God, and it is in the interests of fostering that faith that evidence of God's power can be expected."[28] It may be the case that some within the Church may question the efficacy of the prayers of those not of our tradition. Such would be wrongheaded. (Nevertheless, I have run into such a view on occasion.) This miracle extolls the prayer of the "nonmember"—the nonbeliever. It paints them as instrumental to the accomplishment of God's work and will. I'm reminded of the experience of a colleague of mine, who had been hospitalized with a life-threatening illness. A dear friend of his—a Protestant pastor—visited the hospital, and, as they sat together, asked his LDS friend if he could pray over him. The Mormon graciously accepted this great act of faith by his non-LDS friend. And, in the end, my colleague recovered. The point is that God hears and answers the prayers of all who are sincere—regardless of what their religious tradition is. And, in our hours of need, we would do well to enlist the aid (in fasting and prayer) of our non-LDS, as well as our LDS, friends. God heard Darius, and He will surely hear the prayers and petitions of each of His faith-filled children, regardless of their denomination.

While there are a number of applications that can be drawn from this miracle, an important one is embracing the present circumstances while awaiting God's promises for the future. For this story reminds us:

> Hope does not reside in any human, however powerful, but in God alone. The story of Daniel offers hope, not a remedy. The reader is asked to grasp hold of that hope not as the sure and certain means of deliverance but as an attitude to life. Any finely constructed doctrine would have foundered on the rock of present experience. Only the belief in resurrection ([Daniel] 12:2–3) could give the imprecision of life a more satisfying reply.[29]

In other words, this story leaves us—and each of the participants in the narrative—wondering, how will this turn out? There are no guarantees. Daniel is fortunate, and things seem to work to his advantage; but often that's not the case. And, in the story at hand, no promise was made of redemption. Thus, the king had reason to doubt, and Daniel had reason to doubt.

During the mortal experience, God will save whom He will save. While we can't be very certain about the here and now, we can trust in His promises regarding eternity.

I like John Chrysostom's simple assessment of the meaning of the story, "When things are turning out adversely, then we ought to believe nothing adverse is done but all things in due order."[30] While during our trials, our natural tendency may be to panic, we would do wise to embrace Chrysostom's philosophy and trust that God is in charge and what *should* happen *will* happen—provided we are faithful.

The other two presidents, and many of the princes, were jealous of Daniel's gifts and how the king acknowledged them.

> The penalty of greatness is the envy of inferiors. Those who have good eyesight do not feel pain when the light of the sun shines upon them. But the man whose vision is weak feels distressed when the rays of the "ruler of the day" fall upon him. The pain tells him that he had diseased eyes. But God cannot remove the sun from the heavens on that account. Daniel was the sun in the Persian kingdom, showing to all who came under his influence what a good ruler really was. But the intense light of his character was too strong for men whose conduct he thus condemned and who were thus made painfully conscious of their own shortcomings. "Who is able to stand before envy?" (Prov. xxvii. 4).[31]

Daniel fell prey to what all great leaders do: the envy and wrath of lesser men. During the Spanish Inquisition, it was the practice—before taking one to the stake to be martyred—to clothe him in garments covered with painted devils in order to shame them in the eyes of their fellow citizens. And so the envious often do to their victims; just as the princes and presidents clothed Daniel in the garments of a rebel in order to bring shame upon him before the king. The envious often know no bounds—going to any length to destroy those that they are envious of. Such encounters are inevitably painful and, in the midst of them, one can only do as Daniel did—place all trust in God to see you through.

The fact that Daniel, serving as the equivalent of a prime minister, would take time out of his busy schedule to pray is, itself, a lesson. "Nobody is in greater haste than the driver of an express train, yet he never grudges the time consumed in oiling the wheels of his engine."[32] Regardless of our job, calling, or assignment, we should take time out of each day to keep ourselves spiritually healthy. None of us is gifted enough to do our divine calling—whether that be ecclesiastical leader, employee, spouse, or parent—without the help of God.

NOTES

1.   See Andrew E. Hill, "Daniel," in Frank E. Gaebelein, ed., *The Expositor's Bible Commentary*, vol. 8 (Downers Grove, IL: InterVarsity Press, 1988), 7:81. See also Kelly Ogden and Andrew C. Skinner, *Verse By Verse—The Old Testament Volume One: Genesis through 2 Samuel, Psalms* (Salt Lake City, UT: Deseret Book, 2013), 2:407.

2.   See Joyce G. Baldwin, "Daniel," in *Tyndale Old Testament Commentaries* (Downers Grove, IL: InterVarsity Press, 1978), 127.

3.   One source suggested, "One of the main functions of the satraps and their subordinate governors was to see 'that the king would not suffer any loss' (6:3) in the taxes collected throughout the empire." (Louis F. Hartman and Alexander A. Di Lella, *The Anchor Bible: The Book of Daniel*, vol. 23 [New York: Doubleday, 1978], 198. See also Baldwin, "Daniel," in *Tyndale Old Testament Commentaries*, 128; Judah J. Slotki, *Daniel, Ezra, Nehemiah*, in *Soncino Books of the Bible*, 47.)

4.   Andrew E. Hill, "Daniel," in Frank E. Gaebelein, ed., *The Expositor's Bible Commentary*, vol. 8 (Downers Grove, IL: InterVarsity Press, 1988), 7:78.

5.   Hartman and Di Lella, *The Anchor Bible: The Book of Daniel*, 199. See also Baldwin, "Daniel," in *Tyndale Old Testament Commentaries*, 129; Judah J. Slotki, *Daniel, Ezra, Nehemiah*, in *Soncino Books of the Bible*, 49; Robert A. Anderson, *Signs and Wonders: A Commentary on the Book of Daniel*, in *International Theological Commentary* (Grand Rapids, MI: Eerdmans, 1984), 69. Daniel's triple prayer may have implications for Latter-day Saint temple worship. (See Alonzo L. Gaskill, *Sacred Symbols: Finding Meaning in Rites, Rituals, and Ordinances* [Springville, UT: Bonneville Books, 2011], 231–32. See also pages 215–55.)

6.   See Hill, "Daniel," in Gaebelein, *The Expositor's Bible Commentary*, 7:79.

7.   Ibid., 7:81.

8.   Anderson, *Signs and Wonders: A Commentary on the Book of Daniel*, in *International Theological Commentary*, 70.

9.   Baldwin, "Daniel," in *Tyndale Old Testament Commentaries*, 130; Judah J. Slotki, *Daniel, Ezra, Nehemiah*, in *Soncino Books of the Bible*, 51–52; Anderson, *Signs and Wonders: A Commentary on the Book of Daniel*, in *International Theological Commentary*, 70.

10. See Ephrem the Syrian, "Commentary on Daniel," 6.17, in Kenneth Stevenson and Michael Glerup, eds., *Ezekiel, Daniel*, in *Ancient Christian Commentary on Scripture* (Downers Grove, IL: InterVarsity Press, 2008), 216.

11. Hartman and Di Lella, *The Anchor Bible: The Book of Daniel*, 198.

12. See Aphrahat, "Demonstrations," 21.18, in in Stevenson and Glerup, *Ezekiel, Daniel*, in *Ancient Christian Commentary on Scripture*, 218–19. See also James L. Ferrell, *The Hidden Christ: Beneath the Surface of the Old Testament* (Salt Lake City, UT: Deseret Book, 2009), 257–58.

13. Leland Ryken, James C. Wilhoit, and Tremper Longman III, eds., *Dictionary of Biblical Imagery* (Downers Grove, IL: InterVarsity Press, 1998), 514. See also J. C. Cooper, *An Illustrated Encyclopaedia of Traditional Symbols* (London: Thames and Hudson, 1995), 99; Jack Tresidder, *Symbols and Their Meanings: The Illustrated Guide to More than 1,000 Symbols—Their Traditional and Contemporary Significance* (London: Duncan Baird Publishers, 2006), 58.

14. See Ryken, Wilhoit, and Longman, *Dictionary of Biblical Imagery*, 646. See also Kevin J. Todeschi, *The Encyclopedia of Symbols* (New York: Perigee Book, 1995), 202; Walter L. Wilson, *A Dictionary of Bible Types* (Peabody, MA: Hendrickson, 1999), 318.

15. See Judah J. Slotki, *Daniel, Ezra, Nehemiah*, in *Soncino Books of the Bible*, 50.

16. Hill, "Daniel," in Gaebelein, *The Expositor's Bible Commentary*, 7:79.

17. Ibid., 7:80.

18. Being elected as governor of California "confirmed for him a . . . long-held feeling that God had chosen to play a guiding role in his life." (See Paul Kengor, *God and Ronald Reagan: A Spiritual Life* [New York: ReganBooks, 2004], 129.) One of Reagan's biographers wrote, "During his time in Sacramento . . . Reagan began to ruminate openly on the presence of God's hand in his political path." Reagan said, "I've always believed there is a certain divine scheme of things. I'm not quite able to explain how my election [as governor] happened or why I'm here, apart from believing it is part of God's plan for me." Those who knew him believed that "Reagan saw himself as . . . 'His [God's] instrument.'" (Kengor, *God and Ronald Reagan: A Spiritual Life*, 130–31.) A prophetic spiritual experience "occurred at the home of Governor Reagan and his wife in Sacramento on a Sunday afternoon in October 1970." In a prayer, Reverend George Otis—speaking for the Lord—said, "If you walk uprightly before Me, you will reside at 1600 Pennsylvania Avenue." (Kengor, *God and Ronald Reagan: A Spiritual Life*, 135–36.) Paul Kengor wrote, "Readers can make of this what they will. But the Reagans and the participants [in the prayer] clearly felt that they had shared some kind of spiritual communication that day, one that spoke to a higher calling for Reagan—this time a very specific one." (Kengor, *God and Ronald Reagan: A Spiritual Life*, 137.)

19. Kengor, *God and Ronald Reagan: A Spiritual Life*, 154; emphasis added.

20. Ibid., 165.

21. Ibid.

22. See ibid., 168. See also page 371n49.

23. Ibid., 164.

24. Ibid., 166.

25. Ibid., 169–70; emphasis added.

26. Ibid., 167.

27. Ibid., 170.

28. Baldwin, "Daniel," in *Tyndale Old Testament Commentaries*, 130.

29. Anderson, *Signs and Wonders: A Commentary on the Book of Daniel*, in *International Theological Commentary*, 72.

30. John Chrysostom, "On the Epistle to the Hebrews," Homily 27.4, in Stevenson and Glerup, *Ezekiel, Daniel*, in *Ancient Christian Commentary on Scripture*, 218.

31. Richard C. Trench, *Miracles and Parables of the Old Testament* (Grand Rapids, MI: Baker Book House, 1974), 199–200.

32. Ibid., 202.

JONAH in the BELLY
of a WHALE

JONAH 1–2

THE MIRACLE

God commanded Jonah to go to Nineveh and call the people to repentance. However, Jonah disobeyed God, and, instead, went to Joppa, where he boarded a ship bound for Tarshish (see Jonah 1:2–3).

While Jonah was below deck sleeping, a massive storm arose and threatened to sink the ship. Those on board tossed overboard cargo—hoping that that would help the ship stay afloat. All prayed to their own god for intervention. When the captain found Jonah asleep, he woke him and said, "How can you sleep thorough this storm? Get up and pray to your God, that He might intervene and spare us" (see Jonah 1:4–6)

The sailors on the ship cast lots to determine who had caused their calamity, and the lot fell on Jonah. And so they asked him, "Who is responsible for this? What is your occupation? Where have you come from?" Jonah informed them that he was a Hebrew who worshipped the god of heaven who made the sea. At this, the sailors became very afraid (see Jonah 1:7–10). Knowing that he had fled from the Lord, they asked him, "Why hast thou done this?" (Jonah 1:10).

The storm got worse and the sea became rougher. The sailors asked Jonah, "What should we do to calm the sea?" He told them the storm was his fault, and that they should throw him into the sea. The men refused, and instead tried desperately to row back to shore, but they could not. Determining that they needed to throw Jonah overboard, they prayed to God, saying, "Lord, please don't hold us accountable for taking this man's life." Then they took Jonah and threw him overboard, and the sea became calm. At this, the men feared God, and offered a sacrifice to him, vowing their allegiance (see Jonah 1:11–16).

God sent a great fish to swallow Jonah, and he was in its belly for three days and three nights (see Jonah 1:17). And Jonah prayed, asking God for forgiveness and pledging faithfulness. At this, the Lord commanded the fish, and it vomited Jonah onto dry land (see Jonah 2:1–10).

BACKGROUND

Ogden and Skinner wrote, "Jonah, whose Hebrew name means 'dove,' was a prophet from Gath-hepher, a small village west of the Sea of Galilee. . . . He probably lived around 800 to 790 BC."[1] It has been suggested that his surname, "Amittai," means something like, "Yahweh is steadfast."[2]

For those who doubt the historicity of Jonah and the events told in the biblical book about him, it is worth remembering that Jesus cited the story of Jonah, at least three times, as evidence that He believed in the prophet and his mission—including Jonah's mission to typify Christ (see Matthew 12:39–41; 16:4; Luke 11:29–30).[3]

One commentator stated, "Tarshish was, in Jonah's day, . . . the western-most point of the known world, and the farthest place from Nineveh . . . that Jonah could find."[4] Jonah's hesitancy to go to Nineveh when commanded to do so may be explained by the fact that the Assyrians were infamous for their barbaric treatment of their captured enemies. They were known to decapitate and mutilate—cutting off noses and ears, and ripping out the tongues of their prisoners. Some actually had their skin peeled off while still alive, and the impaling of prisoners was no uncommon act.[5] Thus, Jonah may have had legitimate reasons for running when God asked him to preach repentance in Nineveh—something that was sure to upset the Assyrians.

As fanciful as the story of Jonah seems to many, on August 21, 1961, the *Ipswich Evening Star* ran an article with the headline, "Man Was Swallowed By Whale—Emerged Alive." The article recounted an event that took place in February of 1891, off the Falkland Islands. An English whaling ship called the *Star of the East* lost two men at sea—one of which was seaman James Bartley. After a short time, young Bartley was given up for dead. Hours later, the whale they had been pursuing was successfully harpooned and its great carcass was hauled to the side of the ship to be dismembered, and its blubber rendered down into oil. The seamen worked into the night, but did not finish their disgusting chore. The next day, when they resumed their work, the sailors noticed what looked like movement in the deceased whale's stomach. They slit it open and found James Bartley inside, doubled up, drenched and unconscious—but alive. For two weeks, he was largely incoherent, but gradually gained back his senses. The stomach acid of the whale took its toll on his skin but, ultimately, he fully recovered. When he described the encounter some weeks later, Bartley spoke of the sensation of sliding down along a smooth passage that was covered with a thick, slimy coating. He noted that though he could breathe, the heat was almost unbearable. Soon he passed out and remembered no more until he awoke in the captain's cabin.[6] Now Bartley was not three days and three nights in the belly of the whale—but he did survive the better part of twenty-four hours. And his personal story suggests that the tale of Jonah is not outside of the realm of possibility.

It is worth noting that, while we typically imagine that Jonah was swallowed by a large whale, "no species is named [in the Hebrew]—there is no whale in the book of Jonah!"[7] Like the King James Version, the Hebrew text simply says he was swallowed by a "great fish" (Jonah 1:17).[8] The Septuagint—or Greek version of the Old Testament—however, specifically uses the word "whale" in reference to the fish that swallowed the prophet; as does Jesus when He references the story (see Matthew 12:40).

The name "Nineveh" means the "abode of Ninus"—Ninus being the person who Greek historians claim founded Nineveh. The city of Nineveh is mentioned in the early postdiluvium days (see Genesis 10:11), though it was not always the capital city of Assyria. Indeed, it would not become its capital until the last few decades of the Assyrian empire. Nevertheless, Nineveh has always been one of Assyria's principle cities.[9] It was located on the east bank of the Tigris River, about 250 miles north of Babylon—near the modern Iraqi town of Mosul.[10]

SYMBOLIC ELEMENTS

Ogden and Skinner pointed out, "In the story of Jonah, the adverbs 'down' and 'up' are [symbolically] significant. Jonah went down to Joppa, down into a ship, down into the sea, down into a great fish. Then he went up out of the fish, up onto the beach, and up to Nineveh."[11] His physical descent has been seen as a symbol of his spiritual decline—and "is obviously intended as contrast to the spiritual ascent of the pagans (sailors/Ninevites) who, from initial ignorance, are coming closer and closer to Yahweh."[12]

Jonah is a well-known type for Christ.[13] That being said, in many ways, he is a poor symbol of the Savior. Jonah disobeys God's commandment, whereas Jesus never did. Jonah runs from God, whereas Jesus always walks with God. Jonah hopes for the destruction of the Ninevites, whereas Jesus ever hopes for the repentance and salvation of the wicked. And yet, Jonah's three days and three nights in the belly of the whale clearly mirror Jesus's three days and three nights in the earth—as the Lord Himself highlighted (see Matthew 12:40). And, just as Jonah's coming forth from the whale's belly brought salvation to the people of Nineveh, Jesus coming forth from the tomb brought salvation to all mankind.[14] Parry and Parry wrote,

> There are other ways Jonah served as a type of Jesus Christ. One outstanding example concerns the time that Jonah slept on the ship during the raging storm. The ship's captain came to him and said: "What meanest thou, sleeper? Arise, call upon thy God, if it so be that God will think upon us, that we perish not" (Jonah 1:6). This parallels the occurrence when Jesus slept in the ship during a great storm and others awoke him and said, "Master, carest thou not that we perish?" (Mark 4:38–39). In one instance, Jonah's invitation to the sailors to throw him overboard was the cause of the storm's ceasing (Jonah 1:3–12), and in the second, Jesus directly caused the storm to cease.[15]

Of course, Jonah made a conscious choice to die—being thrown overboard into the stormy ocean—in order to save the lives of his fellows (see Jonah 1:1–15). This parallels Christ, who would later do the same on our behalf.[16]

While we might be prone to see the fish in this miracle as a symbol of judgment or punishment, that might be a misreading of what is intended. As mentioned earlier in this book, the waters of the ocean often symbolize chaos and death.[17] Thus, the fish here is an apt symbol of the "source of salvation, preserving [Jonah] from the inevitable death by drowning (Jonah 2:1–10; 4:9–11). . . . The fish must be understood symbolically as representing God's grace of deliverance and salvation."[18]

APPLICATION AND ALLEGORIZATION

The main theme of the book of Jonah is repentance. The narrative establishes that God wants *all* of His children to repent; and He wants his prophetic message to go to *all*—not just covenant Israel. *All* are children of God.[19] Jonah is seen as a stumbling block to this divine mission and mandate. "Although God uses Jonah in spite of himself, he is a small-minded, ill-tempered ethnocentrist who thoroughly disapproves of the universal mercy of God. He is the object of satiric ridicule in the [Old Testament] book that bears his name."[20] Jonah's behavior calls us to self-assessment.

Do we seek the punishment of others? Do we dread seeing God bless those who have somehow harmed us? Are we in all ways, partners with God in the salvation of His children; or do we ever act—like Jonah—as stumbling blocks to God's work?

Another application of this narrative is to be found in the fact that Jonah "could not conquer his own personal desire for vengeance (Jonah 4:2)."[21] That vengeful desire for the destruction of those whom he felt had wronged him caused him to disobey God and miss God's grace in his own life. Jonah is depicted as being completely unaware of the parallels that exist between him and the Ninevites. They were rebellious and sinful, and he had sinfully rebelled against God's command by running from his mission. They were forgiven by God, and God had forgiven him—as evidenced by the fish spitting him up on the shore. He is a good example of the hypocrisy we sometimes manifest in our own lives, when we see the bad in others, but can't see it in ourselves; and when we see God bless others, but can't see how good He has been to us.

This miracle is often described as a great story of repentance. A missionary runs away from his mission, and God sends him experiences to bring him to repentance. When the missionary's heart is right, and when he confesses his sins and commits to live God's commandments, then the Lord takes him back and sends him on to fulfill the mission he was originally called to.[22] Perhaps we can see in the story of Jonah the need to quickly forgive those who repent of their failings; and also the need to use those who have repented in meaningful ways in the Church. When Jonah repented of his sin, God immediately put him back to work. Perhaps we should be more prone to do the same.

One LDS source pointed out, "Jonah's refusal to fulfill his calling not only brought him into peril but also brought unbelievers into peril. Is this not symbolic of us in our day when we refuse to fulfill our member-missionary opportunities and obligations or other assignments?"[23] Members often rationalize their poor performance in their callings, thinking, "It's not that big of a deal." Or, "It's only home teaching. They probably don't really care if I come anyway." However, when we neglect to do our promised duties, we rob those whom we were supposed to serve of blessings that it was our assignment to provide. We are God's stewards—His hands. He has entrusted us with the salvation and care of His children. To run from such assignments—or to just ignore them—is to rob others of blessings that God wants them to have, and that they often *really* need. Just as Jonah didn't care about the needs and salvation of the people of Nineveh, you and I show that we do not care about others when we half-heartedly fulfill our callings, or when we don't do them at all. And we also show God that we do not care about Him!

Regarding this unknown species of fish that swallowed Jonah, and God's use of it to bring to pass His will, one commentary on the passage explains,

> There is no suggestion [in the text] that the fish was a special creation [of God just] for the purpose [of saving the prophet], or that Jonah's preservation within it was miraculous. The power of God ensured that the fish was there at exactly the right time.
>
> If it were more widely realized that the miraculous is probably always achieved by God's control over nature, not by contravention of the laws he has placed in nature, we might be able to recognize miracles more easily in our own experience.[24]

In other words, that God intervened is a miracle. However, the way that He intervened may be less miraculous. God had long before created the "great fish" that would swallow Jonah; He did not create it *ex nihilo* at the very moment it was needed to rescue the prophet. In His foreknowledge of all things, God inspired the fish to be in the right place at the right time to see and swallow Jonah. But all of these things are the natural order of life. God directs the smaller details to bring about the greater effect, but there is no need to overturn natural law in order to make this miraculous event happen. Rather, God works within that very law to accomplish His will. If we believe that such is how God traditionally works, then we can see His hand in many of the day-to-day experiences that we have. God is more involved in the general details of our lives than many of us are willing to believe or acknowledge.

In an effort to avoid making Jonah pay for what he has done, the sailors make a valiant effort to bring their ship to shore. However, their struggles prove futile.[25] There may be a symbolic message in this. Sometimes we seek desperately to avoid the consequences of our own actions—the consequences of our sins. But, as this miracle suggests, we cannot do so. If there is a "spiritual fine" to pay, we must pay it. In some cases, that accountability only fully comes to us in the next life, but in others, we must account for our sins here and now and make our restitution—as was the case with Jonah. It is futile to try to escape from God or the consequences of our sins. The Father is not punitive, but He seeks our repentance so that the Spirit of God can be our ever-abiding companion, and so that peace can dwell within our hearts.

Jonah found himself in the belly of the great fish, and therein prayed for God's intervention and redemption (see Jonah 2:7). One commentator suggested that this is a reminder that "the *place* of prayer can neither add to, nor take from, the value of prayer. The body of the fish was a temple to God when prayer ascended to Him from it."[26] God will hear our earnest petitions, regardless of where we are, whether we kneel or stand, whether we pray vocally or silently. There is nothing more melodious to the ears of God than the voice of one of His children sincerely conversing with their Father.

NOTES

1.   D. Kelly Ogden and Andrew C. Skinner, *Verse By Verse—The Old Testament Volume One: Genesis through 2 Samuel, Psalms* (Salt Lake City, UT: Deseret Book, 2013), 2:133. See also Ellis T. Rasmussen, *A Latter-day Saint Commentary on the Old Testament* (Salt Lake City, UT: Deseret Book, 1994), 653; George A. F. Knight and Friedemann W. Golka, *Revelation of God: A Commentary on the Books of the Song of Songs and Jonah*, in *International Theological Commentary* (Grand Rapids, MI: Eerdmans, 1988), 74; Gleason L. Archer, *A Survey of Old Testament Introduction* (Chicago, IL: Moody Publishers, 1964). 295.

2.   See Jack M. Sasson, *The Anchor Bible: Jonah*, vol. 24 (New York: Doubleday, 1990), 69. "Amittai" has also been rendered as "my truth." (See Sasson, *The Anchor Bible: Jonah*, 86.)

3.   See Ogden and Skinner, *Verse By Verse—The Old Testament Volume One: Genesis through 2 Samuel, Psalms*, 2:134; Ada R. Habershon, *The Study of the Miracles* (London: Morgan & Scott, 1911), 75; Leland Ryken, James C. Wilhoit, and Tremper Longman III, eds., *Dictionary of Biblical Imagery* (Downers Grove, IL: InterVarsity Press, 1998), 459; Herbert Lockyer, *All the Miracles of the Bible: The Supernatural in Scripture—Its Scope and Significance* (Grand Rapids, MI: Zondervan, 1961), 142.

4.   James L. Ferrell, *The Hidden Christ: Beneath the Surface of the Old Testament* (Salt Lake City, UT: Deseret Book, 2009), 189. See also T. Desmond Alexander, David W. Baker, and Bruce Waltke, *Obadiah, Jonah, and Micah*, in *Tyndale Old Testament Commentaries* (Downers Grove, IL: InterVarsity Press, 1988), 101.

5.   See Ogden and Skinner, *Verse By Verse—The Old Testament Volume One: Genesis through 2 Samuel, Psalms*, 2:134–35.

6.   See Ambrose John Wilson, "The Sign of the Prophet Jonah and Its Modern Confirmations," in *The Princeton Theological Review* 25, no. 4 (1927): 635–38. See also C. F. Keil and F. Delitzsch, *Biblical Commentary on the Old Testament: The*

Twelve Minor Prophets (Grand Rapids, MI: Eerdmans, 1967), 1:398n1; Archer, *A Survey of Old Testament Introduction*, 302n8.

7. Knight and Golka, *Revelation of God: A Commentary on the Books of the Song of Songs and Jonah*, in *International Theological Commentary*, 89.

8. See Francis Brown, S. R. Driver, and Charles A. Briggs, *The Brown-Driver-Briggs Hebrew and English Lexicon* (Peabody, MA: Hendrickson Publishers, 1999), 185.

9. See A. Kirk Grayson, "Nineveh," in David Noel Freedman, ed., *The Anchor Bible Dictionary* (New York: Doubleday, 1992), 4:1118; H. L. Ellison, "Jonah," in Frank E. Gaebelein, ed., *The Expositor's Bible Commentary*, vol. 8 (Downers Grove, IL: InterVarsity Press, 1988), 7:368; Knight and Golka, *Revelation of God: A Commentary on the Books of the Song of Songs and Jonah*, in *International Theological Commentary*, 74–75.

10. See Sasson, *The Anchor Bible: Jonah*, 71; Alexander, Baker, and Waltke, *Obadiah, Jonah, and Micah*, in *Tyndale Old Testament Commentaries*, 98.

11. Ogden and Skinner, *Verse By Verse—The Old Testament Volume One: Genesis through 2 Samuel, Psalms*, 2:135. See also Knight and Golka, *Revelation of God: A Commentary on the Books of the Song of Songs and Jonah*, in *International Theological Commentary*, 76–77; Alexander, Baker, and Waltke, *Obadiah, Jonah, and Micah*, in *Tyndale Old Testament Commentaries*, 116.

12. Knight and Golka, *Revelation of God: A Commentary on the Books of the Song of Songs and Jonah*, in *International Theological Commentary*, 76.

13. Ryken, Wilhoit, and Longman, *Dictionary of Biblical Imagery*, 459.

14. See Donald W. Parry and Jay A. Parry, *Symbols and Shadows: Unlocking a Deeper Understanding of the Atonement* (Salt Lake City, UT: Deseret Book, 2009), 97. Parry and Parry also wrote, "There are other ways Jonah served as a type of Jesus Christ. One outstanding example concerns the time that Jonah slept on the ship during the raging storm. The ship's captain came to him and said: 'What meanest thou, O sleeper? arise, call upon thy God, if so be that God will think upon us, that we perish not' (Jonah 1:6). This parallels the occurrence when Jesus slept in the ship during a great storm and others awoke him and said, 'Master, carest thou not that we perish?' (Mark 4:38–39). In one instance, Jonah's invitation to the sailors to throw him overboard was the cause of the storm's ceasing (Jonah 1:3–12), and in the second, Jesus directly caused the storm to cease." (Parry and Parry, *Symbols and Shadows: Unlocking a Deeper Understanding of the Atonement*, 86.)

15. Parry and Parry, *Symbols and Shadows: Unlocking a Deeper Understanding of the Atonement*, 86.

16. Ibid., 97.

17. See Ryken, Wilhoit, and Longman, *Dictionary of Biblical Imagery*, 290.

18. Ibid.

19. See Rasmussen, *A Latter-day Saint Commentary on the Old Testament*, 654; Ogden and Skinner, *Verse By Verse—The Old Testament Volume One: Genesis through 2 Samuel, Psalms*, 2:134.

20. Ryken, Wilhoit, and Longman, *Dictionary of Biblical Imagery*, 459.

21. Ibid.

22. See Rasmussen, *A Latter-day Saint Commentary on the Old Testament*, 654; Ogden and Skinner, *Verse By Verse—The Old Testament Volume One: Genesis through 2 Samuel, Psalms*, 2:136.

23. Ogden and Skinner, *Verse By Verse—The Old Testament Volume One: Genesis through 2 Samuel, Psalms*, 2:135. See also Ferrell, *The Hidden Christ: Beneath the Surface of the Old Testament*, 192–93.

24. Ellison, "Jonah," in Gaebelein, *The Expositor's Bible Commentary*, 7:374.

25. See Alexander, Baker, and Waltke, *Obadiah, Jonah, and Micah*, in *Tyndale Old Testament Commentaries*, 106.

26. Richard C. Trench, *Miracles and Parables of the Old Testament* (Grand Rapids, MI: Baker Book House, 1974), 192.

Bibliography

Achtemeier, Paul J., ed. *Harper's Bible Dictionary*. New York: Harper & Row, 1985.

Alexander, T. Desmond, David W. Baker, and Bruce Waltke. *Obadiah, Jonah, and Micah*, in *Tyndale Old Testament Commentaries*. Downers Grove, IL: InterVarsity Press, 1988.

Andersen, Neil L. "Prophets and Spiritual Mole Crickets." *Ensign*. November 1999.

Anderson, Robert A. *Signs and Wonders: A Commentary on the Book of Daniel*, in *International Theological Commentary*. Grand Rapids, MI: Eerdmans, 1984.

Archer, Gleason L. *A Survey of Old Testament Introduction*. Chicago, IL: Moody Publishers, 1964.

Arrington, Leonard J., ed. *The Presidents of the Church: Biographical Essays*. Salt Lake City, UT: Deseret Book, 1986.

Baldwin, Joyce G. *1 and 2 Samuel*, in *Tyndale Old Testament Commentaries*. Downers Grove, IL: InterVarsity Press, 1988.

———. *Daniel*, in *Tyndale Old Testament Commentaries*. Downers Grove, IL: InterVarsity Press, 1978.

Barclay, William. *The Gospel of Matthew*. Rev. ed. 2 vols. Louisville, KY: Westminster John Knox, 1975.

———. *The Revelation of John*. 2 vols. Louisville, KY: Westminster John Knox Press, 2004.

"Because I Have Been Given Much." *Hymns*, no. 219.

Bednar, David A. "Converted unto the Lord." *Ensign*. November 2012.

Benson, Ezra Taft. "Beware of Pride." *Ensign*. May 1989.

———. *The Teachings of Ezra Taft Benson*. Salt Lake City, UT: Bookcraft, 1988.

Boling, Robert G. *The Anchor Bible: Judges*. Vol. 6. New York: Doubleday, 1975.

Boling, Robert G. and G. Ernest Wright. *The Anchor Bible: Judges*. Vol. 6. New York: Doubleday, 1982.

Botterweck, G. Johannes and Helmer Ringgren, eds. *Theological Dictionary of the Old Testament*. Vol. 3. Grand Rapids, MI: Eerdmans, 1978.

Bowden, John, ed. *Encyclopedia of Christianity*. New York: Oxford, 2005.

Bray, Gerald, ed. *1–2 Corinthians*, in *Ancient Christian Commentary on Scripture*. Downers Grove, IL: InterVarsity Press, 1999.

Bromiley, Geoffrey W., ed. *The International Standard Bible Encyclopedia*. Rev. ed. 4 vols. Grand Rapids, MI: Eerdmans, 1989.

Brown, Francis, S. R. Driver, and Charles A. Briggs. *The Brown-Driver-Briggs Hebrew and English Lexicon*. Peabody, MA: Hendrickson Publishers, 1994.

Brown, Matthew B. and Paul Thomas Smith. *Symbols in Stone: Symbolism on the Early Temples of the Restoration*. American Fork, UT: Covenant, 1997.

Brown, Raymond E., Joseph A. Fitzmyer, and Roland E. Murphy, eds. *The New Jerome Biblical Commentary*. Englewood Cliffs, NJ: Prentice Hall, 1990.

BIBLIOGRAPHY

Budge, E. A. Wallis *Osiris: The Egyptian Religion of Resurrection*. New York: University Books, 1961.

Bullinger, E. W. *Number in Scripture: Its Supernatural Design and Spiritual Significance*. Grand Rapids, MI: Kregel Publications, 1967.

Burton, Theodore M. "The Power of Elijah." *Ensign*. May 1974.

Cairns, Ian. *Word and Presence: A Commentary on the Book of Deuteronomy*, in *International Theological Commentary*. Grand Rapids, MI: Eerdmans, 1992.

Carlyon, Richard. *A Guide to the Gods*. New York: Quill, 1982.

Chappell, Clovis Gillham. *The Cross Before Calvary*. New York: Abingdon Press, 1960.

Charlesworth, James H., ed. *The Old Testament Pseudepigrapha*. 2 vols. New York: Doubleday, 1983–1985.

Christensen, Clayton M. *The Power of Everyday Missionaries: The What and How of Sharing the Gospel*. Salt Lake City, UT: Deseret Book, 2013.

Christofferson, D. Todd. "A Sense of the Sacred." *CES Young Adult Fireside*, in *BYU Speeches*. November 7, 2004. speeches.byu.edu/talks/d-todd-christofferson _sense-sacred/.

Cirlot, J. E. *A Dictionary of Symbols*. 2nd ed. New York: Routledge & Kegan Paul, 1971.

Clark, J. Reuben, Jr. In Conference Report, October 1936.

———. In Conference Report, October 1953.

———. In Conference Report, October 1956.

———. *On the Way to Immortality and Eternal Life*. Salt Lake City, UT: Deseret Book, 1961.

Clark, James R., comp. *Messages of the First Presidency*. 6 vols. Salt Lake City, UT: Bookcraft, 1965–75.

Clarke, Adam. *The Holy Bible, Containing the Old and New Testaments . . . with a Commentary and Critical Notes. . . .* 6 vols. New York: T. Mason & G. Lane, 1837.

Cogan, Mordechai. *The Anchor Bible: I Kings*. Vol. 10. New York: Doubleday, 2001.

Cogan, Mordechai, and Hayim Tadmor. *The Anchor Bible: II Kings*. Vol. 11. New York: Doubleday, 1988.

Cole, R. Alan. *Exodus*, in *Tyndale Old Testament Commentaries*. Grand Rapids, MI: Eerdmans, 1973.

Conner, Kevin J. *Interpreting the Symbols and Types*. Rev. ed. Portland, OR: City Bible Publishing, 1992.

Conti, Marco, ed. *1–2 Kings, 1–2 Chronicles, Ezra, Nehemiah, Esther*, in *Ancient Christian Commentary on Scripture*. Downers Grove, IL: InterVarsity Press, 2008.

Cooper, J. C. *An Illustrated Encyclopaedia of Traditional Symbols*. London: Thames and Hudson, 1987.

Cornwall, Judson and Stelman Smith. *The Exhaustive Dictionary of Bible Names.* Alachua FL: Bridge-Logos, 1998.

Cross, Frank Leslie and Elizabeth A. Livingstone, eds. *The Oxford Dictionary of the Christian Church.* 2nd ed. New York: Oxford University Press, 1974.

Cundall, Arthur E. and Leon Morris. *Judges and Ruth,* in *Tyndale Old Testament Commentaries.* Downers Grove, IL: InterVarsity Press, 1968.

Davis, John J. *Biblical Numerology: A Basic Study of the Use of Numbers in the Bible.* Grand Rapids, MI: Baker Books, 1968.

Delitzsch, Franz. *Biblical Commentary on the Prophecies of Isaiah.* 2 vols. London: Forgotten Books, 2012.

Douglas, J. D., ed. *The New Bible Dictionary.* Grand Rapids, MI: Eerdmans, 1967.

Draper, Richard D. *Opening the Seven Seals: The Visions of John the Revelator.* Salt Lake City, UT: Deseret Book, 1991.

Dummelow, J. R. *The One Volume Bible Commentary.* New York: Macmillan, 1965.

Eakin, Frank E., Jr. *The Religion and Culture of Israel: An Introduction to Old Testament Thought.* Boston, MA: Allyn and Bacon, 1971.

Ehat, Andrew F. and Lyndon W. Cook. *The Words of Joseph Smith.* Provo, UT: Brigham Young University Religious Studies Center, 1980.

Eilberg-Schwartz, Howard. *The Savage in Judaism: An Anthropology of Israelite Religion and Ancient Judaism.* Bloomington, IN: Indiana University Press, 1990.

Elowsky, Joel C., ed. *John 11–21,* in *Ancient Christian Commentary on Scripture.* Downers Grove, IL: InterVarsity Press, 2007.

Eyring, Henry B. "Armed with Righteousness." *Ensign.* March 2017.

Fairbairn, Patrick. *The Typology of Scripture.* 2nd ed. Two volumes in one. Philadelphia, PA: Smith & English, 1854.

Farbridge, Maurice H. *Studies in Biblical and Semitic Symbolism.* 1923. Reprint, London: Routledge, 2000.

Ferguson, Everett, ed. *Encyclopedia of Early Christianity.* 2nd ed. New York: Garland Publishing, 1998.

Ferrell, James L. *The Hidden Christ: Beneath the Surface of the Old Testament.* Salt Lake City, UT: Deseret Book, 2009.

Fitzmyer, Joseph A. *The Anchor Bible: The Gospel According to Luke I–IX.* Vol. 28. New York: Doubleday, 1982.

———. *The Anchor Bible: The Gospel According to Luke X–XXIV.* Vol. 28. New York: Doubleday, 1985.

Fontana, David. *The Secret Language of Symbolism: A Visual Key to Symbols and Their Meanings.* San Francisco, CA: Chronicle Books, 2000.

Ford, J. Massyngberde. *The Anchor Bible: Revelation.* Vol. 38. New York: Doubleday, 1975.

Franke, John R., ed. *Joshua, Judges, Ruth, 1–2 Samuel*, in *Ancient Christian Commentary on Scripture*. Downers Grove, IL: InterVarsity Press, 2005.

Frankel, Ellen, and Betsy Platkin Teutsch. *The Encyclopedia of Jewish Symbols*. Lanham, MD: Rowman & Littlefield Publishers, 1995.

Freedman, David Noel, ed. *The Anchor Bible Dictionary*. 6 vols. New York: Doubleday, 1992.

Fretheim, Terence E. *Interpretation: A Bible Commentary for Teaching and Preaching—Exodus*. Louisville, KY: John Knox Press, 1991.

Gaebelein, Frank E., ed. *The Expositor's Bible Commentary*. 12 vols. Grand Rapids, MI: Zondervan, 1976–1992.

Gard, Richard A., ed. *Buddhism: The Way of Buddhism*. New Jersey: Prentice Hall Press, 1962.

Gaskill, Alonzo L. *The Lost Language of Symbolism: An Essential Guide for Recognizing and Interpreting Symbols of the Gospel*. Salt Lake City, UT: Deseret Book, 2003.

———. *Miracles of the Book of Mormon: A Guide to the Symbolic Messages*. Springville, UT: CFI, 2015.

———. *Miracles of the New Testament: A Guide to the Symbolic Messages*. Springville, UT: CFI, 2014.

———. *Sacred Symbols: Finding Meaning in Rites, Rituals, & Ordinances*. Springville, UT: Bonneville Books, 2011.

Ginzberg, Louis. *The Legends of the Jews*. 7 vols. Philadelphia, PA: The Jewish Publication Society of America, 1912–1938.

Greidanus, Sidney. *Preaching Christ from the Old Testament: A Contemporary Hermeneutical Method*. Grand Rapids, MI: Eerdmans, 1999.

Habershon, Ada R. *Hidden Pictures in the Old Testament*. Grand Rapids, MI: Kregel Publications, 1982.

———. *The Study of the Miracles*. London: Morgan & Scott, 1911.

———. *Study of the Types*. Grand Rapids, MI: Kregel Publications, 1974.

———. *Types in the Old Testament*. Grand Rapids, MI: Kregel Publications, 1988.

Hafen, Bruce C. *The Believing Heart: Nourishing the Seed of Faith*. 2nd ed. Salt Lake City, UT: Deseret Book, 1990.

Hall, James. *Dictionary of Subjects & Symbols in Art*. Rev. ed. Boulder, CO: Westview Press, 1979.

Hamilton, Victor P. *Handbook on the Pentateuch*. Grand Rapids, MI: Baker Academic, 1982.

Hamlin, E. John. *At Risk in the Promised Land: A Commentary on the Book of Judges*, in *International Theological Commentary*. Grand Rapids, MI: Eerdmans, 1990.

———. *Inheriting the Land: A Commentary on the Book of Joshua*, in *International Theological Commentary*. Grand Rapids, MI: Eerdmans, 1983.

BIBLIOGRAPHY

Hare, Douglas R. A. *Interpretation: A Bible Commentary for Teaching and Preaching—Matthew.* Louisville Kentucky: John Knox Press, 1993.

Harris, Stephen L. *Understanding the Bible: A Reader's Introduction.* 3rd ed. Houston, TX: Mayfield Publishing Company, 1992.

Hartman, Louis F., and Alexander A. Di Lella. *The Anchor Bible: The Book of Daniel.* Vol. 23. New York: Doubleday, 1978.

Hastings, James, ed. *Dictionary of the Bible.* Rev. ed. New York: Charles Scribner's Sons, 1963.

Hedges, Andrew H., Alex D. Smith, and Richard Lloyd Anderson, eds. *The Joseph Smith Papers, Journals Volume 2: December 1841–April 1843.* Salt Lake City, UT: The Church Historian's Press, 2011.

Henry, Hugh T. *Catholic Customs and Symbols.* Cincinnati, OH: Benziger Brothers, 1925.

Hertz, J. H. *The Pentateuch and Haftorahs: Hebrew Text English Translation and Commentary.* 2nd ed. London: Soncino Press, 1960.

Hess, Richard S. *Joshua,* in *Tyndale Old Testament Commentaries.* Downers Grove, IL: InterVarsity Press, 1996.

Holland, Jeffrey R. and Patricia T. Holland. "The Inconvenient Messiah." *BYU Speeches,* February 27, 1982. speeches.byu.edu/talks/jeffrey-r-and-patricia-t-holland_inconvenient-messiah/.

Holland, Patricia T. "'One Things Needful': Becoming Women of Greater Faith in Christ." *Ensign,* October 1987.

Holzapfel, Richard Neitzel, and Kent P. Jackson, eds. *My Redeemer Lives!* Provo, UT: Brigham Young University Religious Studies Center and Deseret Book, 2012.

Howick, E. Keith. *The Miracles of Jesus the Messiah.* St. George, UT: WindRiver Publishing, 2003.

Hunter, Howard W. "Walls of the Mind." *Ensign,* September 1990.

Journal of Discourses. 1854–1886.

"I Have A Question." *Ensign,* September 1980.

Ifrah, Georges. *The Universal History of Numbers: From Prehistory to the Invention of the Computer.* New York: John Wiley & Sons, 2000.

Jamieson, Robert, Andrew Robert Fausset, and David Brown. *Jamieson, Fausset and Brown's Commentary on the Whole Bible.* Grand Rapids, MI: Zondervan, 1999.

Janzen, J. Gerald. *Abraham and All the Families of the Earth: A Commentary on the Book of Genesis 12–50,* in *International Theological Commentary.* Grand Rapids, MI: Eerdmans, 1993.

Johnson, Luke Timothy. *Sacra Pagina: The Acts of the Apostles.* Edited by Daniel J. Harrington. Vol. 5. Collegeville, MN: The Liturgical Press, 1992.

Johnston, Robert D. *Numbers in the Bible: God's Design in Biblical Numerology.* Grand Rapids, MI: Kregel Publications, 1999.

Josephus, Flavius. *The Complete Works of Josephus.* Translated by William Whiston. Grand Rapids, MI: Kregel Publications, 1981.

Julien, Nadia. *The Mammoth Dictionary of Symbols: Understanding the Hidden Language of Symbols.* New York: Carroll & Graf Publishers, Inc., 1996.

Just, Jr., Arthur A., ed. *Luke,* in *Ancient Christian Commentary on Scripture.* Downers Grove, IL: InterVarsity Press, 2003.

"Keep the Commandments." *Hymns,* no. 303.

Keil, C. F., and F. Delitzsch. *Biblical Commentary on the Old Testament: The Twelve Minor Prophets.* Grand Rapids, MI: Eerdmans, 1967.

Kengor, Paul. *God and Ronald Reagan: A Spiritual Life.* New York: ReganBooks, 2004.

Kherdian, David. *The Buddha: The Story of an Awakened Life.* Ashland, OR: White Cloud Press, 2004.

Kidner, Derek. *Genesis,* in *Tyndale Old Testament Commentaries.* Downers Grove, IL: InterVarsity Press, 1967.

Kimball, Spencer W. In *The Church News, Conference Issues* 1970–1987.

———. *Faith Precedes the Miracle.* Salt Lake City, UT: Deseret Book, 1972.

———. *The Teachings of Spencer W. Kimball.* Salt Lake City, UT: Bookcraft, 1982.

———. *Teachings of Presidents of the Church: Spencer W. Kimball.* Salt Lake City, UT: The Church of Jesus Christ of Latter-day Saints, 2006.

Kittel, Gerhard, ed. *Theological Dictionary of the New Testament.* 10 vols. Grand Rapids, MI: Eerdmans, 1984.

Knight, George A. F., and Friedemann W. Golka. *Revelation of God: A Commentary on the Books of the Song of Songs and Jonah,* in *International Theological Commentary.* Grand Rapids, MI: Eerdmans, 1988.

Koltko, Claire, Natalie Ross, Brittany McEwen, and Jennifer Johnson, comps. *The Eyewitness History of the Church: Journey to Zion's Hill.* Vol. 3. Springville, UT: Cedar Fort, 2006.

Kugel, James L. *Traditions of the Bible: A Guide to the Bible As It Was at the Start of the Common Era.* Cambridge, MA: Harvard University Press, 1998.

Lang, Seán. *European History for Dummies.* West Sussex, England: John Wiley and Sons, 2011.

Levine, Baruch A. *The Anchor Bible: Numbers 1–20.* Vol. 4. New York: Doubleday, 1993.

Lewis, C. S. *Surprised by Joy: The Shape of My Early Life.* New York: Harcourt Brace, 1955.

Lienhard, Joseph T., ed. *Exodus, Leviticus, Numbers, Deuteronomy,* in *Ancient Christian Commentary on Scripture.* Downers Grove, IL: InterVarsity Press, 2001.

Lockyer, Herbert. *All the Miracles of the Bible: The Supernatural in Scripture—Its Scope and Significance.* Grand Rapids, MI: Zondervan, 1961.

Ludlow, Daniel H. *A Companion to Your Study of the Old Testament.* Salt Lake City, UT: Deseret Book, 1981.

Ludlow, Daniel H., ed. *Encyclopedia of Mormonism.* 4 vols. New York: Macmillan, 1992.

Ludlow, Victor L. *Isaiah: Prophet, Seer, and Poet.* Salt Lake City, UT: Deseret Book, 1982.

Mackenzie, Donald A. *Egyptian Myth and Legend.* Whitefish, MT: Kessinger Publishing, 2006.

Madsen, Truman G. *Joseph Smith, the Prophet.* Salt Lake City, UT: Bookcraft, 1989.

Mann, C. S. *The Anchor Bible: Mark.* Vol. 27. New York: Doubleday, 1986.

Maxwell, Neal A. *All These Things Shall Give Thee Experience.* Salt Lake City, UT: Deseret Book, 1979.

———. *Look Back at Sodom.* Salt Lake City, UT: Deseret Book, 1975.

———. *The Neal A. Maxwell Quote Book.* Compiled by Cory H. Maxwell. Salt Lake City, UT: Deseret Book, 1997.

———. "'Plow in Hope.'" *Ensign,* May 2001.

———. *That Ye May Believe.* Salt Lake City, UT: Bookcraft, 1992.

———. *We Talk of Christ—We Rejoice in Christ.* Salt Lake City, UT: Deseret Book, 1984.

———. *We Will Prove Them Herewith.* Salt Lake City, UT: Deseret Book, 1982.

McBrien, Richard P., ed. *The Harper Collins Encyclopedia of Catholicism.* New York: HarperCollins, 1995.

McCarter, P. Kyle. *The Anchor Bible: 1 Samuel.* Vol. 8. New York: Doubleday, 1980.

McConkie, Bruce R. *Doctrinal New Testament Commentary.* 3 vols. Salt Lake City, UT: Bookcraft, 1965–72.

———. *The Millennial Messiah: The Second Coming of the Son of Man.* Salt Lake City, UT: Deseret Book, 1982.

———. *Mormon Doctrine.* 2nd ed. Salt Lake City, UT: Bookcraft, 1979.

———. *The Mortal Messiah.* 4 vols. Salt Lake City, UT: Deseret Book, 1979–1981.

———. *The Promised Messiah: The First Coming of Christ.* Salt Lake City, UT: Deseret Book, 1978.

McConkie, Joseph Fielding. *Gospel Symbolism.* Salt Lake City, UT: Deseret Book, 1985.

McConkie, Joseph Fielding and Donald W. Parry. *A Guide to Scriptural Symbols.* Salt Lake City, UT: Deseret Book, 1990.

McKay, David O. "The Blessings of Adversity." *Ensign,* February 1998.

BIBLIOGRAPHY

———. *Gospel Ideals: Selections from the Discourses of David O. McKay.* Salt Lake City, UT: Bookcraft, 1955.

McKenzie, John L. *Dictionary of the Bible.* Milwaukee, WI: The Bruce Publishing Company, 1965.

McQuade, Pamela. *The Top 100 Miracles of the Bible: What They Are and What They Mean to You Today.* Uhrichsville, OH: Barbour Publishing, 2008.

Merrill, Byron R. *Elijah: Yesterday, Today, and Tomorrow.* Salt Lake City, UT: Deseret Book, 1997.

Millet, Robert L., ed. *Studies in Scripture: Acts to Revelation.* Vol. 6. Salt Lake City, UT: Deseret Book, 1987.

Monson, Thomas S. "Goal beyond Victory." *Ensign,* November 1988.

Moore, Carey A. *The Anchor Bible: Daniel, Esther, and Jeremiah: the Additions.* Vol. 44. New York: Doubleday, 1977.

Morris, Leon L. *Revelation,* in *Tyndale Old Testament Commentaries.* Revised edition. Downers Grove, IL: InterVarsity Press, 1987.

Mother Teresa. *Where There Is Love, There Is God: Her Path to Closer Union with God and Greater Love for Others.* New York: Doubleday Religion, 2010.

Myers, Allen C. *The Eerdmans Bible Dictionary.* Grand Rapids, MI: Eerdmans, 1996.

Nachmanides, Ramban. *Commentary on the Torah.* 5 vols. New York: Shilo Publishing House, 1971.

Ñāṇamoli, Bhikkhu. *The Life of the Buddha.* Onalaska, WA: BPS Pariyatti Editions, 1992.

Nibley, Hugh. *Enoch the Prophet.* Vol. 2 of *The Collected Works of Hugh Nibley.* Salt Lake City, UT: Deseret Book, 1986.

Nyman, Monte S., and Robert L. Millet, eds. *The Joseph Smith Translation: The Restoration of Plain and Precious Things.* Provo, UT: BYU Religious Studies Center, 1985.

Nyman, Monte S. and Charles D. Tate Jr. *The Book of Mormon: First Nephi, The Doctrinal Foundation.* Provo, UT: Religious Studies Center, Brigham Young University, 1988.

Oaks, Dallin H. "Our Strengths Can Become Our Downfall." *Ensign,* October 1994.

———. "Scripture Reading and Revelation." *Ensign,* January 1995.

Ogden, D. Kelly, and Andrew C. Skinner. *Verse By Verse—The Old Testament Volume One: Genesis through 2 Samuel, Psalms.* Salt Lake City, UT: Deseret Book, 2013.

———. *Verse By Verse—The Old Testament Volume Two: 1 Kings through Malachi.* Salt Lake City, UT: Deseret Book, 2013.

O'Gorman, Bob, and Mary Faulkner. *The Complete Idiot's Guide to Understanding Catholicism.* 2nd ed. New York: Alpha Books, 2003.

Olson, Dennis T. *Interpretation: A Bible Commentary for Teaching and Preaching—Numbers*. Louisville, KY: Westminster John Knox Press, 1996.

Packer, Boyd K. "Counsel to Youth." *Ensign*, November 2011.

———. *The Holy Temple*. Salt Lake City, UT: Deseret Book, 1980.

———. *Mine Errand From the Lord: Selections from the Sermons and Writings of Boyd K. Packer*. Compiled by Clyde J. Williams. Salt Lake City, UT: Deseret Book, 2008.

Parry, Donald W., ed. *Temples of the Ancient World: Ritual and Symbolism*. Salt Lake City, UT: Deseret Book, 1994.

Parry, Donald W. and Jay A. Parry. *Symbols and Shadows: Unlocking a Deeper Understanding of the Atonement*. Salt Lake City, UT: Deseret Book, 2009.

Parry, Jay A., and Donald W. Parry. *Understanding the Book of Revelation*. Salt Lake City, UT: Deseret Book, 1998.

Petersen, Mark E. *Moses: Man of Miracles*. Salt Lake City, UT: Deseret Book, 1977.

Propp, William H. C. *The Anchor Bible: Exodus 1–18*. Vol. 2. New York: Doubleday, 1999.

Rasmussen, Ellis T. *A Latter-day Saint Commentary on the Old Testament*. Salt Lake City, UT: Deseret Book, 1994.

———. *An Introduction to the Old Testament and Its Teachings*. 2 vols. Provo, UT: Brigham Young University, 1972.

Read, Lenet Hadley. *Unveiling Biblical Prophecy: A Summary of Biblical Prophecy Concerning Christ, the Apostasy and Christ's Latter-day Church*. San Francisco, CA: Latter-day Light Publications, 1990.

Reynolds, George, and Janne M. Sjodahl. *Commentary on the Book of Mormon*. 7 vols. Salt Lake City, UT: Deseret Book, 1955–61.

Ricks, Stephen D., Donald W. Parry, and Andrew H. Hedges, eds. *The Disciple as Scholar: Essays on Scripture and the Ancient World in Honor of Richard Lloyd Anderson*. Provo, UT: Neal A. Maxwell Institute for Religious Scholarship, 2000.

Ricks, Stephen E. and John W. Welch, eds. *The Allegory of the Olive Tree*. Salt Lake City, UT: Deseret Book, 1994.

Ricoeur, Paul. *The Symbolism of Evil*. Boston, MA: Beacon Press, 1969.

Roberts, Alexander, and James Donaldson, eds. *Ante-Nicene Fathers*. 10 vols. Peabody, MA: Hendrickson Publishers, 1994.

Roberts, B. H., ed. *History of the Church of Jesus Christ of Latter-day Saints*. 7 vols. Salt Lake City, UT: Deseret Book, 1978.

Robinson, Gnana. *Let Us Be Like the Nations: A Commentary on the Books of 1 and 2 Samuel*, in *International Theological Commentary*. Grand Rapids, MI: Eerdmans, 1993.

Robinson, Stephen E. *Believing Christ: The Parable of the Bicycle and Other Good News*. Salt Lake City, UT: Deseret Book, 1992.

Bibliography

"Rock of Ages." *Hymns*, no. 111.

Runciman, Steve. *A History of the Crusades.* 3 vols. New York: Cambridge University Press, 1988.

Ryken, Leland, James C. Wilhoit and Tremper Longman III. *Dictionary of Biblical Imagery.* Downers Grove, IL: InterVarsity Press, 1998.

Sakenfeld, Katharine Doob. *Journeying with God: A Commentary on the Book of Numbers,* in *International Theological Commentary.* Grand Rapids, MI: Eerdmans, 1995.

Sasson, Jack M. *The Anchor Bible: Jonah.* Vol. 24. New York: Doubleday, 1990.

Schaff, Philip, ed. *Nicene and Post-Nicene Fathers.* First Series. 14 vols. Peabody, Massachusetts: Hendrickson Publishers, 1994.

Schaff, Philip, and Henry Wace, eds. *Nicene and Post-Nicene Fathers.* Second Series. 14 vols. Peabody, Massachusetts: Hendrickson Publishers, 1996.

"Schistosomiasis." *World Health Organization.* January 2017. Accessed July 26, 2017. www.who.int/mediacentre/factsheets/fs115/en/.

Shelley, Bruce L. *Church History in Plain Language.* 2nd ed. Nashville, TN: Thomas Nelson Publishers, 1995.

Sheridan, Mark, ed. *Genesis 12–50,* in *Ancient Christian Commentary on Scripture.* Downers Grove, IL: InterVarsity Press, 2002.

Singer, Isidore, ed. *The Jewish Encyclopedia.* 12 vols. New York: Funk and Wagnalls Company, 1906.

Skinner, Andrew C. "Serpent Symbols and Salvation in the Ancient Near East and the Book of Mormon." *Journal of Book of Mormon Studies* 10, no. 2 (2001): scholarsarchive.byu.edu/jbms/vol10/iss2/8.

Slotki, Israel W. *Kings,* in *Soncino Books of the Bible.* London: Soncino Press, 1978.

Slotki, Judah J. *Daniel, Ezra, Nehemiah,* in *Soncino Books of the Bible.* London: Soncino Press, 1978.

Smith, Joseph. *Teachings of the Prophet Joseph Smith.* Compiled by Joseph Fielding Smith, Jr. Salt Lake City, UT: Deseret Book, 1976.

Smith, Joseph Fielding. *Church History and Modern Revelation.* 2 vols. Salt Lake City, UT: Deseret Book, 1953.

Smith, Mick. *The Book of Revelation: Plain, Pure, and Simple.* Salt Lake City, UT: Deseret Book, 1998.

Speiser, E. A. *The Anchor Bible: Genesis.* Vol. 1. New York: Doubleday, 1964.

Spencer, Carolynn R. "Learning to Cope with Infertility." *Ensign,* June 2012.

Sperry, Sidney B. *The Spirit of the Old Testament.* 2nd ed. Salt Lake City, UT: Deseret Book, 1980.

Spurgeon, Charles Haddon. *Daily Devotion: January to December with Jesus.* Editora Dracaena: Santa Catarina, Brazil, 2015.

———. *Spurgeon's Sermons.* 10 vols. Grand Rapids, MI: Baker Book House, 1996.

Bibliography

———. "The Withered Fig Tree." Sermon delivered September 29, 1889. Accessed July 26, 2017. www.romans45.org/spurgeon/sermons/2107.htm.

Stevenson, Kenneth, and Michael Glerup, eds. *Ezekiel, Daniel*, in *Ancient Christian Commentary on Scripture*. Downers Grove, IL: InterVarsity Press, 2008.

Stuy, Brian H., comp. *Collected Discourses*. 5 vols. Burbank, CA: B. H. S. Publishing, 1987–1992.

Swift, Charles L. *"I Have Dreamed a Dream": Typological Images of Teaching and Learning in the Vision of the Tree of Life*. Doctrinal dissertation, Brigham Young University.

Talmage, James E. *The Articles of Faith*. Salt Lake City: Deseret Book Co., 1984.

———. In *Conference Report*. October 1931.

Taylor, J. Glen. *Yahweh and the Sun: Biblical and Archaeological Evidence for Sun Worship in Ancient Israel*. Sheffield, England: JSOT Press, 1993.

"To the Point." *New Era*, February 2016.

Todeschi, Kevin J. *The Encyclopedia of Symbolism*. New York: Perigee Trade, 1995.

Top, Brent L., Larry E. Dahl, and Walter D. Bowen. *Follow the Living Prophets: Timely Reasons for Obeying Prophetic Counsel in the Last Days*. Salt Lake City, UT: Deseret Book, 1993.

Trench, Richard C. *Miracles and Parables of the Old Testament*. Grand Rapids, MI: Baker Book House, 1959.

Trent, Kenneth E. *Types of Christ in the Old Testament: A Conservative Approach to Old Testament Typology*. Bloomington, IN: CrossBooks, 2010.mckay

Tresidder, Jack. *Symbols and Their Meanings: The Illustrated Guide to More than 1,000 Symbols—Their Traditional and Contemporary Significance*. London: Duncan Baird Publishers, 2006.

Tuttle, A. Theodore. "Developing Faith," *Ensign*, November 1986.

Tvedtnes, John A. "Elijah: Champion of Israel's God." *Ensign*, July 1990.

Uchtdorf, Dieter F. "Learn from Alma and Amulek." *Ensign*, November 2016.

Unger, Merrill F. *Unger's Bible Dictionary*. Chicago: Moody Press, 1966.

Vawter, Bruce. *On Genesis: A New Reading*. New York: Doubleday, 1977.

Webb, Stephen H. *Mormon Christianity: What Other Christians Can Learn From the Latter-day Saints*. New York: Oxford University Press, 2013.

———. "Mormonism Obsessed with Christ." *First Things Magazine*. February 2012. www.firstthings.com/article/2012/02/mormonism-obsessed-with-christ.

Webb, Stephen H. and Alonzo L. Gaskill, *Catholic and Mormon: A Theological Conversation*. New York: Oxford University Press, 2015.

Wells, Evelyn. *Nefertiti*. New York: Doubleday, 1964.

Wenham, Gordon J. *Numbers*, in *Tyndale Old Testament Commentaries*. Downers Grove, IL: InterVarsity Press, 1981.

Williams, Paul L. *The Complete Idiot's Guide to the Crusades*. Indianapolis, IN: Alpha Books, 2002.

BIBLIOGRAPHY

Williamson, Lamar, Jr. *Interpretation: A Bible Commentary for Teaching and Preaching—Mark*. Atlanta, GA: John Knox Press, 1983.

Wilson, Ambrose John. "The Sign of the Prophet Jonah and Its Modern Confirmations." *The Princeton Theological Review* 25, no. 4 (1927): 630–42.

Wilson, Walter L. *A Dictionary of Bible Types: Examines the Images, Shadows, and Symbolism of Over 1,000 Biblical Terms, Words, and People*. Peabody, MA: Hendrickson, 1999.

Winston, David. *The Anchor Bible: The Wisdom of Solomon*. Vol. 43. New York: Doubleday, 1979.

Wirthlin, Joseph B. "Shall He Find Faith on the Earth?" *Ensign*, November 2002.

Wiseman, Donald J. *1 and 2 Kings*, in *Tyndale Old Testament Commentaries*. Downers Grove, IL: InterVarsity Press, 1993.

Wood, Leon J. *The Holy Spirit in the Old Testament*. Grand Rapids, MI: Zondervan, 1976.

Woodward, Kenneth L. *The Book of Miracles: The Meaning of the Miracle Stories in Christianity, Judaism, Buddhism, Islam*. New York: Simon & Schuster, 2000.

Yorgason, Blaine M. *I Need Thee Every Hour: The Joy of Coming to Christ*. Salt Lake City, UT: Deseret Book, 2004.

Young, Brigham. *Discourses of Brigham Young*. Compiled by John A. Widtsoe. Salt Lake City, UT: Bookcraft, 1954.

Young, Edward J. *The Book of Isaiah: A Commentary*. 3 vols. Grand Rapids, MI: Eerdmans, 1992.

Zornberg, Avivah Gottlieb. *The Particulars of Rapture: Reflections on Exodus*. New York: Doubleday, 2001.

INDEX

Index

INDEX

INDEX

ABOUT *the* AUTHOR

ALONZO L. GASKILL is a professor of Church history and doctrine. He holds a bachelors degree in philosophy, a masters in theology, and a PhD in biblical studies. Brother Gaskill has taught at Brigham Young University since 2003. Prior to coming to BYU, he served in a variety of assignments within the Church Educational System—most recently as the director of the LDS Institute of Religion at Stanford University (1995–2003).

Scan to visit

www.alonzogaskill.wordpress.com